U.S. Population Age 85 and Older, 1900–2050 (in millions)

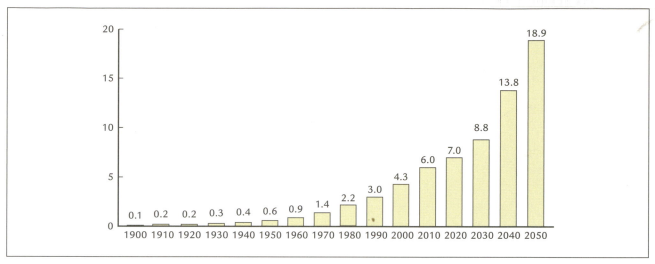

Source: Hobbs, Frank B. with Bonnie L Damon (1996). "65+ in the United States." *Current Population Reports*, P23-290: 2–8.

Labor Force Participation Rate by Sex, 1950–2009, and Projected, 2009–2016

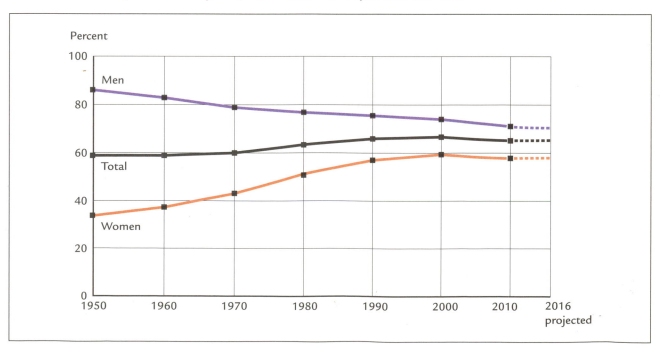

Sources: Occupational Outlook Quarterly, Winter 2001–2002. Washington, DC: U.S. Department of Labor, Bureau of Labor Statistics, p. 39; "Employment Projections." U.S. Department of Labor, 2007. Online: http://www.bls.gov/emp/emplab05.htm.

Why Do You Need This New Edition?

You need the new edition of *Diversity in Families* to understand the rapid changes in today's family life.

This family text treats diversity as the norm, while highlighting how race, class, and gender produce varieties of familial relationships. The 9th edition of this award-winning text includes the following new features:

1. The effects of the Great Recession on families.

2. Families in the Great Depression and differences by race, class, and gender.

3. The effects of globalization on family life.

4. Parental time with children, including marital employment and time with children.

5. Expanded coverage of immigrant families, including second-generation immigrants.

6. The latest research on today's work/family realities, including the high commitment workplace, the work/family experience of single mothers, and the growing care sector of the economy.

7. Mate selection, marriage, and technology.

8. The latest on communication and the sexual relationship in marriage.

PEARSON

Diversity in Families

NINTH EDITION

MAXINE BACA ZINN

Michigan State University

D. STANLEY EITZEN

Colorado State University

BARBARA WELLS

Maryville College

Allyn & Bacon

Boston   Columbus   Indianapolis   New York   San Francisco   Upper Saddle River
Amsterdam   Cape Town   Dubai   London   Madrid   Milan   Munich   Paris   Montréal   Toronto
Delhi   Mexico City   São Paulo   Sydney   Hong Kong   Seoul   Singapore   Taipei   Tokyo

Publisher: *Karen Hanson*
Editorial Assistant: *Alyssa Levy*
Associate Editor: *Mayda Bosco*
Marketing Manager: *Kelly May*
Executive Marketing Assistant: *Gina Lavagna*
Senior Production Project Manager: *Patrick Cash-Peterson*
Manufacturing Buyer: *Debbie Rossi*
Cover Administrator and Cover Designer: *Joel Gendron*
Editorial Production: *Elm Street Publishing Services*
Composition: *Integra Software Services Pvt. Ltd.*
Photo Researcher: *Alan Zinn*

Credits in this textbook appear on appropriate page in text or on page 537, which constitutes an extension of the copyright page.

Many of the designations by manufacturers and sellers to distinguish their products are claimed as trademarks. Where those designations appear in this book, and the publisher was aware of a trademark claim, the designations have been printed in initial caps or all caps.

Library of Congress Cataloging-in-Publication Data

Zinn, Maxine Baca, 1942–
    Diversity in families/Maxine Baca Zinn, D. Stanley Eitzen, Barbara Wells.—9th ed.
      p. cm.
    Includes bibliographical references and index.
    ISBN 978-0-205-69307-8
    1. Families—United States. 2. United States—Social conditions—1980– I. Eitzen,
D. Stanley. II. Wells, Barbara. III. Title.

HQ536.Z54 2011
306.850973—dc22

2009051272

10 9 8 7 6 5 4 3 CKV 14 13 12

Allyn & Bacon
is an imprint of

www.pearsonhighered.com

ISBN-10: 0-205-69307-5
ISBN-13: 978-0-205-69307-8

We dedicate this book to the teachers, students, and scholars who are rethinking family life to meet the challenges of the diverse and changing social world.

brief contents

contents

Themes of the Book

The ninth edition of *Diversity in Families* reflects the critical tradition of family sociologists, economists, and historians whose scholarship is structuralist, feminist, and humanist. Several assumptions guide our inquiry. To begin, the understanding of families requires that we demythologize the family, the most myth-laden of all our social institutions. We must separate, for example, the reality of how families are structured from the ideal images of "the family" that are commonly portrayed. The demythologizing of the family also requires that we examine the diversity of contemporary families.

An important aspect of our focus is the critical examination of society. We ask questions such as "How do families really work?" and "Who benefits under the existing arrangements and who does not?" This critical stance is based on the assumption that the social world is humanly made and therefore not sacred. Thus a keen sociological analysis demystifies and demythologizes social life by ferreting out existing myths, stereotypes, and dogmas. This means, for example, that families must be examined not only from middle-class, White, male viewpoints, which have dominated the scholarly study of the family, but must be viewed from other vantage points as well. Several bodies of new scholarship are considered throughout this book to show how family organization and experience vary by social class, gender, race, and sexuality.

Conventional research and public policy have long treated families as closed units that can be understood in isolation from outside influences. In sharp contrast, this book assumes that families are not the "building blocks of society" but are, rather, the products of social forces within society. The material conditions of people's lives, for example, shape attitudes, behaviors, and family patterns. The structure of a society's economy affects which family members work outside the home, the lifestyles of family members, how material needs are met, the opportunities for children, and even how the labor and decision making will be divided. Clearly, too, the economic rewards of occupations are key determinants in family diversity.

Contemporary patterns of social inequality influence family formation and family relations. Wealth, race, gender, and sexuality produce diverse family forms and household arrangements. Economic conditions and social inequities in the United States make family life difficult. This does not mean that families cannot be warm and loving places but rather that structural conditions sometimes preclude this ideal. In short, these structural arrangements produce a range of family configurations. Important in our view is that differences are the consequence of structured social inequality rather than the result of family values. This structural perspective does not mean, however, that we ascribe to a rigid structural determinism. There is a dialectic between social structure and human response. Family members do not simply respond to their changing situations. To the contrary, people are agents and actors, coping with, adapting to, and changing social structures to meet their needs. Women, men, and children actively produce their family worlds. This process is called **human agency.** We stress both social structure and human agency in this book.

This examination of families also assumes that they must be understood in historical context. What happens to families today is a continuation of what has been happening to them over time.

The Framework

Several organizing principles guide the analysis of families in this new edition. We call this framework "structural diversity." It differs from functionalism, the dominant paradigm of the 1950s, 1960s, and 1970s. Functionalism posited a monolithic model of the family, in which the nuclear family was viewed as the basis of societal organization and cohesion. The nuclear family was considered essential for the proper socialization of children and for the division of labor that enabled women and men to perform their social roles in an orderly manner. Families that deviated from the standard arrangement were thought to be deficient.

The structural-diversity approach challenges the old paradigm on every dimension. Our framework views all families in society as shaped through their interaction with social structures. We explore the close connections between the inner dynamics of family life and the structural forces that shape all families, albeit in different ways. As an example, this edition includes a section in Chapter 4 on the effects of the Great Recession on families.

Our coverage of the nation's various family arrangements is not simply for cultural appreciation. We want to understand why families are diverse.

To summarize, the structural-diversity framework incorporates the following themes (these are elaborated more fully in Chapter 1):

1. Families are socially constructed and historically changing.

2. Family diversity is produced by the same structures that organize society as a whole.

3. Families are embedded in and shaped by interconnected systems of race, class, and gender.

4. Family diversity is constructed through social structure as well as the actions of family members.

5. Understanding families means challenging monolithic ideas that conceive of the family in idealistic ways.

Other Features of the Text

The demythologizing of families is a central theme. To draw students into each topic, chapters begin with common myths about families, many of which students may believe, and contrast these myths with reality. The chapters themselves are clearly organized and written, with many examples of contemporary interest to bolster the analysis. Boxed features focus students' attention on key concepts and trends:

1. **Inside the Worlds of Diverse Families** looks inside microstructural worlds to put a human face on some of the rhythms, textures, and conflicts of everyday family life.

2. **Researching Families** presents the main approaches and methods sociologists use in their studies.

3. **Families in Global Perspective** offers an international view of families, with selected illustrations that have both global and domestic implications.

4. **Technology and the Family** explores the effects of new technologies on different features of family experience.

5. **Emergent Family Trends** provides a look at new family patterns and the meaning they have for future families.

Chapter reviews summarize the main points to help students assimilate the material. And finally, photographs, drawings, and cartoons illustrate many of the ideas and concepts in the text. Relevant websites have been added at the conclusion of each chapter.

New to This Edition

Just as families are socially constructed, so, too, is the scholarship on families. As society experiences major "earthquakes," social science thinking about families is undergoing "seismic shifts" as well. These new intellectual developments have required major revisions of the previous edition. Most significantly, we have sharpened the focus on the macro and micro and emphasized human agency in the analysis. Each chapter has been reorganized to make the themes of the book more explicit. Each chapter includes material on demythologizing, macro (societal forces) impinging on the micro (families), diversity in families, and human agency.

Supplements

INSTRUCTOR'S MANUAL AND TEST BANK (ISBN 0205810640)

Revised by Michael Hillary of the University of Wisconsin, each chapter in the manual includes the following resources: chapter overview; new to this edition; chapter outline; classroom activities and projects; and video and film suggestions. The Test Bank consists of true/false, multiple choice, and essay/discussion questions.

The Instructor's Manual and Test Bank is available to adopters at www.pearsonhighered.com.

MYTEST (ISBN 0205773729)

This computerized software allows instructors to create their own personalized exams, to edit any or all of the existing test questions, and to add new questions. Other special features of this program include random generation of test questions, creation of alternate versions of the same test, scrambling question sequence, and test preview before printing.

The MyTest is available to adopters at www.pearsonhighered.com.

POWERPOINT PRESENTATIONS (ISBN 0205778143)

The PowerPoint slides provide dozens of ready-to-use lecture outlines and include the line art from the text. They are available to adopters at www.pearsonhighered.com.

MYFAMILYKIT

MyFamilyKit is an online resource that contains book-specific practice tests, chapter summaries, audio and video activities, writing and research tutorials, and access to scholarly literature on families through Research Navigator. MyFamilyKit is available with *Diversity in Families,* Ninth Edition, when a MyFamilyKit access code card is shrink-wrapped with the text.

Acknowledgments

We thank Alan Zinn, the picture editor, whose skills and creativity bring life and diversity to our approach. Maxine Baca Zinn thanks Paula Miller of Michigan State University for research assistance. Barbara Wells is grateful for the research assistance by Rachel Bowlin, Brynn Dailey, Kate Deininger, Rachel Foreman, and Maggie Williams. We also thank the following reviewers whose contributions to the preparation of this edition were extremely helpful: Ali Kamali, Missouri Western State University; Michelle Melendres, Mount St. Mary's College, Los Angeles, CA; and Brenda S. Zicha, Mott Community College, Flint, Michigan.

Finally, we wish to thank several special colleagues and friends who have influenced our thinking and helped us sometimes so subtly that they and we were unaware of their contributions at the time: Margaret L. Andersen, Bonnie Thornton Dill, Elizabeth Higginbotham, Steven Gold, Pierrette Hondagneu-Sotelo, Michael A. Messner, Kathryn D. Talley, Doug A. Timmer, and Lynn Weber.

Maxine Baca Zinn
D. Stanley Eitzen
Barbara Wells

chapter **1**

Images, Ideals, and Myths

Families today are very different from what they used to be. They are more diverse and more likely to be formed outside of marriage than in the past. They include a complex array of domestic arrangements, and they are more easily fractured. Family members spend less time together, and parents have less influence over their children. These changes are not unique to the United States. Indeed, they have global dimensions. Throughout the world, every industrialized country is experiencing the same changes. Women's growing economic independence, widespread divorce, and cohabitation have made marriage optional for many people.

Family change and diversity are now highly charged issues, under fire from many quarters. In recent years, no political theme has electrified domestic politics more than the purported breakdown of the family. Some believe that current developments are symptoms of growing social decay. They think the growing diversity of family forms signals the decline of the family and the moral fabric of society. Why do so many lament the state of the family? Why is "family" such a bitterly contested battleground? These are disquieting questions that highlight the public anxiety surrounding the state of contemporary families. In the current climate of rapid social change these questions have become politicized, with competing views of the family vying for public attention.

In this book we present a sociological view of family life in the United States. We ask students to call into question existing social arrangements that many people consider sacred. This requires us to expose the images and myths that influence our perceptions and to replace them with a more inclusive view of families and the social transformations that provide a context for family change. When we understand that families are embedded in larger social and economic structures, we have a more constructive frame of vision for making sense of today's rapid changes in family life.

To begin, we need to be aware that the family is as much a cultural symbol as it is a social form—as much idea as thing (Holstein and Gubrium, 1999:29). Most family images make it difficult to think about family life objectively. As much as we want to be objective, our perceptions are guided by cultural visions of family, by our own family experiences, and, paradoxically, by the very familiarity of family life. Virtually everyone has a family. "Everyone considers himself or herself an expert on his or her own families, yet we are too close to our families to see them dispassionately" (Rosenfeld, 2007:6).

Many social conditions prevent us from being analytical about families. Not only are families familiar and commonplace, they are also mystified. Mystification is the deliberate misdefinition of family matters or "complicated stratagems to keep everyone in the dark" (Laing, 1971:77). This distorts family realities. As a result, we often misunderstand family processes in general and we even have misconceptions about our own families. Objectivity is thus obscured by two different qualities—familiarity and mystification.

Other obstacles that handicap the goal of objectivity are sacredness and secrecy (Skolnick, 1987:58). Families have myths, secrets, and information-processing rules that determine the kinds of communication that goes on—what can be said and, more important, what cannot be said. Families filter information about the outside world and about their own rules of operation. "Secrets" occurring in the realm of interpersonal relationships can occur in any family, remain hidden for decades, and have unsettling, even destructive implications when they are revealed (Brown-Smith, 1998; Imber-Black, 2000).

The family is not merely a social institution; it is a sacred label with strong moral connotations. At the same time, it is the most private of all society's institutions. "Equating family life with the private sphere grants a great deal of autonomy from neighborhood gossips and government regulations" (Hansen, 2005:5). The saying that "a family's business is nobody's business but their [sic] own" is not merely a statement about the right to family privacy; it symbolizes "decency" and other qualities a culture holds dear (Newman and Grauerholz, 2002:16). It also reflects the cultural value of family sacredness. The norm of family privacy gives the family an elusive quality that exists alongside its familiarity. In contemporary Western society, the family is, to use Erving Goffman's (1959) term, a "backstage" area, where people are free to act in ways they would not in public. This accounts for the deceptive quality of family relations. Much of the intimacy of family life remains hidden behind "frontstage" performances—behavior to maintain a proper appearance in front of others (Berardo, 1998; Goffman, 1959). Privacy results in "pluralistic ignorance": We have a backstage view of our own families, but we can judge others only in terms of their frontstage presentations. Often we have "inside" interpretations of other families' "outsides." However, the gap between public norms and private behavior can be wide.

The ideals that we hold about "the family" color not only how we experience family life but also how we speak of our experience. This is not

"Family" evokes a feeling of warm, caring, and psychological nurturance.

unique to our society. Anthropologist Ray L. Birdwhistell (1980) has found that most societies exhibit a gap between family ideals and family realities—between what people *say* about their family behavior and the *real behavior* that takes place in families. This distinction between ideals and behavior, between "talk" and "action," is one of the central problems in the social sciences (Mills, [1940] 1963:467). As we study the family, we cannot ignore the tensions between the way families *are* and the way we *would like them to be*. According to historian John Gillis, "we all have two families, one that we live *with* and another we live *by*. We would like the two to be the same, but they are not" (Gillis, 1996:viii).

Many images surrounding the U.S. family limit our understanding of family life. They distort the real character of life within families. This chapter narrows the gap between family imagery and family reality. We examine the images, ideals, and myths that shape our perceptions of families and our expectations of what our lives should be inside our own families. Then we provide a sociological framework for looking behind the facades of family life. This framework sets the stage for the chapters that follow.

 # Images and Ideals

"Family" in U.S. society is a symbol, a visual image that speaks to us through the senses, including smells, tastes, textures, motions, and sounds from our own remembered experiences (Tufte and Meyerhoff, 1979:11), as well as through our dreams and longings about what family should be. For roughly 150 years before 1960, most Americans shared a common set of beliefs about family life:

> Family should consist of a husband and wife living together with their children. The father should be the head of the family, earn the family's income, and give his name to his wife and children. The mother's main tasks were to support and facilitate her husband's career, guide her children's development, look after the home, and set a moral tone for the family. Marriage was an enduring obligation for better or worse. The husband and wife jointly coped with stresses. Sexual activity was to be kept within the marriage especially for women. As parents, they had an overriding responsibility for the well-being of their children during the early years until their children entered school; they were almost solely responsible. Even later, it was the parents who had the primary duty of guiding their children's education and discipline. (Hamburg, 1993:60)

While these were merely ideals even in 1960, the images they evoke remain with us. They are found in public rhetoric—"in the discourse of politicians, social commentators, and moral leaders; in the talk of everyday interactions, and in movies, television shows and books" (Pyke, 2000:241).

Even in today's world, the cultural ideal of family remains unaltered by dramatic family transformations of the past few decades. The ideal is the presumably stable, two–biological parent, male-breadwinner, female-homemaker family of the 1950s (Demo, 2000:17). In addition to prescribing family structure, the family ideal contains notions about the appropriate values, norms, and beliefs that guide the way families relate to one another (Pyke, 2000:241). "Family" is a warm and happy realm: two heterosexually married adults and their children living together comfortably, and going about their lives in mutually satisfying and harmonious ways. "Family" embodies love, caring, and physical and psychological nurturance in a self-sustaining, nuclear family form—set apart from the troubled world.

The family is quintessentially the private (and some feel the only contemporary private) opportunity for vulnerability, trust, intimacy, and commitment; for lasting pleasant and peaceful relations; and for fullness of being in the human realm. The family thus is located as the physical site for a vast (and repressed) range of human expression, the valid arena (and again perhaps the only arena) in which quality of life is a concern. It is in the family that we find the opportunity for authentic personal life (Tufte and Meyerhoff, 1979:17–18).

At least three distinct images of the family have emerged: the family as haven, the family as fulfillment, and the family as encumbrance.

Family as Haven

This "family as haven" image of a refuge from an impersonal world characterizes the family as a place of intimacy, love, and trust in which individuals may *escape* the competition in modern society. Christopher Lasch (1977:8) has named this image a "haven in a heartless world" and described it as a glorification of private life made necessary by the deprivations experienced in the public world. The image has two distinct themes: love and protection. The sentimentalized notion of the family as a refuge from the cruel world reached its fullest expression in the Victorian period (Millman, 1991:136). The family was idealized as a repository of warmth and tenderness (embodied by the mother) standing in opposition to the competitive and aggressive world of commerce (embodied by the father). The family's task was to protect against the outside world. As the nineteenth century passed, the ideal family became "a womblike inside" to be defended against a corrupting outside (Kenniston, 1977:11).

Family as Fulfillment

The protective image of the family has waned in recent years as the ideals of family fulfillment have taken shape. Today the family is more compensatory than protective. It supplies what is vitally needed but missing in other social arrangements. If work does not provide excitement and stimulation, individuals can turn to their family lives for personal fulfillment. The image of family life today is one of intimacy: spouses, lovers, and even children making us feel alive and invigorated. In short, the family brightens up a social landscape that might otherwise seem gray (Demos, 1979:57). Today's ideal of intensive parenting—large amounts of quality time spent interacting with children—is seen as both critical to children's development and intrinsically fulfilling for parents (Bianchi et al., 2006:126).

The image is still that of a haven, but now it is a haven of primary fulfillment and meaningful experience. The modern emphasis on "self-actualization" and never-ending change in adulthood places more value on being able to choose freely than on commitment. Today, we no longer speak of "true love" as a love we would die for, or die without. Rather, we talk of love that is "meaningful" or "alive" because it involves "honesty" and it stimulates us to discover ourselves and to change (Millman, 1991:140). Self-fulfillment, enjoyment, and rejuvenation—the essential qualities of modern family life—may be contrasted with an older morality of duty, responsibility, work, and self-denial. Duty has been replaced with the obligation to *enjoy* family life. The "fun" morality expressed currently by the advertising industry glorifies the family united in pursuit of common activities that are enjoyed by all.

Family as Encumbrance

Loading the family with compensatory needs has created still another image—this one negative. The anti-image of the family is new. For the first time in U.S. history, we blame the family for inhibiting our full human development. This view calls for *freedom from* domestic relationships. Some research has found that workers escape demanding and stressful family relations by spending more time in the workplace and less time at home (Hochschild, 1997).

This image also views family relations as inhibiting the quest for a full experience of self. In a culture in which the "restless self" must be kept unfettered, flexible, and ready to change, attachments must be broken when they no longer permit continual development (Millman, 1991:142–143).

Monogamous marriage can become boring and stultifying. After all, variety is the "spice of life." Responsibility for children can compound the problem. The needs and requirements of the young are so constant, so pressing, that they leave little space for adults who must attend to them. "Spice" and "space" are, in fact, the qualities for which we yearn. In this anti-image, the family severely limits our access to either one (Demos, 1979:58).

Images and Reality

These three images of family life are different faces of reality. In each image the family is the primary institution through which the goals of personal growth and self-fulfillment are achieved. The differences lie in the effects of family on the individual. In the first and second images the effects are beneficial; in the third they are adverse. What do these images omit, and what kinds of distortions do they foster? All three images separate the family from society, creating, in Demos's words, "a sense of inside out in which the family is not experienced in its own right but in relation to other circumstances and other pleasures" (Demos, 1979:58).

Although family imagery has undergone great changes in recent decades, family and society remain polarized. The family still represents a symbolic opposition to work and business. Relations inside the family are idealized as nurturing, whereas those outside the family—especially in business and work—are seen as just the opposite. Families symbolize relationships of affection and love that are based on cooperation rather than competition (Collier et al., 1982:34).

Popular images of relationships between husbands and wives and between parents and children are overwhelmingly positive, typically of biological mothers and fathers playing with children or a family sharing a holiday dinner or going on vacation. Where are the other images of family life, such as sibling rivalry, divorce, or other common family conflicts? (Ferguson, 2007:2)

Outside circumstances increasingly produce inner family conflicts. Social and economic conditions in the larger society make it difficult to attain the idealized family experience. For example, as women have joined the paid labor force in great numbers, husbands *and* most wives have jobs and families. As they pursue demanding careers or work at jobs with long hours, they may have little time or energy to devote to the family. (See Box 1.1.) For women, the difficulties of balancing work and family are widely recognized, and the image of "superwoman" has become a new cultural ideal. The superwoman who appears repeatedly in magazines and on television commercials meshes her multiple roles perfectly. If she has children, she is a supermother, able to work 40 hours a week, keep the house clean and neat, entertain, keep physically fit by jogging or taking aerobics classes, and have a meaningful relationship with the superfather, who

BOX 1.1 Emergent Family Trends

These Days, the Picture-Perfect American Family Just Doesn't Exist

With the debut of the Palins before a nation-wide audience, a presidential campaign that was supposed to be about the economy, Iraq or even race has unexpectedly become—for a little while, at least—a conversation about family. But even before the surprising news of 17-year-old Bristol Palin's pregnancy, the Obamas, Bidens, and McCains had spent an inordinate amount of precious convention time introducing us to their loved ones: videos, scripted shout-outs, smiling tableaus as the confetti came down. Both parties clearly thought that it was crucial for the candidates to show how deeply they value their family lives.

But if the candidates wished to convince viewers that their families were just like ours, they were undone by a 21st-century reality: There is no typical family anymore—at least not in terms of who lives in the household and how they are related. Alaska Gov. Sarah Palin noted as much. While introducing her clan to a cheering crowd of the Republican faithful, the GOP vice presidential nominee said, "From the inside, no family ever seems typical. That's how it is with us."

In fact, the diversity of American households was the unspoken lesson of both conventions, as four strikingly different kinds of families came into view. First, the Obamas. The Democratic nominee's half-sister, Maya Soetoro-Ng, spoke to the Denver crowd, highlighting his biracial family background, dominated by an often single mother and a largely absent father. Obama's wife Michelle also took a powerful turn at the podium, focusing on her husband's biography but also playing up her own high-powered career and modest roots. The Bidens were introduced to a national audience that week as well, a stepfamily formed after the tragic death of the senator's first wife. With the McCains, we see another stepfamily, formed this time after the senator's divorce. Their family also includes Bridget, a daughter adopted from Bangladesh. And the Palins bring to the stage two working parents with five children, including a pregnant teenager and an infant with Down syndrome.

Divorce itself is not new to the presidential politics—Ronald Reagan and John F. Kerry both campaigned with second wives by their sides—but never has such an extraordinary range of family histories been center stage.

A HALF-CENTURY AGO, WHEN THE TWO-PARENT, breadwinner-homemaker, first-marriage family was at its peak, all of the candidates would have conformed to the same mold. In the 1950s, iconic TV shows—the ones that you can still find while channel-surfing—celebrated the Cleavers and their ilk. Ward went to work and earned enough so that his single paycheck could keep June, Wally and the Beaver happily provided for at home. Sentiment against divorce in public life was so strong that New York Gov. Nelson Rockefeller's presidential aspirations were stymied in 1964 because he had recently divorced and remarried.

But the Cleavers are only available in reruns now, and the prominence of the breadwinner-homemaker family rapidly declined in the last third of the 20th century. Married women moved into the workforce, divorce rates rose, and more children were born outside of marriage.

That traditional family unit has been replaced by a wide variety of living arrangements. Today, only 58 percent of children live with two married, biological parents. Many others live with stepparents or with single parents. Even having a pregnant teen in the home is not that unusual: About one out of six 15-year-old girls will give birth before reaching age 20, according to the National Center for Health Statistics.

The candidates seemed to realize that none of their families is typical in the old sense. None of them tried to look like the '50s family. Instead, they focused on being "typical" in a different, 21st-century sense: They worked hard to show us how emotionally close they are.

Over the past few decades, the emotional rewards of family life have become more important to Americans, as compared to the rewards of bringing home a paycheck or raising children. In a 2001 national survey conducted by the National Marriage Project, more than 80 percent of women in their 20s agreed with the statement that it's more important "to have a husband who can communicate about his deepest feelings than to have a husband who makes a good living."

Personal satisfaction, the feeling that your family is helping you grow and develop as a person, communication, openness: These are the kinds of criteria people use in evaluating their family lives. Practical concerns still matter, but if that's all that holds your family together these days, people may view it askance. Given the demographic diversity of American families, emotional closeness, not who the Census takers find in your home, has become the new gold standard.

And so all four aspiring first and second families, despite their differences, appealed to the voters in much the same way. Each wanted to show how much support

(continued)

(Box 1.1 continued)

and warmth they provide to one other. What matters here is not whether your current wife is your first or second but whether you draw emotional strength from her. So Obama refers to his wife as "my rock" and McCain says of his wife, Cindy, "she's more my inspiration than I am hers." What matters is not whether your teenage daughter is pregnant but whether you provide loving support to her. So Palin and her husband issued a statement assuring the nation, "As Bristol faces the responsibilities of adulthood, she knows she has our unconditional love and support." What matters is being a loving, devoted father, even after the tragedy of losing one's spouse. So Biden's son Beau introduced his father to the Democrats in Denver as "my friend, my father, my hero."

This is not to say that the modern family is a free-for-all, choose-your-own-Thanksgiving-guest-list adventure for everyone. Social conservatives, for instance, still hold the family to stricter moral standards, social conservatives tend to disapprove of divorce except in cases of infidelity or desertion. They teach their children to abstain from sex until after marriage. But the religious right's reaction to the news of Bristol Palin's pregnancy shows they are willing to embrace a family that deviates from their ideals if the parents are willing to support each other and their children through difficult times. As former Baptist preacher, Arkansas governor and GOP presidential candidate Mike Huckabee said during the convention, "People of faith aren't people of perfection."

WHAT IS IMPORTANT TODAY, IN OTHER words, is not who you live with—and how you're legally bound to them—but rather how you feel about them.

Apart from the race and gender hurdles being trampled, the 2008 campaign has also shown that Americans, whether from red or blue states, have embraced a broad definition of what constitutes a family. Some traditionalists may lament the decline of the first-marriage, single-earner households. But diversity, in this case, has clear virtues. Would we really want to go back to an era when a divorce disqualified a person from running for president?

Of course, Americans' tolerance for family diversity still has limits; many voters, for instance, find it difficult to accept gay and lesbian unions. In 2004, Mary Cheney, the lesbian daughter of Vice President Cheney, sat in the audience with her partner as her father delivered his acceptance speech at the Republican convention. But the couple did not join the rest of the Cheney family on stage afterward and did not sit with the vice president when President Bush delivered his speech the following evening.

If the trend toward embracing greater diversity continues, however, convention stages a generation from now could easily look quite different from this year's. We could all be watching as a gay or lesbian candidate shouts out to his or her "rock" or "inspiration": a same-sex partner, smiling from the VIP box.

Source: Cherlin, Andrew J. "Public Display" (2008) *The Washington Post National Weekly Edition* (September 15–21): 25–26.

is both productive and nurturing and who shares fully in the work of running the household. Such superparents have quality time with their children (Galinsky, 1986:20). This upbeat image of the modern superfamily that "has it all" obscures the different and often contradictory requirements imposed by work systems and family systems.

Popular cultural images no longer describe family life, if indeed they ever did. Nevertheless, the general public clings to romanticized images of the family. Even though family images often contrast with most family forms and practices, we persist in thinking about the family as a peaceful harbor, a shelter in the storm. This vision of family life has amazing staying power even if the underpinnings that allowed it to exist have eroded (Casper and Bianchi, 2002:xvi; McGraw and Walker, 2004:174). Sociologist Dorothy Smith calls the idealized family image the **Standard North American Family (SNAF),** an ideological code that distorts family reality and glorifies the two-parent family model (Smith, 1993). The image of an insular group consisting of two parents and children is a class- and race-specific ideal, which ignores the reality of family life in many sectors of the population. Social and economic forces make the ideal inaccessible to all, yet the two-parent family is the universally expected family form (Baca Zinn, 1990; Hansen, 2005:4).

The symbolic families that shape our thinking are misleading when they become standards against which we measure ourselves. They become normative (in the sense of obligatory) and operate as models affecting a great range of action and response. Not only is the symbolic family the measuring rod that shapes public policy; it guides internal evaluations of our own success and failure as family members.

We live in an "information" society filled with images and messages. Much of the vast flood of imagery deals with family life and is aimed at families. The mass media entertains us with endless dramatizations of family normality and deviance. From scenes of domestic perfection exhibited on television by the Cleavers, the Bradys, and the Huxtables, we have been indoctrinated with im-

The mythical monolithic model.

ages of a family life that never existed (Taylor, 1992:64). Certainly, we are past the days of the perfect mom and all-wise dad. Today's television families are infinitely more realistic. Soap-opera families and programs like *The Simpsons, Everybody Loves Raymond, George Lopez*, and *Family Guy* present the nitty-gritty of family life: money problems, divorce, sex, and sibling rivalry. There have also been popular television shows in recent years about urban single people: *Seinfeld, Friends, Sex and the City, Will and Grace*, and *Two and a Half Men* (Lichter and Qian, 2004:1). Although today's television shows reflect diverse family structures, the families we "live by" continue to shape our expectations. We *expect* families to be happy and harmonious, to soothe away the cares of life outside the home. Disappointments in the home then become a source of inadequacy when family life fails to measure up to the imagined harmony of other families (Lerner, 1982:141; Scanzoni, 2004). Stephanie Coontz, the author of *The Way We Never Were* (1992), a book about family images, myths, and half-truths, finds that guilt is a common reaction to the discord between images and reality:

> Even as children, my students and colleagues tell me, they felt guilty because their families did not act like those on television. Perhaps the second most common reaction is anger, a sense of betrayal or rage when you and your family cannot live as the myths suggest you should be able to. (Coontz, 1992:6)

To question the idea of the happy family is not to say that love and joy cannot also be found in family life. Rather, the idealized fantasy overlooks the tensions and ambivalence that are unavoidable in everyday life. Despite the problems resulting from the "family harmony" image, this model is presented to the public by science, art, and the mass media. Even more critical, the model is used by our legal and social experts and by the nation's policy makers. The result is that the family is an "impossibly overloaded, guilt creating institution" (Birdwhistell, 1980:466).

The Mythical U.S. Family

Family images are a composite of several closely related but distinct myths about the family. **Myths** are beliefs that are held uncritically and without examination or scrutiny (Crosby, 1985). These myths are bound up with nostalgic memory, selective perception, and cultural values concerning what is typical and true about the family. We will address the most prevailing myths that are popularly accepted as true in our society. In subsequent chapters we call into question the prevalent beliefs and folk wisdom that, if left unchallenged and unanswered, will become even more entrenched in the American mind as "the way families are." In this book, we use new knowledge as a "reply to myth" (Crosby, 1985): that is, as a way of challenging the commonly held myths about families in society.

The Myth of a Stable and Harmonious Family of the Past

Most people think that families of the past were better than families of the present. In our collective imagination, families in past times were more stable, better adjusted, and happier. There are two reasons for this flawed belief. First, we tend to be selective about what we remember. In other words, we romanticize the past. Second, extraordinary changes in family life *have* occurred over the past few decades. A backward-looking approach makes it seem as if the families of the twenty-first century are in serious trouble. However, public anxiety about families is not new:

> One thing that never seems to change is the notion that family is not what it used to be. Families past are presented to us not only as more stable but as more authentic than families present. We imagine their times to have been the days when fathers were fathers, mothers true mothers, and children still children. Families past are invariably portrayed as simpler, less problematic. We imagine them not only as large but as better integrated, untroubled by generational divisions, close to kin, respectful of the old, honoring the dead. (Gillis, 1996:3)

Contemporary families cannot measure up to romantic notions about "family values."

On closer examination, this glorified family is a historical fiction that never existed (Coontz, 1999a). Such nostalgic images of "traditional" families mask the inevitable dilemmas that accompany family life.

Two points must be made about the stubborn myth of a vanished family past. First, family historians have found that there has never been a golden age of the family. Families have never been perfect. Across time, families have experienced outside pressures and internal family conflicts. There has always been desertion by spouses, illegitimate children, and certainly spouse and child abuse. Divorce rates were lower, but this does not mean that love was stronger in the past. Many women died earlier from pregnancy complications, which kept divorce rates lower and which meant that many children were raised by single parents or stepparents, just as now. Divorces were relatively uncommon also because of strong religious prohibitions and community norms against divorce. As a result, many "empty" marriages continued without love and happiness to bind them.

To judge marriage of the past as better than contemporary marriage is to ignore historical changes. We expect more of marriage than did our forebears, but this fact makes modern marriage neither better nor worse, only different. Our challenge is to avoid nostalgia for a mythic past and examine the real problems facing today's families (Mintz, 2004). Chapters 2 and 3 examine the new social history of the family, which provides a far different picture of the past.

The Myth of Separate Worlds

The notion that family is a place to escape from the outside world is "the myth of separate worlds" (Kanter, 1984). It makes a distinction between "public" and "private" realms with family as the "haven in a heartless world." Here, social relations are thought to be different from those in the world at large. This myth assumes that families are self-sufficient units relatively free from outside social pressures. Families that are not self-sufficient are judged inadequate.

The idea that family is set apart from the world at large developed during industrialization (Zaretsky, 1976). In response to new economic demands, families certainly changed as communities loosened their grip on family life (see Chapter 2); yet families remain deeply linked to economic and political structures.

The idea that families exist in opposition to the rest of the world is a false dichotomy with contradictory expectations. Although we want the family to protect us *from* society, we also expect families to prepare us *for* society. The myth of separate worlds is ambivalent. On the one hand, the family is considered a private world, protecting its members from the outside, especially from the trials of work. On the other hand, families are expected to adapt to the conditions of work, to socialize children to become competent workers, and to provide emotional support to workers to enhance their effectiveness. The myth of separate worlds ignores the many ways in which the wider society impinges on family functioning. Families shape themselves in response to the demands of jobs, careers, schools, and other social institutions.

In our family lives we feel family strains from conflicts posed by the relationship between family and broader social systems, yet the *popular* conception of the family remains that of a special enclave, detached from the outside world. This split vision is rooted in certain social realities. Modern society does demarcate public and private spheres, with the family representing the quintessentially private arena. The vision of the family as a private reserve, however, does not prevent society from intruding on every aspect of family life. There are close and sometimes combustible connections between the internal life of families and the organization of paid work, state-organized welfare and legal systems, schools, and day care centers (Thorne, 1992:5). Family life is constantly squeezed by the demands of these and other institutions. This is why we must reject the assumption that the family is a "haven in a heartless world." It cannot function as a haven when outside forces encroach on it (Lasch, 1975).

The myth of separate worlds leads to the belief that the family survives or sinks by its own resources and fitness—a kind of **family Darwinism** that blames families for structural failure (Polakow, 1993:39). This myth ignores the harsh effect of economic conditions (e.g., poverty or near-poverty), unemployment and underemployment, and downward mobility or the threat of downward mobility. It ignores the social inequalities (due to racism, sexism, ageism, homophobia) that distribute resources differently.

Although the family is under pressure to appear freestanding, all families are entangled with other social institutions—the workplace, the welfare system, and the schools. Agencies and people outside the family have taken over many functions that were once performed by the family. Children, for example, are raised not only by their parents but also by teachers, doctors, social workers, and television. A study of the family commissioned by the Carnegie Corporation more than three decades ago found that parents have less authority than those with whom they share the tasks of raising their children. Most parents deal with persons from outside agencies from a position of inferiority or helplessness. They must compete with "experts," who are armed with special credentials, who are entrenched in their professions, and who have far more power in their institutions than do the parents (Kenniston, 1977).

Just as societal changes have weakened parents' authority, so have other large-scale changes revealed flaws in treating family and society in opposition. Globalization and the changes it produces in the economy, the workplace, and the nation-state are among the most important forces shaping family life today (see Chapter 4). Global forces affect families in profound ways. For example, increasingly global job markets produce uncertainty for workers and their families as jobs are outsourced (Karraker, 2008:19). Globalization creates greater mobility in the search for work (see Chapter 12). It increases nonstandard work schedules, and it makes for longer work hours for most workers. Political globalization undermines the ability of nation-states and their various governmental agencies to control their own economy, the very nature of their jobs, and the income needed for family maintenance. And as Edgar explains, globalization threatens family control of its members. With the anonymity of the World Wide Web, the global networks of interacting strangers, and the freedom of workers to move as markets require, globalization forever alters the life course and interpersonal relationships of millions around the world (Edgar, 2004). Such trends heighten the connections between families and other structural forces.

The Myth of the Monolithic Family Form

We all know what the family is *supposed* to look like. It should resemble the 1950s Ozzie and Harriet form. This uniform image has been imprinted on our brains since childhood, through children's books, schools, radio, television, movies, and newspapers; through the lectures, if not the examples, of many of our parents; and through the speeches, if not the examples, of many of our politicians. Invariably, the image is of a White, middle-class, heterosexual father as breadwinner, mother as homemaker, and children at home living in a one-family house. This monolithic image of "the normal American family" is a stick against which all families are measured (Pyke, 2000:240). This model represents a small proportion of U.S. households. Less than 10 percent of households consist of married couples with children in which only the husband works. Dual-income families with children made up more than twice as many households. Even families with two incomes and no children outnumbered the conventional family by almost two to one (AmeriStat, 2003c; Lichter and Qian, 2004:1).

The mythical model of the typical U.S. family embodies three distinctive features: (1) the family is a nuclear unit; (2) it consists of mother, father, and their children; and (3) it exhibits a gendered division of labor. The first two features are closely related. The nuclear family is separate from society and independent from kin. It consists of a married couple and their children living in a home of their own. The third distinguishing feature of "the family" is its assumed sexual division of labor: "a breadwinner husband, freed for and identified with activities in a separate economic sphere, and a full-time wife and mother whose being is often equated with the family itself" (Thorne, 1992:7).

Although this family type now represents a small minority of U.S. families, major social and cultural forces continue to assume this singular form. In reality, "this is an age of increasing family diversity" (Marks, 2006:62). It now makes more sense to talk about "types of families" (Mabry et al., 2004:93). Contemporary family types represent a multitude of family formations including single-parent households, stepparent families, extended multigenerational households, gay and straight cohabiting couples, child-free couples, transnational families, multiracial families, lone householders with ties to various families, and many other kinds of families (see Box 1.2). The tension between this diverse array of family groupings and the idealized 1950s family creates disagreement about what makes up families. The question of what constitutes a family, where its boundaries are drawn, and who does or does not belong to it at any point in time triggers many more questions. In fact, there is no consensus among social agencies, professionals, and ordinary people on what currently constitutes a family (Aerts, 1993:7; Beck and Beck-Gernsheim, 2004:449). Even our nation's most prominent political figures do not live in picture-perfect families. (See Box 1.1.)

One way of moving beyond the distortions in the monolithic model is to distinguish between families and households. **Family** refers to a set of social relationships, while **household** refers to residence or living arrangements (Jarrett and Burton, 1999; Rapp, 1982). To put it another way, a family is a kinship group, whereas a household is a residence group that carries out domestic functions (Holstein and Gubrium,

BOX 1.2 Emergent Family Trends

The New Demographics of Families

It is clear from U.S. Census projections that U.S. families are changing. It is also clear that, despite the fact that we have been aware that these changes have been coming for the past 20 years, family scientists have done little in the area of theory development to help us understand how to address these emerging families. Some of the most important issues that researchers need to address center on understanding what the new families will look like. However, one problem with the area of family studies is that we are still using theory and theoretical constructs from the 1950s in the twenty-first century to explain behaviors that are unique to this era. For example, recent trends in U.S. families suggest the following about families of the near future:

- At least one-half of all children will spend at least one-quarter of their lives in female-headed households.

- The new families will experience severely limited economic growth and growth opportunities.

- The new families will be characterized by a semi-extended family form made up of fictive kin with some ties to the family members' original homelands.

- The new families will more than likely live in households that have two primary languages for at least two generations.

- The new families will involve at least a definite recognition of sexually variant relatives and/or parents.

- The new families will consist primarily of people of color.

- The new families will have social customs, beliefs, attitudes, and communication forms that researchers have not previously examined using the current theoretical constructs.

- The new families will have unique adaptations to currently mainstream religious beliefs—they may not all be Christians.

- The new families will probably have some form of major involvement with governmental institutions (e.g., immigration, homeland security, criminal justice, public welfare, and social services), not by choice in most cases.

- The new families will be stigmatized in part because we in the scientific community will fail to adapt our research and theories as necessary to understand these families.

Source: Webb, Farrell J., "The New Demographics of Families." In *Sourcebook of Family Theories and Research*, Vern L. Bengston, Alan C. Acock, Katherine R. Allen, Peggye Dilworth-Anderson, and David M. Klein (eds.). Thousand Oaks, CA: Sage Publications, 2005, p. 101.

1999:31). A good example of the importance of distinguishing between family and household is the restructuring of family obligations and household composition after divorce (Ferree, 1991:107). Family members do not always live in the same households. When separation and divorce break the bonds between mother and father, bonds between children and parents can remain intact. Consequently, an increasing number of families extend across two or more households, generations, marital and legal statuses, blood ties, and even continents! People may live apart and still be in the same family. Therefore, household and family may overlap, but they are not the same thing. People may share a household and not consider themselves a family, and people may feel like a family while not living together (Bridenthal, 1981:48). (See Figure 1.1 on changes in households between 1970 through 2005.)

Although family relations and household arrangements today are more varied than at any time in history, diversity is not new. Throughout history, major social forces have created a wide range of family configurations. Today, the changes most responsible for the proliferation of family types are (1) global forces causing families and their members to cross geographic, social, and cultural borders in search of employment, (2) women's unprecedented participation in the labor force, (3) new patterns in marriage and divorce; and (4) a decline in the number of children women bear. These developments have added to the emergence of new family types.

Perhaps the most striking change in the national profile of families is the rise in mother-only households and the poverty that often accompanies them. The vast majority of single-parent households are maintained by mothers. Patterns of gender inequality in the larger society contribute to "the feminization of poverty," the growing impoverishment of women (and their children) in U.S. society. Many children will not experience the idealized two-parent household during major portions of their childhood years. Less than 50 percent of children in the United States live in "traditional nuclear families" that have two biological parents married to each other, full-blown siblings only, and no other household members (Demo et al., 2005).

A growing trend toward the maintenance of households by persons living alone or with others to whom they are not related has also contributed to a greater variety of living arrangements. Factors contributing to the surge of nonfamily households include the increased tendency of young adults to move away from home at an early

Figure 1.1
U.S. Household Types, 1970 and 2005

Source: Mc Falls, Joseph A. Jr., *Population: A Lively Introduction*, 5th ed. *Population Bulletin.* 62 (1). Washington, DC, Population Reference Bureau, March 2007, p. 18.

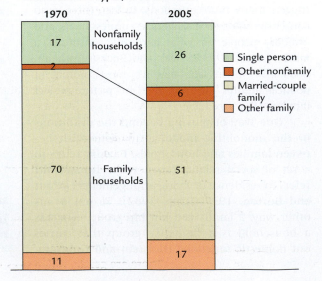

U.S. Household Types, 1970 and 2005

age, postponement of marriage, the continued high rate of divorce, and increasing numbers of elderly persons living alone.

Economic and demographic forces are creating other changes as well. The shifting racial and ethnic balance of the population is also transforming U.S. family patterns. At the beginning of the twentieth century, fewer than one in five Americans belonged to a racial or ethnic minority. Today, racial ethnics make up one-fourth of the U.S. population. They will account for one-third of the population in the year 2030. Some of the most significant differences between various minority groups and dominant groups involve variations in family and household structure (Schwede et al., 2005). As the United States grows ever more diverse in racial and ethnic composition, family diversity will remain evident. One type of family—made up of U.S.-born Whites—is becoming less dominant, and the future characteristics of the family will increasingly be influenced by what immigrant and minority families look like and do (Lichter and Qian, 2004:2; Marks, 2006) (see Chapter 4). Race and class are important structural factors underlying the diversity of family forms (see Box 1.2).

Research confirms that the United States has never had one distinct family form. What emerges when we refer to the U.S. family is a vast array of possible *families* (Elliott and Umberson, 2004:34). This has led some social scientists to conclude that "the American family" does not exist:

> The first thing to remember about the American family is that it doesn't exist. Families exist. All kinds of families in all kinds of economic and marital situations, as all of us can see.... The American family? Just which American family did you have in mind? Black or white, large or small, wealthy or poor, or somewhere in between? Did you mean a father-headed, mother-headed, or childless family? First or second time around? Happy or miserable? Your family or mine? (Howe, 1972:11)

The Myth of a Unified Family Experience

Partly because we glorify the family, we assume that family members experience the family in the same way—that family and individuals are merged and that they have common needs, common experiences, and common meanings. This conception of "the family" as a unified group is a "glued together family" (Sen, 1983, cited in Ferree, 1991), treated as if it were a single unit with a single set of interests.

New research has cut through romantic assumptions about family and household unity, showing that women, men, and children experience their families in different ways. The best way to understand "within-family diversity" is to "decompose" the family—that is, to break it down into its essential components (Mitchell, 1966). Two key components of all families are the gender system and the age system. These two systems produce different realities for men and women as well as for children and adults. These systems shape every activity that has to do with daily family living, such as the division of household labor, leisure activities, the giving and receiving of nurturance and emotional support, decisions about consumption, and employment. In addition, age and gender often produce different and conflicting interests among family members. This means that family experience varies dramatically for children and adults and for women and men (Wolfe, 1990).

Jessie Bernard's classic work on marriage revealed that every marital union actually contains two marriages—his and hers—and that the two do not always coincide (Bernard, 1971). Researchers who ask husbands and wives identical questions about their marriages often get quite different replies, even to fairly simple, factual questions. The family as a **gendered institution** (Acker, 1992) is one of the most important themes in family research. There are gender differences in every aspect of family living, including decision making, household division of labor, and forms of intimacy and sexuality. Similarly, divorce affects female and male family members differently. Girls and boys experience their childhoods differently as there are different expectations, different rules, and different punishments according to gender. **Patriarchy** is the term used to refer to social relations in which men are dominant over women. Patriarchy in the larger society gives shape to a family system in which men are accorded more prestige and more privileges and in which they wield greater power.

Knowing that family experiences vary by gender, we can better understand the problems associated with the image of the family as a harbor from life's storms. The family is idealized as a personal retreat, yet for most women it is a workplace, a place of domestic labor and child care. For whom, then, is the home a refuge—a nurturant haven? Barrie Thorne has provided the following answer:

> For the vast majority of women, the home is a place of considerable work, even when they are employed full-time out of the home. Researchers have found that women work in and out of the home an average of fifteen hours more than men each week, which adds up to an extra month of twenty-four-hour days a year. (Thorne, 1992:18)

Caring for families and caring about them is strongly gendered. Adult women are providers of care but less likely to be recipients of such care. Far more than men, women are the caretakers and the caregivers that maintain family bonds (Aldous, 1991:661). A full understanding of family life requires that we attend to multiple experiences, multiple voices, and different family realities.

The Myth of Family Consensus

The idealized picture of family life is flawed in still another way. It assumes that families are based on "companionate" or "consensual" relations—in other words, on a harmony of interest among family members. This myth neglects a fundamental family paradox. Family life can be contentious due to the following conditions: (1) power relations within the family; (2) competitive aspects of family relations; (3) new patterns of work and leisure, which lead to different activities for family members; and (4) the intense emotional quality of family life.

Cultural mythology has it that the family is a place of love and solidarity. The reality is that people do not always find nurturance and support in their families. Like workplaces and other social arenas, families are themselves sites of negotiation, exchange, power, conflict, and inequality (Cohen and MacCartney, 2004:186). Behind closed doors, the other face of the family may be the opposite of the myth. In marriage, for example, the political reality of husband–wife relationships is evident in household division of labor, in family decision making, and "in extreme form in incidents of wife abuse" (Thorne, 1982:13). Parents' disproportionate power over their offspring produces family strains at all social levels.

Recognizing the political underpinnings of family life does not discount the solidarity and support found within the family realm. Families are sites of deep contradictions. Disagreement, competition, and conflict can coexist with order, stability, and cooperation (Mabry et al., 2004:95). Love and conflict often become entangled, creating an "arena of struggle" between family members (Hartmann, 1981).

Although we commonly romanticize the family as a place where all is shared and where nobody measures, research reveals that money matters are a common source of family strife (Funderberg, 2003). According to Marcia Millman, there is probably more counting in families than in other settings:

> In many ways, families display the same hard traits of the market. One sees this expressed in the ways we use money, often unconsciously, to control children, punish estranged spouses, measure a parent's true feelings for us, buy freedom from relationships, or stop a partner from leaving. Furthermore, in the family as in the workplace, there is a system of exchange with a perpetual accounting and sanctions for not performing as expected. But because of our image of the family as a place of love and sharing (and our deep wish that it be so) we underestimate the conflicts of interest and rivalries that are common, if not inevitable, and make light of the deadly serious bookkeeping. (Millman, 1991:9)

The emotional quality of family life can produce deep ambivalence because emotional relationships inevitably contain negative as well as positive feelings. This combination of love and antagonism sets intimate relationships apart from less intimate ones. Therefore, ambiguity is an integral part of family experience.

Because intimate relationships are intense, they can create a cauldron-like setting, one that is "overheated by its seclusiveness, specialization, and uniqueness" (Tufte and Meyerhoff, 1979:17). The family may then become less a refuge and more like a prison from which growing numbers of "refugees" (runaway children, permanently defecting

"My family likes to set up our grudges at Thanksgiving, stew over them through December, then take our revenge at Christmas."

adolescents, wives, and husbands) seek escape. Closeness, privacy, and intimacy can also create disorder and distance among family members.

Families may provide emotional support and nurturance for their members, but they may also inspire violence and brutality. Many family specialists argue that it would be hard to find a group or institution in U.S. society in which violence is more of an everyday occurrence than within the family. For example, most murder cases involve relatives or people involved in some intimate way. Violence is not found in all families, but there is an emotional dynamic to family life that can generate violence (see Chapter 10). We must acknowledge this fact if we are to understand the complexity of families in our society.

> Until we admit that families may exhibit the most brutalizing, abusing, dangerous, and inhumane types of interaction patterns as well as loving, caring, protecting, helping, sustaining, and nurturing types of relationships, we will fail to understand the range of human interaction that takes place within families. (Eichler, 1981:384)

Family life is fraught with disparities. Families may provide emotional support for some family members but not for others. Or the support derived from the family may vary by age and gender. Some family members may derive support at great cost to others in the family. In addition, new patterns of work and leisure mean that family members are developing interests and activities that are different from other members of their families. In many cases, this leads to conflicting interests and expectations rather than convergence and mutual support. As a result, the companionship function of families comes under increasing stress (Coates, 2003:197).

Families are paradoxical. They may provide support for their members, but that support is neither uniform nor always present. Lillian Rubin has captured well the duality of family experience: "The family as an institution is both oppressive and protective and, depending on the issue, is experienced sometimes one way, sometimes the other—often in some mix of the two by most people who live in families" (Rubin, 1976:6).

The Myth of Family Decline as the Cause of Social Problems

Partly because of the myths about the past, and partly because the family has changed so much in the last few decades, many social analysts conclude that the "breakdown of the family" is responsible for many societal ills.

> Each day, the media serve up new stories and statistics documenting that marriage is going the way of the horse and buggy, that we are becoming a nation without fathers and that, as a result, children are suffering and society is falling apart. The breakdown of the family is taken for granted as a simple social fact. The only question is who or what is to blame and how can we restore the family to the way we imagine it used to be. (Mason et al., 2003:1)

In recent years, the definition of the family has been the focus of public debates. At the end of the twentieth century, rhetoric about the eroding "traditional family" became broadly accepted as a way of explaining such social ills as poverty, crime, drug abuse, teen pregnancy, and gang violence. In the early 1990s, former Vice President Dan Quayle added to the national anxiety by denouncing television character

Murphy Brown for having a baby without a husband. Declaring that unwed motherhood was destroying the nation, Quayle blamed the 1992 Los Angeles riots on family decline. Although such hysteria has subsided, ideas about family decline and social problems persist (Mintz, 2004).

Welfare reform enacted in 1966 included the goal of promoting the two-parent family. The Personal Responsibility and Welfare Reform Act declared in its preamble that the married, two-parent family is the foundation of a successful society (Scanzoni, 2004:10). According to this logic, the two-parent family is the basis of social order. This family form is extolled as the one in which children are best socialized to become good citizens and in which women and men perform the roles essential to society. Any change in family structure is viewed as moral decline—that is, a loss of "family values." But the debate about declining family values is really about a decline in a particular family *structure* (Dill et al., 1993). The family-values refrain is nothing more than a way of distinguishing the two-parent family from other family types. Single-parent families produced by divorce and unwed motherhood are denounced as selfish practices that are damaging children, destroying families, and tearing apart the fabric of society. Put very generally, the family-decline position is that "as a result of hedonistic individualism, we are letting our 'family values' slip away and what is needed now is nothing short of a moral rearmament on behalf of parental responsibility. From this movement come proposals to make divorce more difficult and to discourage strongly or even punish giving birth outside of marriage" (Mason et al., 2003:3).

Today's public debate about social problems and family decline centers on legalizing gay marriage (see Chapter 8). Even as public acceptance grows and state after state approves same-sex marriage, this debate remains contentious with opponents defending a narrow definition of family. At issue here is not family structure as in the debate about single parents, but family *composition*. Opponents argue that marriage should be restricted to heterosexual couples. They argue that same-sex marriage violates the definition of marriage, is harmful to children, and is harmful to society. As a result, legalizing gay marriage destroys the family and threatens social order. Like the national debates of the last century, this unfolding dispute highlights "the way in which a society defines family and the implications of that definition for membership in families" (Bolte, 2006:175).

What is wrong with the claim that family decline is the root cause of many social problems? This reasoning is flawed in two fundamental respects. First, it reverses the relationship between family and society by treating the family as the building block of society rather than *a product of social conditions.* The notion that changing families threaten society is a form of social reductionism. In this simple model of society, the family is the basic unit, the bedrock of society that "causes political and economic institutions to work or not to work" (Young, 1994:89). In reality, families are *situated within the larger political and economic conditions.* Family units are not responsible for social order (or disorder) in the larger society. Second, it ignores the structural reasons for family breakdown. Those who persist in seeing the current shifts in family life as the source of disarray have it backward (Stacey, 1994). Divorce and single parenthood are the *consequences* of social and economic dislocations rather than the cause, as some would have us believe. Disappearing jobs, declining earnings, and low-wage work have far worse effects on families than the demise of family values. The family-decline approach is blind to the realities of rising inequality, concentrated poverty, and escalating government policies of social abandonment. They reverse cause and effect, thus making single parents a convenient scapegoat (see Chapter 13). The simple solution that we return to the nuclear family at all costs allows the public and the government to escape social responsibilities, such as intervening in the ghettos, building new houses and schools, and creating millions of jobs that we need. This view moves the focus from the larger society to individual family members, who must then devise their own solutions for the social, economic, and technological shifts of our times.

Many proponents of strong family values overstate the evidence that divorce produces lasting damage to children and that children are always better off in two-parent families. Not all social scientists agree that family structure is all that matters. As Arlene Skolnick points out, most researchers take a shades-of-gray position on family structure. The evidence does show that children in divorced, remarried, or unmarried families are at greater risk for a number of problems, but there is little support for the frightening picture painted by many (Skolnick, 1997b:16). Social researchers disagree about the benefits of the two-parent structure over other family types for child well-being. Still, important research holds that divorce and other family changes are not disastrous for children, but should be viewed as family challenges that most children adapt to over time (Elliott and Umberson, 2004:46–47). In fact, the vast majority of children in single-parent families turn out reasonably well. Alan Acock and David Demo, who examined a nationally representative sample of children and adolescents in four family structures, reported few statistically significant differences across family types on measures of socioemotional adjustment and well-being (Acock and Demo, 1994). They found few statistically significant differences in children's well-being in first-married, divorced, remarried, and continuously single-parent families (Demo, 2000:18).

Much of the national discussion about the harmful social and cultural effects of family breakdown is a thinly veiled attack on single mothers. Undeniably, many female-headed families are beset with a disproportionate share of family problems. But neither family structure nor poor family values locks people in a cycle of poverty. Upholding the two-parent family as superior to all other family forms is a way of scapegoating individuals who are adapting to society's changes. Shifts in family life cannot be reduced to moral values.

Healthy families need healthy environments. Many neighborhoods have substandard services such as schools, health care, recreation facilities, sanitation, and police and fire protection. Due to massive economic transformations and various kinds of social disinvestment in the lives of the poor, families across the country are forced to live amid crime, gangs, pollution, drugs, and inadequate housing. These are the real enemies of strong families. The important question to ask about U.S. families is not how well do they conform to a particular image of the family but, rather, "how well do they function—what kind of loving, care, and nurturance do they provide?" (Mason et al., 2003:2).

A New Framework for Understanding Families

The Sociological Perspective

We have seen that the conventional wisdom about the family is often wrong. Popular ideas about family life are often "reductionist" in that they focus almost exclusively on individuals as they perform their family roles (Sprey, 2001:4). This book is different. It is firmly grounded in the sociological perspective for a critical understanding of the nation's diverse and changing families. Our central task is to examine how families reflect changes in society. To understand the full range of families that exist today requires that we examine forces beyond individuals and outside the family. It requires a perspective that examines how families are changing in the context of broad political, economic, and technological shifts. A sociological perspective does this. What is a sociological perspective? How does it apply to family study? Sociology focuses on the interplay between families and other social structures. Because social structures are abstract and often invisible, we must look behind the facades of family life to see how families are organized in socially patterned ways.

Two sociological principles are used throughout this book. The first principle is that there is a close relationship between families and the larger society that shapes them. The second principle requires a critical examination of family and society that questions the existing myths, stereotypes, and official dogma. Let us look at these in turn.

In studying family life we make a distinction between two levels of analysis. The macro level examines the family in relation to the rest of society. Instead of focusing on family roles and relations in isolation from the rest of social life, families are analyzed in reference to societal trends. The macro level of analysis illustrates how larger social systems shape the smaller family systems. For example, we call on macrostructural change to explain why families are far different from what they used to be. A macro level of analysis also looks at how the family as an institution contributes to the organization of the larger society (Kain, 1990:15). For example, the family is a vital part of the economy because it produces both workers and consumers. The family is a primary mechanism for perpetuating social inequality through the interlocking systems of race, class, and gender. This enables us to see how "society makes families and families make society" (Glaser, cited in Billingsley, 1992:78).

The societal level is not the only focus of our inquiry. We also emphasize the interior life of families. The micro level of analysis examines the internal dynamics of family life. In this type of analysis, the family is a "small group in which individuals spend much of their lives" (Kain, 1990:15). In micro analysis we examine the varied "experiences of kinship, intimacy, and domestic sharing" (Thorne, 1992:12). This is where the vital interpersonal dramas of love and domination, of companionship and conflict, of happiness and hatred occur. Of course, intimate family relationships reflect the hierarchies of the larger social world. Understanding families requires that we study both the macro level and the micro level and how each affects the other (see Box 1.3 for a look at the methods sociologists use in doing research on families).

Because our emphasis is on social structure, the reader is required to accept a second fundamental assumption of the sociological perspective: the need to adopt a critical stance toward all social arrangements. We must ask these questions: How does society really work? How do current social and economic changes affect families and the individuals within them? Who has power in society? How does this affect the formation and character of families? Who benefits under the existing social arrangements and who does not? To ask such questions means that the inquirer is interested in looking beyond the commonly accepted definitions of family and society.

The Paradigm Shift in Family Studies

The world today is in the midst of profound social changes in which people are taking apart and renegotiating "what used to be straightforwardly known as 'the family' " (Beck and Beck-Gernsheim, 2004:499). Just as families in the nation and

BOX
1.3

Researching Families

How Do Sociologists Conduct Research on Families?

There are many methods for studying families; each has its own purpose and its own underlying logic that justifies using the method. A widely used distinction is that between **quantitative** and **qualitative methods.**

The most frequently used quantitative method is the sample survey (often shortened to "survey"), which focuses on specific behaviors or attitudes and on factors that are hypothesized to influence them. The researcher designs a measure for each behavior or attitude and each potential explanatory factor. As a simple illustrative example, the researcher might expect that how much education a husband has influences how much housework he does. Education is easily measured in years and housework in hours per week, so a survey questionnaire can be designed for interviewing husbands on these matters. The goal is to understand whether such a relationship between education and housework exists for all husbands in the population; since they are too numerous, the researcher must interview an appropriately selected sample. By using suitable statistical procedures, the researcher can find out whether housework is related to education in the sample and whether the results in the sample can be generalized to the population. Measurement, statistical analysis, and generalization of findings from a sample to a population are the distinguishing features of quantitative research.

Qualitative and quantitative methods sometimes have been regarded as incompatible, but several researchers have used them in a complementary fashion. Nevertheless, combining quantitative and qualitative approaches has not been easy because qualitative methods have a different focus and a different starting point than quantitative approaches. Qualitative researchers begin with the premise that human activity is interpretive activity. That is, we cannot do anything without its having some meanings, and qualitative researchers want to discover meanings—how people interpret what they do. Returning to the previous example, the number of hours a week a husband does housework is of some interest, but of more interest is its meaning to him and to his wife. Does he define what he is doing as "helping" his wife in "her" tasks? Or is he a committed believer in

gender equality who defines housework as something to be shared equally? Or is there some other, less obvious meaning? And how does she define what he is doing? And how do those meanings shape their interactions and relationships?

The qualitative researcher usually begins research with questions in mind rather than with specific hypotheses—questions about how people do things and what those activities mean. There are two main types of qualitative research procedures. One is called ethnography. The ethnographer observes people and talks with them over a period of weeks, months, or years as they interact in their customary round of life. The researcher compares participants with those being studied and records observations in field notes. The second is known by various names—qualitative interviewing, unstructured or semi-structured interviewing, in-depth interviewing. The researcher designs an interview guide with open-ended questions that invite and allow the interviewee to answer in his or her own words. Qualitative research is a process of discovery of the implicit and explicit categories through which people define and construct their interpersonal activity. The researcher then tries to understand those categories in some larger theoretical framework. He or she creates categories that facilitate understanding the meanings in use by those studied. The distinguishing features of qualitative research are conversational and participant observation data, discovering meanings in use, interpreting those user meanings, and creating interpretive categories and concepts that are general enough to serve in studying other groups.

One of the issues in collecting qualitative interview data is whether family members should be interviewed individually or jointly. Individual interviewing is more common. Important ethical dilemmas are encountered in doing qualitative research on families. By its nature, such research seeks to penetrate family privacy in the interest of increased understanding of how families function. The full consequences of this effort cannot be known in advance either by the researchers or by the participants. Researchers should be sensitive to possible hazards to family members.

Source: Handel, Gerald and Gail Whitchurch (eds.), "Introduction to Part II: Research Methods." In *The Psychosocial Interior of the Family,* 4th ed. New York: Walter de Gruyter, 1994, pp. 49–51.

the world are changing dramatically, so is the scholarship on families. As society experiences major "earthquakes," social science thinking about families is undergoing "seismic shifts." Today, new ideas about diversity and social context are sweeping the family field and making it more exciting than ever before (Allen and Demo, 1995; Bengston et al., 2005; Cheal, 1991; Coleman and Ganog, 2004; Mann et al., 1997; Scott et al., 2004).

These new developments have fundamentally changed our knowledge about the way families operate, producing what is called a paradigm shift. **Paradigm** refers to the basic assumptions that scholars have of the social worlds they study. A family paradigm includes basic conceptual frameworks—in other words, models of families in society, and the field's important problems, questions, concepts, and methods of study.

The old family paradigm posited a singular process of family formation. This model was rooted in concerns that shaped the early social sciences—namely, the shift from traditional to modern society. Modernization was thought to produce a standard family type. In the 1950s and 1960s, the notion of a standard family type was an important feature of the dominant paradigm known as structural functionalism. This theory views all social institutions as organized around the needs of society. The family fills particular social needs including socializing the young and providing psychological support to individuals. Talcott Parsons (1955), the major sociological theorist in the United States and the leading family theorist of the 1950s and 1960s, saw the family as a vital element in the larger social system because it provides a haven from the outside world. According to his theory, the modern nuclear family with a breadwinner husband and a homemaker wife and two or more children was the basis of moral order, social unity, and the smooth functioning of society. This family form, organized around a harmony of interests, was essential for the common good through the socialization of children and the orderly division of labor between women and men. Parsons called it "the normal family" (Parsons, 1965). Structural functionalism treated the modern nuclear family as the norm, even though there were many varieties of families in different regional, economic, racial, and ethnic groups (Baca Zinn, 2000:44).

Structural functionalism was flawed. It mistook a historically specific family form as the universal form for families in modern society (Mann et al., 1997:321). This distorted and misrepresented family life because it generalized about families from the experience of the dominant group.

In the past three decades, challenges to the false universalization embedded in structural functionalism have changed our thinking. A flood of new ideas and approaches has produced a shift away from uniformity and changed the field forever. The shift in family sociology has been so pronounced that one scholar calls this stage of development a "Big Bang"—a dramatic period of diversification in family studies (Cheal, 1991:153). Not only are families and households becoming more diverse and fluid in the new century, but *diversity and fluidity are now "normal"* (Beck and Beck-Gernsheim, 2004; Bengston, 2001; Stacey, 1996).

The Structural Diversity Approach

The perspective used in this book draws on a conceptual framework that we call "structural diversity." This framework views all families in society as shaped through their interaction with social structures. The approach goes beyond adding different group experiences to already established frameworks of thought (Andersen and

Collins, 2010). We explore the close connections between the inner workings of family life and the structural forces that shape *all* families, albeit in different ways. Our coverage of the nation's various family arrangements is not simply for cultural appreciation. We want our readers to understand *why* families are diverse. We provide a coherent analysis as well as a new approach. Our approach is based on the premise that families are divided along structural lines that shape their form and functioning. The new perspective on families incorporates the following themes.

1. *Families are socially constructed and historically changing.* Although we think of families as "natural," there is no universal definition of the family. Social history shows that families vary by economic, political, and cultural conditions. Supporting this view are the social constructionist and social structural theoretical approaches. To say that families are socially constructed means that they develop in the context of social and economic realities. Different social and economic contexts define and organize families differently. What seems "natural" depends on time, place, and circumstance. How a family is defined depends on the historical period, the society, and even the social stratum within that society (Coltrane, 1998:1–9). "Stages we take for granted like childhood, adolescence, and adulthood are not timeless entities built into human nature but aspects of the human condition that have been reshaped with historical changes" (Skolnick, 1993:45). The point is that the form and meaning of families, gender, motherhood, fatherhood, or childhood are socially and historically varied.

2. *Family diversity is produced by the same structures that organize society as a whole.* The institution of the family is intertwined with other social institutions including the economy, politics, education, and religion. Families are also integrally tied to systems of stratification and inequality such as class, race, and gender. Both social institutions and social stratification systems divide families along structural lines. They create different contexts for family living through their unequal distribution of social resources and opportunities. Different contexts or "social locations" are what cause differences. Instead of being an intrinsic property of groups that are culturally different, family variation is *structural*. The relationship between opportunity systems and families is central to family diversity. The uneven distribution of work, wages, and other family requirements produce multiple family forms and multiple family experiences (Baca Zinn, 2000). At any particular time, a society will contain a range of family types that vary with social class, race, region, and other structural conditions. Today, global forces also affect families; that is, "every family on earth is more or less touched by global economic and political realities" (Karraker, 2008:8).

   Family diversity can be based on "social relations between dominant and subordinate groups" (Weber, 2001:81). Not only do power relations determine the resources different groups have available for family life, but "there is a direct relationship between the privileged circumstances of some families and the disadvantaged position of other families" (Garey and Hansen, 1998:xvi). Family variation is *relational*. This means that the lives of different groups are linked even without face-to-face relations (Glenn, 2002:14). For example, the histories of racial-ethnic families in the United States were not a matter of simple coexistence with dominant race and class groups. Instead, the opportunities of some families rested on the disadvantages of other families (Dill, 1994). In the twenty-first century, global forces are producing new connections between different family forms in far-reaching parts of the world. The growing demand for paid domestic workers is part of an international division of labor in which women from developing nations leave their families to work for U.S. families and those of other post-industrial countries. The work they do enables women in privileged families to have professional careers even as the maids, nannies, and other caretakers are forced to accommodate their lives to the demands of their labor and live across the world from their own families (Hondagneu-Sotelo, 2001; Parrenas, 2001). This is one way in which globalization is producing new forms of privilege and disadvantage that rest on distinctive family arrangements and on structurally connected "disparities between families in the third world and those in the first world" (Karraker, 2008:99) (see Chapter 12).

3. *Families are embedded in and shaped by interconnected systems of class, race, and gender.* These structures of inequality work together to place families in particular **social locations.** When we examine how families and individuals are positioned within these converging systems, we have a better grasp of different family arrangements and different family experiences. Locational differences in opportunity structures are crucial for the sociological study of families. Not only do race, class, and gender shape families in different ways, their linkages mean that people of the same race may experience family differently depending on their location in the class structure as unemployed, poor, working-class, or professional; their location in the gender structure as male or female; and their location in the sexual orientation system as heterosexual, gay, lesbian, or bisexual (Baca Zinn and Dill, 1996:327).

4. *Family diversity is constructed through social structure as well as the actions of family members.* The structural diversity model stresses larger social forces in shaping families differently. Although society and its structures are powerful, human beings are not simply the product of structural forces. Even in social locations characterized by limited resources, family members can find ways of adapting and thriving.

   A structural analysis must not lose sight of the human beings who shape their families through their own actions and behaviors. Families, after all, are not just molded from the "outside in." What happens on a daily basis in domestic settings also constructs families. Women, men, and children are not passive. They actively shape their families by adapting to, and changing, certain aspects of their social environments. This process is called **human agency.** People often use their families in order to survive. Their ingenuity and agency may result in new family arrangements. In other cases, family inventions are guided by choice as much as survival. Behaviors that family members use in adapting to structural constraints and stressful events are called "family adaptive strategies." If used carefully, the concept of human agency can serve as a sensitizing device (Moen and Wethington, 1992), illustrating meaningful interaction between social actors and their social environments.

5. *Understanding families means challenging monolithic ideas that conceive of the family in idealistic ways.* This differs from past approaches, which were based on studies involving mostly White, middle-class families. This practice distorted the reality of lives within most families, given that the United States has always had a significant portion of families of color and far too many families in poor or working classes (McGraw and Walker, 2004:176). Today, the family field takes various

standpoints into account. Several bodies of new scholarship by and about marginalized groups are documenting multiple family realities. Feminists representing different schools of thought along with various racial and ethnic groups, members of the working class, and lesbians and gays have pressed for a redefinition of "the family." New scholarship about families as they vary by class, race, gender, and sexuality offers powerful alternatives to the old paradigm. The structural diversity model draws from many scholarly fields including history, economics, anthropology, and psychology as well as the new fields of women's studies, African American studies, Latino studies, and cultural studies. Their insights can enhance the sociological perspective and offer vital building blocks for understanding the wide variety of family types in the United States.

Additional Features of This Book

The framework described in this chapter is woven throughout this book. The demythologizing of families is a central theme. Each chapter begins with a list of myths juxtaposed by the facts that are presented in greater detail in that chapter. In addition, the chapters include five distinctive boxes to enhance your understanding of family life.

1. *Inside the Worlds of Diverse Families* looks inside microstructural worlds to put a human face on some of the rhythms, textures, and conflicts of everyday family life.
2. *Researching Families* presents the main approaches and methods sociologists use in their studies.
3. *Families in Global Perspective* offers an international view of families, with selected illustrations that have both global and domestic implications.
4. *Technology and the Family* explores the effects of new technologies on different features of family experience.
5. *Emergent Family Trends* provides a look at new family patterns and the meaning they have for future families.

We hope that you capture some of our enthusiasm for exploring the intricacies and mysteries of families in society.

Chapter Review

1. Families are in upheaval around the world. These changes are confusing to many observers. Although some see this upheaval as a sign of family decline, the real causes of family change lie in larger changes occurring in the nation and the world.

2. Our objectivity as sociologists and students is often obscured by our own experiences and by ideals and myths about the family.

3. Three distinct images of the family can be identified in U.S. society: (a) family as a haven, (b) family as fulfillment, and (c) family as encumbrance. All of these images place family and society in opposition to each other.

4. Six family myths underscore the disparities between idealized and real patterns of family life.

5. The myth of a stable and harmonious family of the past romanticizes the "traditional" families of our forebears. However, new research has found that problems considered unique in today's families also existed in the past.

6. The myth of separate worlds polarizes family and society. In fact, the family is embedded in social settings that affect the day-to-day realities of family life.

7. The myth of the monolithic family form assumes that all families are nuclear in structure; are composed of a father, mother, and children; and exhibit a sexual division of labor featuring a breadwinner father and a homemaking mother. This model accounts for only 7 percent of families in the United States. Because "family" is an idealized concept, sociologists often find it useful to use the concept of "household," which is a domestic unit.

8. The myth of a unified family experience assumes that all family members have common needs, interests, and experiences. Gender and age, however, create different experiences for women and men and adults and children.

9. The myth of family consensus assumes that families operate on principles of harmony and love. These ingredients are present in most families. Nevertheless, this myth ignores the contradictions that are intrinsic to family life due to power relations, financial concerns, different work and leisure patterns, and the intense emotional quality of family life.

10. The myth of family decline blames social problems on eroding family values. This myth ignores the changing economic conditions that produce divorce and single-parent families.

11. This book uses a sociological perspective to analyze families. This analysis requires a critical examination of social relations.

12. Sociologists analyze families at two levels. The macro level examines families in relation to the larger society, and the micro level examines the interpersonal features of family life.

13. The sociological perspective stresses structural conditions that shape families differently, but it does not lose sight of individuals who create viable family lives.

14. In the past, family sociology treated diversity in families as special "cultural" cases. The paradigm known as structural functionalism viewed the nuclear family as the norm.

15. A new paradigm has emerged in the family field. The structural diversity approach treats diversity in families as the norm. The key to understanding family diversity is the structural distribution of social opportunities.

Key Terms

family	13	paradigm	23
family Darwinism	11	patriarchy	16
gendered institution	15	qualitative methods	22
household	13	quantitative methods	22
human agency	25	social location	25
myth	10	Standard North American Family (SNAF)	8

Related Websites

http://www.contemporaryfamilies.org

Council on Contemporary Families. Founded in 1996, with a membership consisting of nationally noted family researchers, mental health and social work practitioners, and clinicians, the Council on Contemporary Families (CCF) is a nonprofit organization dedicated to enhancing the national conversation about what contemporary families need and how these needs can best be met.

http://www.trinity.edu/~mkearl/family.html

Kearl's Guide to the Sociology of the Family. Published by Michael Kearl of the Sociology and Anthropology Department at Trinity University, this award-winning website offers extensive resources on a variety of family topics.

http://www.ncfr.org

National Council on Family Relations. NCFR provides a forum for family researchers, educators, and practitioners to share in the development and dissemination of knowledge about families and family relationships, establishes professional standards, and works to promote family well-being. NCFR publishes three scholarly journals—*Journal of Marriage and Family, Family Relations,* and *Journal of Family Theory and Review*—as well as books, audio- and videotapes, and learning tools.

http://www.childstats.gov

Childstat.gov. This website is provided by the Federal Interagency Forum on Child and Family Statistics (Forum), a working group of Federal agencies that collect, analyze, and report data on issues related to children and families. The Forum has partners from 22 federal agencies as well as partners in private research organizations. The site offers easy access to statistics and reports on children and families, including: family and social environment, economic circumstances, health care, physical environment and safety behavior, education, and health. The Forum fosters coordination, collaboration, and integration of federal efforts to collect and report data on conditions and trends for children and families.

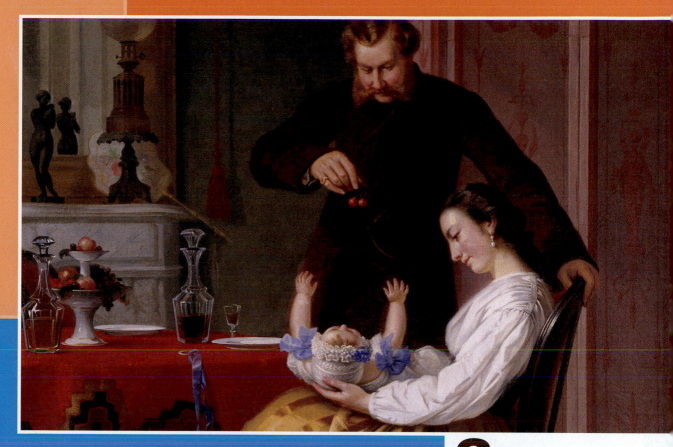

chapter 2

Preindustrial Families and the Emergence of a Modern Family Form

▶ Myths and Realities

Myth	Families everywhere are similar in form because the family is a natural unit, based on the timeless functions of love, caring, and childbearing.
Reality	Families are not merely biological arrangements. Instead, they are social forms influenced by broader social conditions that produce wide-ranging family differences.
Myth	Traditional American families were stable arrangements of many kinfolk living together in large households. Family members all worked together on Grandma's farm. Life was hard but happy, because family members knew their roles and had strong family values.
Reality	This image is what William J. Goode (1983:43) named "the classical family of Western nostalgia." Few examples of this "traditional" family have been found. Grandma's farm was not entirely self-sufficient. Few families stayed together as large aggregations of kinfolk, and most houses were small, not large. Family discord was as common in the past as it is in the present.
Myth	Family life among the Puritans in the New England colonies was disciplined, harmonious, and stable.
Reality	Although the Puritans valued discipline, family life was neither harmonious nor stable. The family was a breeding ground for tension and conflict, especially during the winter, when its members were forced into close and constant contact with each other in small, cramped houses (Henretta, 1973:36). High mortality rates meant stability was hard to achieve. The average length of marriage was less than a dozen years. One-third to one-half of all children lost at least one parent before the children turned 21 (Coontz, 1992:36).
Myth	Premarital sex was unheard of in "traditional" America, when young people, especially girls, were likely to be virginal at marriage and faithful afterward.
Reality	Sexual activity outside of marriage is a time-honored practice. Among the Puritans, fornication and adultery were common in the seventeenth century. Premarital pregnancy is not limited to the twentieth century. In certain communities of eighteenth-century America, 30 to 40 percent of brides went to the altar pregnant (Demos, 1986:6).
Myth	Industrialization replaced the extended family of early America with the nuclear family form.
Reality	Nuclear families did not emerge as a response to industrialization but were brought here by the nation's earliest White settlers.
Myth	Public anxiety about "the crisis of the family" is a recent development.
Reality	The idea that the family is in trouble is as old as the nation itself. The earliest New England settlers feared that children were losing respect for authority and that this endangered the family.

Families are changing in ways that are troubling to many people. Marriages continue to end in divorce, more than half of all mothers with school-age children are in the workforce, family life is more fluid than ever before, and new family forms are on the rise. These trends suggest to some observers that the American family is in decline. Yet popular notions of what is wrong with the family today are based on misconceptions about how families lived in the past. False images of something called "the traditional family" are used both to idealize the past and to lament the present state of the family.

New research has dispelled myths and misinformation about earlier family life. Historical studies have painted a new picture of the history of family life that stands in sharp contrast to our images of the past (Hawes and Nybakken, 2001; Kain, 1990; Ross, 2006). We need to know the basic facts about families of the past for many reasons: One is to better understand our present. Even though U.S. families are far different from what they used to be, many of the new patterns have roots in the past. Throughout history, families have been in flux. Historians refer to these ongoing changes as "domestic revolutions."

> Over the past 300 years, American families have undergone a series of far-reaching domestic revolutions that profoundly altered their family life, repeatedly transforming their demographic characteristics, organizational structure, functions, conceptions and emotional dynamics. (Mintz and Kellogg, 1988:xiv)

Knowing that families have always been swayed by social change is essential for understanding many of the problems faced by today's families.

This chapter uses a broad sociohistorical framework to examine Euro-American or White families in U.S. society over a sweep of two and a half centuries. The chapter shows how larger social structures and processes encompass families and cause them to bend with time. To illustrate this, we focus on family life among the Euro-American colonists, tracing the social forces that, by about 1800, produced a new family form. More important than the precise chronological markings are macro-level changes in the economy. Economic changes in the wider society changed the relationship between families and other institutions, especially the workplace. These changes produced micro-level changes in family organization. The rise of the **"modern" family** traces the historical development of a race-specific and class-specific form. This development was not uniform. There has *never* been one single family form in the United States (Hawes and Nybakken, 2001:1–2). The nuclear family consisting of father, mother, and children living together within a privatized household has often served as the model of family life. But in reality, different social and economic forces created diverse family arrangements within the United States. In every historical period, important race and class differences existed among families. Together, these distinct but connected family forms are part of a larger web of power relations, unequal resources, and struggles over what families "should" be (Coontz, 2008:2). Even though family diversity is as old as the nation itself, an emergent modern family soon became the gold standard against which all families were measured (Pryor and Trinder, 2004).

Spanish family, Culver City, California.

We begin with a brief discussion introducing the field of family history. We then examine Euro-American or White families in the premodern period, extending roughly from the early 1600s through 1800. We devote special attention to the unique connections between families and colonial communities. We then turn our attention to the period of transformation, extending roughly from 1800 through 1850. We look at the shift from an agriculturally based economy to an industrial economy and the consequences for family life.

 # Family and the New Social History

What Is "New" About Family History?

In the past two decades, family history has become an exciting multidisciplinary field. Research by historians, sociologists, demographers, and anthropologists is profoundly affecting our understanding of family life both in the past and in today's global age. Family history is part of "the new social history" that has offered insights about customs and lifestyles of ordinary people during periods of social and economic change.

Social history is new in several ways. Instead of highlighting wars, revolutions, diplomacy, and other dominant events, social historians are interested in uncovering the everyday life of the common person, which includes family matters (Schvaneveldt et al., 1993:101). Social historians also concentrate on differences across social class, race, gender, and region. They are interested not only in the elite, who are the most likely to leave behind letters, diaries, and memoirs; the new social historians also concentrate on the hitherto "voiceless": ordinary people, including immigrants, African Americans and other members of minority groups, women, children, and the elderly, which previously had been little studied (Cooper, 1999:26). Family history gained popularity in the 1960s, first in Europe and then in the United States, as scholars began to challenge long-held theories about the family's historical development. Their work has added a new perspective to family studies by providing an intimate perspective of the roles and relationships of spouses, parents, and children within families over time (Schvaneveldt et al., 1993:101). As family history has become more sophisticated and complex over the last decades, it has become clear that no one family form can be understood outside its context (Coltrane, 2004; Coontz, 2008; Cooper, 1999; Hawes and Nybakken, 2001; Ross, 2006).

Despite these advances, our knowledge about the intimate details of past family life outside the middle class is uneven in the periods we examine in this chapter. The further back we delve into history, the greater is the difficulty in finding such information, because those outside the middle class "usually did not keep diaries or maintain lengthy correspondence; moreover, even if they did, few were preserved" (Degler, 1980:82).

Before we review recent historical findings, a brief discussion of research methods is in order. There is no single historical method. Scholars use a variety of historical methods to do their work. One useful way of discussing historical methods is to describe historical sources and how they are used as the main tools of historians (Schvaneveldt et al., 1993:102). **Family reconstitution** is a tool that reconstructs the lives of individuals. Data are collected from church and community records through a laborious procedure of compiling every available fragment of information about births, marriages, and deaths for all family members (Seward, 1978:42; Vinovskis and Mc Call, 1991). The aim is to reconstruct the family and household patterns of ordinary people who have passed down little information regarding their way of life. Although data on the upper classes have been more readily available, family reconstitution is one way of retrieving information on people whose everyday lives have been hidden from history (Hutter, 1981:72).

Family reconstitution is generally considered to be very accurate, but it is a time-consuming and expensive procedure that is not suited to all problems in

family history. An alternative method is **aggregate data analysis.** This tool involves analyzing records at different points in time in order to develop a picture of trends. Rather than looking at events as they occur in individual families, researchers look at a number of events as they are distributed over time in populations (Gordon, 1983:4). By delving into census records; birth, marriage, and death registers; occupational files; and family letters and diaries, historians have reconstructed the family lives of large numbers of ordinary people in the past. The history of the family has shattered myths and misconceptions about the family in past times and has given us a new picture of family life and social change (see Box 2.1).

Overview of Family History Themes

The most important themes to emerge from historical studies of the family are those of diversity, uneven change, and human agency.

DIVERSITY

Historians have discovered so much diversity that any discussion of "the Western family" must be qualified. Instead of a prevailing type of family at any one time, several types of families were present from the beginning.

> The indigenous peoples who greeted the invaders from across the sea lived under a wide variety of familial arrangements quite alien to the newcomers. The migrants who transplanted themselves to American soil came in many ways and for various reasons—as families and as unmarried individuals, in groups of religious refugees, and as single adventurers seeking fortune or at least an initial stake in life. They came under different conditions of wealth and poverty and in different degrees of freedom and bondage, as lords with vast tracts of land, as gentlemen merchants and planters, as yeoman freeholders with just enough land to build and sustain a family, as renters, as indentured servants, selling four or seven years of their labor for fifty or a hundred acres of uncleared land, and as captive chattel slaves. They set up remarkably different societies, ranging from the compact theocratic communities of New England through quasi-feudal Maryland and the scattered farms and plantations of Virginia, to the largely unorganized back country of the Carolinas. (Scott and Wishy, 1982:2)

BOX 2.1 Researching Families

The Materials of History

Once an area of interest has been identified, historical researchers are faced with the question of relying on existing sources or uncovering previously unknown materials. Definitive data may not be available or, in fact, may be very difficult to obtain. Also, surviving evidence, often consisting of information found in scattered locations, may not be of great help. Thus, available data may not contain the answers the researchers seeks. This is a particularly salient methodological issue, because the careful selection of data is so crucial to good historiography. Family historians have sought creative ways in which to address this problem, but the matter of missing or misleading data still remains as one of the more difficult barriers to establishing definitive responses to important questions. Nevertheless, even as detectives sometimes proceed with only the scantiest of clues, so must historians carry out their research without all of the pieces of the puzzle. It may be necessary for historians to draw from a wide variety of materials as they seek to clarify a research question.

Documents in Archives, Libraries, and Private Collections

Documents constitute the basic source for both traditional and new historians and are defined as any written or oral accounts of human behavior or social condition. Thus, documents not only consist of written and printed materials, such as population censuses, public records, and private papers, but may also include taped interviews.

When family historians conduct research to answer a specific question, and all of the information necessary cannot be obtained from a single document, the use of a number of documents, such as vital statistics, marriage records, tax records, wills, employment ledgers, school rosters, and city registers can yield a composite result. This technique is generally referred to as record linkage, and it is often used with substantial profit, particularly when employing the method known as family reconstitution. Through family reconstitution, profiles of families who lived long ago can be put together to determine structural characteristics and patterns of change.

Letters, being genuine and firsthand, tend to be superior to other material, at least in those respects. Nevertheless, even here there are often problems of content. As people often present themselves differently on paper than they are in real life, the reader is subject to the hidden intent of the writer.

Diaries provide historians with a glimpse into the intimate as well as the public lives of their keepers.

Autobiographies, or memoirs, although very useful to the historian, are problematic for several reasons. When writing for an audience, writers are even less likely than letter writers and diarists to portray themselves candidly. Further, self-knowledge and a good memory are essential for a worthwhile autobiography. Finally, the historian must consider that those who reflect on their own past do so under the influence of the time and situation in which they sat down to relate the details of their lives.

Mission and Church Records

Church records include some of the oldest documents for historical research on families. By and large, historians have diligently searched for data that would indicate the influence of factors such as work and politics on families and societies, yet they have often neglected the impact of religion. Interestingly, religious documents reveal a substantial amount of information about the history of family life in general.

Mass Media Files

Historians traditionally have relied on newspapers as a source of historical data, and often newspapers are the only available source of information on a particular subject. An advantage to using newspapers, and now radio and television materials, is that erroneous assumptions by the public are often corrected by conscientious editors.

Census Data

Census data have long been used by historians to study individual and family trends. Before the nineteenth century, information compiled on public records were often simply lists. It must also be remembered that information contained in such enumerations always reflects the orientation of the person who compiled it. Tax lists could have been drawn up to underestimate or overestimate the number of household members; a military recruiter might have grouped households to facilitate his job; and a household might simply have been described as those who dined together.

Source: Schvaneveldt, Jay D., Robert S. Pickett, and Margaret H. Young, "Historical Methods in Family Research." In *Sourcebook of Family Theories and Methods: A Contextual Approach*, P. G. Boss, W. J. Doherty, R. LaRossa, W. R. Schumm, and S. K. Steinmetz (eds.). New York: Plenum Press, 1993, pp. 102–104.

Chrisman Sisters, Custer County, Nebraska, c. 1880s.

The point is that there have always been a variety of family patterns in the United States. The middle-class nuclear family might have been the ideal, but it has never been universal (Hawes and Nybakken, 2001:2). Even White colonial families were varied, especially in class, gender, and region. Four classes of English men and women made the Atlantic passage: propertyless husbandmen, yeomen farmers, artisans, and common laborers. One in three passengers disembarking in Virginia was a woman, usually in her early twenties; the majority of these women were indentured servants. New England immigrants, in contrast, came more often in family units, two of every three members of which were likely to be women (Ryan, 1983:22).

The principal sources of the population for the original 13 American colonies were Europe and Africa. European sources were mainly the British Isles and other Western European nations. Of the approximately two million White people in the 13 colonies in 1776, the estimate is that 60 percent were English, 17 to 18 percent were Scotch-Irish, 11 to 12 percent were German, 7 to 8 percent were Dutch, and smaller percentages were French, Scottish, Swedish, Irish, Welsh, Danish, and Finnish (Taft, 1936:71–72).

The other principal group to come to America during the colonial period was from Africa. The earliest recorded Africans to come to America arrived in Virginia in 1619 as indentured servants. As slavery grew in the colonial period, thousands were brought by force from different national and tribal groups in western Africa. The first official U.S. Census in 1790 showed a population of 757,208 Negroes, constituting about 19.3 percent of the total population (Vander Zanden, 1966:25–27). However, slaves' households were not recorded in the Census but were combined with those of their masters.

Not listed on the Census returns for 1790 or any other year were the original settlers: the American "Indians," or Native Americans. They may have numbered half a million and were widely and often thinly spread across the American continent. For more than two centuries, devastating European diseases had reduced their numbers, and the relentless and usually violent encroachment of European settlement had pushed them west or into shrinking enclaves. American Indians lived in some 600 societies, with a wide variety of residence and marital rules, representing almost 200 different languages (Larkin, 1988:4). American Indians had diverse marriage and family customs. Before the arrival of European settlers, their family arrangements ranged from simple monogamy to various forms of multiple marriage. Some societies had complex descent systems traced through the maternal or the paternal lines; others were comparatively unconcerned with descent rules (Caffrey, 1991:223; Coontz, 2008:5–6). Most of the Great Plains and prairie Indians were patrilineal. Matrilineal descent was common among many East Coast groups; the Creeks, Choctaws, and Seminoles of the South; and the Hopi, Acoma, and Zuni groups of the Southwest (Coontz, 2000:21).

> But the indigenous peoples of North America all organized production, distribution, and even justice through kin networks rather than adherence to the authority of a territorial state, and did not recognize the private ownership of land by individuals or independent nuclear families. Most Native American societies had a division of labor by gender, but it differed greatly from that of the European settlers. (Coontz, 2008:6)

American Indian family systems and fertility patterns helped maintain the game and forests that made the land attractive to European settlers. But they also made the American Indians vulnerable to diseases brought by Europeans and to the Europeans' more aggressive and coordinated methods of warfare and political expansion. American Indian family systems were devastated by European colonization. Massive epidemics sometimes killed 60 to 90 percent of a group's members, devastated their kin networks, and disrupted social continuity. Many American Indian groups were either exterminated or driven onto marginal land that did not support their forms of social organization. Yet their collective traditions were resilient. Euro-Americans spent the entire nineteenth century trying to eradicate them.

UNEVEN CHANGE

As we look at family life within the context of macro-level changes in the economy, we must also recognize that historical changes never occur uniformly throughout society. Historians have shown that we should not think of family changes as occurring in a linear transition—that is, from one family "type" to another (Coontz, 2001:283). The family type labeled "modern" and linked to the transition from a traditional agrarian society to an industrial society was not universal. In fact, "the modern family" is a historically specific form that applies primarily to Whites. Families in different social classes, races, and immigrant groups all experienced different rates of change, a pattern that can be described as "checkered." This finding belies the existence of any continuous linear pattern encompassing families throughout society moving in the same way to a more "modern" level (Hareven, 1987). In Chapter 3, we examine family diversity by class, race, and gender.

HUMAN AGENCY

As we link the development of families to the history of social and economic change, we must remember that people in the past were not passive objects of historical change. They adapted to social and economic conditions. Historical research has discovered a wealth of information on the varied ways in which families were the products of people's actions. Instead of being a product of their fate, family members took charge of their lives and used their resources in the struggle to survive and to secure their own and their children's future. In going about their day-to-day lives and adapting to changing social conditions, families and individuals called on whatever means they had, including their cultural heritage and the economic resources available to them.

Reconstructing the family lives of ordinary people in the past offers us a view of history "from the bottom up." This gives us an understanding of people's behavior from their own experience and point of view (Hareven, 1987:37).

Family Life in Colonial America

A macro-level analysis is essential for understanding family organization, the lives of individuals, and their connections with the larger community. We must keep in mind that diversity from one region to another was a hallmark of life in colonial America. New England was stable and settled primarily by families, while the Chesapeake region was first settled by single young males (Beals, 1991; Mintz, 2004:38; Vinovskis and McCall, 1991). This regional diversity meant that family life was not the same throughout the colonies. Nevertheless, *the family as an institution* had a unique relationship with colonial society. Historians have found distinctive patterns in household composition, marriage, and childhood. These patterns also provide a framework for looking at families at the micro level, where the internal workings of colonial families differed profoundly from those in later periods.

Agricultural Communities and Families

Early America was primarily rural, and most people were involved in agriculture. For the original settlers of the American colonies, the family was the most important institution in helping them adapt to New World conditions. The English migrants who ventured to New England sought to avoid the disorder of English family life through a structured and disciplined family. They possessed the idea of a **godly family:** a patriarchal institution ruled by the father, who exercised authority over his wife, children, and servants much as God the Father ruled over his children or a king—the "father" of his country—ruled his subjects. This "godly family" conformed to the teachings of the Bible (Mintz and Kellogg, 1988:1). It was a social, political, and economic unit that performed important functions for colonial communities.

The family was the cornerstone of the new society, but colonial communities did not make a sharp distinction between family and society. Family life *was* social life. Boundaries between home and community were almost nonexistent. The family was not private as we know it today, but was a place of work and living that was highly integrated into the community. Colonial communities were strong and cohesive, created to deal with questions of land distribution, taxation, and public works. Communities were much like families, and families were much like communities.

They ran together at many points, and each was a lively representation of the other. Their structure, their guiding values, their inner purposes were essentially the same (Demos, 1986:28).

Families were not set apart from society because most social activities or functions took place in family settings. The most important activities making up the business of daily living were economic. The household was the basic economic unit of the agrarian society. It was the "center of production both for its own consumption and for local barter" (Coontz, 2005:154). Almost all production was done within the household. The goods created were owned and distributed by family members as part of a broader, interconnected community (Coleman, 1998:79). Historians call this mode of production the **family-based economy.** Families provided the goods and services required by their members. Each family provided the market with a commodity. Women, men, and children all worked at productive tasks that were defined by age and sex (Tilly and Scott, 1978:44). The family was a unit of production and exchange. It raised the food and made most of the clothing and furniture for the early settlers. Women, men, and children worked together in the agrarian family economy that supported the colonial population. The colonial family was not only an economic unit; families also provided sustenance, shelter, job training, religious instruction, and care for the young, sick, and elderly (Hawes and Nybakken, 2001:37; Mintz and Kellogg, 1988:1). Historian John Demos describes the range of activities and functions that have since been taken over by specialized institutions:

> The Old Colony family was, first of all, a business, an absolutely central agency of economic production and exchange. Each household was more or less self-sufficient; and its various members were inextricably united in the work of providing for their fundamental material wants. Work, indeed, was a wholly natural extension of family life and merged imperceptibly with all of its other activities.
>
> The family was also a "school." Parents and masters were charged by law to attend to the education of all the children in their immediate care "at least to be able duly to read the Scriptures." Most people had little chance for any sort of education, though "common schools" were just beginning to appear by the end of the Old Colony period.
>
> The family was a "vocational institute." However deficient it may have been in transmitting the formal knowledge and skills associated with literacy, it clearly served to prepare its young for effective, independent performance in the larger economic system. For the great majority of persons—the majority who became farmers—the process was instinctive and almost unconscious. But it applied with equal force (and greater visibility) to the various trades and crafts of the time. The ordinary setting for an apprenticeship was, of course, a domestic one.
>
> The family was a "church." To say this is not to slight the central importance of churches in the usual sense. Here, indeed, the family's role was partial and subsidiary. Nonetheless, the obligation of "family worship" seems to have been widely assumed. Daily prayers and personal meditation formed an indispensable adjunct to the more formal devotions of a whole community.
>
> The family was a "house of correction." Idle and even criminal persons were "sentenced" by the Court to live in the families of more reputable citizens. The household seemed a natural setting for both imposing discipline and for encouraging some degree of character reformation.
>
> The family was a "welfare institution"; in fact, it provided several different kinds of welfare service. It was occasionally a "hospital"—at least insofar as certain men

thought to have special medical knowledge would receive sick persons into their homes for day-to-day care and treatment. It was an "orphanage" in that children whose parents had died were straightaway transferred to another household (often that of a relative). It was an "old people's home" since the aged and infirm, no longer able to care for themselves, were usually incorporated into the households of their grown children. And it was a "poorhouse" too for analogous, and obvious, reasons. (Demos, 1970:183–184)

The preindustrial family, with its permeable boundaries, did not contain an individual's social life. Rather, people lived "in the streets" in the community (Cott, 1979:109). Community members often intervened in family matters. A dramatic example of community intervention was the disciplinary technique called the *charivari*, prevalent in Europe and the United States until the early nineteenth century. The *charivari* was a noisy public demonstration intended to subject wayward individuals to ridicule and punishment.

Sometimes the demonstrations would consist of masked individuals circling somebody's house at night, screaming, beating on pans and blowing cow horns (which the local butchers rented out). On other occasions the offender would be seized and marched through the streets, perhaps seated backwards on a donkey or forced to wear a placard describing his sins. Sometimes the youth would administer the charivari; on other occasions villagers of all ages and sexes would mix together. (Shorter, 1975:219)

People in colonial America were not free to do as they pleased, even in their own families. The larger community—the state—was involved in matters of family living. Thus, for example, disobedient children were not only punished with a thrashing at their father's hands; they were also liable to action by the courts. Colonial magistrates might even remove a child from the care of "unseemly" parents and place him or her in some other family. Or, as a further example, a local court could order the reunion of a husband and wife who had decided to live apart (Demos, 1977:60).

What went on in families was not "their own business" but was, in fact, a community affair. Even "private" matters took place in the presence of lodgers and neighbors (see Box 2.2). This integration of family and society persisted throughout the eighteenth century.

Family Structure and Household Composition

Common wisdom once held that nuclear families emerged as a response to industrial society. Even sociological theory assumed that families of the past were extended. This theory of "progressive nucleation" (Lasch, 1975) assumed that industrialization and modernization replaced the extended family of early America with the nuclear family. However, this belief about the relationship between the family and the Industrial Revolution has been revised. New research shows that the nuclear family was one of several *different* family systems present in preindustrial Europe (Kertzer, 1991:158).

The study that did most to challenge the myth of the preindustrial extended family was Peter Laslett's *The World We Have Lost* (1971). Laslett showed that a golden age of stable extended families is nothing more than wishful thinking. He used family reconstitution techniques to study family structure and household size in seventeenth-century England. By collecting data from parish registers in scattered villages at scattered intervals in time, he demonstrated that most households were nuclear (Vinovskis, 2006).

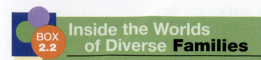

Inside the Worlds of Diverse Families

BOX 2.2

Eighteenth-Century Family and Social Life Revealed in Massachusetts Divorce Records

Nancy F. Cott draws on rich materials contained in divorce records to explore attitudes and practices involved in family relationships. Her findings show that neighbors and lodgers often intervened into couples' affairs.

When men and women of eighteenth-century Massachusetts complained to the court of marital travesties such as desertion, adultery, or neglect, they inadvertently brought these issues to light. Families there experienced none of the isolation or withdrawal from community overseership which presumably characterize the modern family. On the contrary, the divorce records reveal the interconnectedness of family and community, particularly in the form of community members' guardianship over family affairs. Divorce petitioners successfully relied on the proximity and curiosity of neighbors, lodgers, and kin, and on their motives to preserve community norms, in order to obtain material to substantiate their cases. Mary Angel, for example, out walking in Boston with Abigail Galloway one day, saw through an open window her neighbor Adam Air "in the Act of Copulation" with a woman named Pamela Brichford....

Whether avid observers were attempting to uphold community standards by surveillance, when it came to adultery—or simply satisfying their own curiosity—may be a fine distinction. When Mary Cole witnessed Hannah Wales invite a strange man to lie down with her in Boston in 1785, Mary left the room, but later admitted that "Curiosity led her to look thro' a hole in the door, when I plainly saw said man Lying upon Mrs. Wales, his breeches were down..." and the couple was caught in the act. Mary Knight, living with

her husband Russel in William Parham's household in Lancaster, was constantly subject to the Parhams' and their neighbors' observation because they doubted her fidelity. One night William and a neighbor, hearing noises in Mary's chamber, rushed up through a cellar trap door to confront her in bed with a strange man. Mary later accused William of sending the man to assault her and "frame" her in the act of adultery. When the justice of the peace asked William whether he had burst into Mary's room "to find out the man and secure him or not"—for he allowed the man to escape—William replied, "I went into the Room to Satisfy myself whether the sd Russel's wife was such a lewd Person as I suspected—and not to apprehend the Man."

Not only did neighbors know each others' business with predictable small town alacrity. The very circumstances of household life facilitated the intervention of neighbors, and even more readily, of lodgers, into a couple's affairs. The construction and population of houses were respectively so thin and so thick that privacy was hard to come by. Mary Angel, who caught Adam Air in the act, also testified that she "live[d] the next door, where only a thin Partition divided us have often heard him beat...[his wife] & heard her scream in Consequence of the beating." In Katherine and Elijah Cobb's house in Taunton in 1766, only a single wall separated Ruth Cushman's chamber from the Cobbs' and she "had frequent opportunity of hearing their conversation." The presence and transience of servants, hired laborers, nurses, relatives, and other lodgers in households assured numerous omnipresent eyes and ears.

Source: Cott, Nancy F., "Eighteenth-Century Family and Social Life Revealed in Massachusetts Divorce Records." In *A Heritage of Her Own*, Nancy F. Cott and Elizabeth H. Pleck (eds.). New York: Simon & Schuster, 1979, pp. 109–111.

Couples headed households of small nuclear families. Although many households contained servants, the average household did not contain extended kin and was, in fact, relatively small. As this discovery was applied to the American colonies, scholars found growing evidence that colonial families were typically nuclear in structure. The work of two family historians, John Demos and Phillip Greven, makes this point.

John Demos also used family reconstitution tools to study Plymouth Colony, the seventeenth-century Pilgrim settlement. His classic study, *A Little Commonwealth,* analyzed wills, inventories, and official colonial records, as well as physical artifacts remaining from seventeenth-century houses—furniture, tools, utensils, and clothing—to reconstruct family patterns. Demos concluded that the colonial family was *nuclear* rather than extended. A married couple and their children formed the core and most often made up the entire family. While nonkin household members—servants, boarders, and apprentices—were often present, colonial households could be described in terms of simple categories of husband, wife, children, and servants (Demos, 1970:63–67).

Phillip Greven's research on colonial Andover, Massachusetts, during the seventeenth and eighteenth centuries offers more evidence that extended families were the exception, not the rule. He examined four successive generations in Andover, using the family reconstitution method. Greven found that the basic household was nuclear but that families consisted of kinship networks of separate households. He describes these families as "modified extended," somewhere between a nuclear and extended family. First-generation sons who were to inherit land remained in the parental residence, even after marriage. However, households were nuclear in all other respects (Greven, 1970).

Recent studies have addressed such matters as the number of children per family and the average size of the family. Historians disagree about the number of children, but they generally agree that most households were actually quite small (Vinovskis, 2006:272). Demos found that colonial families were larger than families in contemporary society due to the presence of servants, boarders, and lodgers: "What I concluded for Plymouth can be summarized as follows: the average household size throughout the period in question was just under six persons. Typically, this meant a man and his wife and children, and in some cases, a servant or two" (Demos, 1972:56). Where servants were present, households were larger. Looking at summaries of the federal Census for eleven states taken in 1790, Greven found that the presence of slaves could greatly increase the size of a household. Slaves were sometimes listed as members of White families. Because the extent of slavery varied from state to state during the late 1790s, the average family size also varied. Variations ranged from five persons to seven persons per family in 1790. Greven has concluded that the average family in eighteenth-century America was very large in comparison with families in modern America. Still, household size varied.

Both Demos and Greven concluded that families in eighteenth-century America were smaller than our stereotypes assume but larger than today's families. As we use family history to correct the myths about extended families of the past, we must be careful not to substitute a new dogma about the nuclear family. While some historians emphasized the long-standing predominance of the nuclear family, others now demonstrate a kernel of truth in earlier generalizations about the decline of extended families (Coontz, 2001; Cooper, 1999). No doubt some families were extended in form. But because life spans were shorter in the past, comparatively few families had enough members to reside even potentially as a multigenerational household. Even a small number of extended-family households represented a high proportion of all such potential arrangements (Coontz, 2001:81).

The research on the size and composition of colonial families is important. But it tells us little about the quality and texture of family life in past times. Some scholars are critical of research that is limited to the quantifiable part of history. Christopher Lasch, for example, has argued that the study of family structure is not important unless it tells us what different forms *mean* (Lasch, 1975). However, it is always hard to capture the intent and feeling of historical actors (Cooper, 1999:23). Although studies of family size and composition have some limitations, they also offer valuable insights about the internal dynamics of family life. For example, Laslett's study of preindustrial Europe found populations that were overwhelmingly young. Below, he describes day-to-day life amidst ever-present children:

We must imagine our ancestors, therefore, in the perpetual presence of their young offspring. A good 70 percent of all households contained children. This figure is remarkably consistent from place to place and date to date and there were between two and a half and three children to every household with them.…In the pre-industrial world there were children everywhere: playing in the village streets and fields when they were very small; hanging round the farmyards and getting in the way until they had grown enough to be given child-sized jobs to do; thronging churches; forever clinging to the skirts of women in the house and wherever they went; and above all crowding round the cottage fires. The perpetual distraction of childish noise and talk must have affected everyone almost all of the time. (Laslett, 1971:109)

Historians now supplement demographic household data. Demos's work is a good example of this. After gathering certain facts about colonial society, such as evidence of large families and small houses and court records reporting contention among neighbors, he contends that family members turned their "natural hostilities" toward neighbors, thereby avoiding domestic conflict (Demos, 1972:569).

Some scholars are now probing the complexities of premodern households through historical records. As Robert Wells explains:

A simple structural analysis of a seventeenth-century Chesapeake household might provide evidence of a husband and wife and four children living in a household. But with a dynamic perspective, we might learn that this was the second or third marriage for both husband and wife. In addition, the four children, instead of all being born into that particular marriage, might include a child of the father's, a child of the mother's, each from a previous marriage, one child who was the product of this union, and a fourth child who might be an indentured servant or the child of one of the brothers or sisters of the husband or wife who had been taken in either to learn an occupation or because of dislocation in that child's own immediate family. (Wells, 1991:48)

Other historians argue that to capture the meanings of families in past times, we must investigate the myths, rituals, and symbols of family life in different times and places. John Gillis (1996) finds that across the ages, symbolic features of family life have produced a sharp contrast between the families people *want* and the families they *have.*

Wives and Husbands

The early colonists organized their families around the unquestionable principle of patriarchy. Patriarchal authority rested ultimately on the father's control of landed property or craft skills. Children were dependent on their father's support in order to marry and set up independent households (Mintz and Kellogg, 1988:9). In her new study, *Marriage, A History,* Stephanie Coontz (2005) offers the following account of patriarchy in the colonies:

Governor John Winthrop of Massachusetts wrote in the seventeenth century: "A true wife accounts her subjection, her honor, and her freedom." Another New England Puritan urged wives to repeat a catechism that ended: "Mine husband is my superior, my better." (Coontz, 2005:141)

Marriage was a link in a larger system of political and economic alliances (Coontz, 2005:154). Marriages were arranged according to the social and economic purposes of larger kin groups. Marriages across social boundaries were not permissible, given the firm colonial hierarchies of rank and order. Among the wellborn, a suitable marriage was one made or arranged as an economic and social alliance, ensuring that the son or daughter remained in the station to which he or she had been bred. Or it was an arrangement that would secure, and perhaps enhance, the status and fortune of the family as a whole. But property was no less important to the making of marriages of more ordinary people. Among the less well off, who and when one married depended on economic circumstances such as the well-being of the family, the number of sons and daughters who had to be settled, or whether their labor was still needed in the family. The size of the dowry or settlement, as well as the timing of the marriage, could vary greatly among siblings. In places where, either by law or by tradition, primogeniture (the transfer of the family estate to the eldest surviving male) held sway, the eldest son stood to receive the greatest portion (Scott and Wishy, 1982:5). For both women and men, marriage was a central event in life.

The husband-father, or patriarch, enjoyed sole authority over all family members, matters, and property. Because he was responsible for the welfare of the family through succeeding generations, he owned all the property that would ensure its survival. This reinforced his authority and allowed him to exercise control over individual members and govern in the best interest of the household (Hawes and Nybakken, 2001:37). A wife was to be her husband's helpmate, not his equal (Mintz and Kellogg, 1988:11). As a wife, a woman became involved in mutual family duties and responsibilities. She was subordinate to her husband and often acted as his second-in-command, but everyone else in the family was subordinate to her in "the great chain of being" (Caffrey, 1991:230).

Historian Steven Mintz, describes surviving artifacts that symbolize a patriarchal society:

> A prime symbol of male dominance lay in the fact that he sat in an armchair, whereas other family members sat on benches or stools. In letters, husbands seldom asked their wives for advice; they generally addressed their wives in their correspondence with condescending terms such as "Dear Child," whereas women addressed their husbands as "Mister" and signed their letters "your faithful and obedient wife." (Mintz, 2006:13)

Although marriages were based on social and economic rather than on romantic considerations, romantic love was not wholly absent from colonial society. In Europe, too, love was present but was not directly or consistently linked to courtship and mate selection (Adams, 1980:68) (see Box 2.3). Marriage was, for the most part, a relationship in which the husband agreed to provide food, clothing, and shelter for his wife, and she agreed to return frugal management and obedient service. To "act like a man" meant to support one's wife (Cott, 1979:120).

Actual relations between spouses were more complicated than the ideals suggest. According to Mintz and Kellogg, both marital love and marital violence were present in the colonies:

> It was not unusual to find mutual love and tenderness in Puritan marriages. In their letters, Puritan husbands and wives frequently referred to each other in terms suggesting profound love for each other, such as "my good wife...my sweet wife" or "my most sweet Husband." Puritan court records further reveal that wife abuse is not a recent development. Between 1630 and 1699, at least 128 men were tried for abusing their wives. (Mintz and Kellogg, 1988:11)

Families in Global Perspective

Marriage in Seventeenth-Century England and Ireland

In seventeenth-century England, Samuel Pepys's cousin was exceptionally blunt about his motives for marriage. He asked Pepys to help him find a wife to replace his sister, who had kept house for him until her death, specifying that he wanted a widow without children but with a good income. She should be sober and industrious and not someone who would make great demands upon his time.

Marriages based "too much on love" were cause for comment. In the late seventeenth century the nephew of a Yorkshire businessman remarked disapprovingly that his uncle was "the strangliest inchanted and infatuated in his first marriage that I think ever any wise man was."

People valued love in its proper place. But it is remarkable how many people still considered it a dreadful inconvenience. In the 1690s Elizabeth Freke, wife of the sheriff of Cork, Ireland, thought her husband's plan to marry their son to the daughter of an earl was too ambitious, but she went ahead and arranged the meeting. To her great annoyance, her son not only was smitten with the girl but had the poor judgment to show it, thus weakening his family's bargaining position in negotiations over the financial settlement. The girl's parents, Freke wrote crossly, "found my son so taken with the young lady that they would have made us . . . paymasters to the young company." But Elizabeth was not intimidated. "I cared not to be frightened out of my money, nor my son either," she recorded, and the match fell through, "though my son was bitterly angry with me for it."

Some seventeenth-century parents were more indulgent toward their children's personal preferences than Lady Freke. But when they weren't, they rarely felt a need to justify their intransigence or cloak it in concern for their children's long-term happiness. And even individuals who believed that love was a vital part of marriage defined love in ways that were very different from the mutual esteem and reciprocal obligations that most modern couples wish for. Wives, for example, were expected to ignore their husbands' extramarital adventures. In the early sixteenth century Elizabeth Stafford, wife of the Duke of Norfolk, became so angry about her husband's affairs that it caused a family scandal. Her brother wrote to the duke commiserating with him about the couple's deteriorating marriage, which he blamed not on his brother-in-law's infidelity but on his sister's "wild language" and "wilful mind."

Source: Coontz, Stephanie, *Marriage, a History.* New York: Viking, 2005, pp. 139–140.

Throughout the colonial period, there was a shortage of women, especially in the frontier areas. Because women usually married older men, they tended to outlive their husbands. Widowhood was typically short, as women remarried very quickly. A study of marriage in seventeenth-century Maryland revealed that complex family arrangements and family conflict resulted from such marriages:

> Men found themselves responsible for stepchildren as well as their own offspring, and children acquired half-sisters and half-brothers. Sometimes a woman married a husband who himself had previously been married, and both brought children of former spouses to the new marriage. They then produced children of their own. The possibilities for conflict over the upbringing of children are evident, and crowded living conditions, found even in the households of the very wealthy, must have added to family tensions. (Carr and Walsh, 1979:39)

The gender ratio in some ways enhanced the status of women in the colonies by allowing them to perform crucial economic duties. Work for women, whether married or single, was not only approved of; it was considered a civic duty. Wives were expected to help their husbands and received approval for doing extra work in or out of the home:

> The vast majority of women worked within their homes, where their labor produced most articles needed for the family. The entire colonial production of cloth and clothing and in part that of shoes was in the hands of women. In addition to these occupations, women were found in many different kinds of employment. They were butchers, silversmiths, gunsmiths, upholsterers. They ran mills, plantations, tan yards, shipyards, and every kind of shop, tavern, and boarding house. They were gate keepers, jail keepers, sextons, journalists, printers, "doctoresses," apothecaries, midwives, nurses, and teachers. Women acquired their skills the same way as did the men, through apprenticeship training, frequently within their own families. (Lerner, 1979:183)

Although some women worked at occupations outside the home, they were excluded from roles that yielded the most power and privilege (Huber, 1993). The great majority, regardless of age or status, worked in the family setting. Each family provided the market with a commodity that other families needed. The members of the household specialized in different parts of the work of the family. Women's work was an essential part of the colonial economy, even though a sharp division of labor existed between husbands and wives. Men worked outdoors and in the fields, while women worked on the home plot, performing tasks associated with housework and child care. Nevertheless, women's tasks were diverse and endless:

> Over the long term of a lifetime [their tasks] were probably more arduous and demanding than those performed by men. One traveler in 18th century Carolina reported that "the ordinary women take care of Cows, Hogs, and other small Cattle, make Butter and Cheese, spin cotton, and flax, help to sow and reap corn, wind silk from the worms, gather Fruit and look after the House." Looking after the house was itself a heavy task since that included not only cleaning the physical interior but the washing and mending of the family's clothes, preparing meals under the handicaps of an open fireplace and no running water, preserving various kinds of foods, making all the soap, candles, and most of the medicines used by the family, as well as all the clothes for the family. And then, as the quotation suggests, the women had to be ready at planting or harvest time to help in the fields. On top of this, of course, was the bearing and rearing of children. During the colonial years when families of at least six children were common, this task was close to a full job in itself. It was this almost unending congeries of jobs that probably gave birth to the well-known tag that a woman's work is never done. Unlike the work of the husband-farmer, a woman's work went on after dark and at undiminished pace throughout the year. (Degler, 1980:363–364)

Without the labor of women, the economy of the seventeenth century would have been crippled. Although the work was vital, it was done under the heavy dominance of men. According to Coontz, authorities and neighbors were more concerned with wives who challenged patriarchal power than with husbands who abused it:

> Men were so sensitive on this question that they sometimes sued for slander when neighbors gossiped, as they frequently did, that a husband was allowing his wife to usurp his authority. A husband could be fined or ducked in the village pond for not controlling his wife. Even the governor of New Haven colony was once prosecuted and found guilty of "not pressing ye rule upon his wife." (Coontz, 2005:141)

Despite the patriarchal order, women's vital economic role gave them an important position in colonial families and communities and meant that they were neither completely dependent nor powerless (Landry, 2000:20).

Children

One belief about traditional colonial family life that survives the test of evidence is that families reared more children than those of our own day (Demos, 1981:6). Women gave birth to an average of eight children, and the number of children living in a household was three times greater than the number in 1950 (Grabill et al., 1973:379). Families of the premodern period reared large numbers of children, yet household size was not very large because of the high child mortality rate.

Child rearing was a more collective enterprise than it is today, with family behaviors ruled by duty and obligation. Mothers provided care for infants and young children, while fathers were active in the training and tutoring of children (Coltrane, 2004:227). In colonial society, children were dominated by the "three Rs" of repression, religion, and respect (Adams, 1980:72). The prevailing ideology was that children entered the world with original sin. They were inherently devilish and disobedient and therefore in constant need of strict correction. Even newborn infants were embodiments of sin. Cotton Mather, a famous Puritan preacher of the seventeenth century, encouraged parents to discipline their children with the rod or whip, but he urged that blows should not be given in anger but with calm conviction and dedication to the task at hand (Rosenfeld, 2007:126). This exerted a powerful influence on methods of childrearing (Mintz and Kellogg, 1988:15). Together, parents, schools, and churches kept children in subjugation:

In some households [children] were made to stand through meals, eating whatever was handed to them. They were taught it was sinful to complain about food, clothing, or their lot in life. Courtesy of a formal sort was insisted upon. Corporal punishment seems to have been liberally employed. Use was made of birchrods, canes, "flappers" [a leather strap with a hole in the middle], and at school dunce stools and caps and placards bearing humiliating names. (Queen and Habenstein, 1974:306)

From an early age, religious training was grim and constant. Children were required to learn the Bible by reading it chapter by chapter. This pattern of discipline was consistent with the prevailing view of children as miniature adults. In colonial society, childhood was not a life stage in the same way that it is today. Here is how Demos describes the world of the colonial child:

His work, much of his recreation, and his closest personal contacts were encompassed within the world of adults. From the age of six or seven he was set to a regular round of tasks about the house or farm (or, in the case of a craftsman's family, the shop or store). When the family went to church, or when they went visiting, he went along. In short, from his earliest years he was expected to be or try to be a miniature adult. (Demos, 1977:64)

Many historians contend that children in the colonies were miniature adults. A classic work by Phillippe Aries, *Centuries of Childhood* (1965), popularized the idea that childhood is a recent social creation and that for most of human history, a distinct phase of childhood did not exist. Historians disagree on this point. Some recent scholars of the colonial family have continued the idea that children were treated as miniature adults. Other scholars have questioned this interpretation by pointing out that the New England Puritans were aware that children had different abilities and temperaments from adults and that child rearing should be molded to these differences (Juster and Vinovskis, 1987:201; Vinovskis, 2006).

Children in the colonies were not sentimentalized. Many children were parented by a variety of adults who were not their biological parents (Pryor and Trinder, 2004:323). It was common to send young children or adolescents to live in other people's homes in order to work or learn a trade. Many children as young as seven lived apart from their parents for a period of time (Mintz, 2006:12). This practice of "putting out" children indicates an attitude far different from the attachment to children that was to develop in later periods. For some children, early development depended a great deal on caretakers other than parents: siblings, neighbors, or masters. Child abuse was a common feature of poor children's lives in this period (Polakow, 1993:15).

Social class and regional differences made childhood in the colonies highly diverse. In the eighteenth century, outside of New England, child rearing was more

Flax Scutching Bee, 1885. Rural families included resident servants and kin.

genteel. Daniel Blake Smith found an affectionate mode of child rearing in the Chesapeake plantations of Virginia and Maryland:

> The wide open and uncrowded plantation environment, with land abundant and vices scarce, allowed planters to raise their children under more optimistic and permissive assumptions about childhood and parental conduct. Obedience and respect for parental authority remained important for the development of strong character and stable family life, but parents placed considerably more emphasis on developing a child's, and especially a son's, freedom of movement and sense of personal autonomy.
>
> Chesapeake households were often complex units with servants and kin living on the plantation, making constant parental supervision of children unnecessary. Indeed, one senses from the letters and diaries of the period that children were allowed, and perhaps encouraged, to explore their immediate environment with little parental supervision. (Smith, 1983a:220)

The Emergence of Modern Family Life

Modern family life, with qualities distinctly different from those in colonial society, emerged at the end of the eighteenth century and the beginning of the nineteenth, in the years between the American Revolution and about 1850. These years cannot be taken precisely. Historians use decades, whole centuries, and the categories "premodern" and "modern" in reference to an imaginary boundary line set at roughly the year 1800. We should think in terms of a transitional process in which the end of one stage and the start of the next are fully merged (Demos, 1986:xi, 26). Even then, the shift was slow and varied by class, race, gender, and region (Kain, 1990:34). Table 2.1 summarizes the distinctive characteristics of family life during this period.

Unlike the colonial period, the time of transition was not a unique period of American history. Instead, it was part of the passage from an agricultural to an industrial economy. The rise of the modern family accompanied the shift from production in the home to a market economy. Many aspects of family life changed as workers were drawn off the farm into the factories. Households became smaller and more

Table 2.1   Colonial Families and Emerging Modern Families

Dimension	Pre-Revolutionary War Family	Post-Revolutionary War to 1850 Family
Economy, Family, and Society		
Economy	Family-based economy	Family-wage economy
Community linkages	Family and community interpenetrated	Development of boundaries around family
Social control	Community involvement in family matters	Family no longer subject to control by outsiders
Household Composition		
Structure	Nuclear	Nuclear
Members	Husband, wife, children, servants	Exodus of nonfamily members from household
Wives and Husbands		
Marriage	Based on economic considerations	Based on romantic considerations
Division of labor	Women's and men's work converged in the household economy	Separation of men's commercial labor and women's domestic labor
Role of women	Wide ranging with community obligations	Domestic caretakers
Status of women	Subordinate to patriarchal head of household	Subordinate to patriarchal head of household
Children		
Dominant ideology	Children require harsh discipline	Children require affection

private. Marriage was based on love and companionship. Families turned inward and became idealized as the domain of women and children.

Industrialization and Families

The War for Independence produced a new nation with a distinctly "modern" family form. Critical family transformations were aspects of macro-level social, economic, and demographic transformations that were reshaping all aspects of life in the new society (Mintz and Kellogg, 1988:xviii).

Social, economic, demographic, and cultural factors all gave rise to new family patterns. The shift from an agricultural to an industrial economy changed the location of productive work and produced a physical separation of the family and the workplace. Households could no longer sustain themselves by making, growing, or bartering goods. Now families acquired what they needed in the commercial economy. Work was done at central locations such as factories and shops. This trend led to the new concept of "going to work" (Jones, 1982:2) and created the **family-wage economy** (Tilly and Scott, 1978:104). In the family-wage economy, goods and services were produced *outside* the household. Workers earned their living outside the home, and families were supported by their wages.

As goods and labor moved out of the household and into the commercial economy, the family lost many of the functions it had in colonial society. No longer was the family a workshop, church, reformatory, school, and asylum. Activities were relocated to factories, schools, churches, and other nonfamilial settings. Families became increasingly private, set apart from society by distinct boundaries. The family took on the functions of the individual development of children, preparing them to make their way in the world (Hawes and Nybakken, 2001:6). This made the family a "personal" realm—a fortress of protection against the outside world. Aries describes this "emotional revolution":

> Previously, feelings were diffuse, spread over numerous natural and supernatural objects, including God, saints, parents, children, friends, horses, dogs, orchards, and gardens. Henceforth, they would be focused entirely within the immediate family. The couple and their children became the objects of a passionate and exclusive love that transcended even death. From that time on, a working man's life was polarized between job and family. But those people who did not go out to work (women, children, old men) were concerned exclusively with family life. Nor was the division between job and family either equal or symmetrical. Although there was, no doubt, some room for emotional involvement at work, the family was a more conducive setting; whereas the working world was subject to constant, strict surveillance, the family was a place of refuge, free from outside control. (Aries, 1965:229)

In the colonies, when families were the center of production, work and family were bound together. But with the separation of family and work activities, the family turned inward and took on "domesticity, intimacy, and privacy as major characteristics" (Hareven, 1976a:198).

As work and home became separate, a division of public and private spheres emerged along with a new conception of the family. The family became the private sphere. Families were no longer public domains. They became private domains where family activities were observable to fewer and fewer people. Individuals were less subject to social control by nonfamily members as the "audience" of family behavior changed. This fostered individual rights.

Demographic changes were another powerful force for the transformation of family life. (The following is dependent on Mintz and Kellogg, 1988:xix.) Such fundamental characteristics of a population as age distribution and the proportion of the sexes exert strong influences on the size and composition of families, the marriage rate, the death rate, the birth rate, and other features of family life. Two key demographic changes were critical. The first was a gradual reduction of birth rates within marriage. Beginning in the last quarter of the eighteenth century, U.S. women began bearing fewer children, spacing children closer together, and ceasing childbearing at earlier ages. Smaller families meant that parents could invest more emotional and financial resources in each child. A second demographic change was a gradual aging of the population. This meant that a growing proportion of the population began to experience aspects of family life less well known in the past.

Agency, Adaptation, and Change

The emergence of modern family life was tied to broad processes of social and economic change. But we should be careful not to fall back on a totally structural analysis of the shifting family. Two themes are important in this regard: (1) People

Broadside advertising for women operatives, 1859. With industrialization, poorer women transferred their traditional home occupations to the factory.

[1870]

75 Young Women

From 15 to 35 Years of Age,

WANTED TO WORK IN THE

COTTON MILLS!

IN LOWELL AND CHICOPEE, MASS.

I am authorized by the Agents of said Mills to make the following proposition to persons suitable for their work, viz:—They will be paid $1.00 per week, and board, for the first month. It is presumed they will then be able to go to work at job prices. They will be considered as engaged for one year, cases of sickness excepted. I will pay the expenses of those who have not the means to pay for themselves, and the girls will pay it to the Company by their first labor. All that remain in the employ of the Company eighteen months will have the amount of their expenses to the Mills refunded to them. They will be properly cared for in sickness. It is hoped that none will go except those whose circumstances will admit of their staying at least one year. None but active and healthy girls will be engaged for this work, as it would not be advisable for either the girls or the Company.

I shall be at the Howard Hotel, Burlington, on Monday, July 25th; at Farnham's, St. Albans, Tuesday forenoon, 26th, at Keyse's, Swanton, in the afternoon; at the Massachusetts' House, Rouses Point, on Wednesday, the 27th, to engage girls,---such as would like a place in the Mills would do well to improve the present opportunity, as new hands will not be wanted late in the season. I shall start with my Company, for the Mills, on Friday morning, the 29th inst., from Rouses Point, at 6 o'clock. Such as do not have an opportunity to see me at the above places, can take the cars and go with me the same as though I had engaged them.

I will be responsible for the safety of all baggage that is marked in care of I. M. BOYNTON, and delivered to my charge.

I. M. BOYNTON,

Agent for Procuring Help for the Mills.

were not passive victims of change—they engaged in various activities that gave them control over their lives; and (2) not only did the modern family emerge from large-scale economic developments, but changes in the family itself also shaped the emerging social order. Two historical examples make these points.

RESPONSES TO THE DILEMMA OF DECLINING LAND

By the end of the seventeenth century, fathers were losing control of landed property and productive skills. New forms of industrial capital were replacing land as a major source of wealth. This gave many children new opportunities to live away from their parents and permitted greater freedom from parental authority. At the same time, rapid population growth, combined with the practice of dividing family lands among all sons, resulted in plots too small to be farmed viably. This weakened paternal control over heirs. In many older settlements, high birth rates gradually outstripped the amount of cultivable land. Some communities grew by 5 or 6 percent annually, and the number of surviving sons proved to be greater than the resources necessary to establish viable farms. Colonists adapted their family arrangements by devising strategies to meet this dilemma:

> In some instances family homesteads were simply subdivided among all sons. In others fathers encouraged sons to migrate to newer communities where fresh land was available or else converted inheritances into some form other than real estate, such as formal education, an apprenticeship, or a gift of money. In still other cases such as Andover and Dedham, partible inheritance tended to give way to primogeniture; the bequest of land to the eldest son. And in other instances whole families moved to areas with abundant land....In Chebacco, a little village on the Massachusetts north shore, families combined a variety of strategies. First and second sons typically remained in the community, while younger sons migrated to newer areas. To balance the conflicting desires to preserve the family's estate, to allow most children to remain in the village and to provide a legacy for each child, families adopted a complex system of inheritance. (Mintz and Kellogg, 1988:18)

HOW FAMILIES SHAPED SOCIETY

Just as social changes transformed the family, the family also played an important part in adapting different classes to the new social order. Storekeepers, merchants, financiers, and entrepreneurs constituted a wealthier class with material abundance and comfort. But there were also more propertyless workers in the city and countryside. These new inequalities affected family organization. Bernard Farber (1973) studied merchant, artisan, and laboring families of the 1800s. He found that commercialization affected the social classes in different ways. For example, in the merchant class, family alliances fostered entrepreneurship. Relatives were given positions of trust, capital was pooled in family partnerships, and family alliances were created through marriage. These practices fostered a sense of cooperation, and they produced other results as well. First, business decisions sometimes caused merchants to question the motives of relatives (who were also their partners). Second, family coalitions contributed to political factions as well. These factions often became separate worlds, each with its own set of business arrangements and intermarriages among first cousins and between sets of siblings (Farber, 1973:103).

The artisan class played a different role from that of the merchant class in the development of business enterprise. The artisans' industry was still largely home-based. It provided a place for socializing children well suited to the pursuit of business. Families took on relatives as apprentices. Specialized occupations were then transmitted from one generation to another among relatives who remained in the same general locale and were expected to help one another in time of need. In this way, strong, stable, extended family relationships persisted in the artisan class long after the merchant families had fragmented themselves into many smaller units (Farber, 1973:105–106).

The laboring class, made up of "strangers" to the community, contributed to the day labor of the economy. Laborers' flexible family arrangements provided the economy with a pool of geographically mobile laborers, who were then exploited by the merchant and artisan classes.

Household Size and Composition

Premodern households had included a variety of nonkin: apprentices, servants, orphans or children from broken homes, and dependent members of the community placed there by town authorities. From the late eighteenth century on, apprentices slowly disappeared from U.S. homes, as did servants, except in upper- and middle-class families (Hareven, 1976a:194). The spread of wage labor replaced apprenticeships. Young workers were no longer obligated to live in their masters' homes, but began to live in distinctly working-class neighborhoods (Coontz, 2005:146; Mintz, 2006:18). The transition to a market economy produced a new class of urban wage workers. As artisans, craftsmen, boarders, lodgers, and others left family settings and moved out into the commercial economy, households became smaller.

Wives and Husbands

The rise of the modern family was accompanied by profound changes in women's and men's roles. Marriage became a private relationship between two individuals rather than a link in a larger economic system. Where marriage was once viewed as a unit of work and politics, it was now viewed as a place of refuge from work, politics, and community obligations (Coontz, 2005:145).

Individuals were encouraged to marry for love. Marriage was transformed into an emotional bond between two individuals. When people in the nineteenth century spoke of the purpose of marriage, they were most likely to refer to "love" or affection as the basis of the attraction between marital partners and the beginning of family formation (Degler, 1980:19). A content analysis of magazines published in the latter part of the eighteenth century revealed that romantic love was thought to be the basis of an ideal marriage (Lantz et al., 1968).

When production shifted outside the family, women's and men's roles became more and more different. Increasingly, men left the home each day to go to work, whereas their wives stayed home. "The midday meal, when an entire family gathered together was now replaced by the evening meal" (Mintz, 2006:18). Men's and women's activities were split into the male world of work and the female world of the family. Married women lost many traditional "productive" economic roles. Coontz describes the changes:

> The husband, once the supervisor or the family labor force, came to be seen as the person, who by himself, provided for the family. The wife's role was redefined to focus on her emotional and moral contributions to family life rather than her economic inputs. The husband was the family's economic motor, and the wife its sentimental core. (Coontz, 2005:146)

Middle-class women, especially, concentrated on keeping house and raising children. According to the new conception of women's roles, their task was to shape the character of children, making the home a haven of peace and order, and exert a moral and uplifting influence on men (Mintz and Kellogg, 1988:xix). Women's household labor took on new social meaning:

> While the good wives of the past produced prosaic and essential goods—home-spun clothing, simple foodstuffs, crude soaps, candles and dyes—eighteenth-century women and especially those who resided in commercial centers labored over more refined, if not ornamental creations—chintz curtains, decorated rugs, embroidered coverlets. The diaries and correspondence of urban middle-class women also indicated that they were less involved in both their husbands' business activities and the neighborhood barter system than were their foremothers. (Ryan, 1983:80)

Women's definition as homemakers and caretakers rather than as workers was strongest in the middle class. Here, the home acquired a sentimental quality; it was viewed as a retreat where meaning and satisfaction were to be found.

> Women's activities were increasingly confined to the care of children, the nurturing of husband, and the physical maintenance of the home. Moreover, it was not unusual to refer to women as the "angels of the house," for they were said to be the moral guardians of the family. They were responsible for the ethical and spiritual character as well as the comfort and tranquility of the home. In that role they were acknowledged to be the moral superiors of men. Husbands, on the other hand, the ideology proclaimed, were active outside the home, at their work, in politics, and in the world in general. In fact, it was just this involvement of men in the world that made them in need of women's moral guidance and supervision. (Degler, 1980:26)

We must keep in mind that changes were gradual and they varied from class to class. The family as a retreat was more characteristic of middle-class families than of working-class families. Yet women still faced strenuous work in the home that filled their working hours and were needed for survival. Most women faced long days of labor, hauling water and coal or wood for their stoves and shopping daily for food. Even women in the emerging middle classes spent hours each day making and mending clothes as well as cooking, baking, doing laundry with hired help, and cleaning the house (Thistle, 2006:21).

When female occupations such as carding, spinning, and weaving were transferred from home to factory, the poorer women followed their traditional work and became industrial workers. Many families retained their rural economic base while daughters went to work in factories. These women had to meet the demands of the new work system outside their homes and to balance these obligations with traditional domestic and family tasks. Consequently, they retained some continuity between their earlier traditions and their new work experience (Hareven, 1976b; Lerner, 1979).

On the other hand, the middle-class family experience was characterized by a sharp distinction between home and workplace, a role segregation between husband and wife, and limiting of women's activities in the home, along with a glorification of their domestic roles as housekeepers and mothers. The women of the middle and upper classes now used their time for leisure pursuits. They became "ladies" (Hareven, 1976b).

Children

As families became increasingly private and as gender domains became more separate, a new conception of children and childhood began to emerge. Children were now seen as different from adults. Among other things, they were now considered more innocent. Childhood was perceived much as it is today, as a period of life worth recognizing, cherishing, and even extending (Degler, 1980:66). Now, for the first time in this society, the child stood out as a creature distinct from adults: someone with special needs, talents, and character. Around 1800, children started to appear in clothing that was distinctly their own. They were also spending more and more time at play among groups of their peers (Demos, 1977:72).

By the middle of the nineteenth century, a middle-class upbringing differed dramatically from the premodern pattern. Instead of shifting back and forth between their parents' homes and work experiences as members of other households, a growing proportion of children were continuing to live with their parents into their late teens and twenties. Childhood and adolescence began to be viewed as a distinct stage of growth and development in which young people were prepared for eventual emergence into adulthood (Mintz and Kellogg, 1988:58–59). Children were born into families that were White or Black, poor or rich, farmers or wage earners. Their experiences were determined largely by the class and status of the family into which they were born. Few written historical sources have been found on the attitudes of working-class parents toward children in the period of transition. Nevertheless, the limited amount of child labor in the economy at this time suggests that working-class parents saw childhood as a special and different status (Degler, 1980:69).

The most telling evidence of this new view of children—indeed, this new social category—was the publication of books about child-rearing methods.

> For if children were innocent and natural it followed that parents should learn how to care for them, love them, and instruct them properly. And so in the years after 1820 large numbers of advice books on child-rearing came off the presses in Britain and the United States. As one authority on the history of child-rearing remarked, parents thought they "were remiss if they did not obtain and study the expanding body of literature on child rearing." He quoted one mother early in the 19th century as writing "There is scarcely any subject concerning which I feel more anxiety than the proper education of my children. It is a difficult and delicate subject, the more I feel how much is to be learnt by myself." Significantly, he concluded, this interest in child-rearing literature "was a new phenomenon" in the 19th century. (Degler, 1980:68)

Other tangible measures of the new status of children were books designed for children themselves and a decline in the corporal punishment of children (Degler, 1980:68–72). Not only do historians find a new outlook toward children in this period; some argue that the modern family took hold with the discovery of the child, a social category separate from adults (Aries, 1965). Not all scholars agree on this point. Still, childhood was transformed by the reorganization of work and domestic life.

The new view of childhood went hand in hand with the separation of families from the larger society. In colonial times, children were reared in communities by various community members, including their parents. As families became privatized, however, parents were left to bring up children on their own. The family became a child-centered haven set apart from economic and political concerns (Coltrane, 2004:227). In fact, the new conception of children gave the private family a new reason for being, a justification that remains to the present.

Challenging a Uniform Definition of the Family

Even as the modern family form emerged, it was limited by race and class. Not all groups were entitled to family life. During the seventeenth century, slaves had few opportunities to establish a stable and independent family life. As their population grew and African slaves were forcibly sold to serve as a labor pool, slave society

As middle-class family life adapted to industrialized society, women and the home acquired a sentimental quality.

developed with its distinctive African American kin forms. Among American Indians, from the Pueblo to the Cheyenne, both matrilineal and patrilineal family structures existed, expressing further diversity and cultural forms. While early American forms varied widely, however, a uniform *image* of family has dominated historical sensibilities and public memory (Polakow, 1993:25). This monolithic image is traceable to the patriarchal structure of the New England colonies and the emergence of the "modern" family. This stubborn image has long upheld one family form as the norm and the yardstick for judging other family forms. In the next chapter, we examine the varied family arrangements that emerged as U.S. history pressed forward.

Chapter Review

1. Common knowledge about families in the past is pure myth. The most persistent myths stem from false images of the "traditional" family nestled in a golden past.

2. Findings from the new field of family history have taken a long time to reach the public. Nevertheless, the work of social historians has confirmed a rich mosaic of past families.

3. White middle-class families are idealized and used as a measuring rod for all families, even though social and economic realities gave rise to a range of family arrangements.

4. In the early colonial period, Euro-American families were economic units in which all members had productive roles. This arrangement is called the family-based economy.

5. The family-based economy integrated women's, men's, and children's productive labor. Families were patriarchal. At the same time, women played an important role in the colonial economy.

6. During the colonial period, families and communities were highly intertwined. Families performed the economic, political, religious, and educational functions for society.

7. After 1800, social and economic changes produced gradual changes in family living. As the industrial economy developed, families were transformed from integrated work units into specialized domestic units that were separate from the surrounding communities.

8. Industrialization removed productive labor from the household and transferred family functions to other specialized institutions.

9. As industrialization separated the workplace from the home, the family-wage economy developed. In the family-wage economy, goods and services were produced outside of the household, where workers earned wages to support their families.

10. The family-wage economy produced a sharp distinction between women's and men's work, especially in the middle class. The family withdrew from the world of work and became a retreat from the outside world. The household became a setting for the care and socialization of children and for the emotional support of adults.

11. Throughout history, ordinary people developed a variety of family strategies for adapting to changing social conditions.

Key Terms

aggregate data analysis   33

family-based economy   38

family reconstitution   32

family-wage economy   48

godly family   37

"modern" family   31

Related Websites

http://www.nwhp.org

The National Women's History Project. An educational nonprofit organization founded in 1980 The NWHP's mission is to recognize and celebrate the diverse and historic accomplishments of women by providing information and educational materials and programs.

http://frank.mtsu.edu/∼kmiddlet/history/women.html

American Women's History: A Research Guide. This website provides citations to print and Internet reference sources, as well as to selected large primary source collections. It also provides information about the tools researchers can use to find additional books, articles, dissertations, and primary sources.

http://www.academic-genealogy.com

Genealogy and Family History Internet Web Directory. This is a professional genealogy and family history worldwide humanities and social sciences mega portal, connected to thousands of related subsets, with billions of primary or secondary database records.

The Historical Making of Family Diversity

■ **The Great Depression and Family Change**
   BOX 3.4   Researching Families: Did Race, Class, and Gender Matter in the Great Depression?

Chapter Review
Key Terms
Related Websites

▶ # Myths and Realities

Myth	The industrial revolution changed all families by separating them from the world of work.
Reality	Although middle-class families were separated from the world of work, most families did not experience this separation.
Myth	Historical development produced a nuclear family form that was not tied to kin. Kin networks were less efficient than the nuclear family, which was better suited to industrialization.
Reality	First, the nuclear household predated industrialization. Second, kinship ties in the late nineteenth century and the early twentieth century persisted because they were effective in the modern industrial system.
Myth	Families that did not conform to the "standard" model (nuclear in form, with a breadwinner father and a homemaker mother) were exceptions to the rule.
Reality	The breadwinner father/homemaker mother form that developed during industrialization was one of many family forms that emerged in the new society.
Myth	European immigrant families broke down as the old ways clashed with the new in America's industrial cities.
Reality	The immigrant family system made settlement possible in the new society.
Myth	Slavery destroyed African family systems and left a legacy of social problems.
Reality	Although their families were frequently disrupted, slaves rebuilt various family structures that enabled them to cope with enslavement.
Myth	People of Mexican origin were simply another immigrant group, disadvantaged by their traditional family ways.
Reality	The U.S. takeover of Mexicans on their own land in the mid-1800s and the labor migration that followed disrupted family patterns. Nevertheless, family flexibility sustained people of Mexican origin in the United States.

Conventional wisdom about family history assumes a "straight-line" or linear pattern of development with a "modern" family at the end. But even as the breadwinner father and homemaker mother form was taking shape among *some* groups, it was a family type that was found only in certain settings in North America. Other social contexts gave way to diverse family forms.

This chapter highlights the divergent character of family development. We examine the influence of the political economy and labor on family life. The threads of diversity, uneven change, and social agency become thicker in this chapter as we trace family development across time and social context.

First, we pick up on developing industrialization to show that social change is seldom universal in its effects. The new industrial economy had different effects on women, men, and children in different social classes. The theme of uneven change stands out as we contrast the experiences of the White working class with those in the White middle class. We turn, then, to immigration and racial control in the making of family history.

While the conventional histories of these groups and their families often feature diversity themes, they treat racial and ethnic families as special "cultural" cases that are different from a standard form (Baca Zinn, 1994). Instead, we take a **structural diversity approach** to show that social change is never one-directional. We show that diverse families are not merely cultural artifacts. They are shaped through their interaction with social structures (the structural diversity approach is discussed in Chapter 1). We consider the impact of immigration on the family patterns of White European immigrant groups who entered the United States voluntarily during the nineteenth century and at the beginning of the twentieth century. We examine the impact of racial domination on family life. We draw primarily from the historical experiences of African Americans and Mexican Americans, groups incorporated into our society through force and conquest. We conclude the chapter with a very brief look at family dislocations in the Great Depression.

Diverse contexts led working-class families and racial and ethnic families along different paths from that of White middle-class families. Racial domination and different labor structures produced different family forms. Structural forces required a range of domestic adaptations on the part of industrial workers, slaves, and agricultural workers. These adaptations were not *exceptions* to the rule; they were, instead, variations created by mainstream forces. As a result, the idealized modern family was not a luxury shared by all. "Even though it was a legally, economically, and culturally privileged family form that conferred advantages to those who lived in it" (Coontz, 2001:83), those advantages were not evenly distributed. Those outside of society's privileged groups share a historical pattern. Their families were often devalued, degraded, and destroyed. At the same time, the theme of human agency is especially powerful here. Family historians have given us rich accounts of how people subordinated by class and race used their families to survive and create a history and a place in the United States.

Industrialization and Family Life

Family life was fundamentally changed during the period of industrialization. The mill towns that grew up along the streams of the Northeast and the steam-powered factories served to dismantle the family-based economy (Ryan, 1983:116). As increasingly more goods and services were produced for profit outside the home, the family-wage economy developed.

This period in U.S. history was critical. The nation's economy was transformed from an agricultural system to one based on capitalist industrialization. With industrialization, cities grew rapidly, fueled by rural migrants and, most significantly, by wave after wave of European immigrants. During this period, the frontier was expanded to the West Coast. These developments occurred unevenly and had different effects on families in various segments of society. As Stephanie Coontz explains, social changes made families more diverse:

> The changes that helped produce more "modern" family forms, then, started in different classes, meant different things to families who occupied different positions in the industrial order, and did not proceed in a unilinear way. The "modernization" of the family was not the result of some general evolution of "the" family as early

sociologists originally posited, but of diverging and contradictory responses that occurred in different areas and classes at various times, eventually interacting to produce the trends we now associate with industrialization. (Coontz, 2000:24–25)

New Work Arrangements

The crucial era of transition to capitalist industrialization in the United States occurred in the decade before the U.S. Civil War. The most basic changes produced by the industrial revolution revolved around the reorganization of work and the allocation of different kinds of work to various groups within society. An important feature of capitalist industrialization was the development of sharp distinctions between a *middle class* whose wealth was based on business and industry and an industrial *working class* whose labor produced that wealth (Ehrenreich and English, 1978). Different levels of pay, prestige, and power that resulted from various positions within the economy produced great inequalities.

Another transformation was the separation of the workplace from the home. More and more production was moved from the household to larger centralized shops, factories, and industrial establishments. Households became self-contained economic units that were more dependent on outside wages (Glenn, 2002:73). This shift, with men becoming wage workers and women staying home to care for the house and children, became sharper in the early decades of the nineteenth century (Osmond, 1996).

Of course, there were varying shapes of industrialization (Coontz, 2000:22). Two concepts help us understand how the new division of labor in the industrial economy took different forms in the middle class and the working class. These concepts are *social production* and *social reproduction*. The term **social production** refers to the creation of goods—in other words, the varied ways in which people make a living, producing commodities (goods and services) on the job. **Social reproduction** refers to the maintenance of people—in other words, the work of caring for families in the home. This includes the maintenance of life on a daily basis, including food, clothing, shelter, and emotional activities (Amott, 1993:12; Brenner and Laslett, 1986:117; Glenn, 2002:73). Capitalist industrialization changed the relationship between social production and social reproduction. These two forms of work became increasingly divided in the new economy. Before industrialization, both social production and social reproduction occurred in domestic settings. Here, family members were engaged simultaneously in maintaining daily life and in the creation of foodstuffs, clothing, shoes, candles, soap, and other goods consumed by the household. With industrialization, production of these basic goods gradually was taken over by capitalist industry. Social reproduction, however, remained largely the responsibility of individual households (Glenn, 2002:73). The new economy meant that families were now required to have workers in both settings.

Many social critics viewed industrialization with apprehension. They romanticized family life and came to see the family as a haven in a heartless world (Budig, 2004:418). In the middle class, the family developed boundaries that separated it from the larger society, and it became a distinct sphere for women. While men's activities were increasingly focused on the industrial and competitive sphere of work, women's activities were confined to the care of children, the nurturing of the husband, and the physical maintenance of the home (Degler, 1980:26; Wharton, 2006). This complementary arrangement was possible only where men earned wages high enough to support the whole family. However, vast differences among men's earnings meant that many wives were forced into the public world of work. The new social order had different implications for families in different social classes.

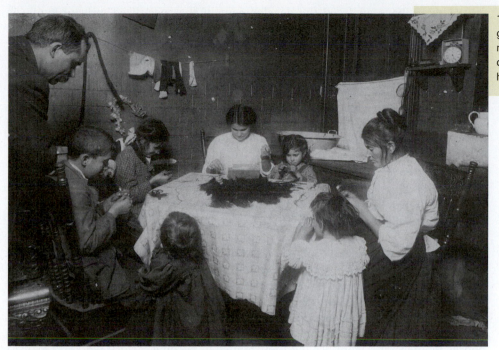

1910 Lewis Hine photograph of immigrant mother and children doing piece work in home.

Work and Family in Industrial Society

THE DOCTRINE OF TWO SPHERES

The division between public and private worlds led to a new prescribed division of labor by gender to carry out production and reproduction. Men were to follow production out of the household, while women were to remain responsible for reproduction at home (Glenn, 2002:74). This was the doctrine of two spheres. The ideology was accompanied by new beliefs about women's moral superiority. Women were thought to be "angels of the house" and spiritual guardians of the family.

The idealization of the women's sphere, called the **cult of true womanhood,** is described by historian Barbara Welter:

> The attributes of True Womanhood, by which a woman judged herself and was judged by her husband, her neighbors, and society, could be divided into four cardinal virtues—piety, purity, submissiveness, and domesticity. Put them together and they spelled mother, daughter, sister, wife-woman. Without them, no matter whether there was fame, achievement, or wealth, all was ashes. With them, she was promised happiness and power. (Welter, 1973:372)

From today's vantage point, Coontz views the glorification of women's piety, purity, and domesticity as a compensation for their exclusion from the expanding political, legal, and economic opportunities of the day (Coontz, 2005:162). The new ideology controlled women, narrowed their options, and lowered their status. True womanhood was to be found in home and in church. Even within the home, women's influence was limited. A husband's authority was supposed to be absolute in all major family decisions. By contrast, a wife's authority was exerted *symbolically*. Indeed, her great virtue was submissiveness and obedience to the will of her spouse, and her role was that of a comforter (Demos, 1977:68).

Scholars have analyzed the development of the specialized, private family in capitalism as oppressive to women (Zaretsky, 1976). As industrial work became increasingly alienating, the new sphere of personal life became more important for individuals. Women were assigned responsibility for maintaining the private refuge, and they were largely restricted by that responsibility. Home was a sanctuary in which women could be sheltered from the turmoil of economic and political life. It was the place where husbands could escape the materialistic preoccupations of the market economy (Coontz, 2005:156). The family life that developed in this "cult of domesticity" was very different for women and men:

> The male sphere encompassed the rational and active ideal, while females represented the humanitarian and compassionate aspects of life. When these two spheres were brought together in marriage, they produced a perfect, well-rounded whole. (Coontz, 2005:156)

The cult of true womanhood was an *ideal* that not all groups could achieve. It did not apply to women of the developing industrial class. Those women were often required to join their husbands (and often their children) in earning money for sheer family survival (Caffrey, 1991; Osmond and Thorne, 1993:610; Wharton, 2006). Historian Gerda Lerner (1979) has argued that the cult of true womanhood became a class ideology, a vehicle whereby middle-class women could distinguish themselves from poorer women who were leaving their homes to become factory workers. As class distinctions sharpened, social attitudes toward women became polarized, and the image of "the lady" was elevated to a status symbol. The cult of true womanhood served as a means of preserving class distinctions. Elite and middle-class White women had privileges that neither women nor men of other classes possessed. Although "home" was the proper sphere for the expression of true womanhood, much of the household work was done by servants, leaving some leisure for ladies to pursue other interests (Mullings, 1986:49). Motherhood and domesticity were elevated as virtues for White women. White men were seen as requiring and deserving a wife's services, and White children were viewed as valued future citizens to be nurtured and protected. In contrast, the caring that Black women performed for their families was not deemed worthy of protection (Glenn, 2002:75).

Although domesticity was idealized for all classes of White women, many were hardly in a position to be "ladies." For example, women on the Overland Trail to California and Oregon between 1842 and 1867 longed for a return of the separate spheres. On the long journey, they performed both women's and men's work, but they viewed the work as only temporary, and indeed they fought to preserve for themselves a separate women's sphere (Faragher and Stansell, 1979).

WOMEN AND INDUSTRIAL WORK

Unlike middle-class women, working-class women in the 1800s were engaged in both social production and social reproduction. Most women lived in households in which the role of full-time homemaker was an unattainable luxury. They bore and raised children during most of their lives. They engaged in both domestic caretaking in the home and wage labor outside the household, mostly in disagreeable and often hazardous jobs in factories and sweatshops (Coleman, 1998:75; Osmond and Thorne, 1993:611). When the New England textile industry began in the first decade of the nineteenth century, the economy was still mostly agrarian and men were fully engaged in farming and independent artisanry. Mill owners actively recruited the only readily available labor force: single young White women from farm families (Glenn, 2002:74).

Women's traditional household tasks were among the first productive activities to be transferred to the factory. Traditionally, female production became the first large industries of the capitalist market, including yarn and textile production (spinning, weaving, bleaching, and dying); shoe-binding; palm leaf and straw weaving; food processing; comb and button making; and the production of ready-made clothes (Coleman, 1998:80). When a group of Boston businessmen drew up plans for cotton mills along the New England waterways in places such as Lowell and Waltham, Massachusetts, they designed female boardinghouses as well as spinning, weaving, and warping rooms. This model of early American industry recruited a workforce of young farm girls from throughout New England. The Hamilton Company in Lowell was typical. By 1835, around 85 percent of the machine tenders were female, 86 percent were native born, and 80 percent were between the ages of 15 and 30. In the large and small textile mills that grew up throughout New England and the Middle Atlantic states, women workers were almost always in the majority. Only shoe manufacturing rivaled textiles in scale of organization and level of productivity. Both industries employed at least as many women as men, and often more women. The development of heavy industries that employed great numbers of males, especially mining and metal working, would await the post–Civil war period (Ryan, 1983:121).

Wage earning was essentially a domestic obligation; wages earned belonged to families. Research on wage-earning women from 1900 to 1930 points to the intensive family loyalties of working-class girls:

> Although they were generally more successful in school than boys, daughters left school for work or to assist at home about as frequently as their brothers. They worked at dull, ill-paying jobs more steadily than adolescent boys; they usually surrendered their entire wage to their mothers—males often returned only a portion of their pay; and they had more household responsibilities than wage-earning sons. Investigators often reported tension between parents and daughters in working-class families, especially over spending money and social freedom, but most daughters stayed essentially obedient; they remained in the parental home, they surrendered their wages, they compromised with parents on standards of behavior. (Tentler, 1979:89)

As industrialization advanced, women continued to inhabit a separate labor market. Then, as today, low-income family life required cooperation and sharing between the sexes and generations. Family was a defense against underclass oppression. Thus, to many working-class women it appeared extremely desirable for the family breadwinner to be the man (Osmond and Thorne, 1993:611).

THE FAMILY WAGE

In the early nineteenth century, working-class men began agitating for a "family wage": an income sufficient to support the family at a decent standard, a so-called American standard of living. The ideology assumed that all women would sooner or later become wives, making it legitimate for women to be cut off from the sphere of the cash economy and become financially dependent on their husbands (Coontz, 2005:156; Glenn, 2002:82; May, 1990:277). Although the family wage was an important victory of the labor struggles of the late nineteenth and early twentieth centuries, it glorified gender differences—women's homemaking and men's breadwinning roles. This justified women's exclusion from the labor force. However, the family wage was limited to White men. Others received wages insufficient to support a family alone. The family wage provided a material basis for race and gender domination:

> A "man's wage" did not apply to men of color, who were not accorded respect as heads of households. Thus, for example, black men's earnings were not assumed to cover support for a non-employed wife and children. Black women, after all were viewed as laboring bodies. Additionally, the standard of living of blacks and other people of color was assumed to be lower than whites. (Glenn, 2002:82)

CHILDHOOD AND ADOLESCENCE

Industrial capitalism and growth had far-reaching consequences for children's lives. No single pattern of childhood marked the nineteenth century. Instead, there were multiple childhoods that differed by class, ethnicity, gender, and region. Family historian Steven Mintz has found that at no point in American history was childhood more diverse than in the mid and late nineteenth century. Class differences were stark:

> For the urban middle class, increasing economic affluence allowed parents to provide an extended, protected childhood; but for the laboring classes, a sheltered childhood was impossible. The demands of a market economy made their children indispensable economic resources, whose labor could be exploited in new ways. Unlike their middle-class counterparts, children in laboring families were expected to repay their parents' sacrifices by contributing to the family economy. These children worked not because their parents were heartless, but because their labor was essential to their family's survival. (Mintz, 2008:96)

Nevertheless, the family as an institution became more child centered. The new conception of children as separate and different from adults went hand in hand with the doctrine of two spheres. The ideal was for children to be reared by women within the domestic setting. Although women had always reared children, in the nineteenth century child rearing was defined as a woman's special task. This concept was reinforced by the industrial changes that were placing women's duties in the home. The separation of family from work also exalted children and raised domesticity within the family to a higher level of respectability (Degler, 1980:73).

In the middle classes, childhood was now viewed as a distinct stage in the life cycle. Changes in the economy and the family were giving way to adolescence—a new life stage. The concept of adolescence emerged in the last two decades of the nineteenth century. As families moved away from production and as the population shifted from rural to urban settings, the concept of adolescence gradually took shape. Urban settings provided circumstances that allowed young people to be brought together and to form a distinctive youth culture (Demos and Demos, 1973:209).

Industrial capitalism changed parent–child relationships. In the family-based economy, children had been little workers who were trained as apprentices. In the new economy, a son's fortune depended on his performance in the labor market and a daughter's fortune on her success in the marriage market and her husband's success. Parenting in middle- and upper-class families became a distinct social and familial activity intended to prepare children for success in economic competition:

> ... [T]he parenting of a son came to mean teaching him to be a self-seeking competitive individual, instilling in him the drive to succeed and the belief in his ability to do so.... The parenting of girls changed with that of boys for it meant, first and foremost, preparing them to be mothers and wife/supporters to these new individuals. (Matthaei, 1982:108)

BOX
3.1

Families in Global Perspective

Discarding Infants in Nineteenth-Century France

In her illuminating study of abandoned children in nineteenth-century France, Rachel Fuchs (1984) argues that the widespread abandonment of infants and young children was part of the very fabric of the culture and the corresponding lifestyles of the poor and destitute. For mothers it was "a radical solution to the social, psychological, and above all economic pressures the woman faced.... They abandoned the baby, because to keep the infant meant loss of job, income and even life for them and the child." We read in Hugo's *Les Misérables* how Fantine is forced to abandon her little daughter Cosette in this way.

Abandonment constituted part of the "social question" that preoccupied France as late as the eighteenth and nineteenth centuries; for the rising tide of destitute abandoned children threatened the state as they grew up to form the "dangerous classes." The desperate conditions of poor mothers and their children illuminate not only state policies toward children but also "nineteenth-century French attitudes toward unwed mothers, illegitimate children, working class and middle class families, and the peasantry." Social economists saw all forms of deviance as having their origins in the poor and uneducated population.

The late eighteenth century saw a rise in population and growing rates of illegitimacy, so starvation threatened both the rural and the urban poor and abandonment became a problem of enormous magnitude. Hence France began to develop a state policy for receiving and maintaining destitute and unwanted children. Influenced by the secular reformers, a national, secular, state-supported form of public assistance was initiated. The constitution of 1791 proclaimed that the task of the nation was to raise abandoned children and to make useful citizens by training them for the military, for agriculture, and for populating the colonies. Prostitution and vagabondage were the vices most feared by the authorities. Because abandoned children were believed to "carry the most dangerous instincts in their hearts," France's public policy for children developed two strategies: The first institutionalized abandonment through the notorious "tour," and the second disposed of disposable children through the wet-nurse institution.

The "tour"—a revolving cylindrical box in which mothers placed their babies—was built into the walls of hospices and foundling hospitals, a stark symbol of anonymity. It was stipulated by decree in 1811 that each hospice should have one. The cradle swiveled so that the mother who deposited the baby from the street could not be seen on the inside, and a bell would be sounded to announce that a baby had been dropped. Thus "the tour was deaf, dumb and blind. The total anonymity of the mother and baby was assured, unless the mother or her messenger put some identifying tag or note on the infant." This anonymity was believed necessary to avoid abortion and infanticide, but it was controversial since many authorities believed it encouraged immorality and irresponsibility on the part of destitute women. The tour, in essence, centralized child abandonment. It regulated the process by which the state took control of pauper children and fashioned them into useful capital for the state. When its controversial practice was discontinued, French child policy continued to permit the "displacement" of babies to the countryside.

Source: Polakow, Valerie, *Lives on the Edge.* Chicago, IL: University of Chicago Press, 1993, pp. 17–19.

This model of early life was a middle-class pattern. It never existed at all for poor children in this country or for poor children in other societies (see Box 3.1 for a discussion of infant abandonment among the poor in nineteenth-century France). Girls and boys from poor families in the United States were "put out" to labor for wages at unskilled or manual work; they were put to work for the family as much as they had been in the household economy (Cooper, 1999:26; Matthaei, 1982:198). Many urban, working-class children contributed to the family economy by scavenging in the streets, vacant lots, or back alleys, collecting coal, wood, and other items that could be used at home or sold. Others took part in the street trades—selling gum, peanuts, and crackers. Teenage girls were employed in domestic service or making shoes, clothing, and household items inside their own homes or in boarding houses. In industrial towns, young people under the age of 15 contributed an average of 20 percent of their families' income (Mintz, 2004:40) (see Box 3.2). According to Mintz, two

BOX 3.2 **Inside the Worlds of Diverse Families**

Children's Uses of the Streets: New York City, 1850–1860

Unlike today, the teeming milieu of the New York streets in the mid-nineteenth century was in large part a children's world.... Public life with its panoply of choices, its rich and varied textures, its motley society, played as central a role in the upbringing of poor children as did private, domestic life in that of their more affluent peers. While middle-class mothers spent a great deal of time with their children (albeit with the help of servants), women of the laboring classes condoned for their offspring an early independence—within bounds—on the streets. Through peddling, scavenging, and the shadier arts of theft and prostitution, the streets offered children a way to earn their keep, crucial to making ends meet in their households. Street life also provided a home for children without families—the orphaned and abandoned—and an alternative to living at home for the especially independent and those in strained family circumstances. Such uses of the streets were dictated by exigency, but they were also intertwined with patterns of motherhood, parenthood, and childhood. In contrast to their middle- and upper-class contemporaries, the working poor did not think of childhood as a separate stage of life in which girls and boys were free from adult burdens, nor did poor women consider mothering to be a full-time task of supervision. They expected their children to work from an early age, to "earn their keep" or to "get a living"—a view much closer to the early modern conceptions which Phillippe Ariès describes in *Centuries of Childhood* (1965). Children were little adults, unable as yet to take up the duties of their elders, but nonetheless bound to do as much as they could. To put it another way, the lives of children, like those of adults, were circumscribed by economic and familial obligations. In this context, the poor expressed their care for children differently than did the propertied classes. Raising one's children properly did not mean protecting them from the world of work; on the contrary, it involved teaching them to shoulder those heavy burdens of labor that were the common lot of their class, to be hardworking and dutiful to kin and neighbors. By the same token, laboring children gained an early autonomy from their parents, an autonomy alien to the experience of more privileged children. But there were

certainly generational tensions embedded in these practices: Although children learned independence within the bounds of family obligation, their self-sufficiency also led them in directions that parents could not always control. When parents sent children out to the streets, they could only partially set the terms of what the young ones learned there. Street selling, or huckstering, was one of the most common ways for children to turn the streets to good use.... In the downtown business and shopping district, passers-by could buy treats at every corner: hot sweet potatoes, baked-pears, teacakes, fruit, candy, and hot corn. In residential neighborhoods, hucksters sold household supplies door to door: fruits and vegetables in season, matchsticks, scrub brushes, sponges, strings, and pins. Children assisted adult hucksters, went peddling on their own, and worked in several low-paying trades that were their special province: crossing-sweeping for girls; errand running, bootblacking, horse holding, and newspaper selling for boys. There were also the odd trades in which children were particularly adept, those unfamiliar and seemingly gratuitous forms of economic activity that abounded in nineteenth-century metropolises: One small boy whom a social investigator found in 1859 made his living in warm weather by catching butterflies and peddling them to canary owners.

Younger children, too, could earn part of their keep on the streets. Scavenging, the art of gathering useful and salable trash, was the customary chore for those too small to go out street selling. Not all scavengers were children; there were also adults who engaged in scavenging full-time, ragpickers who made their entire livelihoods from all the odds and ends of a great city. More generally, however, scavenging was children's work. Six- or seven-year-olds were not too young to set out with friends and siblings to gather fuel for their mothers. Small platoons of these children scoured neighborhood streets, ship and lumberyards, building lots, demolished houses, and the precincts of artisan shops and factories for chips, ashes, wood, and coal to take home or peddle to neighbors.

Source: Stansell, Christine, "Women, Children, and the Uses of the Streets: Class and Gender Conflict in New York City, 1850–1860." In *Unequal Sisters: A Multi-Cultural Reader in U.S. Women's History,* Ellen Carol Du Bois and Vicki L. Ruiz (eds.). New York: Routledge, 1990, pp. 94–95.

distinct conceptions of childhood emerged: "One conception, the useful childhood, was based on the premise that all family members, including children, should contribute to a family's support.... The other conception was a protected childhood, sheltered from the stresses and demands of the adult world" (Mintz, 2008:106).

Accordion Households

In Chapter 2 we dealt with myths about "the classical family of Western nostalgia." Industrialization did not create the nuclear family, but it did contribute to household flexibility during certain periods of transformation. Although households after 1830 tended to be nuclear, recent studies have found that the changes were not linear. To correct common misconceptions about family life in the period of industrial expansion, we must once again distinguish between *family* and *household*. Family members were not isolated from kin, although extended kin did not usually live together in the same household. Although households as residential units were predominantly nuclear, family activities were not contained within the household. Family members sustained ties with relatives outside the household even where the residential unit was predominantly nuclear (Hareven and Vinovskis, 1978:15).

Households could expand and contract according to family circumstances. Families could enlarge their households with nonfamily members. At certain points in their development and in response to economic need, families might augment their household composition by taking in boarders or lodgers. When conditions improved, the family would become nuclear again (Modell and Hareven, 1977). Modell and Hareven found that the structure of households of the late nineteenth century varied along the family life cycle. Migration patterns, available housing, and changing economic needs provided contexts for creating "malleable households":

> Boarding in families in industrial America in the late 19th century was the province of young men of age just to have left their parents' homes, and was an arrangement entered into and provided by household heads who were of an age to have just lost a son from the residential family to an independent residence.... [Boarding involved] the exchange of a young adult person and a portion of his young adult income from his family of orientation to what might be called his family of reorientation to the city, to a job, to a new neighborhood, to independence. It was a transition from a family (often rural, whether domestic or foreign) with excess sons or daughters (or insufficient economic base) to one (usually urban) with excess room (or present or anticipated need). And often both the excess room and the present or anticipated economic need can have come from the departure from the household of a newly independent son. (Modell and Hareven, 1977:177)

These accordion households helped families adapt to urban life. They were important in the life cycle of young people as a transitional stage between departing from their parents' families and setting up their own families. The practice of taking in strangers in exchange for pay or services was more widespread during this period than was the practice of sharing household space with extended kin (Hareven, 1977).

Immigration and Family Life

From 1830 to 1930, the United States witnessed two massive waves of immigration. The first wave (the "old" immigration) began arriving in the 1830s and continued through the 1880s, when more than 10 million immigrants arrived. English, Irish, German, and Scandinavian immigrants predominated in these decades. The opening of large land areas beyond the Mississippi and the building of roads, canals, and railroads, along with increasing industrialization, offered new jobs to immigrant labor and opened up new agricultural areas to settlement.

The "new" immigration took place in the years between 1882 and 1930. This great influx of European people saw the admission of more than 22 million immigrants. This period marked the high point of immigration from northern and western European nations and the beginning of a new influx of peoples from southern and eastern Europe, including Italians, Poles, Greeks, Russians, Austro-Hungarians, and other Slavic groups (Dyer, 1979:103–105).

Immigration, which began as a trickle, gradually gained momentum during the nineteenth century and finally became a flood by the beginning of the twentieth century. This extraordinary population movement (the largest in recorded history) was the result of an extraordinary economic expansion (also the largest and most concentrated in American history). Demographers and historians have identified a host of push and pull factors that operated on different groups. In their countries of origin, immigrants were experiencing population explosions and dislocations that provided the major stimulus for emigration. At the same time, industrialization was generating an insatiable demand for labor in the United States. The prospects of economic opportunity on this side of the Atlantic motivated millions of Europeans to uproot themselves. We can hardly overstate the critical role played by immigrant labor in the industrialization of America. In the early stages of industrialization, immigrants performed unskilled labor in mining, construction, and manufacturing. Foreign labor built the industrial edifice:

> By 1910, the foreign-born made up a quarter of the nation's work force, and in many of the industries closest to the industrial center, the foreign-born were a clear majority. In 1910 . . . a survey of twenty principal mining and manufacturing industries found that 58 percent of workers were foreign-born. In coal mines the figure was 48 percent; in iron mines 67 percent; in clothing factories 76 percent; in slaughter and packing houses 46 percent; in tanneries 53 percent; in steel mills 51 percent; in rubber factories 41 percent; in textile mills 49 percent; in road construction 46 percent. (Steinberg, 1981:36)

Immigrant families varied between groups. Europeans from diverse societies who settled in the industrial cities of the Northeast and Midwest were confronted with numerous problems. They faced discrimination, poverty, and many difficulties in reestablishing families (Hutter, 1991:170). These problems led to the faulty conclusion that migration destroyed family life.

The Social Breakdown Perspective

Themes of instability and crisis were common in the earliest works on immigrants and their families. Those studies depended on the reports of reformers and journalists who stressed what they found to be unpleasant—drink, dirt, and desertion—and blamed the immigrants rather than society for their misfortunes (Berrol, 1991:320). Turn-of-the-century research on immigrants was steeped in questions about how migration broke down the old ways of life. Immigrants were thought to be uprooted and unstable peasants without family ties in the new society. Such themes appeared in an influential book written by Oscar Handlin. *The Uprooted* (1951) emphasized the traumatic consequences of immigration for family life. Family disintegration was viewed as an unfortunate consequence of the immigrants' break with the past (Orsi, 2001; Sanchez, 1999:128). The many varieties of families in different ethnic groups were thought to be out of step with the demands of modern society. According to this perspective, when they adopted modern family patterns, the newcomers would be assimilated by the dominant society. Implicit in this approach was a model of a "normal" family against which immigrant families were judged. By emphasizing immigrant culture, the immigrants themselves were wrongly blamed for many social problems that were the result of larger forces such as the economic order (Pyke, 2004:258).

Critics of the "Handlin school" of immigration history found this interpretation to be false on almost all counts. To begin with, immigrants were diverse and their families differed dramatically. More important, immigrants settled in communities with widely differing social and economic structures that produced different family outcomes. The immigrants were not all traditional peasants. Although first-generation immigrants certainly experienced personal and collective cultural traumas, they were neither totally uprooted nor destroyed. Instead, most endured material hardships and emotional stress with remarkable fortitude and dignity (Early, 1983:482).

The greatest misconception about the family life of the immigrants is that their family patterns in the New World were shaped mainly by their Old World cultures. The key ingredients of the old family ways—patriarchal family ideology and kinship orientation—were thought to be obstacles that prevented successful adjustment. A main point in the early studies was that the immigrants' "cultural baggage" could be erased through acculturation. Immigrant families were major targets for reform. Settlement workers sought to Americanize the newcomers by ridding them of their old family ways.

This thinking ignores the key role that families played in migration, recruitment, and settlement. New historical studies offer a very different picture of immigrants and their families. These studies emphasize the responsibility of an exploitative industrial society for the newcomers' plight, which would have been far worse without the supportive family networks in urban communities (Berrol, 1991:320). Families were the basic resource in the adaptation of families to the new environment (Mintz and Kellog, 1988:87). Instead of relinquishing old patterns completely, immigrants "used their cultural baggage to help them control and fashion their own destinies" (Early, 1983:482).

Industrial Work and Immigrant Families

The family was vital in recruiting workers to the new industrial society. Family patterns often carried over to the urban setting and provided continuity between the Old World and the new industrial setting. Immigrants tended to migrate in groups. They moved into neighborhoods with networks of relatives and friends, where others spoke their language and helped them find work.

> Low-paid industrial immigrant workers were forced by economic pressures to live close to their places of work. The particular choice of residence and occupation was strongly influenced by the presence of friends and relatives in a process that has been called "chain migration." Chain migration refers to the connections made between individuals in countries of origin and destination in the process of international migration and to the process in which choices of residence and occupation were influenced by friends and relatives.... Relatives acted as recruitment, migration, and housing resources, helping each other to shift from the often rural European work background to industrial work. (Hutter, 1991:177)

Instead of breaking their kinship ties, families *used* them in the transition to industrial life. A study of southern Italians in Chicago by Rudolph J. Vecoli discovered that solidarity and support rather than disorganization characterized family life after 1800. The *contadini* emigrated in chainlike fashion. After working a while, men would send for their families. In this way, chains of immigration were established between certain towns of southern Italy and Chicago. By 1920, the Italian population in Chicago had reached approximately 60,000. Within their ethnic communities, families retained their traditions and their unity:

> Reunited in Chicago, the peasant family functioned much as it had at home; there appears to have been little of that confusion of roles depicted in [Handlin's] *The Uprooted*. The husband's authority was not diminished, while the wife's subordinate position was not questioned...nor did the extended family disintegrate upon emigration as is contended...[for] the family unit not only includes those related by blood, but those related by ritual bonds as well....The alliance of the families of the town through intermarriage and godparenthood perpetuates a social organization based upon a large kinship group. (Vecoli, 1964:409)

The work patterns of southern Italians were influenced by their culture and the city's occupational structure. Few found employment in Chicago's manufacturing industries because of their aversion to factory work and discrimination against them by employers. Instead, they retained their traditional laboring mode by replacing the Irish in excavation and street work, as they did on railroad and construction jobs throughout the West. Engaged in seasonal gang labor, they developed an institution for distributing employment and other kinds of social support. This was the *padrone* system. The *padrone* was an employment agent who mediated between employers and the Italian laborers. He also assisted them in other ways, easing their accommodation to the new society.

Like working-class women in general, immigrant women often entered the industrial labor force in order to make ends meet. Although they shared the domestic ideal of womanhood, many worked simply to provide for their families. The extent to which immigrant wives worked outside the home varied according to ethnic group, but at no time did more than 10 or 15 percent of the wives of any nationality work outside the home (Degler, 1980:140). French Canadian women continued to work after their marriages despite the expectation prevalent in their culture that married women would remain in the home (Hareven, 1975). On the other hand, southern Italians in Buffalo, New York, opposed women's employment outside the home. Italian women remained in the home, while Buffalo's Irish, Polish, Swedish, and German women were employed as domestics in middle-class homes. Women's preference to remain in the home resulted somewhat from Buffalo's peculiar occupational structure. Unlike many other cities, heavy industry and transportation dominated its economy. The city offered comparatively little in the way of light industrial production for unskilled women (Yans-McLaughlin, 1973:117).

Recent historical scholarship has shed new light on just how immigrants used their traditional family patterns in accommodating to the new industrial settings. For example, a study of French Canadian families moving to Lowell, Massachusetts, in the 1870s reveals a distinctive *family strategy*. Historian Frances Early (1983) found that French Canadian families arrived from agricultural settlements in Quebec, where the family was still the main unit of production. All family members had contributed their labor to the family farm. In Lowell, the immigrants patterned their work on the farm economy by using children's labor to contribute to the

Children from poor families labored long hours in often dangerous conditions.

earning power of families: They sent their children to work. By the age of 13, children worked away from the home: Seven in 10 children ages 11 through 15 held jobs in 1870 (Early, 1983:485). This was an adaptive mechanism based on the family-based economy tradition. It enabled the immigrants to survive in a one-industry textile town:

> They created new family economic strategies based on difficult new realities, and thereby exerted a certain control over their lives. However, the vast majority of French Canadians, if they chose to live and work in Lowell, had to accept the socio-economic configuration of late nineteenth-century industrial-capitalist New England society. In other words, they had to begin their new lives as members of a large, alienated, and often suffering industrial proletariat whose ability to direct and shape the present as well as the future was, indeed, regrettably limited. (Early, 1983:494–495)

The Irish in Massachusetts in the late nineteenth century also adapted to poverty by sending children out to work. John Modell (1978) found that poor Irish families removed their children from school in order to place them in the labor force. When economic conditions improved for the family, children were reinstated in school. The family was not simply a passive recipient of social change. It was, however, a vital resource in adapting to the new society. The immigrant family was primarily responsible for "making it" in America (Hutter, 1991:175). Yet the family traditions of these immigrants were not something passed down from generation to generation. Instead, different groups drew selectively from cultural resources, often creating new "traditions" as they adapted to or resisted changing economic or political constraints and opportunities (Coontz, 2001:82).

Racial Control and Family Life

New Thinking About Minority Families

The mythical "standard family" has produced far-reaching misconceptions. As the yardstick for judging all family forms, images of what is "normal" have clouded our understanding of minority families. Compared to mainstream families, racial minority families have long been seen as dysfunctional—products of ethnic cultures at odds with modern society. Even some social science treatments of family life are based on racialized images of families "handicapped" by their culture.

The African American family in particular has been stereotyped as disorganized and equated with family problems—in other words, the essence of what families should *not* be. The mistaken idea that slavery weakened kin ties and undermined family values gave way to notions of the **matriarchal family,** a form in which power rested in the mother figures, with fathers largely absent from family life. According to this thinking, family disintegration continued into the twentieth century. Black families remained locked in a "tangle of pathology." This was the theme of Daniel Patrick Moynihan's study, *The Negro Family: The Case for National Action* (1965). The Moynihan report identifies the family as the main problem facing African Americans:

> At the heart of the deterioration of the fabric of Negro society is the Negro family. It is the fundamental source of weakness in the Negro community at the present time....Unless this damage is repaired, all the effort to end discrimination and poverty and injustice will come to little. (Moynihan, 1965:5)

According to this reasoning, family weakness created problems for African American people in U.S. society.

Mexican-origin or Chicano families have been stereotyped as disorganized due to backward Mexican traditionalism. As late as the 1960s, the Chicano family was seen as the main cause of Chicano subordination:

> The kind of socialization that Mexican-American children receive at home is not conducive to the development of the capacities needed for advancement in a dynamic industrial society. This type of upbringing creates stumbling blocks for future advancement by stressing values that hinder mobility—family ties, honor, masculinity, and living in the present—and by neglecting values that are conducive to it—achievement, independence, and deferred gratification. (Heller, 1966:34–35)

Such explanations rest on ahistoric concepts of family life (Mullings, 1997:73). They also ignore the impact of larger forces.

New studies expose the flaws in the old cultural deficit frameworks. Families were not shaped by culture alone. Instead, racial groups displayed different family forms in different historical periods. Furthermore, the historical study of African Americans, Chinese, and Mexican immigrants reveals that economic and political constraints produced family patterns that were *different* from those in their countries of origin. Today, we have a better understanding of why the family lives of people of color have never fit the mainstream model.

In this section we examine the myths and realities of family life among racial minorities from the time these groups entered the United States through 1930. Although we draw primarily from the experiences of African Americans and

Chicanos, we also refer to Asian American families. Although each group is distinguishable from the others, racism created similar histories for these groups. Composite portraits of each group reveal important commonalities. Even groups with very different cultures display similar family patterns when they are located in similar circumstances (Glenn and Yap, 1992). Despite the harsh conditions imposed on each group, family life remained strong. People of color developed many family strategies that allowed them to function. These included fluid family boundaries, flexible family roles, and patterns of support in extended kinship structures.

Race, Labor, and Family Life

To understand how race has produced a diverse history for U.S. families, we must follow the theme that runs through our historical discussion—namely, that family forms emerged in relation to specific forms of labor that different groups provide in society. Throughout this chapter we have seen the way in which a group's assignment to *certain kinds of work* shapes its members' everyday lives. "In any society the distribution of power and prestige is largely determined by the work people do" (Huber, 1993:43). From the founding of the United States and throughout its history, "race has been a fundamental criterion in determining the kind of work people do, the wages they receive, and the kind of legal, economic, political and social support provided for their families" (Dill, 1994:166). This historical fact stands out when we examine the placement of people of color in the labor structures of the U.S. economy.

The United States started out as a colonial economy that offered raw resources and land to European and American capitalists. To develop the economy, capitalists needed labor, which was always in short supply. The presence of racially defined groups in the United States is tied to this demand for labor. Most were brought to the United States for the express purpose of providing cheap and malleable labor. Although European immigrants were also welcomed as a source of low-wage labor, they were incorporated into low-wage economies of the North (Glenn, 1992:177).

In her study of U.S. labor from 1870 to 1930, *Unequal Citizenship,* Evelyn Nakano Glenn (2002) shows how racial inequalities were used to build the capitalist economy. Non-White men and women were excluded from "free labor." Various forms of *coercive labor* such as sharecropping and contract labor were reserved for people of color. White elites used their economic and political power to build large, non-White labor forces to do their work of producing wealth.

Throughout U.S. history, racially defined groups were recruited to fill labor needs in economically backward regions: the West, Southwest, and South. In the late nineteenth and early twentieth centuries, Chinese men constituted between a

Unlike European immigrants, the labor status of people of color severely limited their opportunities. Japanese agricultural worker and daughter in California.

quarter and a third of the workforce, reclaiming agricultural lands, building railroads, and working in mines, and were 90 percent of the domestic and laundry workers in California. During this same period, native Chicanos and Mexican immigrants (Mexicanos) were employed as miners, railroad hands, and agricultural laborers in the western states. In the years following emancipation, African Americans were concentrated in agriculture, as well as in heavy construction labor and domestic service in the South.

Past family life must be understood in terms of the coercive labor systems in which these groups were embedded. In these systems—principally slavery and contract labor—the foundations of family life were denied to those at the bottom in order to maximize economic productivity. Sociologist Bonnie Thornton Dill explains how racial-ethnic families were shaped by labor demands:

> In the eighteenth and nineteenth centuries, labor, and not the existence or mainte-
> nance of families, was the critical aspect of their role in building the nation. Thus,
> they were denied the societal supports necessary to make their families a vital ele-
> ment in the social order....In some instances racial-ethnic families were seen as a
> threat to the efficiency and exploitability of the work force and were actively prohib-
> ited. In other cases, they were tolerated when it was felt they might help solidify or
> expand the work force. (Dill, 1994:149–150)

Coercive labor systems prevented people of color from receiving the kind of legal, economic, political, and social support provided for other families. Racial-ethnic families devised various solutions to sustain their families. One solution was to extend women's work beyond the private family sphere. This created racial differences in how women experienced the public and private spheres. Dill explains why the public-private separation of spheres that developed in the dominant society did not apply to women of color:

> Treated primarily as workers rather than as members of family groups, these women
> labored to maintain, sustain, stabilize, and reproduce their families while working in
> both the public (productive) and private (reproductive) spheres....Long after industri-
> alization had begun to reshape family roles among middle-class White families, driving
> White women into a cult of domesticity, women of color were coping with an extended
> day. This day included subsistence labor outside the family and domestic labor within
> the family. (Dill, 1994:164–165)

Unlike families of the dominant society, racial minorities had no private domestic arena for mothers and children, supported through the productive work of husbands and fathers. The "family wage" did not apply to men of color. Glenn explains that Black men's earnings did not cover the support for a wife and children because Black women were viewed as laboring bodies. Additionally, the standard of living of Blacks and other people of color was assumed to be lower than that of Whites. The racial rhetoric was that they could survive on next to nothing (Glenn, 2002:82).

Systems of racial control systematically disrupted family life (Amott and Matthaei, 1991:16). We are most familiar with assaults on family ties of African Americans under slavery: sale of individuals, slave-master control over marriage and reproduction, and the brutal conditions of family life. Assaults on the family lives of Chicanos and Chinese Americans were common. In both groups, households were broken apart by the demands for male labor (Glenn, 1987:53). Many Mexican American men were employed in mining camps and on railroad gangs, which required them to live apart from wives and children (Barrera, 1979). This was also true for male migrant agricultural workers until the 1880s, when the family-labor system became the preferred mode (Camarillo, 1979). In the case of the Chinese, only prime-age males were recruited as workers, and wives and children had to be left behind. The Chinese Exclusion Act of 1882 not only prohibited further entry of Chinese laborers but also barred resident laborers from bringing in wives and children. This policy was

Mexican workers on the urban rail system in Los Angeles, c. 1903.

aimed at preventing the Chinese from settling permanently once their labor was no longer needed (Glenn, 1987:53). The high concentration of males in the Chinese community prior to 1920 resulted in a split-household family, in which work life was separated from family life and carried out by a member living far from the rest of the household. The split-household form made possible maximum exploitation of workers, because the cost of family maintenance was borne partially by the unpaid subsistence work of women and old people in the home village (Glenn, 1983:14–15).

Despite the harsh conditions imposed on family life by a racial labor system, families did not break down. Instead, people of color created family strategies that allowed them to function. Let us turn to the histories of African American and Chicano families, which illustrate how people of color created strong and viable families.

African American Families in Slavery and Freedom

The earliest studies of African American families were influenced by the research of sociologist E. Franklin Frazier (1939), who argued that slavery and racism crippled African American families by creating unstable female-headed households. In the past three decades, however, *revisionist historians* have given us a new conception of the slave family. They analyze family life as a *positive adaptation* to social conditions (Hattery and Smith, 2007; Mullings, 1997:78; Taylor, 2000). The television version of *Roots,* which emphasized the strong family bonds among slaves, dramatized the new scholarship.

An important historical work in the new social history of slave families was Herbert Gutman's landmark book, *The Black Family in Slavery and Freedom* (1976). Gutman's work was inspired by the controversy following the Moynihan report, especially the idea that the matriarchal family was responsible for African American problems. Gutman used historical evidence to challenge long-held ideas about the predominance of unstable, female-headed families of the past. Gutman examined plantation records and marriage applications during slavery and after emancipation. Instead of high rates of female-headed families, Gutman found that the majority of slave women and men established two-parent households both during slavery and after emancipation (see Box 3.3). The major reason for family breakup during slavery was forced separation through sale. Gutman presents compelling evidence that

Revisionist history has shown that African American families adapted to adverse conditions and endured with remarkable completeness.

family formation continued despite the abuses of slavery. The findings challenged the common portrayal of slave families:

> [T]he alleged inadequacy of the slave father and husband, the absence of male "models" for young slave children to emulate, the prevalence of the "sambo" personality, the insistence that slave marriages usually meant little more than successive polygyny, and the belief that the "matrifocal" household...prevailed among the mass of illiterate plantation field hands and laborers. These misconceptions accompany another erroneous belief: that when slaves did honor the two-parent household they did so either as a result of the encouragement offered to "favored" slaves by owners or because daily contacts between whites and slave servants and artisans (as contrasted to slaves living in "the quarters") permitted these few slaves to "imitate" marriage "models" common among owners and other whites. Implicit in such arguments, none of which rests on significant evidence, is the assumption that such "models" were infrequent among the slaves themselves, an assumption that has encouraged simplified and misleading descriptions of slave socialization and slave culture. (Gutman, 1976:13)

Some historians now question Gutman's analysis that two-parent households were the norm among slaves. These "postrevisionist" scholars reject the notion that a single family form existed among slaves. What slaves did have in common was forced labor and a legal status of property. Beyond that, there was great *variety* in their opportunities to get married and form stable families (Durr and Hill, 2006; Franklin, 1997; Hill, 2005; Taylor, 2000). Conditions such as the region in which plantations were located and the size of plantations gave slaves varying opportunities to form families. We must also recognize

Researching Families

Dispelling the Myths About African American Families

Herbert G. Gutman made ingenious use of quantitative data derived from plantation birth registers, census data, and marriage licenses to document the predominance of the two-parent household during and after slavery. The following table shows that between 1855 and 1880, as many as 90 percent of Black households contained both a husband and a wife.

Percentage of Male-Present Negro Households, 1855–1880

Place and Date	Number of Households	Male-Present Households (%)	Male-Absent Households (%)
Buffalo, NY, 1855	145	90	10
Buffalo, NY, 1875	159	85	15
Troy, NY, 1880	128	85	15
York County, VA, 1865	994	85	15
Montgomery County, VA, 1866	500	78	22
Princess Anne County, VA, 1865	375	84	16
Natchez, MS, 1880	769	70	30
Beaufort, SC, 1880	461	70	30
Richmond, VA, 1880	5,670	73	27
Mobile, AL, 1880	3,235	74	26
Rural Adams County, MS, 1880	3,093	81	19
St. Helena's Township, SC, 1880	491	87	13
St. Helena's Island, SC, 1880	904	86	14

Source: Gutman, Herbert G., "Persistent Myths about the Afro-American Family." In *The American Family in Social-Historical Perspective*, Michael Gordon (ed.). New York: St. Martin's Press, 1983, p. 468.

that *slave agency*—their use of the economic and cultural forces at their disposal—enabled slaves to form a wide variety of family types in the face of oppression (Durr and Hill, 2006; Franklin, 1997; Hill, 2005; Pargus, 2008; Taylor, 2000).

WORK AND GENDER

Slave women and men were laborers on and for the plantation. Sometimes slave labor was gendered. For example, ditching was men's work; sorting cotton was women's work. Exceptions were found in field work when, during the harvest, both sexes worked in hoeing gangs. Advertisements for women slaves often proclaimed their ability to work like men. Women could be found doing the stereotypically masculine work of plowing (Matthaei, 1982:81; Mullings, 1997:82). Away from the fields, however, work was nearly always based on gender. Craft work or skilled work necessary to produce commodities for the plantations was segregated in the same manner as it was among free women and men:

> An elite of slave men was trained as carpenters, coopers, stonemasons, millers, and shoemakers. Some masters used such promotion as a reward for good field work. Slave women were trained for feminine occupations, such as sewing, spinning, and dairy keeping, by their mistress homemaker, by white women bond servants, or by the wife of the overseer. (Matthaei, 1982:91)

Slave women, in addition to their labor on the plantation or in the "public" slave sphere, carried out tasks for their own families where strong gender roles prevailed. Women prepared meals, sewed and washed their family's clothes, cleaned their households, and tended their children. Such domestic tasks were not done by men, who strenuously avoided tasks considered women's work, such as laundry or the care of infants (Thistle, 2006:22). A female slave's work also included being "mammy" to her owner's children; she was, therefore, engaged in mothering two sets of children at once. Thus, the "forced participation of the slave mother in labor outside of her home meant that she lived the double day long before it became common among free families" (Matthaei, 1982:96).

In John Blassingame's collection of two centuries of slave letters, speeches, interviews, and autobiographies, one slave describes the work of his mother, a house servant:

> My mother's labor was very hard. She would go to the house in the morning, take her pail upon her head, and go away to the cow-pen, and milk fourteen cows. She then put on the bread for the family breakfast, and got the cream ready for churning, and set a little child to churn it, she having the care of from ten to fifteen children, whose mothers worked in the field. After clearing away the family breakfast, she got breakfast for the slaves...which was taken at twelve o'clock. In the meantime, she had beds to make, rooms to sweep, and etc. Then she cooked the family dinner, which was simply plain meat, vegetables, and bread. Then the slaves' dinner was to be ready at from eight to nine o'clock in the evening....At night she had the cows to milk again....This was her work day by day. Then in the course of the week, she had the washing and ironing to do for her master's family...and for her husband, seven children and herself....She would not get through to go to her log cabin until nine or ten o'clock at night. She would then be so tired that she could scarcely stand; but she would find one boy with his knee out, and another with his elbow out, a patch wanting here, and a stitch there, and she would sit down by her lightwood fire, and sew and sleep alternately, often till the light began to streak in the east; and then lying down, she would catch a nap and hasten to the toil of the day. (Blassingame, 1977:133)

Slave women's work shaped child-care arrangements. Women organized communal child care in such a way that a few women were responsible for caring for all children too young to work, and women as a group were accountable for one another's children (White, 1990).

Women and men in slavery lived within a gender system that served the needs of plantation owners, yet it was different from the gender system of the dominant society. Women were physical laborers in the public sphere of the plantation. At the same time, they were vulnerable to sexual exploitation. Women slaves had no legal rights to their bodies, their sexuality, or their children. Nevertheless, slave women found ways to resist. They attempted to work in settings that allowed them to be with their families. Not all slaves could control their working conditions. Some mothers murdered their babies to keep them from being slaves. Others resisted through their fertility, by using various contraception and abortion techniques. All of these actions reflect human agency. Anthropologist Leith Mullings calls this transformative work and defines it as the efforts to transform circumstances in order to maintain continuity. "These efforts have spanned the domains of work, household and community" (Mullings, 1997:98).

In contrast to the treatment of women, male slaves were denied manhood in the public sphere of the plantation:

> The slaveholders deprived black men of the role of provider, refused to dignify their marriages or legitimize their issue; compelled them to submit to physical abuse in the presence of their women and children; made them choose between remaining silent while their wives and daughters were seduced and risking death; and threatened them with separation from their family at any moment. (Genovese, 1981:241)

New research offers a fresh look at men in slavery. The slave family did rest on much greater equality between women and men than was the case for White families. Furthermore, slavery produced strong women. However, it did not completely undermine male slaves. According to Genovese, men provided for their families to a greater extent than has been appreciated. Many hunted and trapped animals to supplement the meager food supplied by plantation owners. Slave children usually did have an image of a strong Black man before them. Even when a slave boy was growing up without a father in the house, he had as a model a tough, resourceful driver, a skilled mechanic or two, and other field hands. Some of those men devoted themselves to playing surrogate father to all the children. They told them stories, taught them to fish and trap animals, and instructed them in the ways of survival in a White world. The norm called for adults to look after children whether they were blood relatives or not. Every plantation had some men who played this role (Genovese, 1981:243).

KINSHIP

Strong kinship ties were foremost in the formation of slave families. To understand how families survived enslavement, we must examine kinship—the single most powerful support among slaves (Jones, 1991). Kinship patterns connected unrelated slaves into a family. Even when sales of individual slaves destroyed particular families, kinship networks were recreated. When plantations were initially set up, slaves might be obtained from various sources and would be strangers to one another. Gutman (1976:127–130) found in the records of plantations in Virginia and Alabama that after 30 years, slaves on those plantations had established kinship networks such as those found on older plantations.

Slaves devised various practices for maintaining kin ties. For example, "naming" children after blood kin such as aunts, uncles, and grandparents was a family custom. Sons were often named after their fathers. According to Gutman, naming practices defined the place of the child in slave society and preserved symbolic kinship ties. Slave naming patterns reveal a unique conception of family:

> The names of their children suggest that slaves conceived of their families in a broad sense, including extended kin. Owners, in contrast, saw the nuclear family as the primary unit, perhaps because of its reproductive functions, and established rules to maintain this unit when dividing their estate without regard to preserving the larger net of kinship. (Cody, 1983:441)

Gutman found that marriages endured, that unions were legitimized by rituals such as "jumping over a broomstick," and that fidelity was expected from male and female slaves after marriage.

Following emancipation, large numbers of slaves, often at considerable cost to themselves, came before authorities to proclaim that they were already married. Under slavery, however, legal marriage did not exist. Gutman used plantation birth records to show that female slaves often had their first child outside of slave marriage, and that this was followed by permanent and settled unions. He also uncovered information about marriage and family life in the Freedman's Bureau manuscripts:

> Registers that listed the marriages of former slaves in Washington, D.C., and Rockbridge and Nelson counties, Virginia, between 1865 and 1867 show that models of stable marriages existed among the slaves themselves, not just among their masters, other whites, or free blacks. Some had lived together as husband and wife for more than forty years in slavery. In all, registers recorded the dates of 1,721 marriages: 46 percent in Nelson county, 43 percent in Rockbridge county, and 36 percent in Washington, D.C., had resided together at least ten years. The Washington register tells even more. It listed 848 marriages, and of them only 34 were between men and women who had lived in the District before emancipation. The rest had moved there, probably as families, mostly from nearby rural counties in Maryland and Virginia. Asked by the registrar who had married them, some did not know or could not remember. Others named a minister, a priest, or, more regularly, a master. Most important, 421, nearly half, responded, "no marriage ceremony," suggesting clearly that slaves could live together as husband and wife in a stable (though hardly secure and ideal) relationship without formal religious or secular rituals. (Gutman, 1983:470)

Slave owners used family and kinship ties as an effective control mechanism by threatening to sell insubordinate slaves. But slaves themselves made their kin groupings a setting of human agency. When in need, slaves could depend on family

The Old Plantation, c. 1800, "Jumping the Broomstick."

relations, both real and fictive, to protect them from the dehumanization in slave society. Mothers and fathers instilled in their children self-esteem, a spirit of independence, and various techniques of survival and empowerment (Jones, 1991).

Chicano Families in the Southwest

Families of Mexican descent have been incorporated into the United States both by conquest and by migration. In 1848, at the end of the Mexican War, the United States acquired a large section of Mexico, which is now the southwestern United States. With the signing of the Treaty of Guadalupe Hidalgo, as many as 80,000 to 100,000 Mexicans living in that region became residents of U.S. territory. The U.S. takeover disrupted traditional family life through land displacement of the indigenous people, new laws, and new labor systems.

The military conquest was accompanied by the beginnings of industrial development and by the growth of agriculture, ranching, railroads, and mining in the region. Rapid economic growth in that region resulted in a labor shortage. U.S. businesses recruited Mexican workers to migrate north for work at low wages in railroad construction and agriculture (Portes and Rumbaut, 1990).

Prior to the U.S. takeover and the beginnings of industrial development, Mexicanos, whether natives of northern Mexico or immigrants from southern Mexico, were people of Mexican heritage, largely peasants, whose lives had been defined by a feudal economy and daily struggle on the land for economic survival. This pastoral life was disrupted. With the coming of the railroads and the damming of rivers for irrigation, the Southwest became an area of economic growth, but the advantages accrued mainly to Anglos. Mexicans no longer owned the land; now they were the source of cheap labor—an exploited group at the bottom of the social and economic ladder.

FAMILY LIFE AMID COERCIVE LABOR SYSTEMS

Mexican immigration to the United States increased substantially in the early twentieth century, although immigration from Mexico had already been growing since the late 1880s. The historical study of Mexican immigration allows us to see the great diversity among Mexican immigrant families. "Although many Mexicans migrated from rural villages, other came from cities. Many families migrated as entire units, while others were involved in chain migration. Some immigrants settled largely in Mexican communities along the border; others ventured further inland where the Anglo American population dominated" (Sanchez, 1999:130).

Mexican workers who migrated north for work in the late nineteenth century and later in the first half of the twentieth century often did not settle down permanently:

> The prevailing "ebb and flow" or "revolving door" pattern of labor migration was calibrated by seasonal labor demands, economic recessions, and mass deportations. Although some employers encouraged the immigration of Mexican women and entire families in order to stabilize and expand the available, exploitable work force, many other employers, assisted at times by government-sponsored "bracero programs," recruited only men for an elastic, temporary labor supply, a reserve army of labor that could be discarded when redundant. Employers did not absolutely command the movement of Mexican workers, but employers' needs constructed a particular structure of opportunities that shaped migration. (Hondagneu-Sotelo, 1995:177)

Migratory labor made families highly susceptible to disruption. Historian Richard Griswold del Castillo (1984) provides a powerful historical example of family arrangements among Mexican Americans in southwestern cities during the latter half of the nineteenth century, concluding that a large proportion of households (38 percent) were female headed, even though extended, two-parent families remained the "ideal type." Although migratory labor systems clearly restricted family life, Mexican immigrants extended their families as an expression of family solidarity. Their ability to expand their family organization served them well in surviving the rigors of economic marginality and frontier life. Disruptions and reformulations in family structure were commonplace, but family networks were durable (Griswold del Castillo, 1984; Vega, 1995:5).

Cities in the U.S. Southwest served as focal points for reconstituting the Mexican family constellations and the construction of new families north of the border. Extended family networks were crucial in dealing with migration and in reinforcing Mexican customs and values (Sanchez, 1990:252).

Mexican familism (a strong orientation and obligation to the family) took several forms and served many purposes. The family consisted of a network of relatives, including grandparents, aunts, uncles, married sisters and brothers and their children, and also *compadres* (co-parents) and *padrinos* (godparents) with whom Chicanos actively maintained bonds (Ramirez and Arce, 1981:9). The *compadrazgo* system of godparents established connections between families and in this way enlarged family ties. "Godparents were required for the celebration of major religious occasions in a person's life: baptism, confirmation, first communion, and marriage." At these times godparents "entered into special religious, social, and economic relationships with the godchild as well as with the parents of the child." They acted as co-parents, "providing discipline and emotional and financial support when needed." As *compadres* they were expected to become the closest friend of the parents and members of the extended family (Griswold del Castillo, 1984:40–44).

WORK AND GENDER

Chicano family roles in the early nineteenth century were strongly gendered. As economic hardship forced women and children into the paid labor force, the old pattern of women doing domestic work and men doing productive work began to break down. Historian Albert Camarillo describes how traditional patterns of employment and family responsibilities were altered in Santa Barbara, California:

> The most dramatic change was the entrance of the Chicana and her children as important wage earners who contributed to the family's economic survival. As male heads of household faced persistent unemployment, their migrations to secure seasonal work in the other areas of the country or region became more frequent. In these instances the Chicana assumed the triple responsibilities of head of household, mother, and wage earner. No longer able to subsist solely on the income of the husband, the Chicana and her children were forced to enter the unskilled labor market of Anglo Santa Barbara. The work they performed involved domestic services and agriculture-related employment. (Camarillo, 1979:91)

Entire families entered the pattern of seasonal and migratory field work. Initially, Chicanas and their children were employed as almond pickers and shellers and as harvesters of olives. During the almond and olive harvests, men were usually engaged in seasonal migratory work. There were seasons, however, especially in the early summer, when the entire family migrated from the city to pick fruit. Chicano family labor had become essential for the profits of growers. Families would often leave their homes in Santa Barbara for several weeks, camping out in the fields where they worked (Camarillo, 1979:93). Women confronted severe hardships in raising their families. In the barrios, women's reproductive labor was intensified by the congested and unsanitary conditions. In El Paso, for example,

> Mexican women had to haul water for washing and cooking from the river or public water pipes. To feed their families, they had to spend time marketing, often in Ciudad Juarez across the border, as well as long, hot hours cooking meals and coping with the burden of desert sand both inside and outside their homes. Besides the problem of raising children, unsanitary living conditions forced Mexican mothers to deal with disease and illness in their families. (Garcia, 1980:320–321)

Although women did productive labor, family life was still gendered. As both daughters and wives, Mexican women were instructed to be obedient and submissive to their parents and husbands. Domesticity and motherhood were primary virtues. Whether they labored outside the home or not, they were subject to a sexual division of labor, in which their primary task was to care for their husbands and children. Like other women of color in nineteenth-century America, they were engaged in productive as well as reproductive labor. The wage labor of Mexican-heritage women contributed greatly to family adjustment in a colonized setting (Garcia, 1980). Despite all of these hardships, Chicanos maintained viable families with strong cultural traditions. The Chicano family has acted as a fortress against social displacement by the larger society. Chicanas in particular are described as the "glue that keeps the family together." They have been responsible for preserving Mexican traditions (Sanchez, 1990:251), including birthday celebrations, saints' days, baptisms, weddings, and funerals. Through the family, Mexican culture was sustained.

The Great Depression and Family Change

As the nineteenth century pressed forward, families continued to be molded by different social class and race contexts, even though the ideal of the breadwinner/homemaker family remained. The United States entered the twentieth century in a period of economic transformation from an industrial society to a service and consumer society (see Chapter 4). Families of different social classes and races encountered very different opportunity structures.

The Great Depression of the 1930s profoundly influenced family life. Across the country, men and women were laid off. Wide-scale factory and business closings meant that there were few places where unemployed men could find work. Job competition was fierce. Wages were low. Those who were employed usually earned less than they had a decade earlier. The economic pressures placed on nearly all families during the Depression were harsh and affected family relations and family stability:

> Many people avoided marriage, believing that they could not afford the responsibilities—the marriage rate fell to an all-time low in the early 1930s and stayed low until 1940. The birth rate also fell, as couples were reluctant to add another mouth to feed. The strain of

trying to make ends meet was too much for many married couples to bear—marital conflict increased in the 1930s...The Depression shaped family structures—tearing some families and couples apart, preventing others from coming together, reducing the size of families and households as childbearing was postponed and family members left home looking for work, and increasing the size of other households as adult offspring delayed establishing their own homes by remaining with their parents. The Depression also shaped how couples and families functioned. Not surprisingly, given the financial straits that families encountered, issues involving work and money were paramount. (Coleman et al., 2007)

The Great Depression forced some families to live on the road seeking work.

While nearly all families experienced some deprivation as a result of the Great Depression, the economic burdens were *not* equally shared across the social class and race divides. New research by family historians has found different kinds of dislocations experienced by families—in particular class and racial-ethnic groups. (See Box 3.4,

BOX 3.4 Researching Families

Did Race, Class, and Gender Matter in the Great Depression?

The Great Depression of the 1930s is an iconic period in American history—a period through which each economic depression has since been judged. This fact keeps the Great Depression with us, allowing new generations some level of familiarity with its effects. Unfortunately, these familiarities are generally limited to the premise that the Great Depression increased the number of individuals living in poverty, many of whom were unable to find work. This understanding is far too simplistic. It masks many of the inequalities that existed prior to the Great Depression by treating American society as one of prosperity for all before the economic downturn of the 1930s. These stories also ignore the ways in which social positionings, especially physical location, race and ethnicity, class, and gender shape people's family lives differently, even in periods of economic crisis. Some scholars have addressed this void by creating historical studies that explore how these diverse positionings

produced different experiences for families in the Great Depression.

Winifred D. Wandersee begins to unmask some of these differences in her essay *Families Face the Great Depression (1930–1940)*. In Wandersee's work, this unmasking comes primarily in the form of an extensive literature review, in which she examines prior texts that have been written about the Great Depression. Her literature review provides readers with an accessible synthesis of the seminal works written on this historical period and creates a foundation on which further research can be produced. Her work speaks to the particular ways the Great Depression affected family life in the 1930s and beyond and reveals that the Great Depression affected families differently than it affected other social institutions. She posits that the Great Depression served as a "watershed of family change in the twentieth century" (125). One of the most important trends noted in Wandersee's work are this era's effects on the changing status of women and men, particularly within the context of the family.

Due to the increased economic strain caused by the Great Depression, more and more women were forced to work outside of the home. Wandersee finds that this fact, along with the growing number of government programs available to women, increased women's potential for independence in both the public and private spheres. Although Wandersee does allow that gendered power relations within marital relationships experienced little change due to the Great Depression, she ultimately concludes, "most of the social trends affecting family life [during the Great Depression] appeared to be favorable to women" (134). Wandersee points out that her generalizations "offer only a limited view" and that "class and ethnicity, as well as regional variation, resulted in a diversified experience of economic deprivation" (135).

Julia Blackwelder's book *Women of the Depression: Caste and Culture in San Antonio, 1929–1939* fills this gap by highlighting the complex interplay of structure and agency in a Depression era city. Blackwelder argues against generalizations about the Great Depression. She contends that they are at best unrepresentative and at worst wholly ignore discrepancies caused by families in different social locations. Blackwelder's research gives us an intimate look into the ways the Great Depression affected diverse lives at both the macro and micro levels. The study underscores the fact that the repercussions of the Great Depression were unevenly distributed because it takes place in San Antonio, Texas, which was one of the poorest cities of the time and was also quite ethnically diverse. Although Blackwelder's focus is on Mexican American women living in San Antonio, she documents a wide array of experiences even within the city itself, noting that even the terms "Hispanic," "Anglo," and "Black" "obscure important intra-group differences" (xvii). Blackwelder does use secondary sources in her research, including prior literature that examines the living conditions of families during the Great Depression. However, the majority of her research lies in primary data collection, including interviews and an examination of primary documents such as court records and photos.

One of the clearest representations of the differing impacts the Great Depression had on women, based on their specific social position, is Blackwelder's analysis of the yearly Battle of the Flowers celebration. She notes that even during the worst of times, Anglo girls and women still held fancy lunches, parties, and teas and often purchased extravagant dresses for the parade in hopes of becoming queens or princesses of the celebration. Hispanics and Blacks on the other hand typically only participated in such celebrations as maids, cooks, and seamstresses.

Blackwelder examines not only the structural oppression these women faced but also the individual and group agency they possessed in dealing with economic adversity. Oftentimes these women would share resources, such as housing, food, and caretaking responsibilities, in addition to applying for government assistance and employment to meet the rising demands of poverty.

Ultimately, the Great Depression highlights the ways in which structural and individual opportunities were filtered through the context of complex social positionings. This analysis also reminds us that the culture of abundance alleged to exist before the start of the Great Depression was not a reality for all. Wandersee notes that "racial minorities were systematically marginalized and eliminated from the American dream, the culture of abundance, in such an absolute way that the Great Depression seemed, in a way, irrelevant to their basic problems" (138). Recognizing the dynamic ways the Great Depression affected families gives us a window through which we can begin to debunk simplistic generalities and move closer toward a detailed understanding of how world events affect the lives of diverse individuals.

References

Blackwelder, Julia Kirk. *Women of the Depression: Caste and Culture in San Antonio, 1929–1939.* College Station: Texas A & M University Press, 1984.

Wandersee, Winifred D. "Families Face the Great Depression (1930–1940)." In *American Families: A Research Guide and Historical Handbook* (eds.). J. M. Hawes and E. I. Nybakken. Santa Barbara: Greenwood Press, 1991, pp. 125–156.

Source: Miller, Paula (2009). Department of Sociology, Michigan State University, 2009. This essay was written expressly for *Diversity in Families,* 9th ed.

titled "Did Race, Class, and Gender Matter in the Great Depression?") Even in periods of widespread economic dislocation, class and race remain important foundations for diversity in families.

Chapter Review

1. Industrialization resulted in different labor patterns that affected families in diverse ways.

2. Historical changes did not affect all families in a linear or unidirectional way. Realities such as slavery, immigration, and forced conquest shaped the family experiences of different groups.

3. Throughout U.S. history, race, class, and gender have been important social divisions that made families different.

4. Social production and social reproduction are two distinctive forms of work for the family. Industrialization separated them and drove middle-class women into a cult of domesticity.

5. For most families, the private-public division was only an ideal. Working-class women and women of color did not experience a private life nor a protected sphere of domesticity, because their work outside the home was an extension of their domestic responsibilities. To maintain even minimal levels of family subsistence, most families sent women and children into the workforce.

6. In the 1800s and through the turn of the century, family systems were indispensable in the settlement and adjustment of the European immigrants. Families played a dual role in the massive social transformations of the period: (a) They provided a stable home environment with strong traditions; and (b) they played a major role in labor recruitment and the placement of workers in the factories.

7. European immigrants were integrated into the developing industrial society through wage labor, whereas people of color were historically incorporated into the nation through coercive labor systems. Racial-labor systems made it impossible for people of color to conform to the dominant society's idealized family form.

8. Slavery assaulted and broke up African American families, but it did not destroy the strong kinship system. Instead, slaves drew on both their African heritage and their experiences in this society to recreate multiple family forms.

9. Families of Mexican descent were incorporated into the United States by both conquest and migration. Family life was greatly altered by economic development in the Southwest. Their flexible families and traditional cultures sustained them in the United States.

10. Historical research shows that people can use their families to survive and even challenge social institutions that impinge on them.

Key Terms

cult of true womanhood   61
matriarchal family   72
social production   60

social reproduction   60
structural diversity approach   59

Related Websites

http://www.familytreesearcher.com

Family Tree Searcher. This website allows you to enter your ancestor information to search family trees at multiple online genealogy databases and creates the best searches based on your ancestry free of charge. It also includes tips for researching genealogy online.

http://www.ihrc.umn.edu

Immigration History Research Center. Based at the University of Minnesota, the IHRC promotes interdisciplinary research on international migration, develops archives documenting immigrant and refugee life, especially in the U.S., and makes specialized scholarship accessible to students, teachers, and the public.

http://www.uscis.gov

INS History, Genealogy and Education: Historical Research Tools (Click on "Resources"; "Historical Library"). The U.S. Citizenship and Immigration Services provides several historical research tools to help individuals search their family records through the use of standard immigration and naturalization records that date back to the early twentieth century.

http://www.uscis.gov

INS History, Genealogy and Education: Chinese Immigrant Files (Click on "Resources"; "Historical Library"; "Genealogy"). This USCIS website provides information regarding Chinese immigration to the United States as well as access to public records.

http://www.history.org/Almanack/life/family/essay.cfm

Redefining Family at Colonial Williamsburg. The Colonial Williamsburg Foundation operates the world's largest living history museum in Williamsburg, Virginia—the restored eighteenth-century capital of Britain's largest, wealthiest, and most populous outpost of empire in the New World. "Redefining Family" is the second of six story lines interpreted at Colonial Williamsburg as part of its Becoming Americans theme. It explores the effects of changes in society between Black, White, and Native American families that resulted in the development of new patterns in American family life.

http://www.ellisisland.org

The Statue of Liberty—Ellis Island Foundation. This site provides access to archival information on the more than 22 million passengers and members of ships' crews that entered the United States through Ellis Island and the Port of New York between 1892 and 1924. The passenger archives include passenger records, giving passenger name, date of arrival, ship of travel, age on arrival, and more; original manifests, showing passenger names and other information; and ship information, often with a picture, giving the history and background of each ship that brought the immigrants.

http://feefhs.org/

The Federation of East European Family History Societies. FEEFHS was organized in 1992 as an umbrella organization that promotes family research in eastern and central Europe without any ethnic, religious, or social distinctions. This website provides a forum for individuals and organizations focused on a single country or group of people to exchange information and be updated on developments in the field. While it primarily serves the interests of North Americans in tracing their lineages back to a European homeland, it welcomes members from all countries.

http://memory.loc.gov/learn/features/immig/introduction.html

The Library of Congress: Immigration…the Changing Face of America. This interactive website, hosted by the Library of Congress, provides an overview and introduction to the history of immigration in the United States during the nineteenth and early twentieth centuries. The site includes links to primary sources from online collections of the Library of Congress, interviews with recent immigrants, and recipes with family narratives from around the world.

http://www.digitalhistory.uh.edu/

Digital History. This website was designed and developed to support the teaching of American History in K-12 schools and colleges and is supported by the Department of History and the College of Education at the University of Houston. The materials on this site include a U.S. history textbook; over 400 annotated documents from the Gilder Lehrman Collection on deposit at the Pierpont Morgan Library, supplemented by primary sources on slavery; Mexican American, Asian American, and Native American history; and U.S. political, social, and legal history; and reference resources that include a database of annotated links, chronologies, an audio archive including speeches and book talks by historians, and a visual archive with hundreds of historical maps and images.

chapter 4

Macro Forces Affecting Families: The Economy, Immigration, and Aging

▶ Myths and Realities

Myth	Families are the building blocks of society.
Reality	Families are shaped by specific historical, social, and economic conditions. That is, structural conditions shape families more than families shape societies.
Myth	The dominant family form—intact nuclear household with male breadwinner, full-time homemaker wife, and their dependent children—has persisted over the past 50 years or so.
Reality	"The [institution of] the family has changed more in the last 10 years than any other social institution" (Bianchi and Spain, 1996:5). "Today, many family forms are common: single-parent families (resulting either from unmarried parenthood or divorce), remarried couples, unmarried couples, stepfamilies, foster families, extended or multigenerational families, and the doubling up of two families within the same home. Women are just as likely to be full- or part-time workers as full-time homemakers" (Ahlburg and De Vita, 1992:2).
Myth	Deindustrialization has affected families uniformly across the social classes.
Reality	Deindustrialization has most profoundly reshaped working-class and middle-class families. The poor have always had to adjust to and cope with economic hardship.
Myth	Latino immigrants are a homogeneous group, as are Asian immigrants.
Reality	Within each category there is a wide variation by country of origin in economic resources, educational attainment, poverty rate, and modal type of family.
Myth	The study of culturally diverse families is the study of "others" (i.e., people in families that are different from the mainstream).
Reality	There is no dominant family form against which families are measured and judged. Alternative family forms do not reflect deviance, deficiency, or disorganization. Rather, they reflect adaptations to specific structural conditions.
Myth	The cultural norms emphasizing patriarchal men and submissive women are found uniformly in Latino and Asian American families.
Reality	The degree to which patriarchy is found in Latino and Asian American families depends on structural factors. It is affected by family arrangements induced by the migration process and/or the economic resources of women.
Myth	With a relatively low fertility rate, the proportion of old people in the U.S. population remains relatively stable.
Reality	A low fertility rate translates into a smaller proportion of children in the population. With the elderly living longer and relatively fewer children, the proportion of the elderly population will increase.

amilies are not isolated units free from outside constraints. On the contrary, individuals bring to their family relationships perspectives, needs, and problems gained from their nonfamily roles and experiences. Their activities in organizations and social networks outside the family—at work, at school, at church and other voluntary associations, and at play—have profound influences on what occurs in families. More fundamentally, families are embedded in a society in which governmental laws and policies, economic forces, population dynamics, institutional racism and sexism, and prevailing ideologies have both direct and indirect effects.

The previous two chapters demonstrated the ways in which social factors have transformed family life historically in the United States. This chapter focuses on the way the structure of contemporary society shapes families and the individuals within them. We examine three societal "earthquakes" and their effects on families: the changing economy, the new immigration, and the aging of society. The present generation is in the midst of social changes that are more far-reaching and are occurring more rapidly than at any other time in human history. The purpose of this chapter is to understand these macro social forces and how they affect social life—especially families.

Globalization, the Structural Transformation of the Economy, the Great Recession, and Families

The Industrial Revolution, which began in Great Britain in the 1780s, was a major turning point in human history. With the application of steam power and, later, oil and electricity as energy sources for industry, mining, manufacturing, and transportation came fundamental changes to the economy, the relationship of people and work, family organization, and a transition from rural to urban life. In effect, societies are transformed with each surge in invention and technological growth. Peter F. Drucker describes the historical import of such transformations:

> Every few hundred years in Western history there occurs a sharp transformation. We cross…a "divide." Within a few short decades, society rearranges itself—its worldview; its basic values; its social and political structure; its arts; its key institutions. Fifty years later, there is a new world. And the people born then cannot even imagine the world in which their grandparents lived and into which their own parents were born. We are currently living through just such a transformation. (Drucker, 1993:1)

For example, the shift from private capitalism to industrial capitalism had profound effects on families (Zaretsky, 1976). In the early stage of capitalism, nuclear families were the unit of production. Each family was a self-contained economic enterprise, with parents, children, and employees working together to produce a product. Although the family was organized hierarchically and strictly disciplined, marriage was understood to be an economic partnership based on common love and labor. With the rise of industrial capitalism, however, the production of goods was removed from the home and shops to factories. The work of men and women was separated, with men working away from home in a highly coordinated, strictly disciplined, bureaucratic, and impersonal environment. "Industrial capitalism required a rationalized, coordinated and synchronized labor process undisturbed by community sentiment, family responsibilities, personal relations or feelings" (Zaretsky, 1976:47–48). Working in such settings, men looked to their families as havens—as places of shelter, caring, and emotional attachment. Women, freed from working in the family enterprise, were expected to devote their full attention to the nurturing of family members. Zaretsky's thesis is that the changing conditions of capitalism affected families dramatically. In effect, the particular form of the family found in society is socially determined, because it arises out of definite social conditions.

The United States is now in the midst of a new transformation, one fueled by new technologies and applications (e.g., superfast computers; the Internet as a distributor of information, goods, and services; fiber optics; biotechnology; the decoding of the human genome; and cell telephony). These amazing scientific breakthroughs have had and will continue to have immense implications for commerce, international trade, global politics, and at the individual level employment opportunities, pay and benefits, and family formation. In Drucker's words:

> The next two or three decades are likely to see even greater technological change than has occurred in the decades since the emergence of the computer, and also even greater change in industry structures, in the economic landscape, and probably in the social landscape as well. (Drucker, 1999:54)

Globalization

Among other changes, the new technologies have, most significantly, magnified the connections among all peoples across the globe (the following is dependent in part on Eitzen et al., 2010, Chapter 8). The Internet makes worldwide communications instantaneous. Money moves across political boundaries with a few keystrokes. Low wages in one country affect wages elsewhere. A drought in one part of the world drives up prices for commodities everywhere, while overproduction of a product in one region brings down the prices of that product elsewhere. A collapse in the stock market of one nation has ramifications for financial markets around the world. Movies, television, and advertising from one society affect the tastes, interests, and styles in other places. Polluted air and water cross national borders. Deforestation in the developing nations has a major effect on climate everywhere. Global warming, caused by the burning of fossil fuels, changes climates, generates megastorms, and increases the spread of tropical diseases around the world. A disease such as HIV/AIDS left Africa some 50 years ago and now infects 33 million people worldwide and 1.2 million in North America (World Health Organization, 2008). There has been a dramatic increase in migration flows, especially from poorer to richer nations. With sophisticated weapons systems, no nation is immune from assault from other nations or terrorist acts by revolutionary groups.

Each of these is an example of globalization, which involves the processes by which everyone on Earth becomes increasingly interconnected economically, politically, culturally, and environmentally. Connections among peoples outside their tribes or political units are not new, but the linkages now are increasing geometrically, with few, if any, groups unaffected. We concentrate here on economic globalization.

Although trade between and among nations is not new, global trade entered a new phase after World War II. What have evolved are a global trade network, the integration of peoples and nations, and a global economy, with a common ideology: capitalism. Former colonies have established local industries and sell their raw materials, products, and labor on the global market. The United States emerged as the strongest economic and military power in the world, with U.S. corporations vitally interested in expanding their operations to other societies for profit. Tearing down tariff barriers has accelerated the shift to a global economy. The North American Free Trade Agreement (NAFTA) and the General Agreement on Tariffs and Trade (GATT), both passed in 1994, are two examples of agreements that increased the flow of goods (and jobs) across national boundaries. In 2005 President Bush signed the Central American Free Trade Agreement (CAFTA), which institutes a Western Hemisphere-wide version of NAFTA.

The globalization of the economy is not a neutral process. Decisions are based on what will maximize profits, thus serving the owners of capital and not necessarily workers or the communities where U.S. operations are located. In this regard, private businesses, in their search for profit, make crucial investment decisions that change the dynamics in families and communities. Most significant are the corporate decisions regarding the movement of corporate money from one investment to another (called **capital flight**). This shift of capital takes several forms: investment in plants located in other nations, plant relocation within the United States, and mergers. While these investment decisions may be positive for corporations, they also take away investment (disinvestment) from others (workers and their families, communities, and suppliers).

Structural Changes in the United States Because of Globalization

FROM MANUFACTURING TO SERVICES

The U.S. economy was once dominated by agriculture, but in the twentieth century, while agricultural productivity increased, the number employed in agriculture declined precipitously. Manufacturing replaced agriculture, representing a **structural transformation of the economy.** Now we are undergoing another transformational shift—from an economy dominated by manufacturing to one now characterized by service occupations and the collection, storage, and dissemination of information. Reflecting this shift, the United States has lost more than one-fifth of its factory jobs since 2000 to about 13.0 million in 2008 (Greenhouse, 2009:13; Bureau of Labor Statistics, reported in Manning, 2009). Accompanying this decline, as workers left manufacturing jobs for other jobs, workers have lower wages, less job security, and fewer benefits such as health insurance and pensions.

The transformation from manufacturing to service occupations in the U.S. changed the nature of work. *The Office*—TV comedy.

The United States is shifting to an economy based on ideas rather than physical capital. Most of the manufacturing by U.S. transnational corporations is now done in low-wage economies. This migration of jobs takes two forms: offshoring and outsourcing (Friedman, 2005). **Offshoring** is when a company moves its production to another country, producing the same products in the same way, but with cheaper labor, lower taxes, and lower benefits to workers. **Outsourcing** refers to taking some specific task that a company was doing in-house—such as research, call centers, accounting, or transcribing—and transferring it to an overseas company to save money and reintegrating that work back into the overall operation.

This move to low-wage economies has three negative effects on U.S. workers. First, many have lost their jobs. Second, the wages of those production workers who have not lost their jobs remain relatively low because if they seek higher wages, their employers threaten to move the jobs elsewhere. And, third, workers' unions have been weakened because they, too, have lost clout. When workers had strong unions, the wages and benefits were enough for a middle-class lifestyle.

The new economy has shifted the demand for workers from physical labor to cognitive abilities, thus benefiting more educated workers. The best educated and trained usually benefit with good jobs, benefits, and opportunities. The less educated do not benefit in such a climate. While the New Economy has benefited the more educated workers, they, too, are threatened by global trends. Now, white-collar jobs, just as manufacturing jobs, are being done by cheaper labor in other countries as U.S. corporations seek to improve their profits (Armour and Kessler, 2003).

> An explosion of new technologies—including e-mail, digitization, the Internet, broadband technology, scanners, communication satellites, undersea fiber-optic cables, and videoconferencing—has made it convenient for business to move white-collar jobs overseas.... Now, radiologists in India are analyzing X-rays for Massachusetts General and other hospitals. Five hundred engineers in Moscow are helping Boeing design and build aircraft, as Boeing lays off engineers in the United States. The Bank of America moved 1,000 technical and back-office jobs to India while cutting 3,700 jobs in the United States. (Greenhouse, 2009:203)

This phenomenon of outsourcing has three roots. First, there is the worldwide communications revolution spawned by the Internet. Second, there is a supply of qualified workers in English-speaking countries, most notably India but also the Philippines, Barbados, Jamaica, Singapore, and Ireland. And, third, these workers are willing to work for one-fifth or less the salary of comparable U.S. workers. The professionals affected by outsourcing are software engineers, accountants, architects, engineers, designers, and x-ray technicians. Also negatively affected are lower-level white-collar professionals such as customer service representatives, telemarketers, record transcribers, and those who make airline and hotel reservations.

The Great Recession (2007–?)

PRELUDE TO THE ECONOMIC CRISIS

As the economy shifted away from manufacturing to services and information/knowledge some sectors of the economy faded in importance or even died. These sectors, known as **sunset industries** (e.g., steel, tires, shoes, toys, and textiles), closed thousands of plants since 1975, with tens of millions of jobs lost permanently. Other jobs moved to low-wage economies, putting millions more out of work. Workers who did not lose their jobs in this environment were typically insecure about keeping their jobs. Moreover, weak unions, plus the competition from low-wage economies, led many U.S. corporations to reduce or eliminate their benefits (health insurance, retirement) to workers. Wages were also negatively affected. "The income of a man in his 30s is now 12 percent below that of a man his age three decades ago" (Reich, 2008: para 6). Put another way, "the peak income year for the bottom 90 percent of Americans was way back in 1973, when the average income per taxpayer, adjusted for inflation was $33,000. That was nearly $4,000 higher than in 2005" (David Cay Johnston, cited in Herbert, 2009a: para 9).

Thus, the transformation of the economy, at least in the short run, marginalized millions, increased unemployment, drove social mobility downward, and made many millions insecure about their jobs, health care, and retirement. To cope with these problems, employees worked more hours a week, putting in 350 more hours a year than the average European; more women worked in the labor force (70 percent, almost double the percentage in 1970); and families went deeper into debt with credit cards, car loans, college loans, and home equity loans. The average American with a credit file owed $16,635, not counting mortgages (Palmer, 2008). Families were also buying homes because home values had risen for half a century, most steeply from 1997 to 2006 when they rose by an inflation-adjusted 85 percent) (Zuckerman, 2008). This price appreciation tempted many to speculate, "flipping" recently purchased houses for a quick profit. Others took advantage of easy credit to refinance by taking out second mortgages in order to remodel their homes or to purchase "big ticket" items such as automobiles and boats.

> Homeowners, armed with easy credit, snapped up properties as if they were playing Monopoly. As prices soared, buyers were able to afford ever-larger properties only by taking out risky mortgages that lenders were happily approving with little documentation or money down. (Gandel and Lim, 2008:90)

Mortgage market lenders, therefore, encouraged this housing "bubble." About 20 percent of home loans in 2005 were "subprime"—that is, loans sold to people with questionable credit records. These loans went disproportionately to African Americans and Latinos, many buying homes for the first time. They were offered no-money down loans, with what appeared to be low interest rates. The "low" rates were for the first two years, but then the loans increased substantially when the "variable rate" clause (found in the fine print of the loan contract) was enforced. The Federal Reserve was responsible to prohibit practices that were unfair or deceptive, but it did not.

Add to this mix the reckless and irresponsible dealmaking on Wall Street, which involved an intricate, intertwined system of loan brokers, mortgage lenders, Wall Street trusts, hedge funds, offshore tax havens, and other predators (Hightower, 2007; see also Moyers and Winship, 2009). For example, subprime loans were bundled and sold to third parties. These "derivatives" were financial contracts between a buyer and a seller that derive value from an underlying asset, such as a mortgage or a stock. This allowed banks and insurance firms to leverage their assets by as much as 40 times the value of the underlying asset. In the case of subprime mortgages, this was "financial alchemy that turned low-quality mortgages into trillions of dollars of high-priced derivatives" (Karabell, 2009:35). The government stood by without interfering with the market when it indulged in these reckless ventures. There were five financial agencies at the federal level that could have regulated these practices but did not because they assumed the financial players would police themselves (Hightower, 2007).

THE ENSUING ECONOMIC CRISIS

These forces converged in 2007 creating a "perfect storm" of economic devastation. It began when subprime borrowers began defaulting on their mortgages. That sent housing prices tumbling, unleashing a domino effect on mortgage-backed securities (Gandel and Lim, 2008). Banks and brokerages that had borrowed money to increase their leverage had to raise capital quickly. Some, like Merrill Lynch and Bear Sterns, were forced to sell their assets to other banks at bargain rates (Bear Sterns was sold to J. P. Morgan for $236 million, down from its value of $20 billion a year earlier). Others, like Lehman Brothers, failed. The stock market dropped precipitously. Credit dried up. Business slowed, causing companies to lay off workers by the tens of thousands. What was happening in the United States affected markets elsewhere, causing a worldwide recession and a further slowing of business activity here and abroad. The result was the worst economic downturn in the United States since the Great Depression of the 1930s. Let's consider the contours of the crisis, beginning with unemployment. [This chapter was written in mid-2009, in the middle of the Great Recession. Thus, please note that the numbers and their magnitude will change and that what appear to be trends may weaken in time while others strengthen.]

Job Insecurity   Since the 1970s, retaining a job has become more precarious (Kalleberg, 2009). This trend accelerated in the recent recession as some six million American workers lost their jobs from late 2007 to May 2009. The official government's unemployment rate jumped from 4.6 percent in mid-2007 to 9.4 percent in May 2009, the highest rate in 25 years. The rate of 9.4 percent represents 14 million people, but this underreports the actual number of unemployed. The official statistics do not include the more than 3.7 million people who work part-time but want to work full-time and the 8.1 million who are out of work but are not actively looking for work. If those were to be included, then 9.4 percent would become 16.2 percent, or more than 25 million Americans (Healy, 2009; Holahan, 2009). Given the severity of the economic downturn, the official unemployment rate is likely to rise further.

Hidden in the official unemployment rate are important differences by race, class, and gender (Goodman and Healy, 2009). When the unemployment rate was 8.5 percent in March 2009, the rate for Whites was 8 percent, the rate for Blacks was 15 percent, and the rate for Latinos was 11.4. By educational level, those with less than high school had a rate of 14.8 percent, high school 9.3 percent, and a college degree or higher 4.4 percent. The official male unemployment rate was 10 percent, while the figure for women was 7 percent, reflecting massive cutbacks in male-dominated professions such as manufacturing (Healy, 2009) where the job decline had lasted 37 consecutive months by March 2009.

The families of the unemployed are profoundly affected (see Box 4.1). A family may have to live on the income of one spouse or on unemployment insurance, if qualified. In either case, the family has considerably less discretionary income. It may require finding cheaper housing or even going bankrupt.

Housing Woes   The value of homes grew rapidly in the new millennium, reaching a peak in 2006. By this time many homeowners were on the financial edge as they purchased overvalued houses, assuming their value would increase even more. But the housing bubble burst, causing values to decline precipitously—losing $4 trillion in value from 2005 to the end of 2008 (*Economist*, 2009b:47). The newly unemployed found they could not meet their monthly payments. Those who purchased subprime mortgages were especially vulnerable. By 2009 some 1.5 million homes, owned

BOX 4.1   **Inside the Worlds of Diverse Families**

Layoffs Can Stress Family Ties

The gloomy economy is affecting more than the unemployment lines. It's also having a dramatic impact on many families nationwide.

Unemployed professionals are suddenly becoming stay-at-home parents. Pink slips are triggering marital woes. College students have dropped out, taken jobs, or moved home because their parents can't foot their tuition bills. Some young couples are postponing having children because of job problems.

After earning a six-figure salary and almost all his family's income, Ed Simon was laid off in March from his sales and marketing management job at a consumer products firm. His family is still reeling.

His wife, Lori, used to work a half day so she could be home with the kids. Now she's working more, and Simon is Mr. Mom to Ari, 13, and Daniel, 7. Instead of taking business trips and managing a department, he spends his days clipping coupons and attending parent-teacher conferences.

"It's provided a whole lot of conflict. Now I'm telling my wife she has to spend more time with the kids," says Simon, 43, of Princeton, NJ. "It's a complete role reversal, and it's very tough. My wife comes home, and I'm at the kitchen sink saying, 'You have no idea how hard this is.'"

Mounting research suggests there's a strong connection between economic swings and family stability. These are some of the major trends:

Family time is affected

Research indicates that a failing economy forces many working parents to put in longer hours on the job, leaving them with less time for their children. That's because layoffs have intensified job pressures by leaving fewer employees to shoulder the workload. As a result of longer hours, 7 of 10 Americans feel they don't have a healthy balance between work and life, according to a May survey by Expedia.com.

But while the work day may be longer for those with jobs, a growing number of parents are experiencing the opposite extreme—they've been laid off, and that means they're staying home.

Long-term unemployment has been spreading fastest in families with young children, according to a study by the Children's Defense Fund in Washington, DC.

The proportion of families with an unemployed parent jumped by nearly a percentage point to 6.6 percent from 2000 to 2001 because of the economic slump that began early in 2001, according to the Department of

Labor. In an average week in 2001, 4.8 million families had at least one member who was unemployed—a rise of 665,000 families from 2000.

They're fathers like Rich Miller, 48, who found himself out of work in May 2002, when the New York office of his advertising agency closed. Miller started his own media placement company, Smarter Media, and tends bar on the weekends to help make ends meet.

It's been tough on his marriage. Says Miller, "The financial issues add an additional strain and magnify other problems. It's changed our life."

But he can also work from home, which means more time with his 8-year-old son, Joshua. "He does appreciate the time we have together," says Miller of Hamilton Square, NJ.

Parental involvement can be shaped by economic trends. A U.S. Census Bureau report found that fathers had more time to spend with their preschool-age children during the recession in 1990 and 1991. But as the economy picked up and job opportunities became more abundant, dads were less likely to provide care.

Working parents feel stressed

While the quantity of family time in some cases increases, the quality often suffers. Unemployment leaves jobless people worrying about money and finding work, while those in the labor force wrestle with job insecurities.

That tension spills into the home. Working women with young children are most likely to say they have little time to relax, according to a 2002 *USA Today/CNN/Gallup* poll.

"People are working under double anxiety," says Niels Nielsen, author of *Princeton Management Consultants Guide to Your New Job*. He founded an unemployment support group, JobSeekers, and started a human resources and general management firm, Princeton Management Consultants. "They're working longer hours and dealing with the prospect of being laid off. The family feels the strain. It's a double whammy."

Relationships have more pressures

Job relocations, unemployment, and financial concerns are testing many marriages. More than 70 percent of unemployed workers say family stress has increased since they lost their jobs, according to a poll by the National Employment Law Project.

Financial worries also take a toll. Calls about financial matters to counselors at ComPsych, a Chicago-based employee assistance provider, were up 58 percent in 2002. The majority of calls were for problems such as debt and bankruptcy instead of the typical calls they get for subjects such as money management advice.

Jim Holmes, 42, and his wife, Susan Smith, 40, were both unemployed for about two months last year. Shortly after they relocated from Los Angeles to Seattle for his wife's job, she was laid off, and he was still looking for work.

Today, Holmes is a planner with the city, and his wife is teaching and doing research at the University of Washington. While the stretch without an income gave them extra time with their children, Max, 11, and Sabrina, 6, it also was a time of worry.

"We had a good time together," says Holmes, of Issaquah, WA. "But it was stressful at the same time.... You'd worry about how it affects [the children's] lives."

While tensions may mount, research suggests a difficult economy actually tends to depress divorce rates. The reason: Couples have fewer financial resources, making it more cost-efficient to stay together. The divorce rate (which is shaped by numerous factors, including the economy) dipped from 4 percent in 2000 to 3.9 percent in 2002, according to the National Center for Health Statistics.

"It usually takes another job for a spouse to leave," says Carl Steidtmann, chief global economist at Deloitte Research in New York. "Divorce is an expensive proposition for a lot of people, and in a down economy you wait for a better time."

Many are new to unemployment

Many of the families affected by the economy are college-educated professionals with years of career experience. About 35 percent of workers unemployed for six months or longer in 2002 were over 45 years old, according to an analysis by the Economic Policy Institute (EPI) in Washington. About 18 percent of the long-term unemployed had college degrees, and 20 percent were executive, professional, and managerial workers.

"These are people who aren't accustomed to being unemployed," says economist Jeffrey Wenger. "What kind of coping strategies do they come up with? Because you've had such a stable environment for a long time, it's possible to have family friction."

There are other spillover effects of a downturn. One-third of unemployed workers have had to interrupt their own or a family member's education, according to a recent National Employment Law Project study of laid-off workers. And one in four has moved in with a family member or into other housing....

Source: Armour, Stephanie (2003a). "Layoffs Can Stress Family Ties." *USA Today* (June 27): B1–B2.

mostly by African Americans, were lost through subprime foreclosures. Many either walked away from their now unaffordable mortgages or, after missing payments, were foreclosed on by lenders. So, too, were more affluent owners, who, strapped by unaffordable mortgages, now owed more on their mortgages than what their homes were worth. About 12 million mortgage holders (20 percent) owed more on their properties than what they were worth. This created a downward spiral, decreasing home values further. Foreclosures rose 79 percent in 2007 and another 81 percent in 2008 to a record 2.3 million households (Gross, 2009). Put another way, in 2008, a householder lost her/his home every 13 seconds (Mosley, 2009). In early 2009, nearly one in eight mortgage holders were either delinquent in their payments or in foreclosure. Looking forward from 2009, an estimated six million families could lose their homes by the end of 2012 (Mooney, 2009).

Renters are not immune from the nation's housing crisis. They might experience several different kinds of problems caused by the economic crisis (Armour, 2008a). First, when owners of apartments are foreclosed on, their renters are evicted even though they have been paying their rents. According to the National Low Income Housing Coalition, renters make up an estimated 40 percent of families facing eviction because of foreclosure (Fireside, 2009). Those who are evicted usually lose their security deposits and any prepaid rent. Second, homeowners forced into foreclosure are becoming tenants, which drives up rents. Third, the cost of renting in many areas of the country is high, as demand exceeds the supply. The median monthly rent in 2008 for 12 metropolitan areas was $1,368. Approximately one in four renters pays more than half their income on rent (rents exceeding 30 percent are considered by the government to be unaffordable). Similarly, 37 percent of homeowners with mortgages are spending 30 percent or more of their before-tax income on housing.

This housing problem is especially acute for low-income families, for whom there is a critical shortage of affordable housing. The dwindling supply of affordable housing for the poor and working poor represents a long-term trend (the following is from Timmer et al., 1994:18–24). Since the 1970s, rents have increased and the stock of low-income housing has shrunk. Well over a million single-room occupancy (SRO) hotels have been torn down. SROs and other low-cost rental housing have disappeared because of several related trends. The first trend is gentrification (the process of converting low-income housing to condominiums or upscale apartments for the middle and upper-middle classes). The second trend is urban developers and real estate interests increasing their profits (e.g., slumlording and buying up properties for speculation have depleted the low-income housing stock). The third trend is federally financed urban renewal projects demolishing blighted properties in poor and working-class neighborhoods but failing to replace the housing because funds for that phase were lacking.

Financial Decline   As noted earlier, the average inflation-adjusted income for workers is lower now than it was in the 1970s. The decline is most significant for the nation's hourly work force, which totals 76 million, or 52 percent of all workers (Uchitelle, 2008). James Lin and Jared Bernstein of the Economic Policy Institute have calculated what they consider a modest standard of living for housing, food, child care, transportation, health care, taxes, and other necessities (Lin and Bernstein, 2008). The cost for a family of four in 2008 was $48,778. About 30 percent of U.S. families were below this threshold.

Consider just the losses that occurred in 2008 (Marquardt and Shinkle, 2009):

- Stock market value declined by $7.3 trillion.
- Standard & Poor's 500 lost 38.5 percent, its worst fall since 1937.
- Mutual funds, on average, lost 38 percent.
- Household wealth dropped $11.1 trillion (18 percent) (Bajaj, 2009).
- Americans lost over $1 trillion in their 401(k)s (retirement savings). Individuals who had contributed to 401(k)s for 20 years or more, lost an average of 20 percent of value, even after counting the money they had added through the years (Ridgeway, 2009).
- Over an 18-month period, the investments of public pension plans—the retirement security for 22 million police officers, firefighters, teachers, and their survivors—lost a combined $1.3 trillion (Byrnes and Palmeri, 2009).
- From the start of the Great Recession to May 2009, 2.4 million workers lost health insurance they were getting through their jobs.

In summary, surveys reveal that more than 24 million Americans shifted in 2008 from lives that were "thriving" to ones that were "struggling" (Page, 2009). A 2009 Kaiser Health Foundation survey revealed, for example, that more than half of American households had cut back on health care in the past year because of concerns about costs (reported in Bawley, 2009). Similarly, many Americans ignored seeing dentists during the recession (Marcus, 2009).

Personal Bankruptcies The current economic crisis—with rising unemployment, plummeting home values, staggering stock market losses, and increased indebtedness—has added to the usual reasons for bankruptcy (medical catastrophe, financial missteps, and divorce). From March 2008 to March 2009, about 1.2 million debtors filed for bankruptcy, an increase of 46 percent from the year earlier (Baker, 2009). In 2009, a record number of consumer loans (4.2 percent) were falling delinquent or into default, meaning the loan holders were only a step or two away from bankruptcy.

A major source of bankruptcy is the inability to pay for catastrophic health care needs. Employers have increasingly cut back on their contribution to health insurance, either dropping coverage altogether or decreasing their obligation by introducing high-deductible health insur-

A major source of bankruptcies is the inability to pay for catastrophic health care needs.

ance. One tactic by employers is to hire workers as independent contractors because these workers do not receive company-paid benefits such as health insurance, family leave, and retirement (in 2009 there were more than 10 million such workers). Many workers cannot afford the $12,000 or more for health insurance when their employers do not supply it, at least in part, leaving more than 48 million Americans without health insurance in 2009. Of course those who lose jobs also lose their health insurance. Since the cost of health care is so expensive (e.g., a heart bypass costs $200,000; a premature baby costs close to $1 million), the uninsured are just a catastrophic illness or accident away from economic ruin. The Public Broadcasting System reported that 700,000 households go bankrupt each year because of medical bills (PBS, "Frontline," 2009).

Downward Social Mobility

The "American dream," in effect a middle-class dream, is that one's family will own a home, own at least one late-model car, and be able to provide college education for the children. Through the 1950s and 1960s, increasingly more Americans realized this dream as average real wages (i.e., wages adjusted for inflation), family incomes expanded, and the economy created new jobs and opportunities. The result was that many Americans after World War II were able to move up into a growing and vibrant middle class. This trend peaked in 1973, and since then families have tended to either stagnate or decline in their level of affluence. The transformation of the economy, fueled by globalization, had the effect of shrinking the middle class as the gap between the "haves" and the "have nots" increased. This trend accelerated with "The Great Recession," which began in 2007, with unemployment rates climbing dramatically, personal debt rising, and the housing bubble bursting. All of this happened while the costs for health care, college, consumer goods, and transportation continued to rise. As a result, many middle-class families plunged in income and resources, thus moving down in social class. Some declared bankruptcy. Some were forced from their homes and had to relocate. Some families became poor, hungry, and even homeless.

Hunger The poorest among us are suffering the harshest effects of the economic decline. Already on the economic margins, they have been pushed down even further. The welfare "safety net," which has eroded since 1980, was further cut by the welfare reform of 1996, which ended the idea of welfare as an entitlement. Many states also reduced the welfare safety net.

> Despite soaring unemployment and the worst economic crisis in decades, 18 states cut their welfare rolls last year, and nationally the number of people receiving cash assistance remained at or near the lowest in more than 40 years. (DeParle, 2009: para 1)

Here are some facts about hunger amid the economic crisis:

- Since late 2007, the number of people receiving food stamps increased by 4.6 million, nearly 17 percent (Center for Budget Priorities, reported in Herbert, 2009b).
- In 2008, nearly one in eight Americans (36.2 million adults and children) were "food insecure," meaning they had difficulty getting enough food, due to a lack of resources (*The Nation*, 2008).
- In 2006, the demand at food banks across the country increased by 30 percent from 2005 (Bosman, 2009).
- By early 2009, some 16.5 million children received free school lunches, up 6.5 percent from the previous year. Another 3.2 million students received reduced-priced lunches.

This surge in the number of hungry in the United States exemplifies the struggle by the new poor to cope with their desperate situations.

> The message is simple. Ever more Americans need food they can't afford. As tough economic times take their toll, increasing numbers of Americans are on tightened budgets and, in some cases, facing outright hunger. As a result, they may be learning a lot more about food banks and soup kitchens than most of them ever wanted to know.... Families who just months ago didn't even know what a food bank was and would never have considered visiting a food pantry now have far more intimate knowledge of both.... Other formerly middle class Americans who have never dealt with, or even thought about, food insecurity before simply don't know whom to call or where to turn. (Turse, 2009: para 1, 4)

The New Homeless The extent of homelessness is difficult to measure because those without a permanent home may be doubling up with relatives, sleeping in vehicles, and the like, and not using shelters. Thus the numbers of the homeless understate the actual count. Given that caveat, the official number of homeless prior to the Great Recession was about 1 in 400 Americans (750,000) without a home on any given night, and about 1.6 million Americans experienced homelessness at some point in a given year. Around 40 percent of the homeless population consisted of families, typically single mothers and their children.

During the Great Recession millions more Americans were at greater risk of becoming homeless. Some 9.6 million families were spending more than half of their income on housing. Foreclosures brought evictions, even for renters when their apartment buildings were foreclosed. The newly unemployed could not make their mortgage payments or their rents. Costly medical care put some in bankruptcy. As a result, according to the National Alliance to End Homelessness, as many as 3.4 million Americans were predicted to be homeless in 2009—a 35 percent increase since the recession started in December 2007 (Vestal, 2009). Unlike the traditional homeless, composed mostly of the long-time poor and near poor, the new homeless included the "working poor, who were among the hardest hit by the collapse in subprime mortgages. But others [were] middle-class families who scarcely expected to find themselves unable to afford homes" (Armour, 2008b:2B). See Box 4.2.

CONSEQUENCES OF THE GREAT RECESSION FOR FAMILIES

Living through this economic crisis, families have had to cope with uncertainties about jobs, retaining an adequate income, keeping their homes, losing savings, and paying for health care. The poor have always been insecure, but now even middle-class families fear that they are but one illness or one job loss away from catastrophe. Members of these families are faced with a number of choices for dealing with these critical issues. Let's consider a few of these.

Marriage Bond   Finances are a common source of marital unease even in the best of times. *Money* magazine, in a 2006 study, found that 84 percent of those surveyed said money created tension in marriage and that 15 percent fought about money several times a month (reported in O'Connor, 2009). Marriage partners may differ on questions such as the degree of risk in investments, whether to buy lavishly or

BOX 4.2   Emergent Family Trends

The Economic Homeless

By Emily Bazar

PINELLAS COUNTY, FL.—Jim Marshall recalls everything about that beautiful fall day.

The temperature was about 70° on November 19, the sky was "totally blue," and the laughter from a martini bar drifted into the St. Petersburg park where Marshall, 39, sat contemplating his first day of homelessness.

"I was thinking, 'That was me at one point,'" he says of the revelers. "Now I'm thinking, 'Where am I going to sleep tonight? Where do I eat? Where do I shower?'"

The unemployed Detroit autoworker moved to Florida last year hoping he'd have better luck finding a job. He didn't, and he spent three months sleeping on sidewalks before landing in a tent city in Pinellas County, north of St. Petersburg, on February 26.

Marshall is among a growing number of the economic homeless, a term for those newly displaced by layoffs, foreclosures, or other financial troubles caused by the recession. They differ from the chronic homeless,

the longtime street residents who often suffer from mental illness, drug abuse, or alcoholism.

For the economic homeless, the American ideal that education and hard work lead to a comfortable middle-class life has slipped out of reach. They're packing into motels, parking lots, and tent cities, alternately distressed and hopeful, searching for work and praying their fortunes will change.

"My parents always taught me to work hard in school, graduate high school, go to college, get a degree, and you'll do fine. You'll do better than your parents' generation," Marshall says. "I did all those things....For a while, I did have that good life, but nowadays that's not the reality."

Tent cities and shelters from California to Massachusetts report growing demand from the newly homeless. The National Alliance to End Homelessness predicted in January that the recession would force 1.5 million more people into homelessness over the next two years.

Source: Bazar, Emily (2009). "Tent Cities Filling up with Casualties of the Economy." *USA Today* (May 5): excerpt from pp. 1A–2A.

frugally, to buy or rent, how much debt to incur, and so on. Hence, there is the potential for marital friction any time. *Money* magazine surveyed couples *before* the Great Recession. When faced with a financial crisis such as unemployment, eviction, or bankruptcy the level of strain and stress increases dramatically.

How do these financial strains affect the current divorce rate? The results are mixed. Money troubles may draw some couples closer as they work together to find solutions. But money matters can also break a marriage. The divorce rate may not reflect the actual number of couples who wish to separate because of their financial troubles. They may continue to live together (in the same house) because they cannot sell it in the sour economy. Or, they may not seek a divorce because they cannot afford the legal costs, which are especially high (up to $30,000) in a contested divorce involving child custody.

Fertility   Delaying marriage is a common response to the economic crisis, when jobs and income are so uncertain. The cost of renting or buying a home also constrains prospective married partners, some of whom still live with their parents to save on housing costs. The greater the delay of marriage, the fewer children will likely be born to that union.

Children are expensive. As noted in Chapter 9, the cost of raising a child is huge. According to the Department of Agriculture, a baby born in 2006 will cost middle-income parents $260,000 by the time the child reaches 17. In tough economic times, couples likely will delay having children or limit the number of children. There is some early evidence that couples are cutting back on family size. For example, the number of men seeking vasectomies (male sterilization) increased with the downturn (Alderman, 2009). Also, the sale of family planning products such as condoms and female contraceptives were up (Gregory, 2009). A birth rate decline in the Great Recession has a historical parallel in The Great Depression of the 1930s, when the birth rate fell sharply, resulting in a "Birth Dearth."

What Does It Mean to Families That Move Down from the Middle Class?   The economic transformation and the Great Recession have had dire consequences for many in the middle class. Katherine Newman describes the experience of the downwardly mobile middle class (see Box 4.2 for the methods employed by Newman):

> They once "had it made" in American society, filling slots from affluent blue-collar jobs to professional and managerial occupations. They have job skills, education, and decades of steady work experience. Many are, or were, homeowners. Their marriages were (at least initially) intact. As a group they savored the American dream. They found a place higher up the ladder in this society and then, inexplicably, found their grip loosening and their status sliding.
>
> Some downwardly mobile middle-class families end up in poverty, but many do not. Usually they come to rest at a standard of living above the poverty level but far below the affluence they enjoyed in the past. They must therefore contend not only with financial hardship but with the psychological, social, and practical consequences of "falling from grace," of losing their "proper place" in the world. (Newman, 1988:8)

Thus, individual self-esteem and family honor are bruised. Moreover, this ordeal impairs the chances of the children—as children and, later, as adults—to enjoy economic security and a comfortable lifestyle.

In terms of agency, many downwardly mobile families find successful coping strategies to deal with their adverse situations. Some families develop a tighter bond to meet their common problems. Others find support from families in similar situations or from personal kin networks. But for many families, downward mobility adds tensions that make family life especially difficult. Failure in the work world typically affects relationships between breadwinners and spouses, sometimes stretching emotional bonds beyond the breaking point. The loss of one's home and the process of relocation terminate attachments to friends and a neighborhood and a way of life, often causing alienation and anger, which are sometimes directed at family members. Children, so dependent on peer approval, often find intolerable the increasing gap in material differences between themselves and their peers.

Many families who experience a slide in their standard of living attempt to camouflage their deteriorating situation with lies and cover-ups. These tactics sometimes place heavy demands on family members, and relationships among them tend to grow more strained. The result is that many members of families facing downward mobility experience stress, marital tension, depression, anxiety, hypertension, high cholesterol, and high levels of alcohol consumption. Newman has suggested that these pathologies are somewhat normal, given the persistent tensions generated by downward mobility. Many families experience some degree of these pathologies and yet they somehow endure. But some families disintegrate completely under the pressure, with serious problems of physical abuse, incapacitating alcoholism, desertion, and even suicide (Newman, 1988:134–140).

Shifting Family Forms   The economic crisis has caused many families to change (see Box 4.3 for the larger picture concerning shifting family forms). Housing woes and unemployment, for example, have led many young people or even middle-aged couples to move back in with their parents, other relatives, or friends for extended periods (doubling up).

> As pink slips proliferate and foreclosures multiply, more families are rolling out the welcome mat—sometimes hesitantly—to give shelter and support to relatives in need. The American dream of living under a roof of one's own is being downscaled. Now some displaced residents long simply to have a room of one's own.... According to the 2007 U.S. Census, 3.6 million parents live with adult children, up from 2.3 million in 2000. Almost 3.5 million siblings live with a brother or sister, up from 3 million. And more than 6.5 million people share quarters with other relatives, up from 4.8 million. Their ranks continue to grow. (Gardner, 2009: para 3)

With the economic downturn, more and more children are being raised by their grandparents. In 2007, there were 4.7 million children—or 6.5 percent of American children—living in households headed by a grandparent (up from 3 percent in 1970) (Lagnado, 2009). These grandparents provide a safety net for their children's children when their children cannot provide for them. But these grandparents, typically, are struggling during the Great Recession with the loss of retirement savings because of the stock market crash and the resulting loss of 401(k)s and IRAs. "It will take the typical 55-year-old employee two extra years in the workforce simply to recoup 2008's losses..." (Brandon, 2009:40). The added load of dependent grandchildren coupled with much less retirement income has severely eroded their "golden years."

Another family form emerging from the economic crisis is the married couple that lives in the same house even though the individuals no longer want to live together. They continue to live together because it is too costly to maintain two homes. So they build walls, real and imaginary, to create separate spaces for each in the same larger space—still married, still living together, but living apart emotionally.

Of every five jobs lost, men have lost four of them during this economic crisis (Reed, 2009). This has significant ramifications for families.

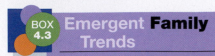

BOX 4.3 Emergent **Family** Trends

The Shift from the Modern Family to the Postmodern Family

Judith Stacey's important research on working-class families documents the difficulties that families face with changes in the economy and the changes in families as a result. Her description reveals much about changing families. (The following is taken from Stacey, 1990, 1991, 1996.)

The prevailing family form in U.S. society in the 1950s was an intact nuclear household composed of a male breadwinner, his full-time homemaker wife, and their dependent children. In 1950 some 60 percent of U.S. households fit this pattern, whether children were present or not. Although this family form was clearly dominant in society, its prevalence varied by social class. The pattern clearly prevailed in working-class households, for example, but was much less likely among the poor, where women have always had to work outside the home to supplement family income.

This model for the family, which Stacey calls the modern family, was disrupted by the destabilizing effects of globalization and deindustrialization on jobs in the United States and the challenges of women to traditional ways. Stacey found that working-class families, especially the women in them, created innovative ways to cope with economic uncertainty and domestic upheavals. In effect, these women were and are the pioneers of emergent family forms. Stacey calls these new family forms postmodern because they do not fit the criteria of a "modern" family. Now there are divorce-extended families that include exspouses and their lovers, children, and friends. Households now expand and contract as adult children leave and then return home only to leave again. The vast majority of these postmodern families have dual earners. Many families now involve husbands in greater child-care and domestic work than in earlier times. Kin networks have expanded to meet economic pressures. Parents now deal with their children's cohabitation, single and unwed parenthood, and divorce. The result is that only 7 percent of households now conform to the "modern" family form. According to Stacey,

> [n]o longer is there a single culturally dominant family pattern, like the modern one, to which the majority of Americans conform and most of the rest aspire. Instead, Americans today have crafted a multiplicity of family and household arrangements that we inhabit uneasily and reconstitute frequently in response to changing personal and occupational circumstances. (Stacey, 1991:19)

Significant in this shift is that working-class families are not clinging to the old "modern" family form. Indeed, they are leading the way toward new forms. Again, according to Stacey,

> [My research findings] shatter the image of the white working class as the last repository of old-fashioned "modern" American family life. The postmodern family arrangements I found among blue-collar people in Silicon Valley are at least as diverse and innovative as those found within the middle class. (Stacey, 1991:27)

It is important to note that these postmodern family forms are new to working-class and middle-class families as they adjust to globalization and deindustrialization, but that they are not new to the poor. The economic deprivation faced by the poor has always forced them to adapt in similar ways: single-parent families, relying on kin networks, sharing housing costs, and multiple wage earners among family members.

Behind that cold statistic is an often heated rearrangement of the family dynamic. With gender roles and responsibilities being radically defined, wives now face the added pressure inherent in being the sole breadwinner while also retaining their household responsibilities. Meanwhile, husbands must reconstruct their definition of contributing to the family enterprise, often swapping a paycheck for a broom. (Della Cava, 2009:D2)

Women becoming the primary earners in families has another implication because their wages are usually lower than the wages of men. Thus, this transformation of households has the further result of lowering families' standard of living.

SHRINKING CONSUMPTION

The Great Recession has caused many families to adjust their lifestyles downward. Many are adjusting their behaviors even though their economic situations have not

"Frankly, we're just keeping our heads above water."

changed, motivated by fear over the future of the economy (Mui, 2009). "Not spending, even if you have money, has become the new national norm" (Horowitz, 2009:1A). These are some indicators of contraction of consumption:

- In 2008 consumer spending for durable goods such as automobiles decreased by 10.8 percent. Spending for nondurable goods such as clothing fell by 4.2 percent (Mandel, 2009).

- Consumers are buying products to do activities personally that they once paid others to do (called "insourcing") such as sewing, hair care (e.g., dyeing), car washing, housecleaning, and landscaping (Mui, 2009).

- Replacing part of the lawn with a vegetable garden is on the rise as is the sale of canning and freezing supplies (Gibbs, 2009).

- The business of thrift stores is booming as people buy used clothing, furniture, and household items rather than purchase new and more expensive items. A related indicator of the new thrift is that these stores are running low on these goods because they are receiving fewer donations as people are using their items longer (Stone, 2009a).

- An indication that more of us are "keeping our stuff" is that the intake at landfills has fallen off as much as 30 percent (Schulte, 2009).

- There is a boon for pawnshops and consignment stores as first-time customers seek cash and bargain hunters are looking for high-end items at reduced prices (Keen, 2008).

- Vacation travel is down. Airlines have fewer passengers. Cruise ships are less full. The sales of gas-guzzling SUVs are lower than the sales of gas-sipping vehicles.

- A 2009 survey by *Time* magazine revealed that people are cutting back on entertainment (eating out, attending sporting events, going to the movies, gambling, and health clubs) because of the cost since the downturn began (Gibbs, 2009).

This shift to thrift brought about by the Great Recession likely will have consequences beyond the inevitable recovery (Herbert, 2009a; Rampell, 2009). A lot of people will be economically desperate for many years. Pessimism will replace optimism as people remember unemployment and the rapid declines in the stock market and housing values, and they will fear the future. This shift to thrift has two additional consequences. Positively, it leads to families saving rather than spending beyond their means. In 2009 the savings rate—the percentage of after-tax income that people do not spend—had risen to above 4 percent, from virtually zero (in 2005 it was a negative 2.7 percent). This has a negative side, however. The growth of the economy has relied on consumer spending. "Sustained increases in household saving would cause a difficult period of restructuring for the American economy, which has become increasingly driven by consumer spending" (Rampell, 2009:para 8). As Americans cut back, what will replace the demand? Companies will likely retrench by cutting back on expenses (wages and benefits to workers), laying off workers, and reducing research and development. Thus, the retrenchment brought on by the Great Recession will be sustained.

The Transformation of the Economy Reshaped by the Great Recession

Globalization, with its offshoring and outsourcing, and the shift from an industrial economy to one based on technology and knowledge has transformed the economy. This transformation will be reshaped further because of the Great Recession. The excesses leading to the recession will likely shift the economy from a mostly laissez-faire capitalism to a more regulated capitalism. Peter Grier argues that when the recession is over, the economy will be different.

This is a given: the BC economy (the one we had Before the Crash) had too much of many important things. Too much debt. Too much consumption. Too much speculation in complicated financial instruments by bankers blind to the bubble inflating around them. That's not coming back. (Grier, 2009: para 10)

. . . .

You don't have to be a futurist to foresee that in the coming new economy just about everyone in the private sector, from consumers to financiers, will be looking to get the most they can for their dollars. You can sum the situation up in two words: "value rules." (Grier, 2009: para 12)

Living through the Great Depression scarred two generations (the grandparents and great grandparents of today's college students), teaching them first hand the importance of thrift. As a result, they tended to live frugally throughout their lives. They drove automobiles until they wore out. They purchased used items and fixed them. They sewed their own clothes and mended and patched them as needed. They harvested vegetables from gardens. When they purchased new items, they were useful, not fancy. To some extent, that pattern is recurring now. To cope with financial contraction due to the Great Recession, more and more families are fixing up, making do, and reusing. A 2009 Pew Research Center survey found that the recession has changed people's minds about what items are defined as "necessities." The Center found that 80 percent of Americans were cutting back in their purchases (reported in Jayson, 2009a). In effect, this serious recession has changed what people value.

A 2009 *Time* magazine survey revealed that most people (61 percent) feel that even when prosperity returns, they will continue to spend less than they did before (Gibbs, 2009). In other words, they will continue their new frugal habits.

In the old days of two years ago, the thrill was in the extras—the heated steering wheel or the size of the second shower in the master bedroom suite. Now it's in the percentage discount from the previous list price. (Grier, 2009: para 12)

If the "New Frugality" continues after the recession, this change will have ramifications for the economy. The "full-price" marketplace will shrink, while the secondary markets (e.g., eBay) that sell used goods will surge. Industries whose growth depends on planned obsolescence will retool to build products that last. These and related changes will affect jobs as they cause a decline in some industries and an increase in others ("creative destruction"). There will be short-term dislocations as the economy shifts and families adjust to cope with these changes. Grier concludes: "Crises can accelerate trends that were already remaking a nation's economic order. The Panic of 1873, for instance, helped propel the U.S. into the modern Industrial Age. This recession is likely to be no different" (Grier, 2009: para 30).

The New Immigration and the Changing Racial Landscape

Another societal "earthquake" that is shaking up society and families is massive immigration. This demographic force—the new immigration—is challenging the cultural hegemony of the White European tradition; creating incredible diversity in race, ethnicity, language, religion, and culture; rapidly changing the racial landscape; and leading, often, to division and hostility.

Historically, immigration has been a major source of population growth and ethnic diversity in the United States. Immigration waves from northern and southern Europe, especially from 1850 to 1920, brought many millions of people, mostly Europeans, to the United States. In the 1920s, the United States placed limits on the number of immigrants it would accept, the operating principle being that the new immigrants should resemble the old ones. The national origins rules were designed to severely limit the immigration of eastern Europeans and to deny the entry of Asians.

The Immigration Act amendments of 1965 abandoned the quota system that had preserved the European character of the United States for nearly half a century. The new law encouraged a new wave of immigrants, only this time the migrants arrived not from northern Europe but from the Third World, especially Asia and Latin America. Put another way, 100 years ago Europeans were 90 percent of immigrants to the United States; now 90 percent of immigrants are from non-European countries, mostly from Latin America and Asia. The result, obviously, is a dramatic alteration of the ethnic and racial composition of the U.S. population. The size of the contemporary immigrant wave has resulted in a highly visible and significant number of U.S. residents who are foreign-born (38.1 million in 2006 [12.6 percent], compared to 19.8 million in 1990; see Figure 4.1). Of the foreign-born in the United States, 34 percent were naturalized U.S. citizens, 35 percent legal immigrants and temporary visitors, and 31 percent unauthorized (Martin and Zurcher, 2008:9).

About one million immigrants enter the United States legally each year. Another estimated 525,000 unauthorized immigrants enter and stay (an estimated 1.5 to 2.5 million people enter the United States illegally each year, but most return to their native countries either voluntarily or by force if caught by the Immigration and Naturalization Service) for a net gain of about 1.53 million immigrants annually. Although the number of immigrants who enter clandestinely is impossible to determine, the best estimate is that about 11 million unauthorized foreign nationals resided in the United States in 2006. Roughly 80 percent of these undocumented immigrants are Latinos (and two-thirds of the Latinos are Mexicans). The number of

Figure 4.1

Foreign-Born Population: 1900–2006 (millions)

Source: U.S. Bureau of the Census, 1993. *We the Americans... Foreign Born* (September):1; and Martin, Philip, and Gottfried Zurcher, 2008. "Managing Migration: The Global Challenge." *Population Bulletin* 63 (March): 9.

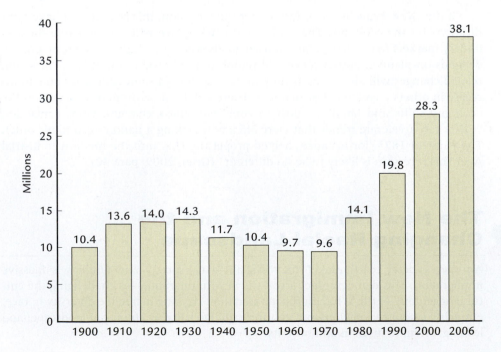

unauthorized immigrants declined in 2008 and 2009 due to tougher enforcement and border control and the very slow U.S. economy and rising unemployment, making jobs more uncertain.

The settlement pattern of the new immigration differs from previous flows into the United States. Whereas previous immigrants settled primarily in the industrial states of the Northeast and Middle Atlantic region or in the farming areas of the Midwest, recent migrants have tended to locate on the two coasts and in the Southwest. Asians have tended to settle on the West Coast; Mexicans, while predominantly in the Southwest, have also located across the country, from urban Chicago to rural Kansas. Other Latinos are scattered (for example, Cubans in Florida and Puerto Ricans and Dominicans in New York).*

California is a harbinger of the demographic future for the United States. As recently as 1970, California was 80 percent White, but since then it has become uniquely affected by immigration. The result is that Whites now constitute a numerical minority (41 percent in 2007, with 37 percent Latino, 12 percent Asian, and 6 percent African American) (Schrag, 2007). One-fourth of California's schoolchildren are studying English as a foreign language. "In another generation Latinos will be an absolute majority, and there will be 2 million fewer non-Hispanic whites than there are now" (Schrag, 2007:18). For example, Los Angeles has the largest population of Koreans outside Korea, the biggest concentration of Iranians in the Western world, and a huge Mexican population. Languages spoken by the diverse population of southern California include 88 languages and dialects. Greater Los Angeles has more than 50 foreign-language newspapers and television shows that broadcast in Spanish, Mandarin, Armenian, Japanese, Korean, and Vietnamese. For example, in the 90706 zipcode lies Bellflower, where 38 languages are spoken (Mohan and Simmons, 2004).

For all this diversity, though, California, especially southern California, is becoming more and more Latino. California holds nearly half of the U.S. Latino population and well over half of the Mexican-origin population. Latinos are expected to surpass Whites in total California population by 2025 and become an absolute majority by 2040 (Purdum, 2000).

Similar concentrations of Latinos are found in Arizona and Texas. Historian David Kennedy argues that there is no precedent in U.S. history for one immigrant group to have the size and concentration that the Mexican immigrant group has in the Southwest today.

> If we seek historical guidance, the closest example we have in hand is in the diagonally opposite corner of the North American continent, in Quebec. The possibility looms that in the next generation or so we will see a kind of Chicano Quebec take shape in the American Southwest, as a group emerges with strong cultural cohesiveness and sufficient economic and political strength to insist on changes in the overall society's ways of organizing itself and conducting its affairs. (Kennedy, 1996:68)

Demographic Trends and Increasing Diversity

The United States is shifting from an Anglo-White society rooted in Western culture to a society with three large racial-ethnic minorities, each of them growing in size

---

*Note that there is a wide diversity among immigrant groups. For example, while there are over three million Latinos living in Florida, they come from several ethnic backgrounds: Cubans, Puerto Ricans, South Americans, Central Americans, Mexicans, and Dominicans (*USA Today*, 2008).

while the proportion of Whites declines. Five facts show the contours and magnitude of this demographic transformation:

1. *About one-third of the people in the United States are African American, Latino, Asian, or Native American.* The non-White population is numerically significant, comprising 33.2 percent of the population in 2005 (up from 15 percent in 1960), and more than one-third of all children in the United States are non-White. Three states have non-White majorities (California, New Mexico, and Hawaii). Minorities make up the majority in six of the eight U.S. cities with more than a million people—New York, Los Angeles, Chicago, Houston, Detroit, and Dallas.

2. *Racial minorities are increasing faster than the majority population.* While non-Whites are now one-third of the population, by 2023 a majority of children (under 18) will be from a minority background (U.S. Census estimate, reported in Yen, 2009); they will surpass Whites among working-age Americans by 2039, and by 2042 minorities will exceed the White population in size (Roberts, 2008).

3. *African Americans have lost their position as the most numerous racial minority.* In 1990, for the first time, African Americans represented fewer than half of all minorities. In 2000, Latinos surpassed Blacks for the first time. By 2005, Latinos outnumbered African Americans 42.7 to 39.7 million. By 2050 Latinos will comprise an estimated 29 percent of the U.S. population and African Americans about 13 percent (see Figure 4.2). This demographic transformation will make two common assumptions about race obsolete: that "race" is a "Black-and-White" issue and that the United States is a "White" society (Chideya, 1999).

4. *Immigration now accounts for a large share of the nation's population growth.* Immigration accounts for more than 40 percent of the population growth since 2000. Today 12.5 percent of current U.S. residents are foreign born. The Census

Figure 4.2

Changing Makeup of the U.S. Population

Source: El Nasser, Haya (2008)."U.S. growth sport by 2050." *USA Today* (February 12): 3A.

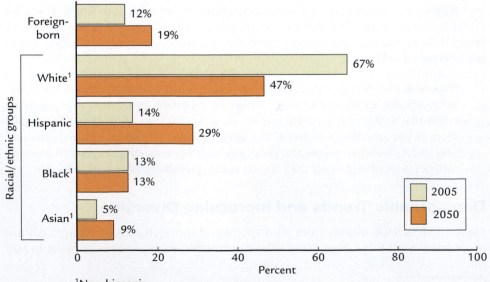

How components of the U.S. population are projected to change by 2050:

[1]Non-hispanic
Note: American Indian/Alaska Native not included.
Source: Pew Research Center

Bureau estimates that the Latino and Asian populations are growing at more than 10 times the pace of the White population (reported in El Nasser and Grant, 2005). Immigration accounts for over a third of the current population growth directly and adds more indirectly, as first- (those foreign-born) and second-generation (children of the foreign-born) Americans have more children on average than the rest of the population.

5. *New patterns of immigration are changing the racial composition of society.* Among the expanded population of first-generation immigrants, the Asian-born now outnumber the European-born, and those from Latin America, especially Mexicans, outnumber both. This contrasts sharply with what occurred as recently as the 1950s, when two-thirds of legal immigrants were from Europe and Canada.

These trends signal a transformation from a White majority to a multiracial/multicultural society:

[Sometime around the year 2042], whites will become a "minority." This is uncharted territory in this country, and this demographic change will affect everything. Alliances between the races are bound to shift. Political and social power will be re-apportioned. Our neighborhoods, our schools and workplaces, even racial categories themselves will be altered. (Chideya, 1999:35)

The pace of these changes is quickening. During the 1990s, while the White population increased by 2 percent, the African American population rose by 12 percent, the Native American population increased by 15 percent, the Asian and Latino populations each increased by 58 percent. One consequence of this is that across the United States, an estimated 84 percent of the foreign-born spoke a language other than English at home. Slightly fewer than half spoke Spanish; about 18 percent spoke Chinese, Tagalog, Korean, or other Asian language; and 17 percent spoke French, German, Italian, or another European language (Martin and Midgley, 2006:25).

Structural Diversity of Immigrant Families

There is a wide-ranging diversity of immigrant families (this section depends in part on Pyke, 2008). Some speak English (from such English-speaking countries as the Philippines, India, or Belize), but most of the new migrants do not. Some live in ethnic enclaves with others from their native land, while others live apart. Some families have separate housing arrangements, and others live with other immigrant individuals or families as a strategy to cope with high rents and low wages. Most come to work in the United States as menial laborers, but others come as professionals with special skills. Some arrive as legal immigrants while others come illegally ("undocumented immigrants," see Box 4.4). Some families immigrate as intact units, some even as two- or three-generation families. Other husbands or wives migrate alone to support the family back home or to find employment and housing to support the eventual arrival of other family members. This type of *transnational family* is a common pattern among undocumented immigrants from Mexico, Central America, and the Caribbean. Typically, a husband leaving his family behind has characterized this family form, but recently more mothers, both single and married, have left their children behind with kin or husbands because of the demand for the low-cost labor of immigrant women. Sometimes children immigrate without parents, constituting another form of transnational family. These "**parachute children**" arrive to pursue

BOX 4.4

Emergent Family Trends

The Family Work of Undocumented Workers

Research by the Pew Hispanic Center shows how much certain industries in the United States rely on undocumented workers. The report estimated that Mexicans make up 58 percent of the illegal immigrant population and Central Americans about 20 percent. Among the Center's findings:

- Almost a quarter (24 percent) of people working in private households as maids, nannies, and other household workers are undocumented immigrants.

- About half (47 percent) of the 2.5 million U.S. farmworkers are undocumented workers.

- Nine percent of restaurant employees are undocumented workers.

- Seventeen percent of those in the business services industry, which includes maintenance workers and employees in mailing houses and credit reporting companies, are undocumented.

- Six percent of workers in construction and manufacturing are undocumented.

These data reveal how important undocumented workers are to the U.S. economy. Most important for our purposes is that a significant number of affluent households are dependent on undocumented workers for child care and home maintenance. Many of these women who take care of other people's children in U.S. society have left their own children behind in their country of origin to be taken care of by family members or others. The result is that mothers are minding other mothers' children both here and there (this is called "the nanny chain" or the "globalization of mothering").

Sources: Kong, Deborah, "24 Percent of Domestic Help Undocumented." *Associated Press* release March 22, 2002; *USA Today* (2002). "Quarter of Household Workers Called Illegal." (March 22): 3A; Hochschild, Arlie Russell (2000). "The Nanny Chain." *The American Prospect* (January 30): 32–36; Parreñas, Rhacel Salazar, *Servants of Globalization: Women, Migration and Domestic Work.* Stanford, CA: Stanford University Press, 2001, p. 2.

---

educational opportunities not found in their homeland. Often children of affluent families, these children live on their own or with relatives or host families.

A common reason for immigration is when family members arrive (either legally or illegally) to reunite with their husband/wife/father/mother/children in the host country. When family members arrive at different times, this is called **chain migration.**

It is important to note that while immigrant families share some general characteristics, there is great diversity. Actually,

[t]hey are distinguished more by diversity than homogeneity. In fact, among all ethnic groups in America today, native and foreign born, immigrants from different source countries account for both the highest and lowest rates of education, home ownership, poverty, and fertility. Thus difference in region of origin not only contributes to cultural, linguistic, and ethnic diversity among immigrants, but also is an indicator of social and economic status. (Guendelman, 2003:251)

Let us examine, briefly, the special circumstances of the two categories whose numbers dominate recent immigration—Latinos and Asians.

LATINOS

In 1970, about 1 in 20 Americans was Latino. In 2005, this proportion had risen to about one in seven, and by 2050 the Latino population is expected to triple to over 100 million (approximately 30 percent of the population) (Pew Research Center, reported in Aizenman, 2008).

Mexicans, Puerto Ricans, Cubans, and other Latino groups differ from each other by history and the timing and conditions of their arrival in the United States (the following is taken primarily from Baca Zinn and Wells, 2000). They differ in size, with Mexicans outnumbering the other Latino groups. They vary in social class. Puerto Ricans and Mexicans are the most economically disadvantaged Latino groups, whereas Cubans are much more likely to be economically advantaged and educated. Some are recent immigrants, either legal or undocumented. Others are descendants of families who have lived in the southwestern United States for over 300 years. Fertility (birth) rates, too, vary by country of origin, with Puerto Ricans and Mexicans having the highest rates and Cubans the lowest. This pattern is also found for percentage of unmarried and teen mothers, with Puerto Ricans having the highest percentage and Cubans the lowest. For birth outcomes, Puerto Rican babies have the highest incidence of low birth weight and infant mortality (Guendelman, 2003). This rate differs according to recency of immigration, with first-generation migrants having the highest rates, followed in order by second- and third-generation migrants. Overall, 31 percent of Latino households have five or more people (with 42 percent for households headed by an immigrant from Central America), compared with 12 percent among non-Hispanic Whites (Barone, 2001; Lollock, 2001).

Latinos are more likely to separate or divorce than are Anglos, but they do so at a lower rate than African Americans. This relatively high rate of family dissolution appears to be related to social class, with the conditions necessary for the maintenance of long-term stable marriages present in the middle class but absent in poor families (Fernandez-Kelly, 1990:185). Cubans, the most affluent Latino category in the United States, have over three-fourths of families intact, compared to only about half of Puerto Rican families (the poorest and most likely to be unemployed Latino category).

Diversity is also found within each Latino group, demonstrating a major theme of this book: "Families are understood to be constructed by powerful social forces and as settings in which different family members adapt in a variety of ways to changing social conditions" (Baca Zinn and Wells, 2000:253). Some examples demythologize common stereotypes of Latinos.

- Strong kin networks are believed to be a defining feature of the Latino population. Studies have found, however, that kinship networks are not monolithic, depending on distinctive social conditions, such as immigrant versus nonimmigrant status and generational status. First-generation Mexican Americans, for example, have smaller social networks than do their second-generation counterparts. Contrary to a common assumption that familism fades in succeeding generations, Carlos G. Velez-Ibanez (1996) found that second- and third-generation Mexican Americans have highly elaborate family networks actively maintained through frequent visits, ritual celebrations, and the exchange of goods and services.

- Latino families are typically viewed as settings of traditional patriarchy because of machismo, the cult of masculinity. Research has found, to the contrary, that there is considerable variation in family decision-making and the allocation of household labor, ranging from patriarchal role-segregated patterns to egalitarian patterns. In general, the more resources and autonomy that Latinas have outside the home through employment, the less patriarchal are the home arrangements. This relationship is impeded, however, for families embedded in dense familial social networks, which tend to promote traditional gender segregation (Coltrane and Valdez, 1993; Hurtado, 1995).

- Not only is there variation among Latinos, there also can be differences within a given Latino family—parents and children, women and men—as they experience family life differently. For new immigrants, family adaptation to new conditions is not a unitary phenomenon. School-age immigrant children generally become competent in English more quickly than their parents, resulting, sometimes, in the children's assuming adult roles as they help their parents negotiate the bureaucratic structures of their new social environment (Dorrington, 1995). Immigration may also create formal legal distinctions among family members. For example, undocumented Central American couples are, by definition, "illegal aliens," yet their children born in the United States are U.S. citizens. This results in a **binational family** (see Chapter 12 for an extended discussion of transnational families).

ASIAN AMERICANS

In 1970, Asian Americans numbered 1.4 million (1.5 percent of the total U.S. population). They now represent more than one-third of all legal immigrants and are growing rapidly, reaching 15.2 million (5.04 percent of the population) in 2007. The nation's 8.4 million foreign-born Asians now make up 23 percent of the nation's immigrants.

Asian Americans are often characterized as one group because of their seemingly common ethnic origins in Asia and their similar physical appearance. However, to classify them as a single group masks great differences among them. The term "Asian American" embraces at least 28 subgroups. Asian Americans are diverse in religion, language, income, education, occupational skills, and immigration experience (Ishii-Kuntz, 2000). The largest Asian American groups are Chinese (about 23 percent of all Asian Americans), followed by Filipino (17 percent), Japanese (6.9 percent), Vietnamese (10 percent), Korean (10 percent), and Asian Indian (18 percent). Among the rest are such ethnic groups as Laotians, Kampucheans, Thais, Pakistanis, Sri Lankans, Indonesians, and Hmong.

There are some interesting findings concerning Asian American families. First, the number of divorces in this group is lower than the U.S. average, especially among first-generation immigrants. Among the various Asian American groups, Japanese Americans have the highest divorce rate. For the number of households headed by a woman, Asian Indians have the lowest rate, while the Chinese, Filipino, and Korean rates are higher than for the United States in general. The fertility rate for Asians is the lowest of all racial categories in the United States. The most economically disadvantaged groups (Vietnamese, Cambodians, Laotians, and Hmong) on average have much higher fertility rates than other Asian immigrants. Japanese Americans and Chinese Americans, however, have much lower fertility rates than found in the general U.S. population. Foreign-born Asian women rarely have children out of wedlock, but the rate doubles for U.S.-born Asian American women (Lee, 1998:19). Finally, interracial marriage (that is, marriage outside one's racial group) is more likely among Asian Americans than among African Americans and is as likely as found for Latinos (Lee, 1998). Of the various ethnic categories, Japanese are the most likely to marry outside their group. Women in all Asian categories consistently outmarry at a higher rate than Asian men, by about two to one. With regard to intermarriage, Asian Indians are the exception to the other Asian groups, having much lower intermarriage rates. Of those relatively few interracial marriages involving Asian Indians, men are much more likely than women to be exogenous (**exogamy** is marrying outside one's group).

The diversity among Asian American families reinforces a major theme of this book—that family forms are shaped by social forces and social location. To reiterate, "Asian American family experiences are diverse because they have been influenced by such factors as socio-economic status, immigration history, generational status, age, gender, and nativity, to name a few" (Ishii-Kuntz, 2000:276). With these structural variables in mind, let us demythologize two common stereotypes of Asian Americans.

■ Many Americans believe that Asian Americans are the model racial minority, scoring high in relative income, educational attainment, and other measures of success. This assumption, however, does not reflect the diversity found among Asian Americans. Whereas most of the pre–World War II Asian immigrants were peasants, the recent migrants vary considerably by education and social class. On the one hand, many arrived as educated middle-class professionals with highly valued skills and some knowledge of English. For example, in 1995, when 23 percent of the total U.S. male population had at least a college degree, 49 percent of Asian Indian men, 42 percent of Filipino men, and 35 percent of Chinese men in the United States were college graduates. In sharp contrast, among other groups, such as Southeast Asians (Cambodians, Laotians, and Hmong), only 3 percent of men had a college degree or higher (Waters and Eschbach, 1995:433). These immigrants arrived as uneducated, impoverished refugees. These initial disparities among Asian groups upon entry into the United States are reflected in the differences in income and poverty level by ethnic category. Asian Americans, taken together, have a poverty rate about double the rate for Whites, although Japanese and Asian Indians have very low poverty rates and are above the national average in income and educational achievement. (Only 6 percent of Indian immigrants, for example, lived below the poverty line in 2000.) The Southeast Asian groups are the most economically disadvantaged, with high poverty rates.

■ It is widely assumed that Asian American families are patriarchal, emphasizing men's superiority and women's obedience to their husbands. Research has found, however, similar to the experience of Latinos, that traditional gender inequality is related to husbands' and wives' differential earning power and gaps in educational attainment. When Asian American women have educations equal to their husbands and contribute significantly to the family income, the relations between wives and husbands are more egalitarian (Ishii-Kuntz, 2000). Also, recent immigrants are more traditional in their gender roles than are those in succeeding generations, reflecting the effects of greater exposure to the mainstream culture.

To summarize, the shape of Asian American families, like that of all families, is the consequence of

the members' daily interaction with each other and with people in the outside world. Just because one is born into an Asian American family does not mean that one's values, beliefs, and family experiences will be identical to those of other Asian Americans. Rather, these experiences are constructed by social and historical situations that surround the families because these situations provide the concrete resources and constraints that shape family interactions. (Ishii-Kuntz, 2000:277)

The Effects of Immigration on Immigrant Families

There are a number of possible consequences of migration for immigrant families. We concentrate on three: (1) the loss of ethnic identity in the new society, (2) family acts of agency, and (3) the effects on family dynamics.

ETHNIC IDENTITY: THE UNITED STATES AS A CULTURAL MELTING POT?

Martin and Midgley sum up the universal dilemma for immigrants:

> There is always a tension between the newcomers' desires to keep alive the culture and language of the community they left behind, and their need and wish to adapt to new surroundings and a different society. (Martin and Midgley, 1999:35–36)

Assimilation is the process by which individuals or groups adopt the culture of another group, losing their original identity. A principal indicator of assimilation is language. In 2000, slightly fewer than one in five Americans (17.9 percent) age five and older spoke a language other than English at home. Overall, foreign-language speakers grew by about 15 million during the 1990s (Frey, 2002:20). Assuming the experience of earlier immigrants to the United States, it is likely that the shift to English usage will take three generations—from almost exclusive use by newcomers of their traditional language, to their children being bilingual, and their children's children (third-generation immigrants) being monolingual English speakers (Martin and Midgley, 1999). According to the Pew Hispanic Center, in 2007, for example, 23 percent of adult first-generation Latinos said they could carry on a conversation very well in English, compared to 88 percent in the second generation and 94 percent in the third (reported in Gorman, 2007).

If the past is a guide, the new immigrants will assimilate. "Our society exerts tremendous pressure to conform, and cultural separatism rarely survives more than a generation" (Cole, 1994:412). But conditions now are different.

An argument countering the assumption that the new immigrants will assimilate as did previous generations of immigrants is that the new immigrants are racial-ethnics, not Whites. The early waves of immigrants (post-1965) were mostly White Europeans. Over time these groups were absorbed into the "melting pot" of society's mainstream because jobs were relatively plentiful and they did not face racial antipathy. Today's immigrants, however, face a different reality. A commonly held assumption (the reasoning of the culture of poverty) is that when new immigrants do not assimilate easily or if they continue to be poor, it is their fault. Their culture (traditional family patterns such as patriarchy and familism) just does not fit with the standards of "normal" family life based on the White, middle-class norms of U.S. society (Baca Zinn and Wells, 2000). Thus, blame for many social problems and resistance to assimilation is placed on the immigrants, thereby "ignoring the impact of larger forces, such as racism and the economic order, that limit opportunities for success and present barriers to assimilation" (Pyke, 2008:212).

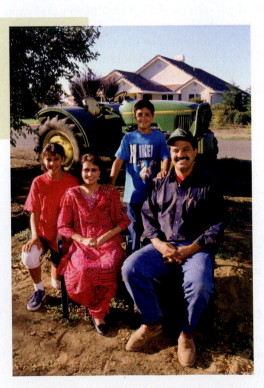

New patterns of immigration bring into question traditional views of the U.S. as a melting pot. Sikh American family outside their home on a farm near Yuba City, California.

The current political mood is to eliminate affirmative action (as California did in 1997) and to reduce or eliminate social programs that help to level the playing field so that the poor and minorities might have a fair chance to succeed. Some legislation is especially punitive toward recent immigrants, particularly the undocumented. Such public policies cause new immigrants to have a more difficult time assimilating than did their predecessors, should they wish to do so.

Another factor facing this generation of migrants is that they are entering the United States during a critical economic transformation and, since 2007, an economic crisis where the middle class is shrinking and the working class and the working poor face difficult economic hurdles. A possible result is that the new immigrants, different in physical characteristics, language, and culture, will become scapegoats for the difficulties that so many face (Powers, 2007). Moreover, their opportunities for advancement will be limited by the new economic realities. Sociologist Herbert J. Gans (1990) argues, for example, that the second generation of post-1965 immigrants likely will experience downward mobility compared to their parents because of the changing opportunity structure of the U.S. economy.

The 11 million undocumented immigrants in the United States can never assimilate. Their illegal status keeps them on the margins in menial jobs and outside the societal mainstream.

The issue of immigrant adaptation to the host society is complex, depending on a number of variables. Min Zhou (1997) describes a number of these critical variables, including the immigrant generation (i.e., first or second), the immigrants' level in the ethnic hierarchy at the point of arrival, what stratum of U.S. society absorbs them, and the degree to which they are part of a family network.

Immigrants who move to the United States permanently have four options regarding assimilation. Many try to blend into the United States as quickly as possible. Others resist the new ways, either by developing an adversarial stance toward the dominant society or by resisting acculturation by focusing more intensely on the social capital created through ethnic ties (Portes and Zhou, 1993). The fourth alternative is to move toward a bicultural pattern (Buriel and De Ment, 1997). That is, immigrants adopt some patterns similar to those found in the host society and retain some from their heritage. Although the concept of a bicultural pattern appears to focus on culture, the retention or abandonment of the ethnic ways depends on structural variables (Kibria, 1997:207). These variables include the socioeconomic resources of the ethnic community, the extent of continued immigration from the sending society, the linkages between the ethnic community and the sending society, and the obstacles to obtaining equal opportunity in the new society.

Immigration and Agency

Immigration can be forced (e.g., the slave trade) or freely chosen. Immigration in this latter sense is clearly an act of human agency. Most people in developing countries do not move. Others move, breaking with their extended family, leaving neighborhood and community ties, mostly to improve their economic situations or to flee repression.

Typically, new immigrants face hostility from their hosts, who fear them as competitors or hate them because they are "different," or because of the fear that they may be terrorists. In this latter instance, immigrants from Muslim countries have had to confront considerable hostility and suspicion since the terrorist acts on September 11, 2001. Recent immigrants also face language barriers as they seek jobs. Often, most especially for undocumented immigrants, their initial jobs are demeaning, poorly paid, and without benefits. How do they adapt to these often difficult circumstances? Commonly, migrants move to a destination area where there is already a network of friends and relatives. These networks connect new migrants with housing (often doubling up in very crowded but inexpensive conditions), jobs, and an informal welfare system such as pooling resources in difficult times. Immigrant communities have used these mutual aid networks throughout U.S. history, whether Swedish settlers in Minnesota, Mennonite settlers in Kansas, Irish settlers in Boston, or Mexican and Vietnamese settlers now (Martin and Midgley, 1999).

Because wages are low, all able family members may work in the family enterprise or at different jobs by combining family resources. To overcome various manifestations of hostility by others, the immigrant community may become closer, having as little interaction with outsiders as possible. Some may become involved in gangs for protection. Still others may move to assimilate as quickly as possible.

The Effects of Immigration on Family Dynamics

Under the provisions of the Immigration Act of 1990, gaining immigrant status generally requires a sponsor, who may be a U.S. citizen, a legal resident, a U.S. employer, or, in the case of refugees, the U.S. government. Of these options, the most common route to legal immigration involves a close family member. Thus, for many, immigration to the United States is largely a family affair. Many undocumented immigrants leave their families to work in the United States, hoping to reunite either by returning home or by their families joining them.

The immigration laws, which favor migrants with family connections, have a snowball effect, enhancing the potential for further migration (called "chain" migration), both legal and extralegal.

When family reunification occurs after years of separation, there might be tensions because some family members have had more time to adapt to life in the United States.

> The result can be a family of related strangers who have very different values, needs, and perspectives, and who may not even speak a shared language—particularly when children, who adapt more quickly, are among those who arrived first. Such differences can generate family tensions. (Pyke, 2008:212)

These chaining processes often lead to dense ethnic concentrations in cities, where extended families are closely networked.

> Such spatial concentrations of kin and kith serve to provide newcomers with manifold sources of moral, social, cultural, and economic support that are unavailable to immigrants who are more dispersed and help to explain the gravitational pull exerted by places where family and friends of immigrants are concentrated. (Rumbaut, 1997:7)

Family connections not only make immigration possible; they also help migrants cope with life in a new social setting.

An exception to family-oriented immigration often occurs among undocumented migrants. These are typically young male manual laborers, who leave their families behind for months at a time while they work in the United States. These migrants typically send money home to their families, $25.1 billion in 2008. These transnational families find their family ties stretched across national boundaries, which often causes extraordinary emotional, financial, and physical stress for the family members (Chavez, 1992). (See Chapter 12 for more on transnational families.)

Undocumented immigrants may have families in the United States. This occurs when they bring their families or when they marry U.S. citizens or legal residents. The children of these unions, if born in the United States, are U.S. citizens. This leads to the awkward situation of families that consist of a mix of legal statuses. Leo R. Chavez (1992) calls these families *binational*, because they consist of both undocumented immigrants and U.S. citizens or legal residents.

No family action has greater consequences than a family leaving its home society for a new one. The family's economic situation changes; if family members are non-English speaking, their language is useless outside the immigrant community; their culture is demeaned; their children in time will likely question tradition; and the family members will likely be the objects of discrimination. They leave behind most of their extended family members and friends for an unfamiliar society without familiar social supports (Bush et al., 2005). In addition to these profound consequences, immigration has consequences for family dynamics. Especially important is the impact of migration on gender dynamics.

GENDER DYNAMICS

Immigrants arrive in their country of destination carrying the traditions, norms, and values from their homeland. Among these might be the established patterns of patriarchal arrangements, including rigid divisions of labor for men and women, and power and authority vested in the male heads of households (the following is taken from Pyke, 2008). Typically, having women in the paid labor force is viewed as undesirable. Four aspects of immigration commonly bring patriarchal ideas into question. The first aspect involves men migrating, while their families remain in their home countries. The second aspect involves immigrant women's employment and its effect on gender relations. The third aspect, and related to the second, is the effect women's income has on reducing the power/authority gap between women and men. The fourth aspect involves the changes kinship patterns undergo in immigrants' new setting. We shall consider these in turn.

CASE STUDY: THE RECONSTRUCTION OF GENDER RELATIONS AMONG MEXICAN IMMIGRANT MEN AND WOMEN

Immigrants from Mexico often arrive in the United States in stages (called family stage migration). The typical pattern is for husbands to travel alone to the United States, where they work and save in anticipation of their wives and children arriving later, sometimes years later, for permanent settlement (the following discussion is based on Hondagneu-Sotelo, 1992, 1994). Wives remain behind to run the household.

This migration pattern confronts traditional patriarchy in two ways. First, the longer the spouses are separated, the more independent the women become. While remaining in Mexico, usually with diminished resources, the women devise income-earning activities, take on multiple roles, and become more competent at traditional male activities such as public negotiation. In short, "the long separation fostered by the men's solo sojourns diminished the hegemony of the husbands' authority and increased women's autonomy and influence in the family" (Hondagneu-Sotelo, 1992:404).

Second, access to social networks of women enables women to subvert patriarchal authority by migrating without their husbands' cooperation. Hondagneu-Sotelo compares the experience of families in which the husbands migrated before 1965 with those who migrated after 1965. This date is significant because U.S. legislation granted legal status to many undocumented pre-1965 migrant men by the 1970s. For wives to join their husbands (and also received legal status), they needed the help of their husbands. This dependence, of course, reduced the independence of wives. Their autonomy was also diminished because there were relatively few Mexican immigrant women in the United States to assist them if their husbands did not.

The wives of men migrating after 1965 were not dependent on obtaining legal status through their husbands because obtaining legal status on the basis of marriage was no longer a viable option. Many wives did migrate without the assistance of their husbands, but they did so with the assistance of a network of immigrant women already in the United States. This network of mothers, sisters, and friends generated independence of wives from their husbands.

Hondagneu-Sotelo's research makes the important point that the strong cultural norms that emphasize patriarchal men and submissive women (machismo) are changed not by learning the values of a new society but by "arrangements induced by the migration process itself" (Hondagneu-Sotelo, 1992:394).

The second source of decline in patriarchal arrangements and male dominance derives from the greater economic resources, esteem, and independence that work provides immigrant wives. The effect of wives working varies, depending on social class (e.g., middle-class immigrant families tend to become more egalitarian), country of origin, and other variables. Some wives remain committed to a patriarchal structure. Others live lives of contradiction, having independence in the workplace while remaining subservient to their husbands at home. An interesting result from the overall increase in power of immigrant women is that the loss of power of immigrant men makes them want to return to their country of origin—more so than their wives.

The third and fourth sources of increased power to women are found in the following case study.

CASE STUDY: MIGRATION AND VIETNAMESE AMERICAN WOMEN: REMAKING GENDER RELATIONS

Traditional Vietnamese family and gender relations were based on Confucian principles, which placed women in subordination to men in every aspect of life (the following is based on Kibria, 1990, 1993, 1994). Women married at a young age, entering the household of their husband's father, where their mothers-in-law dominated them. In this arrangement men controlled economic resources, and men controlled women through isolation from their families of origin.

Following the Vietnam War, many Vietnamese migrated to the United States. Several conditions within Vietnamese American communities worked to undermine the bases of male authority found in Vietnam. One of these conditions was downward mobility. Unlike Mexican immigrants to the United States, who rose in economic resources with migration, most Vietnamese who migrated before 1975 shifted from their middle-class occupations in Vietnam to largely unskilled, low-status, and low-paying jobs in the United States. Their difficulties with English and continuous discrimination tended to keep them low in status.

One consequence of this downward mobility was that Vietnamese men and women became more equal. Women were low status in Vietnam; now, with migration, men and women shared low status in the United States. Husbands in Vietnam earned the income for the family. In the United States the husband's income was often insufficient, so he became dependent on the income of his wife and children.

Another disruption from the traditional patterns was a change in kinship networks. Family ties in Vietnam were based on the husband's family. In the United States, given the scarcity of relatives, Vietnamese migrants adapted by creating flexible kinship networks that involved the husband's kin, the wife's kin, and **fictive kin** (close friends incorporated into family groups). This reconstruction of kinship had some special advantages for women.

One consequence of the more varied and inclusive nature of the kinship network was that women were rarely surrounded exclusively by the husband's relatives and/or friends. As a result, they were often able to turn to close fictive kin and perhaps members of their families of origin for support during conflicts with men in the family. Another condition that enhanced the power of married women in the family was that few had to deal with the competing authority of their mother-in-law in the household, because elderly women often did not leave Vietnam (Kibria, 1994:254–255).

The situation for Vietnamese women, however, did not lead to full equality with men. Kibria notes that while migration enhanced women's power, the women remained attached to the old male-dominant family system because it offered them economic protection and gave them officially sanctioned authority over the younger generation. Kibria summarizes this contradictory situation:

> Migration to the United States has thus had a complex, somewhat contradictory, impact on the status of Vietnamese immigrant women. On the one hand, migration has weakened men's control over economic and social resources and allowed women to exert greater informal family power. At the same time, the precarious economic environment has heightened the salience of the family system and constrained the possibilities for radical change in gender relations. (Kibria, 1990:21)

The New Second Generation

There were more than 16 million children under age 18 living in immigrant families in 2007 (the following is from Mather, 2009). These children account for 22 percent of all children in the United States and are the fastest-growing segment of the population. While racial-ethnic minorities will become the numerical majority in 2042, the immigrant population under age 18 will reach that milestone by 2023. These children in immigrant families are also overrepresented among the poor (21 percent, compared to 17 percent among nonimmigrant children). This means that they are at greater risk than nonimmigrant children to drop out of school, to bear children as teenagers, and to have poor health.

There are several sources of tension and conflict between the generations in immigrant families. First, the second generation tends to be fluent in English, while their parents are not. In 2007, almost half of the children of immigrants spoke English well but lived in families where parents had difficulty speaking English. Moreover, because parents are dependent on there children's fluency in English, there is a loss of parental authority as the children manage transactions and family finances. The parents feel that this gap restricts their ability to pass on to children their ethnic language and culture. Second, there is also a generational breach as the children do not see the applicability of the parents' experiences in the old county to theirs in the United States. Third, second-generation children, influenced by their peers and television tend to view their own families and their ethnic practices as abnormal and deficient. All of these factors lead to a fourth source of intrafamily tensions and conflict as the second generation clashes with parents over such ethnic practices as arranged marriage, dating, and independence. Daughters experience this more than do sons because parents tend to be more lenient with boys when it comes to passing on ethnic traditions.

These tensions between immigrants and their children would seem to increase the likelihood that second-generation youth would look outside their ethnic groups for dating and marriage partners. However, researchers have found a converse trend (the following is from Gowen, 2009). Although the rates of interracial/interethnic marriages have increased overall, the rate of Latinos and Asians marrying partners of other races has declined in the past two decades. The reason is that the growing immigrant population has expanded the pool of potential same-ethnic partners. As a result "The number of native- and foreign-born people marrying outside their race fell from 27 to 20 percent for Hispanics and 42 to 33 percent for Asians from 1990 to 2000" (Gowen, 2009:35).

ELDERLY IMMIGRANTS

Elderly immigrants usually are legal immigrants who reunite with their children who are U.S. citizens. Typically, they are poor and do not speak English. Thus, they are dependent on family members for financial support, housing, and dealing with the norms of the new society. The elderly reciprocate by providing child care, cooking, and home maintenance. The dependence of the elderly on their children works against traditional respect for elders found in their ethnic cultures. Instead, the elderly are often submissive and defer to the needs of their children.

 # The Aging of Society

The population of the United States is experiencing a pronounced change in its age structure—it has become older and is on the verge of becoming much older. In 1900 about 1 in 25 residents of the United States was 65 years or older. By 1950 it was about 1 in 12. In 2000, 1 in 8 was 65 or older, and by 2030 the ratio will likely be around 1 in 5, with more people over 65 than under age 18. In effect, by 2030, when most of today's college students will be around 50, there will be more grandparents than grandchildren. "The Senior Boom is coming, and it will transform our homes, our schools, our politics, our lives and our deaths. And not just for older people. For everybody." (Peyser, 1999:50).

The Demographics of an Aging Society

In 1950 there were about 12.2 million Americans age 65 and older. By 2010 the number had more than tripled to 40.0 million. Two forces, a falling birth rate and advances in medicine, have joined to make the 65-and-older category constitute the fastest growing segment of the U.S. population, increasing twice as fast as the population as a whole. Also noteworthy is the rapid increase in the "old-old," that is, those age 85 and older. In 1950 there were 600,000 in this category, compared to 4,300,000 in 2000, a sevenfold increase. In 2030 there will be an estimated 8,500,000 age 85 and over (12 percent of the elderly). By 2050, this number is expected to be 18.9 million or 23 percent of all elderly Americans (see Figure 4.3). In 2007 some 79,000 Americans were at least 100 years old. Because of continued advances in medicine and nutrition, it is expected that the number of centenarians will increase to about one million by the middle of the twenty-first century.

Because racial minorities have a lower life expectancy than do Whites (African Americans, for example, live about six fewer years), they form a smaller proportion of the elderly category. Whites are overrepresented among the elderly population (i.e., in 2006, about 83 percent of the elderly population was White, compared with only 6 percent Latino and 8 percent Black) (U.S. Department of Health and Human Services, 2007b). It is expected that non-Whites will be one-third of the elderly population by 2050 (with Latinos being the largest elderly minority after 2028).

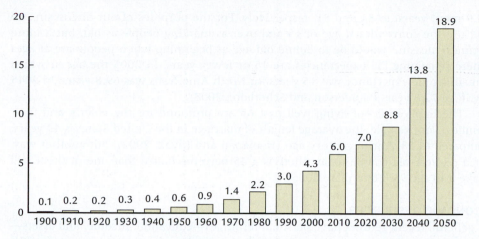

Figure 4.3

U.S. Population Age 85 and Older, 1900–2050 (in millions)

Source: Hobbs, Frank B. with Bonnie L Damon (1996). "65+ in the United States." *Current Population Reports*, P23-290: 2–8.

There are several reasons for minorities being underrepresented among the elderly. The gap for Latinos is explained in part by immigration, because most immigrants are young adults. But the primary reason for the relatively low proportion of minorities among the elderly, compared to Whites, is that they do not live as long because large numbers do not have health insurance, they receive poor health care, and they often work at physically demanding and sometimes dangerous jobs. Most important, the elderly who are racial-ethnics are disproportionately poor.

Older women outnumber older men by a ratio of three to two. As age increases, the disparity becomes greater—for those age 85 and older, there are about five women to every two men. By age 100 and older, four of five are women. Because of pensions coming through work and widows' benefits from Social Security depending on husbands' lifetime income, elderly women who had not worked outside the home are much more likely than elderly men to be poor (a 13 percent poverty rate compared with 7 percent for men). African American and Latino elderly women have an even higher probability than their male counterparts of being poor.

Geographically, some states and communities have disproportionately more older residents. One-fourth of all elderly Americans live in three states—California, Florida, and New York. Many states with a high concentration of older people are rural states, where there has been a large outmigration of young people. Most elderly people remain in their communities after retirement ("aging in place"), but those who move tend to migrate to the favorable climate found in the Sun Belt states (Florida, California, Arizona, Nevada, and Texas). Those who migrate are not representative of the elderly: They tend to be younger and more affluent than those who stay in their home communities.

The Consequences of an Aging Society on Families and the Elderly

Society considers the elderly as those persons 65 years of age and over. This arbitrary chronological age was set by Congress in 1935 as the age when Social Security benefits would go into effect. At that time 65 was old because the average life expectancy was 62. In 2006, however, the average life expectancy at birth was 77.85 (74 years for males, compared to 79 years for females). Under current mortality conditions, women who reach 65 will, on average, live 19.2 more years and men will live

15.9 more years, to 84 and 81, respectively. For the purposes of our discussion, we will use the conventional age of 65 and over as marking people as old, but a more accurate measure would be to define old age as beginning when people are at ages where remaining life expectancies are 15 or fewer years. In 2005 the age at which remaining life expectancy was 15 years for North Americans was 69.8 years. In 2045 it will be 72.8 years (Sanderson and Scherbore, 2008).

The implications of living well past 65 are profound for the elderly and their families. For example, the average length of marriage in the United States is 43 years, compared to 28 years a century ago (Hooyman and Kiyak, 2002). Put another way, for a 65-year-old couple today, there is a 45 percent chance that one of them will make it to age 95 (Fetterman, 2006).

ECONOMIC RESOURCES

In general, recent retirees have personal resources—education, income, and assets—unknown to previous cohorts. A significant minority of retirees are comfortable, with time for leisure, opportunities for rewarding and productive activity, and a decent standard of living. Many have benefited from sharp rises in the real estate market, resulting in extraordinary wealth, which ultimately they will pass on to their fortunate heirs. Some benefited, too, from the stock market boom of the 1990s. However, the steep recession that began in 2007 led to many older people losing more than half the value of their retirement nest egg. Others have lost pensions or have had their pensions reduced by their long-time employers. As a result of this severe financial shrinkage, many older workers have had to reconsider their plans, sometimes returning to employment or continuing to work beyond their original time table for retirement.

The elderly who are members of a racial or ethnic minority typically have relatively few economic resources. Having worked at low-paying jobs, their Social Security payments are usually low. In terms of net worth, the typical non-Hispanic White household has seven times as much (including home equity) as the typical household of color (Sklar, 2003:56).

Elderly racial-ethnics are disproportionately poor, typically more than double the poverty rate for elderly Whites. This relative lack of resources for racial minorities translates into a reduced likelihood, compared to Whites, of their receiving adequate health care and, if needed, living in nursing homes with full-time skilled nursing care under a physician's supervision.

Social Security is the only source of income for about half of retired people and a major source of income for 80 percent of the elderly in the United States. Since the introduction of Social Security in the 1930s, this program has been a significant aid to the elderly. Social Security has reduced poverty significantly among the elderly—from 35.2 percent in 1959 to 10.1 percent in 2005. "Without Social Security income, 54 percent of America's elderly would live in poverty" (Wellstone, 1998:5).

Despite its considerable strengths, the Social Security program has several serious problems that place a disproportionate burden on certain categories of the elderly and on some portions of the workers paying into the program. An immediate problem is that not all workers are covered. Some groups of workers are unable to participate because they work for states with alternative retirement programs. Also, legislation has specifically exempted certain occupations such as agricultural workers from Social Security.

For workers who are eligible for Social Security, there are wide disparities in the benefits received. The amount of benefits depends on the length of time workers have paid into the Social Security program and the amount of wages on which they paid Social Security tax. In other words, low-paid workers receive low benefits during retirement. Thus, 30 percent of the elderly who depend almost exclusively on Social Security benefits live below the poverty line. These are typically people who have been relatively poor during their working years or are widows.

LIVING ARRANGEMENTS AMONG THE ELDERLY

The living arrangements of the elderly vary considerably by age, sex, race, and marital status. Slightly more than 7 out of 10 elderly men live with their spouses, compared to about 4 out of 10 elderly women. About 30 percent (10.7 million) of all noninstitutionalized older persons in 2006 lived alone (78 percent were women). This is the result of the greater longevity of women and the social norm for men to marry younger women. Thus, to the extent that isolation is a problem of the aged, it is overwhelmingly a problem for elderly women (U.S. Department of Health and Human Services, 2008).

Elderly Japanese and Chinese Americans are more likely than elderly Whites to live in their children's homes (Kamo and Zhou, 1994). African American and Latino women are more likely to live with relatives compared to White women. Compared to White and Latino men, older African American men are more likely to live alone and less likely to live with a spouse (U.S. Department of Health and Human Services, 1999:24).

Two demographic trends—increased life expectancy and few children per family—increase the likelihood of elderly parents living with their adult children. These trends result in a **beanpole family structure**—a vertical, four-generation family structure.

> In the decades to come, individuals will grow older having more vertical than horizontal linkages in the family. For example, vertically, a four-generation family structure has three tiers of parent-child relationships, two sets of grandparent–grandchild ties, and one great-grandparent–great-grandchild linkage. Within generations of this same family, horizontally, aging individuals will have fewer brothers and sisters. In addition, at the level of extended kin, family members will have fewer cousins, aunts, uncles, nieces, and nephews. (Bengtson et al., 1990:264)

A variation of the beanpole family structure is the three-generation household, called the **sandwich family structure,** where parents care for their parents and their children. The 2000 Census was the first U.S. Census to ask who lives in one household; results showed that 4 percent of households (3.9 million) had three or more generations living together (cited in Della Cava, 2006).

There are several reasons families make the decision for the elderly to live with their children. It may be that the elderly persons cannot function alone or are too poor to handle the economic demands of living alone. In that case, they must either move in with their children or move into a nursing home, which many resist. The decision may be driven by the wish of both parties to be together with shared responsibilities (e.g., the elderly may take care of babysitting, cooking, cleaning, and other chores, while their children take care of the added finances). The arrangement can be satisfactory or it may be difficult, because the elderly or their children or both may resent the lack of privacy and the erosion of independence, or there may be disagreements over disparate lifestyles.

The 2000 Census found that a total of 1.78 million older people lived in households—either their own or one of their children's—where there is a grandchild present. About 450,000 of these grandparents had the primary responsibility for their grandchildren who lived with them.

An elderly parent living with a family can have positive and negative implications.

About 43 percent of today's seniors will use a nursing home during their lifetime (Greenwald, 1999). At any one time about 4 percent of the elderly live in longterm care institutions, usually nursing homes. The percentage increases dramatically with age, ranging from 1.3 percent for persons 65–74 to 4.4 percent for persons 75–84, and 15.4 percent for persons 85 and older (U.S. Department of Health and Human Services, 2007a). The residents of nursing homes, therefore, are typically over 75, female, White, and currently unmarried—usually widowed. The economically advantaged are not as likely as their less affluent age cohorts to be institutionalized, and if they are institutionalized, they are apt to be in private nursing homes and to receive better care.

PAYING FOR HEALTH CARE

Of all age groups, the elderly are the most affected by ill health. These problems escalate especially from age 75 onward, as the degenerative processes of aging accelerate. Consider the following facts:

- Although the elderly comprise only about 13 percent of the population presently, they consume more than one-third of all health care in the United States.
- The elderly are four times as likely as the nonelderly to be hospitalized. When hospitalized, they stay an average of about three days longer than the nonelderly.
- The medical expenses of the old are three times greater than those of middle-aged adults, yet their incomes are typically much less.
- The elderly account for more than one-third of all spending for prescription drugs.
- One in eight who are 65 years old or older has Alzheimer's disease. By 2030 the number will have doubled to one in four due to the aging of the population (Hyman, 2008). The incidence of Alzheimer's disease, the leading cause of dementia in old age, rises sharply with advancing age—from less than 4 percent of those age 65–74 to almost half (47 percent) of those age 85 and older (Neergaard, 2000).

- Osteoarthritis, the degeneration of protective tissues around the body's joints, afflicts about half of those age 65 and older. At present this disease costs the U.S. economy more than $86 billion a year in lost productivity and direct medical costs. With the elderly population expected to double in 25 years, the costs to society and individuals will increase rapidly as well (Fackelmann, 2006).

- The cost of long-term care is prohibitive. The average cost of a year in a nursing home in 2008 was $213 a day or $77,745 annually (SmartMoney.com, 2008), and in some cities it is much higher (e.g., in 2005 it was $109,648 for a semi-private room in New York City) (Fetterman et al., 2006).

Fidelity Investments estimates that a 65-year-old couple retiring in 2006 will need about $200,000 to cover health costs that are not covered by Medicare. That estimate does not include the cost of over-the-counter drugs, dental services, or long-term care (cited in Block, 2006). Because Medicare does not pay for most long-term care, long-term care insurance is expensive, and Medicaid will help only after the patient's resources are exhausted, resulting in many elderly being impoverished.

Medicare, begun in 1965, is the health insurance program for those 65 and over. Everyone is automatically entitled to hospital insurance, home health care, and hospice care through this program. For an additional modest fee Medicare offers a supplemental medical insurance that helps pay for doctors' bills, outpatient services, diagnostic tests, physical therapy, and medical supplies. Overall, Medicare is financed by payroll taxes, premiums paid by recipients, and a government subsidy.

There are three major problems with Medicare. First, it is insufficiently financed by the federal government. Second, only about half of the elderly's health care bills are paid through the program, leaving them with substantial costs. The affluent elderly are not hurt because they can afford supplemental health insurance. The poor are not hurt because they are also covered by Medicaid, a separate program financed by federal and state taxes that pays for the health care of indigent people. The near-poor, however, do not qualify for Medicaid, and they cannot afford additional health insurance. A third problem with Medicare is that physicians feel that the program pays them too little for their services. As a result, many physicians limit the number of Medicare patients they will serve, some even refusing to serve any. Thus, some elderly people have difficulty finding a physician.

Role Transitions

The elderly in society encounter a number of major role transitions—from work to leisure, from marriage to widowhood, from independence to dependence, and from living to impending death.

RETIREMENT

Most of us work all of our adult lives and then, between the ages of 60 and 70, we exit the work role for a life without work. While the idea of retirement is appealing and many have no problems adjusting to it, for some people this is a difficult transition, posing many challenges. It involves a loss of identity (i.e., one's work was the center of who he or she was and who others thought they were) and a loss of meaning and personal achievement. Moreover, being deprived of the work setting decreases social contacts. Also, it says to others "I am old," which in U.S. society means "I am no longer important." Finally, this significant life transition often means less income, which may require changing homes (downsizing for lower maintenance but also lower cost), and reducing spending on clothing, travel, and various leisure activities.

Retirement can have beneficial or detrimental effects on marital quality (Myers and Booth, 1996). On the positive side, retirement means more time together for the spouses. If they can afford it and are in good health, they can engage in travel and other activities of mutual interest. However, after 40 years or so of being away from each other while one or both worked outside the home, the dramatically increased time together might be seen as an intrusion into each other's space and a source of irritation. Because husbands are typically older than their wives, they will probably retire earlier than their spouses. This leads to difficulties with the household division of labor, because many husbands resist doing their fair share of the housework, even though they have the time.

WIDOWHOOD

Although becoming a widow or widower is theoretically possible at any time, the probability, of course, increases with age, and the likelihood is that women will experience this role transition more than men. Prior to age 65, most women and men are married. Eighty percent of men ages 65 to 74 are married, compared to 55 percent of women. For those 85 and older, only 13 percent of women are married, compared to 53 percent of men (Himes, 2001). A special problem for widows is the decrease in income, which is exacerbated by economic downturns.

Widowhood, as a social disruption, is more difficult for men than for women. A summary of the relevant research shows that widows, when compared to widowers, have more friends, are more self sufficient (e.g., doing household chores), have fewer health problems, and are less distressed and depressed (Cooney and Dunne, 2004).

FROM INDEPENDENCE TO DEPENDENCE

A major transition for the elderly, especially for the old-old, is a shift from independence to dependence. Adulthood is a time of financial and social independence from others. Toward the end of life, however, many elderly persons have to give up driving a car, a major symbol of independence. Because of physical or mental health reasons, they often are cared for by family members or care professionals or placed in institutions. This is a huge shift, one that is often difficult for the elderly as well as their caregivers. A study sponsored by the Kaiser Family Foundation found that more than one-third of those caring for aging parents were concerned about juggling caregiving with their other responsibilities. More than one-fourth worried about having enough time for their spouse or partner; and 25 percent worried that caregiving interfered with their time with their children. Thirty percent also had missed work as a result of elder care (reported in *USA Today*, 2000).

IMPENDING DEATH

In 1900 the average life expectancy was 50 years, with infectious diseases the most common cause of death. The median age of death now is 78 and the leading causes of death are heart disease, cancer, and stroke (this section depends largely on Meier and Morrison, 1999). Advances in the treatment of atherosclerotic vascular disease and cancer have turned these previously rapidly fatal diseases into chronic illness with which people often live for several years before death. This means that the elderly with terminal diseases become progressively more dependent on care by others— most often family members and typically women (spouses, adult daughters, and daughters-in-law). Thus, the majority of an older person's last years and months are spent at home in the care of family members, with hospitalization or placement in a nursing home occurring only near the very end of life.

The elderly and their kin are well aware that death draws nearer with advancing age. How do elderly individuals, their spouses, and their children prepare for this event? Do they avoid thinking and talking about it? Or do they actively prepare for the inevitable by preparing a will that settles the estate and disburses personal effects, by preparing a living will (declaring, legally, that unusual efforts to keep the dying person alive shall not be taken), and by making funeral and burial arrangements? As the patient nears death, family members and health care providers "often have to negotiate difficult, often wrenching decisions about the use or discontinuation of such life-prolonging technologies as feeding tubes, ventilators, and intravenous fluids" (Meier and Morrison, 1999:6).

Responses by the Elderly: Human Agency

Being old is difficult for many. People who were once attractive, active, and powerful may no longer be so in old age. Most must live on restricted incomes that become more constricted by inflation or depleting investments. They must face chronic health problems, pain, and impending death. Many are isolated because they have lost a spouse and their children live at a distance. Some elderly people, especially the poor and those in many nursing homes, live lives of desperation and hopelessness.

After studying the elderly for 15 years, Bernice Neugarten and her associates delineated four major personality types among people age 70 and over (Neugarten, 1980). The majority of the elderly retain *integrated* personalities. They function well, are intellectually able, and have competent egos. Another category, the *defended*, is composed of achievement-oriented people who continue to work hard. They fight the aging process by not giving in to it and by remaining very active. *Passive-dependent* people, in contrast, have essentially given in to the inevitability of aging. They become inactive and depend on others. Finally, a relatively small proportion of the elderly are *disinterested* (disorganized). These people have experienced a deterioration of their thought processes. They may be confused, disoriented, forgetful, childish, and paranoid.

These personality types reflect responses to being old, a devalued status in the United States. Being considered old by society and by oneself is a catalyst that provokes the individual to respond in characteristic ways. However—and this is the crucial sociological point—the elderly are reacting to socially structured inequalities and socially constructed definitions, not to age as such. In a different cultural setting in which status increased with age, observers would likely find different personality types and responses.

Some researchers have argued that senior citizens respond to the aging process by retreating from relationships, organizations, and society (called **disengagement**). This behavior is considered normal and even satisfying for the individual, because withdrawal brings a release from societal pressures to perform and conform. Other researchers have quarreled with disengagement theory, arguing that many elderly people are involved in a wide range of activities.

The majority of the elderly do remain active until health problems curtail their mobility and mental acuity. A striking number of them are politically active, attempting to change some of the social conditions especially damaging to them. Faced with common problems, many are joined in collective efforts both locally and nationally. Several national organizations are dedicated to political action to benefit the elderly. Most significant is the American Association for Retired Persons (AARP), with more than 40 million members. Some other major groups are the National Committee to Preserve Social Security and Medicare, the National Council of Senior

Citizens, the National Council on Aging, the National Caucus of Black Aged, and the Gerontological Society. These organizations work through lobbyists, mailing campaigns, advertising, and other processes to improve the lot of the elderly in the United States.

As the elderly increase in numbers, their sphere of influence will increase as well (Confessore, 2002). In 2000 the elderly accounted for 22 percent of the voting public; it is estimated that in 2038 they will make up 34 percent of the electorate. Thus, there will be strong and coordinated efforts by the elderly for more generous Social Security and Medicare systems. Seniors, if history is a guide, will likely oppose higher taxes and school bond expenditures. Future politics, then, will probably be characterized by generational tensions: younger generations fighting against higher taxes to fund the elderly and fighting for school taxes for children's education and seniors resisting them on both fronts. The tensions will be not only generational but also racial (Peyser, 1999). This is because the younger generation, which is asked to pay the bills for the older generation, is increasingly multiracial and multiethnic, whereas the 65-plus population is overwhelmingly White.

The Three Structural Transformations of Society

This chapter focuses on three major transformations occurring in society—one economic and two demographic: the changing economy, the new immigration, and the aging of society. These macro forces have huge consequences for society, communities, families, and individuals.

Contemporary economic forces have brought about a fundamental transformation in the nature of work. The global economy, networked through new technologies in communications and transportation and the emergence of a few large transnational corporations, moves capital and jobs around the world and within the United States to where wages are the lowest. This phenomenon, coupled with the shift within the United States from a manufacturing to a service economy, has profoundly affected the distribution and type of jobs.

Fewer and fewer workers are engaged in mass assembly-line production, jobs that once paid well and had good benefits. Many assumed that new jobs in the service sector and along the information superhighway and in cyberspace would absorb those downsized from changing industries. This has occurred but to only a limited extent, because the skills required are very different from those of the industrial age, and these high-tech corporations also downsize their workers as they automate and use low-cost labor worldwide. As a result, only 35 percent of displaced workers have found work that has equaled or surpassed their previous wages and benefits. In effect, the economic transformation has caused millions of workers to transfer from well-paying jobs to lower-wage jobs, to temporary or contingent work, or to no work at all. Also, the unskilled and semiskilled workers either have been left out or work at low wages without benefits. Thus, many in society must deal with insecurity and downward mobility. Many wives join their husbands in the labor force to supplement family income. This has consequences for childbearing (whether to have children, the timing and spacing of children), child care, and the division of labor within families.

The transforming economy, with its massive changes, has made many families insecure. These insecurities have been exacerbated by the Great Recession.

One aspect of the global economy is the movement of people (immigration) generally from poor societies to rich societies. The consequence for the United States is a racial transformation, with most of the recent immigrants coming from Latin America and Asia. Most of these immigrants arrive without the work and language skills to fit into a knowledge society. Past immigrants have succeeded economically, but the current realities of the economic transformation increase the likelihood that they will be left on the margins. Moreover, the political climate has fostered the elimination of affirmative action and other compensatory programs to aid minorities, as well as the downsizing of public supports to the poor, and the neglect of urban blight and inner-city schools. All of these occur as racial minorities move toward becoming the numerical majority by mid–twenty-first century.

In addition to the external demographic force—immigration—there is an internal population shift—the growing proportion of the elderly—that has and will continue to have dramatic effects on U.S. society. This increase in the dependent population places pressure on workers and families to provide for them. Their growing political power will affect public policies, the politics of elections, and the political dynamics of certain states and regions.

The consequences of these three powerful macrosocial forces are many. The most significant consequence for us to consider is how these structural conditions shape families, as the following chapters will demonstrate.

Chapter Review

1. The economy of the United States is in the midst of a major structural transformation. This fundamental shift is the consequence of several powerful converging forces: (a) the globalization of the economy, (b) technological change, (c) capital flight, and (d) the shift from an industrial economy to a service/information/knowledge economy.

2. These forces combine to create considerable discontinuity and disequilibrium in society. In particular, they have reduced the number of jobs providing a middle-class standard of living and have expanded the number of lower-standard-of-living jobs. This results in increased job and benefits insecurity, a shrinking middle class, and downward social mobility for many.

3. These difficulties have been magnified by the Great Recession. Wages for the employed are stagnant and their benefits reduced or eliminated. Unemployment has risen sharply. Investments in stocks and home buying have declined precipitously, causing high rates of foreclosures and bankruptcies. The economic decline has increased the numbers of individuals and families who are "food insecure" and homeless.

4. Tough economic conditions have caused couples to delay marriage and if married to delay

childbearing. Financial woes are a major source of marital discord. The bond for some couples may be strengthened as the partners work together to find solutions. Many others find their bonds weakened or severed by difficult economic times.

5. Downward mobility from the middle class causes personal difficulties, such as loss of self-esteem and self-blame. Economic insecurity is related to stress, marital tension, depression, and high levels of alcohol consumption.

6. The economy affects the shapes of families. During the Great Recession more adult children have moved back in with their parents. More children are being raised by their grandparents. With men more likely to be fired than women, more families now have wives as the primary breadwinners, which affects family dynamics. Behaviors have changed, too, as limited resources or the threat of unemployment has affected patterns of consumption.

7. The transformation of the economy from one based on the production of goods to one based on technology and knowledge is itself being transformed by the Great Recession. The excesses leading to the recession will likely shift a primarily laissez faire

capitalism to an economy characterized by regulated capitalism. Changing consumption patterns (the "new frugality") will affect industries and employment. In short, the economic crisis will accelerate trends that will remake the nation's economic order.

8. The second societal upheaval that is shaking up society and families is massive immigration. This wave of immigration differs from previous waves because the immigrants come primarily from Latin America and Asia, rather than Europe.

9. There is great diversity among recent immigrants. Included are legal and undocumented immigrants. There are transnational families (some members in the United States while others remain in the country of origin). There are binational families, where the children born in the United States are citizens of the United States while the parents are not. These families also vary in housing arrangements, skill levels, familiarity with English, and the number of generations represented.

10. Racial and ethnic diversity (the browning of America) is increasing, with the influx of about 1.2 million immigrants and differential fertility. The non-White population will be equal in size to the White population soon after 2050.

11. The two fastest growing minorities—Latinos and Asian Americans—are each heterogeneous groups with wide differences by ethnicity in poverty rates, fertility rates, income, and education.

12. Conditions for new immigrants are, for the most part, difficult (hostility from others, language barriers, and demeaning and underpaid jobs without benefits). In response, migrants tend to adapt by moving to a location where there is a network of friends and relatives (moving in with relatives, pooling resources, and helping others in need). To overcome low wages, all able family members work. To overcome hostility from others, the immigrant community closes ranks.

13. Research on Mexican and Vietnamese immigrants shows that the immigration process itself reduces traditional patriarchal relations in families.

14. There are several sources of tension and conflict between the first and second generations in immigrant families. First, the second generation is more or less fluent in English, while their parents are not, resulting in parents being dependent on their children in many situations. Second, children often do not see the applicability of their parents' experiences in the old

country to theirs in the U.S. Third, the second generation tends to view the ethnic practices of their parents as abnormal and deficient. And, fourth, the generations clash over such ethnic practices as arranged marriage, dating, and independence.

15. The third societal upheaval that has profound consequences for families is the extraordinary growth in the proportion of the U.S. population age 65 and over. In this age category, women outnumber men, and minorities are underrepresented. Although the elderly are not disproportionately poor, the elderly who are women, minorities, or who live alone are disproportionately poor.

16. The Social Security program is the only source of income for about one-half of retired people and a major source of income for 80 percent of the elderly. Medicare is the universal health insurance program for the elderly.

17. The likelihood of the elderly living with their adult children will increase because of greater longevity. The common result for families will be a beanpole family structure—that is, a vertical, four-generation family structure.

18. The elderly face four major role transitions—from work to leisure, from marriage to widowhood, from independence to dependence, and from living to impending death.

19. For most elderly people, dying is a relatively long process because of advances in the treatment of disease and the medical ways to prolong life artificially. This relatively slow process often results in many months of dependence on family caregivers, usually women.

20. The elderly respond to this stage in the life cycle in several characteristic ways. They may withdraw from social relationships (disengagement); they may continue to act as they have throughout their adult lives; or they may become politically active to change the laws, customs, and social structures that disadvantage them.

21. The major consequence of the convergence of these three powerful forces—the structural transformation of the economy, the changing racial composition of society because of immigration, and the aging of society—is their effects on family forms, such as dual-worker families, transnational families, beanpole structure families, and older people living with their adult children who care for them.

Key Terms

assimilation   116

beanpole family structure   125

binational family   114

capital flight   92

chain migration   112

disengagement   129

exogamy   114

fictive kin   120

offshoring   93

outsourcing   93

parachute children   111

sandwich family structure   125

structural transformation of the economy   92

sunset industries   93

Related Websites

http://opr.princeton.edu

Office of Population Research, Princeton University. OPR is a leading demographic research and training center. The office has a distinguished history of contributions in formal demography and the study of fertility change. In recent years there has been increasing research activity in the areas of health and well-being, social demography, and migration and urbanization.

http://factfinder.census.gov

American Factfinder. This website is managed by the U.S. Census Bureau and is designed to help its users quickly and easily access such information as basic demographic facts, geographic comparison tables, detailed tables, custom tables, data sets, and reference maps related to the U.S. population as well as Puerto Rico.

http://www.prb.org

Population Reference Bureau. PRB provides up-to-date and timely reports on such issues as population, health, and the environment, both within the United States as well as globally.

http://www.nia.nih.gov

National Institute on Aging. NIA, one of the 27 Institutes and Centers of the National Institutes of Health, leads a broad scientific effort to understand the nature of aging and to extend the healthy, active years of life. In 1974, Congress granted authority to form NIA to provide leadership in aging research, training, health information dissemination, and other programs relevant to aging and older people. Subsequent amendments to this legislation designated the NIA as the primary Federal agency on Alzheimer's disease research.

http://www.caregiver.org

Family Caregiver Alliance. Founded in 1977, FCA was the first community-based nonprofit organization in the country to address the needs of families and friends providing long-term care at home. It now offers programs at national, state, and local levels to support and sustain caregivers.

www.epi.org/content.cfm/webfeatures_indicators

Economic Policy Institute: Economic Indicators. EPI is a nonprofit, nonpartisan think tank that seeks to broaden the public debate about strategies to achieve a prosperous and fair economy. This page provides links to their analyses of the most recent economic reports.

http://www.urban.org/immigrants

The Urban Institute: Immigrants. This website, sponsored by the Urban Institute, provides links to a variety of current reports related to immigration and the integration of immigrants in the United States.

http://www.nilc.org

National Immigration Law Center. Since 1979, NILC has been dedicated to protecting and promoting the rights of low-income immigrants and their family members. In the past 20 years, NILC has earned a national reputation as a leading expert on immigration, public benefits, and employment laws affecting immigrants and refugees.

http://www.wedo.org

Women's Environment Development Organization. WEDO is an international organization that advocates for women's equality in global policy. It seeks to empower women as decision makers to achieve economic, social and gender justice, a healthy, peaceful planet, and human rights for all. Through the organization's program areas—Gender and Governance, Sustainable Development, Economic and Social Justice, and U.S. Global Policy—WEDO emphasizes women's critical roles in social, economic, and political spheres.

http://www.econop.org

Economic Opportunity Initiative. The EOI is a nonpartisan, nonprofit, public policy institute, started in 1998, to define the policy debate on the issue of economic security. It focuses on concerns shared by middle-class families and low-income workers. The EOI develops new public policies to create ladders for low-income people to move into the middle class and to plug holes so that middle-class families do not fall into poverty. EOI is an activist, progressive, and majoritarian institute. Its work is spread through media outreach, public dialogue, and policy initiatives that address the shared economic security concerns of middle-class and low-income workers.

http://www.unicef.org

United Nations Children's Fund. UNICEF is mandated by the United Nations General Assembly to advocate for the protection of children's rights, to help meet their basic needs, and to expand their opportunities to reach their full potential. UNICEF is nonpartisan and its cooperation is free of discrimination. In everything it does, the most disadvantaged children and the countries in greatest need have priority. UNICEF aims, through its country programs, to promote the equal rights of women and girls and to support their full participation in the political, social, and economic development of their communities.

http://www.nassembly.org/fspc

Family Strengthening Policy Center. The Family Strengthening Policy Center was created with support from the Annie E. Casey Foundation as part of the Foundation's Neighborhood Transformation/Family Development and Making Connections initiatives. The Center aims to make family strengthening a priority by mainstreaming neighborhood-based, family-centered practices, programs, and policy. The Center's objective is to promote family policy that contributes to family economic and social empowerment.

http://www.hsph.harvard.edu/globalworkingfamilies

The Project on Global Working Families is a research team founded and directed by Dr. Jody Heymann at the Harvard School of Public Health. The team has studied and documented the experiences of working families in North America, Europe, Latin America, Africa, and Asia. The Project focuses on how the globalization of the economy affects parental working conditions and social supports, their impact on children's health and development, and the public and private policy solutions available. In their years studying the conditions of working families worldwide, Dr. Heymann and the Project on Global Working Families staff have developed extensive experience in conducting policy-based research domestically and internationally.

Class, Race, and Gender

Myths and Realities

Myth	An advanced, upwardly mobile society such as the United States gives rise to a common family form.
Reality	The United States produces great inequalities in the resources people need for family living, and this creates variation in families.
Myth	Cultural preferences and poor lifestyles keep minority families from advancing.
Reality	Racial-ethnic family forms are often adaptations to race and class discrimination in the wider society.
Myth	Families are women's worlds, where female control of domestic activities gives them the power they lack in other settings.
Reality	Families are part of a wider system of male power, giving men privileges largely at women's expense.

Twenty-first century families in the United States share some common features. All families must acquire provisions for daily living. They must do the work of feeding and caring for family members. All families must make decisions, use leisure time, and engage in countless other activities that fall within the realm of family life. Beneath the similarities, there are far-reaching differences in *how* these family activities are carried out.

This chapter examines how different family arrangements are related to social inequalities. First, we introduce class, race, and gender as structural conditions that produce different contexts for families. We then analyze class, race, and gender separately. First, we examine each system by discussing conventional thought about inequality and family. We then explain why much conventional thought about families is flawed. We use our structural diversity framework to show how class, race, and gender produce different social opportunities and diverse family arrangements. We pay particular attention to the various layers of contexts that shape the daily life of families.

The theme of this chapter is that *all* families are embedded in the systems of class, race, and gender. This is key to understanding family life.

Class, Race, and Gender as Structural Inequalities

Class, race, and gender are macrostructural systems that profoundly affect microstructural family worlds. Of course, many other conditions produce inequalities as well, including age, family characteristics, and place of residence (see Table 5.1).

Table 5.1   People and Families in Poverty by Selected Characteristics: 2007

Characteristics	Below Poverty Percentage	Characteristics	Below Poverty Percentage
People		18–64 years	10.9
Total	12.5	65 years and older	9.7
Family Status		**Nativity**	
In Families	10.8	Native	11.9
Householder	9.8	Foreign born	16.5
Related Children under 18	17.6	Naturalized citizen	9.5
Related Children under 6	20.8	Not a citizen	21.3
In unrelated subfamilies	38.1	**Region**	
Reference person	36.5	Northeast	11.4
Children under 18	40.5	Midwest	11.1
Unrelated individuals	19.7	South	14.2
Male	17.1	West	12
Female	22.2	**Families**	
Race		Total	9.8
White	10.5	**Type of Family**	
White, non-Hispanic	8.2	Married couple	4.9
Black	24.5	Female household, no husband present	28.3
Asian and Pacific Islander	10.2	Male household, no wife present	13.6
Hispanic origin	21.5		
Age			
Under 18 years	18		

Source: DeNavas-Walt, Carmen, Bernadette D. Proctor, and Jessica C. Smith, U.S. Census Bureau, *Current Population Reports*, P60-235, Income, Poverty, and Health Insurance Coverage in the United States: 2007, U.S. Government Printing Office, Washington, DC, 2008, p. 13.

Although many characteristics are associated with family diversity, class, race, and gender are most important. They organize society as a whole and create varied environments for family living.

A structural perspective emphasizes the following points:

1. Class, race, and gender are forms of stratification that foster group-based inequalities.
2. Class, race, and gender influence family life through their distribution of social resources and opportunities.
3. Class, race, and gender are relational systems of power and subordination.

4. Class, race, and gender do not stand alone. They work *together* to place families and individuals in different social locations, which produce diverse family patterns.

5. Class, race, and gender are systems of subordination that shape family life, yet the family can also be a place to resist inequality.

Let us look at these points.

The phrase **social stratification** refers, in essence, to structured inequality. The term *structured* refers to stratification being socially patterned. This means that inequalities are not caused by biological, cultural, or lifestyle differences. Of course, class, race, and gender can also refer to individual characteristics, but they are built into society's institutions in ways that produce advantages and disadvantages for entire groups of people. A crucial feature of social stratification is that groups are socially defined and then treated unequally. Social stratification rests on *group-based* inequalities (Collins, 1997). When groups are differentiated as inferior or superior, we have stratification.

The systems of stratification—class, race, and gender—produce different life chances. **Life chances** refer to the chances an individual has throughout his or her life cycle to live and to experience the good things in life. Stratification systems also place individuals and families in different social locations. Different social locations produce different family dynamics and diverse family arrangements. For example, low incomes often create high levels of kin involvement and extended family forms, even when the nuclear family is idealized (Cohen and MacCartney, 2004:182; Gerstel and Sarkisian, 2008; Schwede, 2005). Not only do families reflect the inequalities of their social locations, but families themselves transmit resources and opportunities to their members. For example, privileged families transmit wealth and status to their members, while others transmit unequal life chances. A common example is the disproportionate odds of poverty experienced by single mothers and their children. Both privilege and disadvantage are organized through family units (Cohen and MacCartney, 2004:182).

Class, race, and gender are structures of power as well as systems that distribute social resources. They structure the ability of the affluent to dominate the poor, of men to dominate women, and of Whites to dominate people of color (Feagin and Feagin, 1997:26–27). These hierarchies of domination and subordination are not just rankings of social resources—who has more income or prestige. They are power relationships (Weber, 1998:305). They structure the experiences of *all families,* albeit in different ways (Baca Zinn, 2000). Social locations of opportunity and oppression are *relational.* This means that different family forms in society are interdependent. Even without face-to-face relations, the privileges of some classes are associated with the disadvantages of other classes (Glenn, 2002:14). The existence of power relations between families in different social locations means that men and women from dominant race, class, and gender groups play a part in and benefit from the oppression of others.

The hierarchies of race, class, and gender do not stand alone. They are interconnected systems of inequality. Economic resources, the bases of class, are not randomly distributed but vary systematically by race and gender. For example, people of color and women have fewer occupational choices than do White males. People of color and women often experience separate and unequal education and receive less income for the work they do, resulting in different life chances.

"Luck, son, is when preparation meets nepotism."

These systems of inequality form a **matrix of domination** (Collins, 2000) in which all individuals and families exist. These interconnections have several important implications (Baca Zinn and Dill, 1996). First, people experience race, class, gender, and sexuality differently depending on their social location in these structures of inequality. For example, people of the same race will experience race differently depending on their location in the class structure as poor, working class, professional/managerial class, or unemployed; their location in the gender structure as male or female; and their location in the sexuality system as heterosexual, gay, lesbian, or bisexual. These systems of inequality create an imbalance of power *within* families as well as *between* families.

Despite the shaping effects of class, race, and gender, families can serve as sites to resist and survive inequality and hardship. Family members themselves may pull together to make ends meet, support each other, and even challenge domination to improve their lives. The actions of family members often represent strategies to deal with social inequality.

Class, race, and gender all play a part in creating varied environments for families. Viewing families as they are patterned by different opportunities, resources, and rewards embedded in society gives us a different understanding of family diversity. Conventional thought explains family differences in terms of group cultures, values, and behaviors. The structural diversity framework agrees that families in different race, class, and gender categories often have distinctive values. But this framework pertains to family life as it operates in social contexts that include power relations between dominant and subordinate racial and class groups as well as power relations between women and men.

Class

Social class is a complex concept that centers on the distribution of economic resources. That is, when a number of people occupy the same relative economic rank in the stratification system, they form a **social class.** There are no clear-cut boundaries, except perhaps those delineating the highest and lowest classes. A social class is not a homogeneous group, given the diversity within it, yet there is some degree of identification with other people in similar economic situations. Also, people have a sense of who is superior, inferior, or equal to them (Eitzen et al., 2010:253).

The class system in the United States is marked by striking differences in income. Income is the amount of money brought into a household in one year (Andersen and Collins, 2010b:71). Table 5.2 shows the average household income for each fifth of the population from 1970 to 2007 in 2007 dollars. This illustrates the growing income gap between the bottom fifth and the top fifth of the population. However, it is open to different interpretations of how income inequality is maintained.

Sociologists agree that there are social classes and that money is a central criterion for classification. However, they disagree on the meaning of class for people and on how to define class. Although this oversimplifies the debate, there are two different ways to think about class. Each approach gives us a distinctive view of family.

The Cultural Approach

Some sociologists use the terms *income, occupation,* and *education* as fundamental indicators of social class, with *occupation* as central. Occupational placement determines income, interaction patterns, opportunity, and lifestyle. Each class is viewed as having its own distinct culture. Lifestyle is the key feature of social class. Each class is viewed as having its own culture. According to this reasoning, each class has values,

Table 5.2   **Share of Aggregate Income by Each Fifth of Households, 1970, 1980, 1990, 2000, 2004, 2007**

Percentage Distribution Of Aggregate Income						
Year	Lowest Fifth	Second Fifth	Third Fifth	Fourth Fifth	Highest Fifth	Gini Index*
2007	3.4	8.7	14.8	23.4	49.7	0.463
2004	3.4	8.7	14.7	23.2	50.1	0.466
2000	3.6	8.9	14.9	23.0	49.6	0.460
1990	3.9	9.6	15.9	24.0	46.6	0.428
1980	4.3	10.3	16.9	24.9	43.7	0.403
1970	4.1	10.8	17.4	24.5	43.3	0.394

*The income inequality of a population group is commonly measured using the Gini index. The Gini index ranges from 0, indicating perfect equality (i.e., all persons having equal shares of the aggregate income), to 1, indicating perfect inequality (i.e., where all of the income is received by only one recipient or one group of recipients and the rest have none).

Source: DeNavas-Walt, Carmen, Bernadette D. Proctor, and Jessica C. Smith, U.S. Census Bureau, *Current Population Reports*, P60-235, Income, Poverty, and Health Insurance Coverage in the United States: 2007, U.S. Government Printing Office, Washington, DC, 2008, p. 9.

attitudes, and motives that distinguish its members from other classes. These orientations stem from occupations and income (Collins, 1988b:29), which then give rise to class-differentiated family patterns.

The cultural approach to class views the occupations of the middle class as orienting them to success and self-direction. Upper-middle-class "careers" require initiative and self-direction, whereas working-class jobs require workers to follow orders. Although these lifestyles stem from specific occupational experiences, comparisons between the classes usually turn out to be *deficit* accounts of lower-status families. Not only are these characteristics insulting, but they are also conspicuously lopsided, implying that lower-class people fail because something is missing in their families (Connell et al., 1982:27). Lower class people are believed to be unmotivated and incapable of deferring gratification, and as a result unable to improve their condition (Miller and Riessman, 1964). Poor families are often described in negative terms: as apathetic and fatalistic, responding to their economic situation by becoming fatalistic; they feel they are down and out and there is no point in trying to improve, for the odds are all against them (Kahl, 1957:211, 213). Such ideas about class-specific cultures blame poor families for their failure.

An important concept in this way of thinking about poor families is the **culture of poverty.** The culture of poverty contends that the poor have certain characteristics that set them apart from the rest of society and that these cultural differences *explain* continued poverty. In other words, the poor, in adapting to their deprived condition, are more permissive in raising their children, less verbal, more fatalistic, less apt to defer gratification, and less likely to be interested in formal education than those in the dominant classes. Some believe this deviant culture pattern is transmitted from generation to generation.

The notion that poverty is rooted in culture originated in anthropological case studies of Oscar Lewis (1959, 1966). Based on ethnographies of lower-class family life in Mexico, Puerto Rico, and New York, Lewis argued that the difference between the poor and the nonpoor lies in their values and behaviors. Poverty is more the result of a defective subculture than of physical environment. If poverty itself were to be eliminated, the former poor would probably continue to prefer instant gratification, be immoral by middle-class standards, and so on. This reasoning blames the victim.

The culture of poverty thesis had a significant impact on social policy in the 1960s. Programs arising out of the "War on Poverty" (such as Head Start) were influenced by the concept of a culture of poverty. However, the theory has never been verified (Rank, 2004:475). Today, the culture of poverty theory has gone out of favor. Nevertheless, we find its ideas used in concepts such as the "underclass," a class at the bottom, said to be locked into poverty by a deficit culture.

SHORTCOMINGS OF THE CULTURAL APPROACH

Common values and lifestyles among families with similar occupations, education, and income are real. But placing the emphasis on culture distorts key points. Treating family diversity as the result of cultural differences amounts to little more than a statement of the tautology "Families in different social classes are different because their cultures are different." This may be true, but it is not meaningful. Although subcultural differences are important, they become fully meaningful only when they are related to social and economic conditions.

Cultural explanations of family life in different parts of the class system ignore the institutional practices that are deeply embedded in the social structure of society.

Instead of recognizing how the economic system produces different levels of support for family life, the conventional explanations make each class responsible for its own fate.

Over the years, social scientists have disputed the typical interpretation of poverty. Today, extensive research finds that many so-called cultural factors can be traced to the social and material realities of different class locations. Here, we review evidence from two studies arguing that family life among the poor is not caused by deviant values. The first study was conducted four decades ago by Hyman Rodman (1964). He analyzed many so-called lower-class family traits as *solutions* to the problems lower-class people face in life. Consensual unions and female- or mother-centered households, "promiscuous" sexual relationships, "illegitimate" children, "deserting" husbands and fathers, and "unmarried" mothers are all solutions employed by the lower class to problems they face in life. In his study of the lower class in Coconut Village, Trinidad, Rodman found that marital or quasi-marital relationships were related to persistent economic uncertainties. "Marital shifting" and fluid marital bonds were then acceptable alternatives among lower-class families in U.S. society as well.

> Within the United States, the higher rates of divorce and desertion within the lower class, as well as of "common law" unions and illegitimacy, are indicative of such fluidity. If, as I am suggesting, these lower-class patterns are responses to the deprivations of lower-class life, and if they are functional for lower-class individuals, then we can see the sense in which many of the lower-class family patterns that are often regarded as problems are actually solutions to other, more pressing problems. (Rodman, 1964:68)

More recent evidence against the culture of poverty comes from a large-scale study conducted by social scientists at the University of Michigan. For over 40 years, the Panel Study of Income Dynamics (PSID) has been gathering data on the economic fortunes of families and individuals over many generations. This study raised the following question: Do the poor constitute a permanent underclass out of step with the majority and doomed to continuous poverty? By following families since 1968, the PSID has found that poverty is not a permanent condition for most people (Rank and Hirschl, 2001). Instead, there is a high turnover in the families and households who are poor in any given year. The typical pattern is that families are poor for one or two years and then manage to get above the poverty line (Rank, 2004:470). For the most part, poor families experience short-term poverty spells as they slip in and out of poverty.

Contrary to the myth that the poor are poor because they lack motivation, the PSID shows that people often fall into poverty because of a dramatic change such as the loss of a job or family break-up. Once adjustments are made to those changes, people are often able to climb back out of poverty (Lichter and Crowley, 2002; O'Hare, 1996; Rank, 2000, 2004). (See Box 5.1.)

The experience of long-term poverty varies among population groups. Female-headed families, African Americans, Latinos, and the elderly have longer-than-average poverty spells once they become poor because they have fewer routes out of poverty. These facts show how race and gender are linked to class in producing poverty. The PSID has found little evidence that poverty is the outcome of the way poor people think or that economic success is a function of "good" values and failure the result of "bad" ones.

BOX
5.1

Researching Families

The Panel Study of Income Dynamics: Following Parents and Children for Four Decades

The Panel Study of Income Dynamics (PSID), begun in 1968, is a longitudinal study of a representative sample of U.S. individuals and the family units in which they reside. It emphasizes the dynamic aspects of family economics, demographics, and health. As of 2005, the PSID had collected information about more than 70,000 individuals spanning as much as 37 years of their lives. The study is conducted at the Survey Research Center, Institute of Social Research, University of Michigan.

Starting with a national sample of 5,000 U.S. house-holds in 1968, the PSID has reinterviewed individuals from those households every year since that time, regardless of whether they are living in the same dwelling or with the same people. The study has followed adults as they have grown older and children as they have advanced through childhood, adolescence, and beyond, forming family units of their own. Information about the original 1968 sample individuals and their current co-residents (spouses, cohabitors, children, and anyone else living with them) is collected each year. In 1990, a representative national sample of 2,000 Latino households, differentially sampled to provide adequate numbers of Puerto Ricans, Mexican Americans, and Cuban Americans, was added to the PSID database.

In the early years, the purpose was to find out more about what the policy makers then called the "culture of poverty." Culture-of-poverty theorists believed that lack of motivation and other psychological factors were deeply rooted in the poor and kept many of them isolated from society's mainstream. The panel study measures individual attitudes about achievement, personal effectiveness, and the future with a series of psychological tests. Findings did not support theories that low motivation contributes to poverty. Highly motivated people were not more successful at escaping poverty than those with lower scores on these tests.

If the panel study did not support common ideas about what causes poverty, what did it show? A new and emerging definition of poverty resulted from the PSID, as the data helped transform research on poverty from a static view of poor and rich to a dynamic view in which families experience episodes of poverty. Changes in family living arrangements are an important factor in many of the shifts in and out of poverty. Researchers have found that family structure changes, such as divorces, are as important to well-being as unemployment.

The PSID data have been the only data collected on life course and multigenerational health, well-being, and economic conditions in a long-term panel representative of the U.S. population. Since 1968, there have been more than 2,167 articles, papers, and other publications based on this data. Today, on average, there is one publication using the PSID every 3.9 days.

Today, the PSID continues to collect data on topics including employment, income, health, wealth, housing expenditures, marital and fertility behavior, and philanthropy. Many of these areas have been included in the study since 1968. In 2007, PSID conducted a study of families who resided in the areas affected by Hurricane Katrina.

Sources: Rueter, Anne, "Myths of Poverty," *The Research News.* Ann Arbor, MI: Institute for Social Research, University of Michigan, July–September 1984, pp. 18–19; PSID Home Page, "An Overview of the Panel Study of Income Dynamics" (April 1997), http://www.umich.edu/psid; PSID Newsletter (April 2000), http://www.isr.umich.edu/src/psid/newsletter/news042000.html; "An Overview of the Panel Study of Income Dynamics: Key Contributions of the PSID to the Knowledge Base," http://www.isr.umich.edu/src/ psid/overview.html; McGonagle, Katherine A. and Robert F. Schoeni, "The Panel Study of Income Dynamics: Overview and Summary of Scientific Contributions After Nearly 40 Years" (January 30, 2006), http://psidonline.isr.umich.edu/Publications/Papers/montrealv5.pdf; "The Panel Study of Income Dynamics" (May 31, 2009), http://psidonline.isr.umich.edu.

The Structural Approach

A very different view of class differences in U.S. families emerges when we examine the institutional features of the class system. The structural perspective is critical of the notion that class position rests on people's own efforts and abilities. Such thinking neglects the ways in which social classes serve as the basis for allocating the resources needed for family life. Opportunities are socially structured; that is, they are built into the class system. They are far more important than individual or cultural factors.

Occupations are an important part of the class structure because they link families with resources and opportunities. Those that are highly valued and carry high-income rewards are distributed unevenly. Income has a profound effect on family life. The job or occupation that is the source of the paycheck connects families with the opportunity structure in different ways.

Are occupations, then, the main criterion for social class? The answer to this question depends on which model of social class is used. The first model places families and individuals in social classes according to occupation. Each social class is composed of people who share a similar lifestyle. Each class-specific culture is assumed to shape family life differently. Treating classes as groups of occupations has been a useful way of creating a picture of the class structure in which occupations and their resources and rewards are stratified (that is, divided like a layer cake, with each class or "layer" sharing certain attributes, such as level of income and type of occupation). However, this picture of classes as occupational strata implies that "class" is a static place that individuals and families inhabit, rather than a real-life grouping (Connell et al., 1982:25).

A second model of social class focuses not on occupations but on the distribution of socioeconomic resources that rest on *relationships of power* between class groups. A social class in this view is not a cluster of similar occupations but rather a number of individuals who occupy a similar position within the social relations of economic production (Lareau, 2008; Wright, 2008; Wright et al., 1982). What is important in this model is that class is not merely a relative position in a layer of occupations but a *material condition* that is part of the larger "economic system of production, distribution, and exchange" (Coontz, 2008a:8). Classes are *power* relationships, involving domination and subordination. Some groups have more power than others through their structural control of society's scarce resources. The key, then, is not the occupation itself but the *control* one has over one's own work, the work of others, decision making, and investments. People who own, manage, oppress, and control must be distinguished from those who are managed, oppressed, and controlled.

Both models of social class are important in understanding how class shapes family life. In this section, we refer to families in five categories in order to illustrate two points: (1) that different connections with society's opportunity structure shape families in distinctive ways and (2) that structured power relationships produce advantages for some families and disadvantages for others. Class privileges shape family relationships. **Privilege** refers to the distribution of goods and services, situations, and experiences that are highly valued and beneficial (Jeffries and Ransford, 1980:68). **Class privileges** are those advantages, prerogatives, and options that are available to those in the middle and upper classes. They confer dominance, power, and entitlement (McIntosh, 1992:98). They involve help from "the system": banks, credit unions, medical facilities, and voluntary associations. Class privileges create many differences in family patterns.

Traditionally, the family has been viewed as the principal unit in the stratification system because it passes on privilege (or the lack thereof) from generation to generation. We will see that even though the family is basic in maintaining stratification, life chances are affected by race and gender inequalities as well as by social class. In most families, men have greater socioeconomic resources and more power and privileges than do women, even though all family members are viewed as members of the same social class. While a family's placement in the class hierarchy does determine certain rewards and resources, hierarchies based on gender create different conditions for women and men even within the same family (Acker, 1973).

Gender cuts across class and racial divisions to distribute resources differently among men and women. Therefore, both family units and individuals are important in our understanding of different family experiences. In the following description of family life and social class, we examine how families in different parts of the class hierarchy are connected to society. The following points are important: (1) Class composition and class formation are always in flux. Large economic transformations are producing profound changes in the class system (see Chapter 4). In important areas such as access to higher education, health and longevity, and where people live, the power of class has been on the rise (Scott, 2008:356). Today, economic inequality in the United States is more extreme than at any time since the 1920s (Collins, 2008). (2) The classes as they are described here contain many contradictions. (3) The classes are always being entered and exited by individuals in either direction. (4) Social class is closely related to gender and race. Nevertheless, the class structure does organize families differently. Poverty, stable wage earning, affluent salaries, and inherited wealth create different material advantages, differences in the amount of control over others, and class differences in how families are shaped and how they operate.

The distinction we have been making between family and household helps us understand why family formation patterns differ by social class. Households are economic sites. They support themselves in different ways: through inheritance, salaries, wages, welfare, or various involvements with the hidden economy, the irregular economy, or the illegal economy. These different ways of acquiring the necessities of life produce variations in family life. Economic circumstances involve more than income. Economic circumstances affect every aspect of family life. The following descriptions situate class-based family differences in *structural factors,* that is, factors *outside the family.*

FAMILIES IN POVERTY

The lack of opportunities at the lower levels of the class hierarchy make the nuclear family a difficult arrangement to sustain. Studies over the past four decades show that the poor are more likely to expand their family boundaries in order to stretch the few resources they have. They are more likely to use a larger network of kin than the nonpoor (Rank, 2001:894). The extended network provides services such as babysitting, sharing meals, or lending money. It represents a coping mechanism for dealing with poverty (Gerstel and Sarkisian, 2008).

Poverty reduces the likelihood of marriage. The reason for a great proportion of female-headed households among the poor is that individuals who contemplate marriage generally seek or desire to be economically secure partners. Because poverty undermines the availability of such partners, individuals in these situations are likely to delay or forego marriage (Rank, 2000:309). Many poor women give up on marriage, not because they reject the institution of marriage but because they believe marriage will probably make their lives more difficult. If they cannot enjoy economic stability and gain upward mobility from marriage, they see little reason to marry (Edin, 2000b:130).

These themes are reflected in many studies of the past three decades that show how poverty affects family life. A labor market that fails to provide stable jobs prevents families from lifting themselves out of poverty. The solutions that poor families devise would surprise most nonpoor people. An important addition to the growing body of research on how low-income families really get by is Kathryn Edin and Laura Lein's *Making Ends Meet* (1997). This study, completed before welfare reform, shows what poor, single mothers who are welfare recipients and those who work in low-paid, unskilled job sectors of the U.S. economy must do to survive. Welfare mothers are not an underclass of women with deviant values. Many mothers struggle in low-wage jobs even though they may have been better off on welfare. Over a 12-month period, Edin and Lein found that both welfare mothers and low-wage working mothers experienced devastating hardships. Both groups faced the same fundamental dilemma each month, and they relied on similar kinds of survival strategies to generate the additional money they needed to bridge the gap between their incomes and their expenditures.

> These survival strategies were dynamic rather than static. They resembled a continuously unraveling patchwork quilt, constructed from a variety of welfare- and work-based income; cash and in-kind assistance from family, friends, absent fathers, and boyfriends; and cash and in-kind assistance from agencies. Though welfare- and wage-reliant mothers drew from the same repertoire of strategies, wage-reliant mothers were less likely to rely on supplemental work because they had so little extra time. For the same reason, they relied much more heavily on their personal networks to meet household expenses. Although maintaining this web of social relations took time, the "work" fit more flexibly into working mothers' schedules. (Edin and Lein, 1997:224–225)

This study highlights both the hardships and creativity of poor, single mothers. With the high rate of unemployment and limited social opportunities, poor families must do whatever it takes to survive. Even though they were clever at devising strategies to make up their budget shortfalls, these strategies took a great deal of time and energy. They were highly unstable and sometimes illegal (Edin, 2000b).

In a new study of motherhood and marriage, Kathryn Edin and Maria Kefalas ask the question "Why do poor women have children outside of marriage?" Their findings show how marriage patterns are closely tied to class factors. Neighborhoods without economic stability or community supports make it difficult for childbearing and marriage to go hand in hand. Poor women value both children and motherhood, but they see them differently. For the women in this study, children are a main source of identity and well-being. Yet they avoid marriage to men who do not meet their standards for financial and emotional security. According to Edin and Kefalas, they take marriage so seriously that they are unwilling to risk failure (Edin and Kefalas, 2005).

Since welfare reform was enacted in 1996 (see Chapter 13), many mothers have been dropped from welfare rolls without any other form of financial support. Those who do obtain employment are often in low-earning jobs and find that employment is not necessarily a ticket out of poverty (Hays, 2003; Murray et al., 2002:112). See Chapter 13 for a discussion of the effects of welfare reform on families. Even full-time work is no guarantee of livelihood for many U.S. families. A recent national study has found that 71 percent of low-income families work, but they earn such low income that they are struggling financially (Waldron et al., 2006). Karen Seccombe summarizes the effects of poverty on families: "Impoverished families face a higher degree of stress, disorganization, and other problems compared to more affluent families. Yet poverty is not simply about money. The effects can be far-reaching and devastating within a variety of realms, including work, family, home, health, schools, and their neighborhood" (2007:51) Low-income immigrants who have higher poverty rates than natives are especially vulnerable to these problems (Marks, 2006:52). For families in poverty, survival often means expanding their family boundaries in order to stretch and sustain the few resources they have (see Box 5.2).

BOX 5.2 Inside the Worlds of Diverse Families

How Single Mothers Survive in Poverty

Two studies provide a window on the lives of single mothers living in poverty. One, by Kathryn Edin and Laura Lein, *Making Ends Meet: How Single Mothers Survive Welfare and Low Wage Work* (1997), interviewed mothers prior to welfare reform enacted in 1996. The other, by Sharon Hays, *Flat Broke with Children: Women in the Age of Welfare Reform* (2003), examined mothers after welfare reform. Each study poses different questions. Each offers different perspectives on single mothers in poverty. Yet they both challenge conventional narratives that blame poor mothers for their own plight. Most single mothers in these studies shared a desire to be working, self-reliant, citizens and parents. Each study highlights a range of behaviors women use to make ends meet. Both studies force us to rethink common stereotypes of poor single mothers.

In the following passages, from *Making Ends Meet* (pp. 143–144), Edin and Lein emphasize what they call "survival strategies":

> These survival "choices" were not entirely up to the mother, since other factors, including her personal characteristics and the characteristics of the neighborhood and city she lived in, often limited the range of options available to her. Despite these constraints, however, most mothers said they still had a range of strategies to try.
>
> Some mothers relied on the father of their children or a boyfriend for help. Others relied mainly on their own mother or other family members. In cases where neither a child's father, a boyfriend, nor a relative could help, mothers often relied on an off-the-books job. Some sold sex, drugs, and stolen goods. Still others moved between informal and illegal jobs. When these strategies failed, many went to churches or private charities to get help to pay the light bill or the rent.
>
> Mothers who did not have supportive friends or relatives had to find some kind of side work. But some mothers told us they could not do side work because they had no one to watch their young children. Others could not get a side job because they were disabled, still others did not have the know-how to get an off-the-books job without getting caught by their welfare caseworker; and others lived in small, tight-knit communities where a side job would be hard to hide from authorities.
>
> Mothers who could get neither network support nor side work were the most dependent on churches and private charities. Not surprisingly, these mothers invested a lot of time learning about the range of public and private sources of help available in their communities. Some mothers had a relatively easy time finding out about agencies because members of their social networks offered them guidance or because such services were well publicized. Other

mothers lived in neighborhoods or cities with poor service environments, making agency help more difficult to obtain.

Like Edin and Lein, Hays studied how single mothers survive in poverty. Her book, *Flat Broke With Children* reports on the impact of welfare reform on the lives of poor women and their children. She discovered that despite the challenges of the new laws pertaining to work, women went to great lengths to provide for their families.

Because neither welfare nor work provided a wage adequate to support all the needs of their families, some women were forced to reduce meal sizes for themselves and their families. Some women reported stealing in order to obtain the resources necessary to support their families. Beyond these tactics, many women sought supplemental income by taking second and third jobs. Some single mothers were limited in their ability to work because they lacked the skills to perform the work. Among those who worked, it was also common to work graveyard shifts, weekends, or off hours.

Single mothers often turned to their friends or families for help both with children and finances. In addition to borrowing money from family members, they sometimes moved in with sisters or parents. They also relied on the fathers of their children or boyfriends for support. Single mothers also leaned on the assistance of friends or family to care for their children. At times, they worked out reciprocal arrangements where they watched each other's children during opposite working hours. Some women employed paid caregivers or leveraged after school childcare programs although the added financial demands of these solutions made them less prevalent. Overall, single mothers struggled to secure jobs that provided adequate wages, benefits, and flexibility to allow them to pay for necessities, care for their children, and raise themselves above the poverty line. As a result, they invested time in learning about the variety of public and private services that were available to support them. And they turned increasingly to private charities, churches, food banks, homeless shelters, or housing assistance programs.

References

Edin, Kathryn, and Laura Lein, *Making Ends Meet: How Single Mothers Survive Welfare and Low Wage Work.* New York: Russell Sage Foundation, 1997, pp. 143–144.

Sharon Hays, *Flat Broke with Children: Women in the Age of Welfare Reform.* New York: Oxford University Press, 2003.

Source: Brower, Tracy. Department of Sociology, Michigan State University 2009. This essay was written expressly for *Diversity in Families*, 9th ed.

BLUE-COLLAR FAMILIES

Working-class families are the largest single group of families in the country. As Rubin described the working class in the 1990s,

> [t]hese are the men and women, by far the largest part of the American work force, who work at the lower levels of manufacturing and service sectors of the economy; workers whose education is limited, whose mobility options are severely restricted, and who usually work for an hourly rather than a weekly wage. They don't tap public resources; they reap no benefit from either the pitiful handouts to the poor or from huge subsidies to the rich. Instead, they go to work every day to provide for their families, often at jobs they hate. (Rubin, 1994:30–31)

Blue-collar families depend on hourly wages, which makes them susceptible to layoffs, plant closings, and unemployment (Rapp, 1982). In Chapter 4 we examine the macroeconomic shifts displacing manufacturing workers and creating new vulnerabilities for family life. These economic pressures move working class families even farther from the idealized nuclear family model. Of course, working class families have always been vulnerable to economic fluctuations. Their class position offers little economic support for economic dislocations. As their jobs are downsized or disappear, many working class families must at one time or another live on a combination of wages, unemployment insurance, and social security benefits (Bridenthal, 1981). Like those in the lower class, they may depend on government assistance, food stamps, and various sectors of the irregular economy. For minorities and women in the working class, economic pressures are compounded by racial discrimination and sex discrimination. Minority groups and women heading households are disproportionately found in this category.

Working-class families continue to be stereotyped as "traditional." However, many blue-collar families keep themselves above the official poverty line through wives' employment. By the end of the twentieth century, wives in blue-collar families were likely to be employed outside of the home. Classic studies of working-class families (Komorovsky, 1962; Rubin, 1976) and more recent examinations by Judith Stacey (1991) and Lillian B. Rubin (1994), reveal consistent themes of financial stress and marital strife. Studies conducted in the first decade of the twenty-first century found that family life took place amid precarious financial conditions (Dodson and Bravo, 2005; Hansen, 2005). The current economic downturn has put families at even greater risk "where any unexpected event such as a child's illness or a brief layoff threatens their financial stability. Moreover, divorce is splitting many working-class families" (Perry-Jenkins and Salamon, 2002:198).

Families in this class location struggle creatively, often heroically, drawing on whatever resources they can to sustain the family. Support from kin turns out to be one of the most important solutions to social and economic pressures. Working-class reliance on extended kin is not new. Practically every study of working-class families shows that they interact more with kin than do middle-class families. For example, Mirra Komorovsky's classic study, *Blue Collar Marriage* (1962), revealed that kin relations were the main experience of group membership.

Herbert Gans's study of "urban villagers," Italian American workers in Boston, also painted a kin-based picture of working-class families (Gans, 1962:245). And Lillian Rubin's classic study, *Worlds of Pain* (1976), described the extended family as the heart of social life. Rubin exclaimed that "even in mobile California, the importance of extended kin among working-class families is striking" (Rubin, 1976:197). The classic literature on working-class families shows that the kin network helps families reduce financial stress (Perry-Jenkins and Salamon, 2002). Recent research also highlights strong kinship ties in the lives of working class families (Lareau, 2003). Of course, living in the context of a large and supportive kin network can have both costs and benefits. On the one hand, kin can provide support when times are hard. On the other hand, they also require assistance, and they can be the source of family conflict.

MIDDLE-CLASS FAMILIES

The middle-class nuclear family is idealized in our society. This form, a self-reliant unit composed of a breadwinning father, a homemaker mother, and their children has long been most characteristic of middle-class and upper-middle-class families. Middle-class families of the new century are quite different from the television stereotyped family of the 1950s. Today, many families sustain their middle-class status only through the economic contributions of employed wives (Warren and Tyagi, 2009).

Middle-class families generally receive salaries rather than wages. Their salaries provide them with a stable resource base, a factor that differentiates them from those below. Even more important, the middle class exerts power and control in relation to the working class. Those in the middle class can control their working conditions in a way that the working class cannot (Vanneman and Cannon, 1987). According to Randall Collins (1988b), this power position distinguishes the middle class from the working class. In his distinction, members of the middle class are "order-givers," while members of the working class are "order-takers." This is a useful way of thinking about class as a social relationship. However, gender complicates matters because paid work gives women and men different connections with society's opportunity structures. Some women's jobs seem to be in middle-class sectors, but Collins argues that, in fact, most women's jobs are "white-collar working-class" because they take rather than give orders:

> Secretaries, clerks, and retail sales positions are order-takers, not order-givers. Many of them are also manual workers, operators of machines (telephones, photocopiers, typewriters, word processors) within an office setting. Nurses, who are conventionally classified as professionals, nevertheless tend to be clerical workers within a medical setting and assistants who perform manual work for physicians (although they may sometimes have some order-giver power vis-à-vis patients). Of the most common female occupations, only schoolteachers (5.3 percent of the female labor force) would be considered genuinely middle class by the criterion of order-giving and order-taking. (Collins, 1988b:30)

Gender can create class inconsistencies in middle-class marriages because many middle-class males have married downward to white-collar working-class women.

Families in which both mother and father are breadwinners must find ways to provide care for their children. How families in different class locations do this in the twenty-first century is the subject of a new study by sociologist Karen Hansen. Her research challenges the myths that middle-class families are self-sufficient and disconnected from kin. Even if they are middle class, families with two breadwinners must build social networks to help them care for children. In today's world, they have increased their reliance on kin. Hansen concludes that structural changes have given rise to middle-class families that are "not-so nuclear" (Hansen, 2005).

But even if middle-class families are less kin-oriented than those in the working class, their "autonomy" is shaped by supportive forces in this class location. When exceptional resources are called for, nonfamilial institutions usually are available in the form of better medical coverage, expense accounts, credit at banks, and so on (Rapp, 1982:181). These links with nonfamily institutions are precisely the ones that distinguish the family economy of middle-class families. Class distinctions are often complicated by race:

> Two main things tend to distinguish black middle-class people from middle-class whites. One is the likelihood that many more of their relatives will come to them first for help. The other is that they tend to lack the resources of people who started in the middle class. (Billingsley, 1992:284)

FAMILIES OF PROFESSIONALS

Families in the professional class are likely to merge the spheres of work and family. Leisure activities often revolve around occupational concerns and occupational associates. Studies of corporation executives and their families reveal a strong corporate influence. For example, Rosabeth Kanter's classic study found that both executives and their wives were closely tied to the corporation. Here is her description of "corporate" wives:

> At a certain point in their husbands' climb to the top [these wives] ... realized that friendships were no longer a personal matter but had business implications. Social professionalism set in. The political implications of what had formerly been personal or sentimental choices became clear. Old friendships might have to be put aside because the organizational situation makes them inappropriate, as in the case of one officer husband who let his wife know it would no longer be seemly to maintain a social relationship with a couple to whom they had previously been close because the first husband now far outranked the second. The public consequences of relationships made it difficult for some wives to have anything but a superficial friendship with anyone in the corporate social network. Yet since so much of their time was consumed by company related entertainment, they had little chance for friendships and reported considerable loneliness. (Kanter, 1984:116)

In many professional homes, family life is subordinate to the demands of the husband-father's occupation. Family can be a respite, "dad's place of leisure" (Larson and Richards, 1994). Family can take a backseat to the male involvement in work, success, and striving. Corporate relocation is commonplace. In many cases employers subsidize moves by paying for moving expenses. Commonly, professional employees are relocated repeatedly, "sometimes as often as every two or three years and on average every five to seven years" (Eby and Russell, 2000:4).

Moving to a new community for a job change affects family members in a variety of ways. There may be some benefits from the move, but there are also costs. An employee's family members must give up their previous home, including the physical dwelling and the surrounding community with its offerings of arts, activities, stores, scenery, and so forth. Also, they give up a sense of familiarity, and they give up close proximity to individuals and organizations with whom they were connected and from whom they drew varying levels of resources such as companionship or support. In some cases, this effect is large. In other cases it is small. And the effect often differs for different members of the family (Whitaker, 2005:89). (See Box 5.3.)

BOX 5.3 Emergent **Family** Trends

Women Pay a High Price for Corporate Relocation in Today's Global Economy

The United States has a national job market for employment, especially professional or managerial employment. As more and more companies become national or global, employment possibilities within a company are geographically widespread. People are expected to relocate to other areas of the country or the world in order to take a job, keep a job, or advance in a job. In fact, more than half of all moves in the United States are believed to be work-related, and promotions, new job responsibilities, and even mere job retention are sometimes attached to geographic moves (Hodson and Sullivan, 2002).

Corporate relocation has different implications for men and women. Although the movers are primarily professional middle and upper-middle class employees, this form of work-related family migration is disproportionately male-centered. According to *MOBILITY Magazine,* the monthly publication of the Employee Relocation Council, a trade association for relocation professionals, 83 percent of domestic corporate transferees and 87 percent of international corporate transferees are male (Marshall and Greenwood, 2002). Most are married (84 percent of domestic) and most have children (about 60 percent of each).

We often think of wives in professional middle-class marriages as both privileged and educated and therefore immune to gender discrimination and gender disadvantage. Employee relocation today is one area that refutes that image and where being a woman can exact a high price. To understand how corporate relocation affects women, we must consider gender role expectations. Productive activity, or paid labor, is treated as men's domain while reproductive activity, unpaid labor necessary for the reproduction of everyday life, is treated as women's domain. Even when women work outside the home, they are still responsible for most family and household work. While relocation maintains or improves the situation in the productive realm, it requires that a family forfeit many of the resources of the reproductive realm. Relocated families must give up their homes and the surrounding communities. Also, they must give up a sense of familiarity and the close proximity to individuals and organizations with whom

they were connected and from whom they drew varying levels of resources, such as companionship or support.

To study the relationship between families, work, and community in the new millennium, I talked with 10 women who had been moved for their husbands' jobs (Whitaker, 2005). We spoke about the decision process that preceded their move, the changes they underwent with regard to home and place, and the process of reestablishing a family in a new community. Although the women spoke in terms of "opportunity," it was clear that pressure and guilt influenced them to "go along" with the move. The pressure came from their feelings of vulnerability in the precarious global economy and from the sense that they didn't have the right to stand in the way of their husbands' aspirations. The following statement is representative of the sentiments of several women who followed a transferred husband:

> For me absolutely [there was a time we considered not taking it], but not for him. We talked a lot about it, but at this time I was a stay-at-home mom and the guilt was overwhelming. What exactly did I have to stay in [city] for? Just pretty much because I didn't want to be away from friends and family was the only reason. It was my husband's career, and I didn't have a career then other than being a full time mom....Ultimately this is his career and if I was going to follow him up the corporate ladder then this was what we had to do.

While transferred husbands are engaged with their careers and are immediately immersed in work activities and work communities, their wives are charged with recreating and then maintaining the private aspects of life, the very aspects that are a hidden cost of relocation. One relocated wife said this when she thought about what she was giving up by moving to allow her husband to advance in his career:

> I really loved where we lived. It was a perfect fit. It wasn't right on top of my family but close enough to see them. And the town, they'd just made so many great improvements. It is just a great place to live and I hated to leave. To leave the town, our friends. [My husband] and I, that was like our little family. (Whitaker, 2005)

About half of these professional, educated women gave up their own jobs in addition to taking on the responsibility of reestablishing their families with new networks of support and companionship. Overwhelmingly, the women said that a move was successful only when

(continued)

(*Box 5.3 continued*)

they were connected and supported within their new community. One wife defined a successful move like this:

> To define successful would be that I'm no longer sitting here sobbing, we have made very good friends here that I have called on in bad times and they have helped me out.

Professional middle and upper-middle class individuals may enjoy privileges in the work arena. They tend to have high levels of autonomy and authority on the job and good compensation compared with working-class and low-income workers. But, the individuals and families who are subject to corporate pressure to forgo place to maintain class status in a corporate world are, in fact, wage earners. They often enjoy good salaries and benefits, but most are not independently wealthy where employment circumstances are irrelevant to their abilities to pay their bills, maintain their lifestyles, and provide for their families. Also, the employment stability of professional middle-class managers has evolved in such a way that the privilege of this group may be more tenuous than it once was. While managers' unemployment rates have traditionally been very low, the prevalence of organizational change affects the long-term job-security of managers. Women and men face different costs and challenges, with women bearing a disproportionately large share of the costs and burdens on the home front. Corporations readily ask families to change their homes and their lives, and they rely on women to do the rebuilding.

References

Hodson, Randy and Teresa A. Sullivan. *The Social Organization of Work.* Belmont, CA: Wadsworth/Thomas Learning, 2002.

Marshall, Edward L. and Peggy Greenwood (2002). "Setting Corporate Policy to Meet the Changing Definition of Family." *MOBILITY Magazine,* Employee Relocation Council (April).

Source: Whitaker, Elizabeth Ann (2006). Department of Sociology, Michigan State University. This essay was written expressly for *Diversity in Families.*

In spite of the work pressures that often mold professional families, husbands (and perhaps wives) in careers have both economic resources and built-in ties with supportive institutions. These ties are structural. They are intrinsic to some occupations and to middle-class neighborhoods. Such class-based connections strengthen the autonomy of these families, allowing them to emphasize the nuclear unit.

WEALTHY FAMILIES

Vast economic holdings give elite families control over social resources as well as opportunities and choices not available to other families in society. Although small in number compared to other class categories, the elite have great power and influence through their ownership or control of the major units of the economy. This is class control. Their network of influence in the global economy and their ability to generate additional resources is what distinguishes the elite from the rest of society. "It is not simply bank interest that generates more money, but income-producing property: buildings, factories, natural resources; those assets Karl Marx referred to as the means of production" (Mantsios, 1996:101). Decisions about what is most profitable for them affect what happens to other families in the nation and the world.

Day-to-day family life among the elite is "privileged" in every sense:

> Wealthy families can afford an elaborate support structure to take care of the details of everyday life. Persons can be hired to cook and prepare meals and do laundry and to care for the children. (Stein et al., 1977:9)

Elite family lifestyles are made possible by their control of labor of others—the subordinate classes whose own families must often suffer as they do the work required to support elite privileges. The point is not only that domination and subordination coexist but that the lifestyles of the wealthy cannot exist without denying the rights and privileges of those who serve them.

Compared to other categories of families, relatively little recent data are available on the wealthy. The elite have a distinctive family structure. They are

lineal, ancestor oriented, and conscious of the boundaries that separate the 'best' families from the others. The Social Register (names of upper-class families) is used even today to consolidate upper class repute, support class cohesion, and maintain 'good breeding' in their interest in continuity of lineage. Families are the units within which wealth is accumulated and transmitted. (Eshleman and Bulcroft, 2006:145–146)

Among the elite, "family constitutes not only a nuclear family but the extended family as well." The elite often have multiple households (Rapp, 1982:182)—that is, numerous townhouses and country places. For years, the Kennedy "compound" at Hyannis, Massachusetts, was an obvious case in point, as were the Rockefeller estates (managed by employees). The compound is usually only one of several residences that serve as community centers for extended kin. Multiple residences are not nuclear households in form, nor are they independent entities (Leibowitz, 1978:165). The concerns and much of day-to-day life exist within the larger context of a kinship network. The kin-based family form of the elite serves to preserve inherited wealth. It is connected with national institutions that control the wealth of society.

Elite families are nationally connected by a web of the institutions they control. Families throughout the country are linked by private schools, exclusive colleges, exclusive clubs, and fashionable vacation resorts. Today, the super rich are finding new ways to set themselves apart. They are secluded by gated communities, private banking coalitions, and members-only health clinics (Vencat and Brownell, 2007). In this way the elite remains intact, and the marriage market is restricted to a small (but national) market (Blumberg and Paul, 1975:69). Marriage legally clarifies the lines of inheritance in a way that is less important to those without property (Hansen, 2005:69). But marriage among the elite is more than a legal-emotional commitment. It is a means of concentrating capital and maintaining the in-group solidarity of the class (Langman, 1987:224). Even the division of labor between women and men sustains class solidarity. In the upper class, women's philanthropic work serves a "gatekeeping" function. Their work in private schools, social clubs, and charity functions is vital in preserving the institutions that benefit family and class (Daniels, 1987; Ostrander, 1984).

We have reviewed studies showing extensive class variation in household and family formation. Kinship ties, obligations, and interests are more extended in classes at the two extremes than they are in the middle (McKinley, 1964:22). In the upper extreme and toward the lower end of the class structure, kinship networks serve decidedly different functions, but at both extremes they are institutions of resource management.

Murals in *ethnic* communities reflect their distinct identity within the larger culture.

 # Race

Like the class and gender systems, racial stratification has structural foundations. The meaning and significance of race was fundamentally changed in the beginning of the twenty-first century. The blatant forms of racism that existed in the past have given way to new, more subtle practices (Lewis et al., 2004:4). Nevertheless, racism continues to operate as a system of advantage and disadvantage through its unequal distribution of power. In this section of the chapter, we show that *racial stratification produces diversity in families.*

The racial hierarchy, with White groups of European origin at the top and racially defined groups at the bottom, serves important functions for society and for certain categories of people. It ensures that some people are available to do society's dirty work at low wages. Racial inequality has positive consequences for the status quo: It enables the powerful to retain their power and advantages. Many people think that multicultural attitudes and a "color-blind" climate have replaced old-fashioned racism. Yet many family features among racially defined groups show that racial inequalities persist in today's multicultural world. White groups receive racial privileges in the form of better occupational opportunities, income, and education. Racially defined groups lack the same opportunities as everyone else. This affects family life in important ways.

The different family experiences of racial groups are systematically produced even though races do not exist biologically. What does exist is the *idea* that races are distinct biological categories. But despite the common belief, social scientists now reject the biological concept of race. Scientific examination of the human genome finds no genetic differences between the so-called races. Fossil and DNA evidence shows that humans are all one race, evolved in the last 100,000 years from the same small number of tribes that migrated out of Africa and colonized the world (American Sociological Association, 2003; Angier, 2000; Bean et al., 2004; Mukhopadhay and Henze, 2003). Although there is no such thing as biological race, races are real insofar as they are *socially defined*. In other words, racial categories *operate* as if they are real.

Racial classification in the United States was long based on a Black/White dichotomy—that is, two opposing categories into which all people fit. However, social definitions of race have changed throughout the nation's history. At different points in the past, "race has taken on different meanings. Many of the people considered White and thought of as the majority group are descendents of immigrants who at one time were believed to be racially distinct from native-born White Americans, the majority of whom were Protestants" (Higginbotham and Andersen, 2009:41). Racial categories vary in different regions of the country and around the world. Someone classified as "Black" in the United States might be considered "White" in Brazil and "Colored" (a category distinguished from both "Black" and "White") in South Africa (Bamshad and Olson, 2003:80). In the United States, a Black/White color line has always been complicated by regional racial divides. Today, the rapidly growing presence of Latino and Asian immigrants and resurgence of Native American identification have changed the meaning and boundaries of racial categories (Lee and Bean, 2004b:224; Lewis et al., 2004:5). Their non-White racial status marks them as "other" and denies them many social opportunities (Pyke, 2004:258). Global events also complicate the color lines. Since the terrorist attacks on the World Trade Center and the Pentagon, Arab Americans, Muslims, and people of Middle-Eastern descent (viewed by many as a single entity) are stereotyped as different and dangerous.

In Chapter 4 we discuss current immigration patterns that are profoundly reshaping the U.S. racial landscape. Because most immigrants are people of color, the character of race relations has become more complex (Lewis et al., 2004:6). Sociologists Michael Omi and Howard Winant (1994:55) call this **racial formation,** meaning that society is continually creating and transforming racial categories. For example, groups that were once self-defined by their ethnic backgrounds (such as Mexican Americans and Japanese Americans) are now racialized as "Hispanics" and "Asian Americans." Middle Easterners coming from such countries as Syria, Lebanon, Egypt, and Iran are commonly grouped together and called "Arabs." The U.S. government has changed its racial categories over time. The Census Bureau, which measures races on the basis of self-identification, revised its racial categories for the 2000 Census. For the first time, people were allowed to record themselves in two or more racial categories. Of the U.S. population, 2.4 percent or seven million people identified themselves as multiracial, reporting that they are of two races. This option of choosing more than one race provides a more accurate and visible portrait of the multiracial population in the United States. We can expect that the use of the multiracial option will grow, especially among the younger population. Marrying across racial lines is on the increase, as attitudes toward interracial unions have become more tolerant; 13 percent of U.S. marriages are now interracial (Lee and Bean, 2004a:228). (See Chapter 8.) Already, children are more likely to identify themselves as multiracial than are adults. Four percent of the population under age 18 was identified in more than one racial category in the 2000 Census, twice the percentage of adults (Kent et al., 2001:6; Prewitt, 2003:39).

Despite the past and present racialization of different groups, we tend to see race through a Black/White lens, thereby neglecting other rapidly growing racial groups. At the same time, we think of the dominant group as raceless (McIntosh, 1992). In this view, Whiteness is the natural or normal condition. It is racially unmarked and immune to investigation. This is a false picture of race. In reality, the racial order shapes the lives of all people, even Whites who are advantaged by the system. Just as social classes exist in relation to each other, "races" are labeled and judged *in relation to other races.* The categories "Black" and "Hispanic" are meaningful only insofar as they are set apart from, and in distinction to, "White." This point is particularly obvious when people are referred to as "non-White" (a word that ignores the differences in experiences among people of

Race-ethnic groups are socially subordinate and culturally distinct within society. Muslim American fifth grader showing henna designs for Muslim Ramidan.

color) (Lucal, 1996:246). Race is not simply a matter of two opposite categories of people; it is a range of power relations among differently situated people (Weber, 2001).

How is race different from ethnicity? Whereas race is an invention used for socially marking groups based on presumed physical differences, **ethnicity** is a social category that allows for a broader range of affiliation. Ethnic groups are distinctive on the basis of national origin, language, religion, and culture. Today's globalized world is replete with examples of socially constructed ethnicities. In the United States, people began to affiliate along ethnic lines, such as Italian American or German American, much more frequently after the civil rights movement.

In the United States, race and ethnicity both serve to mark groups as different. Groups *labeled as races* by the wider society are bound together by their common social and economic conditions. As a result, they develop distinctive cultural or ethnic characteristics. Today, we use the concept racial-ethnic groups (or racially defined ethnic groups). The term **racial-ethnic groups** refers to groups that are socially subordinated and remain culturally distinct within U.S. society. It is meant to include (1) the systematic discrimination of socially constructed racial groups and (2) their distinctive cultural arrangements. We saw in Chapter 3 that, historically, the categories of African American, Mexican American, Asian American, and Native American were constructed as both racially and culturally distinct. Each group has a distinctive culture, shares a common heritage, and has developed a common identity within a larger society that subordinates it (Baca Zinn and Dill, 1994).

As we saw in Chapter 4, the growing presence of racial-ethnic groups is changing U.S. society. At the beginning of the twenty-first century, the United States was 70 percent White, 12 percent African American, 12 percent Hispanic, 4 percent Asian American, and 1 percent Native American. Figure 5.1 shows how the racial composition of the United States is expected to change through the year 2050. Terms of reference are also changing, and the changes are contested within groups as well as between them. For example, *Blacks* continue to debate the merits of the term *African American,* while *Latinos* disagree on the label *Hispanic.* In this book, we use such terms interchangeably because they are currently used in popular and scholarly discourse.

Racial-Ethnic Families

Although racial stratification affects families throughout society, we focus here on racialized patterns of family formation among African Americans and Latinos. Our intent is not to limit our understanding about racial stratification to African Americans and Latinos. Instead, the intent is to counter the mainstream approaches that are based on research involving mostly White middle-class families and treating them as the norm. In this chapter, we place African American and Latino families at the

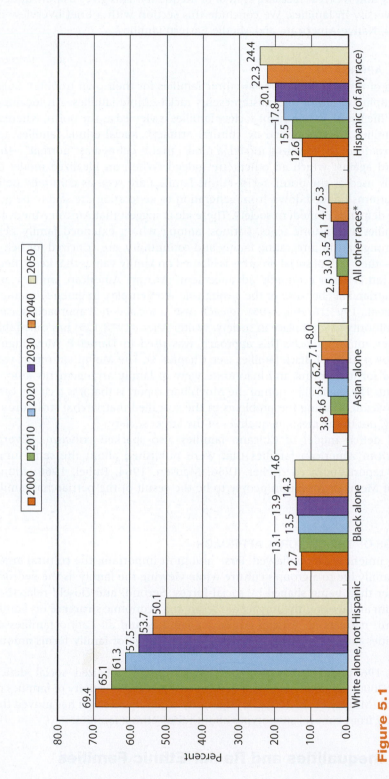

Figure 5.1

Projected Population of the United States by Race and Hispanic Origin: 2000–2050

*Includes American Indian and Alaska Native alone, Native Hawaiian and Other Pacific Islander alone, and Two or More Races.

Source: U.S. Census Bureau (2004). "U.S. Interim Projection by Age, Sex, Race, and Hispanic Origin." Internet Release Date: March 18, 2004.
http://www.census.gov/ipc/www/usinterimproj/.

center of inquiry and we treat race as a system of inequality. This gives us new understandings of diversity in families. We conclude this section with a brief overview of Asian American, Native American, and Middle Eastern families.

THE CULTURAL APPROACH

A long tradition of thought blames racial-ethnic families for their own troubles. Such thought oversimplifies culture and misrepresents racial-ethnic families. An idealized model of family life based on dominant society families is viewed as the norm, whereas racial-ethnic families are thought to be cultural artifacts. Racial-ethnic families are defined as *different* from the idealized model, a model that is defined as "normal"—the cultural standard against which all others are judged. When an idealized model of White families is used as the norm, racial-ethnic families are seen as culturally deficient. Family patterns handed down from generation to generation are said to be out of step with the demands of modern society. These ideas suggest that African American and Latino families are historic relics. Latinos, among whom extended family networks play a strong part in integrating family and community, are criticized for being too "familistic"—their lack of social progress is blamed on family values that keep them tied to family rather than economic advancement. African American families are criticized as "matriarchal" because of the strong role women play in extended family networks (Dill et al., 1993:16; Hill, 2005). In each case, a social deficit approach is used to explain the minority group's place in society. Walter Allen (1978:125) has called this the "cultural deviant" approach. This approach was used in Daniel P. Moynihan's (1965) well-known study of Black families (see Chapter 3). The Moynihan report was widely criticized for its harmful and inaccurate view of family arrangements among Blacks as deviant. The main objection to the Moynihan report is that it is a classic case of blaming the victim, locating the problems in the so-called matriarchal structure of the Black family, not in the racial inequalities of the larger society.

The social deficit model of Chicano families also sparked criticism. Several works on Mexican American families that were published about the same time the Moynihan report appeared (Heller, 1966; Madsen, 1964; Rubel, 1966) found the problems of Mexican American people to be the result of the patriarchal family structure.

SHORTCOMINGS OF THE CULTURAL APPROACH

The cultural argument is deeply flawed. First, and most important, the cultural argument reduces family life to a group's culture while viewing the family as the bedrock of society, rather than being shaped by social forces. Second, and closely related, it blames the victim and ignores the impact of racism and economic structure on family formation. Third, it treats all African American families and all Latino families as monolithic entities rather than acknowledging a wide range of family forms among people of color.

Since the 1960s and 1970s, scholars have roundly criticized social deficit approaches. By 2000, the family field had developed a greater sensitivity of families of color in research (Murray et al., 2001). A large body of family research has moved the family field away from cultural stereotypes about racial-ethnic families.

Structural Inequalities and Racial-Ethnic Families

Social conditions associated with racial inequalities produce aggregate differences between minority and White families. Different racial groups make their homes in neighborhoods that are typically segregated, thus living in "separate societies." An entire arsenal of social institutions creates paths in which families assigned to one group receive better jobs, housing, health care, schooling, and recreational facilities, while those relegated to other groups do worse or do without (Collins, 1997:397). Structural conditions such as segregation, employment discrimination, and poverty make it difficult for minorities to conform to the dominant society's family model.

As minorities make adaptations to structural inequalities, they often develop new forms of family organization and support. For example, extended kinship systems and informal support networks spread across multiple households have long been common among people of color, who spend much more time "helping people they know, especially their relatives" (Gerstel et al., 2002:200; Heard, 2007). Extended families and "fictive kin"—people treated like family even though they are not related by blood or marriage—are found in all racial-ethnic groups and among many immigrants whose family forms often differ from the nuclear family model of biological parents and children. New research on today's immigrants finds "complex households, and fluid residential patterns that compensate for limited economic opportunities" (Schwede et al., 2005). Kinship systems are what organize complex households in which immigrants live. Although these patterns are often thought to reflect ethnic culture, they are not shaped by culture alone. Instead, they are often the result of social inequalities. Extended family structure can be a way of sharing resources denied by the larger society. In saying that family structure is influenced by racial inequality, we should recognize the varied contexts within which different racial-ethnics experience their family lives. While race is important in structuring the immigrant experience, there are no "typical" immigrant families. Immigrants who are racialized, like other racial-ethnic families live in diverse social and economic settings that produce multiple family outcomes. Furthermore, many characteristics of racial-ethnic families *are* culturally unique, such as how their members relate, spend leisure time, and worship. In addition, forms of entertainment, language, and food customs are different from those of families in the dominant society. (See Box 5.4 "We Call Them Cousin Even If They Not Blood").

Nevertheless, racism produces many common characteristics associated with limited economic resources. In the past decade, the research emphasis was on how these conditions affect family structure, especially the shift to family types more vulnerable to poverty (McLoyd et al., 2001). Compared with Whites, people of color have higher rates of female-headed households (see Table 5.3), out-of-wedlock births, divorce, and other factors associated with a general lack of support for family life. In Chapter 3 we saw that minority families have long experienced the juggling of work and family roles for women, single parenthood, extended family relationships, and poverty—conditions that are now affecting more and more families throughout society (Hansen, 2005; Stack and Burton, 1994:42).

Economic hardship among people of color has tended to reinforce the stereotype of poor minority families. However, we must realize that not all people of color are poor. The tendency to view racial-ethnic families as a collection of the problems they face is misleading. Important class variations exist among African Americans and Latinos. By the end of the last century, many well-educated people of color had climbed into the middle class, with incomes, education, and lifestyles similar to those of their White counterparts. They had made considerable advances as professionals, managers, elected officials, and entrepreneurs. In 2007, about 40 percent of African American and Latino families had incomes of $50,000 or more (U.S. Bureau of the Census, 2007b). In becoming the first African American President of the United States, Barack Obama is countering dominant "race" narratives, including those about African American families. Historian John Hope Franklin noted that it was even more important historically and culturally "to have *that family* as first family than to have Obama as president" (Dellinger, 2009:3, emphasis added).

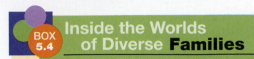

BOX 5.4 Inside the Worlds of Diverse **Families**

"We Call Them Cousin Even If We Not Blood": The Meanings of Family for African Refugee Youth

The immigration experience presents a variety of challenges for youth (Portes & Rumbaut, 1996). Some of these challenges include adjusting to changes in family and gender relations, learning a new language and culture, and constructing new identities within a racially, culturally, and linguistically dissonant "host" society. One of ways scholars investigate migration and adult and youth experiences is to examine family life. Refugee and immigrant families are not merely reactive, but active in developing strategies for coping with the demands of the new society, such as by developing and/or maintaining fictive kin relations. For refugee groups, the various effects of war, prolonged separation from family, loss of family members, and experiences in resettlement camps makes adjustment to life more challenging and can shape meanings of family and how family is defined.

As the definition and meaning of family is socially constructed through a configuration of social inequalities such as of race, ethnicity, class, gender, and nationality, this study explored how eight African (Liberia, Ivory Coast, and Sudan) refugee teenagers living in a midsized, urban community in Michigan define and give meaning to their families. The main question raised was: How do meanings of family shape African refugee youth identity? The data were derived from participant-produced photographs, group discussions, and face-to-face interviews. In the following sections, I document how my informants described the meanings of family through: (1) the value and quality of family ties, (2) the flexibility and inclusiveness of family membership, and (3) the influence of familial expectations.

The Value and Quality of Family Ties

The meaning of family is expressed as a source of belonging from which the teenagers derive a sense of self-love, self-worth, and support in a U.S. context, where they are sometimes reminded that they do not belong. Sibling relationships are particularly important. After Hanna described how close she is with her sisters (e.g., they are always together), Mari, Hanna's sister, explained how she and her sisters responded to the realities of American racism:

Mari: When someone pick on one of us like 'cause my neighbor, the kids are so rude so we show them, we teach them. I know this girl...everyday her dad call us African black monkeys so I was like so what are you. I wasn't thinking of any white good person 'cause I know a lot of white people who are really nice. I wasn't thinking that day

'cause I was sooo mad he called me like African black monkey. I always give respect to all the people and I just started insulting...I am soo pissed off right now... we beat the girl up twice. I beat her up Sunday and Samira [another sister] beat her up Monday.

Hanna: And I beat up, remember I beat her up, remember!

Mari: Yeah. Samira doesn't like talking, but when it comes to family yeah we're in, trust me.

When it comes to family, as Mari said, they are almost "forced" to identify with the family in a collective way in order to respond to U.S. racial discrimination. As previous research has shown, the way youth respond to racial discrimination has implications for the type of racial, ethnic, or cultural identities they form (Waters, 1999).

The "Flexible" Family Form

The informants described family as flexible—that is, close-knit networks of people who are bonded by more than just blood relations. Families are defined by a sense of affection, shared experience, mutual social support, and feelings of group belonging. These kinds of "family members" are also known as fictive kin members. Their identifications with a broad definition of family show their strong sense of inclusivity. That is, the teens include people into their family who were not part of their family when they lived in their countries of origin. Mari, who identified as both Liberian and Ivorian, defined flexible family membership as tied to the value of respect, a "very important cultural value in Liberian society" (Dunn-Marcos et al., 2005:30). She says,

> "...when we gonna respect like older person who is an adult...we call them auntie even if they're not your blood aunties you still call them aunties. Like we call them we call them cousin even if we not blood."

Flexible family relationships are tied to cultural and religious understandings of the family. A clear example of this is illustrated in the following quote:

> You know like Adam and Eve and how they're in the garden the one woman borne all these kids, so in Africa we think when you call them sister you feel close, you feel like your sister and it feels like family when they come over. And, like when somebody ask is this your sister, yeah this is my sister. It kind of feels like wow they go whoa you have a large family but actually they're not [blood related].

From these data, we can ascertain that the meaning of family is socially constructed and is an expression of Pan-African identity—that is, a framing of family relationships that is not unique to their particular country of origin, but to African descendant families.

The Content of Familial Expectations

Familial expectations are incorporated into youth's sense of who they are and who they define themselves to be in the future. The strong familial expectations for academic and career success fostered by close family ties were internalized by my informants. The agreed-upon expectations to embrace the "American Dream" protect them from sources of identity outside of the family, such as gangs. They are not completely rejecting mainstream U.S. middle class ideals, but they are also not shedding the influence of their home cultural orientations. This is an "adaptive identity style," as opposed to an "adversarial" or "ethnic flight" path of forming identities (Suárez-Orozco, 2001). As my informant Kaleb states,

> She [mother] expects us to take of care of each other and be respectful and do good in school. And tomorrow so you can be, so you can become somebody tomorrow, 'cause she doesn't want us to leave Africa and come over and mess around, get bad records and stay over here, we want to go back over there [Africa] and help people over there.

"Becoming somebody" is fundamentally a process of forming an identity in a social way, in which Kaleb expressed his responsibility to a larger social group with connections to Africa. With this, they are also expected to maintain certain aspects of their culture. Kirala explains,

> We eat African food a lot...We have to speak our language every time we around our grandma 'cause she want us to speak it...we have to respect your elders no matter what.

> Every time you see them you have to say hi even if they're far away *you have to say hi*, why because that you have to do it.

In summary, African refugee teenagers' identity formations unfold in ways that are inseparable from their shared meanings of family. This research adds to the growing literature of migration, family, and social identity because it shows that refugee teenagers' sense of identity does not have to be based *only* in racial, ethnic, or immigrant identifications. Their identity can also be grounded in other structures in which their shared meanings of family undergird who they are and what is family.

References

Dunn-Marcos, R., K. Kollehlon, B. Ngovo, E. Russ (eds.). *Liberians: An Introduction to Their History and Culture.* Culture Profile, 19: Washington, DC: Center for Applied Linguistics, 2005.

Portes, A., R. G. Rumbaut. *Immigrant America: A Portrait.* Berkeley, CA: University of California Press, 1996.

Suárez-Orozco, C. Psychocultural factors in the adaptation of immigrant youth: Gendered responses. In *Women, Gender, and Human Rights: A Global Perspective*, M Agosn (ed.). Picataway, NJ: Rutgers University, 2001.

Waters, M. C. *Black Identities: West Indian Immigrant Dreams and American Realities.* New York: Russell Sage Foundation, 1999.

Source: Gjokaj, Linda. Department of Sociology, Michigan State University, 2009. This essay was written expressly for *Diversity in Families*, 9th ed.

Table 5.3 Persons, by Household Type, Race, and Ethnicity: 2007

	Married Couple	Female Household	Male Household	NonFamily Household
Hispanic	59.5	20.9	10.3	9.3
Native Born	58.9	2.5	8.4	8.2
Foreign Born	60.5	15.4	13.1	11
White	66.5	10.8	4.7	18
Black	37.5	38.9	7.3	16.2
Asian	72.3	10	5.9	11.8
Other	54.4	25.1	7.7	12.7
All	61.9	16	6	16.1

Source: Pew Hispanic Center tabulations of 2000 Census and 2007 American Community Survey (3/5/09) Statistical Portrait of Hispanics in the United States, 2007. Pew Hispanic Center Retrieved July 14, 2009, Table 16: Persons by Household Type, Race and Ethnicity, 2007. http://pewhispanic.org/factsheets/factsheet.php?FactsheetID=46.

While some African American and Latino families have improved their life chances, others have been marginalized. There are great disparities in the income levels of White families and Black and Latino families, and the disparities have persisted over time. In 2007, the median income of White households was $53,714. Black median household income was $34,001 while Hispanic median household income was $40,766 (Bishaw and Semega, 2008). Family income differs greatly by family type as shown in Table 5.4.

Although the racial income gap is wide, the racial wealth gap is even wider. White families generally have a greater net worth than Black or Latino families. The net worth of Black households is just a fraction of what White families are worth. This wealth gap is the product of a long history of discrimination in the United States and is perpetuated by family inheritance patterns that pass accumulated advantages and disadvantages from one generation to the next (Collins et al., 2008:14). In their book *White Wealth/Black Wealth,* Melvin Oliver and Thomas Shapiro (1995) define wealth as the command over financial resources that a family has accumulated over its lifetime, along with those resources that have been inherited across generations. In general, White families have greater resources than Blacks for their children and bequeath them as assets at death. Oliver and Shapiro call this "the cost of being Black." One important indicator of a family's wealth is home ownership. Paying off a home mortgage is the way most Americans build net worth over their lifetimes. More minorities are buying homes, but because of discrimination in employment,

Table 5.4   **Median Income by Race and Family: 2007**

WHITE ALONE*	
Married couple families	$73,449
Wife in paid labor force	$87,194
Wife not in paid labor force	$47,772
Male household, no spouse present	$46,000
Female household, no spouse present	$32,850
BLACK ALONE*	
Married couple families	$62,163
Wife in paid labor force	$73,844
Wife not in paid labor force	$39,384
Male household, no spouse present	$35,083
Female household, no spouse present	$24,328
HISPANIC	
Married couple families	$48,144
Wife in paid labor force	$62,129
Wife not in paid labor force	$32,000
Male household, no spouse present	$38,786
Female household, no spouse present	$24,489

Source: U.S. Census Bureau, Current Population Survey, 2007 Annual Social and Economic Supplements, Historical Income Tables. Table F7: Type of Family (All Races) by Median and Mean Income. Detailed tables for each race can be accessed at: http://www.census.gov/hhes/www/income/histinc/incfamdet.html. Accessed on October 21, 2008.

housing, and insurance, they are still less likely than Whites to own the homes in which they live. While two-thirds of all U.S. households were homeowners in 2007, over half of racial minority households were renters (47 percent of Black households, 49 percent of Latino households, and 59 percent of other racial minorities) (U.S. Bureau of the Census, 2007). Rampant racial discrimination prevails in the housing market, even after 40 years of federal fair housing laws (Crowley, 2002:25). African American and Latino households are likely to be located in segregated neighborhoods, where median home values are lower.

African American and Latino families are three times as likely as White families to be poor (see Figure 5.2). In 2007, records show that 24 percent of African Americans and 20 percent of Hispanics were living below the poverty level, compared with 9 percent for Whites (Bishaw and Semega, 2008). Regardless of whether they are living in poverty, most African American and Hispanic families must get by on far less income than White families. Table 5.4 shows clearly that the average income for White families is greater than the average income for Black and Hispanic families. In addition, per-person income for Black and Hispanic families is lower than for White families because Black and Hispanic families have more children (De Vita, 1996:30; Pollard and O'Hare, 1999). This difference in household composition reflects the older age structure of White adults, delayed childbearing, and lower fertility among White couples (O'Hare, 1992:19).

These inequalities reveal that race inequality is in part a class issue, because class is linked to low income. But, many economic inequalities have more serious

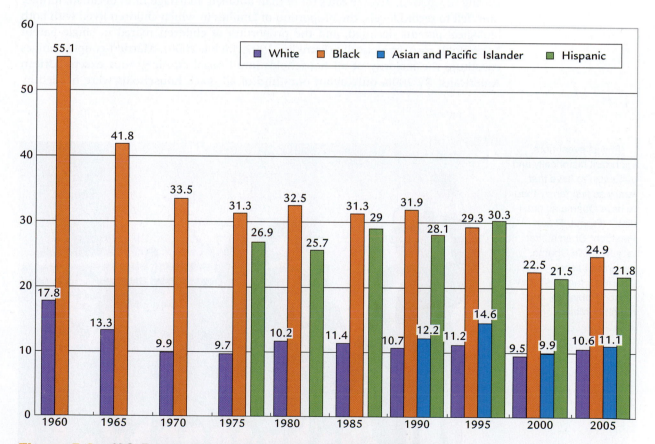

Figure 5.2 **U.S. Poverty Rates by Race and Ethnicity, 1960–2005**

Source: DeNavas-Walt, Carmen, Bernadette D. Proctor, and Jessica C. Smith, U.S. Census Bureau, *Current Population Reports* P60-235, Income, Poverty, and Health Insurance Coverage in the United States: 2007, U.S. Government Printing Office, Washington, DC, 2008, pp. 44–48.

consequences for people of color than for Whites. This shows that economic inequality is racialized. Race and low-class position combined reduce the life chances far more than does low-class position alone.

Let us examine some contemporary realities of African American and Latino families. Rather than using a dominant society family model as the norm, we will examine distinctive family characteristics as they relate to the racial organization of U.S. society.

African American Families in the New Century

The past four decades have brought profound changes in the family lives of Black Americans, including increases in nonmarital child bearing, female-headed households, and children living in poverty. Declines and delays in marriage, along with high divorce rates, have also contributed to distinctive family patterns among African Americans (Taylor, 2001:38). In the next sections, we focus on the connections between structural inequalities and family formation.

MARRIAGE

Although two-parent families were strong during and after slavery, sometime after 1925 the proportion of African American families headed by two parents began to decline, and this decline became more pronounced in the 1960s, 1970s, and 1980s. During this period, divorce rates more than doubled, marriage rates declined, fertility rates fell to record levels, the proportion of families in which children lived with both biological parents declined, and the proportion of children reared in single-parent households rose dramatically (Franklin, 1997; Taylor, 2000). Married-couple families constitute the majority of all households in all racial-ethnic groups except African Americans. By 2000, only about one-third of all Black households were headed by

...[I]t was even more important historically and culturally 'to have *that* family as first family than to have Obama as president.' (From L-R are President Obama, first lady Michelle Obama, daughter Sasha, Obamas's mother-in-law Marion Robinson, and daughter Malia.)

married couples (Lichter and Qain, 2004:15). A much higher percentage (82 percent) of White families were headed by married couples, although this percentage also has slipped over the past two decades (U.S. Bureau of the Census, 1999, 2006d).

African Americans tend to marry later and have higher rates of marital disruption than Whites. In 1980, research shows that 51 percent of persons 18 years and over were married. In 1998, only 41 percent were married. In 2007, only 28 percent of African American women were married and living with their husbands. Over the same period, the percentage of divorced Black persons 18 years and over grew from 8 to 12 percent, and the percentage who had never married grew from 30 to 43 percent (U.S. Bureau of the Census, 1999, 2005d, 2007b). A similar movement away from marriage occurred among White women as well. Still, the change was much more dramatic among Blacks (see Table 5.5).

The marriage gap between Whites and Blacks was just as strong among women without children as it was among women with children. Regardless of parental status, African American women are less likely than those in the general population to be married.

What has caused the movement away from marriage among African Americans? Research points to demographic and economic factors (McLoyd et al., 2001; Taylor, 2000; Tucker et al., 2004). Many social scientists focus on the gender ratio, or the balance of women and men in the Black population. African American women outnumber men in the age range (20–49) when most people marry and start families. Following this reasoning, fewer Black women are getting married because there are too few suitable Black male partners (that is, those with a good education and a job) (Spain and Bianchi, 1996:42). Various social forces undermine marriage among African Americans. African American men of marriageable age have been in short supply due to incarceration, lower levels of education than African American women, death, and unemployment—all symptoms of chronic institutional racism (Root, 2002:71). Structural conditions that produce high levels of men's unemployment, lack of job security, and low incomes make marriage difficult to form and sustain. These conditions produce high rates of female-headed households. Whether

Table 5.5 Martial Status, by Race and Ethnicity: 2007

	Now Married	Separated	Divorced	Widowed	Never Married
Hispanic	50.8	4.1	8.4	3.6	33.1
Native Born	41.6	3.5	10.5	3.7	40.8
Foreign Born	58.4	4.5	6.8	3.6	26.7
White	56.6	1.6	11.7	7.3	22.7
Black	32.8	4.9	12.4	6.9	42.9
Asian	62.5	1.4	5	4.9	26.2
Other	41.8	3	12.7	4.8	37.6
All	53.1	2.3	11.1	6.6	26.9

Source: Pew Hispanic Center tabulations of 2000 Census and 2007 American Community Survey (3/5/09) Statistical Portrait of Hispanics in the United States, 2007. Pew Hispanic Center Retrieved July 14, 2009, Table 15—Marital Status by Race & Ethnicity. http://pewhispanic.org/factsheets/factsheet.php?FactsheetID=46.

they are formed through divorce, separation, or out-of-wedlock childbearing, they are responsible for Black/White differences in marriage patterns.

Social science findings show that economic stressors produce distinctive marital patterns among African Americans. For example, sociologist Robin Jarrett has shown that economic factors play a prominent role in women's decisions to forgo marriage, to bear children outside of marriage, and in some cases to head households. Her interviews with never-married mothers uncovered a range of economic pressures that work against marriage. The prospective mates of Jarrett's informants were generally unemployed, underemployed, or relegated to insecure jobs, including car wash attendants, drug dealers, fast food clerks, grocery store stock and bag clerks, hustlers, informal car repairmen, lawn workers, street peddlers, and street salvage workers. Although most women remained unmarried, this did not preclude strong and stable male/female partnerships existing outside of legal marriage (Jarrett, 1994:40–41). Edin's more recent study of why poor mothers (both Black and White) do not marry found little stigma in remaining single. If marriage could not bring economic stability, poor women found little reason to marry, regardless of race (Edin, 2000a; Edin and Kefalas, 2005). Still, many researchers find that in African American communities, a father's absence from the household does not necessarily mean he is uninvolved in his children's lives. In all racial-ethnic groups, some "single-parent households actually have two very involved parents" (Coontz, 2008a:9).

Marital patterns among African Americans are related to class and race. It is not that African American people per se have different values regarding marriage and family (Furstenberg, 2004; Tucker et al., 2004). Research shows that racial differences in marital patterns are the result of economic differentials between the races. Billingsley's detailed analysis of the variation in Black family structures and social class experience indicates that the higher up in the social class structure families are, the more likely they are to be husband–wife families. They are also more likely to have employed wives to help sustain this status. Social class and family status are directly related (Billingsley, 1992:57).

Based on prevailing economic conditions, social scientists have proposed that marriage is less important than kinship ties for Blacks (Cherlin, 1992, 1999b).

> The Black family is not primarily based on a conjugal relationship or on a single household as in the case of the idealized American family. Rather, it consists of a wide-ranging group of relatives involved in relationships of exchange and co-parenting. (Aschenbrenner and Carr, 1980:463)

This arrangement can be viewed as a protective strategy against the uncertainties of marriage. Marriage involves economic as well as affective relationships. Greater economic support can be provided by a kinship exchange network than by a conjugal bond alone. If we see female-headed households within the context of the larger kinship system, we can appreciate how children and other dependents are cared for when other factors undercut marital unions. Marriage is as much the *result* as the cause of economic security and well-being. If a good job is a prerequisite for a good marriage, then we must understand that marriage itself is a form of class and race privilege.

Because widespread economic marginality threatens long-lasting marriages, African Americans are more tolerant of out-of-wedlock births and informal adoptions. Some scholars have argued that this is one way in which African Americans have managed a relatively high rate of nonmarital births without widespread use of abortions or access to formal adoption agencies sensitive to their needs (Hill, 1977).

SOCIAL SUPPORT NETWORKS

Extended family structure and social support networks among minorities have been consistent themes in social science literature for decades. Scholars have been debating about the extended family in Black communities and whether it is different from that of Whites. One side argues that Blacks have stronger family ties and more kin support that Whites. The other side of the debate argues that kin support has declined, especially in the inner city (Brewster and Padivac, 2006; Rochelle, 1997). Which side is correct? According to the latest research, the answer depends on the kinds of kinship support in question. Using national data, Natalia Sarkisian and Naomi Gerstel analyze extended family support among racial-ethnics and Whites. According to these researchers, their findings provide support for structural rather than cultural explanations of kinship patterns. While they find high levels of family involvement among Blacks and Latinos, they also find important differences in the *kinds* of extended family involvement used by racial-ethnics and Whites. In short, class differences between groups lead to high levels of kin involvement for racial-ethnics. Whites report greater involvement in financial and emotional kin support. Blacks are more likely to count on kin for *practical needs* including child care, household tasks, and rides. Lack of economic resources increases their need for help from kin and boosts their willingness to help in return. (Gerstel and Sarkisian, 2008:451; Sarkisian and Gerstel, 2004:812). Of course, such forms of kin support are only one feature of family organization. Research has consistently documented the fact that Blacks are more likely than Whites to reside in extended-family households (Hill, 1993; Taylor, 2000). Extended-family arrangements involve many forms of support and consist of both kin and nonkin spread over several households—networks of unrelated kin (fictive kin as well as persons in the same household and in separate households).

In a pathbreaking study of ghetto families conducted over three decades ago, Carol Stack revealed that extended-family arrangements are a way of coping with poverty and racism. She found that Black families pooled their limited resources in order to survive and that the urgency of their needs created alliances between individuals. According to Stack, "Kin and friends exchange and give and obligate one another. They trade food stamps, rent money, a TV, hats, dice, a car, a nickel here, a cigarette there, food, milk, grits, and children" (Stack, 1974:32).

While kin networks help compensate for resources withheld by the wider society, they also remain strong among middle-class African Americans. Harriette McAdoo (1978) found that socially mobile Blacks continue to draw on their families for more than financial aid; they depend on them for emotional support as well. Mary Pattillo-McCoy (1999) suggests that the precarious class status of middle-class African Americans ties them closely to their relatives. For African Americans of all social classes, the kin network is a survival strategy.

Current research stresses the role of women in the struggle to maintain family life. For example, caring for other people's children, whether kin or not, is an old tradition. "Othermothers" are women who assist blood mothers by sharing mothering responsibilities (Collins, 1990). According to Collins, othermothers are key in supporting children and in helping blood mothers. Men aren't necessarily absent from these families, but women are central in these resilient networks of grandmothers, sisters, aunts, and cousins that share responsibility for child care (Roy and Burton, 2008).

Similar arrangements are found among other racial ethnics. For example, an Indian "grandmother" may actually be a child's aunt or grandaunt in the Anglo-Saxon use of the term, and extended families may form around complex kinship networks based on conditions other than birth, marriage, or adoption (Yellowbird and Snipp, 2001:129). Asian Americans also have a high proportion of extended families. Therefore, a focus on parents and children alone misses the social and cultural resources that other relatives bring to Asian American families (McLoyd et al., 2001).

INNER CITY FAMILIES AND THE UNDERCLASS DEBATE

Changing household and family patterns have prompted many observers to proclaim a "crisis" in the African American family. Common thought blames a "disintegrating" Black family for the urban underclass. This cultural (and flawed) explanation has produced a national debate over the relationship between family structure and poverty among African Americans. When Bill Cosby recently castigated low-income Blacks for their behavioral deficits, the media revived the long-standing debate (Muwwakil, 2008).

Two distinct models of the underclass now prevail—one cultural, one structural. Both focus on issues of family structure and poverty (see Baca Zinn [1989], Marks [1991], and Jarrett [1994] for elaborations of cultural and structural models of the Black underclass). Cultural models assign the cause of the growing underclass to ghetto-specific behaviors and a lifestyle of out-of-wedlock childbearing. These theories argue that family breakdown and welfare dependence lock inner-city people into a cycle of poverty. This explanation is wrong on many counts. It relies too heavily on cultural preferences and behavioral traits to explain poverty. It falls back on blaming the victim to explain patterns that are rooted in social structure. It reverses cause and consequence: Single-parent families are not the cause of poverty but the *consequence of economic deprivation.* Structural changes in the U.S. economy (examined in Chapter 4) have removed jobs and other opportunities from inner-city residents. This is a better explanation of marriage patterns and family life. This explanation is detailed in William J. Wilson's compelling books, *The Truly Disadvantaged* (1987), *When Work Disappears* (1996), and *More Than Just Race* (2009). According to Wilson, the social problems of the ghetto are caused by economic marginalization. Wilson draws a connection between Black male unemployment, high divorce rates, non-remarriage rates, and the high proportion of children born to unmarried women.

Black men's declining employment has other consequences. Together with high levels of poverty and underemployment, joblessness contributes to the disproportionate number of Black males killed in wars and criminal homicide. This shortage of Black men with the ability to support a family causes many Black women to leave marriage or to forgo marriage altogether. Wilson shows that marriage is itself an opportunity structure that does not presently exist for large numbers of Black people.

The economic foundations of African American families are undermined by changes in the urban economy and the class structure of ghetto neighborhoods. The movement of middle-class African American professionals from the inner city has left behind a concentration of the most disadvantaged segments of the Black urban population. Ghetto residents are socially isolated from both mainstream behaviors and opportunity structures. These forces have led to more unemployment, fewer marriages, more female-headed households, and higher poverty rates among African Americans.

Many scholars agree with Wilson on the causes of family disruption among African Americans, but they argue that this captures only a portion of the problem. Inner-city women are also affected by the new economic realities. They, too, need training, employment, wage equity, and day care. The underclass is not a group of people lacking family values but a group of people who are outside the mainstream of the U.S. occupational structure (Kornblum, 1991:203). This analysis explains how structural changes affect family and household patterns. The reshaping of class, race, and gender systems leave African American women disproportionately separated, divorced, and solely responsible for their children.

When critics lament the state of African American families, they often call for policies that would restore the two-parent family. However, the two-parent family is not a guarantee against poverty for minorities). Although living in a married-couple family generally improves the chances of having high relative income, family structure alone is not responsible for child poverty. "If there were no single parents, Black children would still have much higher poverty rates" (McLanahan and Sandefur, 1994:85). More precisely, for African Americans, emulating the White family structure would close only about one-half of the income gap (Hacker, 1996:309). Raising the life chances of Black children requires changes in the economic status of their parents.

Single parenthood places many families at the social and economic margins of U.S. society. However, we should not use single mothers and their children as the "typical" African American family. This distorts the complex reality of African American families who have created diverse arrangements that depart from dominant forms of marriage, childbearing, and the ideal social organization of families (Hunter, 2006:90). Sociologist Andrew Billingsley argues in his book, *Climbing Jacob's Ladder* (1992), that no one pattern describes African American families. There are both weak families and strong families. Although the dynamics of race are changing in the twenty-first century, racial inequality continues to shape family patterns. But contrary to some strands of thought, Black families are not vanishing. Instead, they are doing what they always do:

> They are adapting as best they can to the pressures exerted upon them from their society in their gallant struggle to meet the physical, emotional, moral, and intellectual needs of their members. It is a struggle for existence, viability, and a sense of worth. (Billingsley, 1992:44)

Latino Families in the New Century

In Chapter 4 we examined the diversity among Latinos. In spite of important family differences among the groups, Latino families show some similarities. In all regions of the United States, Latinos are experiencing many of the transitions facing all U.S. families. Nevertheless, they remain distinctive. The influx of immigrants, together with class and racial inequalities, produce hardships not faced by mainstream families.

A HISPANIC UNDERCLASS?

As the Hispanic presence in the United States has increased in the last decade, poverty rates among Hispanics have remained high. Hispanic children are more likely than White children to be living below the poverty level. In 2007, 28 percent of Hispanic children under 18 were living in poverty, compared to 14 percent of White children.

Among Hispanic groups, Mexicans and Puerto Ricans have the highest poverty rates (22 percent for Mexicans and 24 percent for Puerto Ricans, compared with 13 percent for Cubans). Do high poverty rates and changing household patterns among Latinos mean that they have joined inner-city African Americans to form part of the underclass? In other words, do changes in the economy and jobs have the same effects on Blacks and Latinos? Certainly, the broad changes wrought by economic transformations have affected Latinos. Puerto Ricans have been especially hard hit by economic restructuring over the past three decades. For families of Mexican origin, the conditions that place them in poverty are different. A large proportion of Mexican-heritage families have members in the workforce. The problem is that they are in low-wage jobs and do not earn enough to bring them above the poverty line (Aponte, 2006).

Different economic contexts shape Latino families in different ways. The causes of poverty across Latino communities differ. And different community and family patterns produce a range of responses to poverty. Therefore, the underclass model does not apply evenly to the many diverse Latino barrios across the country. Even in the poorest Latino communities, poverty differs in fundamental ways from the conventional underclass portrait (Moore and Pinderhughes, 1993). For example, Mexicans (both U.S. born and immigrants) have high rates of marriage despite their impoverished circumstances, a pattern called "the paradox of Mexican American nuptuality" (Oropesa et al., 1994). Family structure in Latino barrios is different from African American family patterns in the inner city. In the next section, we focus on Chicanos (Mexican-origin Latinos).

EXTENDED KINSHIP SYSTEMS

Latinos are commonly portrayed as a family-centered group. **Familism**—an obligation and orientation to the family—is depicted as a defining feature of the Mexican-heritage population. Presumably, family relations are more important for Mexicans than for Anglos. This pertains to both the nuclear family and a wider circle of kin—the extended family, which includes aunts, uncles, grandparents, cousins, in-laws, and even *compadres* or co-parents (Alvirez and Bean, 1976:277).

Familism contains four key components. The first component, *demographic familism*, involves characteristics of Chicano families, such as family size. The second component, *structural familism*, measures the incidence of multigenerational households (or extended households). *Normative familism*, the third component, taps the value Mexican-heritage people place on family unity and solidarity. Fourth, *behavioral familism* has to do with the level of interaction between family and kin networks (Ramirez and Arce, 1981).

Compadrazgo is another feature of familism among Chicanos and Mexicans. It encompasses two sets of relationships with "fictive kin": (1) *padrinos y ahijados* (godparents and children) and (2) parents and godparents who become *compadres*, or co-parents. The *compadrazgo* system of godparents enlarges family ties by creating connections between families (see the discussion of *compadrazgo* in Chapter 3).

Familism is a defining feature of Mexican-heritage people. Four generations of women make tamales.

Common thought assumes that extended family ties among the Mexican origin population are stronger than those of all other groups. In fact, studies of extended family groupings are not conclusive. (The following discussion is based on Baca Zinn and Wells, 2000.) Economic changes and the resulting dislocations of Latinos have raised questions about extended family relationships in today's world. Ann Rochelle (1997) analyzed a national sample of minority families and found that extended kinship networks are declining among Chicanos (as well as among Puerto Ricans and Blacks). On the other hand, a large body of past and present research documents long-standing participation in kinship networks. Studies spanning the last three decades have found kinship networks to be important. They operate as a system of cultural, emotional, and mental support (Keefe, 1984; Mindel, 1980; Ramirez, 1980), as well as a survival strategy to maximize resources (Angel and Tienda, 1982; Glick, 1999; Goreman, 2005; Lamphere et al., 1993; Saenz, 2004; Uttal, 1999). Familism among Mexican-heritage adults has been associated with high levels of education and income (Griffith and Villavicienco, 1985) and among adolescents has been viewed as a form of social capital linked with academic success (Valenzuela and Dornbusch, 1994).

Kinship networks are also used in the migration of Mexicans to the United States (Chavez, 1992; Hondagneu-Sotelo, 1994; Portes and Beck, 1985; Wells, 1976). As we saw in Chapter 4, Mexican immigrants use kin to find jobs and housing and to be a buffer against the upheavals associated with migration. This is profoundly important. In contrast to the common view that extended families are mainly a cultural preference, this research helps us understand that among immigrants, family extension is a long-standing adaptation to social and economic marginality. Transnational families and their networks of kin are stretched across space, time, and national borders. This family form is a way of dealing with the challenges of immigration.

Kinship networks among Mexican-origin people are not uniform. There are differences in the kinship groupings of immigrants and nonimmigrants and among different generations. Even though immigrants use kin for assistance, they have smaller social networks available than second-generation immigrants, who have broader social networks available consisting of multigenerational kin (Vega, 1990). Regardless of class, studies have shown that Mexican extended families in the United States become more extensive and strong through successive generations and socio-economic mobility (Velez-Ibanez, 1996:144). Although a cultural perspective would predict that familism fades in succeeding generations, Velez-Ibanez's study (discussed earlier as a refutation of the underclass) finds highly elaborated second- and third-generation extended-family networks actively maintained through frequent visiting, ritual celebrations, and the exchange of goods and services (Velez-Ibanez, 1996).

Are the kinship ties of Latinos in general stronger than those of Anglos? Sarkisian, Gerena, and Gerstel (2007) used data from a national survey to answer this question. Their study found that Latinos are more likely to live with and near kin and to have more face-to-face interactions with them than Anglos. However, they are less likely to give financial assistance and emotional support and more likely to give practical help.

More Racial-Ethnic Diversity in Families: Asians, Native Americans, and Middle Easterners

The family experiences of other groups reinforce a theme of this section—that family arrangements must be seen in the race and class contexts in which they are embedded.

Asian Americans, for example, are commonly seen as the "model minority"—a strong, well-educated, and upwardly mobile group. But this view ignores both the history of discrimination against Asians and the wide differences among different Asian-origin populations (see Chapter 4). The experiences of different Asian immigrant groups (such as Cambodians and Vietnamese) are different from those of other Asian immigrant groups (such as Chinese and Japanese), who have large third-generation populations (Lichter and Qian, 2004:10). Kinship networks are important for all Asian groups, yet experiences related to immigration produce family diversity among Asian-origin families. Recently arrived immigrants who settle in areas with no ethnic enclaves often find it difficult to find jobs and establish family lives (Ishii-Kuntz, 2004).

Native Americans have tremendously diverse family arrangements, representing over 300 tribal or language groups with variability in histories and practices (Walls et al., 2007). In the early nineteenth century, U.S. government policies imposed Western family forms on Indians whose families ranged from simple monogamy to various forms of multiple marriage. But all of them relied on extended family networks for survival and social organization (Coontz, 1999b:xiii). Although good studies of native American families are rare, recent research identifies several unifying pan-Indian principles for modern Indian families. Among these are extended family networks and traditions of respect for elders. Elders, whether biologically related or created kin, are important for children's care and upbringing, contributing to Indian family cohesiveness and stability (Kawamoto and Cheshire, 2004:388; Tongue, 2005).

Middle Easterners have been arriving in the United States since the 1970s, coming from countries such as Syria, Lebanon, Egypt, and Iran. Their ethnic and religious diversity, different levels of education, and places of settlement in the United States make it impossible to generalize about their family arrangements. Even Muslim families are not all the same. The terms "Arab family," "Islamic family," and "Middle Eastern family" each have distinctive meanings and should not be used interchangeably to describe a monolithic family form with static gender roles. Middle Eastern families (both in the United States and abroad) can no longer be viewed in opposition to a mythical U.S. family norm. They face similar globalizing challenges, constraints, and opportunities as other families with respect to matters of gender, marriage, and parenting (Sherif-Trask, 2004:402).

Human Agency and Family Formation

People of color use their families in adapting to their circumstances. Family arrangements have been vital in ensuring survival, and they have also served as a means of resisting social domination (Caulfield, 1974; Cohen and MacCartney, 2004). The concept of **family strategies** (or household strategies) helps us think about some of the ways in which people use their families to cope with the problems in their lives. Instead of responding passively to the outside world, family members can take actions and engage in certain behaviors, including labor force participation, migration, coresidence, marriage, childbearing, food allocation, and education, in order to adapt to changes in the wider society (Wolfe, 1992:12–13). Strategies often differ for women and men. Strategies also change as people use their social locations to shape their family lives.

Strategies are always contingent on conditions in the immediate environment. Different kinds of constraints determine what actions people can take in their own interests. Although racial-ethnic families have adaptive capabilities, they are often restrained by oppression that is systematic and institutionalized. Therefore, family strategies cannot completely solve the problems at hand. Some adaptations can exact a price in family well-being. If individuals and families are able to survive because of unconventional family structures, they also pay enormous costs. For example, **household augmentation** among minorities is a common economic family strategy. But when African Americans, Hispanics, or Asian Americans are forced to double up in households, there may be fewer resources to go around, even though the intent is to add earnings. Ronald Angel and Marta Tienda have studied Black, Hispanic, and White households in which multiple earners had been added. They wanted to know whether additional workers helped buffer the effects of job discrimination. They found that household extension did alleviate some of the harsher aspects of poverty, but it did not lift minority families out of poverty. This means that the extent of income inequality between minority and nonminority groups would be even greater without alternative strategies to compensate for the inadequate earnings of household members (Angel and Tienda, 1982:1377). Many of the family adaptations associated with immigration, including binational families and their networks of kin are age-old "strategies for mustering social resources" (Chavez, 1992:135).

In addition to adapting their household structures, racial-ethnic women and men often use their families politically, as major sources of support in struggling with poverty and other forms of race and class oppression. For example, African American women, Latinas, Native American women, and Asian American women have a long tradition of extending their mothering roles to the realm of political resistance. For example, many Native American mothers weave tribal traditions with a "motherist stance" in fighting together for the survival of their children (Udel, 2001). Nancy Naples (1992) found African Americans and Latinas engaged in different kinds of *activist mothering* for the benefit of the entire community. And in the Chicano movement of the 1960s, the Chicano/Mexicano family was the basis of group solidarity. In *political familism,* the emphasis on family ties was not only symbolic, but also an organizational means of involving entire families in activist work (Baca Zinn, 1975). Families can operate as oppositional enclaves (Roberts, 2009), capable of changing racial structures and even the course of history.

Gender

Gender, like race and class, is a way of organizing social life. Gender inequality is built into the larger world we inhabit. From the macro level of the global economy, through the institutions of society, to interpersonal relations, gender is the basis for dividing labor, assigning roles, and allocating social rewards. Until recently, this kind of gender differentiation seemed natural. However, new research shows that gender is not natural at all. Instead, "women" and "men" are social creations. To emphasize this point, sociologists distinguish between sex and gender. *Sex* refers to the biological differences between females and males. **Gender** refers to the social and cultural meanings attached to women and men.

Gender is not only about women. Men often think of themselves as "genderless," as if gender did not matter in the daily experiences of their lives. Yet, from birth thorough old age, men's family lives are deeply gendered (Kimmell and Messner, 2007).

In the big picture, gender divisions make women and men unequal. Still, we cannot understand the gender system by looking at gender alone. Gender is linked with other characteristics such as class, race, and sexual orientation. These overlapping inequalities produce different gender experiences for women and men of different races and classes. Nevertheless, the gender system ranks women and men differently, and it denies both women *and* men the full range of human and social possibilities. The social inequalities created by gender influence family life in profound ways. In fact, "gender relations and family are so intertwined, it is impossible to pay attention to one, without paying attention to the other" (Coltrane, 1998:1).

Like class and race, there are two main ways to think about gender and family. The first, a **gender roles approach,** treats gender differences as roles learned by individuals. The second approach, a structural or **gendered institutions approach** (Acker, 1992), emphasizes factors that are external to individuals, such as the social structure and social institutions that reward women and men differently. These approaches differ in how they view women and men, in how they explain inequality, and in the solutions they suggest for change. The main difference between the two approaches lies in whether the individual or society is the primary unit of analysis.

The Traditional Gender Roles Approach

Until very recently, most family scholars assumed that the modern nuclear family was the basis of social order in a modern society. According to this view, industrialization made the various components of society more specialized, and it also separated women and men into distinctive roles. Men fill the "instrumental" or breadwinning roles outside the family, while women fill the "expressive" or domestic roles inside the family. Separate gender roles were seen as the building blocks of stable families.

This model of the family was developed by Talcott Parsons and called "structural functionalism." It was the dominant family framework in the 1950s and 1960s. It was based on a family form that was more statistically prevalent in the 1950s than today, but it was not the only family form even then. Today, many of Parsons's assumptions about family life are found in conventional thought and in some strands of family social science (Mann et al., 1997; Smith, 1993).

Shortcomings of the Gender Roles Approach

Throughout the 1970s and 1980s, functionalist theory came into question. Real-world changes in gender and family challenged the old framework. Many scholars argued that this model ignored class and race differences in families even though they were at the core of family life. The gender roles approach made it seem that role division between the sexes was needed for families to operate efficiently. Instead, the critics of this approach charged that role division was not functional at all, but was based on stereotypes of men and women (Andersen, 2009).

The gender roles approach ignores what is most important about roles—that they are unequal in power, resources, and opportunities. When terms such as "sex roles," the "female role," and the "male role" are used in an uncritical manner, male dominance can be easily overlooked (Thorne, 1982:8). Furthermore, ideas about role division in the nuclear family ignore inequality and conflict.

The gender roles approach assumes that the family is defined by its emotional quality. Families are portrayed as havens of intimacy and love. Husband–wife relations are thought to be simply matters of love and agreement. But whether husbands and wives love one another or not, their relations develop within the larger system of male dominance. What is thought to be a private relationship of love is also a social relationship of power. Husband–wife relationships are *political*. Recent research has given us a more complex picture of husband–wife relations. Families are not always havens and may often be settings of conflict. Love between the sexes is complicated by an unequal balance of power.

The Family as a Gendered Institution

Today, sociologists focus on how gender is embedded in the institutions of society. Everywhere we look—the global economy, politics, religion, education, and family life—men are in power. The term *gendered institutions* means that gender is the basis for structuring the relationships between women and men and giving them different positions of advantage and disadvantage in the various sectors of social life (Andersen and Collins, 2010b:77).

Families throughout society are closely bound up with a broad system of gender inequality. In addition, the family is an important foundation of the gender system. Together with other social institutions, the family does the work of creating two dichotomous genders from biological sex. Understanding the institutional basis of gender does not mean that we should ignore interpersonal relationships. Unequal relationships between women and men are built into social processes at all levels of social interaction (McGraw and Walker, 2004:178). How women and men interact, and what they *do* every day in families, is essential in reproducing gender. When we look carefully at everyday family activities, we see how deeply gendered family worlds can be. Few areas of family life are untouched by gender—family tasks, work and leisure, care giving, conflicts and episodes of violence, and decisions about employment and moving are all gendered. Even mundane decisions such as what to watch on television are gendered. Women, men, and children experience the family in gendered ways that vary by class and race.

Patriarchy is the term used for forms of social organization in which men are dominant over women. Patriarchy is interpersonal and structural, private and public; therefore, we distinguish between private patriarchy and public patriarchy. The concept of **private patriarchy** refers to male dominance in the interpersonal relations between women and men; the concept of **public patriarchy** encompasses dominance in the institutions of the larger society.

Patriarchy is connected with other structural forces. For example, its development in the United States is closely tied to capitalism. The United States can be defined as a **capitalist patriarchy.** Capitalism and patriarchy are interrelated in complex ways. They should be analyzed together if we are to understand the position of women (Acker, 1980). Women and men do different work, both in the labor force and in the family, and they have different resources in both of these settings. Men have greater control in both public and private arenas. Their economic obligations in the public sphere ensure that they have control of highly valued resources that give rise to male privileges. Male privilege refers to those advantages, prerogatives, and benefits that systematically uplift men and are denied to women.

Structured gender inequality works with other inequalities such as race, class, and sexuality to sort women and men differently. These inequalities also work together to produce differences *among women* and differences *among men.* Some women are subordinated by patriarchy, yet race and class intersect to create for them privileged opportunities and ways of living (Baca Zinn et al., 2004).

Men are encouraged to behave in a "masculine" fashion to prove they are not gay (Connell, 1992). In defining masculinity as the negation of homosexuality, *compulsory heterosexuality* is an important component of the gender system. Compulsory heterosexuality imposes negative sanctions on those who are homosexual or bisexual. This system of sexuality shapes the gender order by discouraging attachment with members of the same sex. This enforces the dichotomy of "opposite" sexes. *Sexuality* is also a form of inequality in its own right because it systematically grants privileges to those in heterosexual relationships. Like race, class, and gender, sexual identities are socially constructed categories. Sexuality is a way of organizing the social world based on sexual identity and a key linking process in the matrix of domination structured along the lines of race, class, and gender (Messner, 1996:223).

Historic shifts in social forces continue to increase women's labor force participation and change many gender norms. Although there is considerable variation in how different groups of women and different groups of men are placed in society, *men in general* gain privileges at the expense of women. And despite the historical shifts in social forces that have increased women's labor force participation and changed many gender norms, women remain largely in charge of the home—responsible for the unpaid and undervalued work of maintaining family relationships. Both men and women participate in unpaid family work, but women do more regardless of age, race, ethnicity, or marital status (McGraw and Walker, 2004:174). Much of the work that women do in the home remains invisible. Yet recent research has found that women's invisible work sustains family life. For example, not only do women do most household labor, they also do the *planning* needed for household management. They keep a mental account of what needs to be done and they organize and orchestrate the schedules of family members (Amato et al., 2007; Bianchi et al., 2006; DeVault, 1991). Although such work is necessary, it is low in prestige. Apportioning household labor and child rearing (reproductive labor) to women upholds male privilege by freeing men from such responsibilities. Individual males—adults, adolescents, and children—gain leisure time and the opportunity to pursue their own careers or boyhood interests. If wives, mothers, and sisters tend to existence-related needs, such as cooking, cleaning, and taking care of clothing, men gain time at women's expense. (In Chapter 6, we give further attention to household labor.)

The domestic division of labor, in turn, can limit women's occupational activities. Women burdened with domestic duties have less time and energy left over to devote to careers. The gendered division of family labor reinforces the division of labor in the workforce and upholds men's superiority. The interlocking systems of capitalism and patriarchy create a cycle of domination and subordination.

Looking at family activities in terms of power and domination challenges the very concept of "the family" as a unit. Many scholars argue that the image of the unified family is erroneous. As Heidi Hartmann says, the family is a "locus of struggle":

> In my view, the family cannot be understood solely or even primarily as a unit shaped by affect or kinship, but must be seen as a location where production and redistribution take place. As such, it is a location where people with different activities and interests in these processes often come into conflict with one another. (Hartmann, 1981:368)

Hartmann does not deny that families also encompass strong emotional ties, but she concentrates on the ways in which unequal division of labor inside and outside the family generates tension, conflict, and change.

AGENCY WITHIN CONSTRAINT

Although women are subordinate, they are not passive victims of patriarchy. Like other oppressed groups, they find ways to resist domination. Women's resistance takes different forms. It can be subtle or passive. It can also be active defiance of patriarchal constraints. Within patriarchal settings like the family, women negotiate, strategize, and bargain to get what they can in return for their domestic services and subordination. Deniz Kandiyoti (1988) calls these exchanges "patriarchal bargains." Although such bargains do not eradicate women's inequality, they often pave the way for various forms of resistance and control in family matters. In the chapters that follow, we take a closer look at the gendered family and how it varies by class and race.

Chapter Review

1. Class, race, and gender are socially constructed categories that create varied environments for family life.

2. Macrostructural forces press in on families. They determine the resources people in different social locations have available for family life. At the same time, family members themselves are active participants in creating family life.

3. Households are material sites with different ways of acquiring the necessities of life. This creates diverse family arrangements.

4. Two models of social class have different implications for understanding families: (a) conventional explanations of class differences place families into social classes according to occupation and shared lifestyles; (b) structural explanations of class differences focus on society's opportunity structures, which produce advantages for some families and disadvantages for others.

5. According to the culture-of-poverty view, poor families have certain characteristics that set them apart from the rest of society.

6. Contrasting explanations of racial inequality have different implications for understanding families: (a) cultural approaches blame racial-ethnic families for their fate; and (b) structural approaches focus on the socioeconomic system, which creates different contexts for family living.

7. No matter what their structure, White families fare better economically than their minority counterparts.

8. Family structure is a crucial determinant of well-being, because the potential for having two earners in the household increases the likelihood of achieving higher income levels.

9. Inner-city male joblessness has encouraged nonmarital childbearing and undermined the economic foundation of the African American family. This explanation applies more to family changes among African Americans than among Latinos, who require a different model to understand poverty and family issues in each group.

10. Racial-ethnic families in the United States have some important commonalties, including (a) extended kinship networks and multiple households spread across several generations and (b) high rates of female-headed households, out-of-wedlock births, and other factors associated with family disruption.

11. Two views of gender influence our understanding of families: (a) In the first view, gender inequality is a consequence of behavior learned by individual women and men. (b) In the second view, gender is an institutional force closely intertwined with other forms of inequality. In this view, patriarchy shapes families along with other social institutions.

12. Women of all classes and races are subject to patriarchal control, but they experience that control differently.

13. Families are not always cohesive units. Instead, they are settings of power where gendered family roles often produce conflict.

Key Terms

capitalist patriarchy 175	**familism** 170
class privileges 144	**family strategies** 172
culture of poverty 141	**gender** 173
ethnicity 156	**gendered institutions approach** 174

Related Websites

http://psidonline.isr.umich.edu

Panel Study of Income Dynamics. The PSID is a nationally representative longitudinal study of nearly 9,000 families. Following the same families and individuals since 1968, the PSID collects data on economic, health, and social behavior.

http://www.irp.wisc.edu

Institute for Research on Poverty. The IRP is a center for interdisciplinary research into the causes and consequences of poverty and social inequality in the United States. It is based at the University of Wisconsin–Madison. As one of three Area Poverty Research Centers sponsored by the U.S. Department of Health and Human Services, it has a particular interest in poverty and family welfare in the Midwest.

http://www.iwpr.org/index.cfm

Institute for Women's Policy Research. The IWPR conducts rigorous research and disseminates its findings to address the needs of women, promote public dialogue, and strengthen families, communities, and societies. It focuses on issues of poverty and welfare, employment and earnings, work and family issues, health and safety, and women's civic and political participation.

http://www.jcpr.org

Joint Center for Poverty Research. The Northwestern University/University of Chicago JCPR supports academic research that examines what it means to be poor and live in the United States. JCPR concentrates on the causes and consequences of poverty in the United States and the effectiveness of policies aimed at reducing poverty in an effort to advance what is known about the economic, social, and behavioral factors that cause poverty and to establish the actual effects of interventions designed to alleviate poverty.

http://www.legalmomentum.org

Legal Momentum. Founded in 1970 as NOW Legal Defense and Education Fund, Legal Momentum is the nation's oldest legal advocacy organization dedicated to advancing the rights of women and girls. Legal momentum is a leader in establishing litigation and public policy to secure equality and justice for women.

http://pewhispanic.org

Pew Hispanic Center. Founded in 2001, the PHC is a nonpartisan research organization that seeks to improve understanding of the U.S. Hispanic population and to chronicle Latinos' growing impact on the nation. The PHC does not take positions on policy issues. It is a project of the Pew Research Center, a nonpartisan "fact tank" in Washington DC that provides information on the issues, attitudes, and trends shaping America and the world. It is funded by the Pew Charitable Trust, a public charity based in Philadelphia.

http://www.wedo.org

Women's Environment Development Organization. WEDO's mission is to achieve economic, social, and gender justice; a healthy, peaceful planet; and human rights for all. Through its programs on Economic and Social Justice, Gender, and Governance, and Sustainable Development, WEDO emphasizes women's critical role in social, economic, and political spheres.

http://www.aclu.org

American Civil Liberties Union. ACLU works daily in courts, legislatures, and communities to defend and preserve the individual rights and liberties that the Constitution and laws of the United States guarantee everyone. The ACLU also works to extend rights to segments of the population that have traditionally been denied their rights, including people of color; women; lesbians, gay men, bisexuals, and transgender people; prisoners; and people with disabilities.

http://www.nccp.org

National Center for Children in Poverty. The NCCP is the nation's leading public policy center dedicated to promoting the economic security, health, and well-being of low-income U.S. families and children. NCCP uses research to inform policy and practice with the goal of ensuring positive outcomes for the next generation. NCCP promotes family-oriented solutions at state and national levels.

http://www.naacp.org

National Association for the Advancement of Colored People. The NAACP was founded in 1909. Its primary mission continues to be to ensure the political, educational, social, and economic equality of rights of all persons and to eliminate racial hatred and racial discrimination.

http://www.census.gov/pubinfo/www/hotlinks .html

Minority Links for Media. This website is provided by the U.S. Census Bureau and offers links to the latest data on racial and ethnic populations in the United States.

http://www.hsph.harvard.edu/grhf/WoC

Women of Color Web. This site is dedicated to providing access to writings by and about women of color in the United States. It focuses specifically on issues related to feminism, sexualities, and reproductive health and rights. The site also provides links to organizations, discussion lists, and academic tools concerned specifically with women of color.

http://www.coloredgirls.org

Women of Color Resource Center. Founded in 1990, WCRC is headquartered in the San Francisco Bay Area and promotes the political, economic, social, and cultural well-being of women and girls of color in the United States. Informed by a social justice perspective that takes into account the status of women internationally, WCRC is committed to organizing and educating women of color across lines of race, ethnicity, religion, nationality, class, sexual orientation, physical ability, and age.

http://www.nclr.org

National Council of La Raza. Founded in 1968, NCLR is the nation's largest national Hispanic civil rights and advocacy organization in the United States and works to improve opportunities for Hispanic Americans. To achieve its mission, NCLR conducts applied research policy analysis and advocacy, providing a Latino perspective in five key areas—assets/investments, civil rights/immigration, education, employment/ economic status, and health.

http://inequality.org

Inequality.org. Inequality.org is a nonprofit organization made up of journalists, writers, and researchers whose aim is to provide data and essays on various aspects of inequality in the United States.

http://www.inequality.cornell.edu

Center for the Study of Inequality. CSI fosters basic and applied research on social and economic inequalities, as well as the process by which such inequalities change and persist. The focus of CSI is on developing theory-based and empirically-tested models of inequality that assist not only in understanding ongoing changes in inequality, but also in evaluating public policy and social interventions.

chapter **6**

Meshing the Worlds of Work and Family

▶ Myths and Realities

Myth	In the past three decades, women have poured into the labor force due to their desire for liberation.
Reality	Economic necessity is the primary reason most women have gone to work. Changing values are important, yet most women have jobs in order to support their families.
Myth	Many women have grown so tired of juggling jobs and families that they are returning to domesticity and starting a new homemaking trend.
Reality	Although newspapers and magazines periodically feature stories about the rush back to homemaking, there is no sharp decline in women's labor force participation.
Myth	The division of household labor in U.S. families is nearly equal now, especially in families where husbands and wives have paid jobs.
Reality	While fathers are spending more time taking care of children, working couples still feature a gender gap. Women spend twice as much time on household work as their husbands.
Myth	The rise of dual-earner families has drastically reduced parent-child interaction.
Reality	Today's parents actually spend more time reading, playing, and talking with their children than parents did 25 years ago (Bianchi et al., 2006).
Myth	Now that more mothers are in the workforce, children are taking on a greater share of housework for the collective well-being of the family.
Reality	Children are withdrawing from domestic responsibilities, increasing rather than lightening the burdens on their parents.
Myth	The turn-of-the-century workplace is finally supporting workers' family responsibilities. Soon most workers will be able to take advantage of a wide array of family-supportive programs.
Reality	The family-friendly workplace is more talk than action, with only a small percentage of the workforce currently using flexible work programs.

Macro-level social changes are producing major upheavals in family life. In Chapters 4 and 5 we saw how systems of inequality and other social transformations produce a wide range of family structures: one-parent families, cohabiting couples (both gay and straight) with children, co-provider families, multigenerational families, and transnational families. A great deal of family diversification is related to changes in the workplace. The struggle to integrate work and family is creating deep changes in the day-to-day operation of families.

Juggling work and family is a central concern for most adults. Although there is no typical family form, wives are now more likely than not to be employed. Less than 10 percent of U.S. families are breadwinner-and-homemaker families. A growing portion of families have women as heads of households and sole wage earners. The dramatic rise in women's employment has both positive and negative consequences. Most families are faced with conflicting demands of work and home.

In previous chapters we reviewed the myth of separate worlds, or the belief that work and family are detached. This myth ignores the profound effect the type of job and the level of workers' earnings have on each family member and on the family as a unit.

New research on work and family has sharpened our understanding of how these institutions are interrelated. In the 1990s, work–family linkages became stronger and more important to study than ever before. The study of work and family became a major subfield within sociology. New economic patterns recast the family field in terms of the explicit interdependence of work and family (Dubeck, 1998:4; Gerstel et al., 2002). We have discovered that these two spheres were never as separate from each other as was believed. Furthermore, the concept of work no longer refers only to paid employment outside the home. It also encompasses the variety of reproductive or caring labor that family members do for which they receive no reimbursement—housework, child care, kin care, the nurturing of interpersonal relationships, and activities in the larger community (Baber and Allen, 1992:176). Today, family researchers pay close attention to how women and men manage both paid labor and unpaid labor.

This chapter is divided into several sections. We begin with the macrostructural context to examine the social, economic, and demographic transformations that are changing the work patterns of women, men, and teens in different classes and races. We turn, then, to macro and micro connections between the workplace and families by looking at different kinds of linkages and interactions and how they shape family dynamics. Next we review various forms of family labor that have, until recently, been invisible. Finally, we turn to coping efforts and strategies that family members and some companies have adopted to manage work and family.

The Changing Work Patterns of Women, Men, and Teens

We cannot understand today's families in isolation from changes in the U.S. economy. New employment trends show how larger social and economic conditions are revolutionizing family worlds.

Women's Employment

The increased participation of U.S. women in market work is a story that has been unfolding since the early nineteenth century. In the past six decades, the increase accelerated. In 1940, less than 20 percent of the female population age 16 and older was in the labor force. By 2009, the figure had risen to 60 percent, compared to 72 percent of men (U.S. Department of Labor, 2009a). This means that women now make up 47 percent of the workforce. Although women of all age groups are likely to be employed, women of childbearing age have especially high rates of labor force participation. In 1980, for the first time in the twentieth century, married women's place was no longer typically in the home. In that year, the number of married women working for pay outside the home exceeded the number of married women who were full-time homemakers. Now more than two out of three married women ages 25 to 64 are in the workforce.

Women's labor force participation has grown at a faster pace than men's in recent decades. Between 1970 and the early 1990s, women's numbers in the labor

Table 6.1   Labor Force Participation Rates for Women, by Race, Selected
Years and Projected 2016

Year	Black	White	Hispanic	Asian
1975	48.8	45.9	n.a.	n.a.
1986	56.9	55.4	50.1	57.0
1996	60.4	59.8	53.4	58.8
2006	61.5	59.3	56.1	57.6
2016	63.1	58.8	57.8	58.7

Source: "Employment Projections," U.S. Department of Labor, 2007, Table 3. Online: http://www.bls.gov/emp/emplab05.htm.

force increased twice as fast as those of men. At present, women's rate of labor force participation is holding steady, while men's is declining slightly. Today, as in the past, the proportions of employed women and men vary by race. African American women have a long history of high workforce participation rates, and those rates increased only modestly after World War II. Much greater rates of increase have occurred among White, Asian, and Latina women. In 2006, 62 percent of African American women, 59 percent of White women, 58 percent of Asian women, and 56 percent of Latinas were in the labor force (U.S. Department of Labor, 2007). (See Table 6.1.)

Women's representation in the labor force now approaches that of men. Figure 6.1 shows the convergence of women's and men's rates of labor force participation. It is accurate to conclude that businesses are now—and will continue to be—utterly dependent on the labor of millions of women.

Dual-earner families now outnumber breadwinner/homemaker families by more than two to one. And although the workplace still operates as if households had

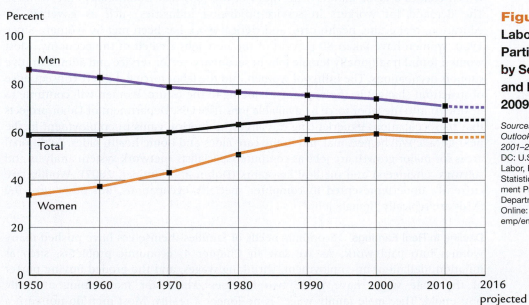

Percent

Figure 6.1

Labor Force Participation Rate by Sex, 1950–2009, and Projected, 2009–2016

Sources: Occupational Outlook Quarterly, Winter 2001–2002. Washington, DC: U.S. Department of Labor, Bureau of Labor Statistics, p. 39; "Employment Projections." U.S. Department of Labor, 2007. Online: http://www.bls.gov/emp/emplab05.htm.

only one full-time worker and the support of a full-time homemaker, no change has had as much impact on family life. Working wives now contribute around 35 percent of their families' incomes and one-quarter of wives in dual-earner households earn more than their husbands (U.S. Department of Labor, 2008b).

Although women are now firmly attached to the labor force, their employment patterns remain different from those of men: Somewhat more of women's work is part-time, part-year, or both, and it is more often interrupted to care for ill, aged, or young family members. Women and men are also differentiated by what they do in the labor market and the sectors of the economy in which they perform their work for pay. These differences are important because they limit women's earning abilities.

The most remarkable trend in women's employment has been the rapid rise in the percentage of married women with children in the paid labor force. Among married couples with children, families in which both parents are working are a large majority of households (U.S. Bureau of the Census, 2008b). All racial groups have experienced an increase in mothers' labor force participation. Despite family obligations, it is more likely than not that women will work outside the home during the years they are raising children. In 1970, 40 percent of married women with dependent children (birth through age 17) were in the workforce. In 2007, 68 percent of married women with dependent children were employed (U.S. Bureau of the Census, 2008b). Increasingly, it is normal for adult women, regardless of parental status, to be employed outside the home.

CAUSES OF INCREASED LABOR FORCE PARTICIPATION

What explains the dramatic changes in women's labor force participation? Three major push and pull factors account for women's new work patterns. First, large-scale changes in the U.S. economy have pulled women into the labor force; second, families have become dependent on women's income, thereby pushing women into the labor force; and third, women themselves find fulfillment in working.

Changes in the Economy   The most important reason for the surge in the number of employed wives has been the transition from a manufacturing to a service economy, which creates a labor market with more of the jobs that traditionally hire women. The demand for workers in service-producing industries such as government, education, real estate, health care, and clerical work has been met by women. Since 1980, women have taken 80 percent of the new jobs created in the economy. Most women found traditionally female jobs in secondary-sector service and administrative support occupations. The influx of women into the labor force is a direct consequence of structural changes in the economy. Looking to the future, women will continue to be drawn into the labor force by available jobs. The U.S. Department of Labor projects that the occupations experiencing the largest numerical gains in employment in the next decade will be personal and home care aides and home health aides. Additional areas for major growth are jobs as computer specialists (network system analysts and software engineers) and medical assistants (Dohm and Shniper, 2007). Women are currently underrepresented in computer specialty occupations, but other growing fields are typically "female jobs."

Decline in Real Earnings   Economic needs of families themselves have pushed many women into paid work. As we saw in Chapter 4, economic problems, such as inflation, deflation, unemployment, shrinking wages, and the eroded buying power of the male wage, have made two incomes crucial for maintaining a family household. The "male family wage" is no longer a reality. Most men do not earn a wage sufficient to support a wife and children. Unless both partners have jobs, many families would be unable to survive economically (i.e., pay the mortgage or the rent). Ironically, over the same time period that men's earnings declined, the demand for consumer goods rose. A social climate of rising expectations for material goods has pressured some women to increase their work hours. It is women's earnings that have allowed many families to achieve what they believe to be an adequate standard of living (Sayer et al., 2005:79).

To a greater extent than ever before, the income level for families with young children is being determined by the extent to which mothers are employed, especially in single-mother families. Three-quarters of women in mother-only families work outside the home to secure adequate support for their children. In 2006, the median annual income of married-couple families in which the wife was in the paid labor force was $82,788, compared with $45,757 for those without the wife in the paid labor force. Women who maintain families alone had the lowest median family income ($28,829) (U.S. Bureau of the Census, 2008b).

Personal Fulfillment   The economy is not the only force driving women into paid work. In the late 1960s and early 1970s, many women began questioning their traditional roles in family and society. The steady rise in the number of women working outside their homes had started to break down the social and ideological barriers to women working. Many women want to do paid work. They want to be rewarded for their work. Work outside the home gives them pride, worth, and identity, and it allows for some economic independence from men (Albelda, 1992:7).

While women work because it is personally satisfying, some women—especially married women with children—work because they realize it is in their best long-term interest to do so. These women recognize the consequences of staying out of the labor force; for example, gaps in work experience may reduce pay and lower occupational status when they do return to the labor force. Lifetime earnings, Social Security benefits, and employer pensions are also reduced (Dex, 2004:446). In this case, women's choices provide an example of human agency. Some women decide to work—in sometimes difficult circumstances—because it protects their earnings potential and promotes their long-term economic security.

PROBLEMS OF WOMEN WORKERS

Despite the massive entry of women into the paid labor force, the economy still restricts women's employment in several ways. Women who live in labor market areas with high unemployment rates or with low demand for labor in typically "female jobs" are less likely to be employed. Problems in securing child care can be another constraint. Many women are unable to work because affordable and adequate child care is simply not available. Others encounter scheduling difficulties. Increasingly, employers seek workforce flexibility—that is, workers who can alter their work schedules to meet the demands of the job. Mothers are especially disadvantaged in this regard because child care providers operate on a fixed-hours schedule and have strict policies for pickup times and other restrictions (Bruinsma, 2006:51). Limited options for child care are especially problematic for single mothers and can create obstacles to their employment. The child-care dilemma, in which parents must find "private" solutions to their child-care needs, is especially acute in the United States. Our government lags behind those of other developed nations in providing child care for the children of working parents (Dex, 2004).

Men's Employment

Recent changes in the labor force itself have altered men's employment patterns as well as those of women. The revolution in paid employment for women coincides with declining employment for men. Since 1960, labor force participation rates among men have edged down gradually from 83 to 72 percent in 2009 (U.S. Department of Labor, 2009a). Declines were steeper for African American men than for White men, with Hispanic men more likely to be in the labor force than White or Black men. Among White men, the declines were importantly due to lower age of retirement, whereas among minorities, the "discouraged worker effect" (the unemployed dropping out of the labor force after an unsuccessful period of job search) on prime working-age males played a greater role. The problem of diminished opportunities for urban minority men (discussed in Chapter 5) has seriously affected their work patterns.

CAUSES OF DECREASED LABOR FORCE PARTICIPATION

Men's work experience is especially affected by three macro-level trends: (1) structural unemployment, (2) the redistribution of jobs, and (3) the low-income-generating capacity of jobs.

Changes in the Economy   Advances in technology and the shift from manufacturing to services and information have had serious consequences in industrial work. Although women have been affected by downsizing, men have been more likely to be employed in hard-hit manufacturing jobs. Men, especially those working in heavy industries, are finding their skills unneeded. Economic survival in these instances depends on unemployment insurance and union benefits (which are short-lived) and their wives' employment. These wives have better luck in finding and keeping jobs because of the growth in the service sector, where the majority of workers is female.

Recent experience illustrates how patterns in employment and unemployment are shaped by assumptions regarding "men's jobs" and "women's jobs." In 2009, as the Great Recession worsened, it appeared that women might soon outnumber men in the U.S. work force. As unemployment rose, it became obvious that many more men than women were losing their jobs. In fact, four out of five workers losing jobs were men. Men were concentrated in industries hard-hit by the recession (Rampell, 2009). The very highest unemployment rates were found in areas in which men hold a large majority of jobs: construction (21 percent unemployment), agriculture (19 percent unemployment), and manufacturing (12 percent unemployment). In contrast, women predominate in areas of the economy with much lower rates of layoffs (for example, health care and education, with 5.4 percent unemployment) (U.S.

"All this family needs is one more worker and we'll be middle class."

Department of Labor, 2009b). Because men are more likely than women to have full-time jobs, employer-provided health care, and higher earnings, the impact of men's job loss on the family economy is severe, even for dual-earner families.

As manufacturing jobs become scarce, young men have increasingly turned to the lower-paying but rapidly expanding service sector. Since 1973, one of the fastest growing occupations for men has been sales. Men's employment in other service occupations (for example, security guards, orderlies, waiters, day-care workers, and janitors) has also increased. The service sector jobs available to men without college degrees generally pay low wages, offer few benefits, and produce limited opportunities for career advancement.

The declining share of men who earn enough to support a family affects family patterns in several ways. Figure 6.2 illustrates that the economic well-being of families is increasingly tied to educational attainment. Since 1970, the earnings of men without a college education—the vast majority of men in the labor force—have fallen. Meanwhile, women's earnings have generally risen (although women's earnings remain considerably lower than men's earnings). One result of men's lower earnings and women's greater economic self-sufficiency is an increasing number of single-parent families. Unmarried mothers may be unwilling to marry men who cannot provide economic stability for their families. Likewise, married women may be unwilling to remain married to men who cannot support them and their children.

Men's shrinking wages have also dealt a serious blow to the "good provider" role. According to Jessie Bernard, with industrialization and the rise of the separate spheres model of gender roles, the "good provider" role became the standard against which masculinity was measured. Men were judged by the standard of living they provided for their families. A wife in the workforce was an admission of the husband's failure as a provider (Bernard, 1984).

Macro-level economic conditions have eroded men's ability to be the sole breadwinner in the family. Most men continue to provide the largest source of income; however, men's share of family income is steadily declining. Increasingly, it is decisions

Highest educational level

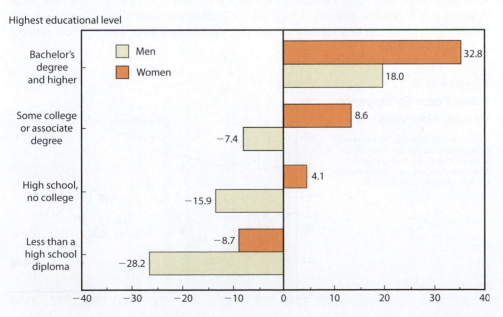

Figure 6.2

Change in Constant-Dollar Median Weekly Earnings from 1979 to 2007 by Educational Attainment and Sex

Note: Data relate to earnings of full-time wage and salary workers 25 years and older.

Source: *Highlights of Women's Earnings in 2007*, U.S. Department of Labor, 2008, p. 5. Online: http://bls.gov/cps/cpswom2007.pdf.

about the extent of women's employment—whether women work and the number of hours they work—that determine whether a family improves its economic position (Bradbury and Katz, 2005).

Teens' Employment

The characteristics of employment among teens make trends somewhat difficult to track. Conventional wisdom has held that youth today work more than they did in the past. In fact, teen labor force participation has declined since the late 1970s (Morisi, 2008). What is most noteworthy is the steep decline in teen's participation since 2000 (see Figure 6.3). This downward trend holds for adolescent employment in both summer months and the school year. Not only are contemporary youth less likely to be employed, but also those who are employed are working fewer hours than in the past. Formal employment rates tell only part of the story, however, because so many adolescents—especially young teens—do "freelance" work, that is, work on a casual, as-needed basis providing services such as lawn mowing and babysitting. Work activity is much harder to measure accurately in freelance jobs than in formal employment. In addition, because child labor laws restrict the age, hours, work activities, and working conditions for children, the employment of youth in illegal employment situations is underreported (Kruse and Mahony, 2000). The statistics presented for teen employment in this section are for youth ages 16 to 19 who have or are looking for formal employment.

Teen workers are a diverse group including high school and college students, recent high school graduates, and high school dropouts. Labor force participation is closely tied to job opportunities provided by the service economy. The top five industries employing teens are eating and drinking places, grocery stores, miscellaneous entertainment and services, construction, and department stores (Aaronson et al., 2006:8). Because many of the jobs offered in these industries pay the minimum wage, teen workers have benefited from recent increases in the federal minimum wage, rising from $5.15 per hour in 2006 to $7.25 in 2009.

One of the principal explanations for teen's decreased labor force participation is related to education. Teens enrolled in school are less likely to be employed than those who are not in school. As rates of high school graduation and college attendance rise, teen employment can be expected to fall. Decreased labor force participation reflects,

Figure 6.3
Labor Force Participation by Age, 1948–2004

Source: Daniel Aaronson, Kyung-Hong Park, and Daniel Sullivan, "The Decline in Teen Labor Force Participation." *Economic Perspectives.* Federal Reserve Bank of Chicago, 2006, QI, p. 3.

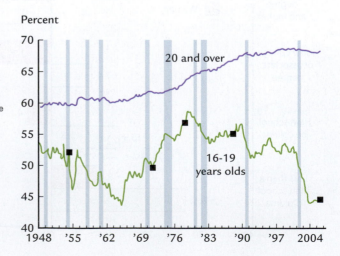

among other things, higher educational attainment. In 2005, 46 percent of 18- and 19-year-olds enrolled in school were employed, while among those not in school, 73 percent were in the labor force (Aaronson et al., 2006:6).

The likelihood of teen employment is related to both social class and race. The same social processes that create obstacles to employment in the adult population are relevant in the distribution of jobs among high school-aged teens. Although we might expect that teens in low-income families would be drawn into the labor force to help their families make ends meet, research finds that 16- and 17-year-olds in higher-income families are much more likely to be employed than youth in lower-income families. Youth in more affluent families are at an advantage because they have reliable transportation to get them to their jobs and most often live in suburban areas with less competition for typical "teen" jobs. Meanwhile, low-income youth in central cities and rural areas compete with unemployed adults for the few available local jobs and lack transportation to get to more plentiful jobs in suburban areas. Because White youth are overrepresented in higher-income categories, they are also more likely to be employed than adolescents of color. In 2005, 38 percent of White 16- and 17-year-olds were in the labor force, while 22 percent of African American and 23 percent of Hispanic teens were in the labor force (Aaronson et al., 2006:6).

What are the effects of employment on high-school students? Is a job a positive or negative factor in the life of an adolescent? Conventional ideas about the benefits of employment suggest that jobs provide opportunities to learn life skills and enhance autonomy (Stringer, 2002). On the other hand, employment may interfere with schoolwork and undermine parental authority as working teens become more economically self-sufficient (Gecas and Seff, 1991; Greenberger and Steinberg, 1986). Furstenberg's (2000) review of research on this topic concludes that the context of employment is vital in determining whether jobs are positive or negative for adolescents. Long hours in unsupervised or hazardous work settings do not promote positive adolescent development. Alternatively, limited hours in a safe and supervised work setting provide a favorable context for learning about the demands of employment and the roles of workers. Positive work experiences may promote responsibility and self-respect for working teens (Furstenberg, 2000:903).

Integrating Work and Family

Many connections and interchanges make it impossible for work and family to be separate worlds. Work shapes family life, and family overlaps with work. The economy provides goods and services for consumption by families. Families use their earned income to buy these goods and services. The economy provides jobs to family members, while the family supplies skilled workers to the economy. Work–family relationships generate difficulties for workers. The term **work–family interference** refers to the ways in which the connections between jobs and family life may be a source of tension for workers and family members (Hughes et al., 1992:32). One of the ways that the work–family relationship is expressed is through **spillover**—that is, the transfer of moods, feelings, and behaviors between work and family settings. Spillover can be positive or negative. Researchers are finding that work-to-family spillover is more negative and more common than family-to-work spillover (Roehling et al., 2003). Spillover appears to be a gendered phenomenon, with men's work stress more likely to affect their family life and women's family stress more likely to affect their work life (Zvonkovic, et al., 2006:149).

Diverse Work–Family Contexts

Just how work and family interact depends on the structural features of each. Job characteristics profoundly affect day-to-day family relations. For example, the demands of professional and managerial occupations, in contrast to those of lower-paid white-collar and blue-collar jobs, pose very different problems for the family. Family characteristics are also important. Is there only one working member, or are there two? Is there only one or are there two parents? These work and family characteristics are important because they set up different work opportunities and demands, as well as different family needs and resources, of both an economic and an interpersonal nature.

Work–family relations also vary because they are linked within a larger society that is stratified by class, race, gender, and sexual orientation. An important new body of research examines how prejudice and discrimination spill over into family life. In analyzing race, it is clear that discrimination in employment remains widespread. Cedric Herring's (2006) study of workplace discrimination against African Americans found case after case of unequal treatment in hiring, promotion, training, and compensation. In addition to these specific areas of discrimination that impact an individual's status of employment, routine acts of day-to-day discrimination also take a toll. The experience of discrimination has clear implications for the stress level and mental health of workers, but we still know little about how workplace discrimination impacts family processes (Marks, 2006:58–59).

Interesting new scholarship begins to clarify the effects of racial discrimination on family life by examining the family experience of African Americans in the military (Lundquist, 2006; Teachman and Tedrow, 2008). The premise for this research is that the military is less racist in organization than society as a whole. This research considers the work and family effects of substantially reducing workplace discrimination. Teachman and Tedrow find that military service reduces the likelihood of divorce among African Americans serving in the Army. They explain their findings as follows: "We attribute the...finding to the fact that the Army has a well-defined career ladder for Blacks that fully integrates them into leadership positions providing role models and positive work environments that reduce stress associated with discrimination and promote stable marriages" (2008:1030).

Sexual orientation shapes the work and family lives of gay and straight families differently. Stephen Marks (2006) points out that the family at the center of the work–family interface is assumed to be a married heterosexual couple with children. For same-sex couples, a number of factors, including workplace discrimination, legal prohibitions of gay marriage, and resistance to accepting gay and lesbian couples as legitimate families, present unique challenges to integrating work and family life.

Work and family connections are complex. They change in both expected and unexpected ways over the life course. Here we focus on how the linkages vary according to the gender of the workers, the requirements of work roles, and the composition of families.

Gender Inequality

Although work and family roles are changing, the gender order shapes everyday relations in the family and the workplace. Both settings impose uneven demands on women and men, and women's demands are higher overall (Milkie and Peltola, 1999). Even the metaphor of "balance" is gendered, with women doing most of the balancing (Moen and Yu, 2000). Not only are women more likely to work part-time, earn less, and receive fewer benefits than men, but they also assume more family responsibility than men and report greater stress in both work and family roles.

The demands of the family intrude more on women's work roles than on those of men. If an emergency or irregularity arises, requiring a choice between the two, the family usually takes priority. For example, when there is a crisis for a child in school, it is the child's working mother, rather than the working father, who will be called on to take responsibility. For husbands, the relationship is reversed. The work role takes priority over the family role. Many husbands take work home with them or use their time at home to recuperate from the stresses they face in the work role. Husbands are expected to manage their families so that family responsibilities do not interfere with their work efficiency and so that families will make any adjustments necessary to the work role. Joseph Pleck (1977) has termed women's and men's uneven relationship to work and family the **work–family role system.** This system represents a partial revision of the separate spheres model for gender roles discussed in Chapter 3, but still reinforces the traditional division of labor in both work and family. This system also ensures that wives' employment does not affect their core responsibilities for housework and child care. Employed wives generally have two jobs, while employed husbands have only one.

The working mother is more likely than the father to care for family emergencies.

The work–family role system perpetuates women's inequality in the workforce. If employed wives have two jobs—work and family—they are perceived as less attractive employees than employed husbands, who are able to be single-focused workers. Marital status frequently has different implications for women and men job-seekers. Schwartz found that married women graduates of the prestigious Wharton School of Business took off their wedding rings before job interviews while unmarried men who were graduates borrowed wedding rings prior to their interviews (cited in Crittenden, 2001:31). For women, a wedding ring raises the prospect of an employee whose commitment to career will likely be compromised by motherhood, while a wedding ring represents maturity and responsibility for men.

Women continue to experience obstacles to promotion to top positions in major U.S. corporations. The Catalyst organization tracks the progress of women in the *Fortune* 500 by counting the number of women in top leadership positions. Although some progress has been made, women remain vastly underrepresented in top leadership. Women make up 47 percent of the U.S. workforce, but held only

Figure 6.4

Catalyst Census of Woman Corporate Officers and Top Earners of the *Fortune* 500 in 2008

Source: Catalyst, *2008 Catalyst Census of Woman Corporate Officers and Top Earners of the Fortune 500* (December 2008). Online: http://www.catalyst.org/file/241/08_census_cote_jan_pdf.

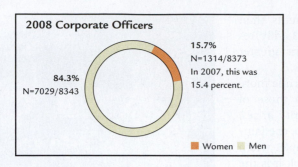

15.7 percent of corporate officer positions (1,314 of 8,343) and 6.2 percent of top earner positions (130 of 2,084) in *Fortune* 500 corporations in 2008. (See Figure 6.4.)

Despite different orientations to work and family, pressures of balancing work and family are increasingly an issue for men as well as women. Fathers' involvement in family life is taking place across race and class. Research on men's family lives offers a contemporary and hopeful perspective on gender equality in family and society. Some men are willing to sacrifice career advancement to share family responsibilities with their wives (Gerson, 1993). Although true "role-sharing" couples remain a minority, men are taking on more of the family workload, a necessary step in the transformation of both the male role and the patriarchal family (Coltrane, 1996).

Significant obstacles remain to achieving a society in which men and women share equally the responsibility for balancing work and family. Persistent culturally prescribed gender roles continue to shape women's and men's work and family behavior in predictable directions. Women's perceived options are frequently influenced by the norm of intensive mothering. Good mothering requires women to be intensively involved in every aspect of their children's lives. Suzanne Bianchi and her colleagues write, "[T]he requirements for effective and good mothering have ratcheted upward at the very time when there are expanded opportunities for women to do other things with their time, such as devoting themselves to fulfilling jobs." Many women resolve this dilemma by limiting their employment when their children are young. This compromise produces "employment histories that are more marginal, more part-time, more sporadic than men's" (Bianchi et al., 2006:175).

For men, responsible fatherhood continues to include assumptions about breadwinning. Nicholas Townsend's *The Package Deal: Marriage, Work and Fatherhood in Men's Lives* (2002) finds that contemporary men view their lives in terms of a "package deal" in which marriage, fatherhood, employment, and home ownership are interconnected. In this package, supporting a family is "crucial to successful fatherhood" (p. 78). Men who do not adequately support their families have failed to be good fathers. The continued linkage between successful fatherhood and the good-provider role encourages men to invest their energies in labor market success and makes the goal of involved fatherhood difficult to achieve.

Work Characteristics

A variety of job characteristics affects families. Two major aspects of work affect family life directly: (1) the level of economic rewards associated with work, and (2) the conditions associated with performing a job. These are structural job characteristics that organize the worker's time, determine when and where one works, and include work hours, travel demands, weekend work, and flexibility in job scheduling (Hughes et al., 1992:32).

THE TIME SQUEEZE

Time is a scarce commodity in U.S. families. As the economy moves steadily to a 24-hour, seven-day-a-week economy, Americans are left with too little time for their families. Long work hours have become a standard part of life for many families. Both women and men now work longer hours than they did 20 years ago. The average U.S. worker now works 1,976 hours per year, 93 hours more than in 1980. In many nations, however, hours on the job have gone down; workers here spend 44 percent more time on the job than Dutch workers and 27 percent more time than German workers (Jacobs and Gerson, 2004). Juliet Schor raised public consciousness of the issue of increased workload in her best-selling book, *The Overworked American* (1991). Recent studies emphasize, however, that long work hours do not characterize the experience of all U.S. workers. Economic restructuring has resulted in a "bifurcation of working time into too-long and too-short work weeks" (Jacobs and Gerson, 1998:447). While the proportion of women and men working 50 hours or more per week has indeed increased, so has the proportion working less than 30 hours. Reducing hours is advantageous to employers because they minimize labor costs by using part-time workers who do not receive benefits. Highly educated professionals and managers are most likely to be overworked while blue-collar and less skilled workers are most likely to be involuntarily part-time (Maume and Bellas, 2001).

What Schor calls a "profound structural crisis of time" is now taking a serious toll on family well-being (1991:5). Gerson and Jacobs propose that the time squeeze may be best understood in terms of "overworked families" instead of "overworked individuals" (2004). A standard 40-hour work week is not generally thought to be an excessive work requirement, but a dual-earner couple with two 40-hour-a-week jobs and two children may experience the total demand on the family to be overwhelming. Over the past 30 years, the most significant change in the relationship between work and family in U.S. society is not increased hours on a particular job, but married women's increased employment. In 1970, the average dual earner couple worked a total of 78 hours; by 2000, total dual earner couple work hours increased to 82 hours. What is most telling is not the rise from 78 to 82 hours, but the fact that in 1970, 36 percent of married couples were dual earners, while in 2000, 60 percent of these households were dual earners (Gerson and Jacobs, 2004). (See Figure 6.5.) When both husbands and wives are employed, families are better off economically, but they are "time poor" (Jacobs and Gerson, 1998).

How do working families handle the time crunch? In *Changing Rhythms of American Family Life* (2006), Bianchi, Robinson, and Milkie examine how the new work–family realities are played out at the household level. Their study, comparing the use of mothers' and fathers' time in 1975 and 2000, clarifies how contemporary

Figure 6.5

Total Hours of Work per Week for Married Couples, 1970 and 2000

Note: Data relate to nonfarm married couples aged 18–64.

Source: Kathleen Gerson and Jerry A. Jacobs, "The Work-Home Crunch." *Contexts* 3 (4) (2004): 29–37.

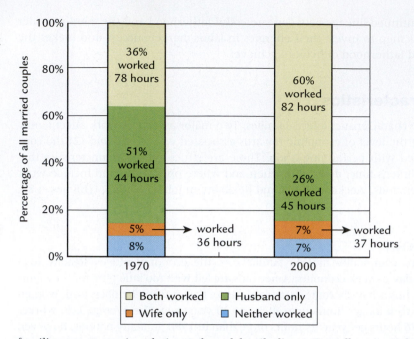

families are managing their work and family lives. Overall, parents have shifted the allocation of their non-working hours in ways that maximize time with their children. Parents are spending more time playing with and reading or talking to their children than was the case 25 years earlier. Parents increasingly include children in their leisure-time activities. This suggests either that leisure-time is becoming more family-oriented or that parents are more likely to include their children in their own leisure activities. Parents have managed to carve out more time for their children despite women's increased labor force participation by spending more hours in multitasking, that is, engaging in multiple activities simultaneously. While interaction with children is up, other types of social interaction are on the decline. For example, married parents spend less time together, the time married women spend in civic activities has declined significantly, and single mothers' time with friends and relatives has dropped markedly. Increasing both hours of paid employment and time with children take a toll on parents. The women and men participating in this research experienced considerable time pressures. All groups of parents reported having too little time for themselves. Married fathers and mothers reported having too little time with their spouses. More than two-thirds of mothers—both single mothers and married mothers—felt like they were multitasking most of the time (Bianchi et al., 2006).

Karen Hansen (2005) finds that middle-class and professional dual earner couples must increasingly rely on kin networks to manage their work and family commitments. Family networks can ease the burden of extended work hours, long commutes, and inflexible child care arrangements by providing support for harried parents or back-up in case of a work or family emergency. In reality, however, many middle-class families have no local family network. Some couples would like to foster non-kin relationships of interdependence and mutual support, but their lives are too overcommitted to allow them to pursue these relationships. Hansen's research counters a dominant cultural assumption that middle-class nuclear families are free-standing, independent households. Conventional wisdom holds that working-class families rely on kin networks of support, but middle-class households are self-reliant. Contemporary shifts in the structure of employment make it increasingly difficult for both middle-class and working-class families to "go it alone."

Lost in cyberspace at mealtime.

TIMING AND SCHEDULING OF WORK

Timing affects the rhythm and quality of daily life directly by determining when, where, and how much a worker can be with his or her family. Some jobs are rigid, requiring employees to punch a time clock, while others are more flexible. With flexible jobs, workers are better able to handle personal emergencies at home, visit with their children's teachers, and the like. Some jobs demand that one be away from home for days or even weeks at a time. This separation requires that one spouse take on a greater share of responsibility for the day-to-day decisions about home and children. Other forms of work-related travel take people away from their families. Some live at a distance from work, losing several hours a day to commuting. A majority of working hours occur from Monday through Friday during the daylight hours. This arrangement permits workers to have greater interaction with spouse and children in the evenings and weekends because their schedules coincide. Other jobs, however, have odd schedules (e.g., working at night, four 10-hour days a week, and swing shifts, in which the work hours rotate from week to week). Many workers are expected to put in overtime hours, either at the workplace or by bringing work home; and many workers take on additional jobs to make ends meet.

The timing of work is a strong determinant of family life. Men's work schedules are important in predicting their involvement in family life. In general, the less men's work schedules overlap with those of their wives, the more likely they are to be involved in caring for their children (Zvonkovic et al., 2006). Theodore Cohen's (1993) research on men's parenting roles found that timing of work was the most important shaper of their fathering activities. The men in his study had to fit children around their jobs. Men's paid work schedules sometimes offered them unique opportunities to engage in more extensive activity with their children:

> Two fathers who worked nights, a third who as a teacher returned home early from work, and a fourth whose job included two weekdays off all associated their work schedules with higher than expected levels of involvement in child care....Thus, whereas some fathers felt that their jobs restricted their parenting activities, others owed their high levels of involvement to their work schedules. In both directions, work became a dominant influence over the nature of men's relationship with their children. (Cohen, 1993:16)

The work schedules of Americans are changing as U.S. society moves toward a 24-hour, seven-day-a-week economy. The standard workweek—that is, a work schedule over weekday, daytime hours—is declining while shift work is on the rise for women and men alike. "Shift work" refers to working evenings, nights, or on a rotating schedule. In less than half of dual-earner households with children do both spouses work a standard work week. An important reason for this new pattern lies in the growth of America's service industries, which require shift and weekend work (Presser, 1999). Shift work can be a strategy for managing child-care needs (Garey, 1999). Nevertheless, shift work often precludes the sharing of routine family activities. As full-time workers and full-time caregivers, parents have little time for leisure, rest, being together, or even sleep (Funk and Hughes, 1996:407). In some circumstances, shift work takes a toll on marriage relationships. For couples with children, nonstandard work schedules increase the risk of separation and divorce (Presser, 2000:108).

Family researchers are assessing the effects of new information technologies on family life. The same computer-based technologies that shape contemporary macrostructural processes of globalization are also reshaping micro-level processes of family life. The work–family interface is being transformed in ways that would have been unthinkable just a decade earlier. (See Box 6.1.)

GEOGRAPHIC MOBILITY

High mobility underlies business and work institutions and, increasingly, the family. Two types of geographic mobility are common in this society: work-related travel and job-related moves and transfers. The large majority of Americans work and live in different places. Commuting extends the workday and requires reliable access to transportation.

Employment-related considerations comprise slightly more than a quarter of all reasons for moving. Some job-related moves occur because individuals must move to find work; others are made to improve an individual's economic and occupational status. Individuals move to find work, for example, in beginning a career after completing school or losing a job because of plant or office closings or cutbacks (Voydanoff, 1987:66). Moving depends largely on the type of job people hold. Doctors, lawyers, and others who rely on local bases of operation have low rates of mobility, while business executives are highly mobile (McFalls, 1998:19).

Success and promotion within a work organization may involve the move to a new geographic location. Migration is a common practice in large corporations, the rationale being that "rising stars" should have varied management experiences and should be familiar with the company's operations in the field. Typically, the case involves a male company executive who is promoted and must relocate. His transfer to a new location often requires his wife and children to pay a heavy price. While husbands often fit into a ready-made work structure complete with colleagues (though not always successfully), wives must find their way around a new community without the status and achievements from their previous community (McCollum, 1990).

Historically, married-couple families have moved in response to husbands' job opportunities. The entry of women into professional and managerial jobs has created new dilemmas for professional couples. Although dual-earner professional couples are more likely to move for men's career opportunities than for women's opportunities, it seems that the historic assumption that the male career takes priority is weakening. Pixley and Moen's study of dual-earning middle-class couples found that one-half of men took advantage of a career opportunity that required their spouse to move or change jobs, while one-third of women took advantage of such an opportunity (2003:199). A person who moves or stays because of a spouse's opportunity, contrary to his or her own optimal economic choice, is said to be "tied." Given current market opportunities, a "tied mover" is likely to be a wife and a "tied stayer" a husband (Spitze, 1991:390).

High levels of geographic relocation can result in family stress (Ammons et al., 1982; Gaylord, 1979; McCollum, 1990). Nevertheless, spouses and children appear to manage. With difficulty, they survive quite well the traumas of moving. These families of geographically mobile executives may even benefit as they pull together because of the disruption.

TYPE OF WORK

Different kinds of work have always had different consequences for families. Jobs vary in wage levels and benefits such as health insurance, Social Security, private pensions, disability, and unemployment insurance. As we move further into the twenty-first century,

BOX 6.1 Technology and the Family

Disappearing Boundaries Between Work and Family

New technologies have blurred the boundaries between work and family and are transforming expectations and assumptions about both realms. Thanks to computers and personal electronics, many employees are expected to be continuously available for work-related communication. Checking the BlackBerry for messages may be the last thing an individual does before going to sleep at night and the first thing in the morning (Conley, 2009). At the same time, workers may use time in the office for personal e-mail and other activities, such as booking hotel reservations for the family vacation.

Middle-class and professional employees experience an increasing interpenetration of their work and family lives. In their ethnographic study of middle-class working families, Charles Darrah (2007) and his coauthors quote one research participant who said that the single rule they had about working at home was "No e-mailing at dinner." These researchers point to the difficulty of categorizing household members' activities as either work-related or family-related. They write:

> Sometimes people were surrounded by family members but lost in cyberspace. Of course, they were still members of the family, but not in the same way as others in the room who were perhaps discussing an upcoming vacation or a relative's health. At other times, individuals were physically apart from their family members, yet firmly "in" the family. A few key strokes on a computer at work could take someone from planning a marketing program for a new product to searching the web for places to park a child after school for a few hours. How people are in their families can change from hour to hour, or even minute by minute. (p. 220)

How will technology reshape family life in the future? Dalton Conley proposes that the future is now. In the book, *Elsewhere, U.S.A.*, he creates a scenario about Mr. and Mrs. 2009 and their children. With his wife away on a business trip, Mr. 2009 and his children sit down for dinner, each with their personal laptops:

> While they eat, Mr. 2009 asks his kids about their day. They chat as each of them keeps one eye on a computer or other communication device. Dad wishes he could be totally engaged and interested, but he simply can't. It's not just that he is constantly multitasking. It's not just that his attention span seems to have shrunk. It's not just that he is more and more worried about work. It's his kids, too: even if he were totally available, they are not. (p. 6)

we see that accompanying the growth of the service sector has been a restructuring of workplace relations. An important change in this regard is the shift "from permanent, long-term ties between workers and employers to short-term, temporary ties" (Wharton 2006:32). This change and the employment-related decisions that follow from it contribute to increasing diversity in work for the U.S. labor force and have serious implications for the families of today's workers.

White Collar and Professional   The classic research on the relationship between white collar or professional work and family life has focused on the father's occupation. In general, higher occupational prestige and income increase marital stability and marital satisfaction. At the same time, the demands of the job sometimes offset the rewards. Although a family benefits monetarily from such success, it may also suffer because of the successful worker's absence or neglect. Arlie Hochschild (1975) observed that "the clockwork of male careers" imposed unrelenting demands. Family obligations must be canceled, interrupted, or postponed if need be. This time-devouring form of work, deeply embedded in the male career model, has generally been the model adopted by career women.

A new direction in employment relations in today's global economy is the high commitment workplace. Although employees, in general, have less job security than in the past, companies still need to motivate and retain their key professional and managerial employees. High commitment workplaces use a model of participatory decision-making that depends on the creative collaboration of key employees who are highly motivated and productive. Employees demonstrate their commitment to their employers by working long hours and allowing work to dominate their lives (Blair-Loy and Wharton, 2004:244; Wharton, 2006). Many employers signal their desire to ease their employees' work–family pressures by providing extensive work–family programs. In many cases, however, the demands of jobs and expectations of supervisors are so high that employees cannot actually do their jobs and use family-friendly policies at the same time.

Blue Collar   Many classic family studies examined how blue-collar working conditions spill over into the family. Especially important contributions are Richard Sennett and Jonathan Cobb's *The Hidden Injuries of Class* (1972) and Lillian Rubin's *Worlds of Pain* (1976). As the titles suggest, these studies found that the characteristics of employment for the industrial working class negatively impact family life. Inadequate resources, monotonous and unchallenging work, unsafe working conditions, dead-end jobs, the unrelenting threat of unemployment, and low self-esteem were found to be associated with men exercising authoritarian control in families, abusing wives and children, and withdrawing from family interaction.

New research on the characteristics of working class employment focuses on inequalities of gender and race. Women constitute a large segment of workers in working class employment. These women are disproportionately working in the "care sector" of the service economy. As a majority of women streamed into the workforce over the past decades, the care that homemakers formerly did—for children, the sick, and the elderly—became market-based work. Because care work continues to be viewed as "women's work," jobs requiring care have lower earnings than other jobs and are disproportionately done by women of color. This "care penalty" has economic consequences for those providing care and their families (Wharton, 2006:32).

Jobs in health and day care occupations requiring responsible workers may not pay a living wage or benefits.

Globalization has created a transnational market in care work. Many jobs in care work are filled by women of color from less-developed nations. U.S. families and communities depend on the care of women who, with few perceived economic options at home, have migrated to the U.S. to work at low wages providing care or domestic labor (Karraker, 2008). We are familiar with outsourcing and offshoring, two global processes that use workers in less-developed countries, earning low wages, to produce inexpensive goods and services for consumers in developed nations. Transnational care work represents a different global process, but has the same central premise. These women leave their homes and families, crossing international borders for low wage work that cannot be moved offshore because it involves providing direct personal services for first-world families. The result is the same because it depends on the cheap labor of third-world workers. Women in transnational employment are among the most marginal workers in the U.S., holding unstable jobs and working long hours in unregulated workplaces.

Professional Satisfaction from Work   Work may or may not be a source of personal satisfaction. In the past, most research focused on fathers' jobs. Today, researchers are asking questions about women's work lives and learning about job conditions that foster greater control. These include having more flexible time and leave options, greater autonomy, and greater control over work schedules (Galinsky and Bond, 1996:102). Chances are that the higher the prestige, the more autonomy; the greater the income received from the job, the greater the importance of work to the individual's well-being. Occupations offering less desirable working conditions offer fewer intrinsic benefits and exacerbate other negative characteristics (Menaghan, 1996:411).

It is unsurprising to find that work–family conflict negatively affects professional satisfaction. In summarizing a large body of research, Thompson and her colleagues write, "[W]ork-family conflict is related to job and life dissatisfaction, depression, anxiety, anger/hostility, hypertension, greater alcohol consumption and substance abuse, and perceptions of a lower quality of life" (2006:287). Researchers generally agree that work-to-family conflict is more common than family-to-work conflict. Further, work-to-family conflict is more closely related to outcomes such as life satisfaction and job satisfaction (Barnett and Gareis, 2006:212).

Substantial work-to-family conflict might be expected in the high-commitment workplaces in which many professionals work. Arlie Hochschild's (1997) research suggests something else. Her study of a *Fortune* 500 company finds that, instead of trying to arrange shorter or more flexible work hours, many women and men are choosing to work longer hours. She discovered a growing tendency for workers to escape family pressures by taking refuge in the efficiency, predictability, and camaraderie of the workplace. For them, work was more like family and family was more like work. Hochschild's provocative conclusions have sparked additional research on the relationship between work and family. Although more research is needed to clarify this dynamic relationship, many studies affirm that work often provides great professional and life satisfaction for both women and men. Extended work hours, however, seem to reflect workplace demands more than employee preferences (Brown and Booth, 2002; Clarksberg and Moen, 2001:1115; Maume and Bellas, 2001).

Although it is generally assumed that blue-collar work produces greater negative carryover than white-collar work, we should caution against this simple generalization. It is difficult to untangle the effects of types of work and social class. Psychologically demanding jobs such as those with high pressure and low support have negative effects and prevent workers from meeting family demands (Hughes et al., 1992:40).

Work demands have a profound impact on how people behave in their families. It is unrealistic to expect that these dynamics can be overcome through individual or family efforts alone; they require, instead, a restructuring of the workplace.

Family Characteristics

Women, men, and children live in a wide range of family forms that must be taken into account when considering work–family linkages. Two-parent families, two-earner families, single-parent families, and other variations have different connections with the workplace. Especially important are the ages of workers; stage in the family life cycle; employment status of workers; number, age, and sex of children; and the presence of aging parents.

DUAL-WORKER FAMILIES: THE DOMINANT PATTERN

Dual-worker families are now the dominant family model among workers in the labor force, with approximately 70 percent of couples as dual-earners (Raley et al., 2006). Whatever their social class, all dual-provider couples confront the challenges of negotiating roles and a division of labor, setting priorities for work and family, and, if children are present, arranging for their care.

Costs and Benefits of Having Both Spouses in the Labor Force   Although research finds that dual-earner families experience tremendous stress, employed wives also have high levels of self-esteem and well-being (Perry-Jenkins and Turner, 2004:158).

How does the combination of marriage, motherhood, and employment affect women? We have seen that for all racial groups, marriage and employment are associated with a higher standard of living for women. In addition, women in co-provider marriages are consistently found to be healthier, less depressed, and less frustrated than wives who are homemakers (Coontz, 1997:67). For more than 20 years, studies have found the health benefits of employment to be significant. Employment connects women to a number of health-enhancing resources, including income, insurance, and social support (Schnittker, 2007:223). It appears, however, that the time pressures involved in fulfilling work and family responsibilities reduce the health benefits of employment for working mothers of young children. The association observed here is clear—stress impacts health status. Still, the overarching relationship between health, work, and family is this: "Women who are employed, regardless of the number of hours they work or how they combine their work responsibilities with family obligations, report better health than those who are not employed" (Schnittker, 2007:234).

Employment is an important predictor of both physical health and psychological well-being among women. Why might multiple roles, typically spouse, parent, and employee, lead to greater life satisfaction? Several studies suggest that multiple roles provide many types of gratification, including a sense of accomplishment, improved interpersonal relationships, opportunities to develop talents and abilities, clear goals and priorities, and a greater variety of experiences (summarized in Thompson et al., 2006). Women's power within the family is greater when they produce income. Some wives who feel trapped by the homemaker role are liberated when they go to work. This is ironic, given the tedious and dead-end jobs they frequently fill, the relatively low pay many receive, and the time crunch they experience. However, these faults may be offset by a new sense of independence and competence, and taking pride in doing a good job and contributing monetarily to the family.

The impact of women's employment on family life has not been uniform. When we assess changes that occur in the family once women enter paid employment, we must be careful not to accept as "universal" the changes that are unique to women in elite professions. Class and race bring different linkages to work and family. Married women in working-class jobs may appear to be far more "traditional" than professional wives—that is, more willing to accept patriarchal authority, less "committed" to their work, and prepared to sacrifice themselves endlessly to family demands. We should be critical of this stereotype because it presents women in elite professions as exemplary, as if their norms, values, and behaviors in "balancing" work and family are superior (Ferree, 1987). The "lesser work commitment" of working-class women might be seen as rational in the context of the characteristics of the work they do. Hansen found that working-class women were committed to labor force participation, but not to a particular job. Their jobs paid low wages, provided no benefits, and offered no "family-friendly" flexibility. Therefore, if a job interfered with family needs, they would quit, assuming that when their family necessity passed they could find a similar job without much difficulty (Hansen, 2005:46).

THE WIFE AS SOLE PROVIDER

While the majority of married-couple families are dual-earner households, in around 7 percent of families the wife is the sole provider (U.S. Bureau of the Census, 2008b). This arrangement reflects a number of different family circumstances. Many wives find themselves in this role as a result of unanticipated economic setbacks. Deteriorating economic conditions pushed wives in many dual-earner couples into the provider role when their husbands were laid off or became victims of corporate downsizing. Women in female-dominated fields such as health care and education have been less vulnerable to job loss than men in male-dominated fields like manufacturing (Tyre and McGinn, 2003:46).

In other cases, though relatively few, wives choose to be the providers while husbands are the homemakers. These arrangements are often experimental, with each spouse taking a turn alternating a career with home and child care. Alternatively, the wife as sole provider may reflect a couple's decision to prioritize the wife's career while resolving work–family time binds. *Fortune* reports that more than one-third of the women on its "50 Most Powerful Women in Business" list have a husband at home full- or part-time (Morris, 2002:80). This phenomenon turns the tables on the conventional assumption that the supportive spouse it may take to get to the top at most companies is a "corporate wife."

Working women may also have husbands who are disabled or retired. Often wives continue working after husbands retire. This occurs with ever greater frequency because increasingly more middle-aged women are in the labor force and because so many men reach retirement age years before their wives do.

SINGLE-PARENT FAMILIES

Today, almost a third of family households with children are maintained by a single parent, nine out of ten of whom are women. Relatively little research considers the work–family interface for single mothers. The labor force participation of single mothers rose sharply in the 1990s with the institution of a new welfare system that required work. (See Chapter 13 for details.) Work–family conflict among single parents is "almost guaranteed" (Riche, 2006:129). While couples negotiate responsibilities for breadwinning, caregiving, and housework, single parents are responsible for all of these.

Single-mother families have the lowest median incomes and experience the highest rates of poverty among all household types. This means that many women strive to be good mothers and good workers without adequate resources to do so. Because many single mothers have low educational attainment and limited work experience, the jobs they are able to secure are frequently low-skilled work in the 24-hour, seven-day-a-week economy. Without a partner to share responsibility for children, these women are the workers least likely to be able to accommodate the nonstandard hours that characterize these jobs (Lleras, 2008). Strong networks of social support play a vital role in reducing the work–family conflict of single mothers.

Ciabattari's (2007) study of low-income single mothers found that work–family conflict has two main consequences for this group: It keeps them out of the labor force and makes it difficult to maintain stable employment. Without reliable transportation and adequate child care, many have no choice but to drop out of the labor force. Irresolvable work–family conflict contributes to poverty and unstable living arrangements for single-mother families.

Invisible and Unpaid Family Work

When most people hear about the massive entry of women into the workplace, their minds turn to one type of work: participation in the paid labor force. Women have always worked in the household, but such labor has not been included in the definition of work. After industrialization divided work and family, men's work evolved into paid labor outside of the home while women's work (regardless of whether they labored outside the home) became associated with unpaid work in the household. This division obscured all of those activities that are done inside the household to keep the family going. Feminists have long argued, however, that "outside" employment is not the only activity that qualifies as "work" (Garey, 1999:41). If we think about work in a more inclusive way, to include any individual effort or activity that produces goods or services of value to others, it becomes clear that a vast amount of unpaid work is done in the family—much of it by women.

Gendered Labor in the Household

Housework is the quintessential example of work that is done inside the family without extrinsic rewards. "We are discussing a set of work activities engaged in daily by many millions of people. Most of them are women, a class of workers who, although socially invisible, collectively devote billions of hours to their work" (Berk, 1988:288).

Household work done each day provides cooked meals, clean clothes, scrubbed floors, and a host of other "commodities." It also reproduces the important rituals that constitute family living. For example, preparing and providing food are important activities in the construction of family life. Not only is meal preparation part of the work of caring; it is also a central ritual that organizes people and activities (DeVault, 1991:263).

Domestic labor maintains families, and it sustains the economy. Without shopping, cooking, housework, and other forms of "care work," the economy would be at a standstill because society requires workers that are "serviced." Women continue to do a disproportionate share of family labor. In recent decades, however, women's hours of household labor have fallen while men's have increased. Sayer, Cohen, and Casper (2005) analyzed time diary data to capture changes in women's and men's weekly hours of housework and childcare since 1965. Box 6.2 shows a decline in women's hours of housework (but not child care), an increase in men's contribution to housework and child care, and an overall decrease in weekly hours allotted to household work, while overall hours in child care increased. While today's working wives benefit from rising expectations about men's contribution to household labor, housework remains principally women's responsibility.

The study of household labor burgeoned in the 1990s and continues to be the subject of substantial research (see, for example, Shelton, 1992; Tichenor, 2005; and reviews in Coltrane, 2000; Gerstel and Sarkisian 2006a; Thompson and Walker, 1991). While some inconsistencies can be found across the results of this large body of scholarship, the following conclusions can be drawn:

1. Family tasks are strongly gendered regardless of whether the wife is employed. Men work on cars and do yard work, home repairs, and household errands, while women do the majority of cooking, cleaning, laundry, mending, and child care.

2. Husbands of working wives spend about one-half as much time on housework as do their wives.

3. When women work longer hours, their household labor decreases while their husbands' tends to increase.

4. Husbands do not share equally in the housework even if the wife works full-time, even if the husband is unemployed, and even if the husband professes that spouses should share equally in domestic work.

Researching Families

BOX 6.2

Using Time Diary Data to Study Trends in Household Labor

In time diary studies, respondents are asked to provide a chronological accounting of the previous day's activities from midnight to midnight, including what they were doing, what time the activity started and stopped, where they were, whether they were doing anything else, and who else was present. We use these data to calculate weekly hours of housework and child care. Considerable research has established that estimates of unpaid work from time diary studies are more accurate than estimates from stylized survey questions such as "how much time do you typically spend in [activity] over an average day/week?"

Trends over time in market work are more readily measured than trends in unpaid work. Federal data collections (most important, the Current Population Survey) monitor paid work on a monthly basis in order to produce estimates of unemployment for the system of national accounts. Work done in the home for one's family has never been included in measures of national wealth, such as the gross domestic product, and therefore the measurement of household work has been far less systematic and frequent.

The federal government is currently collecting time diary information in one module of the Current Population Survey. This is the first federal time diary study conducted in the United States; earlier studies were conducted at the University of Michigan (1965 and 1975) and the University of Maryland (1985 and from 1998 to 1999).

Source: Sayer, Liana C., Philip N. Cohen, and Lynne M. Casper, "Women, Men, and Work." In *The American People: Census 2000,* Reynolds Farley and John Haaga (eds.). New York: Russell Sage Foundation, 2005, p. 83.

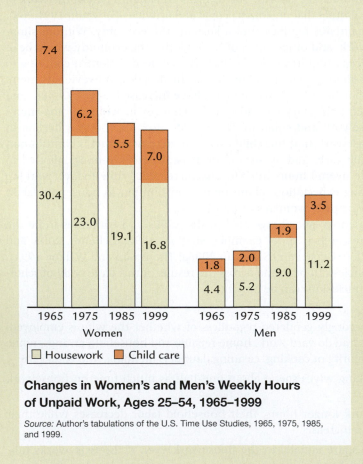

Changes in Women's and Men's Weekly Hours of Unpaid Work, Ages 25–54, 1965–1999

Source: Author's tabulations of the U.S. Time Use Studies, 1965, 1975, 1985, and 1999.

5. Husbands tend to do relatively more housework if they are better educated, and if they are younger.

6. The general pattern of gendered household labor does not vary greatly by social class or race.

Housework carries different meanings for women and men. It is gendered labor, a set of specific tasks that convey social meanings about masculinity and femininity (Ferree, 1991:111; Arrighi and Maume 2000; Risman, 1998). Men and women negotiate work and family responsibilities against the backdrop of the conventional marriage contract. This means that culturally, men continue to be accountable for breadwinning and women for domestic work, regardless of their additional responsibilities (Tichenor, 2005:13–14).

Women's disproportional time in housework, child care, and home management has produced what Arlie Hochschild (1989) calls the **second shift** for employed wives. Hochschild interviewed 50 couples of different classes and races to find out how families attend to the tasks that must be accomplished before and after paid work. She discovered that most women work one shift in their workplace and a second shift at home. Hochschild found that wives devoted more time to housework than did husbands and more time to all forms of family work than did husbands; that performing the second shift left wives much more deeply torn than were their husbands about the burdens of paid work and family work. The additional hours that working women spent on the so-called second shift of housework, Hochschild calculated, add up to an extra month of work each year! Even though social class is important in determining how the household labor gets done (more affluent families can afford to purchase more labor-saving services), Hochschild found that social class, race/ethnicity, and personality gave limited clues about who does and does not share the second shift.

Although gender is paramount in the allocation of household labor, men are doing more housework than they did previously. Research finds men extending their contribution beyond doing yard work and paying the bills to include activities called "core housework" (cooking, meal cleanup, housecleaning, laundry, and ironing). Sayer, Cohen, and Casper found that men increased their time in core housework from one hour per week in 1975 to six hours in 1999 (2005:94). The division of household labor is related to the relative earnings of husbands and wives. This means that co-provider couples are those most likely to share housework, while wives whose earnings are low in comparison to their partners are likely to do a disproportional share of housework (Greenstein, 2000). Tichenor's research reminds us of the continuing significance of gender in predicting the distribution of household labor. In her study of higher-earning women, "gender trumps money" as lower-earning husbands generally did less domestic labor than their higher-earning wives (2005:179).

What do we know about children's contributions to household labor? In general, children do little housework. The assignment of household chores to boys and girls mirrors the traditional gendered expectations about men's and women's work, with girls doing dishes, laundry, and cleaning, and boys doing outside work (Gerstel and Sarkisian, 2006a). Among all children, daughters whose mothers work full time do the most housework. These daughters spend an average of 10.2 hours per week on housework, in contrast to sons' 2.7 hours (Waite and Goldscheider, 1992). It seems that one of the ways working mothers relieve their second shift workload is by requiring their daughters to share it. Research also finds racial differences in children's housework, with Latino and African American children doing more housework than White children (Gerstel and Sarksian, 2006a).

Few families escape the demands of household labor, but some have the resources to hire others to do their domestic work and child care. Some professional lifestyles have long been dependent on the labor provided by domestic workers in private homes (Dill, 1983; Glenn, 1992; Rollins, 1985; Romero, 1992). Today, hiring household help is becoming more common. In 2007, the number of private household workers was 813,000 (U.S. Department of Labor, 2008b). Nine out of ten private household workers are women; they are disproportionately women of color. African American, Asian American, and Latina women have a long history of performing intimate household services for affluent families. Professional women increasingly hire help from a new Latino servant class—women whose own families must accommodate to their work in other people's homes (Hondagneu-Sotelo and Avila, 1997).

How is domestic labor allocated in immigrant families? Research finds that whereas patriarchal norms organize daily household chores, immigration and settlement in the United States can push immigrant men to take on some household responsibilities, especially when their wives enter the workplace (Hondagneu-Sotelo and Messner, 1994).

Nevertheless, women's employment by itself does not produce role-sharing couples among racial ethnics. This is one of the main lessons of Patricia Zavella's (1987) study of Chicana cannery workers in California's Santa Clara Valley. Women's paid work and their family work are both bound up with broader systems of class and racial inequality. Chicana working mothers faced occupational segregation by race and gender on the job and the double day at home. Seasonal jobs in the canneries created temporary shifts in day-to-day family life, but they did not alter traditional marital roles. Although financial incentives kept wives employed, they were workers in a declining industry and were still economically dependent on husbands. These structural conditions supported and reinforced the gendered division of household labor.

Although race/ethnicity does not by itself determine how families organize household labor, minority men generally spend more time on household tasks than White men. Research has uncovered two conditions that are more important than ethnicity in determining the amount of time husbands devote to household labor (Coltrane and Valdez, 1993; Shelton and John, 1993b). Being employed or unemployed together with the relative earning power of husbands and wives shapes the household division of labor. These studies reveal that whereas minority men may have different ideals about men's family work, Black and Hispanic men actually do more housework than White men because they earn less.

Research on the division of domestic labor in lesbian and gay families finds patterns that resemble those in heterosexual families. In Christopher Carrington's (2002) study of lesbian and gay families, one-quarter of couples established an egalitarian pattern of shared housework, while the majority did not. Paid employment structured the organization of domesticity among these couples. Partners with more intensive work demands and longer hours did less housework than partners with less demanding jobs.

The gender-based imbalance in household work has the potential to create divisiveness within marital relationships. Much depends on how women perceive the unequal burden they carry. Neither women nor men define a "fair" division of household labor as a 50-50 split. In a cultural context in which housework is feminized, the unequal burden of household labor is seen as normal by both women and men. Thus despite doing two-thirds of the housework, only one-third of women find their division of household work to be unfair (Coltrane, 2000:1223). Husbands are more satisfied with their marriages and less critical of their wives if their wives do more than their "fair share" of housework. Among wives there is a clear and positive connection between a perceived fair division of family work and marital and personal well-being (Thompson and Walker, 1991:89).

The question, then, is this: As we move further into the twenty-first century, who will be doing the housework? There are indications of change on the horizon. Contemporary trends predict a further convergence in women's and men's participation in household work. F. Thomas Juster says, "We are coming closer and closer to sex-role neutrality in how time is used. The gap will continue to close as society moves closer to the notion that there is not men's work and women's work, but just different kinds of work that is shared by both sexes" (quoted in Peterson, 2002b). The catalyst for change is the ever-increasing number of dual-earner families. Employed wives, especially those who work full-time, have less time, less energy, and less inclination to follow the old ways governing housework (Risman, 1998). And increasingly, there will be less and less rationale to expect them to shoulder an unequal burden.

Other Forms of Family Work

We have redefined work as a social activity that produces "value" even when it is invisible because it is unpaid and done inside the home. This definition includes work other than household labor that is done both within and outside the home. A wide variety of activities that go into creating and sustaining family life have previously gone unrecognized not only as work, but as effort of any sort. For example, Pamela Fishman (1978) calls attention to the **interaction work** that women do to sustain communication with their mates. Arlie Hochschild (1983b) shows how women engage in **emotion work,** the work of trying to find the right feeling, to make and keep everything fine. An example of emotion work is a mother who promotes a positive father–child relationship by offering suggestions for joint activities or by mediating disputes between fathers and children (Seery and Crowley, 2000:119). Current scholarship also includes providing encouragement and support to family members as emotion work (Minnotte et al., 2007).

Other forms of invisible labor have been identified. For example, **consumption work,** which involves selecting goods and making purchases, links the needs of families with products in the market (Weinbaum and Bridges, 1979). Women's invisible and unpaid work often does more than contribute to family well-being; it elevates the family's place in the class hierarchy. Martha Fowlkes (1987) reveals the varied supports, services, and career enhancements that professional men receive from their wives. The volunteer work that upper-class women do in communities is labor that legitimizes the family class position. At the other end of the spectrum, women's invisible work in "family-owned" but husband-controlled enterprises provides access to the middle class. As Ferree notes (1991:110), Cuban, Korean, and Vietnamese family enterprises provide contemporary examples.

Women are involved in still another type of work that sustains family—the work of kinship. **Kin work** includes maintaining contact and connections among kin as well as providing care and assistance to family members in other households. The work of kinship involves taking responsibility for the upkeep and ritual celebration of cross-household kin ties, including visits, letters, telephone calls, presents, and cards to kin, and the organization of holiday gatherings (di Leonardo, 1987:110). It also involves activities such as assisting elderly parents, caring for family members recovering from illness, and helping adult children (most often by providing child care)

(Gerstel and Sarkisian, 2006a). Kin work is like housework and child care: Men in the aggregate do not do very much of it. For working women, kin work is sometimes called the "third shift," because women do it in addition to their "first shift" of paid work and their "second shift" of housework and childcare (Gerstel, 2000:475).

Coping with Work and Family

Family Coping Strategies

COPING AS HUMAN AGENCY

Balancing work and family produces considerable stress and strain. When both spouses are employed, they must manage the competing demands of their work and family roles, which are often contradictory. If they are to construct workable family relationships, they must cope with interference and overload. Although the burdens of work and family responsibilities can strain individuals and families to the breaking point, people are devising adaptive strategies to cope with the stresses of jobs and family responsibilities. This illustrates human agency in operation. At the same time, family strategies always depend on available options (Moen and Yu, 2000). Even though dual-earner families are on the rise, structural patterns are modeled on a breadwinner/homemaker family. Without wider social changes in workplaces, individual family members must devise their own solutions for meeting structurally induced dilemmas.

HOW PARENTS ARE COPING

Coping is "an active process in which individuals manipulate their role expectations and behaviors to deal with stressful situations" (Voydanoff, 1987:189). Research shows that coping (like the other features of family life that we have examined in this chapter) is strongly gendered, with women taking on greater responsibility and men resisting change. A national study of the changing workforce found that women feel more able to cope when they are married and when they have more help at home with chores and child care, mainly from their husbands. "They are also more satisfied with their overall ability to handle problems when they have higher household incomes, which is largely a function of being married; however, women who contribute a higher proportion of family income—that is, single mothers and those whose husbands contribute less—feel that they are coping less effectively" (Galinsky and Bond, 1996:102).

For most working families, housework and child care create the most difficult problems. Parents use a variety of coping strategies for solving these problems. Strategies differ, depending on the resources of couples, on their work schedules, on the demands of their jobs and careers, and on the ages of their children. Common strategies for dealing with work overload and the resultant strain are as follows:

(1) reducing the standards of domestic work; (2) purchasing domestic and childcare services; (3) having other family members (e.g., husbands, children, parents) perform more domestic work; (4) refusing to comply with the demands or requests of greedy employers (with a cost to one's career success, probably most often the woman's); and (5) choosing an occupation (e.g., school teaching) which allows more time for the family (with a cost to one's income, usually the woman's). (Chafetz 1997:120)

Most families rely on several strategies (Haas, 1999). Coping falls unevenly on women's shoulders. Hochschild discovered that couples created **gender strategies** that fit conventional gender beliefs and needs with the realities of women's and men's daily lives. In her study, wives ended up doing most of the coping, yet the couples developed family myths—versions of reality that emphasize "sharing" in order to preserve harmony and camouflage conflict (Hochschild, 1989:17–31).

Although Hochschild found that employed wives devoted more time to housework while their husbands did "more of what they'd rather do," other research has uncovered strategies in which working families are changing the gendered patterns of family labor rather than accommodating to it. For example, shift work is a common solution for solving child-care problems. A study of household and employment patterns among working-class Hispanics and Anglo dual-earner families living in the Sunbelt illustrates how spouses can help one another out:

> If a couple decided to use a "split-shift" day care arrangement, in which each parent took care of the children while the other worked, men tended to do more child-care tasks and, in some cases, more housework. Yet if husbands worked evening or night shifts and their wives worked on day shifts, women could end up doing most of the housework when they were home in the evenings. Child-care arrangements were closely related to the shifts a couple worked. Often there was a tradeoff between housework and child care: if a husband took care of his children, the wife would overlook his lack of responsibility for doing housework. (Lamphere et al., 1993:190–191)

Although more dual-earner families are using split-shift parenting (sometimes called "tag-team parenting") to ease the strains of combining employment with child care, the use of this strategy is not distributed equally among all working families. A closer look at the use of alternating shifts reveals the relationship of coping strategies to social class and gender. **Split-shift parenting** is a strategy used principally by working-class families. The vulnerable economic position of these families does not allow them to relieve work–family tensions by choosing the strategy of reducing work hours. Split-shift parenting generally results in the movement of men into higher levels of participation in family work. The likelihood that fathers are caregivers to their children varies by the mother's work schedule. When parents' work schedules do not overlap, fathers do more caregiving (Barnett and Gareis, 2007:731). Alternatively, dual-earner professional families are more likely to resolve work–family tensions by a reduction in women's work hours. This phenomenon has been documented among part-time women lawyers and physicians (Epstein et al., 2003; Lundgren et al., 2001). In this case, it is women who do the adapting, while no adjustment is required in professional men's work and family responsibilities.

For women, a common way of dealing with work–family overload has been to juggle competing demands by adjusting the timing of events over the life course. This adjustment process is known as **sequencing.** It involves alternating paid work and child raising rather than trying to combine them (Coontz, 1997; Granrose, 1996). After establishing themselves in their career or earning an advanced degree, the women step off the career ladder for a few years to focus on children and home. When their children reach school age, they return to full-time jobs. However, women can pay a high price for having children. When they return to work, many women find that their employers place them on the so-called **mommy track,** which leads to fewer promotions and opportunities for advancement. Although the mommy track has been widely criticized for the way in which it makes women suffer vocationally for bearing the brunt of family responsibilities, there is some evidence that a "daddy track" exists as well. Fathers suffer in promotions and other salary increases when they curtail their work involvement in order to care for children (Waite et al., 1986).

Family-Supportive Government and Employer Responses

Unlike some other countries, the United States has only recently become aware of the complex struggle that most workers face in trying to combine paid work and family work. Only in the past decade or so have political, business, and professional leaders had very much to say about work and family. In the 1990s, the federal government made modest efforts to help families cope with child care through tax credits, programs for subsidizing the child-care costs of low-income parents, and the **Family and Medical Leave Act of 1993 [FMLA].** (Box 6.3 compares U.S. government support for working families with other nations around the globe.)

The FMLA requires employers of 50 or more people to provide 12 weeks of unpaid leave to any worker who has a medical emergency or needs to care for an adopted or newborn child or a seriously ill child, spouse, or parent. FMLA does not cover part-time workers. A total of 41 million workers in the United States—nearly half of the private workforce—are ineligible for family leave under this law. The FMLA of 1993 remained unchanged until 2009, when several points of clarification were added to the original legislation. The 2009 bill also expands military family leave entitlements, permitting eligible employees to take up to 26 weeks of leave to care for a servicemember with a serious injury or illness. In addition, 12 weeks of FMLA leave may be used to assist the families of National Guard or Reserves members on active duty (U.S. Department of Labor, 2009a).

Two major problems identified since the implementation of the Family and Medical Leave Act are these: First, the job-protected leaves provided by the law are unpaid; and second, employers with less than 50 workers are required to provide no leave at all. These provisions create "a 'Catch 22' for most women who earn less [than men] and are clustered in low paying jobs with FMLA-exempt employers" (Dorman, 2001). Nearly two-thirds of those who need a leave are eligible for an FMLA-based leave, but do not take a leave and report that they cannot afford the loss of income (Gornick and Meyers, 2001). Of those who do take a leave, more than half worry about paying their bills (Waldfogel, 2001).

In the absence of a national maternity leave policy, the FMLA has become that policy by default. As a result of the provisions of the FMLA, maternity leaves taken by women in the United States are short. The Commission on Family and Medical Leave reported that the average length of leave "to care for newborns is less than 12 weeks, with a significant proportion less than one week" (quoted in Dorman, 2001). California became the first state to pass paid family leave legislation in 2004. The California Paid Family Leave Insurance Program provides up to six weeks of benefits to employees who take time off work to bond with a new child or provide care for a sick family member; benefits cover approximately 55 percent of lost wages (California EDD, 2005). New Jersey and Washington have now joined California, implementing paid family leave programs in 2009 (Tahmincioglu, 2008). In view of an unresponsive federal government on family policy matters, it remains to be seen whether state-instituted paid family leave plans will become the progressive policy wave of the future.

BOX 6.3 Inside the Worlds of Diverse **Families**

Global Working Families: How Does the United States Measure Up?

The Project on Global Working Families is the first program devoted to understanding and improving the relationship between working conditions and family health and well-being globally. As part of this project, the Work, Family, and Equity Index has been developed to measure governmental performance around the world in meeting the needs of working families. To complete the index, data were gathered from 177 countries that represent a wide range of political, social, and economic systems.

Where does the U.S. have strong work protections?

The U.S. performs well in having policies that ensure an equitable right to work for all racial and ethnic groups, regardless of gender, age, or disability.

U.S. social insurance policies have had marked success in lowering the poverty rates of the elderly [through Social Security and Medicare], although they have been less successful than other affluent nations in protecting children from poverty.

Where does the U.S. lag behind?

Leave around childbearing:

- Out of 173 countries studied, 169 countries offer guaranteed leave with income to women in connection with childbirth. The U.S. guarantees no paid leave for mothers in any segment of the work force, leaving it in the company of only 3 other nations: Liberia, Papua New Guinea, and Swaziland.

- Sixty-six countries ensure that fathers either receive paid paternity leave or have a right to paid parental leave. The U.S. guarantees fathers neither paid paternity nor paid parental leave.

Support for breastfeeding: At least 107 countries protect working women's right to breastfeed; in at least 73 of these the [breastfeeding] breaks are paid. The U.S. does not guarantee the right to breastfeed, even though breastfeeding is proven to reduce infant mortality.

Work hours: 137 countries mandate paid annual leave [paid vacation]. The U.S. does not require employers to provide paid annual leave.

Leave for illness and family care: At least 145 countries provide paid sick days for short- or long-term illnesses, with 136 providing a week or more annually. The U.S. provides only unpaid leave for serious illnesses through the FMLA, which does not cover all workers.

Can we improve conditions for working families?

There is an enormous payoff to improving working conditions—from lowering long-term family poverty to improving population health and education and increasing their associated economic and social benefits. The data does not support the concern that good working conditions lead to job loss; none of these protections is associated with higher unemployment rates on a national level.

Source: Excerpts from Heymann, Jody, Alison Earle, and Jeffrey Hayes (2007). "The Work, Family, and Equity Index: How Does the United States Measure Up?" The Project on Global Working Families. Online: http://www.mcgill.ca/files/ihsp/WFEI2007.pdf.

Corporations offering supports beyond the provisions of the Family and Medical Leave Act do so voluntarily. This means that family-supportive benefits such as paid leaves, child-care assistance, and flextime are offered at the discretion of individual employers. As a result, some categories of workers have generous workplace supports, while others do not. An important concern is the degree to which the absence of government-mandated family benefits is creating a "two-tiered" family benefits structure. First, access to "family-friendly" benefits varies by gender. Ironically, while research finds that flexible work schedules would ease work–family conflict for working mothers, it is fathers who are more likely to have access to flexible hours and are less likely to use them (Christensen, 2006). In a context in which mothers continue to provide the majority of care for young children, it is fathers who work full-time and year-round in the higher status jobs that actually provide these benefits. Second, we find differences among women, with family-supportive benefits far more available to women in high-level professional-managerial jobs than women in low-wage employment (Deitch and Huffman, 2001:103). It seems that employers use attractive family-benefit packages to retain highly skilled women employees, while they find it more profitable to replace women in lower-skilled job slots rather than offer benefits to retain them. Thus, the voluntary nature of family benefits exacerbates existing inequalities in U.S. society.

CORPORATION-SPONSORED WORK–FAMILY PROGRAMS

Corporate work–family programs have expanded since the late 1980s. Many companies are touting their family-friendly policies. But for all the talk about accommodating work and family needs, for most workers life has not changed much at all. Several studies suggest that "the new workplace" is more myth than reality. Family support programs are often public relations gimmicks, costly to implement in an era of heightened global competition.

The 1998 Business Work-Life Study by the Families and Work Institute assesses the implementation of family-supportive policies among U.S. employers. Surveying 1,000 companies with 100 or more employees, the study finds that many family-friendly policies—job sharing, flexible hours, and limited paid leaves—are expanding. Sixty-eight percent of companies allow flextime. Flextime typically allows an employee to choose his or her own work schedule within specified limits. Job sharing is offered by 38 percent of companies. Fifty-three percent of companies now offer some replacement pay to women on maternity leave. The support of child care, however, continues to be meager. Nine percent of companies provide child care at or near the work site and another 5 percent provide subsidies for child care (Galinsky, 2001).

Study after study has identified the importance of job flexibility in facilitating the integration of work and family life (see, for example, Fenwick and Tausig, 2001; Gerson and Jacobs, 2001). A flexible work schedule may include the option to adjust the start and stop times of the workday, take extended breaks, or work at home occasionally. Flexibility reduces work stress because it gives workers an increased measure of control over their lives. "Control by workers over the timing and location of work, while it does not directly solve the time squeeze or address the need for more paid time off, can help workers better manage the often conflicting demands of work and personal life" (Appelbaum and Golden, 2003:80).

Mounting evidence suggests that flexible work schedules are not only good for workers, but they are good for employers as well. For example, analyses of data from the National Study of the Changing Workforce—with a representative sample of more than 3,500 women and men—find that the greater availability of time-flexible work policies is associated with increased loyalty to employers and reduced job-related stress. This translates into fewer absences, fewer days late, and fewer missed deadlines (Halpern, 2005:157, 163). Diane Halpern contends it is time for employers to implement time-flexibility as a strategy for increasing productivity and reducing costs, rather than assuming such policies will be costly to the organization.

Some analyses have shifted the focus from the structure of workplace benefits to the role of workplace culture in creating family-friendly environments. Despite the availability of flexible schedules and family leave, many women fear that using these supports jeopardizes their career advancement (Galinsky, 2001:175). Men are eligible for the same job-protected leave as women under the FMLA, and companies increasingly offer paternity as well as maternity leave. Nonetheless, few men take family leaves. It seems that despite offering family-supportive benefits, corporate culture has changed very little. The employee who is promoted is the single-focused worker who is unimpeded by family matters. Gerson and Jacobs conclude, "Women and men alike thus tend to perceive that family-friendly workplace policies come with costly strings attached. If workers feel confronted with a choice between family involvement and career building, their perceptions are probably well founded" (2001:223).

Corporate policies can reduce or remove some of the stresses for workers who earn a living and raise children. However, work and family benefits will never reach a broad spectrum of workers as long as they are bargained workplace-by-workplace and company-by-company. A national work and family policy seems out-of-reach at present. Demographer Martha Farnsworth Riche believes, however, that slow population growth in the United States may remove current obstacles to policy change in this area. She writes,

> In the long run, American employers may decide that it would be worthwhile to make a two-handed investment to grow the workforce: address the work–family issues that have kept some women out of the labor market and discouraged others from having as many children as they might have liked. Finding suitable work-life solutions for working householders, such as on-site child care, flexible work schedules, or simply helping working parents make the most of their scarce time is doable, if the will to do it is there (2006:138).

Chapter Review

1. Contemporary families across the economic spectrum are being reshaped by changes in the workforce.

2. The number of women in the workforce has increased from under 20 percent in 1940 to 60 percent today. The labor force participation rates of Black, White, and Hispanic women are approaching parity.

3. The most important factors influencing the rising number of women in the workforce are changes in the economy, families' economic needs, and women's fulfillment in their work.

4. Recent social and economic changes are responsible for the demise of men's "good-provider" role. Three structural changes have been most responsible for men's changing work patterns: structural unemployment, redistribution of jobs, and shrinking wages. Men of color and young men have been the most negatively affected.

5. Despite the growth of part-time jobs in the service sector, the rate of teen employment has fallen since the late 1970s.

6. The worlds of work and family overlap and interact. Work and family linkages vary based on the structural characteristics of each. Variance is also created through class, race, and gender inequalities.

7. Work and family roles are strongly gendered. Men's paid employment is taken for granted, but women's paid employment is often seen as problematic.

8. The gender-structured workplace and the gender-structured family take a toll on the well-being of women workers, even though men in all class and racial groups are taking on more of the family workload.

9. Family life is directly affected by two aspects of work: (a) earnings and (b) conditions associated with performing a job.

10. Work–family conflict may be extreme for single mothers because they have sole responsibility for breadwinning, caregiving, and housework.

11. Family characteristics, such as employment status of workers and number, age, and sex of children, shape the work–family interface.

12. Women's labor in the home has been excluded from traditional definitions of work, yet unpaid work contributes to the economy and to the maintenance of daily family life.

13. Housework in most families is strongly gendered. Women do most of it regardless of whether they work for pay. Women in dual-earner families frequently work one shift on their jobs and a second shift at home.

14. In addition to tasks commonly associated with housework, there are many kinds of domestic labor, including interaction work, consumption work, and kin work.

15. Coping with work and family presents real challenges for today's parents. Workers must devise their own solutions for coping with the demands of child care and housework. Sequencing the timing of life events is a strategy women use to manage conflicting demands of work and family. Dual-earner families increasingly use the strategy of split-shift parenting.

16. The traditional workplace is not conducive to meeting the conflicting needs of family members. Although recent changes have heightened public awareness, family-supportive employer responses, such as flexible work schedules, employer-sponsored child care, and flexible benefits, are limited. Some employees find that using family-supportive benefits jeopardizes their careers.

Key Terms

consumption work   207

coping   208

emotion work   207

Family and Medical Leave Act of 1993 [FMLA]   210

gender strategies   209

interaction work   207

kin work   207

mommy track   209

second shift   205

sequencing   209

spillover   189

split-shift parenting   209

work–family interference   189

work–family role system   191

Related Websites

http://wfnetwork.bc.edu/

Sloan Work and Family Research. Based at Boston College, the Sloan Work and Family Research Network is designed to support research and teaching, promote best practices at the workplace, and inform state policy on issues that affect the lives of working families and the places where they work. The website offers a variety of resources to work and family researchers, including a collection of 7,500 bibliographic citations with selected annotations of work and family literature.

http://www.bls.gov/cps/wlf-databook2008.htm

Women in the Labor Force: A Databook. This site is operated by the U.S. Department of Labor, Bureau of Labor Statistics. Links for current data related to women in the labor force are provided.

http://www.working-families.org

Labor Project for Working Families. Founded in 1992, The Labor Project for Working Families is a national nonprofit advocacy and policy organization providing technical assistance, resources, and education to unions and union members on family issues in the workplace including: child care, elder care, family leave, work hours, quality of life.

http://www.workoptions.com

Work Options, Inc. This site offers guidance to working parents and employees over the age of 50 who want to restructure their current job into a telecommuting, part-time, job-sharing, or compressed-workweek arrangement.

http://www.wfbenefits.com

Work & Family Benefits. Founded in 1992, WFB is an employee benefits company that provides comprehensive work-life services, specializing in child care, elder care, and care for people with disabilities. In March 2004, WFB was recognized by Business Insurance as the "Largest Provider of Dependent Care Resources and Referral Services to Employer Clients in the U.S."

http://www.workfamily.com

WFC Resources. This company provides work-life and human capital solutions for employers. WFC Resources has been working to help employers create a workplace that is both supportive and effective, a workplace that ensures that investment in employees pays off, and a work environment with a dual agenda—one that meets business goals and also allows employees to meet their personal goals. The website provides employers with the latest news and information from thousands of trade journals, newspapers and press releases, and experts about the best practices, research, and company experiences that will make a difference.

http://www.brighthorizons.com

Bright Horizons. Founded in 1986, Bright Horizons Family Solutions is the world's leading provider of employer-sponsored child care, early education, and work/life solutions. Conducting business in the United States, Europe, and Canada, it has created employer-sponsored child care and early education programs for more than 600 clients, including 90 of the *Fortune* 500. The organization is committed to providing innovative programs that help children, families, and employers work together to be their very best. Bright Horizons has consistently been the only child care organization named to the "100 Best Companies to Work for in America" list by *Fortune* magazine. In addition, more than half of the organizations on the *Working Mother* "100 Best Companies" list are Bright Horizons clients.

http://whenworkworks.org

When Work Works. When Work Works is a nation-wide initiative to highlight the importance of workforce effectiveness and workplace flexibility as strategies to enhance businesses' competitive advantage in the global economy and yield positive business results. When Work Works is a project of Families and Work Institute (FWI) sponsored by the Alfred P. Sloan Foundation in partnership with The Center for Workforce Preparation, an affiliate of the U.S. Chamber of Commerce, and the Twiga Foundation.

http://www.familiesandwork.org

Families and Work Institute. FWI is a nonprofit center for research that provides data to inform decision making on the changing workforce, the changing family, and the changing community. Founded in 1989, FWI's research typically takes on emerging issues before they crest. The Institute offers some of the most comprehensive research on the U.S. workforce available, including *The National Study of the Changing Workforce (NSCW)*, the largest and most far-reaching study of a representative sample of U.S. workers. The NSCW traces trends in the workforce over the past 25 years and explores topics such as the glass ceiling, changes in men's and women's involvement in family life, the role of technology in our lives, workplace flexibility, and working for oneself versus working for others.

http://www.bls.gov/news.release/famee.toc.htm

Employment Characteristics of Families. Published by the U.S. Department of Labor, this website provides links to current reports related to family employment.

chapter 7

The Social Construction of Intimacy

▶ Myths and Realities

Myth	Sex is a "natural" drive, rooted in biological urges and innate differences between males and females.
Reality	Sexual attitudes and behaviors are shaped by social conditions and cultural meanings that often vary by class, race, gender, and sexual orientation.
Myth	Variations in sexual habits are produced by individual variables such as hormone levels, psychological makeup, and sex role socialization.
Reality	Sexual practices are shaped primarily through social experiences in the social groups to which people belong.
Myth	This society offers us infinite possibilities for falling in love with whomever we wish.
Reality	Our romantic partners and those we marry are people very much like ourselves in class, race, and level of education.
Myth	Abstinence-only education programs have resulted in a major drop in sexual activity among teens.
Reality	A large percentage of teens are still having unprotected sex and engaging in other dangerous risk behaviors. Rigorous research shows that abstinence programs have no significant impact on teen sexual activity.
Myth	Current teen pregnancy rates are skyrocketing in the United States, leading to a sudden epidemic of children having children.
Reality	The rate of teenage pregnancy has decreased by 30 percent since 1990.

Intimacy, like other social relations, is shaped by society. Major social changes have influenced intimate relations among women and men in heterosexual unions and in lesbian and gay relationships. In this chapter we examine intimacy through a sociological lens. We begin by examining the changing historical and social context that gives rise to intimacy as it is defined today. We then look at patterns of courtship and mate selection by connecting them to historical developments. Turning to sexuality, we describe the social conditions that shape our most private behaviors. We look at sexual trends in the contemporary United States. We also consider connections between sexual practices and public health and policy issues. Finally, we turn our attention to the ways in which love and sex are structured by imbalances in structural power, especially those associated with class, race, and gender.

Intimacy in Social Context

Contemporary men and women make decisions about intimacy in a social environment that is confusing and fraught with contradiction. Stevi Jackson writes,

> Ours is a world saturated with sexual imagery, yet one where adults still try to preserve children's "innocence"; where pre-marital and often casual sex is a feature of normal young adulthood, yet where sex education is hedged about with all manner of cautions and prohibitions. This is a world in which gay and lesbian chic can be fashionable while gays and lesbians are being bullied and assaulted in

school playgrounds, at work, and on the streets. Our sexual climate is one where "openness" is valued and where ordinary people's intimate sexual secrets are revealed in detail on television and radio and in the "problem pages" of magazines and newspapers, yet where most young people remain unable to discuss sexuality freely with their parents (2007:12).

This context presents great challenges to young adults (and older adults as well). We live in a society consumed with emotional and sexual intimacy. At the same time, today's social order offers few guidelines for establishing and sustaining intimate relationships (Jackson, 2007). The messages are mixed, while the effects of individual decisions and actions on health, happiness, and well-being are monumental.

Our sociological approach to examining intimacy in its social context has the following assumptions: (1) We experience intimacy at the micro level, yet intimate relations are shaped and given meaning by macro-level forces; (2) human sexuality is not simply a biological drive but is formed by the social system and controlled by those in power; (3) although particular sexual practices are enforced by the dominant society, individuals and groups can resist and take deliberate actions to redefine intimacy as a varied and meaningful part of the human condition.

Over the past several decades, a new emphasis on relationships and sexuality has emerged to create an "intimacy revolution" (Whyte, 1990). This is the result of large social changes that have swept postindustrial societies. The purpose of marriage shifted first from economic necessity to companionship, and now is increasingly focused on personal growth and individual fulfillment through deeper intimacy (Cherlin, 2004:853). Twenty-first century technology, including electronic communication, travel, and improved contraception, offers the opportunity for instant intimacy.

In preindustrial America, work relationships and personal relationships were not sharply divided. In Chapter 2 we traced the separation of public and private spheres. When work moved out of the home, two types of relationships developed. One was personal and private; the other was impersonal and public (Gladin, 1977:33). Since then, social and cultural changes have increased the importance of intimate relationships. Social changes have moved us away from a society in which community, kin, and family groupings were a key means of connecting to others. With the loosening of ties to place and kin, individuals in the modern world make life choices and pursue individual goals of their own. Our social identities are no longer tied to the family collective.

Not only are macro-level forces implicated in the contemporary need for intimacy, they may also shape our mate-selection decisions. Rosenfeld (2007) connects the rise of interracial and same-sex unions in recent decades to the increasing independence of youth from their families and communities. Living independent of parents for a number of years prior to marriage is now the expected life path for young adults. It is during this time that young adults typically make mate-selection decisions. Independent adults who make these decisions at a distance from their families are less constrained by parental disapproval and community norms, and have been more free to form interracial or same-sex unions.

In our global society, identities are fragmented and disconnected. Our private selves are often separated from the public roles we assume. This separation has crucial consequences. The distance between our inner selves and the roles we are playing in work and public life creates the need for intimate relationships—"a private world where we can express our real and whole selves" (Skolnick, 1983:122). Using the theater as a metaphor, Erving Goffman (1959) has also made this point. Life in large, impersonal bureaucracies, whether at work, school, church, or in the community, requires "frontstage behavior"—the formal playing of roles by participants. Intimate relationships permit people to behave as if they were "backstage"—to put "aside the masks we wear in the rest of our lives" (Rubin, 1983:165). To be intimate is to be open and honest about the levels of self that remain hidden in daily life. Intimacy is companionship, emotional bonding, and a process that changes as relationships mature (Mackey et al., 2000:203). Until recently, "courting" served this purpose. Young women and men moved from casual dating to formal commitment and finally marriage. In other words, the participants gradually moved from frontstage to backstage behavior.

In the postmodern world, the intense need for intimate relationships creates a contradiction—the very intensity of emotional and physical intimacy makes the bond increasingly fragile. Individuals burden their relationships with too many expectations. They demand too much of intimacy. A romantic partner must provide all things that family and community once provided. A romantic partner must be all things— "lover, friend, companion, playmate, and parent" (Piorkowski, 2000:37).

Some individuals are indeed successful, but many fall short of sustaining the intimacy required by their partner. This often results in a search for a new partner or partners who will provide the intimacy so intently craved. This is a major source of marital strain and helps account for the high divorce rate in contemporary America.

Heterosexual Courtship and Mate Selection

Macro-level changes have reshaped courtship, moving mate selection from a kin and community orientation to one that emphasizes the individual. The decline of parental influence over children's courting behavior reflects the many changes occurring in the larger society. In the past, when people remained in their community of birth after marrying, the bond of strong kin networks was crucial. With a changing economy, the decline of rural America, changing work patterns, the lure of cities, new opportunities far from home, the importance of education, and the relative emancipation of women, young people began to seek more independence from their parents. One major result of this change was the rise of romantic love as the basis of marriage. This freedom of young people to choose their partners is, as we will see, partly illusory, because relationships are still "arranged" by the status of one's family, colleges and universities, work settings, and other organizational arrangements. Nevertheless, "mate selection" in postmodern societies is highly individualized.

A major break with the past was the emergence of dating. Couples in 1900 got to know each other on the front porches or parlors of parents' homes through a courtship ritual named "calling." A young woman would invite a young man to come "calling" at her home, under her parents' watchful eyes. By the 1920s courting couples began to go out on "dates" without adult supervision. The change from private sphere courting to public sphere dating was significant because its consequence was shifting the role of initiating relationships from women to men. Stephanie Coontz explains, "[Dating] involved money, because when you moved from drinking mother's lemonade on the front porch to buying Cokes at a restaurant, someone had to pay. And because in the context of women's second-class economic status, the boy would have to pay, a girl could not ask a boy to take her out. The initiative thus shifted from the girl and her family to the boy" (2005:200–201). By midcentury,

"I can't wait to see what you're like online."

"going steady" was a regular feature of high school and college life (Coontz, 1992; Kass, 2000).

Rules governing dating were defined by peers rather than by adults. Courting, once a way to select a mate, gave way to dating, which was done for enjoyment. Both courting and dating have taken on new meanings. Researchers now refer to courtship in terms of forming close, sexual relationships but not marriage. Dating, as it was practiced during much of the past century, has gone out of style (Peterson, 2000b). During its initial decades, dating had several goals—namely, pleasure, romance, and learning to relate to the so-called opposite sex. Although traditional dating has been replaced by informal pairing off in larger groups, our culture is still based on the premise that dating provides valuable experience that will help individuals select mates and achieve happy marriages.

Fewer teens date now than in the recent past. Since 1990, the percentage of teens who never date has increased, while the percentage of teens who date frequently—defined as one or more dates per week—has fallen (see Figure 7.1 for the decline of frequent dating). Teen dating is associated with both positive and negative outcomes. Teens who date frequently have been found to have slightly higher levels of self-esteem, perceive themselves as more popular, and have higher levels of autonomy than their peers. However, these teens have more conflict with parents, more depression, and lower academic motivation and achievement than other teens (Child Trends, 2007).

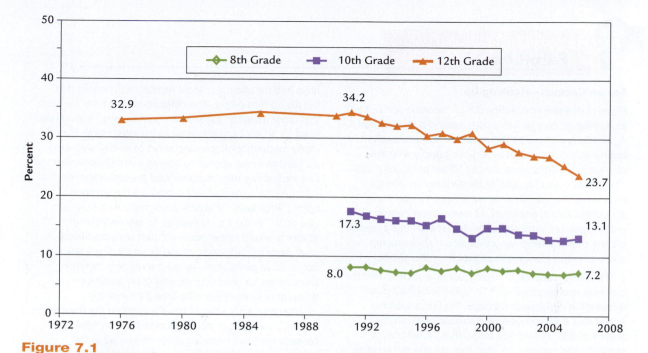

Figure 7.1

Percentage of 8th, 10th, and 12th Grade Students Who Date Frequently, by Grade, Selected Years 1976–2006

Note: Frequent dating is used here to describe youth who report going out on one or more dates each week.

Source: Child Trends, "Dating." Child Trends DataBank, 2007. Online: http://www.childtrendsdatabank.org/figures/73-Figure-2.gif. CHILD TRENDS DATA BANK. ONLINE by Child Trends. Copyright 2007 by CHILD TRENDS INCORPORATED. Reproduced with permission of CHILD TRENDS INCORPORATED in the format Textbook via Copyright Clearance Center.

Adolescents and young people on college campuses typically engage in semiplatonic "group dating," an activity also known as "hanging out" (Annin, 1996). As sociologists Mary Riege Laner and Nicole Ventrone (1998) put it, "hanging out" implies a much more informal kind of interaction than dating. Today, we must use the term "mate selection" cautiously, for choosing a spouse is only one of the many forms that close heterosexual relationships take. The term is no longer useful for describing the variety of premarital relationship experiences (Surra, 1991:54). A prominent feature of the current college campus environment is the casual sex practice of the "hookup." Hookups are casual sex encounters between individuals who have no expectation of a continuing relationship (Paul and Hayes, 2002). While dating involves planning, hooking up is the "fast food of dating" (O'Connor, 2003)—sex with no strings attached. (See Box 7.1.) In a reversal of the old pattern of dating leading to a physical relationship, now a physical relationship might lead to dating (Parker-Pope, 2009).

Online dating is a significant development in contemporary mate selection. Literally hundreds of online dating and matchmaking services promise to help individuals find that "special someone." While younger Internet users are most likely to use these dating services, increasingly, more mature adults are using Internet sites to search for suitable mates. The services offered by dating websites vary from a simple posting of personal profiles to "scientific matching" based on extensive psychological and partner-preference questionnaires. Some dating services are free, but most charge membership fees. Some sites offer both heterosexual and same-sex matching. Many single individuals are drawn to the prospect of accessing a larger pool of potential dates, but there are drawbacks related to the anonymity of this process. One study

BOX 7.1 Researching Families

Sex on Campus—Hooking Up

Reports of a sexual practice called "hooking up" began to surface on college campuses around a decade ago. A hookup is defined as "a sexual encounter usually lasting only one night between two people who are strangers or brief acquaintances" (Paul et al., 2000:76). The practice was thought to be rampant on college campuses, but conclusions were based on personal anecdotes and speculation. In recent years, social scientists have undertaken research that provides a clearer picture of this phenomenon. Elizabeth Paul and her colleagues are pioneers in researching this subject.

The early research confirms just how widespread the behavior has become. In 2000 [Elizabeth] Paul published what colleagues credit as the first academic article that explored college hookups in depth. Her survey of 666 undergrads found that 78 percent of students had hooked up, that they usually did so after consuming alcohol, and that the average student had accumulated 10.8 hookup partners during college. Studies on other campuses produced similar numbers. Researchers at James Madison University found that 77.7 percent of women and 84.3 percent of men had hooked up, a process they said routinely involving "petting below the waist, oral sex, or intercourse." At the University of Michigan, more than 60 percent of students reported hooking up; they said that a typical hookup more often included "genital touching" than "a meaningful conversation."

Skeptics ask whether hooking up is really any different than the one night-stands college students have had for decades. Most researchers believe it is, but it's hard to prove. The difficulty stems from the fact that older research focused on "casual sex," usually defined as an encounter that includes intercourse. Since many modern hookups stop short of all-the-way-sex, it's hard to make apples-to apples comparisons. But the academics say they're convinced the phenomenon has changed. "It's generalized . . . now it's the campus norm," Paul says. "If you're a normal college student, you do it." While it's impossible to say exactly why students would rather hook up than seek traditional boyfriends or girlfriends, students say that greater competitive pressures—to build a resume, position themselves for grad school, and chart a career trajectory—leave them little time for romance.

Now that early studies have quantified the frequency of and sex practices that take place during hookups, researchers are becoming more interested in the emotional aftereffects. Some researchers are doing longitudinal studies that follow the same students from freshman year onward, to see how their attitudes change. For her current research, Paul is asking more questions like: "Do you think your hookup experiences are going to help you be a good relationship partner some day?" The students don't really have an answer. Some researchers worry that hooking up gives students sexual experience but no real relationship experience, which could affect their ability to segue into more adult, committed relationships.

Source: McGinn, Daniel (2004). "Mating Behavior 101." *Newsweek* (October 4): 44–45.

suggests that 30 percent of individuals using these sites may actually be married (cited in Mulrine, 2003:57). In some cases, women have put themselves in danger by posting personal information online or dating a man who was, in fact, a predator using the service with criminal intent.

Research conducted by the Pew Internet and American Life Project shows how important the Internet has become for those seeking romantic relationships: Among the 10 million Internet users who say they are single and looking for romantic partners, 74 percent have used the Internet to advance their romantic interests. Nearly three million adults have either married or entered a long-term relationship with an online dating partner (Madden and Lenhart, 2006:i–ii). The following are some of the key findings from the Pew/Internet Online Dating study:

- Millions of Americans know people who have tried and succeeded at online dating.
- One in 10 Internet users say he or she has personally gone to dating websites.
- A majority of online daters report good experiences with the sites.

- Online daters believe dating websites help people to find a better match because they can get to know a lot more people.

- While some stigma persists, most do not view online dating simply as a last resort.

- There are uses of the Internet beyond dating websites that have woven themselves into the world of romance (Madden and Lenhart, 2006:v).

Variations in "Dating" Practices

GENDER

Gender differences are exceedingly important in today's romantic relationships. In their studies of college dating, Laner and Ventrone originally decided that the words "hanging out" denoted a "nondate." They first surveyed college students about their gendered experience with dating (as if a date were a romantic encounter between two strangers) and then later about their experience with friends who turned into dating partners (to get at the notion of "hanging out"). Interestingly, they found that even today heterosexual "dating" behavior is based on a gendered style of relating. In 1998 and 2000, college students believed that it was still men's responsibility to decide where to go, prepare the car, get money, pick up the date, open the door, pay the bill, and so on. Women-exclusive behavior (regardless of the formality of the "date"/"hang out" session) still included talking with friends about the date, taking extra preparation time, waiting for the date to arrive, and being the recipient (not the initiator) of any affectionate or sexual moves, such as being kissed or having the man put his arm around her (Laner and Ventrone, 1998, 2000).

Of course, the sexual double standard has weakened. Today, many women initiate relationships with men to whom they are attracted. This change has two profound implications. On one side, it creates havoc in many relationships. Some individuals are torn between the traditional standards and new expectations. They are in a quandary as to what are appropriate behaviors: When should a woman take the initiative? Should men never act chivalrous? As relationships form, the parties must now define and redefine the rules.

CLASS

Among young people, the search for romantic partners varies with social class. Structural features account for the different patterns that prevail. In general, the higher the class, the more control parents have over the dating activities of their children. Middle- and upper-class families have more control over desirable resources that they can use (Whyte, 1990:70). The upper class lives in a privileged social world with exclusive neighborhoods, private schools, and country clubs. This social homogeneity continues even during vacations, which tend to be spent in exclusive resorts (Domhoff, 1970). Supervised dances and parties are provided for young people at exclusive schools and country clubs, where social mingling most assuredly occurs among social equals. At 18 years of age, many young women in this class are formally "presented" at expensive galas.

Middle-class youths have more freedom of choice than those from the upper class, but they too are controlled more by their parents than are lower-class youths. Middle-class youths are more likely to attend school, church, and civic-sponsored social events than lower-class students. Middle-class parents are also more likely to move to a different neighborhood or to change their child's school in order to narrow the social choices in the desired direction.

Lower-class youths are less likely to use structured activities for their cross-sex encounters and more likely to gather in streets, bowling alleys, or bars to meet others.

Stratification in the larger society promotes romantic patterns that are based on social class. College campuses no longer serve as marriage marts, since young people now want a prolonged period of freedom before marriage (Hacker, 2003:14). Nevertheless, social resources of potential "mates" remain important. For example, young men are rated according to family background, group memberships, potential occupation, accomplishments, behavior, and appearance. Women are also ranked in terms of their desirability in regard to these characteristics, but with special emphasis on physical beauty and popularity. Decades ago, sociologist Willard Waller (1937) theorized that social stratification shaped intimate relationships. Ranking systems punish those with low status by negatively affecting their self-esteem and increasing their isolation (as seen in shyness, inept social behavior, and refusing to date for fear of rejection). Individuals in each level tend to date within their "dating desirability level." When this behavior occurs, dating partners have relatively equal bargaining power, reducing the potential for exploitation.

Whenever people date outside their stratum, however, the possibility of exploitation increases. According to Waller's "**principle of least interest,**" the person with the least interest in continuing the relationship has the power to control it. Since the high-status person has less to lose by discontinuing the relationship, she or he can make excessive demands on the lower-status partner. The high-status male, for example, can demand more sexual favors from his low-status partner than would be the case if her status were equal or reversed. Similarly, the high-status female can make excessive demands on her lower-status partner for gifts and costly dating activities than she would if the status situation were otherwise. The class hierarchy influences courtship as "people from higher social classes are likely to be viewed as more attractive dating partners than those from lower social classes" (Whyte, 1990:70).

RACE

Because people of color are overrepresented among the poor, their romantic attachments often resemble those found in the lower classes. There are exceptions to this, of course, as the children of African Americans and Latinos who are economically and professionally successful obtain the benefits of class privilege. In many urban areas, for example, there are "coming out" parties for the daughters of the Black elite. These children often attend private schools, and they, like other children of the middle and upper classes, tend to marry late.

Being a person of color often means being situated in social networks and activities that differ from those of Whites. For example, many Mexican American families hold quinceañera rites for young women on their fifteenth birthdays. The quinceañera ritual is the parents' way of introducing their daughter to the ethnic community as a young girl who has become eligible for marriage (Williams, 1990:39).

From high school through college to work settings, dating and mating take place within race- and class-based networks. This is changing, however, due to new organizational arrangements that foster intergroup contact. For example, interracial relationships are likely to form in integrated settings such as the military, colleges and universities, and metropolitan areas (Heaton and Jacobson, 2000).

Interracial dating (or "interdating") is becoming both more common and more accepted in U.S. society (Wellner, 2005). Yancey's national study of adults' dating patterns found that 36 percent of Whites had interdated, as had 56 percent of African Americans, 55 percent of Hispanics, and 57 percent of Asian Americans (2002). Men were more likely than women to date interracially as were individuals who had attended integrated schools. Increases in interracial dating raise the question of the quality of these relationships. How different are these relationships from romantic relationships within a racial group? Both scholars and the general public assume that interracial relationships will encounter difficulties that are related to cultural or ethnic differences (Gaines and Ickes, 1997, cited in Troy et al., 2006). This concern is one of the main reasons parents may discourage interracial dating. Research on this subject is still limited, but the tendency seems clear. In a new study of young adults, Troy and his colleagues (2006) find no differences in relationship quality between interracial and intraracial relationships. This is not to say there are no problems in interracial relationships. What is significant is that "while conflicts might occur in interracial relationships (as in all relationships), partners behave and cope with them in ways that are similar to all relationships" (p. 76). The results of this study, along with others, "challenge the prejudicial view that interracial relationships are fraught with problems" (Troy et al., 2006:76).

Factors in Mate Selection

In some societies the choice of a marriage partner is the exclusive responsibility of the kinship group. This choice is made on practical grounds, with these considerations paramount: Do the two families to be joined have similar social and economic standing? Do the two principals share the same religious values and other important traditions? Does the union make economic sense to the two kinship units?

In contemporary U.S. society, individuals rather than families make the choice of marriage partner, and this choice is governed by such nonpractical considerations as the personality traits, behavior patterns, and attractiveness of the potential partner. Even in our society, however, the choices are not entirely free. The most important norms governing marriage partners have been "*Marry within your own race. Marry someone of the opposite sex*" (Root, 2002:1). Until the U.S. Supreme Court declared them unconstitutional in 1967, some 17 states had laws forbidding interracial marriages. All states prohibit marriage between close relatives (although the definition of "close" varies from state to state). Beyond the legal requirements there are social expectations by peers, family, neighbors, and others in the community that narrow the choices of potential spouses.

Some conventional thinking about appropriate marriage partners is shifting. Despite the continuing presence of the color line in marriage, intermarriage rates have been slowly rising over the past few decades. Less than 1 percent of all U.S. marriages were interracial in 1970, but by 2000 more than 5 percent of marriages were interracial (Batson et al., 2006:658). Intermarriage varies by racial group, ranging in 2000 from 6.1 percent of Whites, 10.9 percent of Blacks, 26.3 percent of Asian Americans, 26.1 percent of Hispanics, and 67 percent of American Indians marrying outside their respective racial group (Nagel, 2003:259–260).

When thinking about the future of interracial marriage, we do well to look at trends in public attitudes on the subject. A series of Gallup Polls shows that the United States has changed its mind on this subject over the past 50 years (Carroll, 2007). In 1958, 4 percent of the population approved of interracial marriage; in 2007, 77 percent of the population approved. Within these results, younger age groups had higher rates of approval. Public opinion, along with other factors, predict that the increase in interracial marriage will continue.

In the study of mate selection, the concept of **assortative mating** addresses the question of who individuals choose as mates. Mate choice in the United States is far from random; instead, clear patterns can be observed in demographic and individual factors among paired individuals. Mate selection research finds positive assortative mating; that is, across the board, in same-sex and different-sex pairings, people choose a mate with traits similar to their own (Jepson and Jepson, 2002; Kurdek, 2003). Individuals date and mate within their class, race, ethnicity, religion, and educational level. This is called **homogamy.** Although ethnicity and religion are playing a less important role in influencing who marries whom, homogamy remains "one of the robust social facts of romantic life" (Schwartz and Rutter, 1998:18).

Exceptions to the general principle of homogamous mate selection can be observed with respect to social class. While most people marry within their social class, the patriarchal structure of society has historically provided women with a powerful incentive to marry a man of higher status (**hypergamy**). Hypergamy is women's principal avenue for upward mobility in societies that prescribe domesticity for women and limit their access to workplace opportunities. Alternatively, in the contemporary context, a professional woman who finds a dearth of possible mates with similar professional standing may be willing to marry a lower status man (**hypogamy**). In short, hypergamy involves marrying upward, while hypogamy involves marrying downward.

One aspect of mate selection that has been studied consistently over time is mate preferences—that is, the qualities women and men think are important in selecting a mate. Groups of young adults have been presented with the same list of 18 characteristics at data collection points between 1939 and 1996. Research participants ranked these characteristics in order of importance. Some shifts in top preferences have occurred over time. In 1939, the men's top three preferences were: (1) dependable character; (2) emotional stability, maturity; and (3) pleasing disposition. In 1939, the women's top three were (1) emotional stability, maturity; (2) dependable character; and (3) ambition, industriousness. By 1996, men's and women's preferences had converged. Both men and women said that their top three criteria in selecting a mate were (1) mutual attraction, love; (2) dependable character; (3) emotional stability, maturity. A number of changes in mate selection preferences can be seen over time. Physical attractiveness has increased in importance while chastity is of declining significance for both women and men. Men are no longer very concerned with women's domestic skills, but for both women and men, the education and intelligence of a potential partner is increasingly important (Buss et al., 2001).

Models for understanding the mate selection process—that is, whether, when, and who an individual marries—were developed prior to the monumental shift that has occurred in women's labor force participation over the past 30 years. An issue currently under discussion in the literature is the importance of women's earning potential in determining their marriage prospects. Many scholars believe that increasingly, both men and women seek partners who are likely to be successful in the labor market (Sweeney and Cancian, 2004). Others suggest that women—now more economically independent—may be less concerned with men's earning potential than in the past. Women who have the ability to be economically self-sufficient may now choose to emphasize men's earnings less than other factors such as physical attractiveness or willingness to do housework (England, 2004; Press, 2004).

At the personal level, some cultural proclivities affect the chemistry between potential spouses. Cultural standards of beauty make certain people more physically attractive and sexually exciting than others. Humans prefer to associate with, date, and mate with facially attractive individuals (Hume and Montgomery, 2001). In addition, most women and men prefer mates with physical characteristics such as tallness, round eyes, buffness for men, and more ample breasts for women

(Chow, 2000:12). A long-standing cultural mandate dictates that the man be older than the woman. Similarly, another long-standing cultural demand has required men to be taller, heavier, and wiser and earn more money than their mates. Cultural prescriptions are, however, subject to change over time. At present, the ideal that men earn more than their women partners is changing. Younger men are increasingly willing to marry women who earn more than they earn (Raley and Bratter, 2004).

Structural Influences on Mate Selection

Patterns of mate selection reveal how influences other than personal ones affect mate choice. The structural composition of the population shapes demographic trends in two ways. First, the availability of marriageable partners (those with qualities that make them desirable spouses, such as the appropriate age or economic circumstances) is limited. Research on sex ratios has found that imbalances in the number of women and men in a given population affect mate choice. When one gender is in oversupply, it becomes a buyer's market for the gender in shorter supply (Root, 2002:71). The undersupply of men among African Americans contributes to mate selection differences between Blacks and Whites. African American females have a much more restricted field of eligibles than White females (if they marry within their racial group).

A second structural influence on mate selection lies in individuals' varied affiliations with different groups. Diverse affiliations provide opportunities to meet and stay in contact with dissimilar others. Summarizing the research, Surra (1991:57) concludes that people marry outside their social group, not because they have a preference for doing so, but because of their multiple and interwoven group affiliations.

Schools play a prominent role in narrowing the choice of eligible partners in terms of social class. Neighborhood schools tend to be homogeneous in social class. In high school, students tend to stratify themselves according to the socioeconomic status of their parents. The tracking system in the schools is highly correlated with social class. This finding is significant because the tracking system formally segregates students, promoting interaction among those preparing for college on the one hand and among those taking technical and commercial courses on the other. Thus students move through the educational system with same-class peers.

College further restricts the pool of eligibles along social class lines. College attendance

BOX 7.2 Technology and the Family

High-Tech Mate Selection

A live video link connected Indonesian and American students for a global-communications course through Indiana University–Purdue University at Indianapolis in the fall of 2005, helping them learn firsthand about topics like listening skills and culture shock.

So when Kanti Winarah, of Jakarta, sent an e-mail message to her American counterparts saying she knew the United States best through its pop music, Sean Crain, of Purdue, was compelled to write back. Pop music, he wrote, is not the best representation of America.

A year later, the two students were engaged.

"The e-mails just got longer and longer, and eventually they got personal," says Mr. Crain, who has since graduated. The couple continued to talk with the help of instant messaging, phone-calling cards, and Skype, the Internet phone service. Eventually Mr. Crain traveled to Indonesia for a few weeks. Then he returned to pop the question.

When they met for the first time, it "wasn't really a nerve-racking experience," he says, although some of Ms. Winarah's friends did worry that he might already be married. He says he has since learned of many other students who have met and courted under similar circumstances.

"There wasn't anything missing" from the courtship, says Mr. Crain, "other than the physical touch—which is nice from time to time, but not crucial."

Next month Ms. Winarah will interview for a U.S. visa, and, if all goes well, she and Mr. Crain will be married in several months, in Indianapolis.

Source: Keller, Josh (2007). "High-Tech Courtship." *Chronicle of Higher Education* (March 23): A6.

is strongly determined by the socioeconomic status of one's parents. Colleges self-select by social class because of the high cost of tuition. Moreover, the colleges and universities are themselves stratified by prestige, cost, and eventual benefit of attendance. Children from the upper classes cluster in the most costly and prestigious private schools. Middle-class young people are most likely to attend state colleges and universities, and those with the fewest resources are most likely to enroll in community colleges. Within a given college, fraternities and sororities play a role in mate selection by social class. These organizations carefully scrutinize prospective members for the right social characteristics (social class, race, and ethnicity).

Despite an ideology that rests on personal choice, the social structural influences on mate selection remain strong. Sociologist Paula England recognizes this dilemma: "I cannot marry someone I never meet, and what neighborhood I live in or what college I attend profoundly affects my pool [of potential partners]" (2004:1036).

Although the structural influences just discussed typically narrow the choice of partners, technology has the potential to increase diversity in the pool of eligible partners by creating global connections. Box 7.2 on page 227 shows how technology facilitates long-distance communication between young adults who just might develop a loving relationship.

Changing Sexual Behavior

Society and Sexuality

Sexuality is an explosive topic. The sociology of sexuality is an emerging area of research that examines how society shapes the expression of sexual desire through cultural images and social institutions—how "organizations like the family, religion, and the state shape and encourage some forms of sexual behavior and not others" (Williams and Stein, 2002:1). Most recently, sociologists have taken a **social constructionist approach to sexuality.** Instead of examining the biological or developmental aspects of human sexuality, this approach "questions the naturalness of the social order and looks for the underlying social motivations and mechanisms that shape human social relations and societies" (Nagel, 2003:5). The social constructionist approach requires that we keep two points in mind: (1) Human sexuality varies across time, space, and the life of any individual; and (2) although sexuality is the site of our most intimate experiences, it is socially controlled and closely bound up with the basic inequalities that configure the structure of society—namely, class, race, and gender.

Sex is grounded in the body, but biology alone does not define human sexuality. If sex were purely natural, we would expect to find uniformity across the world's cultures, yet sexual behavior and sexual desire are incredibly diverse. Activities condemned in one society are encouraged in another; and ideas about what is attractive or erotic or sexually satisfying, or even sexually possible, vary a great deal. Even deeply felt personal identities (for example, masculinity/femininity or heterosexuality/homosexuality/bisexuality) are not privately or solely the product of biology but are created by social, economic, and political forces that change over time. Furthermore, sexuality is situational and changeable, modified by day-to-day circumstances throughout the life course. Sexual behavior refers to the sexual acts that people engage in. Sexual desire, on the other hand, is the motivation to engage in sexual acts—in other words, what turns people on. A person's sexuality consists of both behavior and desire (Schwartz and Rutter, 1998:2).

Although human beings are capable of a variety of sexual expressions, social institutions channel and direct sexual behavior according to what is defined as socially legitimate. Heterosexuality is considered "normal" and natural even though different-sex relations are only one imaginable arrangement of the sexes and their pleasures (Katz, 1990; Messner, 1996). Despite the great variety of sexual practices, there is a dominant sexuality that defines appropriate sexual partners, sexual tastes, and sexuality activities. Heterosexuality is the normative ideal in most contemporary societies (Nagel, 2003:7). Larger forces of social control go to great lengths to define heterosexuality as natural. **Compulsory heterosexuality** refers to the practices that enforce heterosexual behavior as normal and natural while stigmatizing other forms of sexual expression.

When we demystify sexuality, we can begin to see how socially dominant groups use sexuality to their own ends. For example, images about sexuality among African Americans are central to maintaining institutional racism. Similarly, beliefs about women's sexuality operate to maintain gender control. Heterosexuality is the privileged form of sexual behavior. It is protected and rewarded by the state and subsidized through social and economic incentives such as the right to marry. On the other hand, homosexuality and bisexuality are controlled through the denial of marriage. Gays and lesbians are not allowed to marry. This denies them spousal health care benefits and the option of filing joint tax returns (Schwartz and Rutter, 1998:89). (See Chapter 8.) Of course, dominant sexual meanings are being challenged by many social groups, including feminists (both lesbian and straight), gay men, and bisexuals. Through human activism and agency, many are working to change repressive laws and unfair social practices.

Enlarging the Sexuality Frame

Ideas and behaviors regarding sexuality are undergoing rapid changes in the United States and other parts of the world. These changes take on new meanings when viewed sociologically. Understanding why some sexualities are marginalized tells us a great deal about social organization (Epstein, 1994). Gay and lesbian experiences have given us new insights about how sexualities are defined. Homosexuality *and* heterosexuality are social constructions, both at the macro level, where society defines what same-sex relationships mean, and at the micro level, where individuals acquire their own sexual identity (Heyl, 1996:120). (See the discussion of family life among lesbians and gays in Chapter 12.) The terms *sexual identity* and *sexual orientation* refer to how people classify themselves—as gay, lesbian, bisexual, or straight. **Sexual identity** refers to self-classification while **sexual orientation** refers to sexual attraction and desire. Sexual identity and **sexual behavior** may differ, if people identify themselves as heterosexual and desire people of the same sex (Schwartz and Rutter, 1998:26).

In recent decades, social scientists have debated about whether homosexuality has genetic or social origins—on whether it is inborn or shaped by social experience. The debate is between *essentialists* (those who identify biological, or essential, determinants of sexuality) and *social constructionists* (those who emphasize the social conditions leading to the choice of sexual partners). Unfortunately, the debate has polarized nature and nurture rather than seeing them operating in combination. A growing literature provides evidence of a biological basis for homosexuality (for summaries, see Angier, 1991; Burr, 1993; Gelman, 1992; Gorman 1991).

"Do you know its sexual identity?"

Despite the biological facts, sexualities are always social as well. Lesbian and gay identities are a twentieth-century phenomenon, whereas homosexual behaviors are universal and have always been practiced (D'Emilio and Freedman, 1988).

At the same time that scholars are documenting a wide range of sexual experiences, sexual orientation is commonly placed into just two mutually exclusive categories: gay and straight. But because sexuality is comprised of many different elements, including physical, social, and emotional attraction as well as actual sexual behavior, the gay/straight dichotomy masks great variability. Lesbian, gay, straight, bisexual, and transsexual are social roles as well as sexual preferences. Desire is one thing; behaviors and lifestyles are quite another. Sexual orientations are not only a matter of genital activity. They are social creations with identifiable norms and values about sexuality. (See the discussion of same-sex families in Chapter 12.)

The Sexual Revolution

Over the last three and a half centuries, the meaning and place of sexuality in American life have undergone great changes. Sexuality moved from a family-centered reproductive system in the colonial era to a romantic and intimate, yet conflicted, form in nineteenth-century marriage. In the modern period in which sex is highly commercialized, sexual relations are expected to provide personal identity and individual happiness apart from reproduction (D'Emilio and Freedman, 1988). By the 1920s, sexuality had entered the public sphere, becoming a major source of identity and self-discovery. Sexual liberalization continued through the next three decades. "The sexual revolution redefined sexual activity as a right of individuals and not merely as a means for reproduction or even marital intimacy" (Risman and Schwartz, 2002:23). This transformation did not occur overnight. Instead, as Coontz (1992:197) details, the roots of the sexual revolution can be traced to the following social, demographic, and economic changes occurring in the United States:

- The rising age of marriage
- Educational convergence of women and men
- Women's growing autonomy
- The invention of birth control methods that are independent of coitus (first the oral contraceptive pill, introduced in 1960, then the IUD)

- The sheer rise in the absolute number of singles as the baby boom generation reached sexual maturity
- The revulsion of a politically active generation against what they saw as the hypocrisy of their elders

Along with the aforementioned factors, advertising and entertainment media have been important forces contributing to sexual permissiveness. Using sex to sell products is a central and omnipresent feature of mass marketing. Critics accuse many television programs of "sexploitation." Cable television is free to show nudity. Movies are free to display whatever sexual activities they choose, within the guidelines set for each rating category by the movie industry. Advertisers blatantly use sex, even "sexy" poses by preteens, to sell their wares. Popular music, whether country, pop, or rock, is commonly sexual in its message. The media's fixation on sex has served to involve children and youth earlier and earlier in thinking about sex and acting sexually.

Scientific Research on Sexuality

Much of what we know about sex in this society is based on a few surveys in which a sample of people have been selected from the population to answer questions about sexual thoughts and behaviors. Since Alfred Kinsey's pioneering research (1948, 1953), social scientists have asked people about their sex lives. In the years since Kinsey, national women's magazines such as *Redbook* and *Cosmopolitan* and men's magazines such as *Playboy* have done surveys asking people what they do in bed and other places. Sex surveys have shown substantial changes in women's sexual behavior and smaller but significant changes in men's sexual behavior.

Many sex surveys in the research literature are flawed because they sample a narrowly defined group of people. Kinsey's research was based on 18,000 interviews. Although his research did a great deal to break down stereotypes, his landmark study was not based on a representative sample of the U.S. population. Kinsey's respondents were volunteers, a self-selected group, "leading to the suspicion that the more libidinous members of the population were overrepresented and that the incidence of homosexuality in particular was exaggerated" (Robinson, 1994:3).

More than 44 years after Kinsey's study, a team of researchers led by Edward O. Laumann at the National Opinion Research Center completed the nation's most comprehensive sex survey. The 1992 National Health and Social Life Survey (NHSLS) was designed to help researchers learn about the sex lives of U.S. men and women. Based on interviews with nearly 3,500 adults, the study explored the extent to which sexual behavior is influenced by gender, age, marital status, and other demographic characteristics. Among the topics considered by the NHSLS are early sexual experiences, masturbation, contraception and fertility, sexual abuse and sexual coercion, sexual health, satisfaction, sexual dysfunction, and homosexuality. Survey findings are detailed in two books: *The Social Organization of Sexuality* (Laumann et al., 1994) and *Sex in America* (Michael et al., 1994). In 2000, two of the original authors published a new book, *Sex, Love, and Health in America* (Laumann and Michael, 2000), which extends their earlier work. This study differs in several ways from its predecessors. Respondents were randomly selected from a cross section of U.S. households. Even though the sample is far smaller than Kinsey's, the sophisticated sampling techniques make its findings generalizable to the population at large.

The most valuable contribution of the survey is that it looks at sexuality in its *social* context. The finding the authors stress more than any other is that people's sexual choices are shaped by the social networks in which they operate. The study found that most people meet their sexual partners through family members, friends, and acquaintances—in other words, through their social networks. This finding flies in the face of an old image—that of meeting an alluring stranger across a crowded room. This is how the authors of the survey explain how we find our partners:

> People's choices of sexual and marriage partners are severely constrained but also greatly facilitated by their social networks. It's not that you never see a stranger across a crowded room and fall instantly in love. It's more that the stranger you notice will look just like you. This stranger will be of your race, educational status, social class, and probably religion too. The single biggest reason why, of course, is that most of the people in that crowded room are preselected to be alike. The social world is organized so that you will meet people like yourself. (Michael et al., 1994:69)

The following are major findings of the NHSLS:

- Adultery is the exception rather than the rule. Both men and women are remarkably faithful to their partners. Nearly 75 percent of married men and 85 percent of married women say they have never been unfaithful. Over a lifetime, a typical man has six partners, a typical woman two.

- People in this country are divided into three categories according to how often they have sex. One-third have sex twice a week or more, one-third a few times a month, and one-third a few times a year or not at all.

- The incidence of homosexuality is lower than the 10 percent reported by Kinsey and widely reported since then. Just 2.8 percent of men and 1.4 percent of women identify themselves as homosexual or bisexual. Still, 9 percent of men and 4 percent of women report that they have had a sexual experience with someone of the same sex since puberty. While these numbers are surprisingly low, the research team admits that stigmatization probably makes people reluctant to discuss homosexual behavior.

- Married couples have the most sex, they enjoy it most, and they are the most likely to have orgasms when they do. Nearly 40 percent of married people have sex twice a week, compared to 25 percent for singles.

Despite the scientific finding about marital sex, new concerns have arisen about the growing ranks of working couples who seldom have sex. Stress, kids, and jobs are making many working parents too exhausted for sex. Estimates are that 15 to 20 percent of couples have sex no more than 10 times a year (Deveny, 2003). A glut of books now advise couples on rekindling marital sex. Even Dr. Phil says, "sexless marriages are an undeniable epidemic" (Flanigan, 2003:171).

Laumann recently reanalyzed the data to learn more about variations in sexuality by education and life circumstance. He found that being more highly educated is associated with greater sexual satisfaction and that declining fortunes contribute to sexual dysfunction (Herbert, 1999).

The NHSLS makes important contributions to research on the social construction of sexuality. Of course, questions remain about whether people tell the truth about their sexual behaviors. Other shortcomings make the survey too limited to reveal much about subgroups of the population (such as gay Hispanics) and people over age 59 (who were omitted from the survey). Nevertheless, the survey goes a long way toward demythologizing sexual behavior in the United States. More research is needed to shed light on how sexual practices are linked to public health and policy issues such as AIDS and teenage pregnancy, problems that may have worsened because of the public reluctance to confront basic questions about sex.

The Global Study of Sexual Attitudes and Behaviors is the newest research on sexuality undertaken by Edward O. Laumann and a team of international researchers. This research entailed surveying 27,500 middle-aged and older adults (ages 40 to 80) in 29 countries on the subject of the physical and emotional qualities of their sex lives. A major conclusion of the study is that highest levels of sexual well-being are found in Western nations with relatively more gender equality. The greatest sexual satisfaction was found among women and men in these five countries: Austria, Spain, Canada, Belgium, and the United States. In more male-dominant societies, lower levels of sexual satisfaction were found, with East Asia (especially Japan and Taiwan) experiencing the lowest levels and Middle Eastern nations (such as Turkey, Egypt, and Algeria) in the middle (Harms, 2006; Laumann et al., 2006). How might we explain these results? Peter Gorner reports, "Sociologist Edward Laumann, who directed the study, proposes that when relationships are based on equality, couples form sexual habits that are more likely to suit both parties' needs and interests. 'Male-centered cultures where sexual behavior is more oriented toward procreation tend to discount the importance of sexual pleasure for women,' he said" (2006).

AIDS

AIDS was first reported in the United States in 1981 and has since become a national tragedy and a worldwide epidemic (NIH, 2005). Between 1981 and 2007, more than 1,016,000 Americans were diagnosed with AIDS; of that number, 563,000 have died from AIDS-related causes. Currently around 254,000 individuals in the United States live with HIV (but not AIDS). The terminology associated with AIDS and HIV is sometimes misunderstood. The term AIDS (acquired immunodeficiency syndrome) refers to advanced stages of HIV (human immunodeficiency virus). The goal of treatment typically is to treat HIV to prevent or delay the progression of the disease to AIDS (CDC, 2009).

Fear of AIDS has been responsible for changing the sexual behavior of many in the United States. The most common means of transmitting HIV is by having unprotected sex with an infected partner; therefore, an aggressive approach has been taken toward safe-sex education over the last decade. AIDS education changed sexual practices, especially among middle-class gay men. As a result, AIDS cases trended downward after the mid-1990s.

Dramatic declines in AIDS cases and deaths were also due to advances in HIV treatments. Antiretroviral drug therapies, introduced in 1996, have altered the course of the disease for those who have access to this treatment. The progression of HIV to AIDS was slowed for hundreds of thousands of individuals. But because the drugs go only to those who can afford them (or have health insurance that provides them), the drop in AIDS does not occur across the board, but rather benefits those with racial and class privileges. For those receiving the best treatment, "HIV has come to be seen as a chronic, rather than fatal, condition" (Jefferson, 2006:41).

In recent years, the number of new U.S. cases of AIDS has ranged between 36,000 and 38,000 annually. Currently, approximately 456,000 persons live with AIDS. The principal means of HIV transmission is male-to-male sexual contact, injection drug use, and heterosexual contact. Because the most common means of HIV transmission is male-to-male sexual contact, it is unsurprising that the majority of new AIDS cases are among men. In 2007, 73 percent of individuals diagnosed with AIDS were men. Three-quarters of women who were diagnosed with AIDS were infected through heterosexual contact (CDC, 2009).

The incidence of HIV/AIDS is uneven across racial groups. Although AIDS was first diagnosed in gay White men, it has increasingly become a disease of color (Kalb and Murr, 2006:44). African Americans are the racial ethnic group most devastated by the disease. African American men are diagnosed with AIDS at a rate more than seven times that of White men, and African American women are diagnosed at more than 20 times the rate of White women. Although African Americans make up 13 percent of the population, they accounted for almost half of new AIDS cases in the United States in 2007. Hispanics were also overrepresented: Hispanics, who make up 15 percent of the population, accounted for nearly 20 percent of the total number of new AIDS cases (CDC, 2009). African Americans and Hispanics are also overrepresented among the poor.

> The root of the problem [of HIV/AIDS] is poverty and the neglect that comes with it—inadequate health care and a dearth of information about safe sex.... Protecting against HIV isn't necessarily priority No.1 among the poor. "If you're focused on day-to-day survival, you're not thinking about where to get condoms," says Marjorie Hill, of the Gay Men's Health Crisis in New York City. (Kalb and Murr, 2006:44)

Nearly 30 years of AIDS in the United States have taken a heavy toll on this society. Many of us have personal knowledge of this disease; that is, we may know someone—an extended family member, an acquaintance, a community member—who has been stricken with AIDS. A less immediate issue for most of us is the global HIV/AIDS epidemic. More than 25,000,000 people have died of AIDS since 1981, making it one of the most devastating epidemics in human history (UNAIDS, 2005:02). The situation is especially grim in sub-Saharan Africa where 22,500,000 people currently live with HIV/AIDS. See Table 7.1 for a summary of global statistics on HIV/AIDS in 2007.

Table 7.1   Global AIDS: Regional HIV/AIDS Statistics for 2007

	Adults and Children Living with HIV/AIDS	New HIV Cases in 2007	Deaths Due to AIDS in 2007
Sub-Saharan Africa	22.5 million	1.7 million	1.6 million
North Africa & Middle East	380,000	35,000	25,000
South & Southeast Asia	4 million	340,000	270,000
East Asia	800,000	92,000	32,000
Oceania	75,000	14,200	1,200
Latin America	1.6 million	100,000	58,000
Caribbean	230,000	17,000	11,000
Eastern Europe and Central Asia	1.6 million	150,000	55,000
Western and Central Europe	760,000	31,000	12,000
North America	1.3 million	46,000	21,000
TOTAL	33.2 million	2.5 million	2.1 million

Source: UNAIDS/World Health Organization (2007). *AIDS Epidemic Update: 2007.*, p. 7. Online: http://data.unaids.org/put/EPISlides/2007/2007_epiupdate_en.pdf.

Teen Sexuality

Over the course of the last century, young people become sexually active earlier than their parents' generation. Due in part to their freedom from community and parental control, today's young people have more sexual freedom than ever before. We live in a highly sexualized culture that pressures teens to be sexually active.

Data on sexual activity are inexact, but statistics from a number of sources suggest that teen sexual activity has declined modestly over the past decade. In 1991, 54 percent of high school students reported having had inter-

"You'd better ask your grandparents about that, son—my generation is very uncomfortable talking about abstinence."

course; in 2007, 48 percent of teens reported having had intercourse (50 percent of boys and 46 percent of girls). According to the latest data, the median age for first intercourse is 16.9 years for boys and 17.4 years for girls (Kaiser Family Foundation, 2008). New research has found that while the average age of first intercourse hovers at about 17, there is some variation by race and gender in the percentages of teens who have intercourse during their high school years. Among 15- to 19-year-old females, African Americans are most likely to say they were sexually experienced (defined as having had intercourse at least once), followed by Hispanics and then Whites (Child Trends, 2008).

The National Survey of Adolescents and Young Adults, conducted by the Kaiser Family Foundation (2003), is an important study of the sexual activity of teens and young adults. This research asks young people in the United States detailed questions about their knowledge and attitudes toward sex and sexual health. The report's key findings show that young people are more concerned about sex and sexual health than any other issues in their lives. Other findings from the survey:

- Young people report considerable pressure to have sex.
- A third of adolescents have engaged in oral sex, but one in five are unaware that oral sex can transmit sexually transmitted diseases.
- Many young people remain reluctant to discuss sexual health issues with partners, family, and health providers.
- Young people report that alcohol and drugs often play a dangerous role in their sex lives.

Research finds that many teens who have never had sexual intercourse are having oral sex, which they do not count as "having sex" (Peterson, 2000b). One explanation for increases in oral sex is that some teens view it as an abstinence measure that allows them to preserve their virginity (Curwood, 2006).

Sex education in schools is a controversial topic. After 1996, federal support for sex education shifted from comprehensive sex education to abstinence education programs. Federal funding for abstinence-only programming totaled almost $1.3 billion between 2001 and 2009. When states accept funding through these programs, educators are generally prohibited from providing students with information about contraception or safe-sex practices (Santelli et al., 2006).

An obvious flaw of abstinence-only programming is that this method can protect youth from pregnancy, sexually transmitted infections (STIs), and HIV only if individuals do indeed abstain from sex. In 1998, the U.S. Department of Health and Human Services funded a rigorous, multiyear evaluation of abstinence education (Trenholm et al., 2008). The study measures the effects of abstinence education by comparing the sexual activities of teens who had participated in abstinence programming with a control group of matched teens who had not. Their research question was: Were teens who had participated in the programming more likely to be sexually abstinent than teens who had not had access to the programming? The study measured sexual behaviors for several years after participation in the abstinence education program. Figure 7.2 shows the results on this question. Abstinence programming had no significant impact on teen sexual activity. This research is consistent with a growing body of research pointing to the ineffectiveness of abstinence education. In fact, no systematic program evaluation shows abstinence-only education to effectively delay first intercourse among teens (Santelli et al., 2006).

As a long-term strategy, abstinence education seems unrealistic in the current social context. Premarital intercourse is the norm rather than the exception among all groups. This includes adolescents who have taken public "virginity pledges," that is, have pledged to abstain from sex until marriage. Research finds that 88 percent of married "pledgers" had sex before marriage (Santelli et al., 2006). Many are concerned that when teens fail at remaining abstinent, they will lack the information they need to prevent pregnancy and STIs. Health professionals generally support

Figure 7.2

Estimated Impacts of Abstinence Education Program on Reported Number of Sexual Partners

Source: Christopher Trenholm et al., "Impacts of Abstinence Education on Teen Sexual Activity, Risk of Pregnancy, and Risk of Sexually Transmitted Diseases." *Journal of Policy Analysis and Management* 27(2) (2008), p. 268.

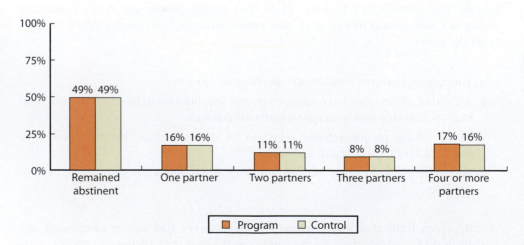

comprehensive sex education programs that provide information on abstinence, contraception, and condoms.

The transition from the Bush to the Obama administration signaled a major change in sex education policy in the United States. President Obama's 2010 budget shifts the federal emphasis from abstinence education to teen pregnancy prevention (Jayson, 2009b). The Obama administration's proposals are compatible with the priorities of comprehensive sex education advocates who favor educating on the effective use of contraceptives and safe-sex practices (Cohen, 2009).

Teenage Childbearing

In some societies over time, teenage childbirth has been a normal reproductive pattern. Over the past several decades, however, this pattern has been viewed as a major social problem. Particularly in the United States, which has the highest rates of adolescent pregnancy among Western industrialized nations, the issue has prompted broad social concern.

What is the best way to think sociologically about teenage childbearing? Is it a matter of morality, fertility, or poverty? Is it an epidemic? Is it a social problem? For whom? Under what circumstances? Answering these questions requires that we become skeptical about some basic assumptions about teen pregnancy. In her book, *Dubious Conceptions* (1996), sociologist Kristin Luker argues that parenthood among teens is not the problem we think it is. Her point is not that there is no problem at all but rather that the "facts about pregnancy among teenagers are based on a fundamental misunderstanding of the problem" (Luker, 1996:13). In the quarter century between 1960 and 1985, teens' sexual activity and their rates of pregnancy rose, but their rates of childbearing declined, largely as a result of greater access to abortion (29 percent of teen pregnancies end in abortion). Although the U.S. teenage fertility rate rose briefly between 1986 and 1991, it has declined by nearly one-third since 1991. This means that even as concerns about teenage childbearing grew over the course of three decades, the probability that a teenage woman from virtually any race or class would become a mother actually diminished!

Why is there a discrepancy between levels of concern and actual demographic trends? First, the teenagers of the 1960s were members of a baby boom generation. This group was so large that even with a smaller percentage becoming mothers, the absolute number of babies born to teenagers went up. This made teenage childbearing more visible than it had been before. At the same time, birth rates among older women were declining, and doing so more quickly than the birth rates among teenagers. As a result, births to teenagers began to comprise a larger percentage of total babies born than in the past (Astone, 1993:9).

The real source of alarm about teenage birth rates in the United States is closely tied to changes involving race, gender, age, and poverty (Luker, 1996:13). Even though teen childbearing occurs in other societies, the United States has high rates compared to other countries. (See Box 7.3.) Because teenage childbearing is increasingly concentrated among the inner-city poor, it is viewed by many as a racial problem, associated in the public mind with stereotypes of poor, young Black women. Research does reveal racial differences among teen birth rates. Hispanics are now more likely to have a teen birth than are African Americans.

BOX 7.3   Families in Global Perspective

Teen Birth Rates Around the World

The birth rate refers to the number of live births per 1,000 women in a particular year. Demographers compute the birth rates for women of various ages, racial-ethnic groups, and nationalities.

The 2006 teen birth rate was 41.9. Is this number high or low? One way of answering that question is to look at birth rates over time. The U.S. teen birth rate for 1970 was 68.3, and it was 53.0 in 1980. In 1990 it was 59.9. The rate has gone down by 30 percent since 1990. How low today's rate is perceived to be depends on the comparison year.

Another way of approaching the U.S. teen birth rate is to reference it to the rates for other countries. The following table illustrates that teen birth rates vary widely across the globe. Comparatively speaking, teen mothering is more common in U.S. society than in most other societies worldwide.

Teen Birth Rates Around the World (from 2006)

Japan	3	Australia	15
Switzerland	4	Ireland	17
Netherlands	5	Morocco	19
Italy	6	United Kingdom	24
China	7	Romania	33
Germany	10	Turkey	39
Czech Republic	11	Egypt	41
Kuwait	13	United States	42
Canada	13	Thailand	42
Poland	13	Chile	60
Israel	14	Mexico	66

Source: World Bank, "Reproductive Health." *World Development Indicators 2008.* Washington, DC: World Bank Publications, 2008, pp. 102–104.

Figure 7.3 shows racial differences in the teen birth rate and changes in the birth rate between 1991 and 2006 by race-ethnicity. This figure also shows something new on this subject: After 14 years of annual declines, the teen birth rate rose from 40.5 per 1,000 teens ages 15 through 19 in 2005 to 41.9 in 2006 (Moore, 2009).

Conventional thinking presumes that early motherhood dooms young mothers and their children to a life of poverty, but many sociologists challenge this assumption. They argue that although teenage pregnancy correlates with poverty, it does not cause poverty. Most teen mothers were poor before becoming pregnant. Further, many teen mothers improve their economic circumstances and move out of poverty. Furstenberg's longitudinal study of low-income, mostly Black, teen mothers found that by the time these women were in their mid-30s, the vast majority were in the work force and had incomes above the poverty line (2003:30).

Early motherhood makes young women vulnerable. Having a baby poses barriers to completing high school and good job possibilities. At the same time, we must

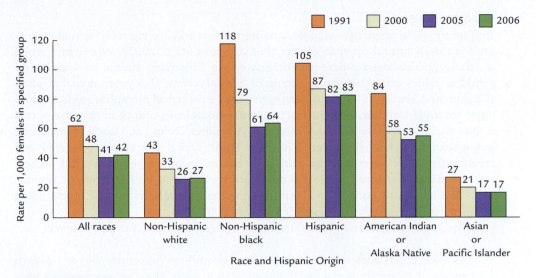

Figure 7.3

Birth Rates for Teenagers 15–19 Years by Race and Hispanic Origin: United States, 1991, 2000, 2005, and 2006

Source: Joyce A. Martin et al., "Births: Final Data for 2006." *National Vital Statistics Reports* 57(7). U.S.D.H.H.S., 2009, p 5.

acknowledge that poverty presents similar obstacles, especially among the urban poor. Youth who attend overcrowded, underfunded schools in communities without jobs will also encounter obstacles to economic success. Sociologist Frank Furstenberg, Jr., has studied teen childbearing for several decades. The urban Black teen mothers he studied ended up being only slightly worse off than women in comparable situations who were not teen mothers. He concludes that

> [T]he long-term costs of teen childbearing…were only modest. No doubt, some of the women would have achieved more and at an earlier age had they been able to delay their first birth, but because of their poor circumstances before pregnancy, they still would have encountered many of the same economic and social barriers to rising up to the middle class. In some situations, according to the mothers' own accounts, having a child helped to galvanize their motivation to succeed and surmount the challenges created by early parenthood. (Furstenberg, 2003:31)

Differentiated Forms of Intimacy

In this chapter, we have examined intimate relations in the context of wider social conditions. Gender, class, race, and sexual orientation shape intimate behaviors and experiences. In this section we look more closely at some of the ways in which intimacy reflects social inequalities. Far from being personal and private, our intimate experiences are shaped by imbalances in structural power.

Gendered Love and Sex

The most significant dimension of sexuality is gender. It relates to the biological and social contexts of sexual behavior and desire (Schwartz and Rutter, 1998:2). Women and men often want different things from heterosexual love and sex.

HIS AND HER SEX

Despite the wide range of sexualities among women and among men, sexual experience is closely bound up with gender (Williams and Stein, 2002). Where and when do these gender-based differences originate? An important stream of sociological thinking frames sexual behavior in terms of "sexual scripts" that guide sexual conduct (Gagnon and Simon, 1973). This perspective uses a theatrical metaphor (as Goffmann does) for understanding social interaction. Individuals learn scripts, in this case sexual scripts that incorporate society's informal guidelines, rules, and social norms and guide sexual conduct (Escoffier, 2007:62). These sexual scripts are gendered and create different relationship trajectories: "men are socialized to initiate and orchestrate sexual interactions, whereas women are socialized to be restrictors or responders, simultaneously concerned about harming their sexual reputations and fulfilling men's sexual needs" (Dworkin and O'Sullivan, 2007:105).

The gendered nature of sexual experience becomes obvious in adolescence:

> As a boy enters adolescence, he hears jokes about boys' uncontainable desire. Girls are told the same thing and told that their job is to resist. These gender messages have power, not only over attitudes and behaviors...but over physical and biological experience. (Schwartz and Rutter, 1998:4)

The double standard that "men care more about sex, while women care more about love" captures both the historical reality and the current imbalance in intimate relations. This imbalance comes into view when we examine happiness and relationship transitions (transitions from single to dating, dating to cohabiting, and cohabiting to marriage). Men experience the greatest increase in happiness in the transition from single to dating status, while women's biggest increase in happiness is the transition to marriage. Laumann and his colleagues explain the difference like this: "Apparently, for never married men, happiness appears to be associated with simply being in a sexual relationship, while for women, level of commitment appears to be more important" (2007:186).

Images and statistics show that women and men have distinct patterns of sexual expression (see Figure 7.4). One difference is that men tend to be more casual about sex. They can more easily compartmentalize their feelings about sex and love, while women view sex as more of a bonding experience. In Lillian Rubin's words, women depend on the emotional attachment to call up the sexual, while men rely on the sexual to spark the emotional (Rubin, 1983:102).

Study after study finds that women stress the emotional relationship and men stress performance. For example, researchers in one study asked their informants

> to fill in the blank in a sentence that read, "A penis is to a man what a _____ is to a woman." Men had no trouble with the task, almost all referring either to a clitoris or a vagina. Women, by contrast, resisted giving any simple answer, objecting that it was not a matter of one tiny organ but far more diffuse—that is, for them sex was only one outlet to express and experience a better, deeper feeling of intimacy. No man in the study spoke in terms of intimacy: sex for them was a matter of drive, vigor, and technique. (cited in Rossi, 1994:27)

This imbalance of love and sex in intimate relationship stems, in part, from the separate and unequal socialization experiences of girls and boys. In their separate worlds, boys learn about genital sexuality and masturbation, while girls learn about love and the importance of boys (Gagnon, 1983:164).

Compared to boys, young girls do not engage in an upsurge of experimental, impersonal, and autoerotic sexual activity during adolescence. More than girls, boys

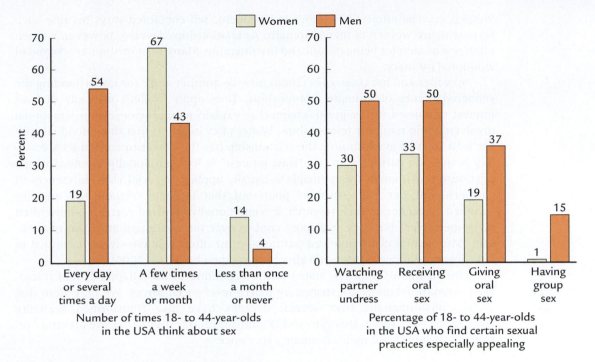

Figure 7.4
Sex and Gender

Source: Judith Mackay, *The Penguin Atlas of Human Sexual Behavior*. New York: Penguin Putnam, 2000, p. 21.

arrive at a non-relationship-based experience of sexual feelings and encounters. As Karin Martin found in her research on adolescent sexuality, girls feel pressure to have sex. Often they "give in" to keep their relationships with their boyfriends, while boys seek sexuality to affirm their masculinity (Martin, 2002).

Gendered socialization experiences predict differences in women's and men's sensibilities about love and sex. Andersen identifies a wide gender gap in attitudes about sexual behavior among young adults (2006:81). A survey of more than 260,000 freshmen entering college in 2005 found that 58 percent of men agreed that "it is all right for people who really like each other to have sex, even if they have only known each other a very short time," while only 34 percent of women agreed (Pryor et al., 2005:56, 76).

The double standard creates problems for men because it demands that they be skilled, experienced, and competent in sexual matters. For adult men, this has three main negative effects: (1) It perpetuates sexual ignorance, (2) it prevents them from discussing sex with their partners, and (3) it prevents seeking help when a sexual problem does occur. According to psychologist Joseph LoPiccolo, the blame for mythical male sexuality rests in advertising, television, and the mass media:

> If we look at the type of male who is used as a status model to sell everything from cars to beer, he is clearly an achieving, strong, unemotional, expert, and highly competent man. Many of the male role models we see in novels and television similarly do not include men who cry, who are vulnerable, need help, and have egalitarian, communicative relationships with women, especially in regard to sex. (LoPiccolo, 1983:48)

Women may be attracted to men's independent, self-contained ways because such ways reassure women of men's strength. As relationships develop, however, women often resent men for being distant and invulnerable. Many relationships are devoid of emotional intimacy.

Sprecher and her colleagues (2006) provide another angle for understanding the gendered nature of intimate relationships. They apply Waller's principle of least interest (discussed earlier in this chapter) to explain men's lower level of emotional involvement in romantic relationships. Waller's key insight is that the individual with the least interest in continuing the relationship has the power to control it. A corollary is that the partner who has "least interest" is less emotionally involved in the relationship. Although this principle is usually applied to social class differences in partners, Sprecher and coauthors point out that intimate relationships are also stratified by gender. In their research, less emotionally involved partners—most often men—perceived that they had more control over the continuation of the relationship. More emotionally involved partners—most often women—were presumed to have fewer desirable relationship alternatives (Sprecher et al., 2006).

One of the assumptions stated at the beginning of this chapter is that micro-level intimate relations are shaped by macro-level social forces. We note here that social transformations over several decades have also transformed sexuality (Laumann et al., 2007). Dworkin and O'Sullivan (2007) summarize the literature on shifts in women's and men's intimate experience:

> Researchers argue that contemporary femininity has outgrown anachronistic notions of sexual passivity and responsiveness to men's advances to include assertiveness in sexual initiation, pleasure-seeking, influencing or coercing reluctant male partners, and negotiating safer sex. . . . Researchers have also documented how men have internalized shifts in contemporary masculinity in a manner that pushes male sexual scripts beyond sex as a conquest or instrumental outcome to include emotionality, commitment, and love. (2007:106)

Some feminist scholars argue that sexuality is the arena in which male dominance and female subordination are produced and reproduced (Dworkin, 1981; MacKinnon, 1989). While men's control of women's sexuality has been an important issue for many feminists, others caution against characterizing women simply as victims. In thinking about this issue, we must take into account both the positive changes in intimate heterosexual relationships just summarized and also acknowledge that many women's lives continue to be blighted by unwanted sex and unintended pregnancies. This debate dramatizes the complexity of sexuality, which many women experience as a contradictory mix of pleasure and danger. The debate also raises questions about social structure and human agency. To what degree are women's sexualities shaped by larger social forces (including male dominance), and to what degree are women "agents," expressing themselves sexually in many ways?

HIS AND HER LOVE

Most individuals experience at least one love relationship in the course of their lives. To be in love is to be in a special world that centers on a relationship of two people. Romantic love is essentially, but not exclusively, sexual. It is a complex social and psychological state involving thoughts and feelings that provide humans with a powerful sense of intimacy and self-worth. Poets, novelists, and social scientists have disagreed on the nature of love—on whether it is trivial and selfish or ennobling and enriching. Undoubtedly, it can be any of these and can encompass different emotions with different meanings and consequences.

Do women and men differ in what they expect from love as well as in their styles of being in love? Women's greater interest in love has structural origins. Social historians have helped us identify how these differences are socially created. As economic production became separated from the home and from personal relationships, women's and men's roles became polarized (see Chapters 2 and 3). Love became "feminized" with the rise of capitalism, and women became responsible for the emotional management of marriage and family relationships (Baber and Allen, 1992; Cancian, 1987). Men were assigned the duties of the larger world and were defined by their responsibilities in the public setting. Therefore, love could be secondary, a less important part of men's life.

Even today, many studies show that women's and men's styles of love are different. Women work harder at love and at staying attractive and interesting to their partners (Rubin, 1983). Women, more than men, closely attend to, scan, and scrutinize their experiences of love. They do what sociologist Arlie Hochschild (1983a:255) has called "emotion work" or "feeling work"; that is, they work on their emotions and feelings to coincide with what "should" be felt. They do this in order to control and direct love relationships in a "useful" direction. In contrast, men tend to fall in love more quickly and less deliberately than women:

> Men, having a more romantic notion of love, cast a different map over their experience than do women. This sets up different expectations about "what might happen" and affects how men attend to experience. The romantic rendering of love suggests a less managerial, more passive stance toward love. Romantic love is by its nature something that cannot be controlled; it occurs automatically, "at first sight," and is predestined. Love feelings are in a particular way ascribed, not achieved. Indeed, the data suggest that men manage and work on love less. On the other hand, women understand love more as something which can, in its nature, be managed and indeed they seem to perform more feeling work upon it. By deromanticizing love, women appear to professionalize it more. Why? (Hochschild, 1983a:255).

The answer Hochschild provides is that young men hold hegemony over the courtship process, while at the same time women, for economic reasons, need marriage more.

Gendered love styles bolster men's power over women. Because our society defines love in a feminine way, women's emotional expressiveness and their connections with and dependence on others are readily acknowledged. But men's acceptance of love, which emphasizes instrumental activities, conceals their dependency on close relationships. This gives men greater power in intimate relationships (Cancian, 1987).

Same-Sex Orientation and Intimacy

Variance from the societal norm of heterosexuality was legally prohibited until 2003, when the Supreme Court ruled that gays are "entitled to respect for their private lives." In *Lawrence v. Texas,* the court struck down a Texas law banning sodomy, thus affirming the Constitution's guarantee of a right to privacy. Justice Anthony M. Kennedy declared that the state cannot demean the existence of gay men and women or "control their destiny by making their private sexual conduct a crime" (Greenhouse, 2003:1).

Although many still regard same-sex intimacy as morally deviant, it is important to remember that such views are shaped by the dominant society's ideas about what is "normal." Heterosexuality is only one form of sexual/emotional expressiveness. Therefore, we must not generalize about intimacy from the experiences of heterosexuals alone. Because gay and lesbian identities are stigmatized, the social context in which intimacy occurs for same-sex couples is markedly different from that of heterosexuals.

Drawing generalizations about intimacy in same-sex relationships is difficult for a number of reasons. First, no reliable data exist on numbers of gays and lesbians in the U.S. population; second, no research uses representative samples of gay and lesbian populations; and, third, sexual behavior in same-sex couples has not been widely studied (Kurdek, 2004). Nonetheless, there are some general patterns that emerge from the literature.

While the experiences of gay, lesbian, and bisexual individuals are unique, one of the most consistent research findings is the degree of commonality in the relational experience of same-sex and heterosexual couples. The following characterization of same-sex intimacy also describes heterosexual couples:

> For both lesbians and gay men, sex is typically satisfying. There is a reciprocal association between sexual satisfaction and relationship satisfaction; each can enhance or detract from the other. Sexual satisfaction is linked to sexual frequency. In long-term couples, the frequency of sex decreases over time. (Peplau et al., 2004:366)

Lawrence Kurdek compared gay and lesbian couples to childless, married heterosexual couples on a large number of variables known to be associated with relationship quality. He found few overall differences between members of gay and lesbian couples and heterosexual couples. A few differences, however, are noteworthy: Gays and lesbians reported more personal autonomy than members of married couples; lesbians reported higher levels of equality in their relationships than did heterosexual women; members of gay couples indicated less commitment than members of married couples; members of lesbian couples reported higher relationship satisfaction than did married couples. An additional significant difference is that gay and lesbian couples received less support from family members than did married couples and relied more on friends than did married couples (Kurdek, 2004).

A challenging approach to thinking about the relationships of lesbians and gay men is to analyze them in terms of gender rather than sexual orientation. Gender exerts a great influence on the intimate relationships of lesbian and gay individuals, often a greater influence than sexual orientation. In this respect, "lesbians resemble heterosexual women just as gay men are similar to heterosexual men" (Risman and Schwartz, 1988:135). Lesbians establish ongoing love relationships earlier than gay men and are more likely to commit to a homosexual identity within the context of an intense emotional relationship, whereas gay men do so within the context of their sexual experience. In general, emotional attachment is the most significant aspect of relationships for lesbians, but sexual activity is most important for gay men. Sexual exclusivity is the norm for most lesbian relationships, but not for most gay-male couples who typically have many more one-time-only sexual partners than do lesbians (Levine and Evans, 1996: 130–131; Peplau et al., 2004).

Social Class and Intimacy

The conditions under which sexuality and love are experienced also vary with social class. Since Kinsey, other research studies on the premarital sexual activities of Americans have found consistently that certain categories of young people tend to be overrepresented among the sexually active. African Americans and teens from lower socioeconomic backgrounds have sex earlier than Whites and those from higher socioeconomic backgrounds (Martin, 2002:149). Kinsey found, for example, an inverse relationship between socioeconomic status and premarital sexual activity—the higher the socioeconomic status, the lower the rate of sexual permissiveness. Using educational level as the indicator of status, he found that males and females with only an eighth-grade education began their coital behavior five or six years earlier than high school and college graduates (Kinsey et al., 1948:550).

Differences in sexual behavior by social class are becoming less clear. Nevertheless, many studies have found differences in the way sexuality is defined and experienced. Is one class's normal behavior another class's deviance? To test this idea, Raymond Eve and Donald Renslow conducted an exploratory study based on a sample of 72 college students who filled out questionnaires about sexual behavior. The study did find that the actual occurrence of different varieties of sexual behavior (and fantasies about these behaviors) is often related to social class. The higher the respondents' socioeconomic status, the greater was the likelihood that they were willing to accept a wider variety of sexual expression as normal (Eve and Renslow, 1980:97).

The NHSLS discovered that sex is very much class-coded. Put broadly, the poorer segments within society incline toward an unadorned, no-nonsense, silent approach to sex, while the more affluent practice a more self-conscious, elaborate, even-mannered sexuality, especially when it comes to masturbation, oral sex, and foreplay (Robinson, 1994:22). A striking finding is that oral sex is most popular among better-educated Whites and less popular among less-educated Blacks (Michael et al., 1994:139). Another striking finding is at odds with the generalization that men surpass women in their number of sexual partners. In some class groups, women's sexual patterns are converging with those of men. Summarizing research on young women in a postboomer world, Paula Kamen claims that "White, middle-class, college-educated women in their twenties have had more sex partners than any other group of women" (Kamen, 2002:43).

LOVE AND SOCIAL CLASS

Little information exists on love relationships in various parts of the class structure. Although the American ideology of love is held by most people regardless of their social location, there are class differences in the resources required to sustain the ideal. Not only do the social networks that surround couples differ; the impact of economic resources also creates differences in "loving" experiences. Intimacy in marital relationships is also affected by economic conditions. In the 1970s Lillian Rubin asked working-class wives and middle-class wives what each group most valued in their husbands. She found that middle-class women valued intimacy, sharing, and communication more than working-class wives.

> Does this mean, then, that working-class women are unconcerned about the emotional side of the marriage relationship? Emphatically, it does not. It says first that when the material aspects of life are problematic, they become dominant as issues requiring solutions; and second, that even when men are earning a reasonably good living it is never "taken for granted" when financial insecurity and marginality are woven into the fabric of life. (Rubin, 1976:94)

The Great Recession provides contemporary evidence for the relationship between intimacy and economic conditions. Dorfman asked, "Will the Tanking Economy Ruin Your Sex Life?" He interviewed a cross-section of sex therapists and psychologists who did connect economic woes to mounting sexual problems. Sex educator Amy Levine finds the effects to be gendered, with "some men, notably those feeling insecure, having erectile problems, while women, due to decreased sexual desire, postpone sex" (Dorfman, 2009).

Race and Intimacy

A sociological perspective on sexuality shows that sex is as closely connected to race as it is to gender and class. Just what does race have to do with sex? Differences of color, culture, and ancestry create clear sexual boundaries. In other words, racial boundaries are also sexual boundaries. According to Joane Nagel, race and sexuality join together

> to form a barrier to hold some people in and keep others out, to define who is pure and who is impure, to shape our view of ourselves and others, to fashion feelings of sexual desirability, to provide us with seeming "natural" sexual preferences for some partners and "intuitive" aversion for others, to leave us with a taste for some ethnic sexual encounters and a distaste for others. (Nagel, 2003:1)

Throughout U.S. history, powerful sexual stereotypes have been central in creating and sustaining the racial hierarchy. Historically, Black women have been associated with an "animalistic, 'wild' sexuality" that expressed itself in promiscuity (Collins, 2005:27). Meanwhile, Black men were viewed as hypersexual beings who were predisposed toward violence and in need of control. In the United States, slavery and racial segregation depended on a discourse of deviant Black sexuality to justify the subordination of people of African descent (Collins 2005:32).

Today, gender and sexuality figure strongly in racial stereotypes. Latinos are stereotyped as "naturally" sexual: Women are "hot tamales" or sexual firebrands (Ortiz, 2000), while men are "machos," an image that conjures up rough, swaggering men who are abusive and oppressive to women. Asian American men are characterized as asexual, whereas Asian American women are represented as sexually available: demure, diminutive, and deferential—the "Lotus Blossom" stereotype (Espiritu, 1997:88).

Not only are African Americans stereotyped as hypersexual, but Black sexuality is a basic, if seldom-acknowledged ingredient of White racism. This is the paradox of the sexual politics of race in the United States. As Cornel West puts it, "behind closed doors, the . . . sex associated with black people is often perceived to be more intriguing and interesting, while in public spaces talk about black sexuality is virtually taboo" (West, 2004:456).

Although sexual and racial boundaries are closely linked, interracial sexual contact has been a hallmark of American history. "The U.S. sexual color line has been crossed, but it has also continually been policed—both formally and informally (e.g., lynching and castrations)" (Nagel, 2003:22). Despite the current trends in multiracial dating, the sexual marketplace is still a minefield for people of color. Their choice of intimate partners is defined by a racial hierarchy that places Anglo/White people at the top. In a world of racial divisions, colorblind attraction is a racial privilege.

CONTEMPORARY DIFFERENCES IN SEXUAL BEHAVIOR

When it comes to sex and relationships, race and class structure patterns of intimacy for people of color. Different patterns of sexuality among people of color are not deviant. Instead, structural features account for the differential patterns that prevail.

Studies agree that African Americans become sexually active earlier than Whites. How can we explain this? Joyce Ladner (1971), a social scientist who has investigated poor Black women, has argued that there is a strong Black culture that is different from that of the dominant White middle class. The Black community has a unique culture because of some African customs that have survived and because of adaptive responses to discrimination.

Patricia Hill Collins (2005) takes Ladner's argument further to point out that relationships with socially subordinated men will be different than relationships with more socially privileged men. In Western societies, gender relations and the sexual relationships that follow have been framed in terms of a strong men–weak women model. This model derives from White men's privileged position in society; their authority in the public sphere carries over to the private sphere. Meanwhile women's secondary status carries over to the private sphere where they are expected to be submissive and passive. African American gender relations are frequently critiqued as epitomizing a strong woman–weak man model and viewed as deviant. What is often missing is the realization that private issues of sexuality and gender relations are connected to public issues of race (2005:35).

In thinking about the strong men–weak women model of gender relations, Shirley Hill clarifies how this model depends on men's opportunities for achievement and success. She argues that as much as African Americans may "buy into" dominant social norms about male–female relationships, their marginalized status in society does not allow many to conform to these norms. According to societal rules about courtship, men are expected to be "aggressors, protectors, proposers, and providers," while women are cast in passive roles, gaining male attention mostly through "physical attractiveness, sexuality, and coyness" (Hill, 2005:95). In contemporary U.S. society, social class and racial disadvantage have created another set of realities for African Americans:

> Heroic efforts aside, black men have often found themselves unable to shield women from the hostilities of the public arena, foot the entire bill for dating, or provide economic support for their families. Black women have had to fend for themselves, work outside the home, and rely on female kinship networks for support, and they have thus developed a strong sense of independence (Hill, 2005:95).

We see here that social context shapes the sexual behaviors of poor minorities and shapes them differently than sexual behaviors of the more privileged majority. The behaviors of those who are poor and people of color are structured in unique ways that are conditioned by poverty, discrimination, and institutional subordination.

Elijah Anderson's study (1990) of life in an inner-city neighborhood shows how poverty creates its own sex code. Young men and young women scramble to take what they can from each other. Sexual conquests result in pregnancies, and girls often have little to lose by having a child out of wedlock. Anderson argues that the situation must be viewed in its social and political context—as a manifestation of urban poverty.

Sexual activity among the poor may be encouraged because it serves as a substitute for other forms of gratification that cannot be fulfilled. Ladner (1971:212) has argued that this takes two forms. On the one hand, sex can provide one with a sense of identity and worth. "Some girls engage in premarital sex because it provides them with a sense of belonging, of feeling needed by their boyfriends." Sex can also be viewed as a system of exchange. "Often in the absence of material resources (such as money to purchase gifts for a boyfriend's birthday, etc.) sex becomes the resource that is exchanged."

The gender ratio among African Americans gives men great power over sex. As Robert Staples has put it,

> the system inherently favors men. With an effective sex ratio of three black women to every male, the females have little, if any, bargaining power where men have such a large number of women from which to choose. In a sense, black women often find themselves in the position of sexually auditioning for a meaningful relationship. After a number of tryouts, they may find a black male who is willing to make a commitment to them. (Staples, 1978:19)

Black men are hardly alone in their exploitation of women for sex. Many men, in all racial and class categories, are similar in the selfish, peer-oriented nature of their sexual behavior. Thus, Staples contends that Black men and White men are much more united in terms of the meaning of sex than are Black men and Black women.

Gloria Gonzalez-Lopez's (2005) study of the sex lives of heterosexual Mexican immigrants illustrates that sexuality and sexual expression are created in particular social contexts. Migration and settlement in the United States resulted in a "reinvention" of sexuality for the women and men she interviewed. Immigrants encountered the struggle to earn a living and experienced the risk of AIDS. They also found job opportunities and participated in community networks of support in which they were educated about sex and became more confident about their sexuality. As a result, patterns of experience and expectations about sex changed. The following provides an example of how women's employment may result in a revision of a couple's sex lives:

> "You came over here and you changed," Azalea's husband told her, claiming that her behavior in the bedroom had changed since they left Mexico City and she became an L.A. apartment manager. "He can be kind of machista, but I don't put up with it any more," said Azalea. "I can support myself, I can live without a man. So now I have sex only if I want to, not just because he wants to." (Gonzalez-Lopez, 2005:188)

We know far less about intimacy among racial ethnics than we should, given the growing proportion of Americans who are people of color. Two facts account for the lack of social science information about love in the lives of people of color: (1) stereotypes that portray racial-ethnic women and men as more sexual and therefore less capable than Whites of controlling animal instincts (Jagger and Rothenberg, 1984:385) and (2) the prevailing ideology of love as a White, middle-class emotion. The study of love should not be restricted to privileged categories but should be linked to social and cultural factors throughout class and racial hierarchies.

Claiming Control of Intimacy

Because intimacy is socially constructed, it offers the possibility for agency, change, and growth. One of the most important developments leading to greater agency in sexual behavior is the ability to separate sexuality from reproduction (Baber and Allen, 1992:81). This has given many women a wide range of options and enabled them to seek intimate relationships based on equality rather than male dominance (Giddens, 1992). A just society would guarantee "basic individual human rights including the rights to choose their own sexual, romantic, and marital partner, as well as to choose one's own sexual practices (as long as they are consensual

"Sex brought us together, but gender drove us apart."

and do not harm others)" (Schwartz, 2000:215). People throughout society are struggling to transform intimate relationships and to enhance pleasure and love. The sexual revolution is occurring on many fronts. People in all walks of life, both young and old, homosexual and heterosexual, are questioning the old definitions of sex and love. Just as lesbians, gays, and other sexual minorities challenge the narrow definition of sexuality, women and men in all walks of life are creating new patterns of intimacy that work for them.

Chapter Review

1. Intimate relations are shaped by social structure and social stratification.

2. Postmodern societies create intense needs for intimate relationships.

3. Courtship is affected by the changing economy, urbanization, and job and educational opportunities away from home. For most of U.S. history, parents controlled the courtship patterns of their offspring. Today, personal choice is the primary determinant.

4. "Dating" and courtship patterns vary in different social contexts, especially those of class and race.

Class- and race-based courtship patterns are due largely to the stratified social worlds in which young people live.

5. Mate selection does not occur entirely through free choice, even in contemporary U.S. society. Homogamy governs mate selection. Factors such as social class, race, and religion limit choice.

6. Sexual orientation is linked to power. Heterosexuals have more institutional power and resources than gays, lesbians, and bisexuals. Although human beings are capable of various

modes of sexual expression, social institutions enforce compulsory heterosexuality.

7. As lesbian and gay individuals have emerged into the mainstream of society, new understandings of sexuality have been developed.

8. Human sexualities vary from one culture to another, within any one culture over time, over the life course of women and men, and between and among different groups of women and men depending on class, race, ethnicity, region, and sexual orientation.

9. Sexual behavior in the United States has changed from a family-centered reproductive system in colonial days to a romantic sexuality in the nineteenth century to a modern sexuality with sexual relations as a source of happiness and personal identity by the 1920s. Over the next several decades, social changes made sexuality an individual right.

10. The 1992 National Health and Social Life Survey is the most comprehensive representative survey ever done of sexual behavior in the U.S. population. This survey looked at sexuality in its social context and found that sexual behaviors are shaped by the social networks in which individuals operate.

11. The number of new AIDS cases has stabilized in recent years. While three-quarters of those newly diagnosed are men, a disturbing trend is the rising rate among heterosexual women. HIV/AIDS is increasingly prevalent among poor people of color.

12. Teenage pregnancy rates have dropped considerably in the past three decades. Still, the United States has the highest rates of teenage pregnancy of any industrialized country—a condition closely related to poor economic opportunities.

13. Research consistently finds similarities in the intimate relationships of heterosexual and same-sex couples. For example, sexual satisfaction and relationship satisfaction are closely related, irrespective of a couple's sexual orientation.

14. Love and sexual experiences vary widely by gender, race, and social class. Research documents that certain categories of young people are overrepresented among the sexually active.

15. Racial boundaries are also sexual boundaries. Both rest on claims that people of color are sexually promiscuous.

Key Terms

assortative mating   225

compulsory heterosexuality   229

homogamy   226

hypergamy   226

hypogamy   226

principle of least interest   224

sexual behavior   229

sexual identity   229

sexual orientation   229

social constructionist approach to sexuality   228

Related Websites

http://www.guttmacher.org

Guttmacher Institute. The Guttmacher Institute is a nonprofit organization focused on sexual and reproductive health research, policy analysis, and public education. It publishes *Perspectives on Sexual and Reproductive Health, International Perspectives on Sexual and Reproductive Health, The Guttmacher Policy Review,* and special reports on topics pertaining to sexual and reproductive health and rights. The Institute's mission is to protect the reproductive choices of all women and men in the United States and throughout the world and to support people's ability to obtain the information and services needed to achieve their full human rights, safeguard their health, and exercise their individual responsibilities in regard to sexual behavior and relationships, reproduction, and family formation.

http://kinseyinstitute.org

The Kinsey Institute for Research in Sex, Gender, and Reproduction. Founded in 1947, the Kinsey Institute at Indiana University is a private, not-for-profit corporation that investigates sexual behavior and sexual health today. Its mission is to promote interdisciplinary research and scholarship in the fields of human sexuality, gender, and reproduction.

http://www.siecus.org

Sexuality Information and Education Council of the United States. Founded in 1964, SIECUS has served as the national voice for sexuality education, sexual health, and sexual rights. Each year, it distributes hundreds of thousands of print and electronic resources to educators, advocates, parents, researchers, physicians, and others working to expand sexual health programs, policies, and understanding. SIECUS also offers specialized assistance to help individuals locate research, write accurate news articles, create sexual health curricula, and build support for high-quality programs in their communities.

http://www.plannedparenthood.org/teen-talk

Teen Talk. Teen Talk is the award-winning Planned Parenthood Federation of America website for teens and is staffed by professionals who are dedicated to providing the information teens need related to sexual health. It is the mission of Teen Talk to provide teens with honest and nonjudgmental information about sexuality in language they can understand with the hope that they will use this knowledge to reduce the risk of unintended pregnancy and sexually transmitted infections.

http://www.biresource.org

Bisexual Resource Center. BRC is a nonprofit international organization that provides education about and support for bisexual and progressive issues. This website makes available a number of BRC publications, as well as other resources about bisexuality and/or bisexuals. In conjunction with commercial distributors, it also provides virtual storefronts to provide convenient access to bi-related books, videos, and recordings. The site also provides links to other relevant sites.

http://www.thetaskforce.org

National Gay and Lesbian Task Force. Founded in 1973, the National Gay and Lesbian Task Force Foundation (the Task Force) was the first national lesbian, gay, bisexual, and transgender (LGBT) civil rights and advocacy organization and remains the movement's leading voice for freedom, justice, and equality. NGLTF, Inc., is a nonprofit organization that works to build the grassroots political power of the LGBT community in order to attain complete equality through direct and grassroots lobbying. NGLTF also analyzes and reports on the positions of candidates for public office on issues of importance to the LGBT community.

http://www.lovethatworks.org

The Institute for 21st Century Relationships: The Foundation of the National Coalition for Sexual Freedom. The Institute for 21st Century Relationships exists to facilitate the fulfillment of the human potential for relating and to support the freedom of consenting adults to discover and to practice the intimate relationship structure that best meets their emotional and human needs. This research and educational organization is guided by distinguished researchers, academics, clinicians, and other professionals and is devoted to studying and educating the public about the various new forms of intimate relationships being chosen in today's world. The group is also dedicated to supporting the proposition that competent adults have a basic human right to choose for themselves the form their intimate relationships should take and to be given education and support to help them make that choice work for them.

http://www.lesbianherstoryarchives.org

The Lesbian Herstory Archives. The Lesbian Herstory Archives of New York City, the largest and oldest Lesbian archive in the world, began in 1973 as an outgrowth of a Lesbian consciousness-raising group at the Gay Academic Union. The website offers a guide to materials that are relevant to the lives and experiences of Lesbians: books, magazines, journals, news clippings, bibliographies, photos, historical information, tapes, films, diaries, oral histories, poetry and prose, biographies, autobiographies, notices of events, posters, graphics, and other memorabilia.

Contemporary Marriages

▶ Myths and Realities

Myth	The typical marriage arrangement in the United States is a couple in a life-long marriage with the husband employed and the wife at home as a homemaker and caregiver to her husband and children.
Reality	There are many variations from the presumed marriage norm, with no one arrangement dominant: Divorce and remarriage are commonplace; dual-earner marriages are typical; in one out of six marriages, the wife is the economic dominant; and some marriages remain childless by choice.
Myth	Each partner in a heterosexual marriage experiences that relationship in more or less the same way.
Reality	Heterosexual marital relationships are gendered, with wives and husbands acting and perceiving differently from each other. Although marriage is generally beneficial to both husbands and wives, husbands benefit more.
Myth	The policy of promoting marriage will improve the economic status of poor women in the United States.
Reality	The economic benefits of marriage vary by social location. Poor women may benefit if they can find an economically viable partner.
Myth	Because of more positive views on gender equality in this generation, husbands and wives in dual-worker families share more or less equally in housework.
Reality	In the average dual-worker family, the husband contributes only about half as many hours to housework as the wife does.
Myth	Successful marriages are alike. That is, there is a cluster of behaviors that identifies successful marriages.
Reality	There is enormous variation among stable marriages.
Myth	Children improve the quality of a marriage.
Reality	Numerous studies find that marital happiness is lowest when children are in the home and highest in homes without children.
Myth	As indicated by the trends of increased cohabitation, marrying later, and high divorce rates, Americans are becoming disillusioned with marriage.
Reality	Marriage remains a vital institution: 90 percent of adults eventually marry; and approximately two-thirds of divorced people remarry.

This chapter examines the institution of marriage in U.S. society. Marriage is an institution in transition. As our society undergoes major transformation, we expect to find (and do indeed find) that patterns of family life, including marriage, will be recast as well. While we strive to understand marriages in their social context, we must not forget that these arrangements are intensely personal. Micro-level interactions and processes profoundly shape the day-to-day lived realities of marriage. This chapter is divided into several parts to capture this duality. The first provides an overview by showing the duality of marriage—the private and the public aspects of this complex social relationship. The second part reviews the facts and trends regarding marriage, revealing its changing nature. The third part examines the benefits of marriage. The fourth part focuses on the micro aspects of marriage—that is, the correlates of marital success, patterns of sexual intimacy, and how decisions are made by married couples. Then we examine strategies for reconstructing gender roles to foster egalitarian marriage. Finally, we address the question of whether marriage is a dying institution.

Marriage: Private and Public Spheres

A fundamental contradiction characterizes marriages in U.S. society. A marriage is a multifaceted bond based on commitment, love, and intimacy. Yet while this relationship is an intensely private affair, it is also shaped by macro forces, such as the law, economics, religion, and gender expectations. Let's look at the private side first.

The Private Nature of Marriage

It is easy to treat marriage as a concrete entity with features as readily observable as any three-dimensional object—with volume, density, and a visible surface. However, a marriage is actually a relationship between two people, not a concrete object. It is a dynamic system that emerges from the actions and interactions of two people who are in many ways strangers to each other, as noted by anthropologist Mary Catherine Bateson:

> We live with strangers. Those we love most, with whom we share a shelter, a table, a bed, remain mysterious. Wherever lives overlap and flow together, there are depths of unknowing.... Strangers marry strangers, whether they have been playmates for years or never meet before the wedding day. They continue to surprise each other through the evolutions of love and the growth of affection. Lovers, gay and straight, begin in strangeness. (Bateson, 2000:3–4)

Each couple creates its unique social organization within the marriage.

The marriage of two "strangers" creates a unique relationship in profound and complex ways. Two individuals with different histories, from different social networks, and (usually) of different genders create a novel household. Within the intimate environment of the marriage and the constraints of society, each couple creates its own unique social organization. As Peter Berger and Hansfried Kellner have said,

> Marriage in our society is a dramatic act in which two strangers come together and redefine themselves.... The marriage partners [embark] on the often difficult task of constructing for themselves the little world in which they will live. To be sure, the larger society provides them with certain standard instructions as to how they should go about this task, but this does not change the fact that considerable effort of their own is required for its realization. (Berger and Kellner, 1975:221, 223)

The couple must work out mutually satisfactory solutions to such crucial areas of potential conflict as the division of labor, decision-making, the spending of money, the use of leisure time, sexual behavior, whether to have children (and, if so, how many and when and how they will be raised), the resolution of conflicts, and much more. Needless to say, couples vary in their ability to achieve satisfactory arrangements in these critical areas of married life.

Macro Influences on Marriage

Marriages do not occur in a vacuum. Both members of the marriage union have expectations of the relationship based on broad cultural prescriptions and proscriptions, their religious beliefs, the norms of their community, and their family background. Thus, while each couple forges a unique relationship, there are patterns across marriages that vary by social class, race, gender, and locality. These patterns involve gendered behaviors, how decisions are made, appropriate sexual behaviors, and the division of housework. Moreover, these relationships are patterned by structural arrangements such as the law, differential job opportunities for men and women, and institutional sexism and racism. This section examines three macro forces that affect the human actors in marriages—the law, religion, and gender.

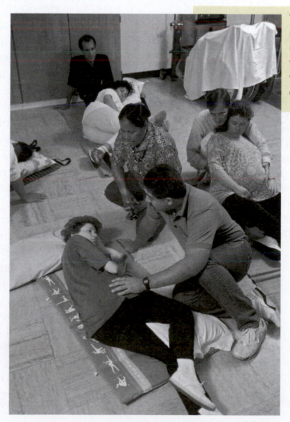

To live a successful marriage, each couple must define what works for them in their shared world. Lamaze birth class.

Families in Global Perspective

BOX 8.1

Legalized Marriages for Same-Sex Couples in Other Societies

Same-sex marriage is now legal in seven countries. European nations have led the way, with the Netherlands the first to legalize same-sex marriage in 2001 and Belgium the second in 2003. In 2005, the governments of both Spain and Canada passed initiatives that allow gay and lesbian couples to marry. In Spain, the legislation was especially controversial because the Roman Catholic Church weighed in with strong opposition. Green (2005) writes that "Pope Benedict XVI... condemned gay marriage as an expression of 'anarchic freedom' that threatens the future of the family." South Africa then legalized same-sex marriage in 2006, and both Norway and Sweden did the same in 2009.

Same-sex marriage is not uniformly accepted across Europe. In fact, approval rates in European Union countries vary widely. A majority of the population approves of gay marriage in European countries that permit it. Examples of other countries' approval rates are France at 48 percent, Ireland at 41 percent, Hungary at 18 percent, and Poland at 17 percent (Lozano-Bielat et al., 2009).

While gay marriage legislation has been contentious where it has been debated and then implemented, the Dutch experience may be instructive. In the Netherlands, the issue has disappeared from public view. Anne-Marie Thus, who married her partner in 2001, says, "We're totally ordinary. We take our children to preschool every day. People know they don't have to be afraid of us." Interestingly, while individuals with strong religious beliefs frequently oppose same-sex marriage most vehemently, Ms. Thus finds that her marriage has created greater acceptance of same-sex relationships among religious people. She says, "When you're just 'partners' or 'living together' they think... you know, every day a new lover. With marriage, the commitment is real, and they believe it" (Sterling, 2004).

THE LAW

Marriage is a legal contract. Each state determines the criteria for a legal marriage within its boundaries. Although there are minor differences from state to state on the legal specifics regarding marriage, there are general principles that are more or less universal in the United States.

Each state stipulates the legal age of marriage, the allowed distance between relatives, health requirements, the length of the waiting period required before marriage, and rules concerning inheritance and the division of property in case of divorce. Although it has been ruled unconstitutional now, states at one time had laws against interracial marriages.

The Issue of Same-Sex Marriages   A perennial rule in state law has been that for a marriage to be legal the couple must be heterosexual (for international variation on this rule, see Box 8.1). Massachusetts was the first state to break from this requirement and legalize marriage for same-sex partners in 2004. Since then, Connecticut (2008), Iowa (2009), Vermont (2009), and New Hampshire (2009) have also legalized gay marriage.

The exclusion of gays and lesbians from marriage has significant negative consequences for these individuals. When same-sex partners are not recognized by the state as legally married couples, they do not receive the legal benefits of marriage. The U.S. General Accounting Office has identified 1,138 federal statutory provisions in which "marital status is a factor in determining or receiving benefits, rights, and privileges" (2004). These legal benefits of marriage are found in a number of categories including Social Security, veterans benefits, employment benefits, taxation, and immigration. This means a surviving partner in a gay or lesbian committed relationship is not eligible to receive Social Security benefits or other pensions. For similar reasons, a partner in a same-sex relationship cannot receive health benefits from his or her partner's company health plan, unless the company provides for same-sex domestic partner benefits (as do such corporations as Microsoft, IBM, Walt Disney, Honeywell, and Boeing). Gay and lesbian couples are also vulnerable in life-threatening situations because their relationships have no legal standing. Committed couples sometimes use advance-planning documents like wills, powers of attorney, and living wills to ensure that their partners are able to make decisions about their well-being in times of emergency or crisis (Riggle et al., 2006:758).

Most states exclude same-sex couples from the benefits and protections that married heterosexual couples enjoy under state law. An increasing number of states do, however, grant all state-level spousal rights and responsibilities (such as inheritance, property transfers, medical decisions, insurance, and filing joint state income tax returns) to gay and lesbian couples. These states are California, Nevada, Oregon, and Washington (all permitting domestic partnerships, as does Washington, DC) and New Jersey (permitting civil unions) (Human Rights Campaign, 2009b).

The federal government has not supported initiatives for legal recognition of same-sex relationships. In 1996, Congress passed the Defense of Marriage Act (DOMA), which denies federal recognition of same-sex marriage and allows states to refuse to recognize same-sex unions licensed in other states. This act makes same-sex legally-married couples ineligible for the federal benefits of marriage, such as Social Security Survivors Benefits. The DOMA also has significant implications for federal data-gathering agencies, especially the U.S. Bureau of the Census. In gathering data from legally-married same-sex couples, the U.S. Census must edit the relationship status of the respondents from "spouse" to "unmarried partner." The language of DOMA does not permit federal agencies or bureaus to categorize these partners as "spouses" or "married" (O'Connell and Lofquist, 2009:2).

The 2003 Massachusetts Supreme Judicial Court ruling that led to legalizing same-sex marriage was very controversial, both within the state and nationally. At the heart of the ruling was the court's decision that the state constitution "forbids the creation of second-class citizens" (Burge, 2003). The landmark decision permitting legal marriage for same-sex couples provided new opportunities and raised new questions. Lannutti's (2005) research in Massachusetts, prior to the implementation of the new law, asked gay and lesbian individuals how legalizing same-sex marriage would impact the LGBT (lesbian, gay, bisexual, and transgender) community. Nearly all research participants mentioned the importance of legal equality; they believed legal equality would provide them first-class citizenship, financial benefits, and enhanced family security. A gay man stated,

> Being able to get married means that I will be able to take care of my partner, like making medical or other types of decisions for him, if something horrible happens or when we are older because everyone will have to recognize me as his partner.

Another respondent added this perspective:

> Having same-sex marriage, and calling it marriage especially, makes the discussion about gay relationships a legal one, not a religious or moral issue. This shows everyone that we are citizens, we pay taxes, and we have to be treated the same as everybody else. So, this isn't about marriage, it's about equal rights.

While some men and women were ambivalent about the impact of legalized same-sex marriage on the gay-lesbian community, many believed it would reduce homophobia in society. One individual said,

> It would be nice if marriage made straight people, in general, like gay people more, but I think it will really matter when you look at it in the smaller scale, like looking at families. If you get married, your straight family will be able to better accept and integrate your partner in the family because being married is something that is easier for them to understand and accept. (Lannutti, 2005:9, 15)

The issue of same-sex marriage prompts the reexamination of the institution of marriage in U.S. society (Lampman, 2003). The gay marriage debate raises this question: Is the key element in marriage the sexuality of the partners or their commitment to each other? U.S. society has, in the past, chosen to define marriage narrowly, as a heterosexual union. Thus, the state has supported loving relationships—but only for heterosexuals. The events of the next few years will demonstrate the degree to which the institution of marriage will be further extended to include same-sex couples across the United States.

Common-Law Marriage Some people erroneously believe that long-term heterosexual cohabitation relationships move into the category of common-law marriage after the passage of a specified period of time. They believe that lengthy cohabiting relationships eventually have the legal benefits and obligations of marriage. In fact, the requirements for attaining a common-law marriage are quite particular. Only nine states and the District of Columbia recognize common-law marriages contracted within their borders. The specific requirements vary by state, but in general the key requirements are that a couple agrees to be married, lives together, and represents themselves to others as a married couple. Recommended ways of demonstrating that a common-law marriage exists include these: the woman takes the man's surname, the couple refers to their marriage in conversation with others, and the couple files joint tax returns, owns property jointly, and holds joint bank accounts (National Conference of State Legislatures, 2009). Common-law marriage cannot be exited as informally as it can be established—common-law marriage may be ended only by a legal judgment of divorce.

RELIGION

By definition, religions constrain their members to behave in particular ways. Thus, as Tim Heaton has said, "religious involvement creates a context, not only for indoctrination into a particular theology, but also for socialization regarding normative expectations" (Heaton, 1986:249). This normative aspect of religion has profound consequences for behaviors within marriage. Almost universally, religions prohibit sexual relationships outside of marriage. Many religiously conservative groups oppose both same-sex relationships and same-sex marriage. Those religions within the Judeo-Christian tradition limit marriage to one spouse at a time. Some religions do not permit remarriage after a divorce. Some oppose the use of contraceptives. Many formally oppose abortion. Some encourage large families—most notably, the Roman Catholic Church and the Mormon Church. Some religious groups use Scripture to justify patriarchy within a marriage. The clearest example of this in the past decade or so occurred in 1998 when the Southern Baptist Convention amended its statement of belief to include a declaration that wives should submit themselves graciously to their husbands' leadership and that husbands should provide for, protect, and lead their families.

Obviously, the more intense one's commitment is to a religious ideology, the more control that ideology will have on one's behavior. When a couple shares that ideology, their marital behaviors will be shaped by the moral authority of their religion. For example, conservative gender ideology is compatible with the theological beliefs of conservative Protestants. Therefore, it is not surprising to find that conservative Protestant wives do more housework than their nonevangelical counterparts (Ellison and Bartkowski, 2002:950).

SOCIETAL GENDER EXPECTATIONS

As each couple creates a marriage that is its own unique social organization, society's gender expectations shape the roles the partners are likely to embrace. The existing gender order—in this instance, as it relates to what society expects of women and men in marriage—constrains men's and women's perceived options by defining the boundaries of what is acceptable, appropriate, and advantageous for husbands and wives. Thus women and men typically construct the contours of their marriages from a limited range of perceived choices.

In the nineteenth century, industrialization produced the separate spheres model of gender roles in which women specialized in the domestic realm of home and children and men specialized in breadwinning. In this context, women and men entered into the marriage relationship with an unquestioned set of roles and responsibilities that each would fulfill. The husband would work outside the home and provide for the family's material needs, while the wife would take care of the home, raise the children, and provide for the emotional needs of the family members. He would achieve and she would support. Power would be asymmetrical, with the husband in charge. This model became a cultural ideal that shaped men's and women's marital aspirations and expectations for several generations.

Today's men and women make marriage and family-related decisions in a very different context. Contemporary U.S. society has undergone a profound shift in gender expectations for men and women. Macrostructural social and economic changes drew women into the labor force and have now produced a convergence in women's and men's gender roles (Amato et al., 2007). Over time, society's views about women's "proper place" have changed. As Amato and his coauthors note, "The American public now views women's economic contributions to family life as being not only acceptable, but also desirable" (2007:140). The new model of marital relations is less patriarchal and more egalitarian. Increasingly, husbands and wives expect to share responsibilities for breadwinning, parenting, housework, and household decision-making. This is not to say that traditional marriages no longer exist. They do. But the traditional breadwinner–homemaker model of gender roles is not the gender division of labor most couples aspire to enact in their marriages. Contemporary society provides today's couples the opportunity to create marriages with gender roles their grandparents might scarcely recognize.

Gender—deeply embedded as it is in the processes and practices of the institution of marriage—plays a key role in shaping women's and men's marital experiences (Acker, 1992:567). It is worthy of note that social class and race/ethnicity also shape access to and experience in marriage.

Recent Trends

For most of U.S. history, Americans have shared with virtual unanimity the following cultural beliefs (Cuber et al., 1975):

- Adults should be married.

- Marriage is a life-long commitment.

- Married couples should have children.

- A wife's place is at home as nurturer, mother, and caretaker.

- A husband's role is provider and decision-maker.

Although many still hold fervently to these traditional beliefs, the behaviors of contemporary couples often contradict them. This raises the question, "To what degree do U.S. marriages now conform to these traditional ideals of what family life should be?" The statistics on contemporary marriages in the United States show a gap between the traditions of marriage and reality. Actually, only 7 percent of U.S. households fit the model of the father as sole breadwinner and the mother staying home to raise their children. Cohabiting households are nearly as likely to include children as are married-couple households (38 percent compared to 43 percent) (U.S. Bureau of the Census, 2009a). Almost two-thirds of married-couple families are dual-earner households, and 12 percent of all households are family households headed by women (U.S. Bureau of the Census, 2008b, 2009a). This section surveys the statistical evidence on contemporary family patterns. Figure 8.1 shows the composition of U.S. households in 2008. (See Figure 12.1 for changes in the composition of households between 1970 and 2008.)

Unmarried Adults

The "unmarried" category is on the rise. Unmarried adults, as a demographic category, refers to individuals who have never married, are divorced, or are widowed (Fields and Casper, 2001:9). Unmarried adults live in a number of different household arrangements: They may live alone, with roommates, with an unmarried partner as a heterosexual cohabiting couple, or with a same-sex partner in a gay- or lesbian-couple household (for more details on these categories, see Chapter 12). People living alone now make up more than one-fourth of all households. The proportion of never-married women and men between the ages of 30 and 34 is more than triple the percentage of never-married single people in this age group in 1970. Of special note, demographers estimate that 25 percent of African American women will never marry, nearly three times the rate for White women. This gap reflects social developments, such as the shrinking pool of African American men that African American women would consider good partners, which is the result of disproportionately high unemployment, incarceration, and homicide rates for African American men.

Figure 8.1

Composition of U.S. Households in 2008 (percent distribution)

Source: U.S. Bureau of the Census, "America's Families and Living Arrangements: 2008." Online: http://www.census.gov/population/www/socdemo/hh-fam/cps2008.html.

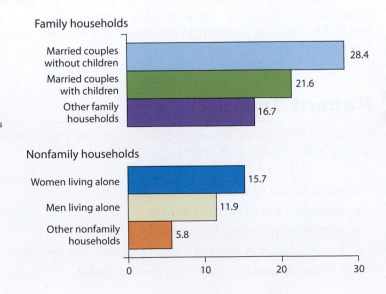

Because federal law does not recognize same-sex marriage (and most states do not permit it), a long-term relationship between same-sex couples is defined by the U.S. Census Bureau as a cohabitation arrangement. The U.S. Census estimates the number of gay or lesbian couple households to be around 750,000 (O'Connell and Lofquist, 2009). Because known homosexual individuals face discrimination, many keep their same-sex committed relationships secret. Thus, Census estimates are expected to understate the actual numbers of gay or lesbian households.

Heterosexual cohabitation continues to increase in the United States. In 2008, the number of heterosexual unmarried-couple households was approximately 6.8 million (38 percent of all unmarried-couple households include a child under 18), up considerably from 1.6 million couples in 1980 and 523,000 in 1960 (Peterson, 2000a; U.S. Bureau of the Census, 2009a). More than half of first marriages are now preceded by cohabitation (most cohabiting couples either marry or split up within 18 months). About half of cohabiting couples do marry each other. Ironically, cohabiting couples who marry have a somewhat higher divorce rate than those who marry without having lived together (Amato et al., 2007).

Less marriage has implications for the lives of children. Approximately 40 percent of all children will spend some time living with their mother and her cohabiting partner before they are age 16. Some will begin their lives in such a family. Others will be born to single mothers who later enter a cohabiting relationship. Still others will see their mothers enter such a relationship after a divorce. These data reflect profound changes in family forms.

> At the end of the twentieth century, the rapid increases in cohabitation and unmarried childbearing have dramatically altered family life in the United States (and, indeed, in most Western societies). Family boundaries have become more fluid and ambiguous, and the significance of marriage as a life-course marker in society appears to be declining. (Bumpass and Lu, 2000b:5)

Unmarried couples cohabit for a number of reasons. Some are in same-sex relationships. Some want to share expenses. Some lack the financial stability to take the step of marriage. Some choose this option as a prelude to marriage. Others are older and do not want to lose financial benefits by marrying (Block, 1999). In this instance, many older couples choose cohabitation over matrimony because pensions are based on the status of being a widow or widower. Some estate plans are set up on the condition that the surviving spouse remain unmarried. And Social Security benefits can differ depending on the amount of assets someone holds singularly or jointly in a marriage. For example, Social Security regulations require seniors to remain below certain fixed income and asset levels to qualify for governmental benefits such as Supplemental Security Income and Medicaid. The combined incomes and assets of a married couple often exceed these limits. Moreover, recipients of Social Security, by staying single, are less likely to pay taxes on their Social Security benefits. Single individuals with incomes less than $25,000 receive their benefits tax-free, while the limit for married couples is $32,000—just $7,000 more than singles (IRS, 2009). By not marrying, the cohabiting couple can earn an additional $18,000 while retaining tax-free benefits. Thus, it is advantageous not to marry although continuing to live together as a couple.

Age at First Marriage

Marriage is still very much the norm, with about 90 percent of the population eventually marrying. However, the number of marriages occurring annually has been trending downward since the mid-1980s, and the marriage rate has declined as well. The marriage rate—the number of marriages in a year per 1,000 population—declined from 10.6 in 1982 to the current low of 7.3 in 2006 (U.S. Bureau of the Census, 2008b). The lower rate is partly explained by delayed marriage; that is, people are marrying later. In 1960, the median age at first marriage for men was 22.8 years and for women 20.3 years. This contrasts with the 2008 statistics of 27.4 years for men and 25.6 years for women (U.S. Bureau of the Census, 2009a). Examined another way, the percentage of U.S. women between the ages of 20 and 24 who had not yet married more than doubled, from 28 percent in 1960 to 76 percent in 2007. Figure 8.2 shows the historical trend for age at first marriage for more than 100 years. Most significant, these data show that the age of first marriage for women is now at its highest point since data were first collected on this subject in 1889.

Philip Blumstein and Pepper Schwartz's summary of the major consequences of this trend remains relevant today:

> Delaying marriage gives a woman more opportunity for advanced education and training, reduces the number of children she will have, and ultimately gives her more independence and flexibility in making life choices. Its secondary effect is to give exactly the same advantages to her husband. (Blumstein and Schwartz, 1983:31)

Hispanic women marry earlier than women of other racial or ethnic groups. In 2000, 42 percent of Hispanic women ages 20 to 24 were married. This compares to 33 percent of both American Indian and White women, 23 percent of Asian American women, and 17 percent of African American women (Lichter and Qian, 2005:179).

Family Size

Earlier we noted that marriages are expected to result in children. Several facts suggest that this expectation has undergone some changes. Some couples have chosen to remain childless, an almost unheard-of alternative just a generation ago. Although it

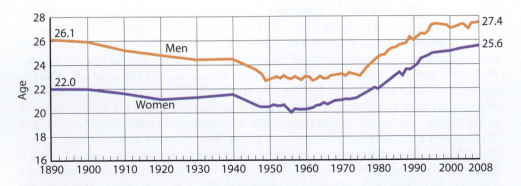

Figure 8.2
Median Age at First Marriage by Sex: 1890–2008

Source: "Marital Status and Living Arrangements: March 1998," *Current Population Reports*, Series P-20.514. Washington DC: U.S. Bureau of the Census, 1998; "Estimated Median Age at First Marriage, by Sex: 1890 to the Present" Table MS-2. U.S. Bureau of the Census, 2009. Online: www.census.gov/population/socdemo/hh-fam/ms2.xls.

is impossible to predict with any accuracy because people do change their minds, it appears that about one in six women will never have children. Moreover, couples who choose to have children are having fewer of them than at any time in U.S. history (see Chapter 9). The result of these trends is that the average household is now 2.6 persons per household, compared to 3.1 some 30 years ago. Household size varies by race/ethnicity, with the size of White households in 2008 at 2.5, African American households at 2.6, Asian American households at 2.8, Latino households at 3.3, and others, including multiracial households at 2.8 (U.S. Bureau of the Census, 2009a).

Interracial or Interethnic Marriages

Interracial marriage was illegal in a number of states until 1967, when the U.S. Supreme Court overturned **miscegenation laws** in 16 states, most of them southern. Those laws reflected the social norms of the time, that marrying someone outside one's race or ethnicity or even religion was wrong. But these age-old barriers are breaking down as the demographic landscape is changing from White to more and more non-White. National polling organizations find that the U.S. public increasingly accepts interracial marriage. A 2003 Gallup poll registered the highest approval rating ever—86 percent of African Americans, 79 percent of Hispanics, and 66 percent of Whites would accept the marriage of a child or grandchild to someone of a different race (Lee and Edmonston, 2005:3). There were 3.1 million interracial marriages in 2000, up from 1.5 million in 1990. Expressed as a percentage of all marriages, interracial marriages increased from 2.9 percent of the total in 1990 to 5.4 percent in 2000 (Lee and Edmonston, 2005:11). While some are calling this trend "the beginning of the blend," the overwhelming tendency remains to marry within one's race (**homogamy**), with almost 95 percent of all marriages between partners of the same race.

A recent report by the Population Reference Bureau draws these conclusions about racial and Hispanic intermarriages in the United States:

- Younger and better-educated Americans are more likely to intermarry than older and less educated Americans.

- Whites and Blacks have the lowest intermarriage rates, while American Indians, Hawaiians, and multiple-race people have the highest.

- About one-fourth of Hispanic couples are inter-Hispanic (that is, Hispanics married to non-Hispanic partners).

- Black men are more likely to intermarry than Black women, while Asian women are more likely to intermarry than Asian men. Men and women from other racial groups are equally likely to intermarry.

- More children are growing up in either interracial or inter-Hispanic families. Between 1970 and 2000, the number of children living in interracial families increased nearly fourfold—from 900,000 to more than three million—while the number of inter-Hispanic families increased nearly threefold—from 800,000 to two million (Lee and Edmonston, 2005:7).

The extent of interracial marriage depends on a number of factors, not the least of which is availability. When social contact is restricted by race, interracial marriage is rare. Social contacts among racial groups depend on the race relations in a community and the extent of residential and school segregation. A primary reason for higher rates of intermarriage among the more educated is that men and women with higher educational attainments are more likely to live in racially integrated neighborhoods and to have more interracial contacts in the workplace. "[E]ducation opens the door of opportunity for greater interracial contact, friendship, romance, and marriage" (Batson et al., 2006:670).

African Americans are least likely to marry outside their racial group. Greater barriers continue to exist to Black/White marriages than to marriages of Whites to other racial minorities. Lichter and Qian (2005) attribute this pattern to greater neighborhood segregation among Blacks and more racial discrimination toward Blacks than other racial-ethnic groups in U.S. society. Analyses of intermarriage among the Black population seldom take diversity within this population into account. Blacks in the United States—an increasingly diverse population—include U.S.-born African Americans, West Indians, Africans (foreign-born), Puerto Rican non-Whites, and others. Batson and her colleagues found that U.S.-born African Americans were more likely than are other groups of Blacks to marry or cohabit with Whites. The typical pattern involved a Black man and a White woman (2006:658).

Intermarriage patterns among immigrant groups differ from those of their U.S.-born counterparts. A recent study of Latinos found that for all groups analyzed—Mexicans, Puerto Ricans, Cubans, and Central Americans—immigrants were much more likely to marry individuals from the same national origin group than were U.S.-born Latinos (Qian and Cobas, 2004:233). This pattern illustrates that intermarriage is related to the process of the assimilation of immigrants into the society that has received them. Intermarriage is sometimes viewed as the final step in the process of assimilation and would be expected to occur after economic and residential assimilation (Gordon, 1964, cited in Lichter and Qian, 2005:191).

Life Span and Marriage

A critical difference between this and earlier generations is that people now live much longer. Between 1920 and 2005, for example, the life expectancy for women increased by 25 years—from 55 to 80 years. And men's life expectancy increased by 21 years—from 54 to 75 years. This dramatic increase in longevity means that now couples have the potential to live approximately 50 years together, the last 25 of which are free of child-rearing responsibilities. This shift has contradictory effects on marital relationships. On the one hand, there is more time to build an enduring bond that provides for mutual sharing and happiness as the needs of each are met in a growing commitment to the relationship. More realistically, though, people often change through the life cycle, with alterations in personality, identity, and needs. With longer life spans, there is the greater possibility of people growing apart. The type of partner one required at the age

Couples have the potential to live together for fifty years or more.

of 25 may be quite different from the type desired at 50 or 70. This new longevity is one explanation for the relatively high divorce rate. Clearly, understanding contemporary marriages requires examination of the different and changing forces that act on the relationship throughout the life cycle.

DIVORCE

The divorce rate accelerated in the 1970s and peaked in 1981 at 5.3 couples divorcing per 1,000 people in the population (for an elaboration on divorce, see Chapter 11). Since then, it gradually declined and in the late 1990s stabilized at around 4.2 couples divorcing per 1,000. In recent years the divorce rate has fallen further, with the 2006 divorce rate at 3.6 couples per 1,000 population (the lowest rate since the early 1970s) (U.S. Bureau of the Census, 2008b). About half of all marriages are expected to eventually end in divorce. The divorce rate varies by race and ethnicity. African American couples are more likely than White or Latino couples to divorce. At current rates, as many as two-thirds of all recent African American marriages will end in divorce. By the age of 16, only about one out of every three White children, compared with two out of every three African American children, will experience the dissolution of their parents' marriage.

REMARRIAGE

About half of all marriages in the United States involve a second or higher-order marriage for one or both of the marriage partners. Remarriage has been common throughout U.S. history, but until the last 50 years or so, the typical remarriage followed widowhood (see Chapter 11). Now more than 90 percent of remarriages involve either a bride or a groom who was divorced. The majority of divorced persons remarry: 3 out of 4 men and 6 out of 10 women eventually do so (Hetherington, 2002).

Several variables affect the probability of remarriage. The age of women is crucial, with older women much less likely to remarry than younger women. The remarriage prospect of younger women with children is less than it is for younger women without children. Race is also significant. African Americans, for example, are much less likely than Whites to remarry. Whereas two-thirds of White women remarry, only about one-third of African American women do so. This, of course, is another reason why African American women are more likely than White women to head households that have children under the age of 18 with no husband present. About one-fifth of all existing marriages include at least one previously divorced spouse. This strong propensity for divorced persons to remarry suggests that people are not disillusioned with marriage as such but with a specific spouse.

 # Are There Benefits to Marriage?

Although most adults affirm the value and importance of marriage, the marriage-related behaviors of U.S. women and men point to the declining significance of marriage as a social institution. Trends such as increased rates of cohabitation, later age of first marriage, more children born outside marriage, and a high divorce rate suggest that women and men orient their lives less and less around marriage. How do we as a society respond to the trends that have reshaped family life over the past several decades? One of the responses to changing marital behavior is a "marriage movement" that seeks to strengthen marriage by raising public awareness of the

BOX 8.2   **Emergent Family Trends**

Uncle Sam Wants You . . . to Get Married?

Well not exactly, but Uncle Sam would like you to consider it. If a new government-funded advertising and education campaign is effective, your generation may be on the leading edge of a trend toward more marriage.

The U.S. Department of Health and Human Services is funding a marriage-promotion media campaign targeting young adults, ages 18 to 30 (Jayson, 2009a). This initiative, launched in February 2009, uses the conventional advertising media of TV and radio, but also reaches out in cyberspace with videos on YouTube and ads on Facebook and MySpace. In addition, a website, TwoOfUs.org, provides information and resources about relationships with Q & As, articles, videos, and podcasts. This interactive site offers discussion boards and "quick polls" that invite site visitors to weigh in on a current issue. A recent question was: Has the recession put stress on your relationship? Answer choices: (1) Yes; (2) No; and (3) What recession? (TwoOfUs.org, 2009).

The premise is that promoting marriage is a kind of public service campaign, much like government-sponsored anti-smoking or "Don't Drink and Drive" advertising. The purpose of these is to encourage the public to avoid actions that put themselves or others at risk. In similar fashion, the goal of this $5 million, four-year initiative is to encourage young adults to consider marriage as a choice that benefits themselves and others.

Paul Amato is a sociologist who advises the organization directing this initiative. Dr. Amato says, "We're not telling people 'Get married,' but [we're telling them] 'Don't underestimate the benefits of marriage' " (Jayson, 2009a).

benefits of marriage and providing marriage education. The marriage movement is made up of family scholars and therapists, educators, policy-makers, and religious leaders who have proposed a number of strategies for improving marriages and reducing divorce (Amato et al., 2007:244). The federal government is a strong partner in promarriage initiatives. A major component of the overhaul of the welfare system in 1996 was marriage promotion (see Chapter 13). More recently, in 2006 President Bush signed a bill that provided $750 million over five years to support marriage-related initiatives ($100 million per year for marriage programming and $50 million per year for responsible fatherhood programs) (Jayson, 2009a). See Box 8.2 for a federal initiative targeting young adults.

From the perspective of some family scholars, the benefits of marriage are clear-cut, and encouraging more and better marriages is good for individuals and society. This group is guided by research findings in two major areas. First, research finds that married individuals are healthier, happier, and better off financially than the never married, the divorced, and the widowed (Waite, 1995). Second, some research concludes that "a large proportion of marriages that end in divorce are *not* deeply troubled, and that many of these marriage might be salvaged if spouses sought assistance for relationship problems, remained committed to their unions, placed their children's well-being ahead of their own, and stayed the course through difficult times" (Amato et al., 2007:246).

The perspective articulated above represents one side in a debate between family scholars about the meaning and substance of family change. Amato and his coauthors (2007) frame this debate in terms of two perspectives, the marital decline perspective and the marital resilience perspective. The marital decline perspective, and the pro-marriage initiatives that follow from it, assumes that excessive individualism has weakened marriage with negative results for individuals and society. On the other hand, the marital resilience perspective assumes that changes in the institution of marriage represent adaptation to social change, and entail few serious negative results for individuals and society (Amato et al., 2007:4–7).

The Benefits of Marriage

Individuals marry for a variety of reasons. These include the obvious ones, such as the desire for companionship and intimacy. This section focuses on other benefits that derive from being married (the following is primarily from Waite, 1995, 1999, 2000; Waite and Gallagher, 2000).

To begin, the marriage relationship promotes healthy behaviors. Research shows that the unmarried are far more likely than the married to die from all causes, including heart disease, stroke, pneumonia, many kinds of cancer, cirrhosis of the liver, automobile accidents, murder, and suicide. There are many reasons why marriage promotes better health. When the married are compared with the unmarried and the divorced of the same age, the married, especially husbands, are less likely to engage in risky behaviors such as excessive drinking, drinking and driving, substance abuse, and multiple sexual partners (smoking, however, is unaffected by marital status, except that pregnant women are likely to quit cigarettes). Divorce is associated with a return to bad habits, whereas remarriages drive down drug and alcohol use once again (Schwartz, 1997). Waite and Gallagher (2000) posit that marriage affects health by providing individuals, especially men, with someone who monitors their health and who encourages self-regulation. Moreover, the support by a spouse, usually the wife, helps individuals deal with stressful situations and to recover more rapidly from surgery and other health problems. It is, perhaps, unsurprising to find that married men live up to five years longer than single men (Kulman, 2005:77).

The married have better mental health than the unmarried. Summarizing the research, Waite and Gallagher say, "Married men and women report less depression, less anxiety, and lower levels of other types of psychological distress than do those who are single, divorced, or widowed" (2000:67). Their interpretation of the research findings is that

[n]ew marriage partners together create a shared sense of social reality and meaning—their own little separate world, populated by only the two of them. This shared sense of meaning can be an important foundation for emotional health. Ordinary, good-enough marriages provide the partners with a sense that what they do matters, that someone cares for, esteems, needs, loves, and values them as a person. No matter what else happens in life, this knowledge makes problems easier to bear. (Waite and Gallagher, 2000:75)

Marriage also enhances the sex lives of the partners. Waite and Gallagher, after surveying the research, conclude that "[m]arried people have both more and better sex than singles do. They not only have sex more often, but they enjoy it more, both physically and emotionally, than do their unmarried counterparts....Marriage, it turns out, is not only good for you, it is good for your libido too" (Waite and Gallagher, 2000:79).

The married have more economic resources (income, pension and Social Security benefits, financial assets, and the value of their primary residence) than the unmarried. This economic advantage stems from the increase in productivity by husbands (compared to unmarried men) and the fact that both spouses in so many marriages are now in the labor force. The greater economic advantages of married couples explain many of the benefits that Waite and others associate with the marriage bond itself. With greater affluence comes better nutrition; better access to private dentists, physicians, psychiatrists, and hospitals; a greater likelihood of living in a safe neighborhood; more travel and quality leisure; and the opportunity to experience the good things in life. So it may not be the marriage bond itself that generates better emotional and physical health for the partners, but the greater resources generated.

Health and wealth differentials between the married and the unmarried raise the issue of protection versus selection. Does marriage, for example, protect individuals from poor health, or are healthy men and women with wholesome lifestyles more likely to be selected as marriage partners? Selection may explain some of the differences, but researchers conclude that marital protection is responsible for some of the better outcomes we find for the married (Kim and McKenry, 2002; Murray, 2000).

Waite (1995:498) argues that there are four factors surrounding marriage that make it cause the aforementioned outcomes: (1) The institution of marriage assumes a long-term contract, which provides the couple with social support by imposing social and economic costs on those who dissolve the union; (2) marriage assumes the sharing of economic and social resources, which is a form of coinsurance, protecting the partners from unexpected events; (3) married couples benefit from economies of scale (that is, two can live almost as cheaply as one in terms of transportation, electricity, telephone, appliances, residence); and (4) marriage connects people to others, to social groups, and to other social institutions. These connections provide individuals with a sense of obligation to others, which gives life meaning beyond oneself.

The Benefits of Marriage Reconsidered

Marriage matters. Married people have more resources, are better networked, and are healthier, leaving little doubt that marriage is beneficial. But we must evaluate this generalization cautiously. Obviously, not all marriages are advantageous to the partners. Some marriages are abusive. Some partners are abandoned by their spouses. Some marriages are empty of love and caring. Clearly, the emotional needs of the partners are not being met in these marriages. The relatively high divorce rate is ample evidence that marriages are not blissful for millions of couples. But let's go beyond these obvious negatives. Consider, first, the generalization that marriage is beneficial economically. Recent research finds the economic benefits of marriage to be uneven; that is, they differ by social class and race.

Many women are interested in accessing the economic benefits of marriage described by Waite and others. The problem many encounter, however, is the difficulty of finding economically attractive marriage partners. Working-class and poor women's potential mates are generally men of the same social class. Wells and Baca Zinn found in their study of White rural families that marriage did not enable rural men with meager labor market credentials to find jobs with pensions and other benefits. Married working-class and poor couples sometimes had more common debts than assets, and their primary investment was frequently their residence—a mobile home that was depreciating in value (2004:76).

Women are generally reluctant to marry men who are jobless or who have unstable employment. The likelihood that cohabiting couples anticipate they will eventually marry depends on men's socioeconomic circumstances (Manning and Smock, 2002:1081). Women are much less likely to expect to move from cohabitation to marriage when their partners have low educational attainment and low earnings.

The economic transformations of the past three decades are closely associated with what has been called the "retreat from marriage" (Lichter et al., 2002). A society that produces an increasing proportion of low-wage, unstable jobs is a society that is likely to have less marriage because economic insecurity discourages marriage and makes existing marriages less stable. The obstacles to achieving economic stability through marriage are especially difficult for people of color. Poverty rates for minorities continue to be much higher than for the White population. A recent report from the U.S. Census found that poverty rates for African Americans, Hispanics, and American Indians ranged between 2.5 to 3 times the White poverty rate. Even more sobering is the finding that poor African Americans are more than three times as likely as Whites to have incomes less than half of the poverty threshold (DeNavas-Walt et al., 2006). Without adequate resources, poor couples experience added stress as they have difficulty meeting basic family needs for shelter, clothing, health care, and safety. "In communities where men have historically had limited ability to be breadwinners, the decline in employment has brought an increase in domestic violence, alcoholism, and other problems associated with joblessness" (Dill, 1998:B8). Lower wages or underemployment, more common to racial minorities than to Whites, requires working longer hours, which means less companionship and more pressure on the marital bond.

U.S. government efforts to encourage marriage as the solution to the economic troubles of poor women are questioned by many. Recent research suggests marriage promotion efforts are somewhat disconnected from the daily realities and priorities of women raising children in concentrated poverty (Boo, 2003; Edin and Kefalas, 2005; Huston and Melz, 2004). Kathryn Edin and Maria Kefalas found that the poor Black, White, and Puerto Rican women they studied placed their children at the center of their lives. They had high expectations for marriage, hoped to be married one day, but were willing to forgo marriage for the present. For many women, past relationships had been threatened by infidelity, substance abuse, and criminal activity. These women were uninterested in marrying the wrong man. Edin and Kefalas conclude, "[P]oor women consider marriage a luxury—one they desire and hope someday to attain, but can live without if they must. Children, on the other hand, are a necessity" (2005:210).

While many poor women may indeed be better off after marriage, critics of government-funded marriage promotion initiatives point out that the "supply" of available men with decent jobs is far lower than the "demand" for economically stable partners. Moreover, "employed men are not looking to rescue someone from poverty"; increasingly, men too are looking for economically attractive spouses, that is, a wife who will herself have good employment prospects (Coontz and Folbre, 2002).

The evidence documenting the economic benefits of marriage is strong; nonetheless, as we have seen, marriage turns out to be more economically beneficial to some groups in society than others. Daniel Lichter and his colleagues conclude:

> [T]he call for policies that promote marriage arguably is at cross purposes with macroeconomic trends that have eroded the economic underpinnings of marriage for those most in need. Marriage in the absence of stable employment and a family wage is no economic panacea; at the same time, marriage has arguably become a "luxury" available mostly to middle-class and affluent women with the best marital prospects. Clearly, if marriage benefits society and becomes an important social goal, then effective public policy will require a much better understanding of the changing personal incentives and structural constraints that affect marriage, especially among disadvantaged women. (2002:254)

Finally, we must be cautious about some of the assumptions undergirding the marriage promotion agenda. The first is that children's well-being is enhanced by growing up in a married-couple household. Gregory Acs points to the real possibility that "children in 'marriage-promoted' families may be in a lower quality home environment than the average child with married parents today" (2007:1327). A single mother's wedding may produce a low quality marriage, difficult stepfamily relations, and disruptions to a child's living environment that may negatively affect his or her well-being. Second, we must question the assumption that more marriage is unequivocally good for society. In fact, married couples—immersed in their own private worlds—are less

"We can't find a compromise between a life of quiet desperation and life in the fast lane."

likely than unmarried individuals to be involved in networks of support for extended family members and less involved with neighbors and friends. As ironic as it may sound, promoting marriage as a way to benefit society may actually undermine community (Gerstel and Sarkisian, 2006b:21).

HIS AND HER MARRIAGE

Gender is a crucial factor in evaluating the benefits of marriage. Each marriage is the creation of a new social unit. The two members of this unit—in which the interaction is intense and the feelings intimate—do not, strange as it may seem, always share the same interpretations and reap the same rewards from their shared life. The fundamental reason for this is that the two members in a marriage differ by gender. Society, through the socialization process and through various institutions, imprints girls and boys, women and men with the customary expectations and behaviors deemed appropriate for each gender within a marriage.

By dissecting the family, we see that the sex–gender system structures women's and men's family lives differently. One of the most useful ways of understanding this is Jessie Bernard's concept of "his" and "her" marriages. Bernard's classic work (1972) on marriage revealed that every marital union actually contains two marriages, which do not always coincide.

The Husband's Marriage   Marriage affects men and women in somewhat different ways. While married men and women are healthier, wealthier, and live longer than the unmarried, men receive greater health benefits than women from marriage (Waite and Gallagher, 2000:163). Coontz offers this explanation: "A man in a bad marriage still gets some health benefits compared with single men because even a miserable wife tends to feed her husband more vegetables, schedule his medical checkups, and shoulder much of the housework and the emotional work that make life function smoothly" (2005:310).

Another advantage is that husbands, in general, receive more social support in commitment and caring from their spouses than they return. Men do, in general, work more hours outside the home than their wives, but the workload is rarely equal when housework, child care, and emotion work are tallied.

The Wife's Marriage   Waite's research shows that wives generally benefit from marriage, but less so than husbands. Unequal outcomes are explained, in part, by research showing that "[m]en benefit from marriage more than women do because men benefit from the status of being married regardless of the emotional quality of the marriage. Wives' benefits, however, appear to depend more on the quality of their unions" (Nock, 2001:770). Women in troubled marriages are likely to experience health-related problems such as depression and immune-system breakdown (Hetherington, 2002:62). The stress of a long-term unhappy marriage leaves women at increased risk for heart attacks after menopause (Elias, 2004).

Wives are relatively disadvantaged in marriages; typically, they have to deal with patriarchy (the dominance of the husband) and their secondary status at home, at work, and in society. A full-time homemaker does the family's "dirty work"—cooking, cleaning, and other household chores that she may interpret as drudgery and even demeaning. Her wishes are secondary to those of her breadwinning husband. Two-career families generate stressors for wives as they, typically, work full-time and still do the majority of the housework. When children are added, mothers devote much more time and emotional energy to their children than fathers do. "The failure of men to share housework and child care with their partners…is a primary source of overload for working mothers and a major cause of marital conflict.…Marital dissatisfaction and divorce frequently originate when modern parents backslide into traditional roles after the birth of a child" (Coontz, 1997:109–110). The problem is especially acute for employed housewives who work "three shifts": a day job, family and household chores at night, and relationship maintenance (Peterson, 1993).

To summarize, the generalization that marriage is beneficial to the spouses is too facile. We can only answer the question "Who benefits from marriage?" by examining the social location of the partners in a marriage. This means including the social class and race/ethnicity of the spouses. And we must include the lesson of Jessie Bernard that every marriage union is actually two marriages. In effect, then, marriage matters; but the degree to which it matters is affected by social class, race, and gender.

Micro Aspects of Marriage

In addition to the dynamics of gender, the partners in a marriage must deal with three issues on an ongoing basis: communication and other correlates of marital success, sexual intimacy, and decision-making.

Marital Success

Studies of marriage have uncovered some of the diversity in the quality of modern marriages. A classic study by John Cuber and Peggy Haroff (1965) revealed that enduring marriages differ in important ways from one another, and they differ as well from the ideals of happy marriages. The intent of these researchers was to study "normal" couples rather than those in crisis. Their sample represented the upper end of the occupational distribution, and they interviewed 437 U.S. women and men between the ages of 35 and 50. One of the most widely quoted findings of the study is its description of five types of enduring marriage. Cuber and Haroff discovered enormous variation within a group of stable marriages among people of similar class positions, thus destroying the myth that happy families are all alike (Skolnick, 1983:276).

- *Conflict-habituated marriages* centered on tensions, arguments, and fights. Conflict in these marriages was not always readily observable to outsiders, but it was always present in various forms including nagging, quarrelling, sarcasm, put-downs, and even physical combat (although it may not include that). A conflict-habituated way of interaction could last a lifetime.

- *Devitalized marriages* involved couples who were once in love but had drifted apart over the years. They remained together in a relationship bound by duty.

- *Passive congenial marriages* were those in which love was not expected, but the marriage provided stability for the couple to direct their energies elsewhere.

- *Vital marriages* differed greatly from the forgoing types in that spouses shared true intimacy in all important life matters. Husbands and wives found their central satisfaction in the life they lived with and through each other.

- *Total marriages,* the fifth type, were like the vital relationship with the important addition of being more multifaceted. Such marriages involved couples who were completely absorbed in one another's life activities, often including their work. (Cuber and Haroff, 1965:43–65)

Cuber and Haroff's successful U.S. marriages were by no means all happy, but they remained intact. Are they successful if they remain intact, or is there more to marital success?

There are two measures of marital success. The first is marital stability (the subject of Chapter 11). This variable is easily measured because it refers to the simple and objective reality of whether the marriage is intact. The problem, as illustrated by some of the marital types delineated by Cuber and Haroff, is that this is not necessarily an indicator of marital quality because one or both of the partners in an intact marriage may not find the relationship satisfying at all, yet they do not separate.

Marital quality, the focus of our discussion here, is the other measure of marital success. This refers to the ways in which the husband and wife describe and evaluate the character of their relationship. This subjective and therefore elusive evaluation of marriages goes to the heart of the matter. The questions directed by researchers to spouses involve such matters as the degree of conflict, success at conflict resolution, extent of shared activities, feelings of happiness, communication patterns, sexual behaviors, and financial planning.

A new study by Paul Amato and his colleagues uses two national surveys to compare marital quality in 1980 and 2000 (2007). In 2000, they found less couple interaction, but also less marital conflict and marital problems than in 1980. They found unchanged both marital happiness and how "divorce-prone" couples were. Women evaluated their marriages less positively than men in both 1980 and 2000 (Amato et al., 2007).

THE CORRELATES OF MARITAL QUALITY

Literally hundreds of studies have examined marital quality, and their findings are summarized here.

Shared Social Characteristics   Research has shown consistently that spouses who are alike in the social characteristics of socioeconomic status, religion, race, age, and intelligence (i.e., they are homogamous) tend to have marriages that are higher in quality than those who differ on these dimensions. The underlying explanation for the relative success of **homogamous marriages** is that persons who share similar characteristics adjust more easily to each other and are more likely to agree on values, politics, and religion, thus increasing the chances for harmony. Marital homogamy has decreased in the United States in recent years (Amato et al., 2003:3).

Economic and Personal Resources   The higher the income, education, and occupational status of the couple, the more they are likely to evaluate their marriage as good. Well-educated partners have better communication skills, less depression, and a stronger sense of personal control than their less-educated counterparts (Amato et al., 2003:3). Sometimes a positive evaluation of one's marriage may not reflect happiness per se but rather a convenience that both affluent spouses find important to their well-being. Randall Collins (1988b) has suggested that success itself can hold a marriage together, given the economic incentives to do so. Couples lower in the class system have more reason to separate, which, in fact, they do.

Dual-Earner Couples   Both spouses in the labor force may have contradictory effects on marital happiness. Positively, working wives have better mental health (e.g., better self-concept, less depression). Dual-career couples are more able to live a middle-class lifestyle. Also, having more discretionary income than single-career marriages alleviates one major source of marital stress. On the negative side, wives' employment may result in conflicts about the division of household work or create child-care dilemmas. A common solution—split-shift parenting—means that spouses spend little quality time with each other.

The relationship between dual-earner households and marital quality has been found to be associated with wives' job satisfaction. Women's negative feelings about their jobs spill over and negatively affect marital quality. This relationship has implications for social class. Middle class women in fulfilling careers have higher job satisfaction (and higher marital quality) than working class women who work in unsatisfying jobs to help their families make ends meet (Amato et al., 2007).

We also see that women's increased entry into professional and managerial jobs has implications for marital quality. The time commitment required to succeed in these jobs may require long work hours that interfere with family necessities. The proportion of wives working extended hours (more than 45 hours weekly) has increased markedly over the past 20 years. Wives' extended hours of employment are associated with lower marital quality (Amato et al., 2003).

The Division of Household Labor   The division of labor at home is another factor in marital quality (see Chapter 6). Wives spend on average about twice as much time on routine household tasks as their husbands. This two-thirds/one-third relationship represents a decrease in women's hours of household work and a slight increase in men's hours since the 1960s (Artis and Pavalko, 2003).

Satisfaction with the division of household work is an important predictor of marital quality. Wives' dissatisfaction with the division of household work creates considerable marital conflict. It is not surprising that wives who work outside the home tend to resent their husbands who work only half as much as they do on household maintenance. Husbands often resent the escalating demands of their wives to engage in housework because they are (in nearly three of four marriages) making the larger income. Men sometimes believe that primary breadwinners have the right to opt out of housework. Husbands, at least the more traditional ones, even when they do only half as much household work as their wives, may also resent it because what they are doing is much more than their fathers did.

The share of housework that husbands do relates to marital quality in a way that is, when we think about it, unsurprising. Wives' marital quality is higher when husbands do a greater share of housework, but among husbands, doing more housework is associated with lower marital quality for them. It seems reasonable to conclude that no one really enjoys doing housework (Amato et al., 2007:166).

When wives evaluate the division of housework to be fair (although "fair" does not usually mean that husbands are expected to share the work equally), marital quality is enhanced. "Satisfaction with spousal help is positively associated with positive marital interaction, marital closeness, affirmation, and positive affect; it is negatively related to marital conflict, thoughts of divorce, negative affect, and depression" (Coltrane, 2000:1224).

A study of the perceptions of interracial couples about the fairness of the division of household work, child care, and other matters in their relationship found that wives had a stronger sense that the relationship was not fair to them than did their husbands. Perceived unfairness was associated with poor marital quality. The researchers conclude, "In many ways the results validated the perspective often stated by spouses in interracial marriages that their marriages are like every other" (Forry et al., 2007:1546).

Role Fit   The term *role fit* refers to the degree of consensus between the spouses on decision-making, the division of household labor, spending money, and issues involving children, such as how many to have, when to have them, and how to discipline them. For example, the marriage of an egalitarian woman and a traditional man is likely to result in poor role fit. Disagreements about appropriate partner roles and responsibilities tend to produce considerable conflict and resentment, and often result in dissatisfaction with the relationship.

Social Class   Couples vary by social class in what their expectations are for husbands and wives in a marriage. As men's and women's work and family roles have converged, the overall trend is toward more egalitarian marriage relationships (Amato et al., 2003:9). Nevertheless, the consistent research finding is that working-class couples are more likely than middle-class couples to accept the traditional gender roles in marriage (Perry-Jenkins and Polk, 1994).

Children   There is a consistent curvilinear relationship between family stage and marital quality. Marital quality is usually higher in the preparental and postparental years of the marriage and lower when children are present in the household. Studies spanning 50 years have found this U-shaped pattern of marital satisfaction among couples who become parents (Twenge et al., 2003). Children doubtless enrich couples in many ways, but marital quality tends to suffer nonetheless. A major reason for this is that time once devoted to the marital relationship now is directed toward the child or children. Children are costly, and the resulting economic stress may also lead to marital stress. The problems of children, especially older children (e.g., school performance, social relationships, sexual behavior, and adolescent rebellion), are crucial concerns and may produce tension between spouses.

Research also shows that marital quality tends to suffer when a child has special needs (e.g., is hyperactive) or is disabled in some way. Especially difficult is a situation in which the parents must take care of their child throughout the couple's life. Factors affecting marital quality are the strength of the marital relationship before the birth of their disabled child, the severity of the child's handicap, the availability of a support network, including health and education services, and the economic resources of the family.

Some analyses of marital quality and children compare the marital satisfaction of parents and nonparents. In general, parents report lower marital satisfaction than nonparents. "The difference in marital satisfaction is most pronounced among mothers of infants (38 percent of mothers of infants have high marital satisfaction, compared with 62 percent of childless women)" (Twenge et al., 2003:574).

Life Cycle   Marital quality appears to decline over the life cycle. Norval D. Glenn (1998) evaluated the quality of marriages based on individuals' reports of marital happiness. He found that the percentage of individuals who say that their marriages are "very happy" goes steadily and appreciably downward for at least the first 10 years of marriage. Although the evidence is conflicting, in some cases there appears to be some increase in satisfaction when the children leave home and the couple is more financially secure. In general, however, there tends to be a loss of intimacy in marriages over time. For many couples marriages become devitalized. The frequency of sexual intercourse and other forms of physical intimacy diminishes, the number of shared activities declines, and the frequency and quality of communication drops.

Bradbury, Fincham, and Beach (2000) conclude in their review of the marital satisfaction literature from the 1990s that, "on average, marital satisfaction probably does not follow a U-shaped function over the marital career, as was once believed, but instead drops markedly over the first 10 years of marriage on average and then drops more gradually in the ensuing decades" (p. 965). Because most married couples have children, the research findings presented here on life cycle as a correlate of marital quality seem to contradict some of the conclusions drawn in the previous section on children. This disparity serves to illustrate both that marital quality is a complex construct and that family scholars use diverse approaches in conceptualizing and measuring it.

Communication in Marriage

Marriage is the most intimate of relationships. The partners in marriage must continually define and redefine their relationship through communication. Noller and Feeney write, "[I]t is important to remember that the essence of the marital relationship lies in the day-to-day-interactions in which married couples engage. Marital interactions are, of course, immensely varied, sometimes dealing with the more mundane aspects of married life, and sometimes involving highly emotional issues that may be either positive or negative in tone" (2002:1–2). How a couple communicates predicts how successfully they will cope with the highs and lows of married life.

"When did our relationship move from the bedroom to the kitchen?"

Considerable research shows that one of the factors associated with marital stability and marital satisfaction is the quality of communication between the partners. Both particular interaction patterns and specific characteristics of the communication, especially the level of positivity and negativity, are related to relationship quality in this research (Christensen et al., 2006:1029). As one might assume, positive communication is associated with relationship satisfaction and stability, while negative communication is associated with relationship dissatisfaction and instability (p. 1030).

A number of studies consider the partners' styles of interaction. This work looks at the impact of positive and negative "affect" on couple interaction. In general, affect refers to a feeling or emotion; in this discussion we are interested in the display of affect in marital communication. Positive affect includes interest, validation, affection, humor, and enthusiasm. Negative affect can be broken down into two categories, a low-intensity negative affect category: domineering, whining, anger, fear/tension, and sadness; and a high-intensity negative affect category: contempt, belligerence, and defensiveness. See Table 8.1 for descriptions of these categories. The relative amounts of each type of interaction predict overall relationship quality. A high level of positive and enjoyable interaction maintains and promotes marital satisfaction while negative interaction erodes satisfaction with the relationship (Kim et al., 2007:70). Thus, satisfying relationships tend to be characterized by more acceptance,

Table 8.1   **Descriptions of Types of Positive and Negative Affect**

Types of Affect	Descriptors
Positive affect	
Interest	Elaboration seeking, involved, positive energy
Validation	Understanding, acceptance, paraphrasing
Affection	Tenderness, caring statements, compliments
Humor	Amusement, joking, laughing, wit
Enthusiasm	Happiness, pleasure, anticipation, positive surprise
Low-intensity negative affect	
Domineering	Lecturing, patronizing, talking over partner
Whining	Complaining, high-pitched voice
Anger	Irritation, annoyance, raised voice, impatience
Fear/tension	Fidgeting, discomfort, nervous laughter
Sadness	Passivity, sighing, pouting, crying
High-intensity negative affect	
Contempt	Sarcasm, insults, hostile humor
Belligerence	Taunting questions, unreciprocated humor, testing limits
Defensiveness	Excuses, countercomplaining, aggressive defense

Source: Kim, Hyoun K., Deborah M. Capaldi, and Lynn Crosby, "Generalizability of Gottman and Colleagues' Affective Process Models of Couples' Relationship Outcomes." *Journal of Marriage and Family* 69 (February): 58.

tenderness, and laughter, while troubled marriages are much more likely to be debilitated by complaining, irritation, and insults.

In addition to the general point made earlier about the significance of positive and negative patterns of interaction, many family scholars point to one especially corrosive pattern of communication in couple relationships: the demand/withdraw pattern of interaction. "In this conflictual pattern, one partner tries to discuss a relationship problem and is often critical and demanding, whereas the other tries to avoid discussion and is often defensive and withdrawn during discussion" (Christensen et al., 2006:1030). The demand/withdraw pattern is a gendered pattern of interaction, with women more often in the demanding role and men more often in the withdrawing role. Many researchers have speculated about the gender dynamics at work in this pattern of communication. Christensen and his coauthors point out that women are more likely to be in the demanding role because they are the ones who more often desire changes in the relationship. In general, it is women, more than men, who are seeking change in their partners. Three broad areas of change that many wives desire in their partners are these: "increased involvement in housework, increased involvement in child care, and increased closeness" 1031). Men who do not wish to change in the directions their wives request may withdraw from the conversation to avoid discussing the issue.

The demand/withdraw pattern of interaction reflects men's and women's uneven experience of marriage and their unequal power in the relationship. The existing arrangements in most U.S. households with respect to housework and child care favor men. When wives try to get husbands to do more, they may complain and apply pressure on their husbands. By withdrawing from the conversation, a husband avoids an argument and also avoids doing more at home. The demand/withdraw pattern has been found to be a strong predictor of marital distress and, in fact, of separation and divorce (Christensen et al., 2006). A couple's patterns of communication provide important cues as to the long-term viability of their marriage (see Box 8.3).

The discussion thus far has focused on the quality of a couple's communication. The quantity of communication is also important in sustaining intimate relationships. Spouses with time-intensive careers, dual-earner couples with children, and partners with long-distance relationships may find themselves with too little time to communicate about significant family, household, and personal matters. Quantity of communication generally refers to the "frequency of contact," the "length of interaction," or "time spent together" (Emmers-Sommer, 2004:401). Susan Roxburgh asked this question to a sample of employed married men and women: "What would you most like to change

BOX 8.3   Technology and the Family

Using Technology to Study Marital Interaction: Results from the "Love Lab"

Dr. John Gottman and his colleagues have studied thousands of married couples at the Family Research Laboratory (nicknamed the Love Lab) at the University of Washington. Their research uses technology, including video cameras, electrocardiograms, electromechanical transducers, polygraphs, and pulse-monitors to analyze how couples interact, particularly in response to conflict. Researchers study not only the verbal content of the couple's conversation but also their facial expressions, vocal tone, and physiological responses in these videotaped interaction sessions. Physiological responses such as sweat rates and heart rates provide an important component of this multidimensional analysis. Using observational and other data, Gottman has been able to predict with 90 percent accuracy which couples will divorce.

An important finding in Gottman's research is that anger is a less destructive force in marriage than many marriage therapists have believed. Expressions of anger may result in long-term gains in marital satisfaction. Instead, he identifies four other destructive patterns in marriage—what he terms "the Four Horsemen of the Apocalypse"—criticism, contempt, defensiveness, and "stonewalling" (listener withdrawal). The extent to which these negative modes of interaction are present in marital interaction is predictive of divorce.

Sources: Gottman, John M., James Coan, Sybil Carrere, and Catherine Swanson (1999). "Predicting Marital Happiness and Stability from Newlywed Interactions." *Journal of Marriage and Family* 60 (February): 5–22; Kantrowitz, Barbara and Pat Wingert (1999). "The Science of a Good Marriage." *Newsweek* (April 19): 52–57.

about the time you spend with your spouse?" The most common response was related to increasing the amount of time spent together (Roxburgh, 2006:540). While researchers view communication quality as most significant in predicting satisfaction with the relationship, quantity of communication is important in facilitating positive relational outcomes (Emmers-Sommer, 2004:409).

Gay and lesbian couples, like their heterosexual counterparts, have to negotiate their roles, work out the division of labor, settle disputes, and develop problem-solving strategies (Galvin and Brommel, 1999). They are at a disadvantage, however, given their marginal status in society. Blumstein and Schwartz (1983) note that young homosexual individuals are denied role models of positive images of long-term same-sex relationships. Society denies them legitimacy. Often they lack a full support network, even lacking one in their own families. Without these social supports, the lesbian or gay couple negotiates each situation without relying on societal expectations or previous gender role models for their answers. This increases the potential for higher tensions within each relationship.

Positive communication represents an obvious gain to relationships. Good communication skills are valuable as couples respond to challenging family circumstances. At the same time, we acknowledge that marital communication does not overcome many structural impediments that strain families—for example, closing factories and lack of health care coverage.

The Sexual Relationship in Marriage

Couples generally say that sex is an important aspect of their marriage relationship. As Elliott and Umberson write, "Sex represents a fundamental way married people can show they love and care for one another. To be sure, there are other ways to show affection, but sex is culturally vaunted as a signifier of love and marital bliss. Thus, it may become a powerful symbol of the relationship" (2008:394). For couples today, satisfying sex and a good marriage are presumed to go hand-in-hand.

In thinking about sexual activity in marriage, we do well to recall (from Chapter 7) the socially-constructed nature of intimacy. How sexuality is experienced and interpreted varies by time and space and reflects particular cultural contexts. In contemporary U.S. society, sexual satisfaction is viewed as one of the main indicators of a happy marriage. Advice on how to keep the "sizzle" in your marriage is widely available in articles in popular magazines and online, on television talk shows, and in marriage-enrichment seminars. Expectations for satisfying sex in marriage are high.

Large-scale national studies find a high level of sexual satisfaction among married heterosexual couples in the United States. For example, the National Health and Social Life Survey (NHSLS) found that 88 percent of married research participants were either extremely or very physically pleased in their relationship (cited in Sprecher and Cate, 2004:240).

There is no doubt that sex matters. The most striking research finding about sex in marriage is the consistent association of sexual satisfaction with overall marital satisfaction. Does this mean that satisfying sex predicts marital happiness, or does a satisfying marriage predict good sex? Many studies hypothesize about the direction of this relationship, but causation is nearly impossible to determine. Sexual satisfaction is also associated with love and commitment. How sexually satisfied partners are in the marriage has implications for feelings of love and their commitment to stay in the relationship (Sprecher and Cate, 2004:241). To use terminology introduced earlier in this chapter, how happy or satisfied individuals are with their sexual relationship is associated with both marital quality and marital stability.

Several studies find that the major factors associated with frequency of marital sex are the length of the relationship and the age of the partners (Willetts et al., 2004:69). As the duration of the marriage and the age of the partners increases, the frequency of sex decreases. For example, in the National Survey of Families and Households (NSFH), married individuals had sex an average of 6.3 times a month. Frequency of sex declined markedly by age group, with couples under age 24 having sex an average of 11.7 times per month and couples age 75 and older having sex less than once a month. It seems that frequency declines sharply over the first few years of marriage and more gradually thereafter (Christopher and Kilser, 2004:373). Decreasing frequency of sex over time is typical in both marriage and cohabiting relationships (Stafford et al., 2004:244).

A couple's sexual relationship may be a powerful source of connection between partners, but it may also be a source of conflict. A commonly expressed conflict in marriage relates to frequency of sex. When couples disagree on this matter, it is most often husbands who desire sex more frequently than their wives, although this is not always the case. Some research concludes that men have stronger sex drives than women, which is said to explain the difference in desire. This conclusion may not actually be very helpful in understanding the characteristics of individual relationships. Pepper Schwartz suggests it is more appropriate to say that many couples have similar sex drives, although there are more men at the high end of the scale and more women at the low end (2004:601).

Elliott and Umberson's (2008) qualitative research on sex in long-term marriages found that three in four couples described conflicts related to sex. Nearly all of these related to frequency of sex, with men outnumbering women wanting more sex by almost five to one. Believing that sexual activity was a gauge of the success of the marriage, couples dealt with this conflict by trying to adapt to their partner's desires. Many of the wives participating in the research worked full-time jobs and were primarily responsible for housework and child care. These women said that the double-day, more than anything else, reduced their sexual desire. They said that "sex is not a priority for them because they are too busy and too tired" (p. 402). One of the husbands interviewed described the mismatch of sexual desire in his dual-earner marriage as follows:

> I think for guys, generally speaking, you know it [sex] is always a priority. For women, obviously it just depends because of wherever they are in their lives. And for Maria [his wife], she was more concerned about the bills, the kids, daily routines, things that needed to get done. Dishes, even dishes or laundry, that kind of stuff, was already a priority first before any leisure time at all or sex, or whatever. (p. 402)

This research raises important issues about studying sexuality. A main theme in the interviews was the "discourse of difference," that is, that men and women believed that conflict about sex was explained by innate differences between women and men. An alternative explanation is that women experienced a gendered sexual time bind. Women, but not men, stated that they lacked the time and energy to desire sex (Elliott and Umberson, 2008). Sexual relations in marriage cannot be analyzed outside the social situations in which they are embedded. Sexual interaction does not exist in a vacuum, but is situated in the larger context of relationships in which intimate partners have a multiplicity of roles and responsibilities that are likely patterned by gender.

Power and Decision-Making in Marriage

Power is defined as the ability of an individual to produce intended results from the behavior of others (Szinovacz, 1987:652). Power in a marriage involves the ability of a wife and husband to influence each other. Research on the balance of power in marriage centers on the significance of gender. Gender has historically been, and continues to be, the most significant determinant of marital power. Evidence of marital power in couple relationships may be seen in interactions ranging from watching TV (and who controls the remote) to family violence as the extreme case (Morgan, 2004:380).

Western civilization has had a long history of **patriarchy**—that is, the idea that ultimate authority (legitimate power) resides in the husband and father. Although norms of male dominance are weakening throughout U.S. society, patriarchy remains a cornerstone in the belief systems of some contemporary religious groups (e.g., Promise Keepers, fundamentalist Christian denominations, and the Mormon Church). In this view, the wife is to be obedient, respectful, and submissive to her husband. In addition, male dominance is sustained and promoted by language, the schools, the media, the law, and politics.

The patriarchal nature of society provides men with "invisible power" in marital relationships (McGraw and Walker, 2004:185). Male dominance is deeply structured into private and public social contexts. Couples negotiate their relationships in situations in which the status quo is already beneficial to men. "[M]en's favored position in society ensures that relationships are already structured as they wish" (Christensen and Heavey, 1990, cited in McGraw and Walker, 2004:186). This means that to advance their interests, women will typically make demands for a change in a couple's existing domestic arrangements (which sometimes leads to the demand/withdraw pattern of interaction). Women frequently have insufficient marital power to effectively challenge the status quo.

The most frequently used measure of marital power in survey research asks husbands and wives who has the "final word" in making key household decisions (the following is from Amato et al., 2007). Joint decision-making is a characteristic of less patriarchal, more egalitarian marriages. Amato and his fellow researchers compared responses about final word decisions in 1980 and 2000. Figure 8.3 shows responses to a question asking if the husband usually has the final word, if the wife usually has the final word, or if neither usually has the final word (equal decision-making). This research suggests a trend toward more shared decision-making and more marital power for wives.

Figure 8.3

Percentage of Husbands and Wives Reporting on Who Has the Final Word in Decision-Making, 1980 and 2000

Source: Amato, Paul R., Alan Booth, David R. Johnson, and Stacy J. Rogers, *Alone Together: How Marriage in America Is Changing.* Cambridge: Harvard University Press, 2007, p. 161.

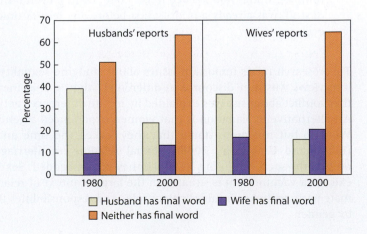

THE DISTRIBUTION OF POWER IN MARRIAGE

The processes of marital power operate in ways that are far from uniform. While the distribution of power in a marriage is generally related to gender, it is, in addition, associated with resources, social class, race/ethnicity, and individual factors.

Resources　The amount of resources each spouse brings to the relationship is important in establishing the relative distribution of marital power. Power tends to accrue to the partner with the highest occupational level, the highest income, and the highest educational level, and to the one most involved in outside organizations. Husbands are more likely than their wives to rate higher on each of these achieved statuses. Because of their secondary status in society, women are limited, typically, to lower-status occupations, with fewer benefits and relatively low wages—all of which reduce their power within families.

The most important resources are economic, involving not only income but also status and prestige based on success in the occupational world. Husbands, typically, are the main providers in families, with only about 20 percent of married-couple families having wives as the primary source of income. Thus, husbands, because of their relative economic clout, have greater power than wives in marriage. It is important to note, however, that employed wives, even when they make less money than their husbands, have increased say in decision-making, less traditional gender role ideologies, and more egalitarian family roles than do nonemployed wives. This relationship between income and power in marriage is buttressed by the study of over seven thousand couples by Philip Blumstein and Pepper Schwartz (1983), who found that in three-fourths of the couples the amount of money one partner earns relative to the other establishes relative power in the relationship.

Blumstein and Schwartz (1983) found one exception to this pattern of partner income determining domestic power. Among lesbian couples, if one partner makes more income than the other it makes no difference in the decision-making and the division of labor in their relationship. This is not true, however, among gay couples, where differences in income between the partners, as in heterosexual couples, translate into power.

Individual couples negotiate the relationship between relative resources and marital power in a gendered context. The continuing salience of gender as a determinant of marital power is illustrated in Tichenor's (2005) study of marital power. While men's power advantage in marriage is frequently attributed to their greater contribution of monetary resources, the same did not hold true when wives had higher earnings than their husbands. She concludes, "Higher-earning wives are unable to trade their substantial incomes for equally substantial reductions in their domestic labor burden" (2005:65).

Noneconomic resources more typically favor wives. These include companionship, emotional support, sex, and home management (meals, purchases, cleaning, maintenance). Wives may use the giving or withholding of these behaviors for power. Ultimately, either spouse may use the threat of divorce to shape the behaviors of the other.

Social Class　Family researchers have studied social class differences in marital power for more than 40 years. Some of the earlier work on marital power described working-class families as "patriarchal" and "traditional," while describing middle-class families as "democratic" and "egalitarian." Many studies have shown that not all working-class or middle-class families conform to these descriptions. The distinction between ideology and behavior is important here. The stereotype of the egalitarian middle-class marriage persists partly because the middle class has a more egalitarian ideology than the working class. Despite egalitarian ideals, however, the husband's career continues to take precedence in many dual-earner middle-class couples. When husbands' careers are seen as more important, wives do not make family demands that would interfere with or compromise men's professional employment. William J. Goode writes of men in this situation, "He takes precedence as a professional, not as a family head or as a male; nevertheless, the precedence is his" (1963:21). Notwithstanding a strong stated preference for equality in marriage—usually defined by dual-earner couples as a shared division of household work and decision-making—the behavior of few middle-class or professional men actually conforms to this ideology (Rosenbluth et al., 1998).

Discrepancies between ideology and behavior are also important in considering marital power in the working class. The "traditionalism" of working-class men must be seen in the larger context of societal patriarchy that upholds male control but distributes unequally the resources needed to exercise control. Recent economic transformations have eliminated many of the high-wage manufacturing jobs that gave working-class men power in their families. Thus, working-class men have lost the economic resources that justified control of family decisions and activities. The mass entry of working-class women into the workforce has required nontraditional patterns of shared responsibility for breadwinning, child care, and household tasks among these couples. The actions of working-class men are frequently more egalitarian than is their ideology.

Race and Ethnicity   We begin this topic by stating the assumption that gendered power in marriage works differently depending on social context (Cowdery et al., 2009:35). Therefore, models of marital power based on White couples cannot be generalized to racial-ethnic couples. And further, we must note that the marital experience within racial groups is diverse. While African American families have been described as less male-dominated and Latino families as more male-dominated than White families, these portrayals are oversimplified accounts of power and authority in minority families. Between-group differences in family patterns are best understood in the context of a society that is stratified by race. Racial-ethnic families encounter a different set of opportunities and obstacles than do White families. These structural differences will affect family interaction, including marital power dynamics.

African American marriages are usually described as more egalitarian than those of other racial groups. An important explanation for this greater egalitarianism is the historic economic marginalization of African Americans in a way that did not permit most to model the breadwinner–husband, homemaker–wife ideal for gender roles in marriage. In comparison to other racial groups, African American wives have the highest labor force participation, and some research suggests African American men do more housework than other men (Hill, 2005). At the same time, other studies describe the effects that the crumbling of many African American communities (including the disappearance of men's work) and increased marital instability have had on contemporary African American marriages. These social changes have impacted the distribution of power in marriage. In research by Cowdery and her coauthors, some African American wives chose to concede marital power to their husbands out of fear that he might leave. Further, "[o]ften women accommodated a man's greater power in the family because of her perception that he was often denied power in the larger society" (Cowdery et al., 2009:25). Marks and his colleagues provide another perspective. They suggest that "Together, We Are Strong," best describes the couple dynamics represented in their study of happy and enduring African American marriages. These couples met the challenges of economic hardships and racial inequality by pulling together to share the load evenly (Marks et al., 2008:180).

Male dominance, or **machismo,** is a popular stereotype associated with Latino families. However, research has challenged the widely accepted notion of Latino men as authoritarian heads of households. Studies spanning more than 25 years find that when Latinas are employed, they increase their power both inside and outside the family (Baca Zinn, 1980; McLoyd et al., 2001; Ybarra, 1977). Still, it is important to keep in mind that not all types of employment offer resources that wives can use to change the traditional balance of power in marriage. This is the conclusion that emerges from Patricia Zavella's study (1987) of Mexican women (Chicana) cannery workers in the Santa Clara Valley of California. Cannery jobs did give wives some leverage in the home, yet, as seasonal, part-time work, their jobs were defined as an extension of their household responsibilities and did not fundamentally transform family roles. The predominant scholarly perspective now is that Latino families (like other families) are flexible and adaptive; gender roles have changed and will be expected to change in response to opportunities and obstacles in particular social and economic contexts (Halgunseth, 2004:343).

Immigration has significant implications for the distribution of marital power for couples migrating to the United States. Immigration involves a process of adaptation to the new society's culture. A study of South American and Central American immigrant couples found that women's opportunities and marital power expanded incrementally over time in the U.S. (Maciel et al., 2009:19). More egalitarian gender norms in the U.S. were frequently women's rationale in pressuring their husbands for change. Colleen, an immigrant from Guyana with eight years in the U.S., said,

> It's a lot different because our parents were living in the colonial days there, where the women did everything. And although the woman worked, the man relaxed. All he did was give [her] plenty [of] kids. So it doesn't work that way with Thomas [her husband] cause I tell him...I'm not going to be washing all your clothes and doing everything else, and you do nothing....This is not the colonial days. You know, it's a new era we're living in. Everybody gotta fetch their own weight. (Maciel et al., 2009:16–17)

Individual Factors Several ascribed characteristics tend to favor husbands over wives. Husbands usually are older than their wives (in excess of two years for first marriages and more for remarriages), and age is related to authority. Also, husbands are almost always taller than their wives, and tallness in U.S. society tends to denote power. Finally, men are physically stronger than women, and this strength gives men the potential for coercive power.

Another ascribed characteristic works to the disadvantage of women. Only they can have children, and research shows that power declines with the birth of the first child and declines further with each succeeding child (Szinovacz, 1987).

In sum, husbands usually have more marital power than wives. First, husbands tend to be the main providers and, by virtue of their gender, age, education, skills, and physical stature, are advantaged in the marital relationship. Although women tend to have less power, certain changes are reducing the impact of men's authority in contemporary marriages. More and more wives are in the labor force; they are thus less dependent economically on their husbands and are developing communication and other assertive skills. Second, as the proportion of family income earned by wives increases, families are becoming more reliant on women's earnings, which gives them power. Third, the gender norms are changing in society. Many couples have developed relationships based on egalitarian principles and shared decision-making.

Reconstructing Gender Roles: Building an Egalitarian Marriage

The context in which couples define the roles and responsibilities of marriage partners has changed dramatically over the past 50 years. The ideal of sharply differentiated spheres of responsibility for women and men has given way to far more egalitarian assumptions. Family scholars have found long-term trends toward supporting shared decision-making in marriage, less gender role segregation, and greater acceptance of mothers' employment (Thornton and Young-DeMarco, 2001:1014).

The present situation represents a considerable shift from the assumptions of the not-so-distant past when there were clear norms regarding the responsibilities of husbands and wives. They lived in separate spheres and led parallel lives. The economic dominance of husbands gave them power in the home. Their domestic chores were gender-specific and less demanding than those of their wives. Wives were responsible for the caring of children and the emotional and expressive needs of their husbands. Although some traditional couples today continue this legacy, for the majority of couples, the old assumptions simply do not fit the realities of the contemporary dual-earner married-couple household.

Although women and men have increasingly embraced egalitarian rhetoric about their preferences in marriage, most have not put these ideals into action. A typical scenario is that couples agree that two earners are necessary to make ends meet or achieve their lifestyle goals. Wives become co-providers, but husbands do not contribute what wives perceive to be a fair share of the household work. Wives resent working at a job and then a second shift at home, while their husbands typically do half as much work at home. In general, what Arlie Hochschild in 1989 called the "stalled revolution" continues; that is, women have been willing to move into the labor force to share the role of breadwinning, but husbands have not made a corresponding move toward sharing responsibility for routine housework and the care and nurturing of children. Couples who do divide the roles and responsibilities of marriage equitably have become the subject of considerable scholarly study (see, for example, Deutsch, 1999; Risman and Johnson-Sumerford, 1998; Schwartz, 1994).

Sociologist Pepper Schwartz has identified a type of relationship in which couples successfully reconstruct gender roles on a genuinely equitable basis. She calls this new type of marriage **peer marriage.**

> Peer couples trade a frustrated, angry relationship with a spouse for one of deep friendship....Theirs is collaboration of love and labor that produces profound intimacy and mutual respect....Above all, peer couples live the same life. In doing so, they have found a new way to make love last....These couples...base their marriage on a mix of equity—each person gives in proportion to what he or she receives—and equality—each has equal status and is equally responsible for emotional, economic, and household duties. But these couples have more than their dedication to fairness. They achieve a true companionship and a deep collaborative marriage. The idea of "peer" is important because it incorporates the notion of friendship. Peer marriages embody a profound psychological connection. (Schwartz, 1994:54, 56)

Schwartz studied peer marriages among same-sex and heterosexual couples and found that their partnerships were based on equality, equity, and intimacy and shared four characteristics:

- The partners do not have more than a 60/40 traditional split of household duties and child raising.
- Both partners believe the other has equal influence over important decisions.
- Both partners feel they have equal control of the family economy and reasonable access to discretionary funds.
- Each person's work is given equal weight in the couple's life plans. Whether or not both partners work outside the home, they do not systematically sacrifice one person's work for the other's.

These peer marriages are, in Schwartz's words, "made, not born" (1994:58). The partners must agree on values, such as the primacy of the relationship over work, and the particulars, such as who does what. The husband must overcome the traditional male role and accept his partner as an equal. He must make their relationship primary, which means that his career becomes secondary. He must accept equal responsibility for the expressive aspects of their relationships (communication, warmth, displays of physical and verbal affection, romance). The wife in a peer marriage must shed traditional female role expectations. She must not accept anything less than equal status. Women are more likely than men to have a vision of a peer relationship. Thus, according to Schwartz, "it is often the woman's responsibility to get across to her partner the relationship style she wants" (1994:58).

As young women and men increasingly espouse nontraditional gender ideologies, we can expect the trend toward egalitarian or peer marriage to continue.

The Future of Marriage: Changing or Dying?

The statistics of marriage show that behaviors are changing—the young delay it, older people often get out of it, and some skip it altogether. These trends have led some social observers to predict that marriage is a dying institution (see, for example, Popenoe, 1993, 2004). But 90 percent of adults will marry, and if they divorce, they tend to remarry. The pessimists are concerned about marriage because it no longer fits the idealized 1950s version, in which people married rather than cohabited, the husband was the breadwinner, and the wife was the homemaker and nurturer of her husband and children. From our vantage point of the first decade of the twenty-first century, the 1950s family does appear to be a relic of the past.

Marriages today are different from what they were 50 years ago because social conditions have changed markedly. The fact that U.S. society is in the process of a "fundamental realignment of gender" has profound implications for marriage (Nock, 2001:774). Over the past 30 years or so there has been a transition from a gender-based division of labor, in which men were in the workforce and women did the domestic work, to one in which household tasks are more contested and the majority of women are now formally employed.

The traditional bargain struck between men and women—financial support in exchange for domestic services—is no longer valid. Men now expect women to help bring home the bacon. And women expect men to help cook the bacon, feed the kids, and clean up afterward. In addition, the old status order that granted men a privileged position in the family is crumbling.... [These] moves toward gender equality have come with a price. Both men and women enter marriage with higher expectations for interpersonal communication, intimacy, and sexual gratification. If these expectations are not met, they feel freer than they once did to dissolve the relationship and seek a new partner. (Furstenberg, 1996:37)

Another stress point affecting contemporary marriages is economic. Globalization and the structural changes accompanying it (Chapter 4) have resulted in downward pressure on wages and corporate downsizing. These changes have created environments for family life that are characterized by greater economic insecurity. The postmodern family—characterized by flexibility and adaptability—has emerged in this context (Stacey, 1996). The new economy does not provide the economic supports that most couples need in order to construct and maintain a stable, lifelong marriage. Thus some couples decide against marriage, and fragile marriages frequently end in divorce.

Family historian Stephanie Coontz insists that contemporary patterns of change in marriage are best understood by taking a longer look at the place of marriage in society (the following is from Coontz, 2005). Historically, marriage served a multitude of economic, political, and social functions. In the past 200 years, however, the idea emerged that marriage could be a vehicle for personal happiness and self-fulfillment. From there, it followed that individuals should have the right to divorce if love faded. According to Coontz, "For 150 years, four things kept people from pushing the new values about love and self-fulfillment to their ultimate conclusion: that people could construct meaningful lives outside marriage and that not everything in society had to be organized through and around married couples" (p. 307). The four impediments to a social transformation of the meaning of marriage were:

- Beliefs about vast inherent differences between women and men.
- Social control, exercised by extended families, that pushed conformity to existing social norms.
- Unreliable birth control and the stigmatization of illegitimate births.
- Women's legal and economic dependence on men and men's dependence on women's domesticity (pp. 307–308).

In recent decades, these barriers have largely been removed. The result has been a sweeping and irreversible revolution in how contemporary men and women organize their private lives.

To conclude, the institution of marriage does occupy a less central place in society than it did in the past. This is not to say that most adults in the United States do not value marriage or aspire to be married. The rewards of marriage—especially love, respect, friendship, and communication—continue to provide strong incentives for women and men to get married, and once married, to stay married (Previti and Amato, 2003:572). Finally, as this and the other chapters point out, marriage (and the family) is not a dying institution but one that is being transformed as society changes.

Chapter Review

1. Within the intimate environment of a marriage and the constraints of society, each couple creates its own unique social organization.

2. Marriages do not occur in a vacuum. Although each couple forges a unique relationship, these relationships are patterned by structural arrangements. Among the macro forces affecting the partners in marriages are (a) the law, (b) religion, and (c) societal gender expectations.

3. Unmarried adults are never-married, divorced, or widowed; they live alone, with roommates, or cohabit as a heterosexual or homosexual couple.

4. The number of marriages is declining, partly because people are marrying later.

5. The median age of first marriage continues to rise for both women and men.

6. Interracial marriages are becoming more common, with about 5 percent of marriages involving partners of different races.

7. With the increase in life expectancy, marriages now have the potential to last approximately 50 years, an increase of 20 years or so from 1920. This new longevity is one explanation for the relatively high divorce rate.

8. The divorce rate accelerated in the 1970s, peaked in 1981, and has declined somewhat since then. At current rates, about half of all marriages will end in divorce. African American couples are more likely than White or Latino couples to divorce.

9. The majority of divorced persons remarry (3 out of 4 men and 6 out of 10 women).

10. Women and men often have different expectations of marriage, and their experiences in marriage differ. Although, generally, both men and women benefit from marriage, men gain more.

11. Although marriage matters for most couples, the benefits are decreased for some poor couples, especially minority poor, who face greater threats of unemployment, underemployment, and lower wages than Whites. There are differences, too, by gender. So marriage matters, but the degree and the way that it matters is affected by social class, race, and gender.

12. Among the correlates of marital quality are (a) shared social characteristics (homogamy), (b) economic success, (c) role fit (i.e., the degree of consensus between the partners on decision-making), and (d) the absence of children. Both spouses in the labor force has contradictory effects on marital quality.

13. A crucial determinant of marital quality is communication. The partners' styles of interaction—especially the degree of positivity and negativity—are important to relationship quality. Both the quality and quantity of communication are important in sustaining marital relationships.

14. Another important factor in marital quality is sexual intimacy. Contemporary U.S. couples view sexual satisfaction as one of the main indicators of a happy marriage. The sexual relationship may be a powerful source of connection, but is sometimes a source of conflict.

15. The distribution of marital power is related to (a) gender, (b) resources (the spouse with the most economic resources typically makes the most important decisions), (c) social class, (d) race, and (e) individual factors (which also tend to favor husbands).

16. Some couples resist the traditional gender expectations for marriage by consciously building egalitarian marriages. In "peer marriages" (whether same-sex or heterosexual), the partners split the household duties and child raising, share equally in the decision-making, have equal access to discretionary funds, and give each person's work equal weight in the couple's life plans.

17. Contemporary marriages are affected by contemporary social conditions. The institution of marriage is not dying, as some observers claim; rather, it is adapting. As a result, marriage is not declining but is being transformed.

Key Terms

homogamous marriages   272

machismo   283

marital quality   272

miscegenation laws   263

peer marriage   284

Related Websites

http://www.projectrace.com

Project RACE. Project RACE advocates for multiracial children and adults through education, community awareness, and legislation. Its main goal is for a multiracial classification on all school, employment, state, federal, local, census, and medical forms requiring racial data. This website provides current and archived news reports as well as links to various other sites of interest to interracial families and multiracial individuals.

http://www.thermotrilogy.com

MarriageSupport.com. Established by Dr. David Sanford, this site provides practical how-to articles and skills-training programs aimed at helping couples learn successful and supportive relationship skills and improve the quality of their relationships.

http://www.abanet.org/family

American Bar Association: Family Law Section. The mission of the ABA Family Law Section is to serve as the national leader in the field of marital and family law. Among the goals the council has adopted to accomplish its mission are to promote and improve the family, to be the preeminent voice on marital and family issues, to improve public and professional understanding about marital and family law issues and practitioners, and to improve professionalism of all participants in the administration of marital and family law.

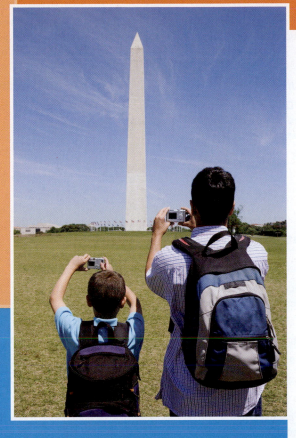

Parents and Children

▶ Myths and Realities

Myth	The parental division of labor is the result of biological imperatives.
Reality	Aside from conception, childbirth, and nursing, parental roles by gender are a social construction, the result of historical, economic, and social forces.
Myth	Contemporary children are similar because they are subject to common parenting styles.
Reality	Parenting styles vary by social class, resulting in children with different traits.
Myth	Children increase marital happiness.
Reality	Research shows that children increase marital happiness in only about one-fifth of marriages.
Myth	Modern fathers share the parenting duties with their working wives.
Reality	Although there are exceptions, the overall pattern is for husbands to leave the child-raising chores to wives. Even among couples who deliberately share parenting equally, mothers do much more of the emotion work than do fathers.
Myth	As more and more mothers enter the labor force, their time with their children decreases.
Reality	Despite the rapid rise in mothers' labor force participation, mothers' time with children has tended to be quite stable over time.
Myth	The socialization process is one-way—children are passive receptors of parental influences.
Reality	Socialization works both ways—children learn from parents and parents learn from children.
Myth	Children raised in nontraditional gender role families are adversely affected.
Reality	Research findings indicate that children raised in families with mothers in the labor force and in which there is a more egalitarian division of labor are not negatively affected.
Myth	Children raised by gay or lesbian parents are harmed in their psychosocial development.
Reality	When the children of gay and lesbian parents are compared with the children of heterosexual parents, there is no difference in their psychosocial development.

In most societies there is a pervasive cultural pressure toward parenthood. There are strong expectations that married couples should not only have children but should also want to have them. Indeed, approximately 85 percent of married couples in the United States have children, and about two-thirds of childless couples want children but are infertile. This chapter examines parenthood, the contours of which have changed dramatically in the past two generations. More children now are being raised in families in which both parents are in the labor force. More children now are being raised by single parents. More children now are being raised by same-sex parents. More children now are being raised by grandparents. More adult children now are living with their parents. And more children now are in households with a stepparent and stepsiblings (a topic discussed in Chapter 11). What are the causes and consequences of these new and pervasive parenting arrangements? In particular, what are the effects of these diverse family forms on the well-being of children? These questions guide our inquiry in this chapter. We begin with a discussion of the social construction of parenting and childhood. Second, we describe various demographic trends regarding parenting in U.S. society. Third, we consider the effects of children on the marital relationship. Fourth, we describe the impact of parents on children. Finally, we examine two significant types of situations in which many contemporary children are raised: dual-earner families and single-parent families.

The Social Construction of Parenting

Typically, we think of families as biological units based on the timeless functions of love, motherhood, and childbearing. Moreover, parenting activities are viewed as "natural" behaviors found universally. This idealized version of the family assumes a gendered division of labor, a husband/father in the workforce, and a wife/mother at home nurturing her husband and children. This image of the family does not fit historical fact nor contemporary reality—only 7 percent of U.S. households currently fit this description—yet it continues to be the ideal. Actually, dual-income families with no children at home outnumber the traditional family by almost two to one (AmeriStat, 2003a). The idealized image is inaccurate because "family forms are socially and historically constructed, not monolithic universals that exist for all times and all peoples, and . . . the arrangements governing family life are not the inevitable result of unambiguous differences between women and men" (Baca Zinn et al., 1997:255).

Supporting this view are the social constructionist and social structural theoretical approaches (the following depends on Coltrane, 1998:1–9). The social constructionist approach argues that what seems "natural" or "real" depends on time, place, and social location. What is sexy, feminine or masculine, or even a family depends on the historical period, the society, and the social stratum within that society. Consider an example provided by Sociologist Scott Coltrane: "Among noblemen in 17th-century France, it was manly to wear perfume, curly wigs, high-heeled shoes, and blouses with frilly lace cuffs. Today, the same attire would be considered unmanly or effeminate" (1998:7). The point is that the meaning of gender (or family, or motherhood, or fatherhood) changes in response to differing cultural and historical contexts. Hence, it is socially constructed. These social constructions are the result of economic and other social forces. In short, people's lives and behaviors are shaped by social forces. As Coltrane says, "Only by looking at the structural constraints people face—such as access to education or jobs—can we understand how cultural definitions and practices governing gender and families have developed" (Coltrane, 1998:3). Summing up this important and sociological way of looking at families, Coltrane states, "In our nostalgia for a mythical past, we tend to envision an ideal family that transcends time and place. In reality, families are very specific forms of human organization that continually evolve and change as they respond to various pushes and pulls" (Coltrane, 1996:22).

To examine the social construction of parenting further, let's consider some related questions: Why is child care and housework obligatory for women and mothers, yet still optional for men and fathers (Coltrane, 1996:7)? Why is being a housewife acceptable and choosing to be a househusband much less so? Why are women who voluntarily release custody of their children to their former husbands defined much more negatively than men who give up the custody of their children to their former wives? Similarly, why do we feel much less incensed when a father abandons his family than when a mother deserts her family? Why does the verb "to mother" include in its core meaning the caring of children, whereas the verb "to father" does not (Shehan, 2003:317)? In short, why are a father's family obligations less important than a mother's?

Biological differences (e.g., genetic programming, hormones, size, strength, and traits such as nurturance and aggressiveness) do not explain these inconsistencies by gender. Beyond conception, giving birth, and nursing the infant, there are no biological imperatives concerning parenting. Mothering and styles of mothering are tied to social rather than biological sources (much of the following is from Glenn, 1994). This assertion questions the presumed universals of motherhood as the most important source of a woman's fulfillment, mothers as nurturers, and even maternal instinct. There are variations on each of these themes, thus belying their universality. A few examples make this point.

We typically assume that the White, middle-class experience is the norm (Collins, 1990). To do so promotes mythology. Bonnie Thornton Dill (1988) shows how mothering has differed historically along racial and class dimensions. Privileged women (usually White), historically, have been able to escape the more difficult parts of mothering by having other women (White working-class women and women of color) do the tedious child-rearing tasks for them. This frees the privileged mothers for leisure or career pursuits while retaining the status of "mother," and forces much less privileged surrogate mothers to spend less time with their own children. In effect, institutional racism and economic necessities required lower-class women to give precedence to the care of the children of others over their own. Thus, the responsibility for their own children often had to be shared with other family members or other women from the minority community. This "shared mothering" or "othermothering" has been and continues to be characteristic in African American communities (Collins, 1990:119–132).

This chain of "othermothering" extends to other societies as well, as noted in Chapter 4. Sociologist Arlie Hochschild (2000) illustrates the globalization of child care as mothers from poor countries hire poor women to take care of their children while they migrate to the United States to work to care for someone else's children for better wages.

> A typical global care chain might work something like this: An older daughter from a poor family in a third world country cares for her siblings (the first link in the chain) while her mother works as a nanny caring for the children of a nanny migrating to a first world country (the second link) who, in turn, cares for the child of a family in a rich country (the final link). Each kind of chain expresses an invisible human ecology of care, one care worker depending on another and so on. (Hochschild, 2000:33)

Another false universal of motherhood is maternal instinct (that is, the assumption that there is a biological imperative of mother love that compels mothers to protect their children from harm against any odds). This is a myth because historians, anthropologists, and sociologists find that mothers do not protect their children universally in all stages of history and across all cultures (Pinker, 1997). Some cultures accept infanticide, usually the killing of girl babies because they are considered a financial burden to the family. Other societies permit the killing of one or all multiple-birth babies because of the belief that animals have multiple births, not humans. There is also the widespread practice in some societies of poor parents selling their offspring as slaves or prostitutes.

Anthropologist Nancy Scheper-Hughes presents an interesting case of accepted infanticide in northeast Brazil. She found that when infants and toddlers from poor families were quite sick from diarrhea and dehydration, mothers could not be convinced to use medicines to save their children. These mothers would not even accept back into their homes those children who recovered on their own. They believed that these children were sickly and fragile and would always be a burden. Thus it was better to let them die, so the family's few economic resources would be more generously divided among the healthy. When this occurred, parents accepted their sickly child's death with stoicism and equanimity. Scheper-Hughes concludes that mother love is not absent (because it is lavished on other children), but that maternal thinking and practices are shaped by overwhelming economic and cultural constraints: "Mother love is anything other than natural and instead represents a matrix of images, meanings, sentiments, and practices that are everywhere socially and culturally produced" (Scheper-Hughes, 1992:340).

As a final illustration of the social construction of parenting, let's look at the changing views of motherhood and fatherhood in the United States during different historical periods. The expectations of mothers and fathers have changed throughout U.S. history, paralleling economic conditions (see Chapters 2 and 3). When the economy was based on agriculture, parenting (and the farm work) was a joint venture for all family members. Child rearing in this historical setting was not the defining characteristic of wives. Mothers and fathers cared for children because both worked at home. So did other relatives because households often included grandparents, older sons and daughters, and perhaps hired help. Fathers were responsible for the educational, moral, and spiritual development of their children. During this era fathers were patriarchs, with complete authority in the home. Child rearing involved instilling submission to authority. There are two interesting differences from the present. First, in divorces involving children, custody was usually given to the father. Second, the literature on child development during colonial times was directed at fathers, not mothers.

During the late eighteenth and early nineteenth centuries, a philosophical movement called the Enlightenment changed child-rearing practices. Fathers were still expected to rule the family sternly, but with more sensitivity than in earlier times.

With the Industrial Revolution, fathers became removed from their children as they commuted to jobs, leaving their wives alone to care for children. In this arrangement fathers became the "sole economic providers" (except for single mothers, poor women, working-class women, and women of color), and mothers became responsible for the educational and moral development of their children. Fathers, on the other hand, became more disengaged from their children, and their direct authority over family members declined. Now the great majority of custody suits ruled against fathers, and the child-rearing literature now placed mothers at the center of families and fathers on the periphery.

Since the 1960s, family life has changed in response to global and domestic economic restructuring. As noted in Chapter 4, wages for working people stagnated or declined since 1973 while the costs of housing, health care, transportation, education, and consumer goods increased, sometimes dramatically. This was also a time characterized by corporate downsizing, contingent work, and declining work benefits. Moreover, the men were much more likely to lose their jobs during the Great

Recession. Thus, in the last generation, mothers in most families have become essential to supplement the economic resources by working in the paid labor market. Moreover, the ideological terrain shifted as various oppressed groups sought equality, including women. Included in this new way of thinking was that women can be fulfilled in a number of ways, not just through mothering. As a result of the economic and ideological changes, there has been a rapid shift in women's employment since 1960, when only one out of four mothers was employed outside the home. Now some 78 percent of mothers with school-age children are in the paid workforce (thus, a shift in 40 years from 75 percent stay-at-home mothers to 22 percent). Now it is acceptable for women to have babies and return to work soon thereafter because their incomes are so necessary for family survival. Now, commonly, child care during the day is shifted from parents to other caregivers, sometimes kin and otherwise to day-care providers, preschool, and school. More fathers are "helping" with domestic chores and child care, but the bulk of these duties is still left to mothers. Thus, in response to changes in the responsibilities of mothers, there is a shift, still slight but real nonetheless, for fathers to move toward more equal partnering in parenting.

Other consequences of so many women working in the paid labor force are that (1) the isolated homemaker is no longer dominant; (2) compulsory motherhood is weakening as more women choose not to marry, postpone marriage, or elect to remain childless; and (3) the relationship between marriage and childbearing is weakening, as increasing numbers of women are becoming parents without husbands.

 # The Social Construction of Childhood

Childhood is not a biological stage of life that is universal and unchanging. Like parenting, it is a social construction, because the experience of childhood varies by time, place, and social location.

> Every aspect of childhood—including children's relationships with their parents and peers, their proportion of the population, and their paths through childhood to adulthood—has changed dramatically over the past four centuries. Methods of child rearing, the duration of schooling, the nature of children's play, young people's participation in work, and the points of demarcation between childhood, adolescence, and adulthood are products of culture, class, and historical era. (Mintz, 2004:36)

Several social forces have changed the way children are raised now compared to earlier times in U.S. history. First, the family used to be a work unit, with each family member a responsible part of the work team. The children worked under careful supervision of one or both parents. Now children, for the most part, are separated from work roles, giving them more leisure time and more time away from parents. A word of caution: The following describes some forces that have affected children of all social classes, but mostly they depict those that affect children of the middle class. Working-class and lower-class children will be considered shortly.

Second, whereas in the past most families lived in rural areas or small towns, now most children are being raised in large cities and their suburbs. This urbanization of families, coupled with children no longer part of the family work unit and having more leisure time, increased the likelihood of children spending more time with and being influenced by peers.

Third, generations ago children were under the almost total influence of their parents. Beginning about a century ago, children became more and more involved in adult (nonparent) organized activities. There was more formal schooling. There was involvement in church activities, Boy Scouts and Girl Scouts, YMCA, YWCA, private lessons, camps, and sports. In effect, these organizational activities segregated children away from their parents more and more hours of the day and increased outside influences on them. Moreover, these modern overscheduled children were losing the spontaneity and creativity of curious children as adults organized more and more of their lives and activities.

Fourth, there have been massive technological innovations that have dramatic effects on the children of today. Contrast what the lives of children must have been before electricity, television, DVDs, cell phones, iPods, computers, YouTube, text messaging, and digitalized games with the lives of children today. Over one-fourth of contemporary two- to four-year-olds, for example, have a television in their bedrooms (Hulbert, 2004). The average child 8 to 10 years old spends six hours a day sitting in front of a television or computer, or playing a video game. Is that child's childhood different from the child reading by a kerosene lamp?

Fifth, family size is much smaller now compared to a century ago. The sharp reduction in the birth rate allows parents now to lavish more time, attention, and resources on each child (Mintz, 2004). For example, today's children are much more likely to have their own bedrooms than those of a few generations ago, where children might even have to share beds. Similarly, children today are more apt to travel with their parents than in earlier generations.

A sixth social force affecting childhood is consumerism. A century ago children did not have many things. Their clothes were often hand-me-downs. They had few toys. Today's children, in sharp contrast, except for the very poor, have many things. Corporate America recognizes the market that children represent, spending $15 billion annually for advertising directed at children. As a result, the average child in the United States sees some 40,000 commercials a year. The spending power of the childhood market is enormous (Chu, 2006; Kelly and Kulman, 2004). For example, "tweens" (those in the 8 to 12 age group) spend $11 billion a year just on apparel (Cohen, 2007).

The demand for things is not only the result of advertising but also the confluence of peer pressure and the behaviors of parents and other adults, which give the not-so-subtle message in the culture that self-worth is measured in what we possess.

Over the past generation or two parenting style has become more flexible and less authoritarian. The social world revolves

Children learn to measure self-worth by their possessions.

around children. As a result, children today are less inhibited and many have a sense of entitlement. They are freer to express their opinions. Actually, their opinions are solicited regarding such things as what to eat, where to go on vacations, and what to buy. They press their parents for more freedom and more consumer goods. They tend to get their way because of the nag factor. "A 2002 survey found that on average kids ages 12 to 17 ask nine times before parents give in, and more than 10 percent of 12- and 13-year-olds reported nagging parents more than 50 times for an item" (reported in Kelly and Kulman, 2004:49). The behaviors of children today are in sharp contrast to the children a century ago when their parents were the authorities to be obeyed or suffer the consequences, usually physical. Children then were, as a consequence, more obedient, more passive, and more compliant than the children of modernity. Now children are indulged with fewer parental controls, but this, too, is changing (see Box 9.1).

The previous description is half right. Generally it describes children of the middle class and, therefore, is incomplete. The experience of childhood differs by social class. Sociologist Annette Lareau (2003) has conducted research that notes the important differences between middle-class children and those from working-class and poor households. Lareau describes how middle-class parents engage in a process of "concerted cultivation" designed to develop a child's talents through arranged activities, while working-class and poor families rely on "the accomplishment of natural growth," where the child's development unfolds more or less spontaneously. In this latter instance, children are left to find their own recreation (e.g., pick-up basketball and makeshift percussion ensembles) rather than in organized sports and formal music lessons. In working-class and poor families, parents do not reason with the child but are more authoritarian. Middle-class parents, in contrast, negotiate with their children.

Each parenting style produces different traits in children, with each having benefits and drawbacks. The following summarizes the differences:

The poor and working-class kids are in many ways more attractive than the middle-class ones. They obey their parents' (relatively infrequent) instructions without whining.... They are creative and skillful in organizing their own activities, including complex games. They are almost never bored. They fight with their siblings much less than middle-class children do—in fact, they rely on their relatives for support and entertainment, and enjoy one another's company. They play happily in groups of mixed ages. Their parents like them to have free time because they don't want them exposed (yet) to the daily grind of adult life.

In contrast, the middle-class kids are immediately bored when not provided with organized activities. They compete for attention with their siblings.... They constantly bargain with adults, including authority figures. They have a pervasive sense of entitlement to expensive goods and individualized services. They lack experience working with others of different ages or solving problems without adult intervention....

Although the middle-class kids are less attractive than the poor and working-class children, their parents' investment will probably pay off for them. These children have precocious skills of verbal expression and negotiation, time-management, and public performance that will serve them well in the white-collar world. They consider themselves entitled to excellent services and demand it [sic] from adults and institutions. Their expectations and behavior are perfectly in synch with those of middle-class professionals (teachers, coaches, and physicians), who respond to their needs. As kids, they are tired and quarrelsome. As grownups, they will prosper. (Levine, 2006:1–2)

BOX 9.1 Inside the Worlds of Diverse Families

Let the Kid Be

By Lisa Belkin

Perhaps you know it by its other names: helicoptering, smothering mothering, alpha parenting, child-centered parenting. Or maybe there's a description you've coined on your own but kept to yourself: Overly enmeshed parenting? Get-them-into-*Harvard*-or-bust parenting? My-own-mother-never-breast-fed-me-so-I-am-never-going-to-let-my-kid-out-of-my-sight parenting?

There are, similarly, any number of theories as to why 21st-century mothers and fathers feel compelled to micromanage their offspring: these are enlightened parents, sacrificing their own needs to give their children every emotional, intellectual, and material advantage; or floundering parents, trying their best to navigate a changing world; or narcissistic parents, who see their children as both the center of the universe and an extension of themselves.

But whatever you call it, and however it began, its days may be numbered. It seems as though the newest wave of mothers is saying no to prenatal *Beethoven* appreciation classes, homework tutors in *kindergarten*, or moving to a town near their child's college campus so the darling can more easily have home-cooked meals. (O.K., O.K., many were already saying no, but now they're doing so without the feeling that a good parent would say yes.) Over coffee and out in cyberspace they are gleefully labeling themselves "bad mommies," pouring out their doubts, their dissatisfaction, and their dysfunction, celebrating their own shortcomings in contrast to their older sisters' cloying perfection.

After all, that is the way it is with parenting—which I bet was never used as a verb before the 20th century, when medicine reached the point where parents could assume their babies would survive. At its core, raising children is about instinct and biology, yes, but on top of that, we build an artificial scaffold, which supports what we have come to think of as parenting truths but are really only parenting trends.

Going way back, the Spartans probably thought they were oh, so modern when they left defenseless infants on wild mountain slopes. So did wealthy Norse mothers who had poor women foster their children, and European aristocrats who employed wet nurses. More recently, as Ann Hulbert chronicles in her book *Raising America: Experts, Parents, and a Century of Advice About Children,* rigid feeding schedules were all the

rage in the United States in the 1920s. The next two decades brought an emphasis on discipline.

In 1946, Dr. Spock came along and told parents to trust their instincts. Later, parents became buddies with their kids, and by the end of the last century, the debate was about the quality versus the quantity of time spent with your children. That was followed by the concept of mothering as an all-consuming identity. Mothers chose their gurus—T. Berry Brazelton (touchy-feely parenting), William Sears (attachment parenting), and John Rosemond (Christian parenting)—then diligently wore their babies in slings and nursed them into toddlerhood, all the while judging (and feeling judged by) those who did not do the same.

After a decade of earnest immersion in parenting, though, the times are ripe for a change. The first sign was the wave of confessionals—from anonymous Web sites like truumomconfessions.com (where mothers admit to transgressions like feigning stomach cramps to steal quiet time hiding in the bathroom) to bylined blogs like the wildly popular dooce.com (where Heather B. Armstrong chronicled her postpartum depression and continues to write about her struggles as the mother of a charming but somewhat high-strung 5-year-old) to memoirs like Ayelet Waldman's (in which she cops to such "sins" as using disposable diapers and loving her husband more than her children).

But in the past few months, a second wave has taken hold—writers are moving past merely venting and are trying to gather the like-minded into a new movement. Carl Honoré is one. He calls it "slow parenting"—no more rushing around physically and metaphorically, no more racing kids from soccer to Suzuki. Lenore Skenazy is another. She calls it "free-range parenting," a return to the days when childhood was not ruled by the fear (overblown, she says, with statistics to prove it) that children would be maimed, kidnapped, or killed if they did something as simple as riding their bikes alone to the park.

By far the most chipper is Tom Hodgkinson, whose book *The Idle Parent: Why Less Means More When Raising Kids* was just published in England, and whose cover—Mum and Dad lounging with martinis while their well-trained toddler sits on the floor mixing up the next batch—illustrates his message that parents should just chill. Pay attention to your own needs, he writes, back off on your children and everyone will be happier and better adjusted.

(continued)

(Box 9.1 continued)

All this certainly dovetails nicely with new economic realities. When you can't afford those violin lessons or a baby sitter to accompany your 10-year-old to the park, you can turn guilt on its head and call it a parenting philosophy. But is it fundamental change? Or is the apparent decline of overparenting (and its corollaries: feelings of competition and inadequacy) actually the same obsession donning a new disguise?

The one constant over the past century has been parents' determination to find the right answers when it comes to raising their children. In this latest chapter, we have replaced the experts who told us what a good parent worries about with experts who tell us that a good parent doesn't worry so much. We may even see parents stop aiming to prove how perfect they are and start trying to prove how nonchalant they are. But worry is worry. The search to keep from messing up goes on.

Source: Belkin, Lisa (2009). "Let the Kid Be." *New York Times* (May 31, 2009). Online: http://www.nytimes.com/2009/05/31/magazine/31wwln-lede-t.html.

Thus, parenting styles vary by social class, shaping children in different and crucial ways. They contribute to the reproduction of class inequality. That is, middle-class children develop traits that lead to success in school and later in jobs and the marketplace, whereas working-class and poor children develop skills that, for most of them, replicate their parents' class positions.

As a final example of the social construction of childhood, let's consider the transition from childhood to adulthood. A common assumption is that one leaves adolescence and becomes an adult by leaving home, finishing school, starting work, getting married, and becoming a parent (Shanahan et al., 2005). In the past, these occurred for most in the late teens or early 20s. But since about 1970 it has taken birth cohorts longer to achieve these markers of adulthood. There appears to be a gap between adolescence and adulthood today not present a generation or two ago. These "twixters" are not children, but they are not adults either. They take longer to finish school, to decide on a career, to marry, and, for many, to leave home.

In the past, people moved from childhood to adolescence and from adolescence to adulthood, but today there is a new intermediate phase along the way. The years from 18 until 25 and even beyond have become a distinct and separate life stage, a strange transitional never-never land between adolescence and adulthood in which people stall for a few extra years, putting off the iron cage of adult responsibility that constantly threatens to crash down on them. (Grossman, 2005:44)

Scholars are now identifying a new stage in the life course between adolescence and adulthood, termed "emerging

"So Dad – Have you given any thought to what you want be when you grow up?"

adulthood" (Arnett, 2000). It is critical to emphasize that this emerging life course stage is a response of young people to structural changes in society such as the postindustrial labor market, the demands for more education (and credentials), and the high cost of education and housing.

Demographic Patterns

Examining a number of demographic factors allows us to describe the changing nature of parenting in the present-day United States. This section considers birth rates over time, differential birth rates by race and socioeconomic status, the facts about those who choose to remain childless, infertility, the trend toward delayed childbearing, and the changing composition of households, including adoption, transracial and transnational adoption, foster care, grandparents raising grandchildren, mixed-race children, children of gay or lesbian parents, the dramatic rise of single-parent households, adult children still living at home, and multigeneration households.

Fertlility

The long-term fertility rate (total childbearing rate) has declined steadily since 1800, when the average woman gave birth to seven children, compared to a current average of two children per woman. This general downward trend obscures four important swings in the birth rate during the past 50 years. The years of the Great Depression (1930–1939) showed a drastic drop, as wives and husbands limited the number of children they had because of the economic hardships and uncertain future during that period. The baby boom that followed World War II (1947–1964) was just that—a boom in the fertility rate (a rate of 3.8 births per adult woman in 1957, compared to 2.1 during the Depression). This was followed by a precipitous decline in the birth rate to an all-time low of 1.7 in 1976. Most recently, however, there has been a slight increase in the fertility rate, to 2.1 in 2007 (see Figure 9.1). This translates to 4,317,119 births in that year. The conditions of the Great Recession beginning in 2007 should reduce the fertility rate, as the Great Depression of the 1930s did.

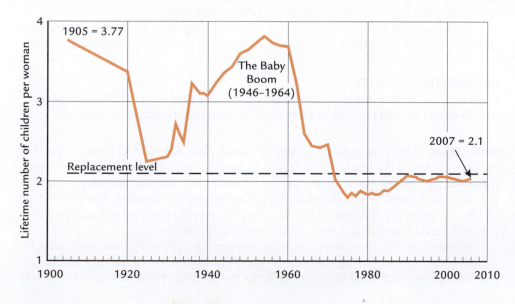

Figure 9.1

Total Fertility Rate (lifetime number of children per woman)

Sources: Caplow, Theodore, Louis Hicks, and Ben J. Wattenberg. *The First Measured Century: An illustrated Guide to Trends in America.* Washington, DC: AEI Press, 2000, p. 85; U.S. Department of Health and Human Services, *Trends in the Well-Being of America's Children and Youth: 2008.* Washington, DC: Office of the Assistant Secretary for Planning and Evaluation, 2008.

The reasons for the relatively low fertility rate today are several. First, marriage tends to occur now at a later age, reducing the number of potential childbearing years for women. Second, the relatively high divorce rate also reduces the number of child-bearing years for many women. Third, the majority of women work in the labor force, which adds to family income and the social status of women. The greater the number of children, the more the career development of women is stifled. Fourth, the economic situation of many families demands two incomes to cover mortgages, car payments, and the other elements of a desired lifestyle. Finally, the number of abortions since the Supreme Court legalized the practice in 1973 (*Roe v. Wade*) has reduced fertility. About one-fourth of pregnancies not ending in miscarriages or stillbirths are aborted. Most women getting abortions are under the age of 25, White, and single.

THE CONSEQUENCES OF LOW FERTILITY

That most family units are relatively small has several important consequences for the family members. The fewer the children, the more family wealth is available to be spent on their health and educational benefits—improving their life chances and the well-being of family members.

Research has shown that small family size is related to positive physical and intellectual endowments for the children. Shirley Hartley (1973:195; see also Blake, 1989) has summarized these findings: (1) In terms of health, height, weight, vital capacity, and strength, all decline as the number of children goes up; and (2) children from small families consistently score higher on intelligence tests than children from large families. Although both large families and lower scores on intelligence tests are related to social class, the explanation for family size and intelligence is not. When family income, or the occupation of the father, is held constant, there is still a substantial decline in IQ with an increasing number of children in the family. This relationship is most likely the result of less parent–child interaction, because, as family size increases, the amount of verbal interactions between parents and their children (such as talking, singing, reading, and playing) is reduced.

Increased marital satisfaction is another benefit of small families. This most likely results from fewer economic problems and because wives and husbands have more time to devote to their relationship. Also, spouses (especially wives) who have few or no children are freer to pursue educational and career opportunities.

At the societal level, sustained rates of low fertility lead to an aging population and a diminished labor force, problems faced by many European countries and Japan.

DIFFERENTIAL FERTILITY

Fertility rates in the United States vary in a consistent pattern by social factors (**differential fertility**), most notably social class, race/ethnicity, and religion.

Social Class   The patterned behaviors by social class are that: (1) the higher the income, the lower the fertility; and (2) the greater the level of educational attainment, the lower the fertility. From the perspective of those with more income and education, the costs of children tend to be perceived as exceeding the benefits. The presence of children negatively affects the chances to complete an education, to pursue a career, to engage in certain leisure activities, and to earn a good income.

In short, as the alternatives grow in number and attractiveness, especially for women, the costs of having children go up. With high educational attainment, career and income potential increase markedly for women. These rewards, then, may outweigh or even replace the rewards of motherhood. This leads to the corollary conclusion that the more prestigious and well-paid the career for a woman, the more deliberately will she restrict family size and maximize time in the labor force.

Another reason for the inverse relationship between social class and fertility is that the more economic resources and educational attainment one has, the later one marries. And there is a strong relationship between the age of the mother at marriage and the pace of subsequent fertility. Lower-class women are more likely to marry soon after high school, whereas middle- and upper-class women are much more likely to complete college first and perhaps even begin a career before marrying. Achieving higher levels of education increases the opportunities to pursue careers, both of which are likely to delay childbearing and, in the long run, to reduce the number of children born to these women.

Generally, the pattern shows that those least able to afford children have more than those who are better able to afford larger families. For example, the 2006 Census revealed that the fertility rates were twice as high among those below poverty (91 births per 1,000) as among those living at 200 percent of poverty (45 births per 1,000) (reported in Kornblum, 2008). Several factors combine to explain this seemingly illogical behavior. First, those with the least amount of education are most likely to hold traditional beliefs, including the acceptance of traditional gender roles and **pronatalism** (the high value given to childbearing). Viewed the other way, the more education a woman has, the more likely she will hold feminist ideals, pursue a career, and limit her childbearing.

In traditional settings, being a mother or father brings social approval from family, friends, and one's religious community. Parenthood facilitates integration into one's kin network and the community. Children may also be considered a benefit to a poor family by supplementing the family income even during their elementary school years. And the poor may desire a large family as a source of retirement security—so that the grown children can support their elderly parents.

Race/Ethnicity   Whites have the lowest fertility rates, followed in order by Native Americans, Asians and Pacific Islanders, African Americans, with Latinos considerably higher than the rest (see Table 9.1). Not shown in this table but significant nonetheless are two additional facts concerning differential fertility. First,

Table 9.1   **Fertility Rates by Race and Hispanic Origin (Births per 1,000 Females Aged 15 to 44) for Selected Years**

Racial-Ethnic Category	1980	1990	2003
All races	68.4	70.9	66.7
White	65.6	68.3	66.4
Black	84.7	86.8	68.9
Hispanic	95.4	107.7	94.1
Asian/Pacific Islander	73.2	69.6	66.6
American Indian	82.7	76.2	59.9

Sources: "Birth and Fertility Rates," Child Trends Data Bank (2005). Online: www.childtrends_databank.org/pdf/79_PDF.pdf; Child Trends Data Bank (2007) (Winter). Online: www.childtrendsdatabank.org/indicators/79BirthRates.cfm.

the fertility rate for foreign-born adult women is about 50 percent higher than the rate for native-born adult women. Second, the fertility rate for any racial-ethnic category masks the diversity found therein. For example, the average number of children a woman will have during her lifetime varies among Latinos, with women of Mexican origin having the highest rate (106.8 in 2004) and Latino women of Cuban heritage having the lowest fertility rate (53.2 in 2004).

An interesting pattern seen over time is that fertility rates by race rise or fall in tandem—for example, the fertility rate for each category was the highest in 1955 and lowest in 1976. This demonstrates that fertility rates fluctuate according to economic and other social factors, regardless of race/ethnicity.

Why is there such a strong relationship between race/ethnicity and fertility? Foremost are the socioeconomic factors—income, education, and occupation—that press the disadvantaged toward pronatalist beliefs and practices. People of color are disproportionately poor, uneducated, unemployed, or, if employed, in the low-paying, low-prestige segment of the economy. Thus, they experience the same pressures and rationales as do other disadvantaged persons to have large families. For example, the total lifetime fertility for Latino women and African American women with only a grade school education is more than double the rate for their counterparts with at least some college. See Box 9.2 for other Latino fertility trends.

A second argument is that people make different sacrifices to get ahead. Because people of color are limited by structural barriers to the normal avenues to success, a common strategy among them has been to have large families. Large families mean more workers. They also make it more likely that the parents, when elderly, will receive help from their children. Also, there is a type of "lottery logic"—that is, as the number of children increases, so does the probability of having a child with unusual abilities (in music or sports, two of the few relatively open areas for people of color) that might lift the entire family out of its marginal economic situation. Thus, large families are a form of adaptation to economic deprivation and a hope to overcome it.

Religion Two generalizations hold for the relationship between religion and fertility. First, people who actively practice a religion tend to have higher fertility than nonreligious people (McFalls, 1998). And second, certain religions encourage high fertility. Traditionally, Catholics have had more children than Protestants, but since the 1980s that pattern has all but disappeared, except for Latino Catholics. Mormons have larger families than non-Mormons. Utah, which is 70 percent Mormon, has the highest fertility rate of the states.

BOX 9.2 Emergent Family Trends

A Shift to Smaller Latino Families

Latinos are the largest racial-ethnic group in the United States. Also, they have the highest fertility rate. But that relatively high rate is declining as more and more Latinas are choosing to have smaller families, resisting the Latino tradition of large families. Recent studies show that (Navarro, 2004):

- The fertility rate for Latinas is declining nationally.

- American-born Latinas have a much lower fertility rate than immigrant Latinas.

- The fertility rate for immigrant Latina women, although relatively high, has dropped 30 percent in the last 10 years, reflecting downward fertility rates in their countries of origin in the past few decades.

The reasons for this downward trend in Latina fertility are several. Foremost, ever greater numbers of Latinas are working outside the home, are obtaining higher levels of education, and are postponing marriage, all of which affect when and how often they will have children. In short, they are increasing their options rather than being limited to the traditional Latina pursuit of motherhood. Second, the lower fertility by second- and third-generation immigrants demonstrates that Latinas are adapting to the lifestyles of other American women. Finally, "in their quest for smaller families, Latina women say quality of life is paramount for those who came from big families themselves and felt crowded and neglected" (Navarro, 2004:29).

Voluntary Childlessness

Despite the strongly held beliefs of most Americans that children are the inevitable and desirable consequences of marriage, some couples choose to remain childless. For most of the twentieth century the proportion of childless marriages ranged from 5 to 10 percent. The percentage of women still childless at ages 40 to 44 (most of whom will remain childless) has increased from 10 percent in 1980 to 20 percent now (Kornblum, 2008). These data include the voluntarily and the involuntarily childless.

Because of the pronatalistic proclivities of Americans, those who reject this prescription often face the stigma associated with being deviant. They are considered by some as less-than-whole persons, emotionally immature, selfish, and lonely. Childless women are more likely than childless men to be negatively stereotyped. This is because motherhood

> is much more salient to the female role than fatherhood is to the male. Whereas masculinity can be affirmed by occupational success or sexual prowess, femininity has traditionally been closely linked with bearing and caring for children, with other roles remaining relatively peripheral. Although the paternal role is also important, it does not have the same centrality that makes motherhood almost a woman's raison d'être. (Veevers, 1980:7)

Given the strong pronatalist ideology and the negative labels that accompany voluntary childlessness, why do some couples choose this "unnatural" option? There appear to be three common paths to this decision. One pattern, found about one-third of the time, is for two persons to make a commitment before marriage that they will not have children. A second pattern occurs with a conscious choice to remain childless after launching a successful career. Childless women 40 to 44 years old, for example, have high levels of education, are employed in managerial and professional occupations, and have relatively high incomes (Hewlett, 2002).

The other and most common route to childless marriages is for a couple to make a series of decisions to postpone childbearing until a time when it no longer is considered a desirable choice. The first two paths explicitly reject childbearing, whereas the latter accepts it in the abstract but never finds it convenient, resulting, finally, in a permanent postponement.

Childlessness affects couples throughout their life course. They, of course, are free from the negatives of childrearing (e.g., the financial costs and restrictions on freedom that are noted later in this chapter), which likely are positive for marital quality. Should divorce occur, childless couples have fewer problems and lower levels of stress, compared to divorcing couples with children. Older couples that remained childless by choice vary in their experiences. Some have regrets; others feel that they made the correct decision. Childless couples replace missing children in their support networks with people other than relatives. Elderly childless individuals rely on siblings and paid supports for daily living (Bulcroft and Teachman, 2004).

Infertility and New Technologies

One in every eight couples is unable to conceive children by natural means (Centers for Disease Control, reported in Arnst, 2006). About 40 percent of the time this is caused by problems with the male partner (having insufficient number of active, healthy sperm, exposure to toxic chemicals, and blocked passages through which the sperm must travel). For infertile women the problem is usually with the failure to release healthy eggs or the blockage of the fallopian tubes.

There are several options for infertile single women, couples, or same-sex couples who cannot become pregnant through regular biological means. These procedures, when successful, are modern miracles that fulfill the wishes of the parent(s). Artificial insemination is a common technique. In this procedure, sperm from the partner or from a donor (often anonymous) is injected into the vagina with a syringe (see Box 9.3). A variation of this is for a woman to freeze her eggs (known as oocyte cryopreservation), preserving her fertility until the time is right (Lehmann-Haupt, 2009). In vitro fertilization, first successfully used in the birth of Louise Brown in 1972, is a procedure used when there is a blockage or scarring of the fallopian tubes. Eggs are removed from the ovaries of the mother or a donor and placed in a petri dish where sperm are added. Fertilization occurs and the fertilized eggs or embryos are transferred to the woman's uterus. Surrogate mothering involves sperm used to impregnate a woman other than one's partner (Ali and Kelly, 2008). A common procedure for women with impaired fecundity is to take fertility drugs. One consequence of this procedure is the increased probability of multiple births. The rate for triplets or more was 29.1 per 100,000 births in 1971. Thirty years later the rate was more than five times that number (about one-third of this increase is due to delaying childbearing until the late reproductive years, which also increases the likelihood of multiple births). Multiple births increase the risks to infants of problems such as preterm births, low birth weight, developmental brain damage, and cerebral palsy. Having twins, triplets, or quadruplets, of course, also increases the economic burden on the household as well as overwhelms the parents with double, triple, or quadruple demands on their time and emotions.

Other issues involving the new reproductive technologies include, first, the cost of the procedures (e.g., one cycle of in vitro fertilization costs $10,000; donor eggs cost $3,000). This results in a class bias, as poor infertile couples and poor same-sex couples are denied the possibility of having children because of their economic situation.

A second issue involves the sex of the offspring. By creating embryos outside the womb, a preimplantation genetic test can determine the sex of the fetus. This raises some questions: Will choosing one gender over another become a new form of sex discrimination? Will it upset the ratio of males to females as has occurred in China (Kalb, 2004)?

A third issue involves obtaining "designer genes" through the careful selection of egg and sperm donors for all manner of desirable traits (e.g., IQ, beauty, height, eye and hair color, athletic ability). An advertisement seeking egg donors in *The Stanford Daily* made this offer: "Egg donor wanted, $35,000 (plus all expenses). Ivy League Professional and High-Tech CEO seek one truly exceptional woman who is attractive, athletic, under the age of 29, GPA 3.5+, SAT: 1400+" (reported in Hopkins, 2006:2A).

The next step in creating "designer genes" is the manipulation of the human genome by inserting certain desirable genes into human eggs. While this has the potential to eliminate hereditary diseases, there are potential dangers. Bioethicist Margaret Somerville asks: "[The human genome is] the patrimony of the entire species, held in trust for us by our ancestors and in trust by us for our descendants. It has taken millions of years to evolve; should we really be changing it in a generation or two?" (quoted in Begley, 2001:52). Another bioethicist, Arthur Schafer, worries about affluent parents-to-be having superior babies. He warns of new social divisions: In addition to the haves and the have-nots, we will have the gene-rich and the gene-poor (paraphrased by Begley, 2001:52).

BOX 9.3 Technology and the Family

Hello, I'm Your Sister. Our Father Is Donor 150

Like most anonymous sperm donors, Donor 150 of the California Cryobank will probably never meet any of the offspring he fathered through sperm bank donations. There are at least four, according to the bank's records, and perhaps many more, since the dozens of women who have bought Donor 150's sperm are not required to report when they have a baby.

But two of his genetic daughters, born to different mothers and living in different states, have been e-mailing and talking on the phone regularly since learning of each other's existence last summer. They plan to meet over Thanksgiving.

The girls, Danielle Pagano, 16, and JoEllen Marsh, 15, connected through the Donor Sibling Registry, a website that is helping to open a new chapter in the oldest form of assisted reproductive technology. The three-year-old site allows parents and offspring to enter their contact information and search for others by sperm bank and donor number.

"The first time we were on the phone, it was awkward," Danielle said. "I was like, 'We'll get over it,' and she said, 'Yeah, we're sisters.' It was so weird to hear her say that. It was cool."

For children who often feel severed from half of their biological identity, finding a sibling—or in some cases, a dozen—can feel like coming home. It can also make them even more curious about the anonymous father whose genes they carry. The registry especially welcomes donors who want to shed their anonymity, but the vast majority of the site's 1,001 matches are between half-siblings.

The popularity of the Donor Sibling Registry, many of its registrants say, speaks to the sustained power of biological ties at a time when it is becoming almost routine for women to bear children who do not share a partner's DNA, or even their own.

"I hate when people that use D.I. say that biology doesn't matter (cough, my mom, cough)," Danielle wrote in an e-mail message, using the shorthand for donor insemination. "Because if it really didn't matter to them, then why would they use D.I. at all? They could just adopt or something and help out kids in need."

The half-sibling hunt is driven in part by the growing number of donor-conceived children who know the truth about their origins. As more single women and lesbian couples use sperm donors to conceive, children's questions about their fathers' whereabouts often prompt an explanation at an early age, even if all the information

about the father that is known is his code number used by the bank for identification purposes and the fragments of personal information provided in his donor profile.

Donor-conceived siblings, who sometimes describe themselves as "lopsided" or "half-adopted," can provide clues to make each other feel more whole, even if only in the form of physical details.

Liz Herzog, 12, and Callie Frasier-Walker, 10, for instance, carry the same dimple near their right eye.

"She looks up to me," said Liz, of Chicago, who was an only child before learning of Callie and six other half-siblings but seemed to have had no trouble stepping into her older-sister role. Finding her brothers and sisters, Liz said, "was the best thing in the world," even if Callie does copy her sometimes, like when Liz got her hair dyed red and Callie did the same. "I wanted blue," Callie said. "But they didn't have blue."

The two girls, who send instant messages to each other frequently, will be spending Thanksgiving with their mothers at Callie's house in Chester Springs, Pa. They had a mini-family reunion with some of their siblings last April, although as Liz's mother, Diana Herzog, notes, "It wasn't really a reunion because no one had ever met before."

Many mothers seek out each other on the registry, eager to create a patchwork family for themselves and their children. One group of seven says they, too, feel bonded by the half-blood relations of their children, and perhaps by the vaguely biological urge that led them all to choose Fairfax Cryobank's Donor 401.

Carla Schouten sent a leftover vial of sperm to another mother who wanted to have a second child and found there was no 401 sperm left to buy. (Banks typically pay men $50 to $100 per sample, and customers pay about $150 to $600 per vial, plus shipping.) In July, Ms. Schouten and her 2-year-old son, Matthys, went camping in Northern California with Louisa Weix, and her Donor 401 twins, Eliza and Julia, who turn 2 next week.

While many donor-conceived children prefer to call their genetic father "donor," to differentiate the biological function of fatherhood from the social one, they often feel no need to distance themselves, linguistically or emotionally, from their siblings.

Several who have met describe a sense of familiarity that seems largely irrational, given the absence of a father, unrelated mothers, and often divergent interests.

"All I can say is, they feel like siblings," said Barry Stevens, 53, a filmmaker who has discovered several

(continued)

(Box 9.3 continued)

half-siblings through research and DNA testing since the release of his 2001 documentary "Offspring," depicting his search for his donor.

If yearning for a sibling is in part a desire to feel less alone, some donor-conceived children may ultimately find themselves yearning for a bit more solitude.

Deb Bash, the mother of a 7-year-old, exchanges e-mail messages often with eight other mothers who have a total of 12 children from the same donor, and she has created a baby book for her son with all their pictures. The siblings, Ms. Bash said, have given her son a way to feel connected to the otherwise abstract concept of a genetic father.

"It's not a phantom person out there any more," Ms. Bash said.

The children already have some uncanny resemblances, she said. "That nurture vs. nature," Ms. Bash added. "Wow, there's just something to that nature."

For Danielle, of Seaford, N.Y., contact with her half-sibling JoEllen has helped salve her anger at what she describes as "having been lied to all my life," until three years ago when her parents told her the truth about her conception. It has also eased her frustration of knowing only the scant information about her biological father contained in the sperm bank profile—he is 6 feet tall, 163 pounds, with blond hair and blue eyes. He was married, at least at the time of his donation, and has two children with his wife. He likes yoga, animals, and acting.

For JoEllen, whose two mothers told her early on about her biological background, it helps just to know that Danielle, too, checks male strangers against the list of Donor 150's physical traits that she has committed to memory.

"It'll always run through my mind whether he meets the criteria to be my dad or not," said JoEllen, of Russell, Pa. "She said the same thing happens with her."

The girls are considering a trip to Wilmington, Del., which Donor 150 listed as his birthplace.

Even as the Internet makes it easier for donor-conceived children to find one another, some are calling for an end to the system of anonymity under which they were born. Sperm banks, they say, should be required to accept only donors who agree that their children can contact them when they turn 18, as is now mandated in some European countries.

That is partly for reasons of accountability. Sperm bank officials estimate the number of children born to donors at about 30,000 a year, but because the industry is largely unregulated, no one really knows. And as half-siblings find one another, it is becoming clear that the banks do not know how many children are born to each donor, and where they are.

Popular donors may have several dozen children or more, and critics say there is a risk of unwitting incest between half-siblings. Moreover, they argue, no one should be able to decide for children before they are born that they can never learn their father's identity. Typically, women can learn about a donor's medical history, ethnic background, education, hobbies, and a wide range of physical characteristics.

More recently, sperm banks have begun to charge more for the sperm from donors who agree to be contacted by their offspring when they turn 18. But they say far fewer men would choose to donate if they were required to release their identity.

Like Wendy Kramer and her donor-conceived son, Ryan, 15, who founded www.donorsiblingregistry.com, many of the site's 5,000 registrants hope that the donor himself will get in touch. But others are happy to settle for contacting their half-siblings, who actually want to be found. As they do, they are building a new definition of family that both rests on biology and transcends it.

"It's so weird to know that you're going to meet someone that you're going to know for the rest of your life," Justin Senk, 15, told his half-sister Rebecca Baldwin, 17, when they spoke on the phone last summer before meeting for the first time.

Justin, 15, of Denver, was the most recent half-sibling to surface in a group that now numbers five. After his newfound family attended his recent choir concert, Justin's mother, Susy Senk, overheard him introducing them to his friends with a self-styled sing-song, "'This is my sister from another mother, and this is my brother from another mother, this is my other sister from another mother,' and so on."

Source: Harmon, Amy (2005). "Hello, I'm Your Sister. Our Father Is Donor 150." *New York Times* (November 20). Online: http://www.nytimes.com/2005/11/20/national/20siblings.html?li=50.

Human cloning takes "designer genes" to the next level. "Cloning involves replacing the female genetic material of an unfertilized egg with a nucleus from a different cell. Thus, the genetic material in the nucleus will be identical to that of the donor, essentially creating a twin born at another time" (Bartels, 2004:494). This would make it possible, for example, for grieving parents to take the DNA of their recently deceased child to clone an exact replica. Cloning could also be used for the creation of spare body parts for research and medical uses. The downside to this technology is voiced by conservative William Kristol and progressive Jeremy Rifkin:

> Humans have always thought of the birth of their children as a gift bestowed by God or a beneficent nature. In its place, the new cloned progeny would become the ultimate shopping experience, designed in advance, produced to specification and purchased in the biological marketplace. A child would no longer be a unique creation but rather an engineered reproduction. (Kristol and Rifkin, 2002:2)

An especially thorny problem involves the legal issues "in establishing parenthood when there may be as many as five people involved: a sperm donor, an egg donor, a gestational mother, and the contracting mother and father" (Stephen, 1999:2). Consider, for example a lesbian strategy where

> an ovum from one woman is fertilized with donor sperm and then extracted and implanted in her lover's uterus. The practical and legal consequences of this still "nascent" practice have not yet been tested, but the irony of deploying technology to assert a biological, and thereby a legal, social, and emotional claim to maternal and family status throws the contemporary instability of all relevant categories—biology, technology, nature, culture, maternity, family—into bold relief. (Stacey, 1998:121)

What if, in such an instance, the relationship is broken and both parties seek custody of the child in the courts? Who is the biological parent? Is it the woman whose egg is fertilized, or is it the woman whose uterus was used to bring the fetus to birth? What about the sperm donor, who could actually be a relative (a common occurrence, with often the brother of one of the lesbian partners donating his sperm): Does he have a claim? Similar questions occur with heterosexual couples who have used reproductive technology to produce a child. There can be later claims by surrogate mothers (whose uterus brought the fetus to term) and by egg and sperm donors. Or there can be claims for the inheritance rights of children conceived posthumously, with frozen sperm, years after the father's death. For example, the Massachusetts Supreme Court ruled in 2001 that posthumously conceived children are entitled to their share of the donor's inheritance. Other questions: "Who has the right to frozen embryos, frozen eggs, frozen sperm? Whose name should appear on the birth certificate the genetic mother, who provided the egg, or the carrier, in whose womb the baby grew?" (Lewin, 2002:1). Clearly, these issues and questions point to a legal and ethical quagmire.

Delayed Childbearing

The age of first-time mothers has risen steadily since 1970, from an average of 21.4 years then to 25.0 in 2006. At least two factors lead to delayed childbearing: the increased age of first marriage and the ever greater likelihood of highly educated women launching their careers before having children. The relationship between age and the delay of a woman's first birth is especially keen for college graduates. Andrew Hacker points out that

> [in 1970] almost three quarters of college women had given birth while they were still in their twenties, and for most of them that meant leaving what might have been promising careers. By 2000, only 36.6 percent were starting babies that early, and many of them had arranged to return to their job. (Hacker, 2003:70)

This trend is producing more newborns at risk for health and learning problems. Research finds that women who postpone motherhood until their mid thirties or later increase the health risk for their babies (e.g., low birth weight, increased chance of premature birth, and learning disabilities) (Elias, 2002).

This shift toward more mature parenthood has several interesting consequences for the parents and children. First, the age gap between parents and their children is significantly greater than it was a generation ago. This may affect the quality of the parent–child relationship. This may be a positive development, as older parents have certain advantages over younger parents, such as more money and more maturity for dealing with the children. On the other hand, older parents, compared to younger parents, may have less patience and a diminished awareness of the needs of the young, especially when children reach adolescence. Second, while older parents will likely be more financially secure, having children later in life places the financial burden of a college education nearer the time of parental retirement, when it may deplete retirement savings. Third, children may push egalitarian couples back toward a more traditional division of labor—husband as provider and wife as homemaker. Aside from the traditional cultural prescriptions, which insist that the father work and the mother stay at home, there are the structural constraints that inhibit a role reversal. In most cases it makes more sense for the father to work because he, typically, makes more money than the mother. Many mothers, however, will continue their careers. Even those who might prefer to stay at home continue to work because their lifestyle depends on two incomes. The result is that more than half of all children under the age of 18 live in homes with fathers and mothers in the workforce. The majority of children, then, spend time away from their parents in child-care centers, in preschools, and with peers—all of which lessen the parental influence on their socialization.

Family Composition

SIZE

Voluntary childlessness and delayed childbearing combine to reduce the size of families. The proportion of couples with no children has risen in the past 20 years, as has the number of one-child families. The result is a gradual shrinking of family size—from an average of 3.14 in 1970 to 2.57 in 2006.

FORM

The demographic trends noted in this chapter and elsewhere in this book have combined to alter the traditional family pattern. The typical family just a generation ago was composed of a working father, a homemaker mother, and their children. Now only a small minority of families—7 percent—meets that description. But for the nation's children younger than 18, about 68 percent of children lived with two parents in 2008 (ChildStats.gov, 2008). As shown in Figure 9.2, slightly more than three-fourths of White children and more than four-fifths of Asian children live with two parents, almost two-thirds of Latino children live with two parents, but slightly more than one-third of African American children do. In each instance the proportion of children living with two parents has declined significantly since 1970. The data in Figure 9.2, while informing about the rise of single-parent households, mask various other family forms—the children raised in stepfamilies, the children with same-sex parents, the children living in grandparent-maintained households, and the percentage of children living with several generations in the same dwelling. An unwelcome trend is the rising share of children, particularly African American children in cities, who are living in no-parent households—living rather with relatives, friends, or foster families without either their mother or their father (Bernstein, 2002).

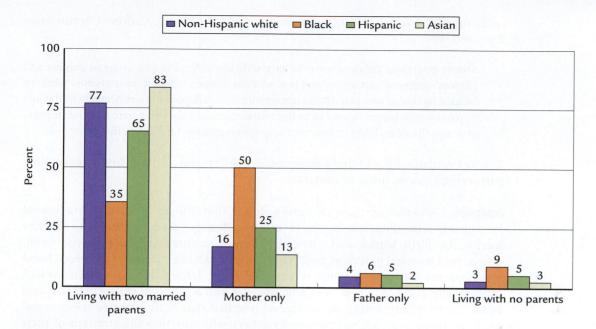

Figure 9.2

Living Arrangements of Children, by Race and Hispanic Origin, 2004

Note: Estimates for 2002 and 2003 by race have been revised to reflect the new OUB race definitions, and include only those who are identified with a single race. Hispanics may be of any race.

Source: Child Trends calculations of U.S. Census Bureau, Current Population Survey, 2004 Annual Social and Economic Supplement. America's Families and Living Arrangements: 2004.Table C-2. Available at http//:www.census.gov/population/www.docdemo/hhfam/cps2004.html

Unmarried Parenting   In 2007 the births to unwed mothers reached an all-time high of about 40 percent of all births (in 1960 it was 5 percent). In the recent past, teens accounted for about half of unwed births, but now they account for less than a quarter. These statistical facts indicate two trends: (1) Fewer unwed births now are due to youthful indiscretions, and more are due to conscious decisions by older women; and (2) many of these infants are born to cohabiting couples, not "single" women. This later trend is significant, because it means that while many children are being raised outside of marriage, they are actually in a two-parent family. The probability of this arrangement varies by race/ethnicity with Latino women and African American women more likely to conceive a child in cohabitation than White women.

Annually, over 400,000 babies are born to teenagers. The nation's highest teen birth rate was in 1957. From 1971 to 2005 there was an overall 34 percent drop in teenage births. Since then there has been a slight rise in teenage births. The overall decline occurred in all racial and ethnic groups. Despite the significant decline in the teenage birth rate, the United States still has the highest adolescent pregnancy rate among developed countries (four times higher than Sweden or France).

Around 40 percent of cohabiting couples have children under age 18 living at home. Usually, these children were born to one or both partners prior to the co-habiting arrangement. About 15 percent of cohabiting couples have at least one child together (Seccombe, 2008:231). How these children fare depends on the situation. Are the children better off living with a single mother, living with a mother and her unmarried partner, living with a father and his unmarried partner, or living with two cohabiting biological parents? Sociologist Andrew Cherlin sums it up this way:

> Simply put, some children seem to have difficulty adjusting to a series of parents and parents' partners moving in and out of their home.... Stable households, whether headed by one or two parents, do not require that children adjust repeatedly to the loss of parents and parent figures or to the introduction of cohabiting partners and stepparents and the new children these partnerships sometimes bring. (Cherlin, 2009:5–6)

The key variable for children's outcome is stability and, lest we forget, cohabiting partnerships can be stable or unstable.

Adoption   Adoption creates a family form that differs from the traditional biologically related nuclear family. It "creates a family that is connected to another family, the birth family, and often to different cultures and to different racial, ethnic, and national groups as well" (Bartholet, 1993:186). Because the blood bond serves as the basis for kinship systems, adoptive family ties have been viewed traditionally as "second best" and adoptive children as "second choice" (March and Miall, 2000; Wegar, 2000). Research has revealed that both adoptive parents and adult adoptees have felt stigmatized by others who question the strength of their adoptive ties.

Adoption is relatively rare, with about 4 percent of Americans being adopted. In an average year in the United States some 120,000 children are adopted. More than one-fourth of these adoptions involve children with "special needs," such as older children or children with mental, physical, or emotional handicaps. Although many adopted children have typical childhoods, on average they are more likely to have problems than nonadopted children. As noted expert David Brodzinsky has suggested, "The experience of adoption exposes parents and children to a unique set of psychosocial tasks that interact with and complicate the more universal developmental tasks of family life" (quoted in Fishman, 1992:46).

Despite this obstacle, most adoptions do work. As Katha Pollitt has observed, "Of course adoption can be a wonderful thing; of course the ties between adoptive parents and children are as profound as those between biological ones" (Pollitt, 1996:9).

Transracial or Transcultural Adoption   This means placing a child who is of one race or ethnic group with adoptive parents of another race or ethnic group. About 15 percent of all adoptions are classified as either of these two types (Shehan, 2003:295). Adoptions, international adoptions, and children being raised in foster homes each increase the likelihood of parents or surrogate parents being of a different race/ethnicity than their children.

About one in six adopted children is of a different race than the head of his or her household. More than 1 in 10 of the nation's adoptees are foreign-born (more than one-fifth from South Korea, followed by China, Russia, Guatemala, Ukraine, Mexico, and India). There are pitfalls with transnational adoption as the process is unregulated domestically or internationally.

Foster Care   Some children are placed in foster care when a court determines that their families cannot provide a minimally safe environment because of physical or sexual abuse, severe neglect, or, in some cases, severe emotional problems. In 2005 there were over 500,000 children in foster care. Foster children are vulnerable because of past and often present circumstances. As a consequence, they are disproportionately vulnerable for dropping out of school, teen pregnancy, drug abuse, and criminal behavior (O'Hare, 2004:13).

Grandparents Raising Grandchildren In 2006 about 5.7 million children (8 percent) lived in a household that included a grandparent. In slightly less than half of these homes, there was no parent present (Child Trends Data Bank, n.d.). Put another way, four million grandparents are rearing their grandchildren, usually grandmother-headed households. This trend toward "skipped generation" households is the result of death, teen pregnancy, divorce, drug use by parents, economic marginality, eviction from housing, the incarceration of parents, child abuse and neglect, mental and physical illness, and changes in welfare that are adding to the pressures on single parents. This family arrangement of grandparent-maintained households is most common in African American households (in the rate, not actual numbers), reflecting the greater likelihood of poverty and single motherhood among them. When both grandparents are raising grandchildren without parents, the families are overwhelmingly White, but when the children move in with a single grandmother, the families are predominantly African American. The children living with only their grandmother are disproportionately poor and tend to be without any health insurance. An Urban Institute study found that among grandparents raising grandchildren, 37 percent had incomes below the poverty threshold, and 66 percent were low-income (less than twice the poverty level) (reported in the *Economist*, 2007b).

Grandparents assuming the parental role are usually stretching meager resources, have reduced freedom, and experience added responsibility. At a time when they should be slowing down, they have the added burdens of providing emotional and economic support, transportation, guidance, and discipline for their grandchildren. The result, typically, is a high level of stress. Although the negatives are real, there are some positives: (1) providing a sense of usefulness and productivity for the grandparents; (2) making the grandparents feel good that they are able to help both their children and grandchildren; and (3) providing a more stable situation for the grandchildren (Giarrusso et al., 2000).

Multigenerational Families More than four million households in the United States (about 4 percent of the nation's households) have three or more generations within them. These households are most common in areas with high immigration, where recent immigrant family members live together for financial reasons and also because of language and other cultural factors.

In another type of multigenerational household, adults are taking care of their aging parents and their children simultaneously (known as the **sandwich generation**). Only a relatively few are caught in this bind because it generally means the combination of two factors exists: having children late in life and having parents who suffer from premature disability (Koss-Feder, 2003).

Older Children Still Living at Home A type of multigeneration family that is on the rise, especially under the conditions of the Great Recession, is one in which adult children, single and married who had lived on their own, move back home to live with their parents. According to the 2008 Census, 30 percent of people ages 18 to 34 live at home with their parents (reported in Trejos, 2009). Some of this so-called **boomerang generation** fit the stereotype of being unfocused, lazy, and immature. The majority, however, have been forced to turn to their parents because of the high cost of education, unmarried parenthood, the loss of jobs and homes (because of the high cost of housing and because they are recently divorced or separated), or because they work at low-wage entry-level jobs.

Mixed-Race Marriages and Children   Over 93 percent of Whites and African Americans marry within their own racial groups, compared with about 70 percent of Asians and Latinos (Kennedy, 2002). Put another way, about 2.5 percent of the married couples in the United States are matches between people of different races (a rise of well over 300 percent since 1970). The result, of course, is biracial children. President Barack Obama is a prime example of a person with mixed race parentage (a Black father from Kenya and a White mother from Kansas). The number of biracial children has increased more than 400 percent in the past 30 years, while the number of all births has increased by just over 18 percent. This difference in growth rate will increase with the continued influx of immigration from Asia and Latin America, the rising trend toward numerical parity between Whites and non-Whites by 2042, and the increasing acceptance of racial intermarriage.

Same-Sex Parents   Estimates of children of gay or lesbian parents vary widely, with various reports putting the number at between 6 million and 12 million (Biskupic, 2003). The existence of same-sex cohabitation, combined with the wish by many committed lesbian and gay couples for children, has resulted in a variety of family forms despite an array of social, legal, and practical challenges. The legality of gay/lesbian parenthood varies from state to state, and the interpretation of the law often varies from judge to judge. In general, the laws and the courts are hostile to same-sex couples gaining and retaining the custody of biological children and adopting children. In 2008, three states (Florida, Mississippi, and Utah) had laws that effectively banned gay couples from adopting. Twelve others allowed same-sex couples to adopt and 35 states were not clear on this issue (Ruggeri, 2008). Countering this trend, a 2006 study by the Evan B. Donaldson Adoption Institute found that a growing number of adoption agencies (60 percent) accept applications from gays and lesbians and that 40 percent of all agencies have already placed children with gay and lesbian parents (Donaldson, 2006).

There are relatively few documented cases of adoption by openly homosexual couples because many adoptions take place in which a single person seeks the adoption while concealing her or his sexual orientation.

Another situation is custody of children by a homosexual parent following a heterosexual marriage. In such a situation judges are likely to give custody routinely to the heterosexual parent, assuming that this is better for the child. For example, Alabama's supreme court ruled 9 to 0 that children are better off with a violent father than a reliable lesbian mother. The chief justice, Roy Moore, wrote in his opinion:

> The common law designates homosexuality as an inherent evil, and if a person openly engages in such a practice, that fact alone would render him or her an unfit parent. Homosexual conduct is, and has been, considered abhorrent, immoral, detestable, a crime against nature, and a violation of the laws of nature and of nature's God. (quoted in Graff, 2002:52)

Many lesbian mothers had children before "coming out" and were awarded custody as women, not as lesbians. The point is that lesbian mothers can, and do, lose custody of their children because of their sexual orientation.

A third method to achieving parenthood is the practice by lesbians of artificial insemination. The partner of the mother in this arrangement often has difficulty in adopting the child. Presently, only 12 states permit second-parent adoptions—that is, gay men and women adopting a child whose parent is the other gay partner. The majority of same-sex parents are women because the courts are more likely to award custody to mothers and because of the lesbian baby boom through artificial insemination.

A final issue: Do children raised by gay or lesbian parents differ from those raised by heterosexual parents? A growing body of research indicates that the children of gay and lesbian parents develop normally, including their sexual identity. Charlotte Patterson, a psychologist, reviewed 30 studies of gay and lesbian parents and concluded that

> despite longstanding legal presumptions against gay and lesbian parents in many states, despite dire predictions about their children based on well-known theories of psychosocial development, and despite the accumulation of a substantial body of research investigating these issues, *not a single study has found children of gay or lesbian parents to be disadvantaged in any significant respect relative to children of heterosexual parents.* Indeed, the evidence to date suggests that home environments provided by gay and lesbian parents are as likely as those provided by heterosexual parents to support and enable children's psychosocial growth (emphasis added). (Patterson, 1992:1036; see also Allen and Burrell, 1996; Cherlin, 2009; Patterson, 2001:119; Patterson and Redding, 1996)

These conclusions are supported but altered somewhat by sociologists Judith Stacey and Timothy Biblarz (2001). They reevaluated 21 psychological studies conducted between 1981 and 1998, which found that children raised by same-sex parents were no different from those reared by heterosexual parents. Their analysis of those studies revealed that (1) the emotional health of youngsters with heterosexual or gay parents is essentially the same; (2) the offspring of lesbians and gays, however, are more likely to depart from traditional gender roles than the children of heterosexual couples; and (3) children with same-sex parents seem to grow up to be more open to homoerotic relations. Stacey and Biblarz conclude that nothing in their work justifies discrimination against gay families or alters their conviction that gays and lesbians can be excellent parents raising well-adjusted children. The key for the healthy emotional growth of children is their empathetic attachment to an adult caretaker, female or male, heterosexual or homosexual. To buttress this conclusion, the American Academy of Pediatrics formally supports gay adoption. So, too, do the American Psychological Association and the American Academy of Child and Adolescent Psychiatry.

There is one special difficulty that children in gay and lesbian families experience, one that is derived from legal discrimination and social prejudice.

> Children of gay parents are vicarious victims of homophobia and institutionalized heterosexism. They suffer all of the considerable economic, legal, and social disadvantages imposed on their parents, sometimes even more harshly. They risk losing a beloved parent or coparent at the whim of a judge. They can be denied access to friends by the parents of playmates. Living in families that are culturally invisible or despised, the children suffer ostracism by proxy, forced continually to negotiate conflicts between loyalty to home, mainstream authorities, and peers. (Stacey, 2003:160)

Earlier in this chapter we considered parenting as a socially constructed phenomenon. The existence of lesbian and gay parents demonstrate this.

Lesbian and gay parents challenge the primacy enjoyed by "traditional" heterosexual marriage and parenthood. They reveal, by their innovation in creating and maintaining families that thrive even in a hostile social environment, that parenting is not an essentialistic or inherently natural experience. Lesbian and gay parents exemplify that families are constructed by a variety of biological, adoptive, and chosen kin ties. (Allen, 1997:198)

Or put another way:

Under postmodern conditions, processes of sexuality, conception, gestation, marriage, and parenthood, which once appeared to follow a natural, inevitable progression of gendered behaviors and relationships, have come unhinged, hurtling the basic definitions of our most taken-for-granted familial categories—like mother, father, parent, offspring, sibling, and, of course, "family" itself—into cultural confusion and contention. (Stacey, 2003:147)

The Impact of Children on Marriage

Probably no single event has more impact on a marriage and on the marriage partners than the addition of a child. This momentous event impacts the career patterns of the parents, the division of housework, the distribution of power, marital satisfaction, and the economic well-being of the unit. Significantly, when spouses become parents, they shift to responding to each other in terms of role obligations rather than as intimates. Interaction patterns shift, as do the patterns of domestic work, communication, and the distribution of power; and the shift is usually toward more traditional gender roles. In effect, then, the addition of a child changes the social organization of the family. To discuss these consequences, this section is divided into four parts—the transition to parenthood, the benefits of parenthood, the costs of parenthood, and gendered parenting.

The Transition to Parenthood

The birth of the first child to a couple brings enormous changes to the parents and their relationship. The structure of their daily lives is altered. The workload of the parents grows with the time devoted to child care. Their living space is more constricted. The freedom the couple had previously is now curtailed severely. The attention that was once lavished on each other is now interrupted by the new arrival. Their lovemaking may become less frequent and more inhibited. There are heightened financial problems. The new mother and new father

find themselves riding the same roller coaster of elation, despair, and bafflement.... [They approached] parenthood full of high hopes and soaring dreams,... [yet] six months or a year after the child's birth they...find themselves wondering "What's happening to us?" (Belsky and Kelly, 1994:4)

Jay Belsky and John Kelly's research on new parents found, among other things, that parenthood presents a fundamental source of tension between the parents. Most couples approach parenthood assuming that the new baby will bring them closer together. In time this often happens, but initially a child has the opposite effect. Couples, even those who consider themselves

as like-minded often find their priorities and needs diverging dramatically when they become parents. Differences in family background and personality also contribute to transition-time marital gaps. No matter how much they love each other, no two people share the same values or feelings or have the same perspective on life, and few things highlight these personal differences as pointedly as the birth of a child. (Belsky and Kelly, 1994:12)

Differences emerge over new concerns, such as whether to minister to every demand of the infant, or feelings intensify over old disagreements about the division of labor, which, with the arrival of a baby, is so relentless.

There is considerable evidence that children have a negative effect on marital happiness. Representative of these findings is the research from a national survey of families (Heaton et al., 1996). The researchers found that the child's influence on marital relationships varies with the age of the child. When parents have very young children, the parents tend to perceive positive parent–child relationships, but these couples spend less time together and have more marital disagreements. Marital stability, however, is greatest in the first five years following the birth of a child. During the early adolescent years, on the other hand, there is a declining closeness in the parent–child relationship and high marital disagreement about children. The researchers also found that the greater the behavior problems of the child, the greater the marital disagreement, the less time together, and the lower marital happiness. They conclude that couples tend to be happiest before the arrival of the first child. This happiness declines with the arrival of a child and reaches a low point as children reach adolescence. Marital happiness increases after the children leave home.

These and other concerns alter marriages. The research of Belsky and Kelly found that the entry of a child into a marriage relationship changes marriage in one of four ways (Belsky and Kelly, 1994:14–15):

1. About 13 percent of new parents are what Belsky and Kelly term "severe decliners." These new parents become so split by their differences that they lose faith in each other and in their marriage. Their communication diminishes, as does their love.

2. Another 38 percent are "moderate decliners." These couples avoid a dramatic falling out, but their love and communication is less than before the birth of their child.

3. About 30 percent of the couples experience "no change." Their marriage neither declines nor is enhanced by their child.

4. Nineteen percent of the couples in Belsky and Kelly's study are "improvers." These couples find that their new child has brought them closer together, increased communication, and enhanced their mutual love.

The tendency for marital satisfaction to decline with the arrival of a baby is mitigated by two factors (research by Philip Cowan and Carolyn Pape Cowan, reported in Council on Contemporary Families, 2009). First, couples who plan the conception jointly are much less likely to experience a serious marital decline. In other words, couples who slid into having a baby without planning or who disagreed about having a baby but went ahead and conceived without resolving their difference will very likely find their marriage rocky after the baby.

Second, marital satisfaction will decrease in couples who do not share in domestic duties after the birth of their child. Typically, after the birth of a child most couples become much more traditional in dividing the chores of housework and child care. This means the women will carry the burden, leading to feelings of tension, depression, and sometimes anger in both partners. Stated positively, couples who plan conception jointly and who establish a collaborative parenting relationship will tend to have happy marriages. In short, babies are not necessarily bad for marriage.

The Benefits of Parenthood

Throughout U.S. history the role of parenthood has been exalted, especially for wives. The assumption has been that a woman's destiny and her ultimate fulfillment is wrapped up in motherhood. This pronatalist belief was fostered by the encouragement of young girls to play at motherhood (e.g., playing with dolls, "playing house"), by children's literature that presented women mainly in nurturing roles, by the Madonna theme in art, and by kinship expectations to marry and have children. The consequence of this usually unquestioned sanctity of childbearing is that today 85 percent of marriages produce children. Although most marriages include children, becoming parents is not a trivial event. The partners in a marriage now add the roles of mother and father to their already complex relationship, and this has profound implications.

The benefits of parenthood are several. First, children can positively affect the marriage bond. The partners share in the miracle of birth, their creation of a common product, their new and enhanced status in two kinship networks, and pride in their offspring's accomplishments. They can experience mutual satisfaction in nurturing the emotional and physical growth of children. The presence of children may also encourage communication between spouses as they share experiences and work through problems.

A second benefit of having children is that it symbolizes a kind of immortality—a link with the past and the future. Related to this is that parents often find it exhilarating to see themselves in their children, as the personality traits of parents, their mannerisms, and their values are passed on and acted out by their children. Third, having children may give the lives of parents a sense of meaning and purpose. This may be especially true for those with low social status. The pride they do not find in their work they might find in their children.

A fourth benefit, and related to the third, is the enhanced status one has as a parent. Parenthood is tangible evidence of one's adulthood to almost everyone—kin, colleagues, friends, neighbors, employers, and community agencies. Fifth, with children there is the ultimate giving and receiving of unconditional love. Sixth, parents can benefit by symbolically recapturing their youth through their children's activities and accomplishments as well as by vicariously having experiences they were denied as children themselves.

A final benefit is that parents are more likely to be integrated into their communities than childless adults (Ambert, 1992). As parents meeting their children's needs, they interact with physicians, teachers, coaches, sitters, day-care providers, and other parents. They become connected to organizations such as schools, churches, sports leagues, children's clinics, and day-care and preschool centers. Children may act as social facilitators as they introduce their parents to the parents of their friends and classmates. Similarly, the children of immigrants who do not know the language of the host country may be the catalysts in connecting their parents with the larger community.

The Costs of Parenthood

While children bring joy to parents, the realistic examination of parenthood requires that we consider the negatives as well as the positives. Almost all of the benefits just listed have a negative side: Children can adversely affect marital happiness, children can have negative personality traits, they may get into trouble, and they may not return their parents' love. Added to these are other emotional costs to parents. They worry about children's safety, physical and emotional development, progress in school, potential negative influences of peers, and the like. When children fail in school or at work, become social misfits, get arrested for driving under the influence of drugs or alcohol, or become criminals, parents tend to blame themselves. Adolescence, in particular, is an emotionally difficult time for parents and children as there is the inevitable clash of wills.

Financially, children are a significant burden. According to the U.S. Department of Agriculture, the average middle-income household could expect to spend a total of $191,000 on the child through age 17 to feed, clothe, house, and educate a child born in 2005 (reported in Ordonez, 2007). Note that this expense is calculated before the costs of a college education and the lost wages for a stay-at-home mom or dad. If these costs are included, raising a child to adulthood costs $1.6 million.

Gendered Parenting

There has been a shift in men's involvement in pregnancy. Just a generation ago, most fathers-to-be were not involved in preparation for the impending birth. Most were not witnesses to the birth. Now, many prospective fathers join their pregnant wives in prenatal classes. These husbands are present at the birth, helping their wives with breathing and other relaxation techniques. They may hold the newborn and present it to the new mother in a significant symbolic gesture. They may even take time off from work to help care for and bond with the infant.

This relatively new involvement of men with pregnancy and birth, however, has not resulted in equal responsibility for child care: "The mother still does most of the work not because she is more nurturing or competent but because the culture ideologically and practically structures women's and men's parenting behavior and the time spent in paid work" (Lorber, 1994:162).

Michael Lamb (1987) divides child care into three components: accessibility, or being on call near the child but not directly engaged in care; direct interaction or one-on-one care, such as feeding, bathing, playing, reading, helping with homework; and responsibility, thinking about the child's emotional, social, and physical development, and making arrangements for such activities as babysitting, doctor visits, and school visits.

Lamb found that in two-parent families in the United States in which mothers did not work outside the home, fathers spent about 20 to 25 percent of the time that mothers spent in direct interaction with children, and about a third of the time in being accessible. They assumed no responsibility for children's care or rearing. In two-parent families where

Research indicates that the key for the healthy emotional growth of children is their empathetic attachment to an adult caretaker.... Same sex couple with twins.

both mothers and fathers were employed thirty or more hours a week, fathers interacted with children 33 percent of the time that mothers did and were accessible 65 percent of the time mothers were, but they assumed no more responsibility for children's welfare than when mothers were full-time homemakers. In fact, the higher proportional level of their day-to-day child care was due to employed mothers' spending less time with the children; it did not reflect more actual time spent with children by the father. (Lamb, 1987; summarized by Lorber, 1994:163; emphasis added)

The parenting pattern, then, is clear—mothers are the primary caregivers, while fathers are passive; mothers spend more time actually doing things to and for their children as well as doing the emotional work of caring and worrying about them. Just as with housework, women are the givers and men the takers.

There are exceptions to this overriding tendency. First, "the overall pattern for all regions, ethnic groups, and religions in the United States was that fathers spend more time with sons than with daughters and were more likely to play with them than do things for them" (Lorber, 1994:163). Related to this bias of fathers for sons, research by two economists found that with the birth of their first child, men work harder— 118 hours a year more if their first child was a boy but only 54 hours more if their firstborn was a girl (cited in Morin, 2002).

A second exception occurs when fathers become the primary parent because of widowhood or divorce. In these instances, single fathers develop relationships with their children that are intimate and nurturing.

A final deviation from the typical male parenting pattern is when couples deliberately share parenting. Here children have two primary caretakers. Parents divide chores and spend time with the children equitably, as noted in the title of a book on shared parenting, *Halving It All* (Deutsch, 1999). This sharing, however, is not as easy as it may appear on the surface. Research has shown, for example, that couples find it easy to divide the work (e.g., changing diapers, giving baths, taking children to lessons) but that mothers tend to do more of the emotion work: "Women feel on call for their children all the time; men do not. Men can more easily distance themselves from their children, letting them cry, not paying attention to their every move, and not thinking about them at work" (Lorber, 1994:166). Thus, parenting often remains gendered even among those who work at overcoming the inequitable arrangements within more traditional couples.

There is a major debate over the consequences of gender egalitarianism of the parents for their children. Conservative scholars claim that contemporary egalitarian lifestyles are undermining families and placing children at risk (Glenn, 1997; Popenoe, 1993). Progressive scholars, in contrast, argue that families are changing but not declining. They see egalitarian marriages as an improvement over traditional families because they provide increased opportunities for adult self-fulfillment, especially equitable arrangements for women (Coontz, 1997; Stacey, 1996).

Family sociologists Alan Booth and Paul Amato (1994), using a 12-year longitudinal study, examined whether nontraditional gender roles among parents are associated with later life outcomes of children. They defined nontraditional families as those in which mothers are employed, fathers contribute to household and child care, and parents hold egalitarian attitudes toward gender roles. Booth and Amato found very little evidence that being raised in nontraditional families had adverse or positive effects on offspring well-being. Adult children from nontraditional families are less likely to live with their parents, they have slightly poorer relationships with their fathers, and they are more likely to have nontraditional gender attitudes. Many aspects of the parent–child relationship are unaffected. The children of nontraditional families are just as likely as those from traditional families to get married and have children, to be happily married, to have positive self-esteem, to experience psychological distress, and to achieve similar levels of education. The authors conclude that

> our evidence does not support the notion that nontraditional families are creating serious problems for their offspring. This is not surprising in that, through history and across cultures, there have been a variety of ways of organizing the family division of labor. Long-term offspring outcomes probably have more to do with economic well-being, parental warmth and competence, social support, and other resources than with family organization. In contrast to the claims of those on the religious and political right, our research suggests that the current trend toward a less traditional, more egalitarian division of labor in the family poses relatively few problems for the youth of today. (Booth and Amato, 1994:874)

Houseknecht and Sastry (1996) compared the well-being of children in four societies, from the least traditional (Sweden), followed in order by the United States, the former West Germany, and the most traditional, Italy. They found that the decline of the traditional family is not associated with the kind of deleterious consequences for child well-being asserted by conservatives.

The Impact of Parents on Children and of Children on Parents

Parents, more than anyone else, interact with their children on a continuing basis and, therefore, have a crucial impact on their children's physical, social, and emotional development. Ideally, parents provide children with communication skills, the interpretation of events and behaviors, identity, a haven in time of distress, a source of emotional attachment, a sense of right and wrong, and skills for competence in the social world.

> When [the child] enters the human group, he is quite at the mercy of parents and siblings. They determine both what and when he shall eat and wear, when he shall sleep and wake, what he shall think and feel, how he shall express his thoughts and feelings (what language he shall speak and how he shall do it), what his political and religious commitments shall be, what sort of vocation he shall aspire to. Not that parents are ogres. They give what they have to give: their own limited knowledge, their prejudices and passions. There is no alternative to this giving of themselves; nor for the receiver is there any option. Neither can withhold the messages conveyed to the other. (Wilson, 1966:92)

Although parents are clearly important socializing agents, this observation must be balanced by the reality that the child is not an empty vessel that the parents fill, but, to the contrary, the child is an active social being who often shapes the parents.

Historically, theories of childhood have focused on children's internalization of and adaptation to their parents' and societal constraints. In this deterministic view, children were believed to be shaped and molded by adults who reinforced proper behavior and punished inappropriate behavior. More recently, less deterministic, more constructionist theories of childhood have been advanced. "In this perspective, children are seen as negotiators and co-creators of their own worlds" (Shehan, 1999:6).

The family's resources and educational achievements affect how children perceive themselves.

In other words, the children are not assumed to be passive receptors of parental influences; rather, influence flows both from parents to children and from the children to parents. The joke that "insanity is hereditary—parents get it from their children" illustrates this point. Parents respond to the smiles, sighs, irritability, and crying of infants. Infants with colic act in ways that exert control over the parents. The gender of infants affects parents as they, typically, treat boys differently than girls, have different expectations according to gender, and structure the play and room environments of children according to gender stereotypes. Other attributes of children—their size, right- or left-handedness, abilities, disabilities, temperament, and personality—are all factors potentially relevant to how parents react to them, as are the unique interests and achievements of children (Alwin, 2004:152). Children may resist the demands of parents, such as toilet training. Younger and older children can manipulate their parents through their behaviors (e.g., showing affection or being difficult). Clearly, the power and authority of parents to form their children is not total: Children are not blank slates to be filled in by parental instruction but rather are active agents in their own construction of knowledge about the world (Kuczynski et al., 1999). This construction will not necessarily be the same as that held by the parents. Thus, children may have insights, children may teach, and children may even lead. For example, older children may pressure their parents to quit smoking, to eat a healthier diet, to use seat belts, and to act more positively toward the environment. In short, children, while being shaped by parents, are also active in shaping their parents. This is known as the bilateral model of parent–child relations (Kuczynski et al., 1999).

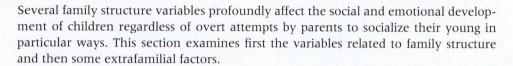

The Structure of the Family Embedded in a Larger Network of Influences

Several family structure variables profoundly affect the social and emotional development of children regardless of overt attempts by parents to socialize their young in particular ways. This section examines first the variables related to family structure and then some extrafamilial factors.

Family Structure

ONE-CHILD FAMILIES

Single-child families are the fastest-growing family unit. In 2004, 17.4 percent of women ages 40 to 44 reported having one child, compared with 9.6 percent of women that age in 1976. Families with only one child now outnumber two-child families (Census Bureau, reported in Stevens, 2008).

Only children are commonly believed to be worse off than children with siblings. They are stereotyped as self-centered, lonely, spoiled, and anxious. These are faulty beliefs, however. Research finds that only children are superior to children with siblings on virtually all positive dimensions including intelligence, achievement, maturity, leadership, health, and satisfaction with friends and family (Blake, 1991).

FAMILY SIZE

With the addition of each child, the resources that a family has for each is diminished. Douglas B. Downey (1995) analyzed data from a national sample of 25,000 eighth graders and found that parental interpersonal resources such as interaction with children and knowing their friends were negatively affected by additional children. Similarly, parental economic resources for their children, such as a personal computer, a place to study, money saved for college, and music or art lessons, were all negatively related to additional children (summarized in Eshleman and Bulcroft, 2006:417–419). Of course, the economic resource problem is minimized when the family is relatively affluent.

BIRTH ORDER

A significant family structure variable affecting the child is ordinal position. As Jerome Kagan has pointed out,

[d]espite the importance of parental behavior, the mere existence of a younger or older sibling in the family is a salient force in the psychological development of the child. The mechanisms that account for these differences do not rest only with the practices and communications of the parents, and, therefore, they are not solely a function of what is normally meant by "direct family experience." Rather, the catalyst of change is simply the introduction of "another," like the introduction of a crystal into

"Here comes trouble."

a cloud to precipitate rain. The "other" is the catalyst that creates uncertainty in the child. In response to that uncertainty, the child alters his beliefs, behaviors, and roles. (Kagan, 1977:53)

Older children have an inherent advantage over their siblings—they have exclusive parental attention at least for a while. This probably explains why, when compared with later-born children, firstborns have a strong tendency to adopt the values of their parents and to be less influenced by peers. They tend to be more achievement oriented, to excel in school, to have higher verbal scores on aptitude and IQ tests (Carey, 2007), and to have high levels of self-esteem. They are even taller and weigh more than later-borns (Kluger, 2007). Female first-borns tend to be more religious, more sexually conservative, and more accepting of traditional feminine roles. These traits accrue from the time they had the exclusive attention of parents and because they want to differentiate themselves from their younger brothers or sisters. Thus, "the first-born is propelled to adulthood by the presence of the younger sibling" (Kagan, 1977:51). Later-born children never have the exclusive attention of their parents. They have the disadvantage of always appearing less competent than the first-born. The result is for later-born children, when compared to first-borns, to be less cautious, more impulsive, and more involved in physically dangerous activities. They are more peer-conscious, more social, and more willing to challenge authority.

SIBLINGS

Related to birth order, and perhaps a more powerful influence on behavior, is the presence of siblings. By the time children are 11, they spend about one-third of their free time with their siblings—more time than they spend with peers, parents, teachers, or by themselves.

From the time they are born, our brothers and sisters are our collaborators and co-conspirators, our role models and cautionary tales. They are our scolds, protectors, goads, tormentors, playmates, counselors, sources of envy, objects of pride. (Kluger, 2006:47)

As a result, brothers and sisters are especially important for teaching how to resolve conflicts or how not to, for educating about the mysteries of the opposite sex, for teaching how to negotiate with parents, and even for steering one another into risky behavior. Regarding the latter, research finds that the existence of an older sibling increases the chances that a younger sibling will drink, smoke, use marijuana, or have sex (reported in Jayson, 2006a). For example, a girl with an older, pregnant teenage sister is four to six times as likely to become a teen mother herself (Kluger, 2006:52).

PRIMARY PARENTS

The question of who does the primary parenting, while seemingly straightforward, is quite complex because there are so many possible variations. These possibilities depend on the number of parents in the household (or even if there are no parents in the "parental" role, such as in households headed by grandparents or foster parents); if there is only one parent, the gender of that parent; the presence or absence of an extended family; parents' marital status; and the sexual orientation of the parents—and each of these may have different effects on children depending on their age (Demo and Cox, 2001). For example, a study of African American children in the Woodlawn community in Chicago distinguished 86 different combinations of adults living in households with first graders (Hunter and Ensminger, 1992). Of crucial importance is the timing and sequencing of changes in children's living arrangements.

The following are some research-based generalizations concerning some of these variations:

- The absence of a same-sex parent for daughters of solo fathers and sons of solo mothers tends to have a negative impact.

- The presence of two adults, even if the second adult is not a legal parent, has been found to diminish adolescent behavior problems.

- Growing up in nontraditional gender role families does not have adverse effects on children (see Box 9.4).

- Children of lesbian and gay parents have normal relationships with peers, and their relationships with adults of both sexes is satisfactory.

- Children do better in stable living arrangements than in transitory ones, even if the stability involves living with a single parent. For example, children experiencing multiple transitions (e.g., from two parents to single parent to parent and stepparent) and experiencing them later in childhood fare poorly compared to those living their entire childhood in stable single-parent families (Demo and Cox, 2001:105).

BOX 9.4 Researching Families

Parental Gender Role Nontraditionalism and Offspring Outcomes

As we have noted throughout this book, the emerging family of the 1980s and 1990s differs significantly from the traditional nuclear family of the 1950s. Now the majority of mothers are in the labor force. Many contemporary mothers and fathers share child-care and household tasks (albeit still unequally for the most part). And the attitudes of spouses concerning gender roles have changed in many families. What, if any, are the outcomes for children raised in families with nontraditional gender roles?

Sociologists Alan Booth and Paul Amato (1994) investigated this question using data from a longitudinal study of a representative sample of 471 parents and their adult offspring. This procedure allowed the researchers to interview children at least 19 years of age in 1992 whose parents had been interviewed in 1980, 1983, 1988, and 1992. Thus, they were able to determine the behaviors and attitudes of parents as their children were being raised as well as how the children were affected as adults. They were interested in the effects of maternal employment, paternal involvement in home activities, and parental attitudes regarding gender roles. In their analysis they controlled for the possible confounding effects of parents' gender and race, mother's education and age, and offspring's age and gender. In other words, they compared respondents similar on a variable to assess whether another variable was making a difference.

When comparing the children of traditional parents with those of nontraditional parents, Booth and Amato found that the latter (1) were more likely to leave home prior to marriage; (2) were less likely to be close to their fathers (possibly because the fathers were not living at home); (3) were similar to the former in ties to close relatives and friends; (4) were just as likely as those from traditional homes to get married and to parent; (5) were the same as the children from traditional families on measures of psychological well-being; and (6) were comparable to their traditional counterparts in educational attainment.

- Children in stepfamilies, compared with those in first-married families, are more likely to experience a broad range of adjustment problems.

Extrafamilial Factors

As parents interact with their children, they are not free from outside influences. A number of work-related factors, for example, affect parents and their interactions with children. Some of these are the level of job satisfaction, promotions or demotions, transfer to a new community, level of pay, work schedules, job-related stress, layoffs or threatened layoffs, sexual harassment at work, job discrimination, and the presence of both parents in the workforce.

The influence of parents on their children is diminished by a number of other outside forces as well. When both parents work, preschool children will be cared for by someone other than the parents. Once children are of school age, the school (i.e., its teachers, policies, and curriculum) becomes an important socialization agent, sometimes in opposition to the wishes of the parents, causing some to move their children to other school environments or to home schooling.

As children grow, they spend less time under the direct supervision of their parents. They are increasingly supervised by others such as teachers, coaches, and youth leaders. Most important, though, is the influence of peers on young people, especially adolescents. Especially disconcerting to parents is that their adolescent children are learning to deal with potentially risky behaviors at the very time peer influence increases (Furstenberg, 2001).

The neighborhoods in which families reside can be mixed in terms of social class and race/ethnicity, but more likely they will be relatively homogeneous—composed of neighbors of the same social class and race/ethnicity. Thus, living in an area of concentrated poverty (such as an urban ghetto) or in affluence (such as a gated suburban community) provides peers with the same backgrounds and privilege, or the lack thereof, in terms of opportunities, well-financed schools, and community services.

The economic resources of families are a crucial factor affecting the outcomes of children. The amount of family income available to children depends on the type of family in which he or she lives (Bianchi and Casper, 2000:27). Most basically, social class position provides for the child's life chances. The greater the family's economic resources, the better the chance to live beyond infancy, to be in good health, to receive a good education, to have a satisfying job, to avoid being labeled a criminal, to avoid death in war, and to live the "good life." On the negative side, this means that millions of U.S. children are denied these advantages because they were born to parents who were unemployed, underemployed, stuck in the lower tier of the segmented labor market, handicapped, victims of institutional racism or sexism, divorced or separated, or otherwise disadvantaged.

Significantly, the family's resources and educational achievements affect the way in which children perceive themselves. These ascribed characteristics (along with race/ethnicity and gender) position children in the perceptions of others, in turn giving children an understanding of their worth. If the family has favored characteristics, children are very likely to gain nourishment from the social power and esteem that come from high social position. But children of the poor and minorities find they are devalued by persons outside the immediate family and kin network; this perception can have a profound effect on their psyches and behavior regardless of the efforts of their parents (Kagan, 1977:35, 47).

Parental Time with Children

Contrary to popular belief, mothers today spend more hours tending to their children than did mothers 40 years ago (the following is from Bianchi et al., 2006; Kendig and Bianchi, 2008; St. George, 2007). Sociologists Suzanne Bianchi, John Robinson, and Melissa Milkie, using four decades of time-diary surveys in which representative samples describe a typical day conclude, "that parents are spending as much—and perhaps more—time interacting with their children today than parents in 1965, the heyday of the stay-at-home mother" (2006:1). This is accomplished through several strategies, including mothers spending less time on housework (use of labor saving devices such as microwave ovens and husbands doing a bit more housework) and parents including children more in their own leisure activities.

There are three types of time with children: (1) primary time, where children are the focus of parents' attention in activities such as reading or playing games; (2) secondary time, which involves helping with homework, working together at preparing a meal, or doing another household chore; and (3) passive time, just being with children. Single mothers spend as much time engaged in primary care as married mothers but they spend less total time with their children than married mothers (Kendig and Bianchi, 2008). Comparing 1975 with 2000, married mothers increased their time with their children while single mothers' total time with their children decreased. This distinction is blurred, however, as more and more single mothers live with the father of their children in a cohabiting arrangement.

Several additional variables affect the time parents spend with their children (Kendig and Bianchi, 2008). First, the greater the economic resources a family has, the better its ability to purchase goods and services that free up time for childrearing. Second, the greater the education mothers attain, the more time they spend with their children and the more often they engage in activities that promote children's cognitive development. Third, employed mothers spend less time with their children than mothers not in the labor force. Fourth, preschool-age children in households increase mothers' child-care time. These factors help to explain why single mothers tend to spend less time with their children than do married mothers. Never-married mothers tend to have younger children than married or divorced mothers. They have less household income. They are likely to have less education and more likely to be employed outside the home than married mothers. Despite the structural locations of single mothers, they, nevertheless, still spend almost 90 percent as much time with their children as married mothers.

Parents and Children in Dual-Earner Families

Since 1960, the rise of women's participation in the labor force has been dramatic. For example, the percentage of mothers in the workforce with children under six years of age increased from around 19 percent in 1960 to over 60 percent in 2009; for mothers with school-age children, the percentage of mothers in the labor force increased from less than 40 percent in 1960 to 78 percent. The year 1987 was a tipping point: That year was the first time that more than one-half of all mothers with babies one year old or younger were working or looking for work.

This phenomenal rise is a consequence of several factors. Feminism has encouraged many women to seek fulfillment in a career outside the home. Wives in many husband–wife households work outside the home to supplement family income, since one-wage families have lost purchasing power since 1973 and since the costs of housing, cars, and college, to name a few expenses, have risen sharply. By 2008 the share of dual-earner family income contributed by women was 44 percent, and 26 percent of women earned 20 percent or more than their husbands (Families and Work Institute, 2008). The rapid rise in the numbers of working women is also a consequence of the growth in the divorce rate and in female-headed households, where their participation in the labor force is an economic necessity.

Working mothers in both categories—single and married—share similar problems, such as low pay (78 cents for each dollar earned by men in 2008); the need to juggle the demands of a job, housework, and parenting; and the need for good child care. One critical difference, however, is that single mothers tend to raise their children with inadequate financial resources, whereas married mothers in the workforce, for the most part, tend to have an adequate financial base.

Maternal Employment and Time with Children

Research contradicts the commonsense notion that mothers in the labor force will spend less time with their children (the following is from Kendig and Bianchi, 2008; St. George, 2007). Despite the rapid rise in mothers' labor force participation, mothers' time with children has remained stable over time. Actually, in two-parent families it has increased. In dual-earner families, mothers spend more time with their children than fathers, but the gap is narrowing. Typically, employed fathers of all ages spend 3.0 hours per workday with children under 13 today, compared with 2.0 hours in 1977. For employed mothers of all ages, the time spent with children has remained at 3.8 hours per workday (Families and Work Institute, 2008).

Social Supports for Working Parents

Dual-earner families and single-parent families (the subjects of the next section) share a common problem—the lack of adequate social supports in the community and workplace to ease the strains of their dual roles of workers and parents. In general, U.S. society is unresponsive to the needs of working parents. Single women especially need supplementary help, such as subsidies for food, housing, health care, and child care, but the government in recent times has restricted and even denied rather than enlarged such supplementary aid to the poor and the near poor. The Great Recession has further reduced government subsidies to needy families.

Places of work have been slow to respond to the needs of their employees who are or who soon will be parents. The traditional organization of work—an inflexible eight-hour workday—makes it difficult for parents to cope with family problems or the conflicting schedules of family members. Many European countries have some form of "flextime" arrangement that allows workers to meet their family and work obligations, but in the United States only about one in six employees has such an opportunity. About 80 percent of industrialized countries offer *paid* maternity leave to women workers (Canada, for example offers 17 weeks). The United States, in contrast, passed the Family and Medical Leave Act in 1993, which permits up to 12 weeks of *unpaid* leave in companies with more than 50 employees (Heintz and Folbre, 2000:63)

More than two-thirds of all children under the age of five are in a child-care arrangement on a regular basis by someone other than a parent. Many of these children are young, since 75 percent of women go back to work by a child's ninth month. The children may attend day-care centers or nursery schools, go to the home of a provider, or be cared for by a relative, neighbor, or babysitter (Zaslow and Tout, 2002). The crucial question is, What are the effects of child care by someone other than parents on children? The common assumption is that a preschool child deprived of maximum interaction with his or her parents, especially the mother, will be harmed. Because this belief is widely accepted, many working parents feel guilty for their assumed neglect.

The relationship between child care and child development is complex, involving sources within the child (e.g., temperament, impairment), factors in the child's immediate environment (such as the quality of relationships with parents), and factors in the child's larger social environment (e.g., neighborhood). Although this complexity prevents us from gaining a full understanding of the relationship between child care and child development, the cumulative evidence from empirical studies does permit some conclusions (the following is from a thorough review of the research by a panel on child care of the National Research Council, as reported by Hayes et al., 1990:47–144 and Belsky, 1991; for findings from other research, see Burchinal, 1999).

1. Young children need to develop enduring relationships with a limited number of specific individuals, relationships characterized by affection, reciprocal interaction, and responsiveness to the individualized cues of young children.

2. There is a normal tendency for children to form multiple, simultaneous attachments to caregivers.

3. Children can benefit from "multiple mothering" if it provides affection, warmth, responsiveness, and stimulation in the context of enduring relationships with a reasonably small number of caregivers (usually assumed to be five or fewer).

4. For children beginning child care after their first year of life, there is little indication of differences in the mother–child relationship. Children beginning full-time child care within the first year, however, increase the risk of insecurity in their attachments to their mothers, compared to children at home full-time with their mothers.

5. Children reared in child care orient more strongly toward peers and somewhat less strongly toward adults than their home-reared counterparts.

6. Child care does not negatively affect the cognitive development of middle-class children, and it has positive consequences for the intellectual development of low-income children (if the child-care programs emphasize cognitive enrichment, as Head Start does).

7. The overall quality of child care (group size, caregiver/child ratio, caregiver training, and educational material available) is associated with children's cognitive as well as social development.

8. The children who experience quality care in their families and child-care environments have the strongest development. Children from low-income families are the most likely to be found in lower-quality care settings; thus, they experience double jeopardy from encountering stress at home and stress in their care environments.

The most comprehensive research on the effects of day care on children was sponsored by the federal government's National Institute of Child Health and Development. Researchers from 14 universities tracked children from birth to age three, comparing those cared for full-time by their mothers with those spending time in day-care centers for varying amounts of time. Among the findings were that children in day care develop as normally and as quickly as children who stay home with their mothers; and children cared for by adults other than their parents have normal cognitive, linguistic, social, and emotional development (Perry-Jenkins and Turner, 2004; Scarr, 1997).

Thus, we conclude that day care under the right conditions can be a positive experience for children. Over three-fourths of preschoolers are cared for on a regular basis by someone other than the parent. Unfortunately, many of these children are in day-care situations that do not meet the standards that lead to positive experiences for children. A key problem is the hiring and retaining of high-quality, well-trained day-care workers. The problem with most day-care centers is that they are underfunded. The average U.S. child-care worker makes one-third the salary of an elementary school teacher. With pay so low and benefits so meager, the annual day-care worker turnover is relatively high and the training expected of workers prior to being hired is minimal. While hairdressers must attend 1,500 hours of training at an accredited school in order to get a license, only 11 states require child-care providers to have any early childhood training prior to serving children in their homes (Children's Defense Fund, 2002). The result, often, is inadequate care.

What should be done to improve day care for the children of working parents? There are two fundamental policy issues involving child care—should the government intervene with subsidies and standards; and if the solution is governmental, then at what level? Conservatives oppose government intervention for several reasons. Some conservatives oppose the government's subsidization of child care because it encourages mothers to leave their homes and children for the workplace.* The Christian Coalition supports this view and is thus opposed to the funding of child care. Others oppose it because of higher taxes. Still others fear government intervention in what they consider issues best left to individual families and the marketplace. Progressives argue that the United States provides the least assistance to working parents and their children of any industrialized nation (Helburn, 1999). As a result, many of our children are neglected. And, as usual, the neglect is correlated with social class, as the affluent can afford the best care for their children and the poor cannot.

The second issue—whether the federal or state governments should help to fund child care—also divides conservatives and progressives. Conservatives seek governmental help at the local and state levels because they fear federal bureaucracy and the universal standards that may not apply to local conditions. Progressives, on the other hand, argue for federal programs because they will ensure that every child, regardless of location, will receive approximately the same benefits. If left to the states, some legislatures and governors will be generous while others will do little, if anything, to provide benefits to the children of working parents. For example, in 2007 New York, Georgia, and Oklahoma had programs that were available to all four-year-olds in participating school districts, irrespective of family income (Eitzen and Sage, 2009:78). But other states provide only minimum help, and some states

---

*There is a major contradiction among conservatives on this point. On the one hand, they strongly favor incentives to encourage middle-class women to forgo employment while their children are young, so that they can care for them at home. At the same time, conservatives approve of government policies such as eliminating welfare to poor mothers (Aid to Families with Dependent Children) and forcing them into the labor force in spite of inadequate provision of early child care (Helburn, 1999:9).

do not provide any assistance for preschool education. Thus, if left to the individual states, the benefits to children will be very uneven at best.

Single Parents and Their Children

About one-fourth of all U.S. children live with just one parent, up from 12 percent in 1970. The disproportionate number of single-parent families headed by a woman is a consequence, first, of the relatively high divorce rate and the very strong tendency for divorced and separated women to have custody of the children. Second, there is the relatively high rate of never-married mothers (in 1960, 5 percent of U.S. babies were born to unmarried mothers; in 2007, 40 percent were). To counter the common myths, the facts indicate that more than three-fourths of out-of-wedlock births are to women 20 and older. Moreover, while the *unwed birth rate* for African Americans and Latinos is higher than for Whites, there are *more unwed births* among Whites than among African Americans and Latinos.

The important question to answer concerning this trend is, What are the effects on children living in mother-only families? Research has shown consistently that children from single-parent homes are more likely than children from intact families to have behavioral problems. McLanahan and Booth's (1991) review of the research on children from mother-only families, compared to children from two-parent families, shows the following:

- They have lower academic achievement. This relationship is more negative for boys than for girls.
- They are more likely to have higher absentee rates at school.
- They are more likely to drop out of school.
- They are more likely to have lower earnings in young adulthood and are more likely to be poor.
- They are more likely to marry early and to have children early, both in and out of marriage.
- If they marry, they are more likely to divorce.
- They are more likely to commit delinquent acts and to engage in drug and alcohol use.

Although these findings are relevant, showing that children of single-parent families are more at risk than children from families with both parents present, most adjust normally. A review of the research concludes the following:

> Most children who experience living in a single-parent family do not get pregnant, drop out of school, or require treatment from a mental health professional.... Such evidence is an important reminder that most children are resilient in coping. Thus, it seems clear that the majority of children from single-parent families proceed along a relatively healthy child development trajectory as measured by key indicators of their academic, social, and psychological adjustment. (Martin et al., 2004:285)

Because 85 percent of one-parent families are headed by a woman, the common explanation for the disproportionate pathologies found among the children of single parents has been that the absence of a male adult is detrimental to their development.

The presence of both mothers and fathers contributes to the healthy development of children (Marsiglio et al., 2001). Also, the absence of a spouse makes coping with parenting more difficult. Coping is difficult for any single parent—female or male—because of three common sources of strain: (1) responsibility overload, in which single parents make all the decisions and provide for all of their family's needs; (2) task overload, in which the demands of work, housekeeping, and parenting can be overwhelming for one person; and (3) emotional overload, in which single parents must always be on call to provide the necessary emotional support (see Box 9.5). Clearly, when two persons share these parental strains, it is more likely that the needs of the children will be met.

The children of a single parent, whether living with their mother or father, can have emotional difficulties because they have experienced the stress, often traumatic, that accompanied their separation from or even the death of one of their parents.

Another reason for the disproportionate behavioral problems seen among children living in one-parent families is that their families, for economic reasons, move more often than two-parent families. Moving is a source of emotional strain as old friends are left behind and children experience social isolation in the new setting.

The stress that mothers face also can have negative effects on their children. Changes in residence require that they, too, leave their social networks and sources of support. These moves are sometimes to disadvantaged neighborhoods, with high rates of crime, poverty, and unemployment, and poor educational facilities. Often mothers in this situation must enter the labor force for the first time or increase their working hours. Such changes add stress to their lives as well as to the lives of their children.

Although the factors just described help to explain the behavioral differences between children from one-parent and two-parent homes, they sidestep a major reason—a fundamental difference in economic resources. As Andrew Cherlin has argued, "it seems likely that the most detrimental aspect of the absence of fathers from one-parent families headed by women is not the lack of a male presence *but the lack of a male income*" (Cherlin, 1981:81; emphasis added). There is a strong likelihood that women raising children alone will be financially troubled (there are exceptions, of course—especially for college educated women who, although not married, have chosen to have children). In 2007, for example, 28 percent of children living in single-parent families headed by a woman were poor, compared with 5 percent of children in two-parent families (DeNavas-Walt et al., 2008).

The reasons for a disproportionate number of poor mother-headed families are obvious. First, many single mothers are young and never married. They may have little education, so if they work, they have poorly paid jobs. Second, many divorced or separated women have not been employed for years and find it difficult to reenter the job market. Third, and more crucial, jobs for women, centered as they are in the bottom tier of the segmented job market, are poorly paid (women, we must again underscore, presently earn about 78 cents for every dollar earned by men). Fourth, half of the men who owe child support do not pay all that they owe, and a quarter of them do not pay anything; those women who do receive child support find that the amount covers less than half the actual cost of raising a child.

The economic plight of single-parent families is much worse for families of color. Women of color who head households have the same economic problems as White women who are in the same situation, plus the added burdens of institutional racism. In addition, they are less likely to be getting child support (their exhusbands, unlike White exhusbands, are much more likely to be poor and unemployed), and they are more likely to have been high school dropouts, further reducing their potential for earning a decent income.

Inside the Worlds of Diverse **Families**

A Single Mother with Children Struggles to Make Ends Meet

Regina Johnson's children are her alarm clock, and they start ringing too early most mornings.

"Mom, I'm hungry!"

"Mom, look what Mark did!"

Such cries punctuate her mornings starting around 8 a.m.

The single mother of three young children would like to stay in bed a while longer, after working until midnight and getting to sleep about 2 a.m.

Instead, Johnson asks what the children want for breakfast and heads to the kitchen. Then it's time to bathe and dress everyone before cleaning their modest central Denver apartment.

The inevitable rough moments of the day crop up: red Kool-Aid spills on the worn carpet. The kids fight over a toy and cry.

All the while, Johnson worries about making ends meet on her $5-an-hour salary as a printer's assistant for Communications Packaging, Inc.

"It's not easy and sometimes I feel like I want to fall apart," said Johnson, 24. "But the kids are here and I know I have to keep them going and keep a roof over their heads."

Michael, 3, nestles his head in his mother's lap in the mid-summer heat.

"He's still kind of sick, and when he's sick, he lays around all day," she says.

Johnson worries about how Michael, Mark, 2, and Paula, 1, will turn out. She acknowledges it's hard to find the energy to play with them as much as she would like.

She feels they will drift toward drugs or crime. Or that they'll grow into the type of kids "who just don't care."

She wonders if they'll be more financially secure than she has been. Johnson would like to buy a savings bond for each child. But money is too tight.

Last month, she mailed the rent about a week late. She can't afford a phone. She's bought herself only one new outfit since the kids were born.

"I don't have a checking account," Johnson said, "I live from paycheck to paycheck. I keep enough to get us by through the week."

She was receiving child-support payments from the children's father. But when he quit his job recently, the $114-a-month checks stopped.

Still, Johnson said he helps out when he can and takes the children sometimes on weekends.

Johnson left home and school in eighth grade because she said her father threatened her. She lived for a while with an uncle, and then with the children's father, whom she never married. When they split, she landed on welfare for brief stints.

"It made me feel like a prisoner," she said. "It wasn't for me. I can't sit around all day. I have to go to work and make my own money."

Besides, Johnson didn't want her children teased as "welfare kids."

She went back to school, earned her General Educational Development degree, and found her first job paying more than minimum wage.

"I was so excited. I felt like things were turning around. It was neat."

But her next thought was where she would find an affordable babysitter. Relatives agreed to watch the children for $5 each per day.

Paula, just up from a nap, comes to sit on her mother's lap.

"I want her to grow up and be a model, lead a glamorous life, wear nice clothes, and see different parts of the world," says Johnson, stroking her daughter's hair. "I don't want her to have kids until she's 25."

And she wants all her kids to finish high school.

"If something happened to one of my kids, I'd go crazy. I don't think I could handle it. I guess I'm real protective."

When she grows depressed over financial matters or the condition of her house, Johnson says the children are her best tonic.

"I got in a better mood after I started playing with them," she says of one recent bout of depression. "They were making me laugh."

Source: Cantwell, Rebecca (1989). "It's Not Easy." *Rocky Mountain News* (August 28): 43.

The financial difficulties of women heads of households are sometimes alleviated in part by support from a kinship network. Relatives may provide child care, material goods, money, and emotional support. The kin network is an especially important source of emergency help for African Americans, but for many women, kin may not be near or helpful.

In summary, the behavioral social costs attributed to the children of single mothers, noted earlier, are, in large part, the result of living in poverty. Lack of income has negative effects on intellectual development and physical health (Guo and Harris, 2000). Living in poverty translates into huge negatives for single mothers and their children—differences in health care (including prenatal and postnatal care), diet, housing, neighborhood safety, and quality of schools, as well as economic disadvantages, leading to a greater probability of experiencing low self-esteem, hopelessness, and despair.

 ## Reprise: The Duality of Parenting

How desirable are children? In the not-too-distant past children were an asset to their families as they worked in the fields, for merchants, or in the shops of their parents. Not too long ago adult children provided a form of retirement insurance by taking care of their elderly parents. However, as we have shifted from an agrarian society to an industrial society and then to a highly technological information/service economy, children are no longer the economic assets they once were. Now they are an economic liability. Moreover, children now often hinder the career aspirations of their mothers, and they can reduce marital happiness. The information in this chapter has focused on the reality of modern parenting, with its risks and liabilities. We should not forget, however, that most adults want children; most adults cherish and celebrate their children. They are fulfilled through parenting. Sylvia Hewlett, upon the birth of her daughter, Emma, penned the following poem, which enunciates what her child means to her and the value of children even in a contemporary world where they no longer are economic assets:

> I glory in her gummy grin which lights up the whole world,
>   and her infectious giggle.
> When she lets loose that bubbling crescendo of pure joy,
>   I stop whatever I am doing and allow it to wash over me.
> Such unstinting, unedited delight cleanses the soul.
>   . . .
> I am deeply grateful for this bonus child,
>   for Emma brings with her special joys and special responsibilities.
> In midlife I am much more in touch with that which is miraculous
>   and glorious in a new life.
> But I am also more in touch with the awesome risks—hers
>   and mine.
> Some are straightforward enough;
> Emma can choke on a pea or drown in three inches of bathwater.
> Others are more complicated.
> I now have another hostage to fortune,
>   one more life that is more precious than my own. And I now know what
>   that means.
> It means a loss of freedom. It means dealing with an undertow of care
>   and anxiety that permeates every hour of every day.
> For I know full well that if I fail to keep my children safe, I will not find life
>   worth living.
> One thing is clear, the loss of freedom is a small price to pay for this, most
>   sublime of earthly connections.

Being a parent, cherishing a child, brings out the better angels of human
nature, drawing upon our most selfless instincts.
For myself it has brought a measure of wisdom, and a great deal of happiness.
(excerpted from Hewlett and West, 1998:xvi–xvii)

Chapter Review

1. Parenting roles by gender—aside from conception, childbirth, and nursing—are not based on biological imperatives. Styles of parenting, expectations of parenting, and behaviors associated with parenting are social constructions, resulting from historical, economic, and social forces.

2. The various aspects of childhood vary by time, place, and social location. Hence, it is a social construction.

3. The long-term fertility rate has declined steadily since 1800. The reasons for the low rate now are (a) marrying late, (b) a high divorce rate, (c) a majority of women in the labor force, (d) two incomes required for many couples to maintain a desired lifestyle, (e) delayed childbearing, and (f) legal abortions.

4. Fertility rates vary consistently by social class and race/ethnicity. The higher the social class, the lower the fertility. In terms of race/ethnicity, Whites have the lowest fertility, followed in order by Asian Americans, African Americans, and Latinos.

5. Those women who chose to remain childless are typically well educated and in professional careers.

6. The availability of reproductive techniques has fundamentally changed the ways families are created. Infertile and same-sex couples have several options for becoming parents other than adoption—artificial insemination, in vitro fertilization, surrogate mothering, and fertilizing drugs.

7. Two factors account for couples delaying childbearing: the increased age of first marriage and the likelihood of highly educated women launching careers before having children.

8. Lesbian and gay parents create and maintain families that thrive even in hostile environments, thus illustrating human agency and that families are socially constructed.

9. The addition of a child affects a marriage dramatically. This event affects the career patterns of parents, the patterns of housework, the distribution of power, marital satisfaction, and the economic well-being of the family.

10. Parenting is gendered, with mothers the primary physical and emotional caregivers. Power tends to become more patriarchal with parenthood.

11. The prevailing view is that parents of young children are all-powerful, shaping their children irreversibly. Although parents are powerful socializing agents, they are not omnipotent for these reasons: (a) The child is an active social being who often shapes the parents; (b) the structure of the family (i.e., two parents, a solo parent [if so, whether that parent is the same sex as the child], ordinal position, and the presence of siblings) affects children and parents in predictable ways; (c) extrafamilial caregivers influence children; (d) peers become increasingly important socializers, especially in adolescence; and (e) social class position determines the child's life chances as well as the child's experiences.

12. Most children live in dual-earner families. The effects of extrafamilial child care are complex and depend on a number of variables: attentiveness and affection of caregivers, the ratio of caregivers to children, the small number of caregivers available, group size, and the availability of stimulating materials. Children from low-income families are the most likely to be found in lower-quality care settings.

13. More than one-fourth of all families with children under age 18 are headed by single parents, and these families are almost always headed by women. Children living in mother-only families (especially boys) are negatively affected in school performance, delinquent behaviors, early marriage, and divorce. These negative probabilities are the likely result of (a) single parents being strained by parental responsibilities, tasks, and emotional overload; (b) children being separated from one of their parents; (c) emotional strains resulting from moving away from friends and neighbors; (d) strains the mothers feel in the labor force; and, most important, (e) economic deprivation.

14. The majority of single mothers have inadequate economic resources. Thus, the social costs attributed to single mothers and their children are largely the costs of poverty.

Key Terms

boomerang generation   311

differential fertility   300

pronatalism   301

sandwich generation   311

Related Websites

http://www.bls.gov/nls/nlsresch.htm

National Longitudinal Surveys. Managed by the U.S. Department of Labor, Bureau of Labor Statistics, this site provides links to numerous government reports regarding youth and employment.

http://www.childrensdefense.org

Children's Defense Fund. CDF began in 1973 and is a private, nonprofit organization supported by foundation and corporate grants and individual donations. CDF advocates for all children, with a special focus on the most vulnerable. It works with elected officials, government agencies, faith groups, and individual activists in an effort to build a nation of families where all children have the support they need to thrive.

http://www.childrennow.org

Children Now. Since 1988, Children Now has championed the needs of children with a successful combination of research and advocacy. Children Now is unique in its bipartisan, strategic advocacy on behalf of the whole child. Children Now is often sought after by policy-makers, the media, business leaders, academics, and parents for its high-quality research and sharp analysis of the full spectrum of matters affecting children. The organization pioneered an annual Report Card on the status of California's children—a publication that has been duplicated in every state, in addition to Puerto Rico and the Virgin Islands. And its Fall Colors reports are the most comprehensive research studies on prime time television diversity.

http://www.childstats.gov

ChildStats.gov. This website provides government statistics and reports on children and their families, especially from the Interagency Forum on Child and Family Statistics.

http://www.childtrends.org

Child Trends. Founded in 1979, Child Trends is a nonprofit, nonpartisan research organization dedicated to improving the lives of children by conducting research and providing science-based information to improve the decisions, programs, and policies that affect children and their families. In advancing its mission, Child Trends collects and analyzes data; conducts, synthesizes, and disseminates research; designs and evaluates programs; and develops and tests promising approaches to research in the field.

http://www.futureofchildren.org

The Future of Children. The Future of Children is a publication of The Woodrow Wilson School of Public and International Affairs at Princeton University and The Brookings Institution. The organization seeks to promote effective policies and programs for children by providing policy-makers, service providers, and the media with timely, objective information based on the best available research.

http://www.pactadopt.org

Pact: An Adoption Alliance. Pact is a nonprofit organization founded in 1991. Pact's goal is to create and maintain the Internet's most comprehensive site addressing issues for adopted children of color, offering informative articles on related topics as well as profiles of triad members and their families, links to other Internet resources, and a book reference guide with a searchable database. The site provides reprints of past Pact Press issues, as well as opportunities to interact with other triad members and to ask questions of birth parents, adopted people, adoptive parents, and adoption professionals.

http://www.adoption.com

adoption.com. This commercial website offers visitors a comprehensive array of information, discussion rooms, and links to relevant sites on every aspect of adoption.

http://www.cfw.tufts.edu

Child and Family WebGuide. This website is provided by Tufts University and is a nonprofit resource. This directory describes trustworthy websites on topics of interest to parents and professionals. All the sites listed on the WebGuide have been systematically evaluated by graduate students and faculty in child development. These sites have been selected from thousands that are available on the Web, based primarily on the quality of the information they provide. The goal of the WebGuide is to give the public easy access to the best child development information on the Web.

http://surrogacy.com

The American Surrogacy Center, Inc. TASC promotes the exchange of information on medical and pharmaceutical treatments, surrogacy alternatives, current legal status, counseling, medical and legal practitioners, agencies and similar societies, as well as providing a forum for those requesting and providing information.

http://www.plannedparenthood.org

Planned Parenthood. Planned Parenthood Federation of America, Inc. (PPFA), is the nation's largest and most trusted voluntary reproductive health care organization. This website is coordinated through PPFA and 48 affiliated Planned Parenthood organizations for the purpose of providing streamlined access to the complete array of sexual and reproductive health information, services, and advocacy and volunteer opportunities available from Planned Parenthood entities nationwide.

http://www.aclu.org/lbgt/parenting

American Civil Liberties Union: Lesbian and Gay Rights: Parenting. Managed by the ACLU, this site provides up-to-date reports and publications regarding lesbian and gay parenting issues and rights across the nation.

http://www.fathers.com

fathers.com. Fathers.com is the premier online resource for everyday dads. Created by the National Center for Fathering (NCF), fathers.com provides research-based training, practical tips and resources to inspire and equip men to be the involved fathers, grandfathers, and father figures that children need.

http://www.fatherhood.org

National Fatherhood Initiative. NFI encourages and supports family and father-friendly policies, develops national public education campaigns to highlight the importance of fathers in the lives of their children, provides motivation for national and local coalition-building, and provides resources to men to help them be better dads.

http://www.fathersnetwork.org

Fathers Network. The Fathers Network provides current information and resources to assist all families and care providers involved in the lives of children with special needs. The Fathers Network is a program of the Kindering Center and is sponsored by Children with Special Health Care Needs Program/Washington State Department of Health, the Paul G. Allen Charitable Foundation, and private donations.

http://www.familyeducation.com

Family Education Network. Launched in 1996 as the first parenting site on the Web, FamilyEducation has become the Internet's most-visited site for parents who are involved, committed, and responsive to their families' needs. Parents find practical guidance, grade-specific information about their children's school experience, strategies to get involved with their children's learning, free e-mail newsletters, and fun and entertaining family activities. FamilyEducation brings together leading organizations from both the public and private sectors to help parents, teachers, schools, and community organizations use online tools and other media resources to positively affect children's education and overall development.

http://www.aecf.org

Annie E. Casey Foundation. Since 1948, the Annie E. Casey Foundation (AECF) has worked to build better futures for disadvantaged children and their families in the United States. The primary mission of the Foundation is to foster public policies, human service reforms, and community supports that more effectively meet the needs of today's vulnerable children and families.

http://www.fci.org

Family Communications. Family Communications, Inc., is a nonprofit organization founded in 1971 by Fred Rogers, as the production company for Mister Roger's Neighborhood. It creates programs and projects for children, their families, and those who support them. Respect for healthy emotional, social, and intellectual development is its core mission. It develops projects in all media, provides education and training for people who work with young children, and consults on issues that affect families.

Violence in Families

▶ Myths and Realities

Myth	The problem of intimate partner violence affects women and men equally. Women and men are equally likely to be abused by their partners.
Reality	According to the U.S. Department of Justice, men are perpetrators in 80 percent of domestic assaults.
Myth	Domestic violence is usually a one-time event, an isolated incident.
Reality	Battering is a pattern in a relationship. Once violence begins, it generally becomes a pattern that is repeated and may escalate.
Myth	Domestic violence, child abuse, and elder abuse occur only in poor, poorly educated, and minority families.
Reality	Domestic violence, child abuse, and elder abuse occur throughout society. Intimate violence is more likely to occur in lower-income and minority households; "violence and abuse, however, are not confined to the poor or blacks" (Gelles and Straus, 1988:43). Physical violence happens in rich, White, educated, and "respectable" families as well as in poor, non-White, and uneducated families.
Myth	Wife batterers and child abusers are mentally ill.
Reality	A small percentage of abusers are mentally ill. "In fact, only about 10 percent of abusive incidents are caused by mental illness. The remaining 90 percent are not amenable to psychological explanations" (Gelles and Straus, 1988:43).
Myth	Battered women stay in violent relationships. If they wanted to leave, they could just pack up and go somewhere else.
Reality	Many abused women do leave their partners permanently despite the fact that leaving may put them in increased danger. Abusive partners may stalk or threaten a woman who tries to leave. Assailants deliberately isolate their partners and deprive them of jobs and opportunities for acquiring education and job skills. This, combined with unequal opportunities for women in general and lack of affordable child care, makes it extremely difficult for women to leave. Despite these obstacles and dangers, many battered women leave their abusers permanently.
Myth	Children who are abused grow up to be abusers.
Reality	There is a greater likelihood that abused children will grow up to be abusive, but "there is absolutely no evidence to support the claim that people who are abused are preprogrammed to grow up to be abusers" (Gelles and Straus, 1988:49).
Myth	Family violence is a minor problem, overall. The instances are few and isolated.
Reality	According to the U.S. Department of Justice, more than 600,000 violent crimes were committed against intimate partners in 2007 (Rand, 2008). Violence in a family context is a substantial threat for couples, children, and the elderly.

The family has two faces. It can be a haven from an uncaring, impersonal world and a place where serenity, love, and security prevail. The family members love each other unconditionally, care for each other, and accept each other. The family provides its members with emotional support; stability; the necessities of food, clothing, and shelter; and the tools to fit into society.

But there is also a dark side of the family. The family is a common context for violence in society. "People are more likely to be killed, physically assaulted, sexually victimized, hit, beat up, slapped, or spanked in their own homes by other family members than anywhere else, or by anyone else, in our society" (Gelles, 1995:450). Statistics on the incidence of family violence in the United States are a matter of social concern. Around 1.5 million women are raped and/or physically assaulted by an intimate partner every year (Tjaden and Thoennes, 2000). Child protective agencies document between 800,000 and 900,000 cases of confirmed child maltreatment every year (U.S. Department of Health and Human Services [U.S. DHHS], 2009). Approximately 450,000 elderly individuals experience abuse and/or neglect in home settings (U.S. Administration on Aging, 1998). The incidence of fatal family violence is noteworthy. More than one in four murders involve family members; half of these involve the use of a firearm (Durose et al., 2005).

Family violence is a relatively new area of research in the field of family social science. It is only since the 1970s that family violence began to be viewed as a social problem in the United States. Sociologists Richard Gelles and Murray Straus were lead researchers on two large-scale national surveys in 1975 and 1985 that mapped the contours of domestic violence in this society. Analyses by Gelles, Straus, and their fellow researchers continue to be widely utilized by current researchers and practitioners in this field. In recent years, scores of additional studies—both quantitative and qualitative in method—have increased our knowledge base dramatically.

Despite more and better data on family violence than in the recent past, the subject remains difficult to examine. This is likely, in part, because we prefer to picture the family "as an arena for love and gentleness rather than a place for violence" (Steinmetz and Straus, 1974:3). Yet the facts of family life in U.S. society cannot be ignored. To disregard them would be to present an inaccurate and unrealistic view of families.

We begin with a discussion of how the phenomenon of family violence is related to violence in the larger society. This sets the macro context for understanding violence in micro settings. We then turn our attention to three main categories of abuse in family relationships: intimate partner violence, child abuse, and elder abuse. For each of these types of family violence, we will consider the incidence, contexts for, and consequences of violence in a family setting.

Families in a Violent Society

One sociological truism is that each of society's institutions (e.g., the polity, economy, education, religion, sport, and family) is a microcosm of the larger society. Each mirrors society and in its own way contributes to the reinforcement of those practices and beliefs that give society its uniqueness. Thus, in our investigation of violence in the family, we must be aware that families do not exist in a vacuum but are shaped by the history, culture, and distribution of power in society. Our thesis is that U.S. society has always manifested and glorified violence. This is not to say that American society is always violent. We argue, however, that society—like the family—has two faces.

America: a symbol of freedom and discussion, rational thought, tolerance of new ideas, equality and justice for all. America: a symbol of violent brawls, unrestrained vigilante activity, forcible suppression of political dissidents or "undesirables," racist attitudes. (Iglitzen, 1972:144)

U.S. Violence Rates in Comparative Perspective

Elliott Currie, the esteemed criminologist, says: "What most distinguishes America from other developed countries is the extent to which Americans are willing to rob, maim, kill, and rape one another" (1998:116). The murder and rape rates in the United States, for example, are at least four times that of other advanced industrial nations. Currie (1998:120–149) suggests several root causes for the disturbingly high levels of violence in the United States, compared to other developed nations.

- Children and families in the United States are far more likely to be poor, and, if they are poor, are more likely to be extremely poor. The links between disadvantage and violence are strongest for the poorest and most neglected of the poor.

- The poor and near-poor receive fewer government benefits to offset problems such as health care and child care. This represents a crucial difference in the United States, compared to its counterparts—our willingness to tolerate extremes of deprivation and social insecurity rather than a sense of collective responsibility for the well-being of others (see Chapter 13).

- Economic inequality combined with racial or ethnic discrimination leads to higher rates of violent crime in the United States.

Institutionally Sanctioned Violence

Violence is promoted in a number of important areas of society. Historically, violence between family members has been legitimized by the law.

In 1824, the Mississippi Supreme Court was the first of several states to grant husbands immunity from assault and battery charges for moderately chastising their wives. Such legal support can be traced back to English common law, which gave husbands the right to strike their wives with sticks no wider than their thumbs—hence the classic "rule of thumb." Similarly, historical evidence indicates legal precedents allowing for the mutilation, striking, and even killing of children as part of the legal parental prerogative. (Gelles, 1990:106)

Although the legal system no longer legitimizes wife beating and child abuse, the criminal justice system often looks the other way. The police and the courts often err on the side of nonintervention. The commonly held assumption is that the privacy of marriage should be upheld.

There are other institutional supports for violence in society as well. Some of these are as follows:

- Congress has rarely limited the right of citizens to own guns, despite evidence that the easy availability of guns, especially handguns, is directly correlated with the murder rate. The result is that approximately 240 million guns are owned by U.S. citizens.

- Corporal punishment—the intentional use of physical force as a method of changing behavior—is widely used by U.S. parents and is legal in every state.

Corporal punishment has become controversial, with 24 countries—ranging from Germany and Sweden to New Zealand and Costa Rica—banning it altogether.

- In education, the U.S. Supreme Court ruled in 1977 that teachers had the right to use corporal punishment if their state legislatures approve. Use of the paddle in schools is legal in 21 states. Paddling in schools is permitted in only two developed nations: the United States and Australia (Dobbs, 2004). A wide-ranging group of professional organizations including the American Academy of Pediatrics, the American Bar Association, and the National Education Association support banning the practice of physically punishing children and youth in schools (Greydanus et al., 2003).

- Schools also promote aggressive, violent sports. The sport with the largest budget and most participation is boys' football. Heavy-contact sports like football are organized around violence. In this sport, players are explicitly taught to be "hitters." Physical aggression produces success on the field and raises a player's status among his peers. The primary long-range concern about sports centered on brutal bodily contact is this: "By applying lessons learned in sports, athletes may perceive violence and intimidation as acceptable means of achieving off-the-field goals and solving problems unrelated to sports" (Kreager, 2007:708).

- Religion, too, supports violence. The Bible states, "He who spares the rod hates his son, but he who loves him is diligent to discipline him" (Proverbs 13.24, Revised Standard Version).

Violence in the Media

TELEVISION AND MOVIES

Violence is glorified both in the movies and on television. The total number of violent acts children view on television over the course of their childhood is staggering. The American Psychiatric Association calculates that by age 18, the average American child will have seen 16,000 simulated murders and 200,000 acts of violence (cited in Brown and Bzostek, 2003:2).

Many studies link exposure to media violence and negative outcomes (both long-term and short-term) for children. Research finds increased aggressive behavior and attitudes, fears or pessimistic attitudes about the world, and desensitization to violence to be correlated with exposure to media violence. Children who identify with aggressive television characters have been found to be more likely to be aggressive as adults. In addition, increased depression, nightmares, and sleep disturbances are associated with viewing media violence (Brown and Bzostek, 2003:2).

PORNOGRAPHY

The widespread dissemination of pornography (a $13 billion industry) is believed to encourage male dominance. A central feature of pornography is the conflation of sex and violence.

> Pornography sexualizes rape, battery, sexual harassment, prostitution, and child sexual abuse; it thereby celebrates, promotes, authorizes, and legitimizes them. More generally, it eroticizes the dominance and submission that is the dynamic common to them all. (MacKinnon, 2007:376)

MUSIC

The lyrics of some popular music, especially rap music, "celebrate violence and contempt for women and legal authority" (Bogart, 2005:243). The Recording Industry Association of America (RIAA) justifies the marketing of music with obscene lyrics by providing parents of today's youth with this explanation: "[This music] scares some parents because of the sexually explicit themes, violence, and strong language so readily available.... Every generation throws a hero up the pop charts, every generation rebels. Your parents didn't like or understand The Who or Jimi Hendrix; you don't like or understand much of your children's music" (cited in Bogart, 2005:252).

VIDEO GAMES

The U.S. home video game industry is huge ($18 billion in 2007). The theme of many of these games is violence.

> Also cause for concern is that video games have become increasingly interactive and incredibly realistic. When a child plays a "first-shooter" game, for example, he not only witnesses graphic violence, he *becomes* the perpetrator. As one retired military officer reports in the film *Game Over*, some of these games are so effective in teaching people how to kill that the army uses them to train soldiers. (O'Toole et al., 2007:298)

LITERATURE AND FOLKLORE

Violence has always been a dominant theme in American literature and folklore. Children's stories and even nursery rhymes are often quite violent. Consider the following familiar examples that describe spouse abuse, child abuse, and elder abuse, respectively:

Peter, Peter, Pumpkin Eater,
had a wife and couldn't keep her;
He put her in a pumpkin shell,
and there he kept her very well.

There was an old woman who lived in a shoe.
She had so many children she didn't know what to do.
She gave them some broth without any bread;
She whipped them all soundly and put them to bed.

Lizzie Borden took an ax
and gave her father forty whacks.
When the job was neatly done
she gave her mother forty-one.

It is important to note that the empirical research linking violent behavior to watching violent movies, playing violent video games, or watching violent pornography is inconclusive. Thus, real-world violence cannot be directly blamed on the media, but media violence is nonetheless socially significant. It desensitizes its observers to the consequences of violence. And perhaps most importantly, it provides continuing evidence that the use of violence is acceptable in this society.

Customs and Beliefs

Many customs and beliefs support violence. For example, males are socialized to be dominant. Parents often encourage their sons to be aggressive. The overwhelming proportion of American parents consider it part of their role to train sons to be tough. They want their boys to play aggressive sports where they have to hit and be hit. Also, boys are encouraged to not back down when challenged.

Adults in our society consider it normal to discipline children by hitting them. Gelles and Straus, the acknowledged experts on abuse in families, say that

in general, the large majority of Americans believes that good parenting requires some physical punishment. Over and over again, when we interview parents about hitting their children, we are told that kids "deserve to be hit" or "need to be hit." Among the thousands of people we have interviewed, it was absence of physical punishment that was thought to be deviant, not the hitting of children. (Gelles and Straus, 1988:27)

In short, our society accepts physical punishment in the family as "normal violence."

Violence and the Social Organization of the Family

Although the family is based on love among its members, the way it is organized encourages conflict (the following is taken from Gelles and Straus, 1979, 1988; Rouse, 1997). First, the family, like all other social organizations, is a power system; that is, power is unequally distributed between parents and children and between spouses, with the male parent typically dominant.

Male dominance has been perpetuated by the legal system and religious teachings. Threats to male dominance are often resisted through violence. Parents have authority over their children. They feel they have the right to punish children in order to shape them in the ways the parents consider important. Also, because marriage is between a woman and a man, this sets the stage for a "battle of the sexes." This may not present a problem in some homes, where there is a basic agreement on gender roles, but for many couples these problems are a constant source of stress. Gelles and Straus summarize the importance of this dimension for understanding family violence:

> The greater the inequality, the more one person makes all the decisions and has all the power, the greater the risk of violence. Power, power confrontations, and perceived threats to domination, in fact, are underlying issues in almost all acts of family violence. (Gelles and Straus, 1988:82)

Unlike most organizations, in which activities and interests are relatively narrow, the family encompasses almost everything. Thus, there are more "events" over which a dispute can develop. Closely related to this phenomenon is the vast amount of time in each day that family members spend interacting. This lengthy interaction increases the probability of disagreements, irritations, violations of privacy, and the like, which increase the risk of violence.

Not only is the range of activities greater in the family than in other social organizations, but the feelings are also more intense. As Gelles and Straus have put it:

> There is ... a greater intensity of involvement in family conflict. Love, paradoxically, gives the power to hurt. So, the degree of distress felt in conflicts with other family members is likely to be much greater than if the same issue were to arise in relation to someone outside the family. (Gelles and Straus, 1979:35)

Family privacy is another characteristic that enhances the likelihood of violence. The rule in our society that the home is private has two negative consequences. First, it insulates family members from the protection that society can provide if another family member becomes abusive. Second, privacy often prevents the victims of abuse from seeking outside help.

Intimate Partner Violence

Violence between husbands and wives, cohabiting partners, and dating couples in the form of beating, slapping, kicking, and rape is relatively common in U.S. society. That such violence occurs between persons whose relationship is supposedly based on mutual love and affection is puzzling indeed.

Intimate partner violence is difficult to define. Researchers simply cannot agree on a common definition. As a result, estimations of this phenomenon vary. The estimates of the incidence of intimate partner violence provided here use the definition used in the National Violence Against Women (NVAW) Survey. This survey, undertaken by the National Institute of Justice and the Centers for Disease Control and Prevention (CDC), is a comprehensive national study of intimate partner violence with a nationally representative sample of 8,000 women. The NVAW Survey defines intimate partner violence to include rape, physical assault, and stalking perpetrated by current and former spouses, cohabiting partners, and dating partners (Tjaden and Thoennes, 2000:5).

The development of the term "intimate partner violence" is noteworthy. Early research and writing in this field centered on violence between married partners, so domestic violence was framed as "wife abuse" or "spouse abuse." As the research literature expanded, however, it became clear that partner violence was an area of concern among cohabiting and dating couples as well. Further, statistics on the rise of cohabitation indicated that a significant proportion of U.S. women and men were organizing their intimate relationships outside of marriage. Increasingly, therefore, scholars frame their research questions and practitioners their outreach strategies in terms of the more inclusive "intimate partner violence." In this section, we generally use the term "intimate partner violence," but occasionally refer to "wife abuse."

Conclusions about the incidence of violence among intimate partners vary based on both who is included within the category of intimate partners and what actions are defined as abusive. Some studies continue to focus on married couples while others exclude dating couples. Some include same-sex partners while others do not. Some researchers define domestic violence to include emotional abuse and threats of physical or sexual violence in addition to physical harm. Needless to say, this variation presents obstacles to making comparisons across studies.

Nonetheless, research consistently shows that intimate partner violence is both a pervasive problem in the United States and a serious public health concern. The findings of the National Violence Against Women Survey allow for the following estimates of the scope of the problem:

- Approximately 33 million Americans have been victims of intimate partner violence at some point in their lifetime.

- Every year, around 1.3 million women and more than 800,000 men are physically assaulted by an intimate partner; many of these individuals are victimized repeatedly.

- In comparing the experience of abused women and abused men, we find that abused women are assaulted more frequently and are more likely to be injured than are men.

- Injuries inflicted by intimate partners are frequently severe enough to require medical care; approximately 550,000 female victims and 125,000 male victims require medical treatment every year. (Tjaden and Thoennes, 2000)

Both women and men are victims of intimate partner violence; nonetheless, ample evidence—including the most recent report from the U.S. Department of Justice—documents that a large majority of domestic violence victims are women. This report, titled *Intimate Partner Violence in the United States*, finds that more than 80 percent of the victims of intimate partner violence are women (Catalano, 2007). The discussion that follows focuses on men's abuse of their women partners. We do not intend to negate the existence of physical violence by women, because it does occur; but since the frequency and severity are so much less than in men's attacks on their partners, the experience of abused women is the focus of our attention.

Violence Against Women

As with other forms of family violence, the extent of woman abuse in domestic settings is impossible to know. First, events of a violent nature generally take place in private, with no witnesses other than family members. Second, battered women are often treated by medical professionals who fail to inquire deeply into the cause of their injuries. Third, victims commonly lie about the causes of their injuries because of shame, out of fear of reprisal, or to protect their partners. Last, many victims do not go to public agencies for help because they have found these organizations to be unresponsive. This situation is especially true of the police and the courts. Tjaden and Thoennes (2000) found that only 27 percent of women reported physical assaults by an intimate partner to the police. For nearly all

I never knew reaching out could make such a difference.

Imagine if we all worked to end domestic violence.

Work to End Domestic Violence Today

WORK TO END DOMESTIC VIOLENCE

For help and referrals to resources near you, call 1-800-799-SAFE.

women who failed to report the incident, the reason given was that they did not think the police could do anything about it.

Although we must be concerned about the reliability of the data, the following are the best estimates of the extent of the abuse of women by their partners.

- Approximately 22 percent of women report that they have been physically assaulted by an intimate partner at some time over their lifetime (Tjaden and Thoennes, 2000).
- Women are the victims in 8 of 10 spousal homicides (Durose et al., 2005).
- Every year, more than 1 million women are stalked by intimate partners.
- Native American and African American women report significantly higher rates of intimate violence victimization than do other racial ethnic groups; at the same time, Asian American women report domestic violence at a rate lower than other groups (comparison groups are Hispanic and White).
- A majority of female victims who obtain a temporary restraining order against their intimate partner report that these orders are violated (Tjaden and Thoennes, 2000).

Contexts for Intimate Partner Violence

SOCIAL CLASS

The connection between intimate partner violence and social class is clear. "Irrespective of the method, sample, or research design, studies of marital violence support the hypothesis that spousal violence is more likely to occur in low-income, low-socioeconomic-status families" (Gelles and Cornell, 1990:75). Although battered women are found in all social strata, they tend to be found in families threatened by economic hardships. This relationship is generally viewed as the outcome of the stresses of poverty or the lack of resources. Managing family life in a context that may include, for example, crowded and substandard housing, unstable work, unreliable transportation, and neighborhood crime is difficult. In such situations, domestic violence against women would be viewed as the outcome of the "pileup of stressors" associated with inadequate resources (Fox et al., 2002:794).

Men's unemployment puts their partners at increased risk for abuse (Tjaden and Thoennes, 2000). Unemployment increases economic strain as bills accumulate and debt rises. In addition, unemployment can be devastating for men who believe it is their responsibility to be the primary provider (Gelles and Cornell, 1990:75).

Social class not only affects women's vulnerability to intimate partner violence; it also shapes how they experience that abuse. Poor women experience abuse as part of a larger context of stressful life circumstances. Abuse is not their only or, perhaps, worst problem they are trying to manage. Kimberly Eby (2004) asked women with abusive partners what the most upsetting or stressful situation was that they were coping with at present. More than half of interviewees identified a problem unrelated to their abuse—for example, health problems, problems with children, and financial concerns.

Poverty—which has been shown to increase the likelihood of abuse—also limits women's range of responses to abuse (Coker, 2005:370). Sufficient material resources are key to escaping an abusive situation; alternatively, inadequate material resources are a primary reason women do not separate from an abusive partner. Donna Coker explains, "Separation threatens women's tenuous hold on economic viability, for without the batterer's income or his assistance with childcare, for example, women may lose jobs, housing, and even their children" (p. 374). In addition, poor women who leave a batterer may experience increased physical danger because they cannot afford to hide from him. The arrest of a battering partner may mean he loses his job and stops supporting his children.

Analyses that consider intimate partner violence in the context of social class illustrate the importance of economic resources in constructing women's vulnerability to family violence and finding ways to escape it. Social programs that provide material resources to women who are victims of intimate partner violence will support them in leaving violent relationships (Websdale and Johnson, 2005).

RACE AND ETHNICITY

The National Violence Against Women Survey (Tjaden and Thoennes, 2000) found that 15 percent of Asian American women reported having been victimized by an intimate partner. For White women, the figure was 25 percent, for African Americans 29 percent, for Hispanics 23 percent, and for Native Americans 31 percent. Women of color have higher rates of poverty and, it seems, heightened susceptibility to abuse. We must, however, view the apparent overrepresentation of people of color among the abusers and abused with caution. First, when demographic and socioeconomic factors are controlled, minorities are no more likely than nonminorities to be violent. In other words, racial differences in domestic abuse have less to do with racial patterns than they do with social class (Johnson and Ferraro, 2000). Second, although official reports of abuse indicate that poor and minority families are overrepresented, *these data tend to distort the actual incidence for these categories.* This is because "the poor run the greatest risk of being accurately and inaccurately labeled 'abusers' " (Gelles and Straus, 1988:43). Also, statistics based on police arrest records may overrepresent minorities and the poor because of differential arrest policies (Barnett et al., 1997:195).

Both structural and cultural factors shape the experience of abuse for diverse groups of women. For example, working-class Native American women respond to abuse from a different cultural context than do middle class White women (see Box 10.1).

BOX 10.1 Inside the Worlds of Diverse Families

Examining Navajo Women's Responses to Abuse

The traditions of many native cultures in the United States have strong taboos against spouse, child, or elder abuse, but a variety of circumstances have at least partially contributed to a breakdown in these traditions. Mary J. Rivers cites "the gap in generational teaching caused by forced attendance at boarding schools, the rise of alcohol and drug abuse, rampant unemployment, the growing presence of TV and radio, and the migration of family members away from the homeland" as factors contributing to the present situation in which high rates of violence against Native American women and children have been documented (2005:83).

Rivers interviewed Navajo women who had been victims of family violence, in some cases both as children and adults. From the standpoint of mainstream society, their responses to that violence might be viewed as surprising. The pattern Rivers found was that most women stayed with abusive partners, despite options to do otherwise. "More tellingly, the talk [about] their men showed little anger, hate, resentment, or desire for retribution. They raised the children of adulterous husbands, gave abusers second, third, and tenth chances, and reconciled with violent fathers and molesting uncles" (p. 86).

Rivers contends that Navajo women's responses to experiences of abuse can only be understood in the context of native culture. The following excerpts center on the cultural significance of the Navajo principle of hózhó.

The key to understanding the women's strength lies in part in understanding the principle of hózhó and grasping its pervasiveness into all aspects of the culture. Hózhó is typically translated in English as "beauty," but the Anglo definition doesn't capture the full Navajo meaning. In this case, beauty refers to balance, to harmony, to inner peace, to a cooperative existence of opposites. There is a balance between earth and people, between earth and sky, between animal and human, and between male and female. The

Navajo believe that every man has a bit of the female in him, and every female has a bit of male in her. Both men and women must honor both sides of themselves; they must not deny one or reject it. Beyond this is the demand that men and women must live together, in harmony.

Hózhó helps us understand the Navajo woman's response to abuse in two ways: first it explains her reluctance to leave her partner. It is disruptive of the essence of hózhó. Leaving her partner disobeys the injunction that man and woman stay together. Second, it offers a plausible explanation for her partner's aberrant behavior; he is out of balance, his hózhó is disrupted, and he needs a sing [a Navajo ceremony] to restore harmony. This is not to say that that the abuser is a victim or ill. He is generally presumed to be responsible for his state. It is merely offered as an explanation for his actions and offers a solution: a sing.

The lesson of hózhó is taught in many different ways, all to reinforce the message that balance, family, and tolerance are more valued than personal happiness, wealth, or fame. This includes balancing each person's male and female sides and maintaining the balance and interdependence of the male–female relationship.

It is tempting to view the Navajo woman's response to the violence in her life as an example of victimization. But it is a disservice to the women to simplify their situation thusly. To be a victim, one must feel helpless. The women in this project do not feel helpless. When they talk of being a Navajo woman, they are describing themselves, and the words they use, "strong," "respect," "hard work," "pride," are not descriptive of the downtrodden. The women who collaborated in this study may not be representative of the entire [Navajo] Nation of women, but they provide a good picture of one segment of the population. They show us, that for some women, it is possible to straddle two worlds, to embrace both one's cultural roots and MTV, to live with the detritus of the Anglo culture and transform the experience into a triumph of will. In order to collaborate successfully with the Navajo to eradicate domestic violence among the tribe and to offer the abused the form of support they need, understanding this point is essential.

Source: Rivers, Mary J. (2005). "Navajo Women and Abuse: The Context for Their Troubled Relationships." *Journal of Family Violence* 20 (3):

Another factor that complicates the issue of race and abuse is immigration status. Women who are recent immigrants are generally less likely to acknowledge abuse and reach out for support (Yoshioka et al., 2003). They may hold traditional gender norms that require a woman to be a good wife and mother and sacrifice herself for the cause of family stability. In addition, they may lack English proficiency. Acculturation results in attitudes less supportive of wife-beating among Asian Indians and positively related to seeking help among battered Hispanic women (West et al., 1998, cited in Yoshioka et al., 2003:172). Immigrant status creates special challenges to women in abusive relationships. Increasingly, feminists and others are advocating for culturally sensitive programming and supports for immigrant women.

It is important to recognize that an individual's vulnerability to abuse is shaped not only by her gender but also by her race (Sokoloff and Dupont, 2005:2). Patterns of racial inequality that shape access to good jobs and decent education also shape women's experience with domestic violence. A relevant question is whether abused African American and White women are equally likely to report their victimization to the police. One study found that abused White women in the sample often relied on police assistance, while none of the African American women wanted their partner arrested or jailed (Richie, 2005, cited in Yllo, 2007:620). The possibility of contact with the criminal justice system raised a set of concerns for African American women that simply were not present for most White women.

INDIVIDUAL AND RELATIONAL CHARACTERISTICS

Several individual and relational factors are associated with violence toward women in intimate relationships. These factors help us understand micro level contexts in which partners are or are not abusive.

Alcohol Abuse   The most common trait associated with the abusive treatment of a woman partner is the excessive use of alcohol. The problem with assuming a relationship between alcohol abuse and partner abuse is that the relationship is not causal, but contributory. Put another way, stress may be the antecedent to both drinking and spouse abuse (Barnett et al., 1997:198; Kaukinen, 2004:466).

Occupation   The relationship between men's occupations and domestic violence is essentially related to the concept of spillover (Fox et al., 2002:805; Melzer, 2002:821). Spillover, as discussed in Chapter 6, is the transfer of moods, feelings, and behaviors between work and family settings. Males in two occupations, both violent, are especially prone toward spousal violence. Statistics show that 4 out of 10 police families experience domestic violence, in contrast to 1 out of 10 families in the general population (reported in Sherry, 2001). Similarly, a Defense Department task force found that the number of domestic violence cases in the military was five times higher than in the civilian population (reported in Cockburn, 2002). Possible explanations for this relationship between a violent occupation and domestic violence include the following: (1) These occupations attract and recruit aggressive and controlling personalities, (2) high-stress jobs lead to intemperate acts, and (3) those recruited into these organizations are socialized to solve problems by acting with physical aggression.

Inadequacy of Male Partners   Battering can be generated by a number of problems a man faces in his marriage, his work, or other situations. These may include financial difficulties, sexual dysfunction, and jealousy. Research on husbands known to be wife abusers has also found that these men tend to be underachievers when compared to their wives. They may be less intelligent, less successful in their jobs or school, or lower in certain status characteristics (occupation and education) compared to their wives. The inability to be superior to one's wife in a male-oriented society apparently leads to the desire to prove one's superiority over her in physical ways (Gelles and Cornell, 1990:77).

Emotional Abuse   What is emotional abuse? A range of behaviors—from ridicule and personal put-downs to humiliation and trying to convince someone he or she is crazy—constitutes emotional abuse. In some cases emotional abuse is experienced in the absence of physical violence (Anderson, 2008). In general, however, emotional abuse is linked to patterns of escalating violence, sexual violence, and potentially lethal violence (Drumm et al., 2009:65).

Family History of Abuse   The intergenerational transmission of violence hypothesis states that exposure to violence as a child is related to involvement in violent intimate relationships as an adult (Gover et al., 2008:1668). Research does find that "adolescents or adults who were exposed to violence within their homes are more likely than others to perpetrate intimate partner violence" (Miller and Knudsen, 2007:46). But at the same time, a "violence begets violence" explanation for spouse abuse is oversimplified. Research finds only a weak relationship between growing up in an abusive family and becoming involved in a violent partner relationship. Thus, we conclude "that while growing up in a violent family may put one at risk for using violence as an adult, the relationship is far from absolute. The fact remains that most adults who grow up in violent homes do not become violent adults" (Stith et al., 2000:641; Lackey, 2003).

In sum, a number of variables are associated with wife beating. Gelles and his associates (1994) provide an overall risk profile: (1) male unemployed; (2) male uses illicit drugs at least once a year; (3) male and female have different religious backgrounds; (4) male saw father hit mother; (5) male and female are cohabiting rather than married partners; (6) male has blue-collar occupation, if employed; (7) male has some high school education; (8) male is between 18 and 30 years of age; (9) male or female uses severe violence toward children in home; and (10) total family income is below the poverty line.

> For households with none of the ten risk markers, the rate of male-to-female severe violence was 14 per 1,000; for households with two risk factors, the rate was…35 per 1,000; for households with seven or more risk factors, the rate was 610 per 1,000, more than 17 times the base rate [34 per 1,000]. (Gelles et al., 1994:10)

Types of Partner Violence

Recent years have seen a breakthrough in the conceptualization of intimate partner violence. (The following is from Johnson, 1995, 2008; Johnson and Ferraro, 2000; Johnson and Leone, 2005). Johnson and his colleagues have argued for the importance of distinguishing between two types of violence—intimate terrorism and situational couple violence. **Intimate terrorism** is defined by "the attempt to dominate one's partner and to exert general control over the relationship, domination that is manifested in the use of a wide range of power and control tactics, including violence" (Johnson and Leone, 2005:323). **Situational couple violence** is defined as "intimate partner violence that is not embedded in such a general pattern of controlling behaviors...but occurs when specific conflict situations escalate to violence" (Johnson and Leone, 2005:324). By definition, the main distinction has to do with the control variable and not the nature or frequency of violent actions. Because these types of violence have varied roots and dynamics, analyzing intimate partner violence as a single phenomenon is not very helpful in understanding it.

Analyses find that intimate terrorism is perpetuated almost exclusively by men, while situational couple violence is only slightly more likely to be perpetuated by men than women. Situational couple violence frequently occurs in contexts in which an argument escalates and one or both partners react physically. The two types of violence have different effects on their victims—with the effects of intimate terrorism much more severe. Women who are victims of intimate terrorism experience violence that is more frequent and more likely to lead to injury. These women are also more likely to experience symptoms of post-traumatic stress disorder, miss work, and leave their partners.

The previous discussion illustrates that gender shapes vulnerability to the worst of domestic violence's effects—that is, susceptibility to intimate terrorism. One might expect that the effects of situational couple violence (sometimes called mutual violence) might be experienced equally by women and men. After all, the incidence of perpetration and victimization appear to be roughly equal (symmetrical) for this type of violence. Anderson's research finds, however, that the negative effects of this more symmetrical type of violence are significantly greater for women. While both men and women victims experience heightened levels of depression and substance abuse, the effects on women are significantly stronger (Anderson, 2002:861).

INTIMATE TERRORISM: POWER AND CONTROL

The type of violence that has come to be called intimate terrorism (or sometimes patriarchal terrorism) has been the focus of research by feminist scholars. These scholars emphasize that partner violence is gendered—that is, who within a couple will be the perpetrator and who the victim, and who will be controlling and who will be terrorized—and can be predicted on the basis of gender. Researchers relying on data collected from battered women (rather than surveys of the population that revealed correlations and probabilities), especially those who have come into contact with the courts, hospitals, and shelters, have emphasized the traditions of the patriarchal family that in the extreme lead to intimate terrorism (Johnson, 1995). This violence is initiated by men as a way of gaining and maintaining absolute control over their female partners and is rooted in patriarchal ideas of male ownership of their spouses. This pattern of total control incorporates the systematic use of tactics that are not physically violent but are nonetheless an exercise of power. The Power and Control Wheel, a widely used resource of the Domestic Abuse Intervention Project, captures how this abuse is patterned to involve the following nonviolent tactics: intimidation, threats, emotional abuse, isolation, blaming, using children, using male privilege, and using economic abuse (see Figure 10.1). The Wheel was developed by abused women through a shelter program in Duluth, Minnesota, in the 1980s and is part of an educational curriculum for abusive men in a widely used batterers intervention program (Domestic Abuse Intervention Project).

Feminist legal scholar Donna Coker describes the link between the act of battering and the institutional patterns that provide the context of domestic male dominance and control.

> Battering may be experienced as a personal violation, but it is an act facilitated and made possible by societal gender inequalities. The batterer does not, indeed could not, act alone. Social supports for battering include widespread denial of its frequence

Figure 10.1

Power and Control Wheel

Source: Domestic Abuse Intervention Project, Duluth, Minnesota. Online: www.duluth-model.org.

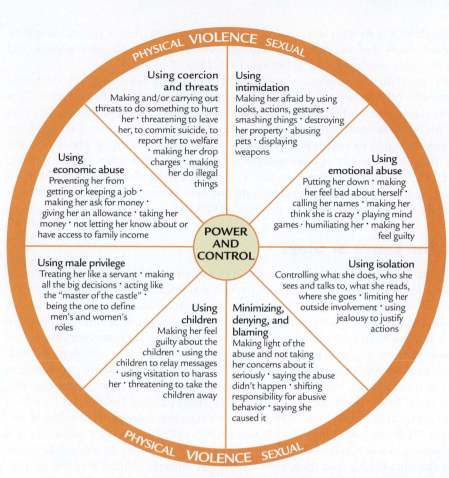

or harm, economic structures that render women vulnerable, and sexist ideology that holds women accountable for male violence and for the emotional lives of families, and that fosters deference to male familial control. Batterers often use the political and economic vulnerability of women to reinforce their power and dominance over particular women. Thus, their dominance, or their attempts at dominance, are frequently bolstered by stigmatization of victims through the use of gender social norms that define the "good woman" (wife/mother). Batterers also take advantage of the vulnerabilities of their victims, such as the victim's economic dependence on the batterer, or on her state as an illegal immigrant, her alcohol or drug dependency, or her responsibility to provide and care for children. (Coker, 1999:39)

For this type of violence, some men feel the need to control "their" women and in the process assert their authority. If the partner resists being controlled, the perpetrator escalates the level of violence until she is subdued. This pattern was observed by Dobash and Dobash, who showed that women in this situation cannot behave in ways to avoid being beaten.

For a woman to live her daily life she is always in a position in which almost anything she does may be deemed a violation of her wifely duties or a challenge to her husband's authority and thus defined as the cause of the violence she continues to experience. (Dobash and Dobash, 1979:137)

The research on the women who seek help from the criminal justice system, hospitals, and shelters finds that the beatings occur on average more than once a week and escalate in seriousness over time (Johnson, 1995:287).

Why are some men intimate terrorists, systematically battering their partners? The correlates related to battering husbands provide some clues. For example, low economic status plus traditional gender role expectations by males also explains wife abuse: "Men whose masculinity is tied to norms of dominance but who do not have the economic status to back up a dominant stance are likely to be abusive to the women they love, either psychologically or physically, and often both" (Lorber, 1994:71). Or, as Gelles and Straus argue, "Perhaps the most telling of all attributes of the battering man is that he feels inadequate and sees violence as a culturally acceptable way to be both dominant and powerful" (1988:89).

Does She Leave or Stay?

A consistent theme of the literature on the abuse of women by intimates has been to ask, "Why do they stay?" Increasingly, however, it is becoming clear that women are not staying with their batterers (Johnson and Ferraro, 2000:956). Newer research focuses on the extent to which women exit violent relationships. Several studies have found that more than half of women who were abused by their partners either left the relationship or negotiated an end to the violence (Campbell and Ramey 1994; Campbell et al., 1998; Herbert et al., 1991). Women do not necessarily make a clean break with their abusers, but may leave and return a number of times before the relationship ends. Researchers are also beginning to conceptualize the process by which women leave. Choice and Lamke frame women's stay/leave decisions in terms of two questions: "Will I be better off?" and "Can I do it?" (1997:290). Their model reflects the decisions a woman makes about whether her overall quality of life will be better without the relationship and then whether she has enough control over her circumstances to leave the relationship.

Despite the decisions of many women to leave their abusers, it is appropriate to observe that many stay in abusive relationships. As irrational as it sounds, many victims choose to stay with their violent partners when they know they are in peril. They do not stay because they are masochists—experiencing some perverse pleasure in being beaten—as has often been alleged. They have difficulty leaving for a variety of social and psychological reasons including fear, hope and love, self-blame, and economic dependence.

FEAR

The most obvious deterrent for an abused woman is that leaving may well increase the danger to her and her children. For the abusive husband, control of his wife is paramount. Obviously, when she leaves he loses control over her. Thus, creating a climate of fear may be effective in keeping her in the relationship. When women leave, some controlling abusers resort to terrorizing or even killing their partners. According to a U.S. Department of Justice study, the victimization rate of women separated from their husbands is three times higher than that of divorced women and about 25 times higher than that of married women (Bachman and Saltzman, 1996).

Research by Anderson and his colleagues (2003) demonstrates the relevance of the fear factor in women's decisions to stay. These researchers analyzed surveys of 400 abused women who had never left their partners or who had returned after separating. Women were asked to indicate the factors that affected their decisions to stay (see Table 10.1). Fear was represented in their decisions in these ways: "fear of being

Table 10.1   If You Never Left Your Mate or Returned to Your Mate After Separating, Check Those Factors Which Affected Your Decision (*n* = 400)

Percentage	Items	Percentage	Items
70.5	Mate promised to change	22.4	I felt I was safer with him, because I knew what he was doing
60.0	Mate apologized	21.9	Threats from mate to find me and kill me
53.8	Love	18.5	Children wanted to go back
46.4	Belief that I should try to make my marriage vows work	18.2	Became homeless
45.9	Lack of money	16.5	Couldn't get a lawyer
40.1	Fear of being alone	14.8	Mate found me
36.7	Fear of mate	14.5	Threats from mate to harm my family
35.5	Mate needed me	13.5	Police didn't help me
35.3	Missed my mate	9.2	Advice from a priest, preacher, rabbi
34.7	Belief that the children would suffer without mate	6.8	Courts wouldn't give me help to make mate stop
32.4	Fear of not being able to survive without mate	6.0	Advice from a counselor
31.2	Threats from mate to kill self	5.3	Mate took children from me
28.5	Nowhere to go or stay	4.8	Shelter was full
24.9	He continually stalked me	2.8	Advice from a lawyer
24.4	Fear that I might lose my children	2.5	Professionals didn't understand my culture
22.5	Advice from family or relatives	2.3	Medical people (doctor, nurse, etc.) didn't give the help to get safe

Source: Anderson, Michael A. et al. (2003). " 'Why Doesn't She Just Leave?': A Descriptive Study of Victim Reported Impediments to Her Safety." *Journal of Family Violence* 18 (3): 154.

alone" (40.1 percent), "fear of mate" (36.7 percent), "fear of not being able to survive without mate" (32.4 percent), and "fear that I might lose my children" (24.4 percent). In addition, threats to the safety of women and their families were intended to make women fearful. Women also cited the following factors: "threats from mate to find me and kill me" (21.9 percent) and "threats from mate to harm my family" (14.5 percent).

HOPE AND LOVE

Abused women may remain with their partners because they are convinced that their husbands will somehow reform. Further, they may continue to love their partner and believe that if the abuse stopped, the relationship would be viable. Many women are simply unwilling to give up on their relationships. The three most commonly cited factors in Table 10.1 for remaining with an abusive partner relate to hope and love.

They are: "mate promised to change" (70.5 percent), "mate apologized" (60 percent), and "love" (53.8 percent) (Anderson et al., 2003:154). These women may believe the myth that it is always best for the children if the parents stay together. This avenue is often encouraged by psychologists, clergy, and friends, who counsel abused wives to keep the family together no matter what the price because they believe it will work out favorably in the long run.

SELF-BLAME

In some cases women remain in abusive relationships because they blame themselves for their maltreatment. In a curious twist of logic, the structure of society not only forces battered women to endure abuse; it also creates a situation in which the victims see themselves, as do others, as the source of the problem. How is it that a woman might come to blame herself for the abusive behavior of her partner? First, self-blame may reflect a context of emotional abuse. Many women report a pattern of control by intimates that includes humiliation, manipulation, and social isolation (Anderson et al., 2003; Strauchler et al., 2004). The goal of the abuser is to destroy "the psychological identity of the victim as her own person, perhaps in an effort to render her incapable of independent thought or deed" (Anderson et al., 2003:153). Second, traditional gender role expectations set women up for blaming themselves when relationships become problematic. Anderson and his colleagues point out that in a patriarchal society, women are socialized into the role of being the primary caretaker of relationships. They describe how social expectations contribute to self-blame: "The victim's role as caretaker squarely puts the blame on her for the failing relationship. This serves to amplify the already burdening blame the abuser puts on her. Internalizing this blame makes it difficult to escape, as she is expected to repair the damage" (Anderson et al., 2003:155).

ECONOMIC DEPENDENCY

Economic concerns are especially important deterrents to leaving the abusive situation. The lack of marketable skills and jobs with decent pay and benefits often trap women in abusive relationships. Women who leave must find a way to pay for housing and provide care for dependent children, usually on low earnings. Kristin Anderson examined the relationship between economic dependence and women's decisions to divorce abusive partners. She found that dependency reduced the likelihood that women would exit relationships characterized by intimate terrorism or those with situational couple violence (2007).

Married women may also fear that their husbands will default on child support payments that would likely be ordered by the court if the couple divorced. If wives have little education and few job skills, they may feel there is no alternative but to stay in their troubled relationship. There is also the difficulty of working and taking care of the children. For middle- and upper-class women, divorce or separation usually means losing the lifestyle and status to which they have become accustomed. For many women who are insecure and have negative self-concepts, it is better to cope with the known than to face the unknown. "Many flee one problem—battering—only to become part of another: 'the feminization of poverty'" (Jones, 1994:200–201).

Domestic Violence in Same-Sex Relationships

Until recently, violence in same-sex relationships was an invisible issue. This invisibility was due, in part, to the myth that domestic violence occurs only between women and men (Ferguson 2007:609). In recent years, however, researchers have begun to study the dynamics of same-sex relationships, including violence (see, for example, Island and Letellier, 1991; Renzetti, 1992; Turrell, 2000). This research finds that rates of physical and sexual violence in same-sex relationships are similar to those in heterosexual unions (Turrell, 2000). As in abusive heterosexual relationships, the explanation seems to center on power and control over a partner. "A desire for power and control drives the abuser to beat, insult, or threaten the victim into submission to her or his wishes" (Elliott, 1996:4). Because the partners are of the same sex, however, the dynamics of gender and patriarchy are missing.

There are some crucial differences between the patterns of violence in heterosexual and homosexual relationships. The first is obvious. The predominant understanding of battering is that men are most likely to be perpetrators and women are most likely to be victims. That understanding is challenged as neither partners in same-sex relationships would be predicted—on the basis of sex—to be more likely to be an abuser. The idea that women are innately nonviolent can make it difficult for lesbians to identify intimate partner violence in their own relationships. Hassouneh and Glass found that the belief that "girls don't hit other girls" initially led some battered lesbians to deny their own victimization in a violent relationship (2008:316). Second, abusers in same-sex relationships have a unique form of control over their victims—the threat of "outing" (i.e., revealing a partner's sexual orientation publicly (against his or her wishes) to family, landlords, employers, or others). Third, abused partners in homosexual relationships are even less likely to acknowledge their abuse than are abused individuals who are heterosexual. Deciding to seek help or intervention may be more difficult for gay men and lesbian women because seeking help as a gay or lesbian victim is tantamount to "coming out of the closet" (Simpson, 2000). Lesbians of color are especially disadvantaged because they—already victims of sexism and racism in society—become triply oppressed in a society that stigmatizes homosexuality (Kanuha, 2005:71).

Gays and lesbians also face unique challenges when they seek a criminal justice response to domestic violence. The police, because of homophobia (this varies by locality, with rural areas more homophobic than urban areas; some cities, such as San Francisco and Seattle, are less homophobic than others), cultural stereotypes, or inappropriate training, frequently respond ineffectively to domestic violence among gay couples (Miller and Knudsen, 1999). The courts also find it difficult to deal with same-sex violence by partners. State statutes concerning domestic violence refer to "spouse" and "battered wife" but have no reference to gay or lesbian victims. In many states, because same-sex unions do not have the legal status of marriage, lesbians and gays cannot get protective orders in Family Court, even though married couples can (Leland, 2000). Gay men and lesbians are more cut off from the usual support systems in society (such as their families, who often reject their homosexuality; the church, which tends to condemn homosexuality as a sin; and the medical and mental health professions, which have a history of diagnosing homosexuality as a mental illness) (Island and Letellier, 1991:100). There are shelters for battered women, but few shelters exist for battered men. In short, same-sex battering victims are even more isolated than battered heterosexuals.

Child Abuse and Neglect

Gelles and Straus have concluded that "with the exception of the police and the military, the family is perhaps the most violent social group, and the home the most violent social setting, in our society" (1979:15). "Adult family members who abuse each other also tend to abuse their children" (Mignon et al., 2002:15). "A small child has more chance of being killed or severely injured by its parents than by anyone else. For children, the home is often the most dangerous place to be" (Collins and Coltrane, 1995:476–477). Child abuse is even more prevalent than intimate partner violence. Every week, child protective services (CPS) agencies receive 60,000 referrals alleging child abuse or neglect; CPS agencies investigated the family environments of 3.5 million children in 2007 (U.S. DHHS, 2009). This problem is reviewed in this section with a focus on the definition, incidence, contexts, consequences, prevention, and treatment of child abuse and the characteristics of abusing parents.

What Is Child Abuse?

What constitutes child abuse? The extreme cases of torture, scalding, beatings, and imprisonment are easy to place in this category. However, there are problems in determining whether many other actions are abusive. For example, one definition of child abuse is violence "carried out with the intention of, or perceived as having the intention of, physically hurting the child" (Gelles and Straus, 1979:136). This definition includes everything from spanking to murder. The problem is that spanking is used by 9 out of 10 parents and is considered legitimate and acceptable behavior. At what point does punishment become excessive? This is an important question for counselors, social workers, health practitioners, and the courts to address because the consequences for children and parents are enormous. To have a definition that is too lax imperils the health and safety of children, and to have one that is too stringent jeopardizes parents who might incorrectly receive the label of "child abuser," have their children taken from them, and even be imprisoned.

To assist in developing consistent definitions for child abuse, the Child Abuse Protection and Treatment Act provides minimum federal guidelines states must use in defining child maltreatment. These guidelines provide four categories of child maltreatment: neglect, physical abuse, sexual abuse, and emotional abuse. Most states include terminology that defines physical abuse as "nonaccidental physical injury as a result of punching, beating, kicking, biting, burning, shaking, throwing, stabbing,

choking, hitting, or otherwise harming a child" (U.S. DHHS, 2008). By this definition, parents who express concern about being labeled as an abuser for the mild spanking of a child should have little to fear from the authorities.

An important development in efforts to more adequately define child abuse is the inclusion of neglect as a type of abuse. While abuse might be perceived to require action, neglect is defined as the "failure to provide for children's basic needs" (U.S. DHHS, 2008). This type of abuse involves a range of behaviors, including the inadequate feeding of a child or lack of provision of sanitary living conditions. These forms of neglect may be just as damaging to children, physically and mentally, as physical aggression. This type of problem is complicated, too, because the neglect may or may not be willful on the part of parents.

We have chosen to use an all-inclusive definition of child abuse: "The distinctive acts of violence and nonviolence and acts of omission and commission that place children at risk" (Gelles, 1976:136). This is consistent with the government's definition in the Child Abuse Prevention and Treatment Act mentioned earlier. We should not be misled, in using this broad definition, into thinking that all the forms of child abuse and neglect are essentially alike, caused by the same sources, and subject to a uniform treatment mode (Gelles, 1976). We generalize about this problem, but the reader is warned that child abuse is, like all social problems, very complex. [In this section, we use the terms "child abuse" and "child maltreatment" interchangeably.]

Incidence of Child Abuse

The precise extent of child abuse and neglect is impossible to know, for two reasons. First, studies of the phenomenon have not used uniform definitions; and, second, the issue is extremely sensitive to the persons involved. To be the perpetrator or victim of child abuse is generally something for which people are stigmatized. Acts of violence and neglect are hidden from society because they occur in privacy. When asked by a survey researcher if they have ever physically abused their children, abusing parents will most likely deny such an act. Thus, many of the statistics are taken from police, teachers, social workers, and medical personnel, who must assume that the children were victims of abuse. Obviously, such subjective observations are subject to error. As one illustration of the problem of subjectivity, authorities commonly view the parents and children of the middle and upper classes quite differently than those from the lower classes. Trained personnel are more likely to label as a victim of child abuse a poor child who has a black eye than a rich child who has a black eye. Also, of course, authorities never see many cases of abuse and neglect. Official statistics, then, always underreport the actual incidence.

Although there are problems with defining and determining the exact incidence of child abuse, the government provides annual statistics. For 2007, the U.S. Department of Health and Human Services reported 794,000 substantiated cases of child abuse and neglect, including the deaths of 1,760 children. The rate of child abuse and neglect in 2007 was 10.6 cases per 1,000 children; this represents a decline from a rate of 12.5 in 2001 (U.S. DHHS, 2009). See Box 10.2 for a description of an innovative program to protect children at risk for abuse.

Contexts for Child Abuse

The reasons for the abuse and neglect of children by parents are complex and varied, involving personal, social, and cultural factors.

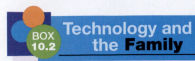

BOX 10.2   Technology and the **Family**

Protecting Children at Risk for Abuse

The Watchful Shepherd program uses electronic monitoring devices to protect children in potentially dangerous family situations. The program provides children with a wrist band that can activate an electronic device installed in their home. This, in turn, activates a computer monitoring system at a 24-hour-a-day response center. Within 10 seconds, dispatchers can make voice contact with the child. The response center staff then notifies 911 or an appropriate local police dispatcher as necessary. The same technology has been widely used with elderly and infirm individuals to signal their need for medical attention.

The Watchful Shepherd website points out that electronic monitoring is an effective tool for child protection service agencies that face a double mission of preserving family unity while protecting children. Social workers with heavy caseloads simply cannot know when intervention in a particular household might be necessary. The following personal story of sisters who were molested and later stalked by their father provides an example of a situation in which the program has been implemented.

> Female siblings, ages 10 and 11, had been molested by their natural father approximately 3 years earlier. Even after separation from the mother and a period of incarceration banished the father from the home, he continued to pose a threat by stalking his daughters and threatening the security of the family. These matters were also brought to the attention of law enforcement but since no actual physical violence had taken place, it was not possible to file significant charges against him.
>
> Nonetheless, the children did experience emotional trauma over the possibility of any irrational actions on the part of the father. The mother also had mental health issues of her own, having been raised in an alcoholic and abusive family. There was also a concern that the mother's string of unstable relationships were not a stabilizing influence on the girls.
>
> It was decided that the Watchful Shepherd program would provide a measure of protection for the children that was not otherwise available within the family structure and would also provide an opportunity for case management workers to view the overall environment. Case workers determined that despite her inherent limitations, the mother did provide emotional support for the children and that the bonding was a significant consideration in preserving this family structure. The children reported that the Watchful Shepherd program enabled them to feel safety and was a potential resource if matters escalated. Overall, the Watchful Shepherd program provided the needed reassurance while agency protective supervision continued in the home. (Watchful Shepherd, "Personal Stories," 2005)

The Watchful Shepherd program is not a panacea for the problem of vulnerable children in potentially volatile home settings. It does, however, seem that the electronic monitoring system serves as a deterrent to child maltreatment in the homes in which it is implemented. In some cases parents have themselves contacted the response center because they recognized they were losing control and feared that, unless they received help, they might hurt their child.

The Watchful Shepherd program was initiated in Washington County, Pennsylvania, in 1993; it now has a presence in several additional states.

Source: Watchful Shepherd (2005). Online: http://www.watchful.org.

PERSONAL FACTORS

The most commonly assumed explanation for abusive behavior toward children is that the perpetrators are mentally ill. This assumption, however, is a myth that hinders the understanding of child abuse (Gelles, 1976:138). In the view of experts, only about 10 percent of maltreating parents have severe personality disorders or psychoses. This is not to say that personal factors are unimportant. Obviously, abusive parents let their aggressive feelings go too far. There are several possible reasons for this. One important reason is that abused children have a higher probability of becoming abusive parents than do nonabused children. In short, violence tends to beget violence. Some caution is advised concerning this relationship, however. The evidence is that about 30 percent of physically abused children grow up to be abusive adults. Although this is much higher than the overall societal rate of between 2 and 3 percent, we must not ignore the fact that 7 out of 10 abused children *do not* become abusive adults (Gelles, 1993:15).

The failure to learn parenting skills may also be the reason that children who have lost a parent, who have been separated from their mothers, or who come from a disrupted home show some tendency to become abusing parents themselves.

Abusive parents, for whatever reason, tend to be more demanding than other parents. Abusing parents demand far higher performance from their children than ordinary parents. What they demand is beyond the capacity of their children even to understand, much less perform. Typically they become angry because the child will not stop crying, eats poorly, urinates after being told not to do so, and so on. In fact, they feel righteous about the punishments they have inflicted on their children. They avoid facing the degree of injury they have caused, but they justify their behavior because they feel their children have been "bad." (Goode, 1971:633)

A relatively common trait of abusing parents is substance abuse. This activity reduces the normal restraints inhibiting aggression in the individual. Parents' alcoholism has long been associated with child abuse. Recent years have seen an increase in reports of child abuse in households in which parents used methamphetamines (Children's Defense Fund, 2005). Substance abuse is also associated with a number of other factors that produce strain and disruption in stable family patterns: greater unemployment, poor health, low self-esteem, isolation, and preoccupation with self.

Finally, a caution from Gelles and Straus: "When our explanations focus on 'kinds of people'—mentally disturbed, poor, alcoholics, drug abusers, etc.—we blind ourselves to the structural properties of the family as a social institution that makes it our most violent institution with the exception of the military in time of war" (Gelles and Straus, 1988:51).

There is a strong propensity among the lay public to explain child abuse (or partner abuse) in individual terms. Although personal factors should not be ignored, social factors are extremely important for an understanding of this complex phenomenon.

SOCIAL CLASS

The Children's Defense Fund states the relationship between social class and child abuse starkly: "Poverty is the single best predictor of child abuse and neglect. Children who live in families with annual incomes of less than $15,000 are 22 times more likely to be abused or neglected than those with annual incomes of $30,000 or more" (2005:113). In fact, rising and falling rates of child maltreatment are closely tied to changes in the poverty rate. Figure 10.2 captures this relationship in recent years. It is

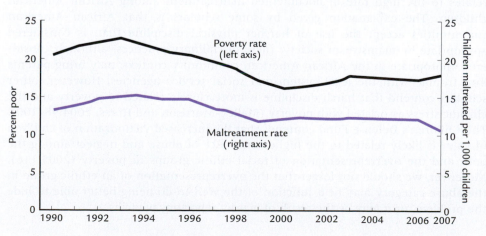

Figure 10.2

Poverty and Child Maltreatment Rates, 1990–2007

Sources: Children Defense Fund, *The State of American Children 2005*, p. 115, 2008, p. 19. Online: www.http://childrensdefense.org; U.S. Department of Health and Human Services, *Child Maltreatment 2007*, p. 38. Online: http://www.acf.hhs.gov.

important to note that most poor children are not abused or neglected. In 2003, nearly 13 million children were poor, but fewer than 1 million U.S. children (representing all social classes) were confirmed as abused or neglected (Children's Defense Fund, 2005:115).

One of the reasons poor parents are more susceptible to charges of child maltreatment is that they may lack the resources to adequately provide for their children's material needs. As a result, they may be charged with child neglect—a type of child maltreatment. Child neglect makes up 59 percent of substantiated cases of child maltreatment (U.S. DHHS, 2009). Thus, in some cases, child maltreatment is not willful or deliberate, but reflects the desperate economic circumstances of many poor households.

While it is appropriate to generalize that children of the poor are more likely to be abuse victims than are children in other social classes, this does not mean that child abuse is rare among families in higher social classes (Straus and Smith, 1990:250). Child abuse is more likely to be underreported in more affluent families in part because wealthier families are simply better able to hide abuse (e.g., they go to private physicians, who may be more reluctant to report signs of abuse in their "respectable" clients than the doctors who treat the poor in general hospitals).

Unemployment is another factor associated with child abuse. This may lead to poverty, low self-esteem because of being a "failure" in a success-oriented society, and depression. The unemployed are also homebound, increasing their interaction with children.

RACE AND ETHNICITY

Government statistics on confirmed cases of child abuse and neglect show varying rates of abuse by race and ethnicity. The Department of Health and Human Services' report for 2007 found the following rates of child maltreatment: African American children had the highest rate of abuse (16.7 cases per 1,000 children); next was American Indian or Alaska Native children (14.2 cases per 1,000), followed by multiracial children (14.0 per 1,000), Hispanic children (10.3 cases per 1,000), White children (9.1 cases per 1,000), and Asian American children (2.4 per 1,000) (2009:25).

These data on child abuse by race and ethnicity should be treated with some caution. What may appear to be determined by ethnicity may actually be explained by social class. One example of the questions raised by these statistics relates to the high rate of documented maltreatment among African American children. The explanation given by some scholars is that African American communities accept the use of harsher physical discipline than is considered appropriate by mainstream society; these disciplinary practices, although considered appropriate in the African American community context, may bring parents into trouble with the legal system and social service agencies. However, other scholars contend that harsh discipline is more closely related to poverty and the chronic stress associated with poverty (Malley-Morrison and Hines, 2004:98–100). The Children's Defense Fund contends that the increased victimization of children of color is likely related to the higher incidence of abuse and neglect among the poor and the overrepresentation of racial ethnic groups in poverty (2005:116). Moreover, we should not forget that the overrepresentation of an ethnic group in the abuse category may be a function of the well-to-do being better able to hide the problem, or it may be the result of bias by reporting agencies.

Despite these problems with the data, we can see variations in the patterns of child abuse. These variations are the result of differences in family structure, differing placements in the opportunity and reward structures of society, and contrasting parenting styles. The relationship between social class and child abuse and between ethnicity and child abuse suggests that child abuse is a result of structural stress (i.e., stress from social sources). Most incidents of abuse appear to be related to a central factor in child abuse—"inadequate resources available to the parent who is charged with the 24-hour-a-day responsibility to raise and care for the child" (Gelles, 1976:139). In a society in which violence toward children is culturally acceptable (as noted earlier), those parents in unusually difficult social circumstances may go beyond the cultural norm.

GENDER

Men are much more likely than women to be the assailants in all forms of family violence except child abuse, in which women are the perpetrators more often than men. Data from many sources, including clinical observations, official reports, and surveys, find that mothers are more likely to abuse their children than are fathers (Gelles, 1997). In 2004, 57 percent of perpetrators in confirmed cases of abuse and neglect were women and 42 percent were men (U.S. DHHS, 2009:68).

Gelles believes that the differences between men's and women's rates of abusive behavior are due, in part, to differences in time actually spent with children. Mothers spend far more time with children, especially young children, than do their fathers (1997:59). Disparities in time spent in contact with children increases the susceptibility of women to abusive behavior. Because patriarchal norms in society still place women in the role of the primary parent, a mother also feels more responsibility and guilt than the father for the failures of her children (Breines and Gordon, 1983:504). Moreover, women are also much more likely than men to be in stressful economic situations (to head households alone, to be poor, and to do less fulfilling and less economically rewarding work).

Gertrude Williams (1980:597) has argued that some additional gender-related issues also promote child abuse by women. In her opinion, a primary reason for child abuse is the pronatalist bias in society. Pronatalism, as discussed in earlier chapters, is the widespread belief that a woman's primary means of fulfillment is motherhood. This ideology forces many women into a role that they may not want. They are also forced into the mothering role by the lack of interesting and well-paid work options and by unwanted pregnancies. Unwanted children born to a woman in a marginal economic situation are prime candidates for abuse and neglect.

LACK OF SOCIAL SUPPORT

The lack of social support is also related to child abuse. The research by Gelles and Straus found that the most violent parents had lived in the community less than two years; belonged to few, if any, community organizations; and had little contact with friends and relatives.

> This social isolation cuts them off from any possible source of help to deal with the stresses of intimate living or economic adversity. These parents are not only more vulnerable to stress, their lack of social involvement also means that they are less likely to abandon their violent behavior and conform to community values and standards. (Gelles and Straus, 1988:87–88)

Consequences of Child Abuse

Many of the consequences of child maltreatment are obvious. More than 1,700 children die annually from abuse. Emergency rooms, clinics, and therapists treat hundreds of thousands more. What is less obvious are the long-term negative consequences of child abuse and neglect. The consequences of child maltreatments can be categorized as health outcomes, cognitive and educational outcomes, and social and behavior outcomes. Literally hundreds of studies have provided evidence on these outcomes. Chalk and her colleagues have summarized the results of this massive body of literature (2002). The following is drawn from their report.

HEALTH OUTCOMES

- Various types of brain injuries are associated with childhood maltreatment, particularly when exposure to physical abuse and neglect occurs in the first three years of life.

- Child and adolescent sexual abuse is associated with the risk of sexually transmitted diseases, including HIV, gonorrhea, and syphilis.

- Abuse and neglect may be associated with physical defects, growth and mental retardation, and speech problems.

- Maltreated children tend to have heightened levels of depression, feelings of hopelessness, and low self-esteem.

COGNITIVE AND EDUCATIONAL OUTCOMES

- Some studies find associations between childhood abuse and neglect and language deficits, reduced cognitive functioning, and attention deficit disorders.

- Both neglected and physically abused children tend to do poorly in school, as evidenced by low grades, low standardized test scores, and frequent retention in the same grade.

SOCIAL AND BEHAVIORAL OUTCOMES

- Antisocial behavior and physical aggression are two of the most consistent outcomes of physical child abuse, along with fear and anger.

- Maltreatment can have a negative impact on children's emotional stability and self-regulation, problem-solving skills, and the ability to cope with or adapt to new or stressful situations.

- Child sexual abuse has been reported as a risk factor for adolescent pregnancy.

- Several studies have suggested a link between childhood victimization and substance abuse in later life.

- Maltreated children are at increased risk for getting into trouble with the law and running away from home.

 **Incest**

We consider incest as a special case of child sexual abuse. The American Medical Association defines child sexual abuse as "the engagement of a child in sexual activities for which the child is developmentally unprepared and cannot give informed consent" (1993:20). Incest is a sexual relationship with a closely-related family member. The legal definition of incest is sexual intercourse between persons so closely related that marriage is prohibited by law. Incest is illegal in all 50 states. Although specific state laws vary, in general, sexual relations between siblings, parents and children, grandparents and grandchildren, aunts/uncles and their nieces/nephews, and sometimes first cousins are prohibited. We restrict our use of the term **incest** to cases of inappropriate sexual contact between a parent (or a person in the parent role, such as stepparent) and a child.

An inappropriate sexual relationship between a parent (or stepparent) and child is the most common type of incest, and that is the focus of this section. Children in these abusive relationships usually interpret the experience as coercive and assaultive. The child is powerless to do anything about it because parents are stronger physically and because children have been socialized to trust and obey their parents. Miller and Knudsen point out that, given the secrecy in which this abuse takes place, "the victim becomes the person responsible for her or his own safety to a degree not found with other types of child abuse or neglect" (2007:168).

The social stigma attached to incest results in further victimization of its survivors. First, stigma results in the underreporting of this offense. Miller (2006) contends that improving the rate of reporting will only occur when social stigma has been reduced. She writes, "The effect of the taboo nature of incest is to play into the abuser's hands—if we turn our backs on an ugly secret, if we refuse to acknowledge a problem exists, it breeds the ability to perpetrate and cover up incidences of incest" (2006:191). It seems that reluctance to acknowledge these experiences is diminishing a bit as celebrities such as Oprah Winfrey, Roseanne Barr, La Toya Jackson, and former Miss America Marilyn Van Derbur have gone public with their stories of childhood sexual abuse. Second, incest survivors frequently experience a lack of support after the abuse ends. Sometimes immediate family members reject the idea that the experience was severe and traumatic for the child involved. This response serves to keep the family secret hidden (Lorentzen et al., 2008). Adults who disclose their childhood experience with incest may experience continued stigmatization by family and acquaintances (Miller, 2006).

Incidence of Incest

Because of the stigma and secrecy associated with incest, accurate statistics on incidence are impossible to obtain. Margaret Andersen, after reviewing the literature, thinks that the most accurate estimate of incest is that "16 percent of women have been sexually abused by a relative by the time they are 18 years old" (Andersen, 1997:177). Incestuous relationships typically last an average of two years. It is important to note that incest occurs throughout the social structure, among all races and religions, and in all geographical areas (Finkelhor, 1993).

Although accurate data on incest are unavailable, the information from reported cases provides some ideas about the incidence of incest by type. We know from various studies that (1) the victims of incest are usually female (a ratio of 3:1); (2) the offenders are almost always male; (3) the median age of first encounter is under 12 years, with the age ranging from a few months to the late teens; (4) 9 out of 10 cases involve father and daughter, stepfather and stepdaughter, or grandfather and granddaughter; of the remaining 10 percent, half are sexual relationships between fathers and sons.

A mother may be aware of incestuous abuse but might not have the power to stop it. She may become a silent bystander because her emotional and/or economic dependence on her husband prevents her from confronting the situation. Particularly in families in which mothers are unusually powerless as a result of battering, disability, mental illness, or repeated childbearing, there is an especially high risk of sexual abuse, especially among daughters who have taken on the household responsibilities (Andersen, 1997:178).

Explanations for Incest

The explanations for incest are varied. There are psychological reasons, such as low self-esteem, immaturity, and **pedophilia** (sexual interest limited to children) on the part of the perpetrators. Some psychological theories misplace the blame for incest. Some blame wives whose lack of sexual interest toward their husbands turns the men's interest to a daughter. Others place the responsibility on the seductive daughter who is competing with her mother. Some have criticized these theories for blaming the victim. They see the source of the problem, rather, in patriarchy. Some feminists point to the research finding that the greater the paternal dominance and authoritarianism in a family, the more likely it is that incest will occur (James and MacKinnon, 1990). In a patriarchal society, male dominance is normal in sexual relations. Judith Herman and Lisa Hirschman (1981) found that many fathers felt no guilt for their aggressive sexual behavior toward daughters. This may result from being accustomed to forcing sex on weaker and unwilling partners, a common condition in a patriarchal family. Thus, "father-daughter incest will disappear only when male supremacy is ended" (Breines and Gordon, 1983:527).

Jane Gilgun connects the problem of incest to inequalities that are part of the structure of family life:

> Families are permeated with inequalities in terms of age, size, gender, developmental level, status, knowledge, and power. Children, in particular, are vulnerable to abuse of power because of their unequal status in relationship to adults. When parents and others with authority over children choose to disregard principles related to justice and care, children have few resources with which to prevent harm to themselves. The behaviors and verbal protests have impact only on those who are receptive to them. (1995:267)

Gilgun notes the lack of a public discourse on the moral dimensions of family life. She believes this absence may partially explain the prevalence of incest.

Unlike the case for spouse abuse, poverty, unemployment, and downward mobility are *not* associated with increased incidence of incest (Finkelhor and Baron, 1986).

Consequences of Incest

The children who are victims of incestuous relationships are negatively affected. The fundamental problem with parent–child incest is the violation by the adult of the child's trust. Parents who pursue incestuous relations with children disregard social norms of parental care, nurture, and protection.

Gilgun's research on this subject involved interviewing incest perpetrators. Her results illustrate both a pattern of manipulation by perpetrators and the vulnerability of child victims. While perpetrators framed their relationships with the children they abused in terms of love and care, their accounts showed how they exercised psychological power over their victims.

> Ironically, their professed love of whatever type was contradicted by many other aspects of their accounts, such as continuing the incest when the children wanted to stop, withholding permission to do ordinary things until the children submitted sexually, and letting others think the children were lying when the incest was disclosed.... Some were cruel in keeping the incest secret. Instilling fear in the children, such as warning that their mothers would leave if they ever found out, was a common tactic. One man let his daughter believe that if she told, her mother—and his wife—would kill him: "A couple of times, [my wife] would say, 'if I ever found you were touching the girls, I'd kill you'.... saying that in front of the victim and the abuser, and the victim feeling close to the abuser, and [the victim] kind of says, 'I ain't, I sure ain't going to say anything because, if I say anything now, Ma will kill Dad.'" (Gilgun, 1995:270, 274)

The experience of incest may affect a victim's physical and mental health well into adulthood. Adult women who were sexually abused as children are susceptible to low self-esteem, depression, and anxiety disorders. Post-traumatic stress disorder is a common diagnosis (Miller, 2006). Long-term physical effects may include migraine headaches, gynecological problems, and epileptic seizures (Browning and Laumann, 1997; Hyman, 2000). Adult–child sexual contact appears to affect the path that women's sexual experience takes in future years. Women who experienced adult–child contact have more sexual partners, are more likely to have a teenage birth, and are more likely to acquire a sexually transmitted infection over their lifetime. In addition, some women experience sexual dysfunction related to desire and response (Browning and Laumann, 1997:550, 552).

Sibling Abuse

Children may be victimized by parents, but they may also be victimized by brothers and sisters. Actually, sibling violence is the most common form of family violence in the United States (Haskins, 2003; Straus et al., 1980). Sibling abuse takes the forms of emotional, physical, and sexual abuse. Sibling abuse has received less attention from practitioners and the authorities than other types of family violence. Frequently parents attribute aggression toward a sibling—either verbal or physical—to "normal" sibling rivalry (Haskins, 2003). How can we distinguish normal sibling conflict from sibling abuse? Vernon Wiehe (1997) provides several characteristics that constitute sibling abuse: (1) there is a pattern of repeatedly hurtful behavior; (2) the roles of perpetrator and victim are carried on over time; (3) the behavior of the perpetrator reflects a negative general attitude toward the sibling; (4) the intent is to harm the victim; and (5) the behavior is inappropriate for the developmental level of the perpetrator (summarized by Mignon et al., 2002:25).

Sibling abuse is most likely to occur in families where there is physical abuse by parents. "In general the more violence experienced by the child, the higher the rate at which such children are violent towards a sibling" (Straus, 1981:5). Other factors associated with sibling abuse include inadequate supervision, marital problems, financial problems, parental mental disorder or substance abuse, and the perpetrator having a negative self-image (Crane, 1997).

Elder Abuse

In the 1960s, child abuse gained attention as a serious family problem. This occurred for spouse abuse in the 1970s. The problem of the battered elderly has, until recently, gone unnoticed. Elder abuse, although certainly not new, has become more of a problem because people are living longer and the numbers of elderly are increasing. This means that as an ever-larger number of adult children must assume a caretaker role, elders are more likely to be physically abused by their children.

What Is Elder Abuse?

As with other types of abuse, definitions of elder abuse used by researchers may differ and legal definitions may vary on a state-by-state basis. Comprehensive definitions of elder abuse (sometimes referred to as elder mistreatment) commonly include the following categories (from U.S. Administration on Aging, 2006):

- Physical abuse, defined as the use of physical force that may result in bodily injury, physical pain, or impairment.
- Sexual abuse, defined as nonconsensual sexual contact of any kind with an elderly person.
- Emotional or psychological abuse, defined as the infliction of anguish, pain, or distress.
- Financial or material exploitation, defined as the illegal or improper use of an elder's funds, property, or assets.
- Abandonment, defined as the desertion of an elder person by an individual who had physical custody or otherwise had assumed responsibility for an elder.
- Neglect, defined as the refusal or failure to fulfill any part of a person's obligation or duties to an elder.

Incidence of Elder Abuse

Accurate information regarding how many elderly persons are subjected to abuse is impossible to obtain. Elderly victims find themselves in a double bind that traps them in an abusive situation in which they feel they cannot notify the authorities.

> The abuser is providing financial and other resources necessary for the victim's survival. Thus, the [elderly victim recognizes his or her] dependency on the abusing caretaker. These battered parents, whose attacks cover an even wider range of abuse than that perpetrated upon children, often refuse to report the abuse for fear of retaliation, lack of alternative shelter, and the shame and stigma of having to admit that they reared such a child. Paralleling the battered wife, these abused old people prefer the known, even when it includes physical abuse, to the unknown, if they seek to leave the situation. (Steinmetz, 1978:55).

As a result, as many as five out of six cases of elder abuse go unreported (National Center on Elder Abuse, 1998). This is because, in addition to the reasons just mentioned, many mistreated elders are homebound and isolated, and thus are unlikely to be seen at banks, senior centers, hospitals, health programs, and police stations (Wolf, 2000:8).

In the last decade, researchers have made some progress in estimating the incidence of elder abuse. The National Elder Abuse Incidence Study investigated the incidence of elder abuse for 1996. This study concluded that 450,000 elderly (60 and older) Americans were abused or neglected in that year. The National Research Council estimates that between 1 and 2 million Americans 65 and older have experienced abuse (2003:9).

CHARACTERISTICS OF VICTIMS AND ABUSERS

The National Elder Abuse Incidence Study (1998) advances our understanding of the phenomenon of elder abuse and neglect by providing characteristics of the elders who are abused and the abusers who injure, exploit, or otherwise harm them.

The Abused   Elderly women are more likely to be abused than elderly men. Women make up 58 percent of the elderly population but are the victims of 76 percent of emotional/psychological abuse, 71 percent of physical abuse, 63 percent of financial/material exploitation, and 60 percent of neglect. Men are the majority of victims of abandonment (62 percent). The oldest elders—age 80 and over—are the group most vulnerable to abuse; this group is abused at a rate two to three times their proportion in the population. A large percentage (nearly 60 percent) of substantiated elder abuse victims have experienced some degree of dementia or confusion; only 10 percent of the elderly population has some form of dementia.

Perpetrators of Elder Abuse   In almost 90 percent of incidents of elder abuse and neglect, the perpetrators are family members, and two-thirds of perpetrators are adult children or spouses. Men are more likely than women to be perpetrators of elder mistreatment. Males are perpetrators of the majority of incidents of abandonment (83 percent), physical abuse (63 percent), emotional abuse (60 percent), and financial exploitation (59 percent). Women are more likely to be perpetrators of neglect (52 percent).

Contexts for Elder Abuse

Although progress has been made in estimating the prevalence of elder abuse, the contexts in which it occurs and the factors that put the elderly at risk for abuse remain poorly understood. A panel of experts in the field has concluded that a large part of the problem is that "early assertions, founded on faulty data (or no data at all), have been frequently repeated and widely believed, despite the lack of evidence" (National Research Council, 2003:88).

The earlier conventional explanation for elder abuse rested on the victim dependence and caregiver stress model. This model holds that adult children are abusive because they are overwhelmed by the role of taking care of a dependent parent or parents. The experts mentioned above, the Panel to Review Risk and Prevalence of Elder Abuse and Neglect, find that the problem with the model is that it fails to explain why elder abuse occurs in some settings and not others. Most elders are not abused, despite the fact that their dependence does produce stress for their caregivers. Newer analyses ask what risk factors raise the likelihood of elder abuse. Here, few factors can actually be validated by substantial evidence, but living arrangements, social isolation, and dementia are clearly implicated as factors associated with abuse. A shared living situation is a risk for abuse; likewise, social isolation—that is, having a poor social network—is associated with increased likelihood of abuse. As was mentioned in the previous section, Alzheimer's disease or dementia puts an elderly family member at increased risk for abuse (National Research Council, 2003:92–94).

Another set of risk factors that have been substantiated is related to personal characteristics of the abusers. Here, mental health, hostility, and alcohol abuse are relevant. With respect to mental health, many studies point to caregiver depression as associated with elder mistreatment; caregiver hostility also puts the elderly at increased risk. Alcohol abuse is commonly found among perpetrators of elder abuse (National Research Council, 2003:94–95).

A final factor to consider in explaining elder mistreatment is the ageism prevalent in society (U.S. Administration on Aging, 2007). This provides an atmosphere in which the elderly are devalued, negatively stereotyped, and subjected to discrimination. To the extent that older people accept these negative definitions of the aged, they may view abusive treatment as deserved or at least as unavoidable. Similarly, if their children accept the tenets of ageism, then they may assume that the elderly deserve their mistreatment.

New efforts are underway to prevent and detect elder abuse through routine screening by medical doctors. The rationale is that elders typically trust their doctors and see them in confidential settings that promote disclosure (Levine, 2003). Several questionnaires have been developed for screening patients aged 60 or older for elder abuse. See Figure 10.3 for the questions used by the Elder Abuse Screening project at the University of Maine's Center on Aging.

Please return finished screen to your doctor.	Circle one	
Has anyone close to you called you names or put you down recently?	Yes	No
Are you afraid of anyone in your life?	Yes	No
Are you able to use the telephone anytime you want to?	Yes	No
Has anyone forced you to do things you didn't want to do?	Yes	No
Has anyone taken things or money that belong to you without your OK?	Yes	No
Has anyone close to you tried to hurt you or harm you recently?	Yes	No

Figure 10.3

Routine Screening Questions for Elder Abuse

Sources: University of Maine Center on Aging, Elder Abuse Screening Protocol for Physicians, 2007, p.13. Online: http://www.umaine.edu/mainecenteronaging/documents/elderabusescreeningmanual.pdf. The elder abuse screen presented in this manual has been adapted from the Hwalek-Sengstock Elder Abuse Screening Test. The original screen and subsequent revisions are discussed in the following two articles: Schofield, M. J., R. Reynolds, G. D.Mishra, J. R. Powers, A. J. Dobson (2002). "Screening for Vulnerability to Abuse Among Older Women: Women's Health Australia Study. *Journal of Applied Gerontology* 21 (1), 24–39; Neale, A. V., M. A. Hwalek, R. O. Scott, M. C. Sengstock, C. Stahl (1991). "Validation of the Hwalek-Sengstock Elder Abuse Screening Test." *Journal of Applied Gerontology* 10 (4), 406–418.

Macro and Micro Linkages

Violence in the family presents the ultimate paradox—the physical abuse of loved ones in the most intimate of social relationships. The bonds between wife and husband, parent and child, and adult child and parent are based on love, yet for many these bonds represent a trap in which they are victims of unspeakable abuses.

Although it is impossible to know the extent of battering that takes place in families, the problem these forms of violence represent is not trivial. The threat of violence in intimate relationships exists for all couples and for all parents and children. For many the threat becomes real as the strong abuse the weak. Violence in the family, however, is not only a problem at the micro level of family units. It also represents an indictment of the macro level—society, its institutions, and the cultural norms that support violence.

All forms of intimate violence occur within a social context. The social context of intimate violence includes a patriarchal ideology that condones and maintains the power of men over women. The social context includes a media barrage with the consistent message that violence solves problems. The social context includes an economy in which poverty, unemployment, underemployment, and corporate downsizing jeopardize millions of families. The social context includes institutional sexism, institutional racism, and institutional heterosexuality, which make life more difficult for certain categories of people, especially limiting the possibilities for women, women of color, and gays and lesbians. The social context includes the breaking up of kin networks as household units move for better opportunities, thus increasing social isolation. These social forces cause and perpetuate violence toward spouses, children, and elders. In short, these social forces create the conditions that foster abuse in intimate relationships. Personal suffering at the micro level, then, is a result of macro forces. However, this type of determinism can be resisted, challenged, and changed. These efforts are the topics of the next section.

Agency

Although the existence of family violence is strongly affected by social forces, individuals acting singly or with others can and do shape, resist, and challenge the forces affecting their lives. Our focus here is on the social movement that emerged in the 1970s whose overarching goal was ending violence against women. This movement addressed the invisibility of the problem of woman abuse and the vulnerability of abused women. It provides a powerful example of the impact of collective action for social change. Since the 1970s, concerned citizens—abused women, feminists, and others—have worked through organizations to change the societal forces that encourage abuse. They have also worked to change laws and procedures to protect the victims of abuse. And they have worked to provide viable alternatives for abused women.

The Women's Movement

The credo of feminists is that domestic violence cannot be treated in isolation. Legal remedies, mediation, or therapy will not work without considering the issues of women's equality and gender subordination (Schneider, 2000:28). Thus, the agenda of the women's movement, through various organizations, has focused on changing society to bring sexual equity before the law, equal pay for equal work, and the end of oppression of women in all areas of society. The women's movement has been successful, although not completely, and each success has helped to reduce violence in families. Most pertinent, out of the women's movement came a movement to provide shelters for battered women.

The Battered Women's Shelter Movement

Beginning in the early 1970s, women's groups (also church groups and other civic organizations) in various communities formed residential sanctuaries for battered women and their children after they escaped an abusive home (Schneider, 2000:11–28). This movement has swept the country, and shelters are now found universally in cities. These shelters typically provide protection, food, clothing, legal assistance, personal counseling, assistance in obtaining welfare, child care, and job counseling. Obviously, when a community provides these services to abused women, many who otherwise would have no place to turn can leave their abusive situations for a safe haven.

Assessing Progress

A careful assessment shows that the antiviolence movement has been successful in raising awareness of the extent of the problem of domestic violence, advancing knowledge, and implementing support services. This is not to say that all women are equally safe in their own homes or have equal access to support services. The successes have been partial. Inequalities of race and class continue to create circumstances whereby the needs of poor women, especially poor women of color, remain unmet. Notwithstanding the challenges yet to be addressed, this movement represents an important example of agency.

Beth Richie describes how the context for woman abuse has changed since the 1970s:

> In the last thirty years, the social change movement organized to respond to the problem of violence against women has made a significant impact on the legislative and moral psyche of the United States. In a relatively short time, numerous victories can be claimed. A wide variety of programs have been created to respond to women who experience domestic violence: sexual assault survivors have access to a range of supportive services; a national hotline has been established to respond to women in crisis; and agencies around the country are held up as model programs that claim an impressive degree of success in securing women's safety.

> - The creation of intervention programs has been matched with a tremendous increase in public policy attention to the issues of violence.
> - Laws designed to protect women have been created; federal and local legislation has been passed to provide resources for programs.
> - Academic and research institutions have been central in creating change by advancing new knowledge in the field.
> - Many programs engage in evaluation research to determine their impact and effectiveness. Each year new training videos, new websites, and new books appear.

What was once a problem hidden deeply within the private sphere is now understood to be a common social problem worthy of social, intellectual, clinical, and political attention. It is safe to say that many women—hundreds of thousands perhaps—are safer today than they were thirty-five years ago because of the work of the anti-violence movement. (Excerpts from Richie, 2005:xv–xvi).

Chapter Review

1. Families reflect the society in which they are embedded. Thus, a violent society—as seen in its history, laws, media, pornography, folklore, and customs—will have violence in its families.

2. The ways families are organized in U.S. society encourage conflict. Conflict occurs through the unequal distribution of power, patterns of male dominance, the intensity of interaction, and privacy.

3. The data on partner abuse, child abuse, incest, and elder abuse are unreliable because the events usually take place in private, physicians treating the battered tend to protect the well-to-do, and the victims often lie about the causes of their injuries because of shame or fear.

4. Despite the unreliability of the data, we do know that woman abuse in domestic settings is a fairly common practice, and we do know some facts about the contexts in which it occurs. It is more probable when (a) families are threatened by economic hardships, (b) males hold traditional gender role expectations, (c) emotional abuse is present, (d) husbands feel inadequate, and (e) husbands came from homes in which they were beaten or in which they observed their fathers beat their mothers.

5. Intimate partner violence may be divided into two general types: intimate terrorism and situational couple violence.

6. Many women are able to take control of their circumstances and leave violent relationships. Reasons for remaining in abusive relationships include fear, hope and love, self-blame, and economic dependence.

7. Comparing the pattern of violence in same-sex relationships with heterosexual unions, we find two commonalities: (a) the rate is about the same, and (b) the explanation seems to center on power/control in both. Important differences are as follows: (a) when the gender of both partners is the same, patriarchy is missing and the typical gendered patterns of abuse do not apply; (b) abused individuals in same-sex relationships are even more isolated than the abused in heterosexual relationships.

8. Child abuse occurs when parents (a) are too demanding, (b) do not have adequate parenting skills, (c) were victims of child abuse, and (d) face economic hardships. Women are more likely than men to abuse or neglect children.

9. Incest, the special case of child abuse involving sexual abuse, usually involves a male perpetrator and a female victim. Just as with spouse and child abuse, the offenders are not all psychotic.

10. Sibling abuse is the most common type of violence within families.

11. Several factors place elderly individuals at increased risk for elder abuse: shared living situations, social isolation, and dementia. Elderly women are more likely to be abused or neglected than elderly men.

12. A number of macro social forces maintain family violence—patriarchal ideology, laws, the media, institutional sexism and racism, and an economy that encourages inequality. These social forces affect families, leading some to be physically violent. Thus, macro forces lead to micro suffering.

13. The abused in families need not be passive and, indeed, most often they are not. Human beings have agency—they can resist, they can cope, they can change social arrangements. Many victims leave abusive situations. Many take their assailants to court. Many join with others to make the problem of family abuse more visible, to change laws and police procedures, and to work for gender equity.

Key Terms

incest 363

intimate terrorism 349

pedophilia 364

situational couple violence 349

Related Websites

http://www.ojp.usdoj.gov/nij/topics/crime/violence-against-women/welcome.htm

Violence Against Women & Family Violence Program. Operated by the U.S. Department of Justice, the mission of the Violence Against Women and Family Violence Research and Evaluation Program is to promote the safety of women and family members and to increase the efficiency and effectiveness of the criminal justice system's response to these crimes. The program's objectives are to estimate the scope of violence against women and family violence, identify their causes and consequences, evaluate promising prevention and intervention programs, disseminate research results to the field, and build partnerships among a wide variety of disciplines to accomplish these objectives.

http://www.mincava.umn.edu

Minnesota Center Against Violence and Abuse. The mission of MINCAVA is to support research, education, and access to violence-related resources. MINCAVA is considered a leader in innovative violence-related education, research, and Internet publishing and now coordinates four nationally and internationally renowned projects.

http://www.dvalianza.org

Alianza: National Latino Alliance for the Elimination of Domestic Violence. Alianza is part of a national effort to address the domestic violence needs and concerns of underserved populations. It represents a growing network of Latina and Latino advocates, practitioners, researchers, community activists, and survivors of domestic violence. Its mission is to promote understanding, initiate and sustain dialogue, and generate solutions that move toward the elimination of domestic violence affecting Latino communities, with an understanding of the sacredness of all relations and communities.

http://www.dahmw.org

Domestic Abuse Hotline for Men and Women. This nonprofit organization provides direct services, support, and referrals to adult victims of intimate partner violence through its website as well as through its crisis hotline.

http://www.childwelfare.gov

Child Welfare Information Gateway. Formerly the National Clearinghouse on Child Abuse and Neglect Information and the National Adoption Information Clearinghouse, Child Welfare Information Gateway provides ascess to information and resources to help protect children and strengthen families. It is a service of the Children's Bureau, Administration for Children and Families, U.S. Department of Health and Human Services.

http://www.human.cornell.edu/fldc

Family Life Development Center. FLDC was established by New York State in 1974. Its mission is to understand and act upon risk and protective factors in the lives of children, youth, families, and communities. As a multidisciplinary unit of the College of Human Ecology at Cornell University, the Center accomplishes its mission through research, training, and outreach. It serves New York State, the nation, and the international community. The current areas of special interest include child maltreatment and family violence, youth development, children in residential care, HIV/AIDS prevention, and military family life.

http://www.unh.edu/frl

Family Research Laboratory. Housed at the University of New Hampshire, the FRL has devoted itself primarily to understanding family violence and the impact of violence on families since 1975. Researchers at the FRL pioneered many of the techniques that have enabled social scientists to estimate directly the scope of family violence, earning them international recognition. The FRL is unusual among research centers in this field because it includes on its agenda *all* aspects of the family, violence, and abuse.

http://www.ncea.aoa.gov/ncearoot/Main_Site/Index.aspx

National Center on Elder Abuse. The National Center on Elder Abuse (NCEA) is a national resource for elder rights, law enforcement and legal professionals, public policy leaders, researchers, and the public. The Center's mission is to promote understanding, knowledge sharing, and action on elder abuse, neglect, and exploitation. The NCEA is administered under the auspices of the National Association of State Units on Aging.

chapter **11**

Divorce and Remarriage

▶ ## Myths and Realities

Myth	High divorce rates mean that marriage is becoming less popular.
Reality	Actually, marriage is still popular. Divorced people overwhelmingly tend to remarry.
Myth	Marriages are much more likely to end in divorce today than a generation ago.
Reality	The divorce rate peaked around 1980 and has been declining ever since.
Myth	Marriage and divorce rates are more or less stable across racial groups in the United States.
Reality	There are differences across racial groups because of social class, cultural, and religious differences.
Myth	Divorces occur throughout the life cycle, with little pattern according to length of marriage.
Reality	Divorces tend to occur early in marriages—about half by the seventh year of marriage.
Myth	Ex-husbands and ex-wives suffer about equally from the consequences of divorce.
Reality	The consequences of divorce are different by gender, with women experiencing more negatives than men.
Myth	Men are more likely than women to initiate divorce proceedings.
Reality	Women are much more likely than men to file for divorce, with the exception of older wives in long-term unions.
Myth	Having learned from their mistakes, remarried couples have more marital success than do couples in first marriages.
Reality	The divorce rate for remarrieds is higher than for first marriages.

Andrew Cherlin, comparing marriage and divorce in the United States with other Western nations, concluded:

I believe that what truly makes American families different is the sum total of these differences—frequent marriage, frequent divorce, more short-term cohabiting relationships. Together these factors create a great turbulence in American family life, a family flux, a coming and going of partners on a scale seen nowhere else. There are more partners in the personal lives of Americans than in the lives of people of any other Western country. The most distinctive characteristic of American family life, then, the trait that most clearly differentiates it from family life in other Western countries, is sheer movement: frequent transitions, shorter relationships. Americans step on and off the carousel of intimate partnerships (by which I mean marriages and cohabiting relationships) more often. (Cherlin, 2009:5)

Although many marriages do not end in divorce, nearly half do. Some marriages become intolerable as they are filled with more and more tension and even violence, as shown in the previous chapter. Some marriages fail because the love the wife and husband once shared diminishes for various reasons. Still other marriages break up because of the relentless strains from economic difficulties. For these and countless other reasons, **divorce**—the formal dissolution of marriage—is a relatively common experience in the United States.

This chapter examines divorce rates (past, present, and future), the correlates and causes of divorce, and the consequences of the divorce experience for the former spouses and their children. Divorce apparently is not a repudiation of marriage, because most divorced persons eventually marry again. We examine this phenomenon of remarriage, looking at the remarriage rates, prospects for marital success, and the role of the stepparent. The final section examines briefly the politics of divorce.

"I have the kids Friday, Saturday, and Sunday. She has them Monday, Tuesday, and Wednesday. Thursday they're free-range."

Divorce Rates

This section examines the historical patterns in divorce, the variables associated with marital breakdown, the sources of the marital strains that lead to divorce, and the predictions for future divorce rates.

Trends in Divorce

Many politicians, clergy, editorial writers, and others have shown great concern over the current high rates of marital dissolution in the United States. Although estimates vary, most scholars agree that between 40 and 50 percent of all first marriages end in divorce (Visher et al., 2003). Various government documents from the Census Bureau ("Marital Status and Living Arrangements"), The Centers for Disease Control and Prevention, and the National Center for Health Statistics, reveal the following patterns for first marriages (summarized in Coontz, 2007):

- One in five marriages end in divorce or separation within five years.
- Couples who separate do so, on average, after seven years and divorce after eight years.
- One in three marriages dissolve within 10 years.
- More than two-fifths (43 percent) of marriages end within 15 years.
- Three-fourths of all divorced men remarry; 6 out of 10 women remarry.

The historical rate reveals three trends. First, the rate has been rising since 1860 (see Figure 11.1), when the refined divorce rate (the number of divorces in a

Figure 11.1   **Annual Divorce Rates, United States, 1860–2005 (divorces per thousand married women age 15 and over)**

Sources: Cherlin, Andrew J. *Marriage, Divorce, Remarriage.* Cambridge, MA: Harvard University Press, 1981, p. 22; Levitan, Sar A., Richard S. Belous, and Frank Gallo, *What's Happening to the American Family?* Rev. ed. Baltimore: Johns Hopkins University Press, 1988, p. 27; and current U.S. Census Bureau documents.

given year per every 1,000 married women) was about 1 to a rate of 17.6 in 2005 (see Box 11.1 for the methodological issues on computing the divorce rate). Second, although the current divorce rate is near its historical peak, it has been declining slowly for the past 25 years. And third, as shown in Figure 11.1 the divorce rate is clearly affected by social and economic conditions. Note, for example, that the rate increased after wars: slightly after the Civil War, more noticeably after World War I, and then dramatically after World War II. Note also that there was a downward shift during the economic depression of the early 1930s and an increase in the prosperous 1970s.

Factors Correlated with Divorce

The probability of divorce is associated with a number of variables, the most significant of which are cohort, premarital cohabitation, age at first marriage, circumstances of the first birth, the presence of children, income, race, religion, and the intergenerational transmission of divorce.

COHORT

A **cohort** is a category of people who were born during the same time period and thus subject to similar social factors as they move through the life cycle. For example, children born in the economic depression of the 1930s are different as adults than children born after World War II. The Census Bureau found, for example, of the first

BOX 11.1 Researching Families

Computing the Divorce Rate

The divorce rate is calculated in several ways by official agencies and the media. Each of these methods is based on certain assumptions that can, in some instances, lead to faulty generalizations.

One method is to count the number of divorces per thousand population in a given year (crude divorce rate). In 1980 there were 5.2 divorces for each 1,000 Americans, compared to a 1960 rate of 2.2 divorces per thousand. In 2006 the rate was 3.6. A major problem with this statistic is that not everyone in the population is at risk of being divorced—that is, if they are not married. A second problem with this measure of divorce is that it is too sensitive to the nation's age distribution. From 1960 to 1980 there was a very large increase in the age group in which divorces are most likely to occur, so this inflated the rate. In future years the nation's population will be aging, and this fact will deflate the divorce rate if this measure is used.

A second method—the divorce/marriage ratio—is the least satisfactory, yet it is a favorite of the popular press. This ratio compares the number of marriages in a given year with the number of divorces occurring in that year. In 1980, for example, there were 2,390,000 marriages and 1,189,000 divorces, giving a ratio of 490 divorces per thousand marriages. Many would misinterpret this to mean that 49 percent of all marriages end in divorce. Such a reading is inappropriate because the ratio compares two quite different populations. It compares the marriages in a given year with the divorces in that year that came from all existing marriages, not just those from that year. Further confounding this measure is that about 45 percent of marriages in a given year are remarriages for one or both spouses.

A realistic measure of divorce reverses the method for the divorce/marriage ratio just mentioned. Instead of comparing the number of marriages in a given year with the number of divorces in that year, this measure (the refined divorce rate) records the number of divorces that occur out of every 1,000 women in a year. If we use this measure, the divorce rate was 9.2 per thousand marriages in 1960, 22.6 in 1980, and 17.6 in 2005.

Sources: Hacker, Andrew (ed.), *U/S: A Statistical Portrait of the American People.* New York: Viking Press, 1983, pp. 106–108; Ritzer, George, Kenneth C. W. Kammeyer and Norman R. Yetman, *Sociology: Experiencing a Changing Society,* 2nd ed. Boston, MA: Allyn and Bacon, 1982, pp. 330–332; Constance L. Shehan, *Marriages and Families,* 2nd ed. Boston, MA: Allyn and Bacon, 2003, pp. 410–412; Saluter, Arlene F., "Marital Status and Living Arrangements." Current Population Reports, Series P-20-380 (May 1983): 3; National Center for Health Statistics, *First Dissolution, Divorce, and Remarriage: United States.* Hyattsville, MD: Department of Health and Human Services (May 31, 2001); Eshleman, J. Ross and Richard A. Bulcroft, *The Family,* 11th ed. Boston, MA: Allyn and Bacon, 2006, pp. 537–540; Dan Hurley (2005). "Divorce Rate: It's Not as High as You Think." *New York Times* (April 19). Online: http://www.nytimes.com/2005/04/19/health/19divor.html.

marriages for women from 1955 to 1959 (very likely born during the Great Depression), about 79 percent were still married 15 years later. For women married between 1985 and 1989 (born soon after World War II and the leading edge of the Baby Boom generation), only 57 percent marked their 15th anniversary (reported in Coontz, 2007).

PREMARITAL COHABITATION

Logically, it would seem that cohabitation before marriage would increase the marital stability for those couples who eventually marry, but research consistently finds that the opposite occurs (for a review, see Amato et al., 2007:73; Faust and McKibben, 1999:484). There are several possible reasons for this seeming anomaly. First, research shows that cohabitors differ from noncohabitors in that they are younger, less likely to adapt to traditional marital expectations, and more approving of divorce as an answer to marital problems. Also, those who are used to greater freedom in the cohabitation arrangement may find marriage too stifling. Cohabitors, too, are more likely to have divorced parents, which leads to higher risks in marriage (see the next section). Finally, cohabitors who marry are more likely to have stepchildren in their relationships, which leads to higher rates of marital dissolution in cohabiting unions.

AGE AT FIRST MARRIAGE

The age at which persons marry plays a major role in whether marriages will remain intact (Heaton, 2002:395), with marriages between younger people having a heightened probability of divorce. A government study found that 59 percent of marriages for women under 18 end in divorce within 15 years, compared to 36 percent of those married at age 20 or older (reported in Peterson, 2001a). There are several reasons for this relationship between youth and marital instability. An obvious one is that teenagers may lack the maturity to handle the responsibilities of marriage. Their youth and relative inexperience in relationships also may lead them to make less sensible choices in marital partners. Those who marry early may not have had sufficient dating experience to develop a clear idea of what characteristics they value in a partner. Couples who marry young have restricted opportunities for college education and tend to have financial difficulties, especially if they have children early. Since premarital pregnancy is a common reason for early marriages, many young people enter marriage for the wrong reasons, have reduced chances for education and income, and are likely to feel prematurely limited in their search for potential spouses. Women especially find that early marriages and parenthood restrict their options, and this feeling increases the potential for resentment and strains, leading to eventual marital dissolution.

CIRCUMSTANCES OF THE FIRST BIRTH

Premarital pregnancy and births increase the risk of divorce. Women who have never married and who either had a premarital first birth or a premaritally conceived, but postmaritally delivered, birth have higher divorce rates after their first marriage than do mothers whose first child was postmaritally conceived (Fine et al., 2005). A quick marriage that often accompanies an unplanned pregnancy works against marital success because the newlyweds may feel that they are trapped with little choice, that the swift arrival of a baby does not give them sufficient time to adapt to married life, and that the timing limits educational and career opportunities, especially for the young women.

THE PRESENCE OF CHILDREN

The presence of children in a family affects marital stability in several ways (from a review of the research literature by Faust and McKibben, 1999:483–484):

- Couples with children are less likely to divorce than childless couples.
- The likelihood of divorce decreases as family size increases, although having more than four children makes couples more likely to divorce than having four or fewer children (Heaton, 1990).
- Divorce rates are lower in families with children under the age of 3, while rates are higher in families with children over the age of 13.

Do these findings mean that the presence of children makes for happier unions? Actually, as noted in Chapter 9, the opposite is more likely the case: Couples tend to be happiest before children and after their children leave the nest. If children do not necessarily increase marital happiness, then what is the explanation for the greater durability of marriages that involve children? There are several possible explanations: (1) Couples at risk of dissolving their marriage may decide not to have children unless their difficulties are mended. (2) Couples with children may be as unhappy as those without, but they may tend to stay together "for the good of the children." (3) Couples with large families have, by definition, been married a relatively long time, and longevity in a marriage increases its chances for survival. In this last instance, when families become too large, the economic and time demands on parents may detract from marital stability.

Research suggests that under certain circumstances the presence of children increases the likelihood of divorce (Faust and McKibben, 1999):

- The presence of children born prior to the marriage increases the likelihood of divorce.

- The presence of stepchildren increases the probability of divorce in second marriages (this relationship will be elaborated later in this chapter).

- Families whose children are exclusively daughters have a higher divorce rate than families whose children are limited to sons (Katzev et al., 1994). This appears to be the result of fathers being more actively involved in child care and family activities when raising sons than when raising daughters.

INCOME

The research evidence indicates an inverse relationship between divorce and socio-economic status. In other words, the lower the income, the higher the probability of divorce (U.S. Bureau of the Census, 2006).

The lack of adequate resources places a burden on intimate relationships. Sudden financial difficulties such as unexpected unemployment also increase the possibility of marital breakdown. Low income, for example, is one of the basic reasons for the high probability that teenage marriages will end in divorce. If, however, these youthful unions have sufficient incomes, the negative effects of youth are moderated.

An important exception to this generalization that income is inversely related to divorce is that wives' earnings are positively associated with divorce rates. In short, when women have independent sources of income, the likelihood of divorce rises.

Evidence for this relationship between one's economic situation and divorce is found in the divorce rate in cities, states, and regions undergoing economic stress. For example, the divorce rate in areas of severe economic downturn, where, for example, steel mills and automobile factories and their suppliers have laid off hundreds of thousands of workers, the divorce rate is higher than in areas of relatively low unemployment rates (Kilborn, 2004). Box 11.2 presents another structural variable—in this instance, war—that dramatically increases the potential for divorce.

While hard times can often strain marriages leading to a surge in divorces, the severe economic situation of 2008–2009 actually had the opposite effect in the short term (Armour, 2009). The reason is that spouses contemplating divorce may have been forced to postpone separating because of the surge in foreclosures, sinking property values, and vanishing home equity, making it very difficult to sell their houses. Thus, spouses in the throes of divorce often did not separate, continuing to live together until the housing market turned around.

EDUCATION

Persons with lower educational achievement, on average, are more likely to divorce than those with higher levels of education (National Marriage Project, 2006). While

Emergent **Family** Trends

A Casualty of War: Divorce

The costs of war are great in the loss of life, physical and psychological impairment to soldiers and civilians, environmental devastation, destroyed infrastructure, money diverted from social spending, and disrupted lives. More specifically, for the Iraq War by early August 2006, more than 2,500 Americans and 40,000 Iraqis had died, more than 20,000 Americans were injured, and the United States was spending $1.5 billion a week. Often overlooked in the tally of war costs are the negative consequences on the intimate lives of soldiers and their spouses that result in a higher than normal divorce rate. Let's consider what we know of the effects of the Iraq and Afghanistan conflicts on the combatants and their spouses.

In 2004, 3,325 Army officers' marriages ended in divorce—up 78 percent from the previous year, and more than three-and-a-half times the number in 2000, before the Afghan operation began. For Army enlisted personnel, the 7,152 divorces in 2003 were up 53 percent from 2003 (Zoroya, 2005). Put another way, from 2001 to 2004 divorces among active-duty Army officers nearly doubled, even though the total troop strength remained stable (Crary, 2005). A notable trend is for a higher rate

for female soldiers than male soldiers. In 2008, for example, more than 7 percent of military females divorced, which is nearly two-and-a-half times that of military males (Erickson, 2008).

As the Iraq war continued, the number of divorces among military personnel also rose, with the number of divorced soldiers rising 5 percent from 2007 to 2008. For the marines, it was up 11 percent (Erickson, 2008).

What accounts for the soaring divorce rate in time of war? First, war means stress from combat, long separations, and, in the case of the Iraq War, a series of redeployments of troops beyond what they had expected. Second, many marriages were rushed into before deployment by relatively young people (where the divorce rate is the highest among the civilian population as well). Third, approximately one-fourth of returning soldiers will experience significant psychological distress due to the inherent stressors of deployment, prolonged separation, persistent fear, chronic uncertainty, unstable finances, and grim consequences of engagement. Common psychological problems include post-traumatic stress disorder, depression, anxiety, alcohol abuse, and drug addiction. (Operation Comfort, 2006: para 2).

this inverse relationship between education and divorce is generally true, highly educated women, just as those women with independent incomes, are more likely to divorce than highly educated men.

RACE/ETHNICITY

The divorce patterns in the United States differ by race and ethnicity. The data since 1960 show consistently that White and Asian marriages are the most stable, Latino marriages less so, and those for African Americans the most likely to end in divorce.

Marital Instability among African Americans   Andrew Cherlin has argued that the differences between African American and White family patterns reflect the life of African Americans today in cities, where their economic lot continues to deteriorate. Cherlin's findings reveal that those African Americans who differ most from Whites are the least educated, have the most unstable work history, and have the least income. In short, marital instability appears to "represent the response of the poorest, most disadvantaged segment of the black population to the social and economic situation they have faced in our cities over the past few decades" (Cherlin, 1981:108). The economic changes accompanying the transformation of the economy especially have placed African Americans at a disadvantage. Many of the jobs that once provided economic stability for African Americans have left the central city areas for the suburbs and the Rustbelt for the Sunbelt, leaving African Americans with lower-paying jobs or no jobs at all. As a result of these and other social factors, African

Americans and Whites differ significantly in occupation and income, with 24.5 percent of African Americans living below the poverty line in 2007, compared to about 10.5 percent of Whites. The average African American household income in 2008 was $38,269, compared to $61,280 for Whites (Rivera et al., 2009); also, African Americans are consistently twice as likely as Whites to be unemployed. Clearly, the disparities between these two racial groups show that African Americans are more likely to experience economic hardships and insecurities that lead to marital disruption. Added to these economic differences are the racial inequities that continuously confront people of color.

Marital Instability among Latinos   The rate of marital instability among Latinos is about the same as the rate for Whites. This is curious, because Latinos share economic disadvantage and discrimination with African Americans. The members of both groups suffer discrimination because of skin color; both groups are disproportionately poor (21.5 percent of Latinos were below the poverty line in 2007; DeNavas-Walt et al., 2008), unemployed, employed in the secondary labor sector, negatively impacted by the economic transformation, undereducated, and more likely to marry at a young age. How, then, are we to account for the marital patterns of Latinos, which approximate more closely the patterns of Whites than of African Americans?

First, we must remember that Latinos are not a homogeneous category. The marital disruption rate for Cuban Americans, for example, is relatively low, while it is quite high for Puerto Ricans.

The most common explanation for the relative stability of Latino marriages is a cultural one. This explanation focuses on the traditional Latino family, which is typically a strong unit embedded in a very significant kin network. Also, Catholicism, the religion of most traditional Latinos, is absolute in its prohibition against divorce. Although these cultural explanations appear to make sense, they are too simplistic because they do not take into account the diversity among Latinos.

Peter Uhlenberg (1972), for example, compared two groups of Latinos— first-generation immigrants in rural Texas and third-generation urban Latinos in California—and found some interesting differences. The first-generation immigrants, although very poor, rarely divorced (having a rate actually less than that found for Whites) because they were extremely traditional in their attitudes and behaviors. Also, these new immigrants tended to stay together because they were aliens in a strange land, with nowhere else to turn for refuge other than their immediate and extended families. The third-generation Latinos in California, on the other hand, had a high rate of unstable marriages, similar to that for African Americans. They were not constrained by tradition but were affected rather by structural variables. Wives in these families were much less dependent on their husbands than were wives in first-generation immigrant families because these third-generation Latino women had more education and better employment. Thus, for them, traditional gender roles were less tenable. Males were relatively weak compared to females because of their low wages and widespread unemployment. This inability of males to be adequate providers, along with the wives' questioning of gender roles, led to strain in marriages. "For a male unable to fulfill his role as economic provider, leaving his family reduces the gap between what is socially expected of him and what is possible" (Uhlenberg, 1972:55–56). Uhlenberg's research is important because it demonstrates that Latinos are not a homogeneous group constrained uniformly by the strong traditions brought from Mexico and by the hold of Catholicism. Moreover, we see that the divorce rate for Latinos is an average that masks the diversity in family experiences among this minority.

Marital Instability among Arab Americans   First-generation Arab Americans tend to maintain traditions and are slow to assimilate. One consequence is a low divorce rate. The reverse is true for second- and third-generation Arab Americans, resulting in the percentage of American Muslims who are divorced rising from 2 to 35 percent in one generation (Chauhan, 2005). Overall, though, Arab Americans have a somewhat lower divorce rate than the U.S. population as a whole (Kayyali, 2006:71). In addition to the reasons for marital disruption among all couples, those that particularly affect Arab Americans are: when one in the marriage is more observant of Muslim traditions than the other and, similarly, when wives are educated and work outside the home. Also, there is a high rate of intermarriage among Arab Americans—over 80 percent of U.S.-born Arabs have non-Arab spouses (Kulczycki and Lobo, 2002). As noted in the following discussion, interracial marriages have a higher divorce rate than intraracial marriages.

Interracial Marriages   Data from the 2000 Census revealed that 7.0 percent of Whites were married to someone from a different racial background, compared to 12.6 percent of Blacks, 30.9 percent of Asians, and 29.3 percent of Latinos. For Asians and Latinos the intermarriage rates are even higher among younger, native-borns (Lee and Bean, 2004a:52–53).

As just noted, interracial marriages have a higher divorce rate than intraracial marriages. Moreover, the type of intermarriage makes a difference. For example, the most common type of Black/White marriage (four times more likely) is for a White woman to marry an African American man, rather than for an African American woman to marry a White man. Among these types, divorce is more likely to occur among those interracial couples who do not follow the typical pattern of a White woman married to an African American man (Collins, 1988a:362).

RELIGION

A 1999 national survey conducted by the Barna Research Group found that 24 percent of all adults have experienced at least one divorce during their lifetime (reported in Matthews, 1999). Concerning religious affiliation, this study found that Jews have the highest divorce rate (30 percent). Among Christian denominations, Baptists have the highest rate (29 percent), those identified as "born again" have a rate higher than the average (27 percent), while those from the mainline Protestant denominations and Mormons are no different than the national average (25 percent). Atheists and agnostics are below the norm, with the same rate (21 percent) as Lutherans and Catholics.

These findings underscore the importance of social, demographic, and economic influences beyond the relative commitment of two people (Carman, 2000). For example, the relatively low rate for Catholics is due, of course, to the unyielding opposition of the Catholic Church to divorce while the higher rate for Protestant denominations is due to their more accepting attitudes of divorce. Although the Catholic divorce rate is lower than the Protestant divorce rate, it is important to note that the rates move in tandem. That is, when the divorce rate is going up in society, it moves upward for both religious categories, indicating the importance of other social factors affecting marriages.

Interreligious couples have higher divorce rates than couples with the same religious beliefs. This indicates that couples who are alike on social variables (homogamy) will have lower divorce rates than those who are different (**heterogamy**). Gender and religion combine for an interesting pattern. The divorce rate is lower when the woman is a Catholic and the man a Protestant than when the man is a Catholic and the woman a Protestant.

INTERGENERATIONAL TRANSMISSION OF DIVORCE

Adult children of divorce are more likely to experience divorce than are adult children from intact families (Amato et al., 2007:23). Sociologists Paul Amato and Danelle DeBoer (2001) examined data collected between 1980 and 1997 from 2,033 married persons and found that among those interviewed in their study parental divorce approximately doubled the odds that offspring would experience the breakup of their own marriages. There are several possible reasons for this tendency. First, the children of divorced parents usually live with their mother, and this often means a decline in standard of living. Children growing up with economic disadvantages are more likely to have lower educational attainment and an increased probability of pre-marital pregnancy, all of which are characteristics associated with a higher divorce rate (McLanahan and Sandefur, 1994).

Second, children experiencing their parents' divorce may have feelings of depression, anxiety, and stress, which may have long-term negative effects leading to poor preparation for marriage.

Third, parents who divorce are not good role models for their children. Those children, by observing the ongoing conflicts between their parents before the divorce, do not learn how to resolve conflicts satisfactorily, and may tend to view divorce as the solution rather than trying to work things out with their spouse.

Fourth, as a result of accepting their parents' divorce, the children from divorced households, more than the children of intact families, are more accepting of divorce as the only way to deal with a troubled marriage.

Finally, the results of Amato and DeBoer's research, just mentioned, provide strong support for the possibility that elevated divorce rates among the children of divorce reflect a loss of faith in the ideal of marital permanence. In other words, the commitment to a lifelong marriage is undermined by their parents' divorce (*Society*, 2003).

There is evidence that divorce has consequences beyond the next generation. In other words, when grandparents divorce, the repercussions may affect not only their children but their grandchildren as well. Amato and Cheadle (2005) analyzed data from a 20-year longitudinal study and found that family problems can persist across generations. Divorce, they found, results in lower educational attainment and problematic family relationships in the second generation, and these outcomes occur in the third generation as well.

Predicting the Future Divorce Rate: Up or Down?

As noted earlier, the divorce rate has steadily risen in the United States since at least 1860, with a dramatic rise from 1960 to 1981, followed by a mild but steady decline from the historic high. In 2009 the divorce rate was at its lowest level since 1970. But what of the future? Is this recent decline the beginning of a downward trend in the rate or at least a leveling off, or only a pause in the long-term upward trend? Although the future is difficult to predict with accuracy, the factors associated with divorce rates indicate that the trend is for divorce to continue its decline or to level off. A word of caution: Divorce rates are based on what has happened to earlier marriages (Kammeyer, 1981; Kammeyer et al., 1990:399). We simply do not know whether this and future generations will follow the patterns of previous generations. With this caveat in mind, let's review first the factors that will have a dampening influence on future divorce rates.

Young adults now are marrying about five years later than in 1980, reducing the number of very young brides and grooms. The later the marriage takes place, the less chance there is of divorce.

A basis for the high divorce rate in the 1970s was the ideological gap between the rise of new feminists and their traditional husbands. Many wives developed a keen awareness of gender inequities *after* they were married. When their challenges to traditional gender patterns were resisted by their traditional husbands, the chances for divorce increased. Although these gender battles are still being fought in contemporary marriages, there is a greater likelihood that both partners are aware during courtship of their future spouse's beliefs concerning gender roles. Thus, there are fewer surprises, and the demands by wives that their husbands participate in household chores and child care are viewed as less threatening and less challenging. As a result, it is argued, gender battles have diminished as a source of marital disruption.

On the legal side, there is a concerted attempt by conservatives to make divorces more difficult to obtain, which, if successful, will bring the divorce rate down. This is a reaction to no-fault divorce laws, which were passed by every state since the 1970s and which made divorces easier and faster to obtain. These laws made it possible for either spouse to cancel a marriage at any time. Some have argued that the divorce rate, which jumped 30 percent since the passage of no-fault divorce laws, is a consequence of those laws. Research substantiates this. One study found that no-fault laws raised the divorce rate by about 15 percent (Nakonezny et al., 1995), but, as Larry Bumpass has argued, no-fault laws "account for a short-term rise in divorce by speeding those cases that were already coming down the pipeline" (quoted in Johnson, 1996:80).

Many states are trying to legislate ways to discourage divorce (that is, bringing back fault-based divorce law). A different legislative strategy with the same presumed outcome is to make marriage more difficult to obtain. Another option with the expressed hope of deterring divorce, passed by the 1997 Louisiana legislature, is a voluntary method called "covenant marriage" (Nock et al., 1999). Arizona enacted similar legislation in 1998 and other states, mostly southern, are considering this attempt to strengthen marriage (Latham, 2000). In Louisiana it works this way: Although couples may opt for marriage as before, they now also have the option of a "covenant marriage." Couples choosing this option must receive premarital counseling and promise to marry for life. Divorces are granted only after counseling and only under certain conditions: (1) The couple has been separated for more than two years; (2) either spouse has committed adultery; (3) a spouse is convicted of a felony and sentenced to prison; (4) a spouse physically or sexually abuses his or her spouse or child; and (5) a spouse abandons the house and refuses to return for at least a year.

Clearly, the enactment of laws making marriage and/or divorce more difficult to obtain will bring divorce rates down. Contrary to the assumption of the proponents of such legislation, however, these efforts will not enhance the quality of marriages. Nor will this legislation increase marriages. What will likely occur is that there will be a greater reluctance to marry, increasing the likelihood of cohabitation as a substitute for marriage.

The number of couples who live together without marrying (cohabitation) has increased twelvefold since 1960 to about 5.4 million couples in 2006 (Fowler, 2008). This dramatic increase in couples living together without marrying is the primary reason why divorce rates have declined in the recent past. This is because many couples who would have married in previous generations and later divorced now live together before marriage. In 2000 some 41 percent of people who cohabited eventually married (Amato et al., 2007:71). If they had not lived together but married instead, the 59 percent who separated without marrying would have been counted in the divorce statistics. Cohabitation has become increasing acceptable in society, which leads to the assumption of even more cohabiting unions and fewer formal marriages in the near term.

There is also a trend toward more stable marriages. For instance, "[m]arriages that began in the 1990s were more likely to celebrate a 10th anniversary than those that started in the 1980s, which, in turn, were also more likely to last than marriages that began in the 1970s" (Stevenson and Wolfers, 2007: para 3).

Historically, economic downturns increase the divorce rate. But the recession beginning in 2008 is deeper than any since the 1930s. There are indications that the seriousness of these current economic times may neutralize the typical trend of hard times leading to divorce, at least in the short term. Dramatic declines in 401(k)s (retirement accounts) and housing values have kept many couples from separating because they cannot afford to. Michigan, for example, the state with the highest unemployment rate in 2009, has a declining divorce rate. A family-law attorney in Michigan, Henry Gornbein, states that "[p]eople have no choice sometimes now except to return to the marriage" (quoted in Luscombe, 2008: 62).

Several trends lead to a **marriage gap** by social class (*Economist*, 2007a). That is, there is a widening gulf between the least educated and best educated in divorce patterns. High school dropouts and those who stopped their education with high school are more likely than their more educated peers to be pregnant at the time of marriage, marry young, have children early, and be limited to low-wage dead-end jobs, all factors leading to a relatively high divorce rate. The well educated and more affluent, on the other hand, are more likely than economically marginal couples to stay married. The data show that people with college degrees are half as likely to be divorced or separated as their less-educated peers (Jefferson, 2008:49). A knowledge-based economy requires an emphasis on education. To the degree that the demand for higher education increases, we can expect the overall divorce rate to decline.

There is a debate on the direction of future divorce rates. While considering the merits of the arguments in this debate, we must remember an important fact: The divorce rate reflects the composite picture of marital instability. Thus, this single rate, whether rising or falling, masks the variation in marital disruption by class, race, and ethnicity.

The Consequences of Divorce for Spouses and Children

The previous section on divorce rates examined divorce in a detached manner, considering divorces in the aggregate rather than as the personal dramas of individuals at the micro level severing the most intimate of relationships. Divorce is an intensely personal event, and this intensity makes the breakup a painful experience, even when both parties want the marriage to end. The uncoupling process begins with feelings of estrangement.

Because virtually all people enter marriage with the expectation (or the hope) that it will be a mutually supportive, rewarding, lifelong relationship, estrangement from one's spouse is typically a painful experience. Estranged spouses might spend considerable time attempting to renegotiate the relationship, seeking advice from others, or simply avoiding (denying) the problem. Consequently, the first negative effects of divorce on adults can occur years prior to final separation and legal dissolution. (Amato, 2001:1271–1272)

Both of the partners in a divorce are victims. Each is affected, in the typical case, by feelings of loneliness, anger, remorse, guilt, low self-esteem, low levels of psychological well-being, depression, and failure. Although ex-spouses tend to share these negative feelings, the divorce experience differs for husbands and wives in significant ways because of the structure of society and traditional gender roles. This section scrutinizes the personal side of divorce—the consequences for ex-husbands, ex-wives, and their children.

"His" Divorce

Ex-husbands have some major advantages and a few disadvantages over their ex-spouses.

IMPROVED STANDARD OF LIVING

Men have the advantage of being better off financially than their former wives. Typically, they were the major income producers for their families, and after the separation, their incomes stay disproportionately with them.

INCREASED PERSONAL FREEDOM

A second benefit that men have over women after divorce is greater freedom. If children are involved, they usually live with the mother (about 85 percent), so most men are free from the constraints not only of marriage but also of child care. Thus, they are more free than ex-wives to date, travel, go to school, take up a hobby, or work at a second job. Especially significant is sexual freedom, since males tend to have more money and leisure time. Moreover, because older men in U.S. society are considered more attractive to younger women than older women are to younger men, men have a much wider selection of dating partners and potential spouses than do women.

PERSONAL ISOLATION

The experience of ex-husbands on some counts, however, is more negative than that of ex-wives. Many divorced men, especially those from traditional marriages, experience initial difficulty in maintaining a household routine. They are more likely than divorced women to eat erratically, sleep less, and have difficulty with shopping, cooking, laundry, and cleaning. And because ex-wives usually have legal custody of the children, ex-husbands see their children only relatively rarely and at prescribed times. Thus, they may experience great loneliness, having lost both wife and children.

The image of liberated ex-husbands as swinging bachelors does not fit many men. Some find dating difficult. They find that women in general have changed or that they themselves have changed. Many men withdraw from relationships because of feeling awkward, or because they fear rejection. They may also be wary over concerns about AIDS or other sexually transmitted diseases.

"Her" Divorce

Contrary to common belief, about two-thirds of divorces are initiated by women (Sweeney, 2002). The only exception is that older wives in long-term unions are less likely than their husbands to file for divorce (Hacker, 2003:27). This is an interesting anomaly, because women benefit less from divorce than men. To be sure, many ex-wives are relieved to have ended an onerous relationship, and some are even freed from a physically abusive one. Some are now liberated from a situation that stifled their educational and career goals. Of course, divorce also frees them to seek new and perhaps more fulfilling relationships. But there are many reasons for women to keep their marriages intact because divorce has several negative consequences for them. (See the "Families in Global Perspective" box for the special problems of divorce among binational spouses.)

PERSONAL ISOLATION

For women, the negatives of divorce outweigh the positives. Women oriented toward traditional gender roles especially tend to feel helpless and experience a loss of status associated with their husbands' identity and status. Divorced mothers who retain sole custody of their children often feel overwhelmed by the demands of full-time parenting and economic survival. The emotional and schedule overloads that usually accompany solo parenting leave little time for personal pursuits. The result is that divorced women often experience personal and social isolation, especially the feeling

BOX 11.3 **Families in Global Perspective**

Divorce in Binational Marriages

Globalization has led to an increasing number of binational marriages as young adults attend schools or work in foreign lands. In the European Union, for example, where 875,000 divorces take place each year, one-fifth of them are binational). Should these marriages sour, divorce—with its division of assets and custody of the children—is complicated by former spouses being from different traditions and laws. Which laws apply—those of the country or state of residence, those of the spouse seeking the divorce, or those of the wife or husband, regardless of who seeks the divorce? Let's consider the situation of child abduction, about two-thirds of which are perpetrated by mothers (two-thirds of the time) when a marriage breaks down (the following is largely from the *Economist*, 2009a). This act is an attempt to retain custody of the children when the laws and traditions are often stacked against them, because they usually have fewer economic resources than men, they are often less knowledgeable about the law and their options, and, in some countries, there is a male bias in the law.

Most advanced industrial nations, plus most of Latin America and a few other countries, have agreed to the 1980 Hague Convention, a treaty that requires countries to send abducted children back to the jurisdiction where they had previously lived. Sounds simple enough, but in practice some signatory nations do not always comply with the agreement. The U.S. State Department lists Honduras, Brazil, Bulgaria, Chile,

Ecuador, Germany, Greece, Mexico, Poland, and Venezuela as showing "patterns of non-compliance." "Anyone in a wobbly marriage with a citizen of these countries might bear that in mind before agreeing to let the children go on holiday there" (*Economist*, 2009a:22). The U.S., too, makes it difficult at times. State and federal laws may clash. Appeals take time and money. While Great Britain offers automatic legal aid to the foreign parent seeking to recover the children, in the United States that parent must rely on her or his own resources and "sorting out these cross-border legal wrangles can be colossally expensive" (*Economist*, 2009a:24).

Then there are countries that have not signed the Hague Convention, such as Japan, China, and Russia. Other than Turkey and Bosnia, no Muslim countries have signed the Hague Convention. *Sharia* law (Muslim law) assumes that "children over seven will be brought up by the father, not the mother, though that is trumped by a preference for a local Muslim parent. So the chances of a foreign mother recovering abducted children from a Muslim father are slim" (*Economist*, 2009a:22).

So questions remain: Can *sharia* law be used as a legitimate argument in the courts of non-Muslim countries? Does the U.S. parent divorcing a spouse from another country have an advantage in a U.S. court? Should the parent in a binational marriage who abducts her or his children be advantaged or disadvantaged in the courts? How is the jurisdiction of the case decided fairly? What can be done to make the disputing parties be treated equally in the courts?

of being locked into a child's world. White women cope less well with divorce than do African American women. Presumably, this is because African American women have better social supports (extended family networks and friendship and church support networks) than do White women (Fine et al., 2005).

Both ex-husbands and ex-wives tend to lose old friends. For the first two months or so after the divorce, married friends are supportive and spend time with each of the former mates. But these contacts soon decline because, as individuals, divorced people no longer fit into couple-oriented activities. This disassociation from married friends is especially acute for women, because their child-raising responsibilities tend to isolate them from adult interactions.

On the positive side, women tend to have stronger family and friendship networks than men. These networks provide support, explaining, in part, why women fare better emotionally than men after divorce (Faust and McKibben, 1999). Moreover, because most women receive custody of their children after divorce, they are more connected to their children than noncustodial fathers.

Those few women who give up custody of their children face a two-edged sword. On the one hand they have lost their children, and on the other they face society's double standard—it is appropriate for divorced men to give up custody of their children, but not for women to let fathers have custody. By giving up their children, these women experience social ostracism and the belief that they are uncaring and unfit mothers.

DECREASED STANDARD OF LIVING

The biggest problem facing almost all divorced women is a dramatic decline in economic resources. Paul Amato, after examining the relevant research, concludes that "overall, mothers' postseparation standard of living [is] only about one half that of fathers" (Amato, 2001:1277). As Lenore Weitzman argues, for most women and children

> divorce means precipitous downward mobility—both economically and socially. The reduction in income brings residential moves and inferior housing, drastically diminished or nonexistent funds for recreation and leisure, and intense pressures due to inadequate time and money. Financial hardships in turn cause social dislocation and a loss of familiar networks for emotional support and social services, and intensify the psychological stress for women and children alike. On a societal level, divorce increases female and child poverty and creates an ever-widening gap between the economic well-being of divorced men, on the one hand, and their children and former wives on the other. (Weitzman, 1985:323)

Research shows, further, that there has been little change in the gender disparity in the economic costs of marital disruption since the 1960s: "The economic costs of marital disruption for young women are as severe today as in the 1960s and 1970s. Both cohorts lose, on average, almost half of their income when marital disruption occurs" (Manning and Smock, 2000).

SOURCES OF INCOME

Depending on the situation, divorced women have one or more of five meager sources of support.

Alimony   One source is alimony ("spousal support"), which is awarded only rarely by the courts (about 15 percent of all cases), usually for a specified brief time. This is generally an option only for the very affluent, who seek to maintain the high standard of living to which they have become accustomed.

Marital Property   A second source of wealth for divorced women is their share of marital property. Of course, for a poor couple who separate, there is essentially no property to divide. Even for a couple somewhat better off, there may not be much to apportion beyond cars and furniture, because the house is likely to have a large mortgage, with payments the wife will not be able to afford.

Presumably, when there is property to divide, the gender-neutral rules that accompanied "no-fault" divorce laws will treat women and men equally. However, as Lenore Weitzman's analysis (1985) has shown, the effect of these laws has been, rather, to deprive divorced women—especially older homemakers and young mothers—of equitable economic settlements. The problem is that the courts assume that, at the time of divorce, husbands and wives are equal. This assumption ignores the economic inequalities created during marriage. The rules do not compensate wives for the years they spent making a home and providing emotional support while husbands moved ahead in their careers. "By far the most important property acquired in the average marriage is its career assets, or human capital, the vast majority of which is likely to be invested in the husband" (Okin, 1989:163). What of the wives' lost educational opportunities, impaired earning capacities, lost job seniority, and lost pension benefits? Judges typically overlook the husband's career assets, which are almost always superior to those of the wife—his salary, pension, health insurance, and potential earning power. Most husbands and wives, in short, are not equal at the time of divorce. Wives are clearly disadvantaged economically in both the short and long term, facts ignored by the supposed fairness of the law.

Child Support   A third source of income for divorced women is child support paid by absent fathers. However, this is not universally granted by the courts or, when granted, actually paid by nonresident fathers. About two-thirds of divorced mothers have child support awards requiring nonresident fathers to pay child support. In many cases, though, the fathers are either entirely or partially delinquent in the payments. According to the Census Bureau, in 2003 only 45 percent of families received their full child support payment (Grall, 2006). The poorer the family, the less likely they are to receive child support. This is related to race, as people of color are the poorest members of U.S. society. Thus, White women are much more likely than women of color to be awarded child support payments. The lack of adequate child support compounds the economic strain on women who have low earning prospects and poor marriage prospects. African American women are especially exposed to these sources of poverty:

> Formerly married black women and their children are especially vulnerable.... They have limited earnings capacity, face bleak prospects of remarriage, and receive less help from noncustodial fathers than do previously married white women. (Furstenberg, 1990:387)

Welfare   Traditionally, welfare assistance has been a possible source of economic support for the economically disadvantaged. Prior to the welfare reform legislation of 1996, about four million women (not all divorced, of course) received Aid to Families with Dependent Children (AFDC) for themselves and their 8.5 million children. Although AFDC was meager, it at least provided some assistance. The 1996 welfare legislation eliminated AFDC and cut various welfare programs by $55 billion over six years (see Chapter 13). Federal welfare monies now are distributed to the states to be administered by the rules of each state (and, if the states elect, by counties), thereby providing less assistance to families than before.

Employment   The fifth source of support for single women is a job. Most of these women, including those with non-school-age children, are employed, but they are disadvantaged in at least three ways. To begin, the average pay for female workers in the United States is about 78 percent of the average pay for males. This relatively meager pay is reduced even further by the necessity of paying child-care costs. Finally, women's work is concentrated either in the secondary tier of the labor market—where job security is tenuous, pay is low, fringe benefits are weak or nonexistent, and the chances for advancement are poor—or in the service sector (e.g., nursing, teaching, sales, and secretarial jobs), where "women's work" is clearly underpaid.

THE FEMINIZATION OF POVERTY

The economic situation for many divorced women is grim. The "**feminization of poverty**" is a reality that reflects in large part the growing divorce rate of the 1960s and 1970s and the relatively high rate since then. But more than just a mere reflection of a high divorce rate, it is the consequence of a sexist society in which women earn much less than what men earn and almost always end up with the children. The no-fault divorce laws have compounded this problem because their assumption "that men and women are equally capable of self-sufficiency after divorce does not reflect labor-market conditions for most women" (Carlson, 1990:441). Add to this that many women do not receive child support, even if it is awarded by the courts, and the decreases in public welfare programs; the conclusion is that the division of winners and losers in divorce is clearly gendered (Bartfield, 2000).

DIVORCE AS AN OPPORTUNITY FOR CHANGE

Before divorce was widely accepted in this society, marriage was literally "until death do us part." Such a lifelong commitment works for many, but for other couples marriage becomes a trap. Love atrophies, partners change, interests diverge, the interaction becomes abusive—for whatever reason, some marriages are not happy unions.

In this sense, divorce allows people to end difficult and sometimes destructive relationships and start anew, rather than be condemned to "life imprisonment" (this section is dependent in part on Ahrons, 1994). Severing a marriage relationship, although traumatic as we have seen, allows each partner to go her or his own way—to find a new partner who meets his or her needs in a cohabiting or remarriage relationship, to move to a different locale and begin afresh, to go back to school, or to change jobs.

This renewal through divorce allows many women to seize the opportunity and develop a new identity, forge ties with others in order to survive, and delight in becoming competent to do things they could not do or were not allowed to do.

"I'm granting your divorce and ordering you both be released back into the wild."

Adjustment after Divorce for Ex-Spouses

The foremost researcher of divorce, E. Mavis Hetherington has tracked nearly 1,400 families and more than 2,500 children for as long as three decades

(Hetherington, 2002; Hetherington and Kelly, 2002). She says, "Divorce is a painful experience. I've never seen a victimless divorce—where the mother, father or child didn't suffer extreme distress when the family broke up" (quoted in Corliss, 2002:40). But the experience can also be life transforming in a positive sense: "Ending a marriage is an experience that for most people is challenging and painful. But it is also a window of opportunity to build a new and better life" (quoted in Peterson, 2002a:2A).

The divorce experience, especially when it involves children, is miserable for most couples (the following draws heavily from Hetherington, 2002). In the early years, ex-spouses must cope with resentment and anger, self-doubt, guilt, the loss of social networks, and stress from being separated from children or from raising them alone. Typically, a gradual recovery usually begins by the end of the second year. And six years after the divorce, 80 percent of both women and men have moved on to build reasonably or exceptionally fulfilling lives. About 20 percent of the women in Hetherington's sample eventually emerged from divorce enhanced and showing competencies that they would never have developed in an unhappy or constraining marriage. Divorced men were less likely to undergo such personal growth following divorce, but the vast majority of them did construct reasonably happy new lives. According to Hetherington's longitudinal research, 20 years after their divorces, ex-spouses fall into one of the following categories (summarized in Peterson, 2002a:2B):

- *Enhanced* (20 percent). Mostly successful at work, socially, and as parents.
- *Competent loners* (10 percent). More emotionally self-sustaining than enhanced ex-spouses, but they do not need a lifetime companion.
- *Good enoughs* (40 percent). Divorce was difficult, but it did not make a lasting impression, good or bad.
- *Defeated* (10 percent). Succumbed to depression, substance abuse, and/or purposelessness.
- *Seekers or libertines* (20 percent). Seekers, typically insecure men, remarry quickly. Libertines, on the other hand, want life in the fast lane, casual sex, and no rules.

In sum, Hetherington found that 20 years after their divorce 7 out of 10 ex-spouses made it through the divorce relatively unscathed.

Children and Divorce

Approximately 65 percent of the divorcing couples each year have minor children, resulting in about one million children affected by new divorces annually. This means that about two-fifths of children—one in every three White children and two in every three African American children—by age 16 will experience the permanent disruption of their parents' marriage. Figure 11.2 shows the percentage of children living in various family arrangements. Most of them will remain with their mothers and live in a fatherless home for at least five years. Most significant, many children of divorce effectively *lose* their fathers (Amato and Booth, 1996). "Ten years after a divorce, fathers will be entirely absent from the lives of almost two-thirds of these children" (Weissbourd, 1994:68). Some are twice cursed by the broken relationships of their parents—about one-third of White children and one-half of African American children whose mothers remarry will experience a second divorce before the children reach adulthood. Figure 11.3 shows the breakdown in living arrangements of children by race/ethnicity for 1970 through 2007. These data reveal that in 2007, 37 percent of Black children lived with both parents, while the majority of White children and Latino children lived in two-parent homes

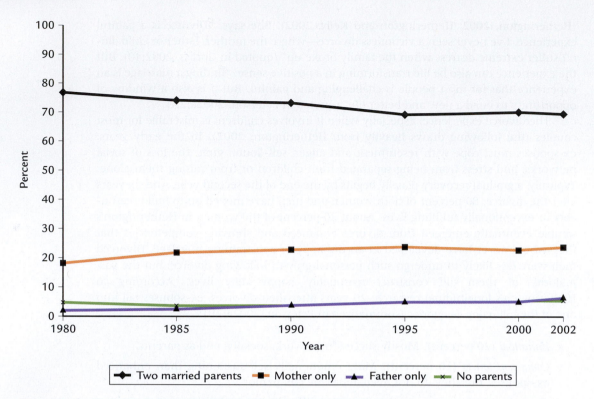

Figure 11.2 **Percentage of Children under 18 by Presence of Parents in Household, 1980–2002**

Note: The category "two married parents" includes children who live with a biological, step, or adoptive parent who is married with his or her spouse. If a second parent is present and not married to the first parent, then the child is identified as living with a single parent

Source: U.S. Census Bureau, March Current Population Survey and Federal Interagency Forum on Child and Family Statistics (2003). America's children: Key national indicators of well-being, 2003. Washington, DC.

(74 and 66 percent, respectively). Also, the proportion of children living in two-parent families declined between 1980 and 2007 for White children (83 to 74 percent), Black children (42 to 37 percent), and Latino children (75 to 66 percent). While two-parent families decreased from 1970 to 2007, the proportion of children living with their mothers in single-parent households increased from 8 to 19 percent for Whites, from 30 to 52 percent for Blacks, and from 20 percent in 1980 to 27 percent in 2007 for Latinos.

The crucial question is, What are the consequences of divorce for children? There is clearly the possibility of emotional scars from the period of family conflict and uncertainty prior to the breakup. Children will be affected by the permanency of divorce and the enforced separation from one of the parents. Most commonly this is separation from their father.

There are the possible negative effects of being raised by a single parent who is over-burdened by the demands of children, job, expenses, and household maintenance. And there are the negative consequences that may result from the sharp decline in resources available to the family when the parents separate. The data are consistent: Female-headed single-parent families, compared to two-parent families and to male-headed single-parent families, have much lower incomes. This severe decline in family resources for female-headed single-parent families produces a number of challenges for children's adjustment, often including moving to a different home and school, eliminating or greatly reducing the probability of a college education, and other alterations in lifestyles.

Proportion of children living with 2 parents by race/ethnicity, 1970–2007

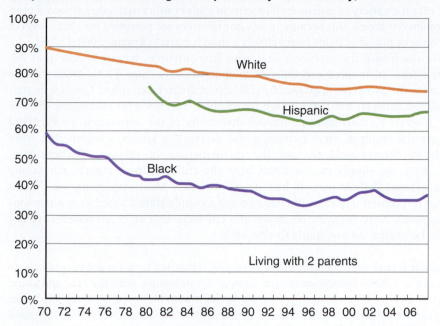

Proportion of children living with mother only by race/ethnicity, 1970–2007

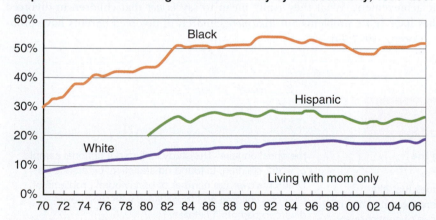

Figure 11.3 **Living Arrangements of Children under 18 Years Old by Race Ethnicity: 1970–2007**

Note: *Persons of Hispanic ethnicity can be of any race; however, most are white. Race proportions include persons of Hispanic ethnicity

Source: U.S. Bureau of the Census. Current Population survey, family and Living arrangements, Historical tables. Online:www.census.gov/population/www/socdemo/hh-fam.htm#ht.

As a result of all of these possible outcomes of divorce, children may experience behavioral problems, decline in school performance, and other symptoms of maladjustment.

Summaries of the research on the consequences of divorce on children reveal that children with divorced parents score lower than children with continuously married parents on measures of academic success, conduct, psychological adjustment, self-concept, and social competence (this section is dependent on the reviews of the literature on children and divorce by Amato, 2001, 2004; Amato and Cheadle, 2005; Fine et al., 2005; Wallerstein, 2003). Although the differences between children from divorced and two-parent families were small, they were consistent. Research also finds that children are better off on a variety of outcomes if parents in high-conflict marriages divorced than if they remained married. But because only some divorces are preceded by a high level of conflict, "divorce probably helps fewer children than it hurts" (Amato, 2001:1278).

Before discussing the problems that arise from divorce, we must note that the long-term effects of divorce are difficult to measure (see Box 11.4). Does divorce actually cause the problems displayed by children of divorced couples? Could it be that these troubled children are being raised by troubled parents who eventually divorce (Cherlin, 1999a)? Hetherington points out that many of the adjustment problems of children are the result of inept parenting and destructive family relations that were present *before* divorce and are not the consequences of divorce (Hetherington, 2002:63). Also, we simply cannot know how the children from a particular family would have fared if their parents had stayed together. Most important, we do not know what the consequences would have been if a couple stayed together in a tension-filled household. Also, we must be aware that children with divorced parents are not doomed to be misfits. As Stephanie Coontz says,

> [w]hile it is true that children in divorced and remarried families are more likely to drop out of school, exhibit emotional distress, get in trouble with the law, and abuse drugs or alcohol than children who grow up with both biological parents, most kids, from *every* kind of family, avoid these perils. And to understand what the increased risk entails for individual families, we need to be clear about what sociologists mean when they talk about such children having more behavior problems or lower academic achievement. What they really mean to say is *not* that children in divorced families have more problems but that *more* children of divorced parents have problems. (Coontz, 1997:99)

BOX 11.4 Researching Families

A New Approach to Researching the Impact of Divorce on Children

Allen Li of the Rand Corporation argues that it is methodologically unsound to compare the outcomes of children of divorced parents with those of continuously married parents. Instead, his research compares the behaviour of children years before a divorce and their behaviour after the divorce. Only then, he argues, can we tell whether children's problems after a divorce were a result of the divorce or a continuation of prior problems resulting from pre-existing conditions of the child's environment. Li's data included all children born to a national representative sample of American women born between 1958 and 1965. These same women were surveyed repeatedly since 1979 and their children since 1988. Some 47 percent of these mothers were divorced by 2002. Li used a 28-item checklist to measure behaviour problems for children between 4 and 15 years of age. Mothers in each biennial survey filled out the questionnaire. The study included a national sample of 6,332 children. Li found no statistical difference between the average number of behavioural problems of divorced children and those living with their never-divorced parents. Li states:

> It is possible that the dissolution of some marriages decreases some children's behaviour problems and the dissolution of others increases children's behaviour problems, so that they cancel each other out, creating the zero effect that I found when I totalled the average effect of divorce. However, for this to be true, one must admit that while certain divorces harm children, others benefit them. My findings contradict the widely-accepted claim that MOST divorces increase children's behaviour problems and that only a tiny minority of divorces do NOT.

Source: Li, Allen (2008). "The Impact of Divorce on Children's Behaviour Problems," Annual conference of the Council on Contemporary Families (April 25–26). The paper can be accessed at: http://www.rand.org/pubs /working_papers/WR489/.

Note this well: Reviews of the studies on the effects of divorce on children find that "the 'large majority' of children of divorce...do not experience severe or long-term problems: Most do not drop out of school, get arrested, abuse drugs, or suffer long-term emotional distress" (Coontz, 1997:100; see Amato and Cheadle, 2005). Put another way, this time by esteemed family researcher Andrew J. Cherlin:

> What divorce does to children is to raise the risk of serious long-term problems, such as severe anxiety or depression, having a child as a teenager, or failing to graduate from high school. *But the risk is still low enough that most children in divorced families don't have these problems.* (Cherlin, 2003:1)

Hetherington's research on 2,500 children found that "after a period of initial disruption 75 percent to 80 percent of children and adolescents from divorced families are able to cope with the divorce and their new life situation and develop into reasonably or exceptionally well-adjusted individuals" (Hetherington, 2002:63). Stated negatively, 20 to 25 percent of the children of divorce do not cope successfully.

With these caveats in mind, let us examine the evidence from research according to the characteristics of the children and their families.

CHARACTERISTICS OF THE CHILD

The age of the child at the time of divorce appears to be related to personal adjustment problems. The younger children are at the time of marital disruption, the more likely they are to have adjustment problems. However, after the initial trauma of divorce, most children are as emotionally well adjusted as those in two-parent families.

The gender of the child appears to be an important variable, with boys being more handicapped by divorce than girls. Boys affected by divorce show more aggression, have a greater need for attention, and are lower achievers in school; when these boys are adolescents, they have more problems than do girls with alcohol and drug use (the studies finding these differences compared boys and girls from divorced homes with boys and girls from intact homes). Boys seem to take about twice as long as girls to adjust to a divorce, and they are more likely to have a relapse during adolescence. Girls, too, are affected, but in different ways. As Furstenberg has put it, "The hazards of divorce may not be greater for boys than for girls—only different. Boys 'act out' in response to divorce, while girls exhibit less socially visible forms of maladjustment" (1990:392).

The seemingly greater resilience of girls to the potential trauma of divorce may, however, be a consequence of the living arrangements made after divorce rather than the divorce itself. Since about 85 percent of children of divorced parents live with their mothers, the negative behaviors of boys may be the result of living with a female rather than a male parent. Boys in families headed by a single mother are less well adjusted than are girls. However, boys living with single fathers are better adjusted than are girls living with single fathers (Seltzer, 1994:241).

Adolescence appears to be a particularly troublesome time for children of divorced parents. They are more likely to begin sexual intercourse at an earlier age, and they are more apt to engage in delinquency, deviancy, and antisocial behavior. The research indicates that all of these behaviors are more the result of living with one parent than of divorce per se. That is, "antisocial behavior is less likely to occur in families where two adults are present, whether as biological parents, step-parents, or some combination of biological parents and other adults" (Demo and Acock, 1991:179). Thus, antisocial behavior on the part of adolescents is more a function of less parental control than the result of the trauma of parents divorcing.

*"I have to be getting back—I'm the glue that holds
my parents' marriage together."*

CHARACTERISTICS OF THE FAMILY

The children of divorced parents face difficult adjustments, and many suffer. We should remember that although the finality of the divorce is important, the conditions and situations leading up to the divorce also might have a negative impact on the children.

> Families that eventually divorce may be different in a variety of ways from those that do not long before marital disruption occurs. They may be more likely to exhibit poor parenting practices, high levels of marital conflict, or suffer from persistent economic stress. Many of the same processes that are often thought to be initiated when marriages dissolve actually antedate the separation event. Our analysis suggests that exposure to these conditions may compromise children's economic, social, and psychological well-being in later life whether or not a separation takes place. (Furstenberg and Teitler, 1994:187)

The size of the family after divorce has been found to be related to maladjustments among the children. The larger the family, the greater is the amount of stress (scheduling and economic demands) experienced by single parents, and this stress may negatively affect children. Also, the more children in a family, the more restrictive are the child-rearing techniques employed by the parent, resulting in possible hostility.

The socioeconomic status of the family is a significant variable affecting the adjustment patterns of children. As we have seen, divorce results in a lower socioeconomic status for families headed by a single mother, and this reduced income and accompanying shift downward in lifestyle have a negative effect on children. Parents of higher socioeconomic status are more likely to assume joint legal custody of their children. This is significant because, compared to fathers whose former wives have sole legal custody, nonresident fathers with joint legal custody spend more time with their children (Seltzer, 1994:242).

Race appears to be significant for children from divorced families. People of color are disproportionately at a disadvantage economically in U.S. society. At divorce, the meager resources are reduced substantially, putting these children further at risk. Moreover, African American children are less likely than White children to experience their mothers' remarriage or informal cohabiting union, which keeps them without a father figure and, typically, from enhancing their economic situations.

Contact with both parents after divorce helps children adjust. Research shows, for example, that children in divorced families do better in joint custody than those who live with just one parent (Peterson, 2002a). Similarly, when parents divorce, their children do best if both parents continue to live in the same general vicinity. Moves away typically separate the child from the father because either the mother moves away with the child or the father moves away alone (Peterson, 2003).

Finally, maternal employment in the labor force is a family-related variable. A single working mother has a negative impact on her children if she goes to work for the first time after the divorce, giving the child an additional feeling of loss and deprivation.

To conclude, we quote from the presidential address to the Population Association of America by family sociologist Andrew Cherlin:

> Whether a child grows up with two biological parents, I conclude, makes a difference in his or her life; it is not merely an epiphenomenon. Not having two parents at home sometimes leads to short- and long-term problems, but not all the differences we see in outcomes are the results of family structure. Some of the differences would have occurred anyway. Moreover, parental divorce...does not automatically lead to problems. Many (perhaps most) children who grow up in single-parent or in stepfamilies will not be harmed seriously in the long term. (Cherlin, 1999a:427)

DISSOLUTION OF SAME-SEX RELATIONSHIPS

Same-sex marriage is legal (as of November 2009) in only four states: Massachusetts, Iowa, New Hampshire, and Connecticut. A few other states allow same-sex civil unions, which offer all of the rights and responsibilities of marriage without the marriage license. Still other jurisdictions have legal unions for same-sex couples but deny some of the rights and responsibilities granted to married couples. Moreover, the federal Defense of Marriage Act (DOMA) limits marriage at the federal level to one man and one woman, and a number of state-passed "mini" DOMAs have made unclear "the extent to which the rights afforded to same-sex marriages, civil unions, or domestic partnerships actually exist outside of the state in which the relationships were sanctioned" (Coltrane and Adams, 2008:223). The result is murky for those in a same-sex relationship who wish to separate. How will the property be distributed? If they have left a jurisdiction where their union was legal to one where it is illegal, must they return to the state where the relationship agreement was made to legally separate? The ambiguity is especially salient for same-sex couples with children (more than one-fourth have a child under 18 with them). One of the partners may have custody of a child from a previous relationship, or the couple may have a child during the current relationship through adoption or artificial insemination. Who will be granted custody and under what conditions? Coltrane and Adams conclude:

> Divorce, available only to a legally married couple, provides for 'legal protection and structural clarity' in property division, child and spousal support, and child custody matters, as established by law and/or precedent. In the absence of formal divorce, the children of same-sex couples will continue to be subject to ongoing uncertainty about their family positions (2008:224).

Remarriage after Divorce

Although there has always been a strong tendency in the United States for the formerly married to remarry, there has been a shift in the pattern in recent decades. For most of American history, people remarried after the death of a spouse but not after a divorce. Even as late as the 1920s, more remarriages occurred after widowhood than after divorce. By 1974 divorce had replaced death as the most common endpoint of marriages (Coltrane and Adams, 2008:210). Now, close to 90 percent of those remarrying are divorced. This increase in remarriage by the divorced is the result of two fundamental demographic facts. The first is that people are living longer, reducing the time of widowhood. Second, this trend is also simply the consequence of the ever-greater proportion of divorced people in the population. Divorce, as we have seen, is common now and is considered a relatively acceptable alternative to an unhappy marriage.

Divorce and remarriage after divorce are now common experiences. The next subsection examines the phenomenon of remarriage, focusing especially on the demographic facts of remarriage after divorce and the unique problems experienced by the partners in remarriage and by their children.

Statistical Facts about Remarriage

Some facts:

- About one third of all Americans will marry, divorce, and remarry.
- Women are less likely than men to remarry if they are older, well educated, and have children (Pann and Crosbie-Burnett, 2005). Overall, 6 out of 10 women remarry, while three-fourths of men remarry.
- About half of all marriages are a remarriage for at least one of the adults (Visher et al., 2003).
- Of the 1.5 million divorced men and women who remarry each year, 61 percent marry divorced partners, 35 percent marry single partners, and 4 percent marry widowed partners (Pann and Crosbie-Burnett, 2005).
- The remarriage rate has declined since the 1960s, but this is likely the result of the increasing rate of cohabitation.
- The risk of divorce is greater for second marriages than for first marriages (Amato et al., 2007). The divorce rate for remarriages is highest in families with children from previous relationships.
- Divorce is likely to occur more quickly in remarriages than first marriages.

The probability of remarriage is affected by several important variables: age, socioeconomic status, race, and religion.

AGE

The older a woman is at the time of her divorce, the lower are her chances of remarrying. As we have already noted, more men than women remarry, and they are more likely than women to marry soon after the divorce. This is because divorced women who seek remarriage are at a disadvantage compared to men, because the size of the pool of potential spouses for these women is relatively small. One reason for this shortage in available men is the shorter life expectancy for men than for women. The second and more important reason for this imbalance is the propensity for men to remarry younger women. Given the sexism present in the occupational patterns of the United States, men generally gain in property, prestige, and power as they age. Therefore, they tend to retain or even improve their attractiveness to women as they age. These differences in the attraction patterns by sex and age result in a great imbalance in the number of eligible marriage partners, as most men marry younger women, and women must therefore marry older men. Consequently, although the male–female ratio is approximately equal in the 45-to-64 age bracket, there are three times as many single, divorced, and widowed women as there are single, divorced, and widowed men in that age category.

SOCIOECONOMIC STATUS

Socioeconomic status is related to remarriage rates. Income, for example, is significant, but the relationship differs by gender. The more money a divorced man has, the more likely he is to remarry. The reverse is true for women. Similarly, among women, remarriage is negatively correlated with their educational level. Those with less than

Oh, that—that's the hard drive from my first marriage."

a college education remarry quickly, whereas those with more education tend to remarry later or not at all. This is most likely because college-educated women have more career options than less educated women and therefore do not have as much pressure to marry for economic reasons. Also, the lower the socioeconomic status, the earlier that first marriage occurs. If women divorce in the average time of about eight years, they will still be in their twenties and thus will have a higher probability of remarrying.

RACE

The race of the divorced who remarry is a significant factor, with African Americans and Latinos remarrying at lower rates than Whites (Amato et al., 2007). Both African Americans and Latinos also remarry later than Whites.

There appears to be a difference in remarriage patterns by race and education. Pamela J. Smock (1990) found in her research that although the likelihood of remarriage did not differ significantly by schooling level for White women, it did for African American women. For African American women, the relationship between remarriage and education is a positive one; that is, those with the worst socioeconomic prospects are the least likely to marry.

RELIGION

A final factor affecting remarriage rates is religion. In the past, most Christian religious groups disapproved strongly of divorce, with varying severity in sanctions for those who defied the doctrines of the church on this matter. The ultimate church sanctions were for the divorced who remarried to be considered adulterers. Most denominations have shifted considerably on this issue and show ever-greater tolerance, even bestowing the church's blessing on remarriages. The exception has been, and continues to be, the Catholic Church, which officially does not recognize remarriage. Thus, the more devout Catholic is more likely to remain in an unhappy marriage and, if divorced, is likely not to remarry or at least to delay remarriage.

The Uniqueness of Remarriage

Marriages following divorces have strengths and weaknesses not found in typical first marriages.

THE ADVANTAGES OF REMARRIAGE

On the positive side, many factors should lead to marital satisfaction and more successful marriages among the remarried. Having chosen badly the first time, people are likely to be more careful in their selection of second partners. When people remarry, they are older and presumably more mature than when they married the first time.

Partners in a remarriage should, when compared to first marrieds, be more tolerant, more willing to compromise, more aware of the need to integrate their different styles of living, and better able to anticipate problems and work them out before they snowball. Moreover, the pooling of economic resources and the greater probability of better-paying jobs usually results in a higher standard of living, especially for women and children. Also, these older partners should be more likely than first marrieds to have worked out their solution to the division of household chores, work outside the home, and other matters concerning gender roles.

Remarriage, just like divorce, offers positive opportunities for growth. Stepfamily researchers Mavis Hetherington and James Bray summarize the possibilities: "Although divorce and remarriage may confront families with stresses and adaptive challenges, they also offer opportunities for personal growth and more harmonious, fulfilling family and personal relationships" (cited in Rutter, 1994:32).

THE DISADVANTAGES OF REMARRIAGE

Although there are advantages to remarriages, these marital unions entail very special problems that make marital success more difficult to attain than in first marriages. As a result, remarriage divorce rates are higher than first marriage divorce rates. Also, second divorces occur on average after five years, compared to eight years for first divorces. There are several reasons why divorce among remarried people is more prevalent and happens more quickly than in first marriages. First, the once-divorced are less likely than the never-divorced to stay in a poor marriage out of fear of social pressure. Second, remarriages, especially those involving stepchildren, have stresses not found in first marriages. Third, the once-divorced individuals in remarriages may be less mature, less responsible, and less supportive than the never-divorced. Their first marriages may have been troubled precisely because of their immaturity, and unresolved personal problems may haunt the second marriage relationship as well. Fourth, the once-divorced may, as a group, be more willing to bail out of a difficult relationship than to try to resolve the problems. And, finally, the remarried person may, as is also sometimes the case in first marriages, marry for the wrong reasons. A man may be overly enthralled by the attentions of a much younger and more physically attractive mate, only to find later that they have little in common. A woman may remarry too soon after a divorce in her eagerness to find economic security, a father for her children, or both, and thus end up with an incompatible partner.

Remarried spouses generally report higher levels of tension, disagreement, and spouse abuse than do spouses in first marriages (Pann and Crosbie-Burnett, 2005). These disagreements typically center on issues related to stepchildren, such as discipline, rules for children, and the distribution of resources to children. The evidence is, then, that the presence of stepchildren tends to lower marital quality for remarried adults. Consequently, remarriages dissolve at higher rates than first marriages.

BLENDED FAMILIES

About 17 percent of all U.S. children under the age of 18 live in a stepfamily household and another 5 percent lived with a parent and the parent's cohabiting partner (reported in Pasley and Moorefield, 2004). There are five times as many stepfathers as stepmothers (Coontz, 2008b). About 5 million of the 11 million households of remarrieds include minor children. The family form created in a remarriage that involves one or more children from the previous marriage of either spouse is called a **stepfamily, reconstituted family, blended family,** or **binuclear family.** This type of family has a special problem with family unity (see Box 11.5) and therefore is at a relatively high risk of divorce. Let's begin with some facts about stepfamilies (Mason, 2003; Pasley and Moorefield, 2004):

- More than 40 percent of all marriages are remarriages.
- One-third of all marriages in the U.S. bring a stepfamily into existence.
- Slightly more than 1 in 10 stepfamilies include biological children from one or both of the partners' previous marriages and biological children from the current partners.

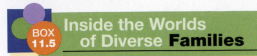

In Stepfamilies, Blending Yours, Mine, and Ours

At first, Christa and Shayne Johnson treated each other with the wariness of two hungry cats who suddenly have to share the same food bowl. Each was eight years old and used to being the only child of a single parent. When those parents were married eight years ago, Shayne and his father moved in with Christa and her mother.

"They were each used to getting all of the attention," said Christa's mother, Mary Lou Johnson, a nurse in suburban Minneapolis. "They weren't real happy about having to wait their turn. They had some very choice names for each other."

For many children, having a new stepparent means gaining new brothers or sisters as well. Sharing with these other children may be the most difficult challenge of all. Giving up the privacy of one's room or the status of being the oldest or youngest child in a family can be as stressful as coping with a new parent. Having stepsiblings forces children to reevaluate themselves.

The teasing, tattling, and tussles that routinely mark sibling rivalry can become a special problem for blended families. Cries of "Mom always liked you best!" have a sharp and bitter edge. Newly married parents find themselves pulled in different directions by their feelings of love and protectiveness for their spouse and their children.

"It caused trouble between my husband and me," Ms. Johnson said, "We were defensive about our respective children when we argued. We never argued about anything except the children."

Such fights are common among stepparents and stepchildren. They reflect the large number of dramatic and subtle changes children must undergo when they enter a blended family. Child psychologists say most parents underestimate the extent and importance of those changes.

"Children in blended families are asked to share, all of a sudden, their room, their toys, their clothes," said Dr. Emily B. Visher, a psychologist in Palo Alto, Calif., who has written extensively about such families. "It's a very dramatic transition, and it's very unsettling."

Teenagers often have more difficulty than younger children adapting to a blended family. Parents wonder if the apparently rebellious adolescent who stays away from the house and who doesn't participate in planned family activities is trying to sabotage the new family.

Often, the problem is not the child's attitude but a conflict between the stage of development of the child and that of the new stepfamily. Adolescent behaviors that would draw little attention in a traditional family—for ex-

ample, not wanting to spend time at home—sometimes become a serious problem for a new stepfamily. When misunderstood or dealt with poorly, they can escalate into conflicts that last well into adulthood.

Among the developmental tasks of adolescence are separating from family and developing an individual identity. It is important that teenagers place some distance between themselves and what they perceive as the dependent behavior of their childhood. Spending time with friends away from home and arguing over parental restrictions are ways of safely testing the turbid waters of adulthood.

The newly formed stepfamily, however, is at a developmental stage much closer to that of a younger child. Parents strive for their new family to be surrounded by symbols of harmony and closeness. The adolescent perceives those same symbols as signs of the very dependence he is trying to escape. The more the parents promote togetherness, the more the teenagers strive for separation, both from their parents and from their new stepsiblings.

High-school seniors and other teenagers who are about to leave home may have a very different reaction to a parent's remarriage than younger adolescents. While a 15-year-old may rebel against the new family, an 18-year-old will often embrace it.

"A child who has one foot out the door may feel relieved that the parent is going to be taken care of," said Dr. Sheldon M. Frank, a psychiatrist in Westchester County and president of the New York Council on Child and Adolescent Psychiatry.

Private space is a major area of conflict for stepsiblings. Arguments over who gets which bedroom or who has to share a bedroom can make some international political negotiations pale by comparison.

Researchers and family therapists generally agree that, although having one set of children move into the house or apartment lived in by the other set of children may be a financial and human necessity, it is likely to lead to bitter territorial squabbles. The children who are already in the house may feel imposed upon and threatened. The entering children may feel out of place.

"When you move into a place where one family has lived, everyone has their own territory staked out," said Mala S. Burt, a social worker in Baltimore and president of the Stepfamily Association of America. "They have to give up some of it to make room for new people."

Birth order becomes confused in blended families, causing additional friction. Children view themselves, in large part, by their position within the family. After a remarriage, a girl who has been the oldest child for 10 years may suddenly have two older stepsisters. A boy who was the baby of the family suddenly loses the advantages of that position to a younger, and perhaps cuter, stepbrother.

Holidays and birthdays can develop an unpleasant edge. Each set of children, unsure of what the new family means for their future, clutches at the past by insisting that theirs is the "right" way to celebrate. Stepsiblings will sometimes divide a Christmas tree in half for decorating, especially on the first Christmas together. One side of the family puts their ornaments on one side of the tree; the other children decorate their half.

Some parents in blended families say holidays and birthdays pose special rivalry problems because of gifts from the noncustodial parents. Dramatically unequal gifts or the lack of a gift from a parent who no longer lives with the child can spark nasty comments and feelings of superiority or inferiority.

"To this day, its hard for us," said Ms. Johnson, recalling how her children would tease each other about the presents they would get from their noncustodial parents. As they became teenagers, however, the tone changed.

"Now my son feels bad for my daughter because she hardly ever hears from her biological father," Ms. Johnson said.

Source: Kutner, Lawrence (1989). "In Stepfamilies, Blending Yours, Mine and Ours," *New York Times* (January 5): B1, B6.

- About 40 percent of adult women will likely reside in a remarried or cohabiting stepfamily household as a parent or stepparent at some time.
- About one-third of children will live in a remarried or cohabiting stepfamily household before they reach adulthood.
- One in three Americans is a stepparent, a stepchild, a stepsibling, or some other member of a stepfamily.
- Sixty-five percent of children living with a stepparent live with a stepfather.

TYPES OF STEPFAMILIES

Stepfather Families   Families composed of a mother and a stepfather are the most common type of stepfamily structure (the following depends on Visher et al., 2003). This type of stepfamily tends to experience less stress than other stepfamilies. Boys respond more favorably than girls to this arrangement. Acceptance by stepchildren is more positive when stepfathers engage in less discipline and control behaviors. The problem of acceptance is difficult, however, for stepfathers. Paul Bohannan and Rosemary Erickson have addressed this problem.

> Stepfathers take on a functioning ingroup. The mother and the children share a common history, the man coming into it has quite a different personal history....The new family has basically two subgroups: the husband and wife are one and the old mother-headed family is the other. Only the wife is a member of both, and for this reason she is pivotal. The mother-cum-children group

"We're saving his toddler clothes for my Dad's new baby."

is one with which the stepfather must deal; the children, in turn, must deal with the husband-wife power bloc. There are four possible outcomes: the stepfather may take control; he may be assimilated into the mother-headed family; both he and the mother-children group can change and reach a new status quo; or he can be driven away. (Bohannan and Erickson, 1978:54)

Stepmother Stepfamilies   Stepmothers have a more difficult time integrating into stepfamilies than do stepfathers because they are expected by their husbands to assume the primary caretaker role (Hetherington and Stanley-Hagen, 2000:187). Also there is the likelihood of a clash between the children's mother and stepmother.

Complex Stepfamilies   This is a situation where both adults have children from a previous marriage living in the household. This arrangement occurs in 7 percent of stepfamilies. The greatest likelihood of redivorce is in complex stepfamilies (Coleman et al., 2000). The greater the number of children, the more likely the couple will divorce.

Stepfamilies with a Mutual Child   About half of all remarriages have a child born to the couple usually within the first two years. Increasing the complexity, about 5 percent of all remarried households have three sets of children—his, hers, and "ours" (Coleman et al., 2000). The addition of a mutual child complicates the dynamics of the family. There is the possibility that parents will devote more attention to their biological child, causing resentments and hostility by the stepchildren. The stepchildren may interpret behaviors by parent and stepparent as an unfair distribution of attention and favors even when these do not exist (Stewart, 2005).

> About 60 percent of remarriages end in divorce, and half of these occur in the first 5 years. However, partners who have a mutual child are less likely to divorce in the first 10 years than those without a child born to the remarriage (this also includes re-marriages without any children present). After 10 years, the rate of divorce is similar for remarriages with and without a mutual child. (Visher et al., 2003:158).

PROBLEMS ENDEMIC TO STEPFAMILIES

Each type of stepfamily must confront a number of dynamic issues (taken from Visher et al., 2003:160–163).

Outsiders Versus Insiders   Successful stepfamilies integrate outsiders into the family unit. Potential outsiders are the stepfather joining an ongoing family of a mother and her children, a woman marrying a man who has custody of his children, or children staying with the noncustodial parent on weekends.

Boundary Disputes   Often children are members of two separate households, resulting in blurred and changing boundaries, negotiated and renegotiated by the adults. Also, within a household there are disputes arising over property rights, space, sleeping arrangements, and privacy.

Power Issues   As in all marriages, there are power struggles between the new partners in a remarriage. Added to this mix are the power issues between the spouses and their ex-spouses. As for children,

> [i]n stepfamilies, children can gain power in the age-old game of "divide and conquer"—a game also played in first-marriage families. However, because their

biological parents now live in separate households and typically do not interact on a daily basis, there is greater opportunity to be successful at this game. If, in addition, the parents maintain only minimal and hostile contact with each other, there exists a built-in system that makes it extremely easy for children to gain tremendous power. "If you don't treat me right, I'll go live with my Dad." "You are really mean! My mother lets me watch TV until midnight." (Visher et al., 2003:162)

Conflicting Loyalties   In stepfamilies, children feel torn apart when their parents no longer live together. The more amicable the relationships between the spouses and their exes, the fewer the children's loyalty conflicts.

Rigid and Unproductive Triangles   Unproductive triangles involve three individuals in a struggle where dyadic relationships are not possible. Visher, Visher, and Pasley (2003:163) suggest four important and potentially destructive triangles:

- Remarried parent in the middle, not allowing a direct relationship between a stepparent and a stepchild.
- Remarried parent and stepparent standing united against a former spouse.
- Child caught in the middle between hostile former spouses.
- Child caught in the middle between mother and stepmother or father and stepfather.

Cherlin argues that the difficulties of couples in remarriages after divorce derive from the lack of societal guidelines for solving many of the common problems of remarried life. These reconstituted families have

> problems for which institutionalized solutions do not exist. And without accepted solutions to their problems, families of remarriages must resolve difficult issues by themselves. As a result, solving everyday problems is sometimes impossible without engendering conflict and confusion among family members. (Cherlin, 1978:642)

The problem is that remarriage, especially when it involves children from one or both of the previous marriages, greatly increases the complexity of familial relationships. There are additional social roles, such as stepparents, stepchildren, stepsiblings, stepgrandparents, noncustodial parents, and the spouses of noncustodial parents—in short, a new type of extended family of "thin kin," as Furstenberg and Cherlin (1991) have labeled it. Society has not provided a useful way to handle these complex social roles. Even the language fails. What does the child who already has a "mom" call his or her stepmother? There is no term in the language to describe a child's relationship to the woman his or her father married after he divorced the child's mother. What are the rights and duties of the child and this woman to each other? Where is "home" to a child whose remarried parents share her or him in a joint custody arrangement? What people constitute that child's "family"? As Cherlin has noted, the absence of clarity in our language about these roles and relationships in families of remarriage "is both a symptom and a cause of some of the problems of remarried life" (Cherlin, 1978:644). Thus, in contrast to the nuclear family, divorce and remarriage have created what anthropologist Bob Simpson has called "the unclear family" (Simpson, 1998:xi).

The complexity in stepfamilies is compounded further by the linkages not only among the remarried couple's household and the household of each former spouse but also with the households of the child's grandparents. The entanglements arise because the new kin in a remarriage do not replace the kin from the first marriage, as they more typically do in a remarriage after widowhood. Rather, in a remarriage, the effect is cumulative. Another problem stepparents create is that they often bring different values, different expectations, and different routines to the reconstituted family. This phenomenon encourages ambiguity and has the potential to add stress to the family relationships. The spouses in the remarriage may find that what they had worked out in the abstract does not work in the real world of the reconstituted family, with differences in what should be the division of labor, in parenting roles (especially in the discipline of children) and the like, creating stresses in the marital relationship.

In summary, society, in its language, customs, and laws, does not provide guidelines for how a remarried couple and their children should solve their special problems. Without sufficient guidelines, each remarried couple must work out for themselves definitions for the obligations of each role. Each couple must learn how to reconcile competing claims for time and resources from their own children, the children they are raising who have an absent natural parent, and the children being raised by an ex-spouse. The complexity of these problems that each couple must work out through trial and error means that many will fail. Family unity will not be achieved, tensions will mount, feelings will be hurt, and relationships will be strained. The consequence is that remarried divorced couples, especially with children from previous marriages, have an increased probability of redivorce when compared to first marriages.

The Outcomes for Stepchildren

Stepchildren are children who have, typically, experienced several major life transitions. They have experienced the divorce of their parents (and the tensions that very likely preceded the divorce), life in a single-parent family following the divorce, and the move into a newly formed stepfamily. In addition, over one-fifth of them will, before they turn 18, experience the divorce of their custodial parent and stepparent. Each of these transitions disrupts child–parent relations as expectations, rules, and boundaries shift (Mason, 2003). Given the ambiguities and strains, these children are especially susceptible to feelings of resentment, anger, and rejection.

The adjustment of children depends on a number of factors. Some parents (biological and stepparent) are more skilled than others in easing the children through these difficult transitions. Some parents are emotionally close while others are disengaged. Stepparents who try to take control too quickly are less successful than those who ease into their parent role.

> Parents' and stepparents' use of authoritative parenting involving warmth, high monitoring, low coerciveness, firm but responsive control and demands, and expectations for mature behavior has been associated with less externalizing and internalizing behavior and greater social and academic competence in children. (Pasley and Moorefield, 2004:322)

The children, too, vary in their willingness to accept the stepparent. The age and gender of the child at the time of stepfamily formation are important in the children's adjustment, with remarriage occurring during early adolescence generating the greatest difficulties (Mason, 2003).

The evidence is that most children in stepfamilies work through these difficult transitions relatively unscathed. However, findings from both the United States and Great Britain suggest that about one-fifth of stepchildren are at risk for negative outcomes (Pasley and Moorefield, 2004).

The Special Case of Remarriage among the Elderly

As the population of seniors grows, so too will the number of elderly who remarry after divorce or widowhood. About 500,000 people over the age of 65 remarry each year, a number that will likely increase in the next decade as the baby boom generation begins reaching retirement age (Coleman et al., 2001). Although remarriage among the elderly is often rewarding in companionship, mutual caring, and pooled resources, it brings a special set of problems that younger remarrieds do not face (the following is from Barton, 1994). Foremost is the problem of money—not so much the lack of money, but who controls the combined assets. Second, and often related to the first problem, are adult children. Daughters are more accepting of the remarriage of their parent than are sons. Sons, it appears, are more concerned than daughters about their inheritance, which is now diluted by the presence of a stepparent. Finally, seniors who remarry often face difficulty because of their differing expectations for the relationship. Men typically remarry because they want someone to cook for them, take care of the home, and take care of them. Women, in contrast, are more interested in the affective parts of the relationship (companionship and romance). Thus, just as in marriage the first time, marriage late in life is typically more difficult for women than for men.

The elderly who find romance after the death of a spouse or divorce may choose cohabitation rather than remarriage (Brown et al., 2006). In 2006 some 900,000 couples age 50 and over chose cohabitation over marriage (a 50 percent increase since 2000). Financial reasons often make cohabitation more beneficial than marriage because of the rules regarding alimony, taxes, and Social Security benefits. As Ashlea Ebeling, reporting in *Forbes* says, "Get married and your future Social Security checks might be smaller. The alimony from you ex, your kids' college financial aid or the survivor's annuity you receive from your late spouse's job might evaporate" (Ebeling, 2007:86).

 ## The Politics of Divorce

There is an ongoing, contentious debate among scholars, religious leaders, marriage counselors, and others over divorce and its consequences for individuals and society. The two positions are summarized by Paul Amato:

> [The family] is the setting in which adults achieve a sense of meaning, stability, and security and the setting in which children develop into healthy, competent, and productive citizens. According to this view, the spread of single-parent families contributes to many social problems, including poverty, crime, substance abuse, declining academic standards, and the erosion of neighborhoods and communities.... In contrast, [others] argue that adults find fulfillment, and children develop successfully, in a variety of family structures. According to this view, divorce, although temporarily stressful, represents a second chance for happiness for adults and an escape from a dysfunctional home environment for children. Poverty, abuse, neglect, poorly funded schools, and a lack of governmental services represent more serious threats to the well-being of adults and children than does marital instability. (Amato, 2001:1270; see also Amato et al., 2007:4–8)

For arguments supporting the conservative position, see Glenn, 1996; Popenoe, 2005; and Wallerstein et al., 2000; for the liberal position, see Coontz, 1992; and Stacey, 1996. (See Box 11.6.)

Amato's review of the accumulated scholarship on the consequences of divorce leads him to conclude that both of these views are one-sided accentuations of reality.

> The increase in marital instability has not brought society to the brink of chaos, but neither has it led to a golden age of freedom and self-actualization. Divorce benefits some individuals, leads others to experience temporary decrements in well-being that improve over time, and forces others on a downward cycle from which they might never fully recover. (Amato, 2001:1282)

BOX 11.6 Emergent **Family** Trends

Stronger Marriages or Serial Marriages?

The marriage failure rate has hovered between 40 and 50 percent over the last two decades. Divorces now are occurring progressively earlier in marriage with one in five first marriages dissolving within the first five years (Bramlett and Mosher, 2001). One response to this impermanence of marriage has been the organized attempt to make marriages and divorces more difficult to obtain. Several state legislatures (Oklahoma, Arizona, Maryland, Florida, and Wisconsin) have started programs to cut the divorce rate. Oklahoma, for example, ties receipt of monthly welfare benefits to the recipients' attendance at marriage workshops (Tyre, 2002). At the federal level, President Bush set aside $100 million in welfare funds for state-run programs that support marriage. In the religious sector, "Marriage Savers," for example, has organized clergy in 146 cities to promote Community Marriage Policies and Covenants, which require engaged couples to take four months of religious marriage-preparation counseling. Evangelical Christians also campaign for state laws permitting "covenant marriage." Louisiana and Arkansas have such laws that allow couples to sign restrictive marriage contracts that make divorce almost impossible (Stacey, 2001). Secular groups such as the Institute for American Values, the Council on Families in America, the Communitarian Network, the National Marriage Project, Focus on the Family, and Smart Marriages work to promote promarriage and antidivorce policies.

Will these efforts bring about a lifetime marriage renaissance or will divorce rates remain high? Pamela Paul in her book, *The Starter Marriage and the Future of Matrimony* (2002), argues that there is a conflict between our

> cultural conception of marriage, which has not changed, and the society surrounding it, which has. We continue to configure marriage in precisely the same way we did fifty

years ago, even though almost none of the factors shaping marriage then still apply. . . . Some will argue that the way to "fix" this problem [high divorce rate] is to pull us back to marriage's original meaning, to force society to adhere to its "traditional" definition. This is neither wise nor pragmatic, and given the shifting definitions of marriage, the very premise is a fallacy. People's lifestyles and their ideas about how they want to live have fundamentally changed; a stricter definition of marriage won't alter that. We're redefining marriage because our lives have changed dramatically. Rather than tug ourselves back to an older definition, we ought to move forward to better survive within the new one (Paul, 2002:265–266).

Pamela Paul suggests that several societal trends make contemporary marriages shorter and less stable. Among these are the following: (1) People are living to an increasing old age, twice as long as 100 years ago; (2) active parenting takes up about 20 years, leaving couples with 45 years or so as a couple; (3) typically, people entering the workforce will have five or six careers over a span of 50 years or so; (4) young people today are the children of the 1970s and 1980s divorce generation; and (5) both spouses are now in the workforce, freeing women from the confines of the home and providing them with the possibility of economic independence as well as fulfilling nonfamilial roles.

In the light of these trends is it realistic to assume that spouses chosen in their twenties will be appropriate for other stages in life? Traditionalists argue that we need high-commitment relationships that keep spouses together regardless of the changes in their lives. At the other extreme are those who foresee a series of "temporary marriages" (a phenomenon called "serial monogamy"), one for each stage in life, or there might be renewable marriages, which get evaluated every five years or so (Ehrenreich, 2000b). Whatever the future, couples will continue to marry. The question is how permanent will that marital bond be?

As for the effects on children, "the fact of the matter is that most kids from divorced families do manage to overcome their problems and do have good lives" (Amato, quoted in Kirn, 2000:78).

The leading conservative treatise on the negative impacts of divorce on children is by Judith Wallerstein and her associates (2000). They argue that the children of divorce suffer greatly from this trauma, with only a minority managing to construct successful personal lives. Consequently, the authors conclude that parents in unhappy, loveless, but low-conflict marriages should stay together for the sake of their children. Family scholar Andrew Cherlin, in his review and critique of this book, questions the research and conclusions of Wallerstein and her colleagues. His conclusion, as did Amato's, takes the middle ground in the political debate over divorce.

> What divorce does to children is to raise the risk of serious long-term problems, such as severe anxiety or depression, having a child as a teenager or failing to graduate from high school. But the risk is still low enough that most children in divorced families don't have these problems.... Wallerstein encourages readers to believe that most of their commitment problems stem from their parents' divorces. But parental divorce isn't that powerful, and its effects aren't that pervasive. To be sure, it raises the chances that children will run into problems in adulthood, but most of them don't. (Cherlin, 2000:68; see also Amato, 2004)

Is Marriage a Failed Institution?

This chapter has considered failed marriages and the attempt by many of those who divorce to create new marriages. The media, religious leaders, and politicians, looking at the statistics on divorce, portray an image of marriage in U.S. society as a failed institution. But we must not lose sight of two facts: (1) Overwhelmingly, most people want to get married. As Margaret Talbot has put it, "The right to divorce is deeply ingrained in American culture precisely because so is the ideal of a mutually fulfilling marriage" (2000:2). (2) The overwhelming majority of those who divorce remarry. Thus, we must conclude that the institution of marriage in the United States is not dying but is, rather, quite alive.

Chapter Review

1. Looking back over the past 100 years, divorce rates have trended upward. The rate is affected by social and economic conditions (up after wars and during prosperity and down during economic depressions). The rate since the late 1970s has declined.

2. Less than one in two contemporary marriages ends in divorce. The probability of divorce is correlated with a number of variables: cohort, premarital cohabitation, age at first marriage, the circumstances of the first birth, the presence of children, economic troubles, race, religion, and whether one's parents were divorced.

3. The factors leading to a prediction of a declining divorce rate are (a) high rates of unmarried cohabiting couples, (b) declining birth rate, (c) increased educational attainment of women, and (d) a diminishing gap between wives and husbands on gender expectations.

4. Divorce gives ex-husbands two major advantages: (a) an improved standard of living and (b) increased personal freedom. There is one major disadvantage: personal isolation.

5. Divorce is much harsher for ex-wives than for ex-husbands. Ex-wives face personal isolation but, most important, they face a significant decline in their standard of living.

6. Although divorce is a difficult experience for both ex-spouses, after six years 80 percent of both women and men have moved on to build reasonably or exceptionally fulfilling lives.

7. About one million children are involved in new divorces annually. About 85 percent will remain with their mothers. How these children adjust to the divorce of their parents is related to their age and gender, family size, the socioeconomic status of the family, whether the noncustodial parent is nearby and involved, race, and the employment of the mother in the labor force.

8. Although divorce is a traumatic event for children, leading to some negative behavioral and emotional problems, the large majority does not suffer long-term distress.

9. Most divorced people remarry—3 out of 4 men and 6 out of 10 women. The probability of remarriage is affected by several variables: age for women, income and education, gender, race, and religion.

10. About 60 percent of remarriages end in divorce.

11. About 40 percent of remarriages after divorce involve one or more children, thus creating reconstituted or blended families. This greatly increases the complexity of familial relationships, linking several households and creating stepparents.

12. Children in stepfamilies have experienced a number of major life transitions. Most adapt, but about 20 percent of these children are at risk for various negative outcomes.

13. Rather than considering divorce as pathological, we should remember that there is also a healthy element to the breaking up of marital bonds. Some marriages are destructive or just are not working for one or both partners. Rather than being condemned to a life sentence in a dysfunctional relationship, the actors break it off. This event leads, potentially at least, to greater personal growth and the establishment of a new relationship that works.

14. There is a contentious debate among observers concerning the consequences of divorce for individuals and society. The conservative position is that divorce contributes to social problems such as poverty, crime, substance abuse, and declining school performance. The progressive position is that although divorce is temporarily stressful, it represents a second chance for happiness for adults and an escape from a dysfunctional home environment for children. The research on divorce and its consequences shows that the reality lies between these two extreme views.

15. The relatively high divorce rate does not mean that marriage is a failed institution. We conclude that the institution of marriage is not dying because (a) most people want to marry, (b) half of all marriages do not end in divorce, and (c) the vast majority of those who divorce choose to remarry.

Key Terms

binuclear family   401

blended family   401

cohort   376

divorce   375

feminization of poverty   390

heterogamy   382

marriage gap   385

reconstituted family   401

stepfamily   401

Related Websites

http://www.divorceonline.com

Divorce Online. Operated by the American Divorce Information Network, Divorce Online provides free articles and information on the financial, legal, psychological, real estate, and other aspects of divorce. Additionally, the site provides a Professional Referral section to assist in locating professional assistance by location.

http://www.divorceabc.com

National Family Resiliency Center, Inc. Founded in 1983, NFRC aims to help children and adults preserve a sense of family, foster healthy relationships, and constructively adjust to change, especially during times of individual and family transitions through a multidisciplinary offering of programs and resources for families and professionals.

http://www.stepfamilies.info

National Stepfamily Resource Center. Housed at Auburn University, the mission of the NSRC is to promote stepfamily education and make stepfamily resources available to all stepfamilies, stepfamily support groups, websites, authors, and publishers; all human-service professionals working with stepfamilies (clinicians, clergy, educators, medical professionals, mediators, financial advisors, family-law and law-enforcement professionals, etc.); and the media.

http://www.stepfamily.org

The Stepfamily Foundation. The Stepfamily Foundation provides counseling, on the telephone and in person, and information to create a successful step relationship. Founded in 1975, the Stepfamily Foundation has pioneered this particular method of counseling. It provides training, information, and counseling to avoid the pitfalls that often stress these relationships.

http://pbskids.org/itsmylife/family/divorce/index.html

It's My Life. Family. Divorce: PBS Kids. It's My Life is an award-winning website funded by the Corporation for Public Broadcasting. In this section of the site, a variety of issues and challenges related to divorce are covered in an engaging and educational manner aimed at children aged 9 to 12.

http://www.nokidding.net

No Kidding! No Kidding! is an all-volunteer, non-profit international social club for adult couples and singles who, for whatever reason, have never had children. With 102 chapters and more than 10,000 members worldwide, the organization is not allied with any sect, denomination, political entity, business, organization, or institution and does not engage in any controversy, and neither endorses nor opposes any causes.

www.fatherhood.org

The National Fatherhood Initiative serves to increase the number of children growing up with responsible fathers in their lives.

chapter 12

Emergent Families in the Global Era

▶ ## Myths and Realities

Myth	Alternative lifestyles are destroying the family.
Reality	New family forms not based on marriage reflect global changes. They are not threatening the nuclear family.
Myth	Being single is a lonely existence, especially for never-married women, who miss out on the best things life has to offer.
Reality	Research belies this stereotype. Never-married women can lead meaningful lives, complete with intimate relations and strong family ties.
Myth	Living together is practicing for marriage. Therefore, cohabitants who later marry have more successful marriages than those who do not.
Reality	Some couples live together to test their compatibility before marriage, but others live together without marriage simply as a nonmarital family form. Couples who live together before marriage are more likely to divorce than those who do not.
Myth	Lesbian and gay partnerships are incompatible with family life.
Reality	Family arrangements are becoming more common in gay communities, as gay men and lesbians establish families of choice, raise children, and create their own kinship networks.
Myth	Today's immigrants to the United States are mostly men who migrate alone or men whose families accompany them.
Reality	Globalization has produced a feminization of immigration, with increasing numbers of women who migrate to the U.S. for domestic and care work. Many of these are transnational mothers whose children remain in their "home" country.
Myth	Commuter marriage is a romantic lifestyle, much like a honeymoon when partners are together.
Reality	Commuter marriage is a difficult alternative, and most commuters are ambivalent about their way of life.

Throughout this book we have examined the social forces that make families diverse. In the last three decades of the twentieth century, domestic arrangements have become more varied as the U.S. population has adapted to evolving technologies, economic changes, and social developments. Twenty-first century families continue to move away from the idealized family model of the 1950s. This chapter is about the growing fluidity of family life in an era of unprecedented change.

First, we set forth the close connections between emerging family forms and larger social trends. We use the social constructionist perspective to set the stage for thinking about today's diversity in domestic life. We show how structural changes are freeing women and men from conventional marriage, enabling them to accommodate their family arrangements to the new social realities they face. We move beyond a simple "lifestyles" approach to see that diversity and change are the central dynamics in family formation. We turn, then, to four domestic arrangements that are the subject of this chapter: singlehood, heterosexual cohabitation, lesbian and gay families, and family arrangements involving separations of space and time.

The Rise in New Family Arrangements

Families in Transition

To understand current trends in living arrangements, we must return to the distinction between households and families (see Chapter 1). (The following is based on Ahlburg and De Vita, 1992:5; Bianchi and Casper, 2000:8; Lichter and Qian, 2004.) The U.S. Bureau of the Census defines a *household* as all people living in a housing unit. A household may consist of one person who lives alone or of several people who share a dwelling. A *family,* on the other hand, includes household members who are related by blood, marriage, or adoption and who reside together. All families comprise households, but not all households are families under the Census Bureau's definition. **Family households** include families in which a family member is the householder—the person who owns or rents the residence. These households can also include nonfamily members such as a boarder or friend. A **nonfamily household** includes the householders who live alone or share a residence with individuals unrelated to the householder, such as college friends sharing an apartment. Some nonfamily households substitute for families and serve many of the same functions. Same-sex couples are one example (Lichter and Qian, 2004:2). The growth of the nonfamily household (that is, persons who live alone or with unrelated individuals) is one of the most dramatic changes to occur during the past four decades, as shown in Figure 12.1.

Figure 12.1

Households by Type: 1970–2008 (percent distribution)

Sources: Fields, Jason (2004). "America's Families and Living Arrangements: 2003." *Current Population Reports*, P20-553. Washington, DC: U.S. Bureau of the Census, p. 4; "America's Families and Living Arrangements: 2008." *Current Population Survey Reports* (2009). U.S. Bureau of the Census. Online: http://www.census.gov/population/www/socdemo/hh-fam/cps2008.html.

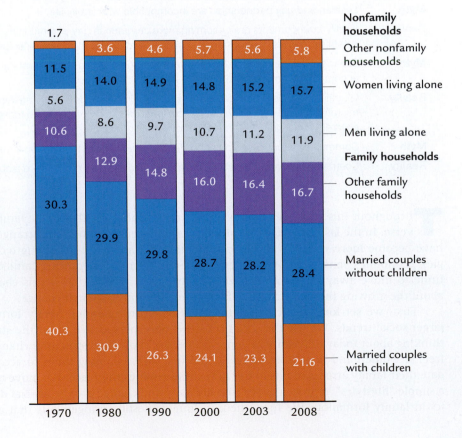

In 1970, 81 percent of households were family households; by 2008, just 67 percent were family households (Fields, 2004; U.S. Bureau of the Census, 2009a). At the same time, nonfamily households, which consist primarily of people who live alone or who share a residence with roommates or with a partner, have been on the rise. The fastest growth has been among persons living alone. The proportion of households with just one person increased from 16 to 28 percent between 1970 and 2008 (Fields, 2004; U.S. Bureau of the Census, 2009a).

Nonfamily households are a diverse group. They may consist of elderly individuals who live alone, college-age youths who share an apartment, cohabiting couples, individuals who delay or forgo marriage, or those who are "between marriages" (Ahlburg and De Vita, 1992:5; Rawlings, 1995:22).

Another dramatic shift in household composition has been the decline in the percentage of married-couple households with children. Two-parent households with children dropped from 40 to 22 percent of all households between 1970 and 2008 (Fields, 2004; U.S. Bureau of the Census, 2009). This downward trend reflects the postponement of marriage and children and the shift toward smaller families. However, household composition varies considerably among different segments of the population. Minorities are more likely than Whites to live in households that include children. In 2007, 35 percent of African American households and 49 percent of Latino households had at least one child under age 18, compared with 31 percent of White households (U.S. Bureau of the Census, 2008b). This difference arises primarily because minority populations tend to have a younger age structure than the White population (that is, a greater share of minorities are in the prime childbearing ages) and minorities tend to have higher fertility rates than Whites (De Vita, 1996:34). In the next decade, the overall composition of households is projected to continue to shift, with a decreasing proportion of family households and continued growth of nonfamily households.

The Global Revolution in Family Life

Current household and family patterns are not the result of overnight changes but a continuation of forces set in motion long ago. These changes are not uniquely a U.S. phenomenon; instead, they have global dimensions. Research of the last two decades has revealed five global trends in family formation:

> (1) women's average age at first marriage and childbirth has risen, delaying the formation of new families; (2) families and households have gotten smaller; (3) the burden on working-age parents of supporting younger and older dependents has increased; (4) the proportion of female-headed households has increased; and (5) women's participation in the formal labor market has increased at the same time that men's has declined, shifting the balance of economic responsibility in families. (Bruce et al., 1995:5)

We are living in the midst of a global revolution in which the old rules of what used to be known as "the family" are changing. All over the world, people are questioning and renegotiating the meaning of the family in an era of radical social change, in what some call a "runaway world" (Beck and Beck-Gernsheim, 2004:499). Today's changes in the family mirror those in the runaway world.

In Europe and North America, many family forms do not have marriage at their core. Marriage is less central in organizing and controlling life course transitions, individual identities, intimate relations, living arrangements, childbearing, and child rearing (Thornton and Young-DeMarco, 2001:1009). Declining proportions of adults are married. Indeed, nonmarriage has risen by 50 percent in recent decades, from 28 percent of the adult population in 1970 to 42 percent in 2007 (U.S. Bureau of the Census, 2008b). Many adults now push beyond current definitions of "the family," choosing to live as a single person, to live with another adult of the same or the other sex without marriage, or to live separately from a spouse. Still, the focus on choice should not ignore the broad social conditions that produce changes in household formation. Emerging domestic arrangements reflect the complex interaction of social structure and human agency. Individual choice is now an important facet of alternative household and family formation, but structural conditions that lie beyond individual choice help explain the long-term trends.

How to Think about Family Diversification

RETHINKING FAMILY CATEGORIES

Many people now choose from a wide range of living arrangements. For others, family adaptations emerge in response to changes and constraints in the external world. Despite the proliferation of family forms, there is little evidence that "the commitment of Americans to children, marriage, and family life has eroded substantially in the past two decades" (Thornton and Young-DeMarco, 2001:1030). Although the standard family has not disappeared, it has "many other forms alongside it and, above all the norm has lost much of its force" (Beck and Beck-Gernsheim, 2004:405). This requires us to rethink the categories we use to sort out the complex array of family relationships in society today.

The family field has long made a distinction between "the traditional family" and "nontraditional alternatives." Although so-called nontraditional families make up a diverse array of forms, they are often seen in *opposition* to the family ideal of the working father, stay-at-home mother, and their children. This dichotomy is less useful for understanding the emergence of new family and household forms. Not only does it oversimplify the incredible array of contemporary family arrangements, but it also miscasts the idealized family as the normal family—the standard from which "alternatives" depart. But how can one family form be the standard when all family forms are adaptations to their social contexts? In fact, the 1950s model was itself made possible by specific social forces. At the same time, other social conditions, such as the growing participation of married women in the paid labor force, rising divorce rates, and the rise of lesbian and gay communities, have led to a variety of domestic arrangements. New family types are no more alternative to what had preceded them than the 1950s (traditional) type was to its historical predecessors. To believe otherwise is to make a false distinction between "traditional" and "alternative" family forms (Nicholson, 1997:28).

Rather than thinking of varied family arrangements as *alternatives* to an idealized traditional form, we should think of all family forms *in their own right*. No family structure is better than others. All families are social forms that emerge in response to different conditions. This gives us a better understanding of today's diverse families. As the larger social world in which families are embedded grows more complex, families, too, become more diverse and fluid. Today, different family forms coexist in society. As individuals move through the phases of their lives, their family and household arrangements are marked by ongoing change.

THE QUESTION OF LIFESTYLES

Past scholarship often used the term *alternative lifestyles* to refer to new family and household arrangements. However, the concept of "lifestyle," which refers to the "relational patterns around which individuals organize their living arrangements" (Stayton, 1985:17), has become less useful. In fact, the concept of "alternative lifestyles" can be misleading in that it must be alternative to something. Alternative lifestyles prompt the question, "alternative to what?" (Fowlkes, 1994:152), presuming a family form shared by most people in society. As the number and significance of families formed outside of marriage have grown in recent decades, scholarship moved away from "lifestyles" to a broader emphasis on nonmarital families. "Although studies of non-marital relationships are not new phenomena, recent data facilitate a broader conceptualization of families than was possible before this decade" (Seltzer, 2001:466).

Throughout this book, we have argued that social and economic forces in society produce and require diversity in family life. Therefore, family variation is not new. What is new is a greater recognition of diversity and ongoing public outcries of groups insisting that "they too are families." These changes have given a new urgency to questions about family diversity. "What makes a legitimate family? Who is entitled to family status and the social support associated with it? Who should or does define appropriate family formation?" (Lempert and DeVault, 2000:6).

Despite the variation in family life, the continuing reality is that "one form of family is the culturally affirmed and socially supported ideal" (Scanzoni, 2004:12). Some family forms are devalued (Sarkisian and Gerstel, 2004:829). For example, female-headed families are often stigmatized, whereas blended stepparent families are more highly valued. When variations are associated with subordinate class and racial categories, they are judged against a standard model and found to be deviant. Many nonmarital living arrangements that appear new to middle-class Americans are actually family patterns that have been traditional within African American and other ethnic communities for many generations. Presented as the "new lifestyles of the young mainstream elite, they are in fact the same lifestyles that have in the past been defined as pathological, deviant, or unacceptable when observed in Black families" (Peters and McAdoo, 1983:288). Many of the family patterns among racial ethnics have been adopted as available and logical life choices in a society that has denied them a full range of resources.

The family and household configurations discussed here represent additional adaptations to those already discussed in previous chapters. Like the variations in family living produced by class, race, and gender inequality, these variations have always existed.

Singlehood, heterosexual cohabitation, lesbian and gay alternatives, and families separated by time and space represent an array of adaptations that cannot be neatly tied to a single cause. They are part of a larger web of economic, demographic, and social trends. Women's economic independence, later age at marriage, and the high divorce rate are some of the trends associated with these forms, but no one explanation covers all of them. Although these arrangements appear to be a heterogeneous mixture of lifestyles, in fact they all embody new definitions of women's and men's public and private roles. Singlehood, heterosexual and same-sex cohabitation, and families separated by time and space expand the traditional boundaries and behaviors associated with gender. Each form, in its unique way, modifies the relational patterns around which women, men, and sometimes children organize their living arrangements. In this way, these domestic arrangements represent adaptations to both particular social arrangements and the times in which we are living. They show how emergent domestic forms are situated and structured in the larger social world. Of course, they do not include all of the new family patterns in today's world. It is impossible to include all present arrangements in one chapter, so we encourage our readers to explore others such as multigenerational families including grandparents, their children, and grandchildren (see Box 12.1) and other broad transformations in family life.

The question "What is a family?" will grow more contested as household and family patterns fall outside the nuclear mold. The U.S. Census Bureau's definition of "two or more persons related by birth, marriage or adoption who live in the same household" fails to include many arrangements in which people live and relate as families; practical and legal considerations require that we modify the conventional definition of the family.

Emergent **Family** Trends

BOX 12.1

Under One Roof

Life for Phillip Doggett of Columbus, Ohio, isn't quite as serene as it was when he retired from the state corrections department—before his daughter and her family moved in, and his mother-in-law, too.

Now Doggett and his wife, Diana, share a bathroom with their two grandsons, ages 12 and 5, who sleep down the hall. The Doggetts' daughter and her husband, Erica and Joseph Blunt, who lost their home to foreclosure last year, sleep in the basement. The living room is a makeshift bedroom for Diana's mother, who's recuperating from surgery.

It's a crowded house for a pair of would-be empty nesters. But the gloomy economy has created unusual living arrangements for the Doggetts and many other extended families across the nation.

A portrait of America's households, drawn from an AARP analysis of U.S. Census data, shows a 25 percent increase this decade in the number of arrangements

with multiple generations living under one roof. That excludes two-generation households of parents and their children under age 18.

According to Stephanie Coontz, author of *The Way We Really Are: Coming to Terms with America's Changing Families*, the driving force was often economics: higher housing costs or the financial constraints of divorce, for example. Caring for an ailing parent also contributed to the shift, as did the growing numbers of immigrants, who tend to live as extended families.

Since the recession took hold, however, families are doubling up at a faster pace, experts say, though figures are hard to come by. Massive job layoffs, home foreclosures and dwindling retirement income are fueling the need to slash expenses by squeezing more family members under one roof.

Source: Fleck, Carole (2009). "All Under One Roof." *AARP Bulletin* (May): 24–25.

Single Life

Single used to mean what people were before they settled down to marriage and family. Today, the question "When are you going to settle down and get married?" no longer applies. Over the past four decades, a growing proportion of adults spent a larger proportion of their lives in a single status and in one-person households. As Figure 12.1 demonstrates, men and women living alone grew from 16 percent of all households in 1970 to 28 percent of all households in 2008. People living alone are now over one-fourth of households; 57 percent are women and 43 percent are men (Fields, 2004; U.S. Bureau of the Census, 2009a). Although women accounted for the larger share of people living alone, the number of men living alone increased at a faster pace. As a result of the rise in single living, there are now substantially more households of those alone than there are of married couples with children. Reasons for the increased numbers of those living alone include more people living independently before marriage; more people, especially women, postponing marriage; a boom in the elderly population due to increases in life expectancy, including many who have lost partners; and the desire for residential independence.

Today, a growing share of adults are unmarried. Since 1970 the postponement of marriage has led to a substantial increase in the percentage of young, never-married adults. The proportion of women 20 to 24 years old who had never married more than doubled between 1970 and 2007—from 36 to 76 percent. The increase was relatively greater for women 30 to 34 years old, quadrupling from 6 to 24 percent. Changes were also dramatic for men—the proportion of men 20 to 24 years old who had never married increased from 55 percent in 1970 to 87 percent in 2007. Although more women and men now live alone for part of their adult lives, most people do marry, at least once. In 2007, a large majority of men and women had been married by the time they were 30 to 34 (71 percent), and among women and men 65 years old and over,

B. Smaller

"I'm surprised I'm still single—I always thought I'd be divorced by now."

96 percent had been married (U.S. Bureau of the Census, 2008b). For younger women and men today, it is plausible to assume that approximately 10 percent will never marry in their lifetime. For those who do marry, approximately 50 percent will divorce, and the surviving marriages will eventually end in widowhood.

The Singles Population

The growing disinclination to marry among people of all ages means that there are many different ways of being single and consequently many different ways to depict the experience of singlehood. In the broadest sense, the term *single* refers to all unmarried adults over the age of 18. This population represents a wide-ranging demographic diversity with respect to age, race, ethnicity, education, occupation, income, and parental status. Singlehood also has different connections to the institution of formal, legal marriage, including as it does those who have never married, together with the divorced, the separated, and the widowed (Fields, 2004; Fowlkes, 1994:153).

Formal marriage no longer organizes life decisions and transitions, as it did in the past. In colonial times, almost all unmarried persons lived in a family environment, either with parents or in the homes of their employers. Only with marriage did they become fully independent members of society. This pattern began to change in the nineteenth century, when increasing numbers of single people worked for wages outside the family and lived in boardinghouses. The dramatic shift, however, occurred in recent years, as divorce, cohabitation, remarriage, and single motherhood all contributed to the growth of the single population (Coontz, 1997:79).

Women's economic independence has had a great impact on the rise of singlehood as a viable option. Many women have jobs that pay enough that the women do not require a partnership with a man to have a decent living. They need not marry for economic support or for social identity. Many women with strong career aspirations have opted for singlehood because marriage and domestic demands greatly lessen their chances for career success. Other social and cultural reasons make marriage less desirable. Marriage may be less necessary for happiness now, because unmarried persons can more readily engage in sexual relationships without social stigma and because the financial security of marriage has been undermined by high rates of divorce. With higher rates of single living, the social stigma of divorce is decreasing (Kantrowitz, 2006; Marks, 1996:917).

Gender, Race, and Class

Slightly more women than men marry sometime over the life course. Still, women are more likely to be alone for some or all of their lives from their middle years on. Fifty million women are now single, in comparison to 43 million men. This is 43 percent of all adult females, up from 30 percent in 1960 (U.S. Bureau of the Census, 2002, 2008b). Of course, the rise in single women encompasses other important trends, and a growing number are being more open about lesbian relationships. Still, singlehood is not always a matter of choice. Demography and culture can combine to create a phenomenon known as the "marriage squeeze." This refers to an imbalance in the number of women and men (who meet certain culturally-determined criteria, such as appropriate age) available for marriage. Because women tend to marry men who are somewhat older than themselves, there are more women than men who are seeking a partner. The older women become, the greater the imbalance. The terminology refers to the idea that some women who would like to be married may be "squeezed" out of the marriage market. Among persons age 65 and older, men are a minority. In the *total* single population, comprising the widowed and divorced together with the never-married, unmarried women begin to outnumber men by the age of 35 (Fowlkes, 1994:154).

The single woman has now come into her own. Not long ago, she would live a temporary existence—a rented apartment shared with a girlfriend or two. Adult life—a house, a car, travel, and children—only came with a husband. Single women often have vast friendship networks that provide rewarding lives without a partner. Today 60 percent of single women own their own homes, more than half of adventure travelers are women, and two in five business travelers are women (Edwards, 2000; Kantrowitz, 2006).

The proportion of never-married adults has increased for Whites, Blacks, and Hispanics. Among Whites, the proportion increased from 16 to 23 percent between 1970 and 2007. Forty percent of Black adults in 2007 had never been married, up from 21 percent in 1970. For Hispanics the proportion rose from 19 to 30 percent during this period (Fields, 2004; U.S. Bureau of the Census, 2008b).

Many would say that fewer Black women marry because there are not enough eligible men. However, many Black women remain single by choice. Sociologist

Elizabeth Higginbotham, who studied the priorities of educated Black women in the contemporary United States, found important class differences in women's life preferences. Women from established middle-class families were expected both to marry and to complete college, but women from lower-middle-class families were expected to finish college before they married (Higginbotham, 1981, 2001).

New thinking on race, class, and household composition is challenging scholars to reexamine long-held assumptions about the connections between marriage and social class. Research by Marsh and colleagues (2007) considers the relationship between the rising population of singles living alone and the growth in the Black middle class. Conventional wisdom holds that the middle class is composed largely of married-couple families. A central concern about the decline of marriage among African Americans has been the assumption that this change also signified the decline of the Black middle class. Many believed that less marriage provided fewer opportunities for African Americans to get ahead. This research finds, however, that the Black middle class increasingly comprises never-married singles who live alone. This dynamic and growing segment of the Black middle class is made up of 25- to 44-year-olds who have college degrees, have higher-than-average incomes, and are home owners (Marsh et al., 2007).

A great deal of research conducted over the past few decades provides a corrective to the myth that never-married women are lonely "old maids." For example, Barbara Simon conducted interviews with 50 never-married women born between 1884 and 1918. She included women of diverse racial, ethnic, and religious backgrounds in her study. Thirty-eight of her 50 elderly respondents (76 percent) actively chose singlehood. Although they gave varied reasons for their choice, the theme of "freedom" from the demands embedded in the wife's role emerged as a major reason to remain single. Intensely involved in the social networks of their jobs and voluntary service, these women were "agents contributing to their own history" (Simon, 1987:38).

More recent research by sociologist E. Kay Trimberger (2005) found important social changes in the lives of single women. Her study of single women over age 35 identifies a *new type* of single woman who is content with her life and with the prospect of remaining single. The women Trimberger studied created their own satisfying lives. They revealed that building a rewarding single life was much like building a good marriage—a process of development, self-discovery, and work. Six important characteristics distinguish the *new single woman:* (1) She creates a nurturing home where she feels physically and emotionally comfortable; (2) her work is satisfying not only financially but also personally; (3) she is comfortable with her sexuality, and she has fostered an empowering relationship to sex or has opted for a sensuous celibacy; (4) she connects with the next generation through the children of friends and relatives, her students, younger colleagues, or volunteer work with young people; (5) she finds emotional intimacy with friends and family; and (6) she builds a supportive community from various areas of her life—from work to politics to religious worship.

Experiencing Single Life

Singlehood's new respectability has not dispelled myths and stereotypes about single people. Stereotypes about singles abound in a society in which marriage is idealized (Mahoney, 2006). In the United States, politicians espouse "family values" and promise to work for America's families. Promoting marriage is social policy. Given the strong profamily ideology, single life is stigmatized and many singles feel disparaged. In her analysis of single life, Bella DePaulo defines singles as people who are not in a serious couple relationship (2006:2). She argues that the cultural belief that marriage is the vehicle to happiness supports the myth that to be single is to be miserable and lonely. Other myths include the idea that singles are immature and self-centered (DePaulo, 2006:94, 107). DePaulo debunks these stereotypes by analyzing the characteristics of the married and single with respect to health, happiness, life satisfaction, and other indicators of well-being. She concludes that single and married people are much more similar than different. When significant differences are identified, the major point to be made is that formerly married individuals may have more difficulties than either married or always-single individuals (DePaulo, 2006:234).

While the likelihood of marriage differs by race and social class, it is right to say that marriage remains a goal for most young women. What happens when the events in one's life do not follow a woman's anticipated life course? In Sharp and Ganong's (2007) study of White, college-educated women who were still single at ages 28 to 34, interviewees expressed uncertainty about their experiences of being never-married women. These women had anticipated lives of marriage with children, most had had serious romantic relationships and considered marriage, but none had married. Women now questioned their relationships and career paths, wondering if they had missed out on the chance for marriage and children. They coped with their ambivalence and doubt in a number of ways, affirming their own value as a potential partner, recalling the flaws in past romances, and focusing on what they had accomplished as single women. One research participant said,

> I have been able to buy a house for myself. I have a reliable, decent car that I am able to pay for by myself. I have a lot of nice jewelry that a lot of people expect others to buy for them. I guess I am okay being single because I enjoy the freedom and not having to explain where I've been when I don't come home after work or if I want to go to three happy hours in one week, I can. Or if I want to spend $50 on two bottles of wine, I could do that. That is what makes it okay. It is just the next level of independence: That I can provide for myself, that I can take care of myself.... Even though I want that extra part [marriage and children] in my life, I don't need it to survive. (840)

This research illustrates the continuing strength of the ideology of the value of marriage despite the sharp rise in singlehood (Sharp and Ganong, 2007:842).

Although singles and their issues have generally been ignored, this group constitutes a large and potentially powerful interest group. Advocacy groups for singles are now questioning the current system of institutionalized supports for married individuals, ranging from federal legislation benefiting the married to the assumptions of the "family-friendly" workplace. The Alternatives to Marriage Project and Unmarried America are two organizations that disseminate information for and about singles online. The Alternatives to Marriage Project is a grassroots organization relying on individuals to contribute their time, energy, and money to work for fairness for unmarried people. The website encourages singles to get involved with the organization by becoming an intern or volunteer, joining a reading group, attending an event, or making a donation (Alternatives to Marriage Project, 2009). Unmarried America is an information service for the "new unmarried majority." This site provides relevant information for singles in areas including politics and the law, taxation, workplace concerns, lifestyle, and health (Unmarried America, 2009).

Single life is difficult to examine, in part, because "single" is used as a marital status category that encompasses everyone who does not have the legal status of "married." To know that someone is single tells us little about his or her residential arrangements or their relationship commitments. A growing number of adults are opting to live by themselves while maintaining a stable relationship. Other "singles" are, in fact, living with a partner without being married. Today, what it means to be single is no longer clear.

Because many single people are actually cohabitants, what it means to be "single" or "married" is changing "as the personal lives of unmarried couples come to resemble those of their married counterparts in some ways but not in others" (Casper and Bianchi, 2002:40). In the next section, we examine how the lives of millions of unmarried women and men do and do not resemble those of married people.

Heterosexual Cohabitation

The term *heterosexual cohabitation* refers to a family formed outside of marriage by sharing a residence. Once considered "living in sin," this arrangement is one of the most important trends in family life. Today, living together is a routine step leading to marriage as well as a variation on marriage. The U.S. Census estimates that approximately 15 million people in the United States live unmarried with a partner. This number includes both different-sex couples and same-sex couples: 6.8 million couples live as unmarried different-sex partners and 750,000 couples live as same-sex partners. This chapter section focuses on heterosexual cohabiting couples; the next section focuses on same-sex couples. Heterosexual cohabiting households increased rapidly from 2.9 million in 1990 to 4.7 million in 2000, and 6.8 million in 2008, an increase of well over 100 percent in less than two decades (U.S. Bureau of the Census, 2009a).

Cohabitation has grown rapidly in all developed countries. In the United States, it has changed the steps in family formation. Sixty percent of all marriages formed in the 1990s began with cohabitation (Teachman, 2003). Looking to the future, there is reason to believe couples will continue to cohabit as a step toward marriage. Surveys of high school seniors show a high rate of approval for premarital cohabitation (see Figure 12.2). Whereas the pattern in the United States is relatively new, it is an old

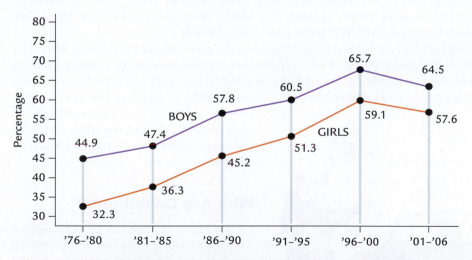

Figure 12.2   **Percentage of High School Seniors Who "Agreed" or "Mostly Agreed" With the Statement That "It is usually a good idea for a couple to live together before getting married in order to find out whether they really get along," by Period, United States.**

Note: From *Monitoring the Future* surveys conducted by the Survey Research Center at the University of Michigan.

Source: "National Marriage Project (2009)." *The State of Our Unions 2008: The Social Health of Marriage in America.* Online: http://marriage.rutgers.edu.

custom in many Scandinavian countries, where about a quarter of all different-sex unions are cohabiting rather than married (Paetsch and Bala, 2004:313).

The Rise of Cohabitation

Noted demographer Larry Bumpass asks, "How has it happened that what was once morally reprehensible has become the majority experience in just two decades?" (Bumpass, 1990:486). Sociologists point to several trends that explain why cohabitation is now a normative step in the marriage process. The trends include the later age at which young people marry, the sexual revolution, new living arrangements after divorce and before remarriage, and increasing individualism and secularization (Bianchi and Casper, 2000; Bumpass and Lu, 2000b; Lichter and Qian, 2004; Seltzer, 2004; Smock, 2000). These developments underlie the growing acceptability of living together. Bumpass explains that

> shacking up was offensive after all, not because couples were sharing cooking and the laundry, but because they were sharing a bed. The revolution in the sexual experience of unmarried persons over the same period has seriously weakened the basis for disapproving of cohabitation. (Bumpass, 1990:486)

Not only have social norms changed, but other conditions also have promoted the increase in cohabitation. The increased independence of single young adults—living away from parents in dormitories and apartments—has opened up new possibilities for women and men. Women's changing roles in the labor market have given them financial and personal options beyond marriage, while men no longer face the same pressures from employers to be married (Goldscheider and Waite, 1991; Rosenfeld, 2007; Smock, 2000). Something else has changed to make living together a common experience. People are much more cautious about entering marriage. Many choose cohabitation because they worry about the possibility of their own divorce (Bumpass, 1990:407; Lichter and Qian, 2004:6).

Still other reasons for cohabitation lie in the economic and emotional benefits it offers. It is a means by which two persons can pool their resources to share the costs of rent, food, and utilities. Even among the elderly, economic incentives may encourage cohabitation and inhibit marriage (Chevan, 1996). In addition, this arrangement provides some of the emotional advantages of marriage with few of its economic and legal restrictions (Spain and Bianchi, 1996:32).

Who Are Cohabitors?

Cohabitation is not new. Throughout American history, some couples have lived together without formal marriage. In the past, the practice was concentrated among the poor. But as cohabitation has become the majority experience, cohabitors are not a distinct population. We could make the case that instead of asking, "Who cohabits?" we might ask, "Who does not cohabit?" (Smock, 2000:4). Although we no longer

provide profiles of those who live together without being married, we can make some generalizations about the social characteristics of cohabitors (McLanahan and Casper, 1995; Scommegna, 2002; Seltzer, 2001, 2004; U.S. Bureau of the Census, 2009a):

- They are mostly young adults. Although cohabitation has risen in all age groups (including older adults), it is most prevalent among women and men under the age of 35. More than half (56 percent) of cohabitors are younger than 35. A substantial number (17 percent) are age 50 and above, and 3 percent are 65 and older.

- A sizable proportion are divorced from a previous mate. Over two-thirds of cohabiting couples include at least one divorced person.

- Increasing proportions of cohabiting couples today include children in their households.

- Today, two out of every five children will live in a cohabiting family at some point during childhood.

The old assumption was that those individuals who cohabit before marriage are somehow different types of people—less traditional, more willing to experiment. However, this assumption tells us little about the social circumstances that go beyond individual choices to facilitate cohabitation. Nor does it provide insight into the properties of the cohabiting partnership itself. A burgeoning body of research seeks to substantiate the advantages and disadvantages of cohabitation for individuals at varied social locations. While some progress has been made in disentangling the complexities of these relationships, cohabitation remains an ambiguous arrangement, often lacking in predictability and clear normative standards. As Thornton and colleagues note, the boundaries between cohabitation and being single, and between cohabitation and being married, can be "relatively fuzzy and arbitrary" (2007:79).

Gender, Class, and Race

Cohabitation is a heterogeneous arrangement. Like other domestic forms, it is shaped by gender, class, and race. For example, gender is an important variable in how cohabitation is experienced. Cohabiting women are younger than cohabiting men. In 2008, 27 percent of cohabiting women and 17 percent of cohabiting men were under 25 (U.S. Bureau of the Census, 2009a). Past research has shown that men tend to view cohabitation in pragmatic terms, with less emotional involvement and less personal commitment than women, who tend to define the arrangement as a step toward a stable, long-term relationship (Jackson, 1983; Macklin, 1983). Women and men often see the relationship differently. Just as marriage has a "his and her" dimension, men and women who cohabit may differ in whether and when they define themselves as living together (e.g., when they moved their clothes to the same place; when they stopped paying rents in two places; when they spent most but not all nights together) (Seltzer, 2004:69). Women cohabitors are more likely than men to desire marriage (Blumstein and Schwartz, 1983; Lyness et al., 1972:308). About one in four unmarried women who are now living with a man do not expect to marry him. The biggest factor in women's expectation of marriage is the man's social and economic status. If she perceives he is not good marriage material, she does not expect to marry him (Healy, 2002). Cohabiting may be a better deal for men than for women if women end up with the responsibilities of marriage without the legal protections. Some research finds that women who cohabit are more prone to depression than married women, especially if children are involved. For women who constantly worry that the union could dissolve, the instability is detrimental to their well-being (Peterson, 2000a:2D).

Compared with married couples, cohabitors tend to be more egalitarian and have less traditional attitudes toward family life. While egalitarian men generally do more housework than do traditional men, we still find among cohabiting couples the strong tendency for household duties to be split along traditional gender lines, with women doing more domestic chores (Blumstein and Schwartz, 1983:148; Seltzer, 2001; Shelton and John, 1993a). The gender gap in housework is, however, smaller than that found among married couples. Cohabiting women do less housework than their married counterparts, and recent evidence suggests that cohabiting men do more housework than married men (Davis et al., 2007:1263). The still unequal distribution of housework is another indication that cohabitation may be more advantageous to men than to women.

The rise in cohabitation is characteristic of all social and economic groups, but it functions differently by social class. For more privileged young adults, the events on the path to marriage are now frequently arranged in this order: "school, career, living together, marriage" (Jayson, 2008). Here cohabitation is part of a long-term strategy for economic success and personal fulfillment. Cohabitation continues to be more common among those who are less economically privileged. For those with less education and more economic constraints, cohabitation may be attractive because it requires less commitment to fulfill long-term economic responsibilities to a legal partner. Thus those with uncertain economic prospects are more likely to cohabit than to marry (Seltzer, 2004:60).

Economic factors have produced a long history of consensual unions among African Americans and some Latino groups. These patterns differ in important ways from the majority patterns (Hunter, 2006). While cohabiting families have risen in all racial groups, rates of cohabitation are somewhat higher among African American and Hispanic couples (Dunifon and Kowaleski-Jones, 2002; Seltzer, 2004). Unlike the large racial differences in marriage, there are more modest racial differences in cohabitation rates. Figure 12.3 shows the racial differences in the proportion of unmarried households to all coupled households. We see that Asian and White couples are least likely to live in unmarried partner households (and most likely to be married).

Is Cohabitation a Prelude to Marriage or a Substitute for Marriage?

Variation in cohabiting unions raises the following question—How should this widely accepted practice be viewed in relation to marriage? In the family field, scholars are debating whether cohabitation is a trial period before marriage, a stage in the marriage process, or a replacement for formal marriage.

Some see cohabitation as simply a new stage in the U.S. courtship process, a now-common premarital step. They argue that cohabitation is an extension of marriage because it allows people to "try out" potential marriage partners. As reasonable as this sounds, some cohabitation patterns raise questions about this perspective. First, not all cohabiting couples anticipate marriage. In fact, cohabiting unions do not last that long—only 1.5 years on average (Bumpass, 1990:487; Bumpass and Lu, 2000b; Seltzer, 2004). Cohabitation before marriage may even increase the risk of divorce (Casper and Bianchi, 2002; Lichter and Qian, 2004; McLanahan and Casper, 1995).

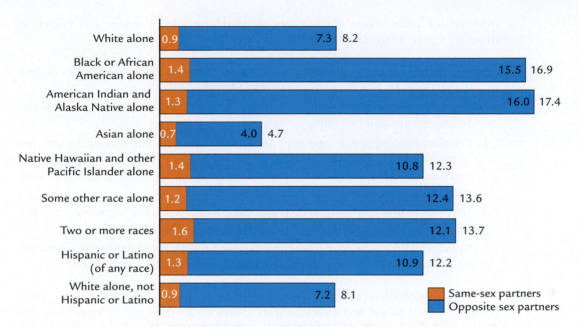

Figure 12.3 Unmarried-Partner Households by Sex of Partners and Race and Hispanic Origin of Householder: 2000

(Percent of all coupled households. For information on confidentiality protection, nonsampling error and definitions, see http://www.census.gov/prod/cen2000/docs/sf1.pdf.)

Note: Percent same-sex partners and percent opposite-sex partners may not add to total percent unmarried-partner households because of rounding.

Source: Simmons, Tavia, and Martin O'Connell (2003). "Married-Couple and Unmarried-Partner Households: 2000." *Census 2000 Special Reports.* U.S. Bureau of the Census (February).

Another perspective holds that cohabitation is not a prelude to formal marriage at all. Instead, it is a family form in its own right for couples who do not necessarily reject marriage but are "less likely to see marriage as the defining characteristic of their family lives" (Seltzer, 2001:470). In many racial-ethnic settings, informal unions are surrounded by standard expectations much like those that apply to married couples. And the fact that minority cohabiting couples are more likely to have children than White cohabiting couples suggests that cohabitation is more of a *substitute for marriage* in minority communities. Among Whites, more cohabitations may be characterized as *trial marriages* (Dunifon and Kowaleski-Jones, 2002; McLanahan and Casper, 1995:29; Phillips and Sweeny, 2005). In a study of planned and unplanned childbearing among unmarried women, cohabitating Hispanics were two times more likely to have a planned birth versus an unplanned birth, suggesting that cohabitation is more integral to the family life of Hispanics than other groups (Musick, 2002:925).

Which of the contrasting views about cohabitation is most correct? Is it a temporary step on the way to marriage, or is it a distinctive family type? Both perspectives are correct. Each captures a different feature of cohabitation with its own purposes and meanings. Given these differences, we must not treat cohabitants as one homogeneous group. Comparisons between cohabiting and noncohabiting couples imply that all cohabiting relationships are alike, which is not true.

Given the increasing numbers of cohabiting couples and the fact that many do not intend to marry their partner eventually, does this mean that the institution of marriage is in jeopardy? Bumpass, after reviewing the evidence, does not think so.

However, he notes several implications of cohabitation for marriage and singleness (from Bumpass, 1990; Smock, 2000):

1. Cohabitation changes the meaning of "single." Singlehood (and the rapid decline of marriage) no longer means unattached living.

2. Marriage is now a less specific marker of other transitions, such as sex, living arrangements, and parenting.

3. Cohabitation requires a new way of marking those unions that eventually become marriages. For some couples, "marriage" began when they started living together, whereas others avoid an unstable marriage by splitting up before they reach the altar.

4. "Premarital divorces" help keep the divorce rate from going higher, since many couples are using cohabitation to test their relationship.

5. Not all cohabitations are part of the marriage process. Some are better characterized as relationships of convenience in which marriage is not an issue.

Does cohabitation provide an opportunity for couples to learn about each other, strengthen their bonds, and increase their chances for a successful marriage? The evidence suggests the opposite. "Premarital cohabitation tends to be associated with lower marriage quality and to increase the risk of divorce even after taking account of variables associated with divorce (e.g., education, age at marriage)" (Smock, 2000:6). Why? Three explanations address this association. The first explanation suggests that people who cohabit before marriage differ from those who do not, and these differences increase the likelihood of marital instability. The second explanation is that there is something about cohabitation itself that increases the likelihood of marital disruption beyond one's characteristics at the start of the cohabitation; in other words, the experience makes people more prone to instability (Smock, 2000:6). Third, new research looks at diversity among cohabitors, finding that certain groups are at greater risk of divorce upon marriage. For example, when cohabitors with nonmarital births married, their marital quality was lower than that of comparable couples who did not have premarital births (Tach and Halpern-Meekin, 2009). Likewise women who have been involved in multiple cohabitations and then marry have much higher divorce rates than women who cohabited only with the man they married (Lichter and Qian, 2008:861).

In sum, it is apparent that U.S. families are not following the path established by some European countries. Most of the evidence indicates that cohabitation is not (yet) becoming an alternative to marriage. Nevertheless, it is redefining family life.

Same-Sex Partners and Families

The emergence of nonheterosexual families is a movement with large social, political, and legal ramifications. Debates about whether same-sex marriage threatens the institution of the family are not limited to the United States. Around the world, legal recognition of same-sex marriage is both supported and resisted. "This is a time of great paradox. Lesbians and gays are simultaneously depicted as pioneering and as a major sign of social deterioration" (Laird, 2003:176). A majority of Americans think that same-sex marriage undermines the traditional family. However, the public has been more supportive of civil unions (entitling same-sex couples to certain rights and responsibilities, but without the full benefits of legal marriage) (Brewer and Wilcox, 2005).

The global transformation of family life has produced landmark legislation for same-sex couples in Scandinavian countries, Belgium, Spain, Canada, South Africa, and elsewhere. In Chapter 8 we discussed the passage of U.S. laws in favor of same-sex marriage. In this chapter, we examine the policy debates surrounding legal rights for nonheterosexual unions. In this section, we limit our discussion to same-sex families themselves—an emergent family form, where new patterns of relationships are being invented (Weeks et al., 2004:341).

In conventional thought, family is a heterosexually based unit, formed through legal marriage between a man and a woman. "It is not surprising that the family as the widely proclaimed 'building block' of society is seen as the antithesis of homosexuality" (Weeks et al., 2004:341). Yet many, if not most, lesbians and gay men express the desire for an enduring love relationship with a partner of the same gender. Research findings suggest that many are successful in creating such relationships. Survey data suggest that 40 to 60 percent of gay men and 45 to 80 percent of lesbians are currently involved in steady romantic relationships (Patterson, 2001:272). It is true that gay rights movements once sought to escape the constraints of a heterosexist institution. In the 1990s, however, procreation, parenting, and kinship among same-sex couples were at the forefront of lesbian and gay struggles for social justice (D'Emilio, 1996). Despite resistance and discrimination, lesbians and gay men are creating families. Not only are gay families here to stay, but family has become a frontier issue in the struggle for gay rights. It may seem odd to identify a family, rather than an individual, as gay. Nevertheless, this historically new category of family is a vital part of family diversification that is now taking place in the nation and the world (Stacey, 1998:118).

Who Is Gay and What Are Gay Families?

Important questions revolve around the numbers of gay men and lesbian women in the United States. These numbers are unknown and perhaps unknowable, because many gay and lesbian individuals never reveal their sexual orientation and live lives that appear to be heterosexually oriented. The common estimates by researchers range from 4 to 10 percent of adults in the total population that are exclusively or substantially homosexual. Pioneering research by Alfred Kinsey and his associates first on men, in 1948, and then on women, in 1953, made it clear that homosexuality was much more common than anyone had suspected. Since Kinsey's studies, the 10 percent figure has been widely used, prompting the phrase "one in ten," meaning that one in 10 persons in the United States is gay or lesbian. In fact, Kinsey argued that it was impossible to answer the question of how many gays and lesbians are in the population. The authors of *Sex in America* (Michael et al., 1994), the book based on the national sex survey (see Chapter 7), explain that the answer to the gay numbers question is subtle and shaded with gray. They give three reasons why we cannot say that a person is gay or not gay: First, people often change their sexual behavior during their lifetime, making it impossible to state that a particular set of behaviors defines a person as gay; second, there is no one set of sexual desires or self-identification that uniquely defines homosexuality; and, third, homosexual behavior is not easily measured. Persecution causes many people to never reveal their sexual orientation (Michael et al., 1994:172).

Problems of definition also apply to gay families because individuals—not families—have sexual orientations. Typically, in families of origin, family members have different sexual orientations. Katherine Allen and David Demo suggest that we can define lesbian and gay families by the presence of two or more people who share a same-sex orientation (e.g., a couple) or by the presence of at least one lesbian or gay adult rearing a child. This definition represents families that are influenced by homosexuality (Allen and Demo, 1995:113). Others refer to lesbian and gay cohabiting couples as families even though they are not considered families according to official definition because they are not legally married (Bianchi and Casper, 2000:10). Although the matter of what constitutes a gay family is important, family researchers extend the discussion to include the following (from Savin-Williams and Esterberg, 2000:199):

- Families in which parents are heterosexual but the children are lesbian or gay.
- Children of lesbian and gay parents and how these children have fared, both psychologically and socially (see Chapter 9).
- Lesbian and gay parents who are making the decision to parent and the relationships they have with each other.
- Public policies that have, with relatively few exceptions, neglected the needs of gay and lesbian families (see Chapter 13).

Many same-sex couples misrepresent their relationships in surveys, and their households come in different shapes and compositions, so "gay families" are difficult to count. We have not had systematic or comprehensive data on gay and lesbian households because the U.S. Census Bureau does not identify the sexual orientation of those it surveys. The totals it provides for same-sex households are the sum of (1) the unmarried partner category when the partner is indicated as the same sex, and (2) the households that identified as married couples, but were reallocated to the unmarried partner category, again when the partner is the same sex (as was discussed in Chapter 8). Thanks to the Census Bureau's recently implemented American Community Survey (ACS), we now have annual estimates of the number of same-sex households and descriptions on a range of characteristics. In 2007, gay and lesbian households numbered approximately 754,000; 52 percent of couples were gay men and 48 percent were lesbians. One in four same-sex couples has children under 18 (O'Connell and Lofquist, 2009). (Figure 12.4 shows U.S. Census counts for same-sex couples from 1990 to 2007).

Gay Couples and Families

The idea that we should go beyond "homosexual lifestyles" to study the *family relations* of lesbians and gays is new even in the family field. "We have yet to reach a point where lesbians and gays are viewed as family members who happen to be gay" (Allen and Demo, 1995:116). Until recently, much of what we knew about gays and lesbians came from classic studies of homosexual partnerships (e.g., Bell and Weinberg, 1978; Blumstein and Schwartz, 1983; Harry, 1983; Peplau, 1981). While there are still many gaps in our knowledge, new analyses of recent data provide a more current portrait of cohabiting same-sex couples than was previously possible (from Gates, 2007; O'Connell and Lofquist, 2009):

1. Lesbian and gay couples have been a highly urban population. This remains true, but many couples are now moving from cities to suburbs. Some major cities (e.g. Atlanta and Detroit) have seen substantial declines in the population of same-sex couples, while surrounding counties have seen significant increases.

2. Many couples include children: 30 percent of lesbian couples and 21 percent of gay couples, compared with 44 percent of married-couple families.

3. Gay and lesbian couples are more highly educated than heterosexual married couples. In 2006, the percentage of households in which both partners had at least a bachelor's degree was 30 percent for lesbian couples, 26 percent for gay couples, and 21 percent for married couples.

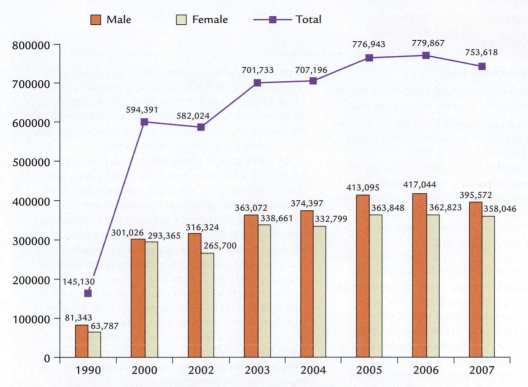

Figure 12.4 **Same-Sex Couples in the United States, 1990–2007**

Sources: Gates, Gary J. (2007). "Geographic Trends among Same-Sex Couples in the U.S. Census and the American Community Survey." The Williams Institute, p. 3. Online: http://repositories.cdlib.org/uclalaw/Williams/census/gates_1; O'Connell, Martin and Daphne Lofquist (2009). "Counting Same-Sex Couples: Official Estimates and Unofficial Guesses." *U.S. Census Bureau Working Papers.* Online: http://www.census.gov/population/www/socdemo/hh-fam.html.

4. Average household income in 2006 was $111,000 for gay men, $95,000 for lesbians, as compared to $91,000 for heterosexual married couples.

5. Same-sex couples are more likely to be White or interracial and less likely to be Asian than are heterosexual married-couple households.

In their classic study, Blumstein and Schwartz (1983) found that lesbian couples and gay male couples faced many of the same issues confronting heterosexual couples who live together, married or not. They must work out issues related to the division of household labor, power and authority, and emotional obligations. Same-sex couples, however, face additional problems. Because of the general antipathy toward homosexuality in U.S. society, gay and lesbian couples function in social settings that may or may not accept their family commitment. They must negotiate their families in varying degrees of adversity, with the possibility of disapproval, rejection, or discrimination around any corner (Laird, 2003:194; Oswald, 2002; Weeks et al., 2001).

Research has long identified *social networks* as the distinguishing feature of same-sex families. Networks are complex systems made up of "chosen" family connections (Weeks et al., 2004). This is what anthropologist Kath Weston's classic study of same-sex families in the San Francisco Bay Area discovered. During a two-year period, Weston conducted interviews and engaged in participant observation with 40 lesbians and 40 gay men from diverse racial and ethnic backgrounds (see Box 12.2). She discovered kinship networks among gays and lesbians who were creating relationships they defined as family. "Chosen" families are formed from networks of friends, lovers, co-parents, children

BOX 12.2 Researching Families

Fieldwork in Gay Communities

Kath Weston describes the methods used in this classic work to study lesbians and gay men in San Francisco.

The fieldwork that provides the basis for my analysis was conducted in the San Francisco Bay Area during 1985–1986, with a follow-up visit in 1987....

With its unique history and reputation as a gay city, San Francisco hardly presents a "typical" lesbian and gay population for study. Yet the Bay Area proved to be a valuable field site because it brought together gay men and lesbians from very different colors and classes, identities and backgrounds.

In addition to the long hours of participant-observation so central to anthropological fieldwork, my analysis draws on 80 in-depth interviews conducted while in the field. Interview participants were divided evenly between women and men, with all but two identifying themselves as lesbian or gay. Random sampling is clearly an impossibility for a population that is not only partially hidden or "closeted," but also lacks consensus as to the criteria for membership. In general, I let self-identification be my guide for inclusion. Determined to avoid the race, class, and organizational bias that has characterized so many studies of gay men and lesbians, I made my initial connections through personal contacts developed over the six years I had lived in San Francisco previous to the time the project got underway. The alternative—gaining entree through agencies, college classes, and advertisements—tends to weight a sample for "joiners," professional interviewees, the highly educated, persons with an overtly political analysis, and individuals who see themselves as central (rather than marginal) to the population in question.

By asking each person interviewed for names of potential participants, I utilized techniques of friendship pyramiding and snowball sampling to arrive at a sample varied in race, ethnicity, class, and class background. While the Bay Area is perhaps more generally politicized than other regions of the nation, the majority of interview participants would not have portrayed themselves as political activists. Approximately 36 percent were people of color; of the 64 percent who were White, 11 (or 14 percent of the total) were Jewish. Slightly over 50 percent came from working-class backgrounds, with an overlapping 58 percent employed in working-class occupations at the time of the interview.

Of the 82 people contacted, only two turned down my request for an interview. A few individuals made an effort to find me after hearing of the study, but most were far from self-selecting. The vast majority demanded great persistence and flexibility in scheduling (and rescheduling) on my part to convince them to participate. I believe this persistence is one reason this study includes voices not customarily heard when lesbians and gay men appear in the pages of books and journals: people who had constructed exceedingly private lives and could scarcely get over their disbelief at allowing themselves to be interviewed, people convinced that their experiences were uneventful or unworthy of note, people fearful that a researcher would go away and write an account lacking in respect for their identities or their perceptions.

To offset the tendency of earlier studies to focus on the White and wealthier sectors of lesbian and gay population, I also utilized theoretic sampling. From a growing pool of contacts I deliberately selected people of color, people from working-class backgrounds, and individuals employed in working-class occupations.

In any sample this diverse, with so many different combinations of identities, theoretic sampling cannot hope to be "representative." To treat each individual as a representative of his or her race, for instance, would be a form of tokenism that glosses over the differences of gender, class, age, national origin, language, religion, and ability that crosscut race and ethnicity. At the same time, I am not interested in these categories as demographic variables, or as reified pigeonholes for people, but rather as identities meaningful to participants themselves.

Source: Weston, Kath, *Families We Choose.* New York: Columbia University Press, 1991, pp. 7–10.

conceived through artificial insemination, adopted children, children from previous heterosexual relationships, and blood kin (in other words, "fictive kin"). The network families that gays and lesbians created in the Bay Area had fluid boundaries, much like kinship organization among sectors of racial-ethnic and White working class families (see Chapters 3 and 5).

Weston's study is important because it challenges the conventional notion that gays and lesbians lack family ties. It also reveals some of the ways in which gays and lesbians are broadening the definition of the family by including domestic partnerships and friendship networks. Joan Laird reports that in some lesbian communities, the boundaries between family, kinship, and community are diffuse. "Although it has been said that you cannot choose your relatives, that is exactly what gay families in devising a new system of kinship do. They choose their families, retaining the familiar symbol of blood and combining it with symbols of love and choice" (Laird, 2003:178).

Are the family dynamics of same-sex families different from those in heterosexual families? Current research on lesbian and gay couples points to a number of similarities and differences between homosexual and heterosexual couples, some of which contradict the prevailing stereotypes. In a study of differences between partners from heterosexual, gay, and lesbian cohabiting couples, Lawrence Kurdek found that close relationships work in similar ways (Kurdek, 2006). For example, lesbians and gay men report as much satisfaction with their relationships as do heterosexual couples. For the most part, they describe themselves as happy. When they do experience problems in their relationships, they often stem from the same difficulties that heterosexuals face—that is, different backgrounds, job-related problems, financial pressures, and friction with extended family networks. On the other hand, the lack of formalized social supports for committed lesbian and gay relationships might lead to higher breakup rates than are found in married couples (Kurdek, 1998). In her summary of research, Charlotte Patterson concludes, "In general, the picture of lesbian and gay relationships emerging from this body of work is one of positive adjustment even in the face of stressful conditions" (Patterson, 2001:271).

GENDER

In Chapter 7 we saw that gender is important in the intimate relationships of lesbians and gays, but in ways that contradict common stereotypes. For example, lesbians are commonly depicted as masculine women, whereas gay men are depicted as effeminate men. In reality, lesbians and gays are not inverts of heterosexuals. Lesbians and heterosexual women are more alike than different, as are gay and heterosexual men. Nevertheless, in the values and behaviors that link love and sex, lesbians and gays have identifiable gender-linked behaviors (Fowlkes, 1994:172). To simplify, "men are like men, and women are like women despite differences in sexual orientation" (Hovedt, 1982:182, cited in Fowlkes, 1994:172).

Studies comparing lesbian, gay, and heterosexual couples find important contrasts in their characteristic patterns of intimacy. Gender shapes domestic values and practices more strongly than sexual identity (Stacey, 1998:139). For example, lesbians have been found to be more sexually exclusive than gay men. Data collected before and after the HIV/AIDS epidemic had attracted public attention revealed that most lesbians experienced monogamous sexual relationships whereas gay men did not (reported in Patterson, 2001:273). The tendency for gay men to be less sexually exclusive than lesbian women parallels the difference in heterosexual males and females. This difference is related to gender role socialization in society, where "males are socialized to engage in sexual behaviors both with and without affection while women are expected to combine the two" (Harry, 1983:226).

Research highlights the effects of gender on relationship quality. There are many coupling issues in which gender "sameness" can be valuable, and other areas in which it can generate problems. Similarly, the issue of gender "differentness" can enrich a couple's life (Laird, 2003:195). Studies find that same-sex couples handle conflicts better than heterosexual couples (Gottman and Levinson, 1999) and that lesbian couples have higher levels of cohesion and adaptability than heterosexual couples (Zacks et al., 1988).

In a major departure from the heterosexual pattern, gay and lesbian couples tend to be egalitarian (Allen and Demo, 1995). Studies have found that heterosexual couples, whether in cohabitation or marriage relationships, tend to accept the traditional gender roles for men and women. In contrast, same-sex couples are much more likely to share in the decision-making and household duties. This was confirmed by Lawrence Kurdek (1993), who found that married, gay, and lesbian couples followed different strategies for allocating household labor. Consistent with the literature, married couples allocated housework primarily on the basis of gender. In other words, wives did most of the housework. Although partners in gay couples and married couples were equally likely to be specialized in task performance, gay couples tended to distribute the pattern of specialization equally so that, unlike married couples, one partner did not do all the work. Partners in gay couples specialized in task performance on the basis of skill, interest, and work schedule, while lesbians typically followed an ethic of equality (Kurdek, 1993).

An important implication of the equality found in homosexual relationships is that, contrary to the stereotype, the partners do not take the role of either "husband" or "wife." The prevailing assumption is that one takes the "masculine" role and is dominant in sexual activities and decision-making, while the other does the "feminine" household tasks and is submissive to the first. Research consistently refutes this "butch/femme" notion, noting that only a small minority of couples reflect the stereotype.

In Chapter 8, we considered how the benefits of marriage might differ by gender. Such an analysis does not apply directly to same-sex couples, but research does find that cohabiting gay and lesbian couples report greater happiness and better health than do single gays and lesbians (Wienke and Hill, 2009).

A Shifting Social Context for Same-Sex Partners

In general, gay and lesbian partners face a "catch-22": Most are legally prohibited from marrying and yet they face discrimination because they are not married. They are denied inheritance rights, Social Security benefits, health insurance, and other employee benefits. Despite national refusal to legally recognize same-sex unions, same-sex couples have won important victories on the state level. In a flurry of legal and legislative activity between 2003 and 2009, same-sex marriage was legalized in five states; five additional states (and the District of Columbia) offer either civil union or domestic partnerships for same-sex couples (see Chapter 8.) This means that 10 states grant all state-level rights and benefits accorded to married couples to same-sex couples (Human Rights Campaign, 2009b). In surveying the movement for gay rights over several decades, it is accurate to say that the movement has achieved considerable success, and the relative success of gay rights initiatives has increased over time (Hull, 2006:7).

The mobilization of activists working for equal employment benefits has occurred as part of the **domestic partner movement.** Although this movement has received far less attention than same-sex marriage, it has been quite successful in obtaining employment benefits for same-sex families. Domestic partners are two individuals who are in a long-term committed relationship and are responsible for each other's financial and emotional well-being. Gay and lesbian workers receive family benefits equal to those of their heterosexual counterparts by one of two avenues. First, if states, counties, or cities have domestic partner legislation, companies whose health care coverage includes spouses, must treat domestic partners as spouses and cover them. Alternatively and more often, individual employers decide to extend benefits to gay and lesbian partners

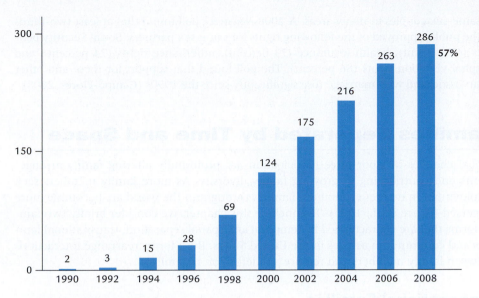

Figure 12.5

***Fortune* 500 Companies Providing Domestic Partner Health Benefits, by Year**

Source: Human Rights Campaign Foundation (2009). *The State of the Workplace, 2007–2008.* Online: http://www.hrc.org/workplace.

independent of statutory requirements as a good business practice to retain valuable employees and from a sense of fairness (Human Rights Campaign, 2009a). National gay rights organizations such as the Human Rights Campaign began devoting resources to workplace issues in the 1990s. As more employers added the benefits through the 1990s, others followed. Now a majority of the largest U.S. corporations extend benefits to domestic partners. In 2008, 286—or 57 percent of *Fortune* 500 companies—provided benefits to employees' same-sex domestic partners (see Figure 12.5). In contrast with the private sector, state and federal governments are moving more slowly to extend equal benefits to gays and lesbians. In June 2009, President Barack Obama signed an executive order extending limited partnership rights to federal workers in same-sex relationships. Gay rights activists expressed disappointment because the most important benefit—healthcare—was not included (Rutenberg, 2009).

The Domestic Partner movement has achieved remarkable success in corporate settings. More than one-fourth of Americans now work for an employer that offers domestic partner benefits, and 90 percent of employers offering domestic partner benefits make them available to both same-sex and different-sex couples. Thus, cohabiting heterosexuals also benefit because many also use these domestic partner plans when they are available. Not only has the gay rights movement transformed our understanding of human sexuality; it is also expanding the definition of what constitutes a family.

The success of the movement for equal employment benefits for domestic partners reflects growing public support for extending the legal rights

"What's the point of being your sidekick if the courts won't recognize it?"

of same-sex couples in many areas. A 2008 *Newsweek* poll found that at least two-thirds of the public approved of the following rights for same-sex partners: Social Security benefits (67 percent), health insurance (73 percent), inheritance rights (74 percent), and hospital visitation rights (86 percent). The poll found that support for these and other rights associated with marriage rose significantly since the 1990s (Campo-Flores, 2008).

 # Families Separated by Time and Space

Global changes in labor force participation are profoundly altering family arrangements and contributing to growing family diversity. As more family members seek employment in market economies, families throughout the world are becoming more dispersed (Bruce et al., 1995). To conclude this chapter, we consider briefly two family forms that are characterized by temporal and spatial separation: transnational families and commuter marriages in the United States. Both forms rearrange interactions between family members and require a redefinition of family.

Transnational Families

As goods, information, and people move across national boundaries, family life is affected in several ways. "An ever-increasing number of families are transnationally networked: they no longer live in just one place, are no longer rooted in just one country, but are developing into intricate wickerwork relationships spread out over several countries or even continents" (Beck and Beck-Gernsheim, 2004:502). The global movement of families is not a minor concern; it is at the very core of our understanding of social life in the twenty-first century.

The forms families take in global restructuring are shaped by the structural inequalities of globalization. In Chapter 4 we discussed some of the family consequences that are emerging from immigration. While reasons for immigration are complex, most individuals and families are economic migrants; that is, they migrate to take advantage of labor market opportunities in other countries. Today's patterns of work and migration are creating a new family form—the transnational family.

Transnational families are families whose members span national boundaries, typically for the requirements of work. In a pattern that is well-known, many families become transnational families as part of the process of family immigration to a new home country. In this case, one family member is sent ahead for the purpose of finding employment and housing in order to support the eventual arrival of other family members or to earn income to be remitted to the family left behind. The majority of these migrant workers are men. This pattern is common among undocumented migrants from Mexico, Central America, Puerto Rico, the Dominican Republic, elsewhere in the Caribbean, and Southeast Asia (Pyke, 2004).

Globalization is now creating new immigration patterns and producing new transnational family forms around the world. The globalization of the market economy has produced a demand for female workers from developing nations to supply low-wage service labor in more developed nations. In the United States, the labor of immigrant women meets the demands for domestic labor and care work in household, business, and institutional settings. That women are increasingly drawn into transnational employment is new, but not really surprising. Jobs in postindustrial service economies have been overwhelmingly filled by women (see Chapter 6). It is understandable, then, that the postindustrial jobs needing to be filled by immigrants are female-typed jobs in the service sector. Thus, a growing proportion of labor migrants worldwide are women, producing what has been called the feminization of international migration (Karraker, 2008:54).

Globalization has destabilized old models of sustaining families, creating greater economic insecurity for many in developing nations. It is economic need that compels women to migrate to developed nations for higher wages than are available in their home countries. Greater economic security comes, however, with family separations and uncertainties of other kinds (Karraker 2008:91).

Women involved in transnational employment are frequently mothers. This means that motherhood is often stretched across national boundaries. **Transnational motherhood** is an arrangement whereby immigrant women work in one country, while their children live in another country. Hondagneu-Sotelo and Avila (1996) studied transnational mothering among Latina domestic workers, where mothers work in the United States while their children remain in Mexico or Central America. Many mothers found that they could best provide for their children by a transnational mothering arrangement because U.S. dollars stretched farther in Central America and Mexico than in the United States. This arrangement is difficult for parents and children, but it is sometimes the only choice if one is to take advantage of better wages in the United States. When these women cross the U.S. border for work, they are embarking not only on an immigration journey but also on a more radical gender transformative odyssey. These mothers are leaving traditional assumptions about women's appropriate roles behind as they become breadwinners and initiate long-distance relationships with their children. They are establishing separations of space and time from their communities of origin, homes, children, and sometimes husbands. In doing so, they must cope with stigma, guilt, and criticism from others (Hondagneu-Sotelo and Avila, 1997:7).

An increasing number of Filipina migrants are also mothering their children from a distance. In more than 100 countries today, Filipinas do housework and other forms of caretaking for more privileged women. At the same time, they hire low-wage women workers in the Philippines to care for the children they left behind. This represents an international division of reproductive labor that extends to family life among (1) middle-class women in receiving nations, (2) migrant domestic workers, and (3) third-world women who are too poor to migrate. The Filipina domestic workers who are "in the middle" of this division of labor suffer the pain of family separation, even as they provide care for other families in postindustrial societies. A paradox of transnational families is that families' economic security is achieved at great costs to family life (Parreñas, 2000, 2007). (See Box 12.3.) Many immigrant mothers of newly born children must send their

BOX 12.3 Inside the Worlds of Diverse Families

Mothering from a Distance

When the girl that I take care of calls her mother "Mama," my heart jumps all the time because my children also call me "Mama." . . . I begin thinking that at this hour I should be taking care of my very own children and not someone else's, someone who is not related to me in any way, shape, or form. . . . The work that I do here is done for my family, but the problem is they are not close to me but are far away in the Philippines. Sometimes, you feel the separation and you start to cry. Some days, I just start crying while I am sweeping the floor because I am thinking about my children in the Philippines. Sometimes, when I receive a letter from my children telling me that they are sick, I look up out the window and ask the Lord to look after them and make sure they get better even without me around to care after them. (Starts crying.) If I had wings, I would fly home to my children. Just for a moment, to see my children and take care of their needs, help them, then fly back over here to continue my work.

Every day Filipina domestic workers such as Rosemarie Samaniego are overwhelmed by feelings of helplessness: They are trapped in the painful contradiction of feeling the distance from their families and having to depend on the material benefits of their separation. They may long to reunite with their children but cannot, because they need their earnings to sustain their families.

Source: Parreñas, Rhacel Salazar, "Mothering from a Distance: Emotions, Gender, and International Relations in Filipino Transnational Families." In *Shifting the Center: Understanding Contemporary Families*, 3rd ed. Susan Ferguson (ed.). Boston: McGraw Hill, 2007, p. 409.

infants "home" to their countries of origin to be cared for by extended-family members. This is a common practice in New York's Chinatown, where immigrants work long hours in garment factories for paltry pay, leaving them no time to care for children (Sengupta, 1999).

Much of the discussion about the children of transnational immigration portrays children as neglected and abandoned (the following is from Karraker, 2008; Parreñas, 2007). This conversation typically assumes a sharply divided gender system in which only mothers can adequately raise a child. A closer look finds that transnational families enact flexible family arrangements in which children are cared for by fathers, maternal grandmothers, or other kin. Transnational mothers provide care for their own children from a distance of thousands of miles through letters and phone calls. Electronic communication allows families to remain in close contact by e-mail and, in some cases, via Skype. (This represents a positive aspect of globalization for these families.) At the same time, the unreasonable demands of employers, the expense of travel, and the constraints of immigration may result in long parental absences, which certainly contribute to negative effects for children. Women are sometimes separated from children for four or five years; absences as long as 10 years have also been documented.

Transnational families reveal the global relationship between families of dominant and subordinate groups. As first-world women were pulled into the labor force, much of the reproductive labor formerly done by women in the domestic sphere became market-based work. Millions of women from poor countries now serve as domestic workers for middle- and upper-class families. While their work supports the professional careers and families of the women who hire them, the arrangement leaves immigrant women of color disenfranchised and living across the world from their own families. The labor of these women reduces the unmet demand for care in developed societies but creates a "care deficit" in less-developed nations. This pattern of female migration reflects a worldwide gender revolution (Ehrenreich and Hochschild, 2002) and a worldwide family revolution as well.

Transnational families require major adaptations in all areas of family life. Children of Mexican farm laborers in a North Carolina labor camp, one of whom is an honor student.

As we think about how immigrant families adapt themselves to the new social and economic realities they face, it is important to keep the following two points in mind. First, transnational families are closely linked with the globalization of economies that create increasing demands for immigrant labor. Second, transnational families require major adaptations in all areas of family life to cope with the problems of immigration and withstand temporal and spatial separation. In restructuring their families, immigrants pay a great price, which we have yet to fully comprehend (Ehrenreich and Hochschild, 2002:3).

Commuter Marriages and Other Long-Distance Relationships

Changes in technology and the workplace have contributed to the growth of commuter marriages and other long-distance relationships (Dainton and Aylor, 2001). Commuter marriages or partnerships are defined as those where dual-career couples set up residences in separate locations, usually in response to the demands of their work (Holmes, 2004:188). Most commuting couples do not see their decision to commute as a matter of choice. Instead, living apart is a necessary accommodation to their careers. Like many innovations, couples view commuting as a temporary lifestyle (Baber and Allen, 1992:38). Not all long-distance relationships are alike. Some couples are together each weekend; others are together only once a month. Some couples are a day's drive away; others fly across the country.

Marital separation is not entirely new. In the past, there have always been circumstances under which husbands and wives lived in different locations. These have included war, military camps, seafaring, and immigration. By the mid-twentieth century, specific occupations such as those of pilots, truck drivers, politicians, entertainers, salespeople, and executives involved distance relationships. These lifestyles have not usually required separate households. Furthermore, in these examples, it is typically the husband's work that separates the couple. And the onus to adapt to an absent husband was on the wife (Holmes, 2004:183). New distance relationships are the result of *women's* professional roles. Most often, wives set up a temporary residence in a different geographic location. Family historian Stephanie Coontz argues that commuter marriage illustrates just how much marriage has changed in recent decades: "There's no longer the assumption that the woman immediately puts her career on hold once she gets married. It's part of an avalanche of evidence that marriage is being reconstructed for the first time in history as a marriage of equals" (Cullen, 2007:64).

Dual-residence couples view the careers of husband and wife as being equally important. Their work and family arrangements promote women's equality by making it acceptable for women to be dedicated to their careers, to individual freedom, and to personal growth. Great effort is required to live this way. Individuals' needs are pitted against family needs, and most commuters are ambivalent about their way of life (Gerstel and Gross, 1987a; Holmes, 2004). Yet most commuting couples feel that the strains in separate living are outweighed by the individual rewards they gain in their careers.

Studies of commuting couples have found both benefits and challenges for those involved. (The following is based on Jackson et al., 2000.) Benefits of commuting include (1) increased sense of autonomy, achievement, and satisfaction; (2) greater self-esteem and confidence; (3) ability to pursue careers without immediate and everyday family constraints, and other opportunities associated with compartmentalizing work and family roles (Chang and Wood, 1996; Douvan and Pleck, 1978; Groves and Horn-Winegerd, 1991).

Commuters tend to compartmentalize their lives into two areas: work and marriage. This may restrict interaction with people outside these realms and impose unique strains on the couple's relationship. While they may be satisfied with their work life, many claim it produces dissatisfying relationships (Holmes, 2004). Unlike the habituated togetherness of most married couples, commuters must work out the patterns of communication, sex, and domestic maintenance during their infrequent visits. This can be a gain for couples as an interacting unit. "They invest themselves heavily in their marital relationship when they are together, and often regard this shared time as a special, important time to concentrate on the relationship. As a result, there is less trivial conflict" (Gerstel, 1977:364). Some relationships are even strengthened by living apart. The separation can offer a balance between separation and togetherness by easing the stress of unrelieved companionship (Douvan and Pleck, 1978:138; Haberman, 2000). A study by Bunker et al. (1992) found greater work–life satisfaction among commuting couples than among dual-career single-residence couples.

The other side of this career-enhancing autonomy includes the following challenges: (1) stresses from trying to balance family and career responsibilities, (2) loneliness and lack of companionship, (3) missing sense of order from the lack of daily proximity, (4) uncertainty about the future of the relationship, (5) lack of understanding of this family arrangement, and (6) hectic schedules associated with greater separation of work and family responsibilities (Dainton and Aylor, 2001; Holmes, 2004; Jackson et al., 2000:23).

Gerstel and Gross (1987b) found that career and family characteristics interact to influence couples' commuting experiences. They identified three types of commuting couples who experience commuting differently based on the length of the marriage and the presence of children:

1. *Adjusting couples.* These were young couples in the early stages of both careers and marriages. They spent a good deal of effort "adjusting."

2. *Balancing couples.* These couples were older and more advanced in their careers, contending more with conflict over the increased child-care and domestic responsibilities of who stays home with the children. They struggled to strike a balance between the demands of their jobs and their families.

3. *Established couples.* These couples were freed from their childbearing responsibilities. At least one partner was well established in a career. With children no longer in the home, they had the fewest stresses and saw the greatest advantages in commuting.

Distance relationships are becoming more common for couples of various racial backgrounds, but little research has addressed the experiences of racial-ethnic couples in this arrangement. Anita Jackson and her colleagues studied African American couples in commuter marriages to see how they managed commuting and how their families and careers were affected. These couples experienced many of the same advantages and disadvantages as noted in studies of White couples (see Table 12.1), but the study also suggests that commuting may have distinctive benefits for African Americans:

Commuting is a strategy for engaging in meaningful work when such opportunities are not in close proximity to one's family residence. For African Americans, this opportunity may be of particular significance considering their long history of oppressed employment opportunities and the finding in this study that commuting was viewed as a way to combat obstacles, such as employment limitations, restrictive assumptions about one's skills

Table 12.1 **Advantages and Disadvantages of the Commuter Lifestyle in the Lives of African American Couples**

Advantages	Disadvantages
Meaningful personal expression	Stress of complex lifestyle
Personal fulfillment	Hectic schedules
Enhanced identity	Driving
Autonomy	Financial hardship
Enhanced family dynamics	Sexual advances
Effective interactions	Alienation and isolation
Quality use of time	Loneliness
Career advantages	Guilt
Combat employment limitations, assumptions, racial stereotypes/oppression	Misperceptions of the lifestyle
	Lack of community

Source: Jackson, Anita P., Ronald P. Brown, and Karen E. Patterson-Stewart (2000). "African Americans in Dual-Career Commuter Marriages: An Investigation of Their Experiences." *The Family Journal: Counseling and Therapy for Couples and Families* 8 (1) (January): 26.

and abilities, and racial stereotypes and oppression. Throughout history, African Americans have traveled long distances from their families to obtain gainful employment, such as during the large migration of African Americans from the rural south to the northern cities in the early part of the 20th century (Staples and Johnson, 1993). Today, with a greater range of educational and occupational opportunities available to them, coupled with a competitive workforce, African American men and women may be choosing to commute in order to obtain not only employment but employment that matches their skills and abilities and is personally meaningful. (Jackson et al., 2000:31)

The Great Recession has precipitated a new rise in commuter marriages (Conlin, 2009). Corporate recruiters report that more couples are willing to consider living apart in the "down" economy. In some cases, new commuter marriages are undertaken with a different set of assumptions than those discussed earlier. In the context of high unemployment and few jobs, some distance relationships reflect a short-term strategy for remaining financially solvent rather than an egalitarian impulse. Some husbands have begun new jobs that will eventually result in a household move, but families who lost home equity in the housing market meltdown may need to delay the move until the real estate market improves. These couples may be dual earners, but in stable economic times, husbands' jobs still determine where the family lives. Commuter marriage is sometimes a short-term adaptation to economic hard times, an extraordinary measure in extraordinary circumstances.

GENDER

Dual residence relationships are a solution to the incompatible demands of career and family, but they create new problems depending on the couple's stage of family and career. Although some commuters as a group view their adaptation as a complex mixture of costs and benefits, women in general tend to evaluate the overall arrangement less negatively. Apparently, the freedom from schedules and household chores and the ability to work without interruption works to the advantage of women more than men. Gerstel and Gross (1987b) found that women increased the amount of time they spent on professional work, but because commuting equalizes the division of domestic responsibilities, men did more household labor than they had done in the past. This made men more dissatisfied with the arrangement.

Still, most studies have found varied sources of strain for husbands and wives (Gerstel, 1977; Gross, 1984; Holmes, 2004; Jackson et al., 2000; Kirschner and Walum, 1978). Distance relationships are gendered. Women are responsible for maintaining relationships. Emotion work "falls mostly to women and this includes not just the relationship to the partner, but the social relationship that surrounds it" (Holmes, 2004:195). Though highly career oriented, these women still give interpersonal relations, as compared to work-related rewards, a primacy in their lives that their husbands do not. Husbands, on the other hand, are less likely to express as much unhappiness about the loss of emotional closeness that living apart can produce. They do feel guilty about not providing the emotional closeness they sense their wives need. But in spite of women's expressed loss of intimacy, wives are more comfortable with the arrangement because it validates their equal rights in work and marriage.

The study of African American couples found that while commuting produced stronger identities for both husbands and wives, gender differences were also present. Commuting strengthened husbands' family provider identities, while wives' new identities centered on their confidence in managing home, career, and travel responsibilities (Jackson et al., 2000:32).

Chapter Review

1. Family boundaries are becoming more ambiguous. Marriage is no longer the basis of family life. This decline has been ushered in by global changes, especially new social practices regarding sex, childbearing, divorce, and women's labor force participation.

2. Emerging family forms have not replaced nuclear families but coexist as increasingly legitimate social arrangements.

3. The rise in new family arrangements shows the importance of both structure and human agency. Social, economic, and demographic changes have created opportunities for individuals to choose from a wide variety of household and family options.

4. A growing share of adults are spending more of their lives in an unmarried status. Approximately 10 percent of adults will never marry. The increased number of singles is rooted in historical circumstances, including the independence from birth families fostered by urbanization and industrialization.

5. Women are more likely to be single than men. Demographic and cultural factors combine to create a "marriage squeeze" that increases the number of single women, including those who are not single by choice.

6. The imbalanced sex ratio among Black men and women creates greater difficulties for Black women desiring marriage than for White and Latina women. New research finds that the Black middle class is increasingly made up of well-educated, never-married singles who live alone.

7. The rise in cohabitation is one of the most important changes in family life. A quarter of Americans have cohabited at some point during their lives. Several possible factors explain the increasing acceptance and practice of a formerly unthinkable phenomenon, including postponement of marriage and the tendency of divorced individuals to choose cohabitation over remarriage.

8. Cohabitation is diverse. For some, it is a prelude to marriage. For others, it is a practical domestic arrangement.

9. Cohabitation resembles marriage in some ways, and it also resembles singlehood. Among minorities, cohabitation often resembles marriage. Common sense suggests that cohabitation would increase the chance for successful marriage, but the evidence shows that it increases the risks for divorce.

10. Many lesbians and gay men establish families of choice, constructing their own network families and thereby expanding the definition of family.

11. Although they lack many formalized supports, same-sex families reveal many of the same dynamics as those within heterosexual families.

12. Gay and lesbian unions are not recognized on the federal level, but a number of states have legalized marriage or offer domestic partnerships for these couples. Employers increasingly provide equal benefits for married heterosexual couples and same-sex partners.

13. New patterns of family dispersal stem from changes in work opportunities in the United States and the world. Transnational families and commuter partnerships are two emerging family forms that require radical changes in family living as women and men adapt to temporal and spatial separation. Immigration creates transnational families, while commuter marriage is the result of U.S. women's increased entry into professional occupations. Both family forms entail difficult costs and strains that accompany women's and men's new roles.

Key Terms

domestic partner movement   534

family households   414

nonfamily household   414

transnational families   436

transnational motherhood   437

Related Websites

http://www.lovemakesafamily.org

Family Diversity Projects. Family Diversity Projects, Inc., is a nonprofit organization devoted to educating people of all ages to recognize, support, and celebrate the full range of diversity. The organization's award-winning photo-text traveling exhibits are designed to help reduce prejudice, stereotyping, and harassment of all people who are perceived to be "different" from the "norm." Through this site, visitors can access samples of their current exhibits as well as find information on how to bring the exhibits to a local venue.

http://www.unmarried.org

Alternatives to Marriage Project. AtMP is a national nonprofit organization advocating for equality and fairness for unmarried people, including people who are single, choose not to marry, cannot marry, or live together before marriage. It provides support and information for this fast-growing constituency, fights discrimination on the basis of marital status, and educates the public and policy-makers about relevant social and economic issues. The group believes that marriage is only one of many acceptable family forms and that society should recognize and support healthy relationships in all their diversity.

http://www.unmarriedamerica.org

Unmarried America. Unmarried America is the membership division of the American Association for Single People. The group promotes the well-being of and fairness for unmarried Americans whether they live with a family member or partner, live with a roommate, or live alone. It conducts research and provides information to members, elected officials, corporate policy-makers, and the media.

http://www.ssc.wisc.edu/nsfh

National Survey of Families and Households. The NSFH was designed to provide a broad range of information on family life to serve as a resource for research across disciplinary perspectives. A considerable amount of life-history information was collected, including the respondents' family living arrangements in childhood, departures and returns to the parental home, and histories of marriage, cohabitation, education, fertility, and employment. The design permits the detailed description of past and current living arrangements and other characteristics and experiences, as well as the analysis of the consequences of earlier patterns on current states, marital and parenting relationships, kin contact, and economic and psychological well-being.

Over 13,000 interviews were conducted nationally in 1987–1988, 1992–1994, and 2001–2003.

http://www.law.ucla.edu/williamsinstitute/home.html

The Williams Institute. This Institute, located at UCLA School of Law, advances sexual orientation law and public policy through independent research and scholarship. The Williams Institute is a think tank that produces high-quality research with real-world relevance and disseminates it to judges, legislators, policymakers, media, and the public. The Williams Institute is a reliable and respected source of information on issues related to sexual orientation.

http://www.familyequality.org

Family Equality Council. The Family Equality Council works to ensure equality for LGBT families by building community, changing hearts and minds, and advancing social justice for all families. The FEC is the new name for the Family Pride Coalition, which for 25 years was the only national nonprofit organization dedicated solely to equality for lesbian, gay, bisexual, and transgender (LGBT) parents and their families. Headquartered in Washington, DC, FEC supports nearly 200 membership-based LGBT parenting groups nationwide with a base of 35,000 supporters. FEC works with state-based and local parenting groups to advocate in favor of family-friendly laws and fight antifamily laws and facilitates understanding and dialogue between parents, teachers, and administrators in order to make schools safe and hospitable for children of LGBT parents.

http://www.unfpa.org

United Nations Population Fund. UNFPA seeks to improve the lives and expand the choices of individuals and couples. Over time, the reproductive choices they make, multiplied across communities and countries, alter population structures and trends. UNFPA helps governments, at their request, to formulate policies and strategies to reduce poverty and support sustainable development. The Fund also assists countries to collect and analyze population data that can help them understand population trends, and it encourages governments to take into account the needs of future generations, as well as those alive today.

http://www.unifem.org

United Nations Development Fund for Women. UNIFEM provides financial and technical assistance to innovative programs and strategies to foster women's empowerment and gender equality. Placing the advancement of women's human rights at the center of all of its efforts, UNIFEM focuses its activities on four strategic areas: (1) reducing feminized poverty, (2) ending violence against women, (3) reversing the spread of HIV/AIDS among women and girls, and (4) achieving gender equality in democratic governance in times of peace as well as war.

http://www.migrantwatch.org

Migrant Rights International. Founded in Cairo in 1994 during the United Nations International Conference on Population and Development, Migrant Rights International (originally formed as the "International Migrants Watch Committee") is a membership organization comprising experts and practitioners in the fields of migration and migrants' human rights, each bringing specialized knowledge and experience in the promotion of human rights of migrants. Members are affiliated with nationally and locally based migrant groups, human rights organizations, trade unions, religious bodies, and legal organizations in different parts of the world.

http://www.hrc.org/

Human Rights Campaign. With over 750,000 members, HRC is the largest U.S. civil rights organization working to achieve gay, lesbian, bisexual, and transgender equality. By inspiring and engaging all Americans, HRC strives to end discrimination against GLBT citizens and realize a nation that achieves fundamental fairness and equality for all.

http://www.irpumn.org/website/projects/index.php?strWebAction=project_detail&intProjectID=1

Institute on Race and Poverty: Commuting Patterns, Minority Suburbanization in U.S. Regions. The IRP, housed at the University of Minnesota, is undertaking an ambitious multiregion analysis of the employment centers, commuter sheds, and minority suburbanization patterns in a series of highly diverse metropolitan regions in the United States. The goal of the project is to be able to compare how different racial groups are faring in regions of various sizes across the United States in terms of mobility and access to jobs. This site provides links to PowerPoint presentations that outline some of the studies' most recent findings.

http://www.longdistancerelationships.net

Center for the Study of Long-Distance Relationships. This website is an online clearinghouse of authoritative information about long-distance relationships for separated couples, researchers, clinicians, educators, and the media. The center is dedicated to providing resources for couples in long-distance relationships and for therapists and researchers who work with geographically separated couples. It also provides information for professors, teachers, and other instructors who teach interpersonal relations or communication sciences. A media section is available for those looking for authoritative information in preparation for stories or articles on geographically separated couples. In addition, the Center's bookstore provides easy access to resources for separated couples.

http://www.gay.com/families

Gay.com: Families. Gay.com is a subsidiary of PlanetOut, Inc., the leading global media and entertainment company exclusively serving the lesbian, gay, bisexual, and transgender (LGBT) community. This website provides links to contemporary issues facing LGBT families in the news and media including parenting, marriage, health, and finance.

http://www.familieslikeours.org

Families Like Ours. Families Like Ours is a national nonprofit adoption exchange providing adoption support and education to pre- and post-adoptive families and professionals that provide permanent families for adoptable children in the U.S. foster care system. The organization's emphasis is with gay and lesbian adoptive families; however, they welcome and encourage the diversity of all family structures. The mission of Families Like Ours is to make change by reducing barriers within the foster care and adoption communities.

http://www.glad.org

Gay and Lesbian Advocates and Defenders. Founded in 1978, GLAD is New England's leading legal rights organization dedicated to ending discrimination based on sexual orientation, HIV status, and gender identity and expression. Providing litigation, advocacy, and educational work in all areas of gay, lesbian, bisexual, and transgender civil rights and the rights of people living with HIV, GLAD has a full-time legal staff and a network of cooperating attorneys across New England. This link provides access to legal tips and information on current cases related to gay marriage and civil unions.

http://www.buddybuddy.com

Partners Task Force for Gay & Lesbian Couples. An international resource for same-sex couples, Partners is dedicated to the proposition that all families deserve equal treatment. They support the diverse community of committed gay and lesbian partners through a variety of media. The website contains more than 400 essays, surveys, legal articles, and resources on legal marriage, ceremonies, domestic partner benefits, relationship tips, parenting, and immigration.

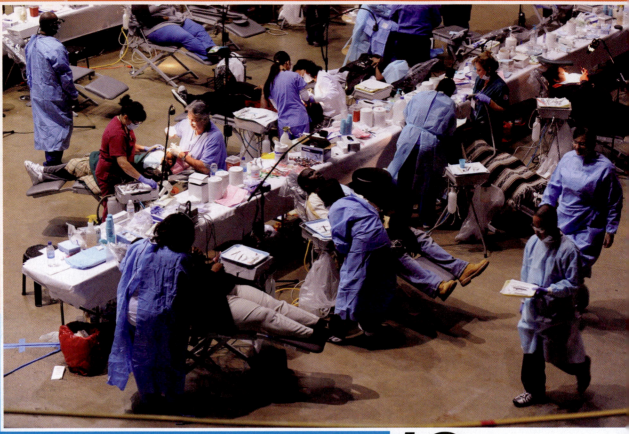

chapter 13

Family Policy for the Twenty-First Century

Myths and Realities

Myth	Making condoms and sex education available to high school students encourages sexual promiscuity.
Reality	Research that compares the sexual activity of students in schools with sex education and the distribution of condoms with students in schools without sex education and no free condoms shows consistently that the former increases sexual safety without any corresponding increase in sexual activity.
Myth	Since abortions became legal, the number and rate of abortions have steadily risen.
Reality	The number of abortions annually has steadied after dropping since 1980. The abortion rate (number per 1,000 adult women) has dropped from over 29 in 1980 to less than 21.3 in 2000.
Myth	Welfare to the poor has risen steadily, and it is a significant part of the federal budget.
Reality	Welfare to the poor has declined dramatically since 1980. Before the welfare legislation was passed in 1996, welfare to the poor constituted about 5 percent of the federal budget. Since 1996 the money spent on the impoverished has declined further.
Myth	Poor people are undeserving because they do not help themselves.
Reality	Research shows that most welfare recipients earn extra money from various informal jobs. Also, there are not enough jobs in many locales, such as the inner cities and rural areas.
Myth	The majority of welfare recipients are African American.
Reality	Whites outnumber African Americans and Latinos among welfare recipients.
Myth	The proportion of children in poverty is lower than the proportion of elderly who are poor.
Reality	The proportion of poor children is almost twice as high as it is for the elderly.
Myth	Because the United States has the world's best medical system, it ranks at or near the top on the basic health indicators for children.
Reality	Compared to other industrialized nations, the United States ranks relatively low in overall infant mortality and ranks last in children covered by medical insurance.
Myth	The money spent on welfare for poor children is a bad investment.
Reality	Research shows that money spent on childhood poverty programs (immunization, prenatal health care, preschool education) saves society many times more money than is spent on welfare.
Myth	Preschool programs for high-risk children are a waste because intelligence is fixed genetically.
Reality	Research shows that preschool programs for at-risk children have long-term positive effects on IQ scores (the earlier the intervention, the better the results).

Two fundamental themes have guided this sociological inquiry of families: Family forms are increasingly diverse, and the forms families take are the products of social, political, and economic forces in the larger society. In this final chapter we ask, What is the role of government regarding families? Should government actions move us back to the "modern family" of a breadwinning husband, his homemaker wife, and their dependent children, or should the government assist families to cope with the social, political, and economic forces that affect them so greatly? These are policy issues that generate considerable heat in today's political climate.

We use Aldous and Dumon's definition of family policy: "family policy refers to objectives concerning family well-being and the specific measures taken by governmental bodies to achieve them" (1991:467). This definition requires clarification. First, most, if not all, government policies affect families—for example, taxes, education, subsidies, minimum wage laws, health, warfare, and welfare. Although this is true to a degree, we concentrate on those policies aimed specifically at families. Second, the United States does not have an official family policy (the Constitution never mentions families). The U.S. government and the state governments have no plan regarding families but rather a potpourri of laws, court decisions, regulations, and policies that lack coherence. This does not mean, however, that an overall family policy is impossible to attain. The government actions concerning family policy address four family functions: (a) family creation (marriage and divorce, childbearing, and adoption), (b) economic support, (c) child rearing, and (d) caregiving (e.g., assistance to the ill, frail, and elderly) (Bogenschneider and Corbett, 2004:453). Third, the very notion of a government plan regarding families is abhorrent to some because it implies government intrusion into family life. President Richard Nixon, for example, vetoed a federal child-care bill because it was, in his view, an unwarranted governmental intrusion into a family concern (Bogenschneider and Corbett, 2004). This reminds us that public policies regarding families often divide Americans along ideological lines.

This chapter begins with a discussion of the ideological fault lines, to use an earthquake metaphor, that divide the public and governmental officials on issues affecting families. This background is important for understanding why the United States as a society takes some actions regarding families and avoids others. The heart of this chapter focuses on five crucial and hotly contested public policy issues: family planning (contraception and abortion), gay marriage, helping the impoverished, meeting the needs of disadvantaged children, and relieving burdens for working parents. The chapter concludes with a personal note—the principles that we believe should guide the formulation of profamily social policies.

The Ideological Fault Lines

Sociologist Andrew J. Cherlin examined families in the United States and the other Western countries and observed that "in none of the other countries has marriage become a social and political battlefield. Nowhere else is the government spending money to promote marriage.…Moreover, nowhere else is the debate about same-sex marriage so fierce" (Cherlin, 2009:3). In sum, people in the United States are rarely neutral about family issues. They respond with passion because family issues are at the heart of religious, political, and philosophical ideologies. Progressives and conservatives are quickly divided over welfare, gay rights, abortion, stem cell research, sex education in schools, condom distribution, parental leave, and the like. These issues are debated with passion in legislatures as conservatives and progressives confront each other with opposing views and solutions.

The Social Conservatives

Social conservatives believe that the family is the basic building block of society. The family is where members' basic needs are met, where children learn their most important lessons, and where individuals are loved unconditionally. The conservative ideology is profamily, but not just any family form. The ideal family is a married couple in a lifelong monogamous relationship; the husband is the disciplinarian and economic provider, while the wife is a homemaker in charge of raising the children (for the intellectual foundations of the conservative position see, for example, Carlson, 2005; Murray, 1984; Whitehead, 1993; Wilson, 1993). As the late Reverend Jerry Falwell, a spokesperson for the moral conservatives, said, "The family is the God-ordained institution of the marriage of one man and one woman together for a lifetime with their biological or adopted children" (Falwell, 1980:104). From this perspective,

> the family is seen as God-given but also as based upon essential biological differences between men, women and children and their differing needs. Women are seen as biologically needing to be mothers and fulfilling themselves through motherhood. Biological mothering is also seen as the foundation of the social role of women, who are the ones "naturally" committed to caring for children. Children are seen as needing family support during a prolonged childhood and parents are seen as those best able to guide their children's moral and social development. (Abbott and Wallace, 1992:10)

The conservatives are alarmed and appalled by what they consider the breakdown of the family. The following facts illustrate the changes in families that frighten conservatives.

- *Premarital sex:* Relatively few young people wait until they marry to initiate sex.
- *Cohabitation:* From 1960 to 2008, cohabitation increased from approximately 500,000 to 5.5 million couples.
- *Abortion:* Abortion is legal; in 2005, 1.2 million abortions were performed in the United States.
- *Out-of-wedlock childbearing:* One-third of all births in the United States—more than a million babies a year—are born to unmarried women.
- *Divorce:* Almost 50 percent of all marriages now end in divorce, and each year more than a million children are affected by their parents' separation or divorce. One in three of us is a member of a stepfamily.
- *Fatherlessness:* Divorce, single parenthood, and desertion translate into an estimated 35 percent of all households with children but without fathers present.
- *Nonparental child care:* More than 6 in 10 mothers with children under the age of 1 year are in the labor force; almost three-fourths of the mothers with children between 1 and 18 years are in the labor force. This requires, of course, that parents entrust their children to other caregivers during working hours.
- *Legitimacy of homosexuality:* Homosexuality is considered a sin, so national, state, community, or corporate policies that legitimate gay and lesbian lifestyles are condemned.

Abbott and Wallace say that

> [t]he [conservative or Moral Right] is best conceptualized as a backlash movement, reacting to social changes that have taken place since World War Two, especially in

the areas of morality, welfare spending and the role of women; ... [it] combines a nostalgia for the past with a zeal to save the [nation] from what is perceived as [its] current economic and moral sickness. (Abbott and Wallace, 1992:19)

Conservatives tend "to blame all of society's ills on the breakdown of the traditional family. Poverty, crime, violence, teenage aimlessness—all are blamed on the purported breakdown of the family" (Mintz, 2003:para 4).

According to the conservative credo, the principal causes of family decline in the past three decades or so have been cultural and political. The primary reason is the decline of traditional family values, which has led to the moral decay of society's members. People are making selfish decisions (e.g., women working in the labor force rather than being full-time mothers, divorcing without seeking reconciliation, or accepting welfare rather than providing for themselves and their family) or behaving immorally (e.g., premarital sex, cohabitation, extramarital sex, abortion, and homosexuality). In short, "[t]he conservative position is that, as a result of hedonistic individualism, we are letting our 'family values' slip away, and what is needed now is nothing short of a moral rearmament on behalf of parental responsibility" (Mason et al., 1998:3).

The members of the moral right are also incensed at government policies that have furthered the decline of the traditional family. Some of these policies are as follows:

- No-fault divorce laws that make divorce easy to obtain.
- The 1973 U.S. Supreme Court decision (*Roe v. Wade*) that made abortion legal.
- Decisions by local authorities to provide contraceptives and birth control counseling and compulsory sex education in the public schools.
- State and local decisions that encourage homosexuality (passage of homosexual rights legislation, granting gay unions legal status, allowing gay couples or lesbian couples to adopt children).
- Policies of the welfare state that encourage people to rely on the state rather than on their own initiative.
- High welfare spending, which causes high levels of taxation, which, in turn, forces married women into the labor market.
- Government subsidies for child care, which encourage mothers to work outside the home.
- The banning of sodomy laws (in 2003 the Supreme Court overturned the sodomy laws in 15 states, thus, in their words, legitimizing gay and lesbian sex and leading eventually to legal same-sex marriage).

POLITICAL ACTION

The political result of the morality crusade is that there is a virtuous "us" and an immoral "them." This moral framing of social troubles means that the morally "virtuous" are convinced of their "rightness" (Morone, 1996). This feeling of moral superiority and certitude results in resistance to negotiation and compromise, and intolerance toward those who are not only wrong but also immoral. The result is a zeal to promote and support traditional values and the traditional family.

Although there is some diversity within this political movement to stop the moral decline and restore the traditional family, at the center it is very organized. The Christian Right includes a number of organized groups that are actively involved in the media and promoting their ideology in Washington, DC, and in the various state legislatures. Some of these organizations are Pat Robertson's Christian Coalition,

James Dobson's Focus on the Family, Beverly LaHaye's Concerned Women for America, Phyllis Schlafly's Eagle Forum, and Gary Bauer's Family Research Council (see Boston, 2006, for the "Top 10 Power Brokers of the Religious Right").

The concern of conservatives about families includes how families are described and analyzed in college textbooks. In a critique of 20 textbooks on family and marriage, sociologist Norval D. Glenn (1997), sponsored by the conservative Institute for American Values, expressed grave concern that each of these textbooks describes the diversity of family forms that have emerged without ample consideration for the negative consequences emanating from them, especially for children. Moreover, these books, according to Glenn, are antimarriage because they minimize the beneficial consequences of marriage to individuals and society. Implicit in Glenn's critique is that current textbooks, ours included, celebrate new family forms while denigrating the modern family of working father, homemaking mother, and their children.

The Progressives

For progressives the traditional family is not a given. Rather, family forms are socially and historically constructed, not monolithic universals that exist for all times and places. The family that conservative writers uphold as "legitimate" is no less a product of social structure and culture; it emerged as a result of social and economic conditions that are no longer operative for most Americans and that never were operative for many poor Americans and people of color (Baca Zinn and Eitzen, 1998; Dill et al., 1993:14).

Thus, one critical difference between the conservatives and progressives is causation: What is the cause of family changes over the past 40 years or so? As we have seen, the conservatives believe that these changes result from a shift in values, accompanied by government policies congruent with these new values. Progressives disagree with that view.

> The [conservatives] have it backward when they argue that the collapse of traditional family values is at the heart of our social decay. The losses in real earnings and in breadwinner jobs, the persistence of low-wage work for women and the corporate greed that has accompanied global economic restructuring have wreaked far more havoc on Ozzie and Harriet Land than have the combined effects of feminism, sexual revolution, gay liberation, the counterculture, narcissism and every other value flip of the past half-century. (Stacey, 1994:120–121)

Because families come in so many varieties, progressives argue also that to speak of "the family" obscures more than it reveals. Families today may be two-parent, single-parent, stepfamilies, gay and lesbian families, and foster families, with different forms within each of these categories. Indeed, 93 percent of contemporary families do not fit the traditional family model held as the ideal by conservatives—two parents, a breadwinning husband and homemaking wife, with their children at home. Also, "different families, located at different points in the American social structure, face different problems and pose different policy challenges" (Mason et al., 2003:1). To focus on an idealized family based on a nostalgic view of the past, as the conservatives do, leads policy-makers in the wrong direction—that is, away from focusing on the actual problems experienced by most families now. Progressives, therefore, seek ways that society might maximize the love, care, and nurturance within various types of families. Some possibilities are subsidized day care, universal health insurance, the legalization of gay and lesbian marriages, programs to help economically disadvantaged children and families, especially economic support for poor single mothers. As an example of the latter, the poverty of single mothers is not a result of never marrying or divorce but a combination of factors, including secondary job markets, low wages, the unemployment, and no health insurance.

The key for progressives is the impact of social forces confronting today's families. These problems have several roots (Mintz, 2003):

- Stable employment is a prerequisite for establishing stable, life-long relationships. Many impoverished women cannot find partners who hold steady, decent-paying jobs. The Great Recession has exacerbated this problem, resulting in a lower probability of marriage and a higher divorce rate by the impoverished, when compared to the more affluent.

- For the more affluent, structural changes in the economy have meant that families need two earners to support a middle-class standard of living.

- A source of stress in contemporary families is the transition away from the rigid gender-based division of labor characteristic of families in the 1950s.

- The familial, economic, and demographic transformations have resulted in a crisis of caregiving. An aging population, adult children moving back home, and an environment of dual-worker and single-parent families has placed great challenges on the nuclear family.

Progressives believe that society, through the government, should come to the aid of families, promoting diversity, eliminating institutional racism and sexism, assisting single mothers, allowing a woman's right to choose whether to have a baby, requiring businesses to give new mothers in their employ paid maternity leave, meeting the basic needs of children, and promoting such policies as universal health insurance.

POLITICAL ACTION

The progressives are much less organized than the conservatives. There is one national organization, the National Organization for Women (NOW), that lobbies in Washington and files lawsuits on behalf of women's rights. Local chapters work for the progressive agenda at the state and local levels. There also are organizations focused on special issues. Most prominent are prochoice organizations such as the National Abortion and Reproductive Rights Action League. There is one progressive media network, Air America Radio.

To summarize, issues surrounding the family divide conservatives and progressives on questions such as these: Is there a preferred family form? Why are family forms changing—is the reason cultural or structural? What actions should be taken to address problems surrounding family issues—are these best left to private choices or are they public choices? If they are public choices, what is the proper role of government? Keep these questions in mind as we address several important family-policy issues, beginning with the two most volatile ones—the legalization of same-sex marriages and issues surrounding family planning.

The Government's Limits on the Definition of Marriage

"Local, state, and national governments, through social and family policies, determine the rights, rules, and benefits for families, thus sanctioning certain kinds of families and ignoring or actively discriminating against others" (Laird, 2003:181). The Supreme

Court, for example, outlawed the ban on interracial marriages in 1967, and the federal government required Utah to prohibit polygamy in order to become a state in 1896.

At the forefront of today's cultural wars is the definition (and legality) of marriage. At issue is whether marriage is limited to a woman and a man or whether it can be between two members of the same sex. For cultural conservatives, making same-sex marriages legal abandons the basic building block of the family and a major source of the traditional family. To allow same-sex marriages legitimates the lesbian/gay lifestyle, which social conservatives consider not only deviant but also immoral.

Referring to same-sex marriage, Robert Knight, director of the Culture and Family Institute, provided this apocalyptic prediction: "When you destroy marriage by radically redefining it, you destroy civilization" (quoted in Lytle, 2003:2A). James Dobson, the founder of Focus on the Family, wrote this: "For more than forty years, the homosexual activist movement has sought to implement a master plan that has had as its centerpiece, the utter destruction of the family. Barring a miracle, the family as it has been known for more than five millennia will crumble, presaging the fall of Western civilization" (quoted in Hertzberg, 2006:30).

From this perspective, the fundamental purpose of marriage is "to uphold and encourage the union of a man and a woman, the framework that is the healthiest and safest for the rearing of children. If marriage stops meaning that, it will stop meaning anything at all" (Jacoby, 2001:4B). This view dominates politics in the United States. For example, President Clinton signed the "Marriage Protection Act" in 1996, which prohibits federal recognition of same-sex marriage and relieves the states of the obligation to recognize gay marriages performed in other states where it might be legal. As of June 2009, some 29 states had constitutional amendments restricting marriage to a man and a woman. In 2006 three state supreme courts—New York, Georgia, and Washington—ruled that same-sex marriage is not permitted in their jurisdiction. In that year, the Senate failed to pass the first step in a constitutional amendment to ban gay marriage.

The Catholic Church, in a formal statement in 2003, strongly opposed same-sex marriages and demanded that all Catholic politicians work to oppose any legislation supporting them (in 2009 there were 136 Catholic representatives and 26 Catholic senators in Congress, and six Catholic justices on the U.S. Supreme Court). Most politicians, whether Catholic or not, find it difficult, politically, to support same-sex marriages.

Progressives support same-sex marriages or at the least "civil unions." Most fundamentally, to allow same sex-marriages provides gays the dignity and privileges of marriage and explicitly affirms their social acceptance in our pluralistic society (see Box 13.1). Moreover, legalizing same-sex marriage provides basic civil equality and social approval to gays and lesbians. If marriage is denied to lesbians and gays, then they are being discriminated against based on their sexuality. And a significant part of the equality that marriage achieves and what gays and lesbians are denied is the more than 1,000 federal protections, such as Social Security benefits, health care, and pension benefits, to the partners in legal marriages.

Second, progressives argue that everyone—gays and straights—gain by legalizing same-sex marriages. Society is not threatened when lesbians and gays commit publicly to lasting and responsible relationships. That promotes stability and reaffirms the sanctity of marriage. Answering the charge that same-sex marriages threaten traditional marriage, gay Congressman Barney Frank of Massachusetts asked, "How does the fact that I love another man and live in a committed relationship with him threaten your marriage? Are your relations with your spouses of such fragility that the fact that I have a committed, loving relationship with another man jeopardizes them?" (quoted in Jacoby, 2001:4B). In short, how can you support marriage in general and exclude gay and lesbian unions?

BOX 13.1 **Inside the Worlds of Diverse Families**

"This is my spouse..."

I received roses from my partner on Valentine's Day. We have spent 21 years making a home, raising children, facing challenges together. And so I wonder why our president wants to ensure that we can never marry.

You see, the person I have loved all these years happens to be the same gender as myself.

Our children are grown now, with families of their own. I nursed them through illnesses, attended school conferences, helped them with homework, encouraged them in sports, scrutinized their boyfriends, trembled through their driving lessons. My partner is their birth mother. They consider me their "second mom." Yet, society and our government relegates me to an inferior role.

I never even enjoyed a stepparent's rights to our children, let alone the possibility of adopting them. Their teachers had more legal rights than I did. Their school would not allow me to be listed as the emergency contact because I wasn't a "blood relative."

Parenting is daunting enough. Marriage could have eased some of the difficulty.

Fortunately, I work for an employer who, 10 years ago, began to provide domestic partner benefits. Yet, when we purchased medical insurance, we discovered another harsh reality for the unwed. My married co-workers enjoy untaxed benefits. We must pay income tax on the imputed value of the insurance, not because we choose to avoid marriage, but because we are legally barred from marrying. While my employer embraces diversity, my government shuns it and increases my tax burden.

After all these years together, the likelihood of our relationship breaking apart is minimal. That is lucky for us because, without marriage, we have none of the protections offered by a legal divorce. I could have lost all rights to visit our children. I devoted my life to them, but no law would assure me continued parental status.

Additionally, we have made absolutely certain every asset we own is placed in our joint names. Unlike married couples, neither of us is guaranteed equity in the case of a separation.

Much more frightening to us than divorce, though, is the inevitability of death. When that day arrives, one of us could be left facing major legal obstacles. Although we have created wills and other necessary documents, I cannot be certain, as any married person can, that my loved one will inherit all our property. There always exists the possibility of contentious family members battling our wishes in court and depriving my partner of our life's possessions. Our marriage could put such fears to rest.

According to a 1997 report by the Government Accounting Office, more than 1,000 legal rights and benefits automatically are granted to married couples. For example, if a married person receives Medicaid assistance for nursing home care, the spouse cannot be forced from their jointly owned home. Married persons can take time off work to care for an ill spouse under the Family and Medical Leave Act. A married person can receive survivor benefits from Social Security when a spouse dies, or inherit a retirement plan without severe tax burdens.

All these rights, and hundreds more, are denied to my partner and me.

While gays in Colorado scored two key victories recently—the House shot down a ban on gay marriage and both houses approved bills to protect gays and lesbians from hate crimes and job discrimination—there's still a lot to be done. There's also no guarantee that Gov. Bill Owens will sign the proposals into law.

Still, my strongest reason for wishing to marry is far less practical than basic rights given to married heterosexual couples. One day, I would simply like to introduce the woman I love not as "my partner, or friend, or co-parent, but as my spouse." By that title, people would recognize the true meaning of our relationship and the depth of our love.

Source: Zimmerman, Ann (2005). "This Is My Spouse..." *Denver Post* (May 11): 7B.

Third, progressives argue that what is defined as a "normal" family is a social construction, its definition shaped by historical and current social conditions. In the words of Stacey and Davenport:

The postmodern family represents no new normal family structure, but instead an irreversible condition of family diversity, choice, flux, and contest. The sequence and packaging of romance, courtship, love, marriage, sex, conception, gestation, parenthood, and death are no longer predictable. Now that there is no consensus on the form a normal family should assume, every kind of family has become an alternative family. Lesbigay or queer families occupy pride of place in this cultural smorgasbord which includes familiar varieties that were historically most prevalent among the poor—such as stepfamilies, unwed motherhood, blended families, bi-national families, divorce-extended kin, cohabiting coupledom, and grandparent families—along with newer developments as at-home fatherhood, deadbeat dads, and open adoption—as well as innovations made possible by new commerce and technology—surrogacy, sperm banks, ovum exchange, genetic screening, gender selection, frozen embryos, and the no-longer-distant specter of human cloning. (Stacey and Davenport, 2002:356–357)

Fourth, the United States trails Canada, Europe, and Scandinavia on gay rights. As of June 2009, gay and lesbian couples have full marriage rights in seven countries, while only 6 of the 50 states allow gays and lesbians to marry legally—Massachusetts, Connecticut, Maine, Vermont, Iowa, and New Hampshire.

Lesbians and gays may enter into registered partnerships ("civil unions") in 15 nations. Civil unions are one step removed from "marriage" but allow same sex partners to have the same legal protections under state law as married couples. In the United States civil unions do not confer federal benefits, such as Social Security. A Gallup poll found in 2009 that 57 percent opposed giving gays the right to marry (reported in Stone, 2009b). Public sentiment on this issue is shifting as young people clearly support gay marriage, the *New York Times* and over 100 other newspapers now announce same-sex commitment ceremonies.

The Government and Reproductive Rights

Contraceptives

The state and federal governments have a long history of involvement in reproductive matters. Historically, some states with Catholic majorities outlawed the use of contraceptives. That prohibition was lifted in 1968 when the U.S. Supreme Court, in *Griswold v. Connecticut*, ruled that a state statute making the use of contraceptives by married couples a criminal offense was unconstitutional. This court decision did not, however, end the controversy.

- About three million pregnancies (approximately 50 percent) in the United States are unplanned, occurring because the people involved misuse contraceptives, use unreliable contraceptives, or do not use contraceptives at all. Among the poor, about three-fourths of pregnancies are unplanned. If the poor wish to use contraceptives, the expense is sometimes prohibitive. For example, a new and effective contraceptive device—Plan B—taken within 72 hours of intercourse, costs $25 to $40 for a two-pill pack. In contrast, a woman in the Netherlands can purchase a year's supply of oral contraceptives for about $8.

Government programs aimed at reducing nonmarital sexual activity have focused primarily on adolescents. Here are some facts about teen sexual behaviors:

- One out of five teens has intercourse before age 15. And 60 percent of U.S. teenagers have sex before age 18.
- More than 50 percent of teens engaged in oral sex.

- Each year, U.S. teenagers bear over half a million children; abortions terminate an almost equal number of adolescent pregnancies.

- The U.S. teen pregnancy rate (7 percent of high school girls become pregnant every year) is almost twice as high as that of Great Britain, three times that of Canada, and four times higher than that of Sweden or France.

- The U.S. HIV rate for young men is three times higher than in the Netherlands. The U.S. rate for teen births is 11 times higher than in the Netherlands. The teen gonorrhea rate is 74 times higher than in the Netherlands (Fox, 2002).

One course of action to reduce the magnitude of these problems is to provide sex education in the schools. There are two opposing views on the focus of such a course. One is to provide students with a comprehensive sequential sexuality education, throughout the grades, which is part of a K–12 health education program, with parental involvement, counseling, and positive peer support. Included in the curriculum are what happens to boys and girls at puberty, how conception occurs, and how to block conception, including the proper use of various types of birth control devices, abortion, homosexuality, and information about sexually transmitted diseases. Conservatives oppose sex education in the schools because they believe that it promotes sexual activity and experimentation.

The preferred option by social conservatives is for schools to promote abstinence only. This has been the policy of the federal government since the 1996 welfare law, which provided federal funds only to those states endorsing "abstinence-only" sex education. Under this legislation, the abstinence programs should teach that sex outside of marriage is likely to have harmful psychological and physical effects. Information about contraception (the pill and condoms) is precluded by the abstinence-only message required by the law. An abstinence-only program emphasizing the unambiguous message that postponing sex until marriage is the only option was promoted by the George W. Bush administration, spending $1.3 billion over the eight years. For states to receive federal funds, the schools within them could not "endorse

Choices in Sex Education

or promote" contraceptives, but talk only about their drawbacks. Moreover, the schools were obliged to inform teens that having sex outside of marriage could harm them mentally and physically. Such programs taught only that sex before marriage was wrong and did not offer any information about birth control or sexually transmitted diseases to students who are sexually active. President Obama changed the direction by shifting most of the money in the fiscal 2010 budget for abstinence-only sex education to teen pregnancy prevention.

Does abstinence sex education succeed in reducing sexual activity and teen pregnancies? Various studies show that the most successful approach is a combination of sex education and abstinence counseling. Abstinence education programs alone do not delay first sex or affect the number of partners or the rates of sexually transmitted disease or pregnancy (for a review of studies, see Jayson, 2008). A Columbia University study found that while abstinence works for some young people,

> it also found that 88 percent of middle and high schoolers who pledge to stay virgins until marriage end up having premarital sex anyway. The bad news is that they are less likely to use contraception the first time they have intercourse. As for students who get comprehensive sex education, they do not have sex earlier or more often, but, although they are reported to practice safe sex more frequently, both groups had the same rate of sexually transmitted infections. (Kelly, 2005:48)

Societies that focus on comprehensive sex education have much better results on a number of measures. While U.S. teenagers are about as sexually active as teenagers in Europe,

> American girls are four times as likely as German girls to become pregnant, almost five times as likely as French girls to have a baby, and more than seven times as likely as Dutch girls to have an abortion. Young Americans are five times as likely to have H.I.V. as young Germans, and teenagers' gonorrhea rate is 70 times higher in the U.S. than in the Netherlands or France. (Kristof, 2005:2)

Obviously, abstinence is the best way for teenagers to avoid pregnancy and sexually transmitted diseases. However, as the *New York Times* editorialized:

> This is a recipe for disaster in a nation that has the highest teenage pregnancy rate of any developed country. It is fine to urge teenagers to "just say no" to sex before marriage, but surely it makes sense to provide them as well with information that could avert pregnancies or protect them from a fatal AIDS infection should they become sexually active. (*New York Times*, 2002:1)

Abortion

Abortion was a common procedure in the United States until the last third of the nineteenth century (the following historical information is from Reagan, 1997). Prior to criminalization, abortions were permitted until the fetus was felt to move in the uterus (about the fourth month of pregnancy). Beginning about 1867, the American Medical Association began a crusade against abortion (ironically, that same organization was instrumental in the legalization of abortion a century later). This state-by-state effort was successful so that by 1900, all states had antiabortion legislation. Sixty years later the situation began to reverse as some state legislatures passed legislation permitting abortions only to save a woman's life. Thus, for most of the twentieth century, abortions were illegal, and countless women sought illicit and often unsafe abortions (as many as 5,000 to 10,000 women died per year following illegal abortions) (Center for Reproductive Rights, 2003).

In 1973, the U.S. Supreme Court, in *Roe v. Wade*, invalidated all state laws against abortion. Most significant, the Court ruled that the fetus is not a person and therefore is not guaranteed the protection and rights provided to persons by the Constitution. This ruling raises one of the most highly charged emotional and political issues in the United States. Prochoice and antiabortion forces clash over whose rights are to be protected—those of the woman or those of the fetus. Abortions are interpreted by one side as a viable option for the woman to control her life and by the other side as murder.

As a result of *Roe v. Wade*, approximately 1.2 million (2005) legal abortions occur per year, ending about 23 percent of all pregnancies. The U.S. abortion rate has been declining since 1980 (the rate then was 29 percent). The annual U.S. abortion rate in 2005 was 19.4 per 1,000 women ages 15 to 44, the highest rate among the developed nations. Here are some additional facts according to the Guttmacher Institute (reported in Jones et al., 2008; Sowti, 2005):

- 47 percent of unintended pregnancies are aborted.

- White women have about 40 percent of all U.S. abortions, African American women 32 percent, and Latino women about 20 percent. But in terms of rates (number per 1,000 adult women), 11 Whites had abortions, compared to 28 for Latinas, and 50 for African American women.

- 6 in 10 women who have abortions are mothers.

- One in five women will have an abortion during her lifetime.

- The majority—56 percent—of women who terminate pregnancies are in their 20s.

- Teenagers have 19 percent of abortions.

- 60 percent of women who have abortions have household incomes below the poverty level for a family of three.

- 90 percent of abortions are performed in the first trimester (the first 12 weeks after the first day of the woman's last menstrual period) with most performed before 9 weeks.

- Fewer than 1 percent of abortions are done after 24 weeks.

The antiabortion forces were incensed by the *Roe v. Wade* decision and have directed their efforts since to weakening or changing it. They have engaged in intense lobbying and have worked hard to elect candidates who favor what they call the "pro-life" position. Especially important in this crusade has been working for the election of presidents who will nominate Supreme Court justices and federal judges opposed to abortion. Antiabortion advocates have also engaged in demonstrations and acts of civil disobedience, including "rescue" squads that harass abortion patients and providers. Occasional zealots have firebombed abortion clinics and murdered workers and doctors at abortion clinics. The hassles and dangers for doctors who perform abortions are so great that many decline to engage in that activity. As a result, the number of abortion providers has plummeted 40 percent since the peak in 1982. Nationwide, 87 percent of counties have no abortion services and the entire state of Mississippi, with a population of three million, has only one abortion clinic.

Following *Roe v. Wade* in 1973, a number of legislative, judicial, and executive actions at the federal level have made abortions more difficult to obtain. In 1976, Congress passed the Hyde amendment, which cut off federal funds for all abortions except for pregnancies resulting from rape or incest or that endangered a woman's life. The Supreme Court has supported this by ruling that a woman, although possessing the right to have an abortion, does not have a constitutional right to have the federal government pay for it. Similarly, a majority of the states now have laws prohibiting the use of tax monies to pay for abortions. In 1989, the Court ruled in *Webster v. Reproductive Services* that the states have the right to prohibit public employees from participating in an abortion. In 1990, in *Rust v. Sullivan*, the Court upheld the administration's right to prevent doctors at federally funded clinics from offering advice on abortion. In 1991, a federal appeals court upheld most provisions of a Pennsylvania abortion law, one of the strictest in the nation. In 1994, the Supreme Court ruled that judges can create carefully drawn buffer zones around abortion clinics to prohibit demonstrators from blocking access to patients and staff members, while at the same time protecting the free speech rights of demonstrators outside the buffer zones. In 2000, the Court, by a 6-to-3 margin, upheld the right of states to restrict abortion protests through "bubble" laws that keep protesters at least eight feet from women entering reproductive health clinics.

Meanwhile the states enacted many measures to restrict access to abortion. Mississippi, for example, has enacted every restriction on abortion possible within the limits set by the Supreme Court (Lerner, 2005; Quindlen, 2005). Among these are (1) a woman must be counseled in person about the procedure and then wait 24 hours; (2) all abortions are prohibited after the first trimester; (3) counseling provisions require that patients be told that abortion may increase the risk of breast cancer [there is no scientific evidence to support that contention]; and (4) a minor must get the consent of both parents to have an abortion (there is one exception—if the minor is impregnated by her father, she needs only the consent of her mother). In 2005, some 52 measures were enacted by various state legislatures to limit access to abortion.

The ideology of the president clearly affects reproductive rights policies. The Reagan and the George H. W. Bush administrations took a number of actions that affected family planning. During the Reagan years, some 16 percent of federal funds for the provision of family planning clinics were cut. Both the Reagan and Bush administrations opposed sex counseling and the provision of contraceptives in the schools. During the 1980s, federal monies for research on the development of contraceptives and educational programs designed to increase their correct usage dropped by about half. The Food and Drug Administration under President George H. W. Bush banned the import of RU-486, the French "abortion pill" that was legal in France and Great Britain. The right-to-life groups called this drug the "French death pill" because it prevents pregnancy after sexual intercourse. The Reagan and Bush administrations also banned the use of federal funds for fetal-tissue research (the use of fetal cells appears promising for victims of Parkinson's disease and could possibly treat Alzheimer's, diabetes, leukemia, and spinal cord injuries).

President Clinton reversed or at least neutralized some of the actions by his predecessors. His appointment of two justices to the U.S. Supreme Court tipped the balance against overturning *Roe v. Wade*. He first permitted the testing of RU-486 in the United States, and later his administration's Food and Drug Administration approved its use. Moreover, the Clinton administration ruled that federal funds could be used for research involving stem cells derived from human embryos. Also, President Clinton vetoed bills that would have outlawed late-term abortions (the so-called partial-birth abortions).

President George W. Bush consistently took the conservative position on contraceptive and abortion issues. He championed "abstinence only" for sex education in the schools. In his first few days in office, he used an executive order to reverse President Clinton's earlier executive order, reinstating a "global gag rule" that denies federal funds to international family-planning groups if they mention abortion anywhere in their program activities (Rayman-Read, 2001). Bush criticized the use of RU-486; he was antiabortion, and he signed new legislation banning partial-birth abortion. In 2006, he vetoed legislation (his first veto in the six years of his presidency) permitting federal financing of stem cell research. The Bush administration withheld $34 million from the United Nations Population Fund, thus depriving poor women worldwide of contraceptive education. Similarly, the United States, along with the Vatican and some Islamic countries, succeeded in deleting strong endorsements of sex education programs by the United Nations.

Moreover, President George W. Bush nominated judges to the federal appellate courts who opposed abortion. Most significant, his two nominees for the Supreme Court—Justices Roberts and Alito—will likely vote against abortions in subsequent cases before the Court.

The election of Barack Obama in 2008 changes the equation once again. He will likely nominate judges and justices more favorable to abortion rights. By executive orders he will overturn many of Bush's antichoice rulings. He has opened the research doors to stem cell research.

Politically, the right to an abortion has gradually been weakened by federal and state laws and court decisions. The public, meanwhile, remains supportive but ambivalent about the issue. Polls show, consistently, that a majority favor upholding *Roe v. Wade*. Yet most support at least some restrictions on when abortions can be performed. A 2006 poll found that 19 percent of Americans said abortion should be legal in all cases; 16 percent said that it should never be legal; 6 percent did not know. That left almost 60 percent somewhere in between, believing that abortion should be legal under certain circumstances (Benac, 2006).

BIAS AGAINST THE POOR

According to the Hyde amendment, mothers on public assistance cannot obtain abortions through Medicaid. Similarly, the Health and Human Services Department under President George W. Bush directed the states that RU-486, like abortions, would be covered by Medicaid only when a pregnancy results from rape or incest or when a woman's life is in jeopardy. Prochoice advocates argue that the federal and state decisions denying public funding for abortions make the abortion option less feasible for those women least able to afford children. Faced with the high cost of an abortion, poor women are either forced to have the baby and keep it, to have the baby and place it for adoption, or to attempt self-induced abortions. The result is that about 4 in 10 poor teens have abortions, compared to 7 in 10 higher-income teens (Goodman, 1995). The irony, of course, is that poor women who want abortions but cannot afford them have their babies and then are vilified for having babies to increase their welfare checks. In terms of social policy, public funding of reproductive services would save dollars.

 **Welfare**

In 2007, some 12.5 percent of the population (37.3 million people) were below the poverty line of $16,530 for a family of three and $21,203 for a four-person family (U.S. Bureau of the Census, 2008b). These statistics were compiled before the ravages of the Great Recession and therefore understate the extent of poverty, homelessness, and hunger now. Since the 1930s, the United States has had a fairly comprehensive welfare program to help those in need. This changed in 1996, when the federal government cut federal aid to the poor and eliminated welfare to poor women with children. Let's first examine the welfare system in place until 1996 and then review the changes and consequences resulting from the recent welfare legislation.

The Shrinking Welfare State

From 1935 to 1996 the United States had a minimal welfare program for those in need. The New Deal under President Roosevelt and the Great Society under President Johnson created the minimum wage, federal aid to education, health and nutrition programs, food stamps, energy assistance, subsidized housing, and Aid to Families with Dependent Children (Moen and Forest, 1999:644–647). Beginning with President Nixon and accelerating under President Reagan, this welfare program was gradually dismantled. This dismemberment quickened appreciably in 1996, when the federal government made welfare assistance to families temporary and withdrew $55 billion of federal aid to the poor.

The Personal Responsibility and Work Opportunity Reconciliation Act (PRWORA) of 1996

The welfare system prior to 1996 needed an overhaul. Its provisions encouraged dependency because recipients who left welfare lost Medicaid. It provided disincentives to work because money earned was subtracted from welfare payments. By leaving the distribution of benefits for many programs to the states, there were wide disparities. And the benefits provided were never enough to lift many people out of poverty. The welfare system, however, did help many on the economic margins to receive enough to get by.

Although this difference is certainly important, the government could do much better if it chose to do so. For example, France and the United States both would have child poverty rates of about 25 percent if it were not for government assistance. With the generous government assistance provided in France, the child poverty rate is just 6.5 percent. The minimal U.S. welfare program, on the other hand, reduced the child poverty rate to only about 17.6 percent in 2007. A strong safety net makes a difference in several important ways, as Stephanie Coontz and Nancy Folbre show:

> The association of single parenthood with poverty is not inevitable. In Canada and France, single mothers—and children in general—are far less likely to live in poverty. Sweden and Denmark, with higher rates of out-of-wedlock births, have much lower rates of child poverty and hunger than does the United States. *The reason for the difference is simple: These countries devote a greater percentage of their resources to assisting families with children than we do.* (Coontz and Folbre, 2002:9; emphasis added).

Conservatives and progressives wanted to reform the welfare system, but rather than reform, in 1996 the Republican-dominated Congress and a middle-of-the-road Democratic president passed a sweeping welfare law that ended the 61-year-old safety net for the poor, completing the "Reagan Revolution" (Watts, 1997:409). The major provisions of this law (as later amended) include the following (much of the description of the new welfare law and its consequences is from the Children's Defense Fund, 1997; Edelman, 1997; Eitzen, 1996; Pavetti, 2000; Schorr, 1997; Watts, 1997):

1. States, through federal block grants, are given a fixed sum of money and considerable flexibility in how to spend it.

2. The law insisted on work. The states were required to demand that parents work within two years of receiving cash assistance, although the states had the right to shorten the period before welfare recipients must work.

3. The law mandated a five-year lifetime limit on the receipt of assistance, which states can reduce if they wish.

4. The law required that unmarried teen parents must live at home or in another adult-supervised setting and attend school to receive welfare assistance. The states again had the option of ending assistance for teen parents who have children outside marriage.

5. Various federal assistance programs targeted for the poor were cut by $54.5 billion over six years. Included in these budget cuts were $27 billion from the food stamp program, $7 billion from the children's portion of the Supplemental Security Income program, $3 billion over six years for child nutrition, and a six-year total of $2.5 billion for social services. Cuts were also made by tightening the qualifying criteria for being defined as a disabled child. Ironically, the narrowed eligibility requirements resulted in the loss of coverage for some children who if they were adults would be considered disabled (Edelman, 1997:48).

6. The welfare law denied a broad range of public benefits to legal immigrants. All legal immigrants were cut off from food stamps, and those who entered the country after the welfare bill was signed were ineligible for federal programs such as Supplemental Security Income and state-run programs such as temporary welfare and Medicaid.

7. The federal money given to the states is now capped at $16.4 billion annually. This is significant because it means that there is no adjustment for inflation and population growth. In effect, by 2002 the states will have considerably less federal money to spend on welfare than they did under the old welfare provisions.

In sum, this new welfare legislation ended the entitlement, which guaranteed that states must give help to all needy families with children. Now assistance for poor families is temporary (Aid to Families with Dependent Children [AFDC] was replaced by Temporary Assistance for Needy Families [TANF]), with parents required to work. With the passage of the 1996 Welfare Act, *The Nation* (a progressive publication) editorialized, "There is now a bipartisan agreement that the United States bears no responsibility for its poorest families" (*The Nation*, 1995:371).

THE CONSERVATIVE ASSUMPTIONS GUIDING CURRENT WELFARE POLICY AND THE PROGRESSIVE RESPONSE

Assumptions from conservative ideology provide the bedrock of the 1996 welfare law. First, there is the assumption that welfare programs establish perverse incentives that keep the beneficiaries from working and encourage them to have babies outside marriage. That is, welfare is so generous that it makes sense to stay on welfare rather than go to work. Moreover, because the benefits increase with each child, women on welfare make the rational decision to have more children. Progressives argue that this reasoning is fallacious because it ignores five facts: (1) The average monthly AFDC payment, accounting for inflation, had withered by almost 50 percent since 1970, yet the birth rate for unmarried mothers soared during this period; (2) the average monthly AFDC payment plus food stamps provided benefits that were much below the poverty line; (3) states with low welfare benefits had higher illegitimacy rates than states with higher welfare benefits; (4) New Jersey's 1993 law that ended the practice of increasing a welfare check when a recipient had another baby did not drive down birth rates among women on welfare (Healy, 1997); and (5) the much more generous welfare states of Canada, Western Europe, and Scandinavia have much lower out-of-wedlock birth rates than found in the United States.

A second assumption of the lawmakers is that when poor people are confronted with a "sink or swim" world, they will develop the motivation and the skill to stay afloat (Murray, 1984). If welfare recipients are forced off welfare, their only recourse will be to work, resulting in productive people rather than parasites. Progressives, however, note that under current societal conditions many of the poor will "sink" even if they want to "swim." There are not enough jobs. Many of the jobs that are available do not lift the poor out of poverty. And many who are being pushed "into the pool" cannot "swim" because of some disability.

Third, welfare dependency is assumed to be the source of poverty, illegitimacy, laziness, crime, unemployment, and other social pathologies. Progressives, however, point to the nations with much more generous welfare systems than in the United States (Canada, Scandinavia, and Western Europe), noting that cities in those countries are much safer and that violent crime is much lower than in the United States, as is the rate of teenage pregnancy.

Fourth, the United States is an individualistic and competitive society. The obvious result of competition and a market economy is inequality, and that is good because it motivates people to compete and weeds out the weak. Following this logic of the conservatives, losers are responsible for their failures. Therefore, it is not the responsibility of society to take care of them. Progressives argue, to the contrary, that the causes of poverty are complex, involving social location (class,

Night class for plumbing trades skills.

race, gender), the changing economy, the lack of good jobs, institutional racism and sexism, the maldistribution of resources for schools, and inadequate pay and benefits for low-end jobs. Thus, a cure for poverty involves much more than greater individual effort and elimination of the welfare system. It requires structural changes in society.

A final conservative assumption underlying the welfare legislation of 1996 is that the able poor must work. Many poor people are labeled as undeserving because it does not appear that they help themselves. That belief, however, is false. It assumes, for example, that welfare mothers are unable or unwilling to work. Research from a number of studies shows that most welfare recipients earn extra money from various activities, such as housecleaning, doing laundry, repairing clothing, child care, and selling items they have made. For example, sociologist Kathleen Harris, summarizing her findings from a nationally representative sample of single mothers who received welfare, says that

> I found exclusive dependence on welfare to be rare. More than half of the single mothers whom I studied worked while they were on welfare, and two-thirds left the welfare rolls when they could support themselves with jobs. However, more than half (57 percent) of the women who worked their way off public assistance later returned because their jobs ended or they still could not make ends meet. (Harris, 1996:B7)

This outside work to supplement welfare is necessary because welfare payments are insufficient to meet their economic necessities. This gap is made up through various strategies (agency), including income-producing work and help from family, friends, neighbors, boyfriends, and absent fathers.

A question arising from the requirement that all welfare recipients work is whether a single mother is "able" to work (McLarin, 1995). Traditionally, she was not considered so. AFDC was created in 1935 with the goal of keeping women at home with their children. The new legislation changed that, forcing poor women with children to work, without training, without jobs, and without child care. Through twisted logic, the same politicians who want poor mothers to work want middle-class mothers to give up their jobs because a stay-at-home mother is positive for children.

Another issue regarding work has to do with its availability. During the Great Depression the federal government provided jobs to the poor. These jobs included constructing roads, bridges, and buildings; planting trees to stop wind erosion; and the like. This government jobs program was successful. The jobs provided society with important projects and needy individuals with income and skill development. The situation is different now. The new legislation mandates that poor people work, but without providing the jobs.

> This punitive overhaul [of the welfare system] sends [welfare recipients] off on their own to secure work in a world of downsizing, layoffs and capital flight. Where are the welfare recipients going to find stable jobs? How can they pay for health insurance and child care when they earn the minimum wage? What will happen to their children? (*The Nation*, 1995:372)

Underscoring one of the preceding points is that working for the minimum wage ($7.25 in 2009) which most former welfare recipients do, gave a full-time worker an annual income that was $1,450 *below* the poverty line for a family of three.

Is Welfare Reform Working?: An Assessment after 13 Years

The 1996 Personal Responsibility and Work Opportunity Reconciliation Act abolished a cornerstone of the New Deal known as the Aid to Families with Dependent Children program. What are the consequences of this major reform of welfare for families over a decade later?

The first six years or so after welfare reform showed positive results. That is, caseloads were cut in half, 60 percent of mothers who left welfare were in the labor force, and real incomes rose by 15 percent (Urban Institute, 2006). But poverty did not decrease at the same rate as welfare participation. That is, while welfare rolls decreased by half, poverty declined only by 15 percent, because so many who were now working were not making wages sufficient to escape poverty (Hays, 2003).

So the results are mixed. What appears as success was not due to welfare reform per se but rather to the booming economy of the late 1990s (Hays, 2003). With the economic slowdown from 2000 to 2003, jobs were more difficult to find and keep and the positive numbers declined. Most significant, many single mothers who left welfare for work moved from the "welfare poor" category to "working poor." Their wages averaged between $7 and $8 an hour, which, while above the minimum wage at that time, still left many families close to or even below the poverty line (Albelda and Boushey, 2006). Moreover, only about half of those leaving welfare had employer-sponsored health insurance. Also, there were new expenses required by work—transportation, clothing, and child care. Left out of the gains from welfare reform are the very poorest of the poor, who have no income

Item: Higher income families seeking assistance...

DAVE GRANLUND © www.davegranlund.com

from either work or welfare. Christopher Jencks and his colleagues found that "some of these mothers were very poor indeed. In the years between 1996 and 2003, roughly one in 10 reported that her total household income was less than $2,500" (Jencks et al., 2006:38). Clearly, welfare reform has not eliminated poverty. Albelda and Boushey conclude:

> Nobody liked the old welfare system. It provided disincentives to employment, treated people poorly, and didn't provide enough income to support a family. But, the current system isn't working very well either. Ten years later, many low-income working families are wondering when we will insist that work should work for families—that jobs pay enough to afford the basics, that they come with health care and access to paid sick leave, and that every parent has access to safe, affordable and enriching child care for their children while they're at work. (Albelda and Boushey, 2006:2)

Then the Great Recession arrived in 2007. Requests for food stamps rose sharply (28 million in 2008, compared to 17 million in 2000). Requests for welfare case loads increased markedly. Unemployment rates doubled in two years, putting the least skilled at heightened risk of losing their jobs. At a time when welfare programs should be expanding to meet the exigencies of the Great Recession, they were curtailed by most states. Recall that one of the provisions of the welfare reform legislation was that the federal government gave each state a fixed amount to be used by each state at their discretion. The states, faced with their own economic crises, sometimes cut welfare programs and used the government to meet other budgetary needs. In 2008, for example, 18 states cut their welfare rolls. "Of the 12 states where joblessness grew most rapidly, eight reduced or kept constant the number of people receiving Temporary Assistance for Needy Families, the main cash welfare program for families with children" (DeParle, 2009:para 4). (See Box 13.2.)

Inside the Worlds of Diverse Families

BOX 13.2

Barriers to Welfare

In 2006, Letorrea Clark was 22 years old, unemployed, and living with her boyfriend in Homerville, a tiny town near the Okefenokee Swamp in southern Georgia, when she discovered she was pregnant. The timing wasn't ideal. Her boyfriend's job at the local can-manufacturing plant supported them both, but his largesse came at a price. The man was controlling, unfaithful, and jealous, a problem only enhanced by the wide array of drugs that filled his freezer. Clark had hit the stash, too, but the pregnancy pushed her to get clean and get out. She slept on a park bench until a friend helped her secure a place to stay.

Desperate, with her due date fast approaching, Clark decided to apply for Temporary Assistance for Needy Families (TANF), better known as welfare.

But when she went to the local Division of Family and Children Services office, a caseworker told her—wrongly—that she couldn't apply until after the baby was born. "They basically said, 'Go get a job,'" says Clark. "I was eight months pregnant."

Gabby arrived by C-section a month later, and Clark brought the chubby newborn home to a sweltering trailer with a busted fridge, no air conditioning, and no running water. (Her ex had reneged on promises to get the water turned on.) Clark got by with help from her church and her landlord, who let her stay for free until she was able to move. Later, she found a job in a day care. But the center docked her paycheck for Gabby's care, an expense the state would have picked up had she been able to get on TANF. Sometimes she'd go home with just $20 at the end of the week.

Clark patched things together with food stamps and $256 a month in child support. But after nine months, Gabby's father stopped paying just long enough for Clark to get evicted. She went back to the welfare office, where caseworkers turned her away, saying–falsely again–that because she'd been getting child support she was ineligible for TANF.

What Clark didn't know was that Georgia, like many other states, was in the midst of an aggressive push to get thousands of eligible mothers like her off TANF, often by duplicitous means, to use the savings elsewhere in the state budget. Fewer than 2,500 Georgia adults now receive benefits, down from 28,000 in 2004—a 90 percent decline. Louisiana, Texas, and Illinois have each dropped 80 percent of adult recipients since January 2001. Nationally, the number of TANF recipients fell more than 40 percent between then and June 2008, the most recent month for which data are available. In Georgia last year, only 18 percent of children living below 50 percent of the poverty line—that is, on less than $733 a month for a family of three—were receiving TANF.

Plunging welfare rolls were big news in the wake of Bill Clinton's 1996 welfare reform, which limited benefits and required recipients to engage in "work-related" activities. Those declines coincided with record numbers of poor single mothers heading into the workplace and a significant drop in child poverty—proof, supporters said, that the new policy was a success. But the reform took effect at a time when unemployment was at a historic low—there were actually jobs for welfare moms to go to. In recent years, by contrast, TANF caseloads have been falling even as unemployment has soared and other poverty programs have experienced explosive growth. (Nearly 11 million more people received food stamps last year than did in 2000.) With the economy settling into a prolonged slump, this trend could be devastating.

Welfare is the only cash safety-net program for single moms and their kids, notes Rebecca Blank, an economist at the Brookings Institution and one of the nation's leading experts on poverty. "One has to worry, with a recession, about the number of women who, if they get unemployed, are not going to have anywhere to turn."

No longer the polarizing, racially tinged political issue it was when Ronald Reagan attacked "welfare queens," the welfare system today is dying a quiet death, neatly chronicled in the pages of academic and policy journals, largely unnoticed by the rest of us. Yet its demise carries significant implications. Among the most serious: the rise of what academics call the "disconnected," people who live well below the poverty line and are neither working nor receiving cash benefits like Social Security disability or TANF. Estimates put this group at roughly 2 million women caring for 4 million children, many dealing with a host of challenges from mental illness to domestic violence. "We don't really know how they survive," says Blank.

Women turned away from TANF lose more than a check. TANF is a gateway to education, drug rehab or mental health care, child care, even transportation and disability benefits—tools for upward mobility. Without those options, some women are driven to more desperate measures. In one of the towns in Georgia where I traveled to research this story, arrests of women for prostitution and petty crime went up as more and more families were pushed off welfare. And women are increasingly vulnerable to sexual assault and exploitation—sometimes, as I discovered, from the very officials or caseworkers who are supposed to help them. In the worst cases, they are losing custody of their children, precisely what TANF was designed to prevent. "I worry a lot about the kids in these families," Blank says. "We don't know where the kids are going."

Source: Mencimer, Stephanie (2009). "Brave New Welfare." *Mother Jones* 34 (January/February): excerpt from pp. 41–42.

The Conservative Solution: Marriage

Conservatives were encouraged by the welfare reform and that so many had left the welfare rolls for work. Still, they wanted more. They have proposed more punitive rules, essentially eliminating welfare.

In July 2003 the welfare reauthorization bill proposed to spend nearly $2 billion over six years to encourage welfare recipients to marry. This proposal, supported by President George W. Bush, would provide money to the states, which would establish services to encourage the formation and maintenance of two-parent families. The goal of this proposal (called "wedfare") is to move families out of poverty. The money would be spent on relationship counseling, marital-enrichment classes, public service campaigns to encourage marriage, and even, should the state choose as West Virginia has done, provide cash bonuses to people on welfare who marry. The logic goes like this: "The families of single mothers are five times as likely to be poor as the families of married couples. Ergo, if single mothers would just get and stay married, poverty would virtually disappear" (Goodman, 2002:5B). Thus, the wedfare proposal reflects the conservative assumption "that failure to marry, rather than unemployment, poor education, and lack of affordable child care, is the primary cause of child poverty" (Coontz and Folbre, 2002:1).

Marriage offers important social and economic benefits. Children who grow up in stable, healthy, married two-parent households are better off than children growing up in some other kind of arrangement. Marriage facilitates income pooling and task sharing to meet family needs. What could possibly be wrong with a promarriage public policy as an antipoverty program?

Critics of the plan argue, first, that marriage is not viable as an antipoverty program. If it were, there would be no poverty among two-parent households, yet 38 percent of all poor children live in two-parent homes. "As for single moms and dads, it's not clear whether they are poor because they are unmarried, or unmarried because they are poor" (Goodman, 2002:5B). Put another way: "Non-marriage is often a result of poverty and economic insecurity rather than the other way around" (Coontz and Folbre, 2002:2).

Second, mothers who are poor, undereducated, and with weak work histories are not prime candidates for marriage. So, too, for their potential mates. Who are they supposed to wed? As sociologist William Julius Wilson has pointed out, in high-poverty areas there are few marriageable men (Wilson, 1996). A study of census data found that more than a third of fathers of children born out of wedlock lacked a college degree; 28 percent were unemployed; and 20 percent had incomes of less than $6,000 per year. Roughly 38 percent had criminal records. The truth is, many single mothers are single because they find their unemployed and undereducated potential partners to be unattractive partners. Do we really want to encourage them to marry unsuitable partners? (Tanner, 2003:1). In other words, "an unemployed couple can't feed their children with a marriage license" (Malveaux, 2002:15A). Family historian Stephanie Coontz and economist Nancy Folbre conclude:

> The notion that we could end child poverty by marrying off impoverished women does not take into account the realities of life among the population most likely to be poor. It is based on abstract scenarios that ignore the many ways in which poverty diminishes people's ability to build and sustain stable family relationships. (Coontz and Folbre, 2002:6)

Third, the quality and stability of marriages matter. Healthy and happy marriages benefit adults and children. But marriages marked by conflict and anger are harmful. "Prodding couples into matrimony without helping them solve problems that make relationships precarious could leave them worse off" (Coontz and Folbre, 2002:2).

A fourth argument against this "marriage proposal" is that young women who marry are more likely than those who stay single to have a second child while still young. This makes them more likely to drop out of school and thus be less employable. Moreover, people who marry at a young age are more likely to experience domestic violence and to separate or divorce than those who marry later, resulting in unstable relationships. An empirical study by sociologists Daniel T. Lichter, Deborah Roempke Graefe, and J. Brian Brown found that poverty rates are substantially higher for women who marry, but later divorce, than for never-married women. "Without also strengthening fragile marriages, marriage promotion initiatives are unlikely to provide a long-term solution to poverty; indeed, they could make matters worse for disadvantaged women if they separate or divorce" (Lichter et al., 2003:80; see also Lichter, 2001).

These researchers conclude:

> In our view, marriage alone cannot substitute for, or replace, other policy prescriptions, such as minimum wage legislation, affirmative action, expansion of the EITC [Earned Income Tax Credit], and education and training programs, which directly rather than indirectly benefit the poor and provide a strong economic foundation for a stable family life. The goal of strengthening families might best be served through a larger package of social and economic policies that promote the marital, educational, and employment aspirations and needs of low-income women and men. (Lichter et al., 2003:81)

The Progressive Solution: A Stronger Safety Net

Implementation of the 1996 welfare legislation had some immediate effects. The welfare rolls decreased dramatically as single mothers took jobs, as 70 percent of AFDC recipients left welfare within two years. But much of this decline in welfare dependency is attributable to the economic boom and resulting low unemployment rates in the late 1990s (12.2 million jobs were added to the economy between 1996 and 2000). But with the economic recession, followed by a jobless recovery from 2001 to 2003, some three million jobs were lost, many in the sectors such as retail trade where low-income single mothers were most likely to work. The Great Recession from 2007 onward had even more dire consequences for the economically marginal. Moreover, a number of social forces, as noted in Chapter 4, have worked to dry up the job market (i.e., the transformation of the economy from industrial production to service/information, the continuous mechanization of work [e.g., robotization], the globalization of the economy with factory and white-collar jobs moving to low-wage societies, and the continuous influx of immigrants into the United States). In other words, the welfare legislation ignored the structural sources of joblessness and poverty and how best to meet the challenges of a rapidly changing economy.

The 1996 welfare legislation, while focusing on the replacement of welfare with work, made no provision for jobs or job training (most of the women who left welfare for jobs had a high school education or less and little if any job experience), and if one found work, no guarantee of a living wage and no assistance for transportation (two-thirds of all new jobs are in the suburbs, while three-quarters of welfare recipients live in central cities or rural areas); and there was only a modest child-care subsidy.

A fundamental flaw in the welfare legislation was that it did not address the real issue—ending poverty. Many of the women who left welfare, even if they found work, remained in poverty. There are programs to help them—food stamps and Medicaid, for example—but the funds for these programs have declined with the state and federal budget shortfalls of the early 2000s. A successful program, the Earned Income Tax Credit (EITC) is a fully refundable tax credit aimed at low-income working families with children. Although the program is helpful, there are at least three problems with it. First, it is closely tied to earnings and phases out steeply after family income reaches $12,460, thus giving a disincentive to two-earner families and the working poor just above the poverty line. Second, the maximum benefit goes to families with two children, which means that low-income families with three or more children do not receive any additional assistance. And, third, it applies only to earned income, thus the poor unemployed receive no benefits. A similar logic, but not pertaining to EITC, determined who would receive the tax relief to parents enacted in 2003. This legislation gave families making more than $26,625 a tax credit of $400 per child. Denied by this plan were the almost 12 million children from families making less than the $26,625 (Klein, 2003). Thus, the poor and near-poor were denied this benefit while the nonpoor received the payments.

Exacerbating the situation is the pressure to reduce the already frayed safety net even more. After September 11, 2001, when terrorists killed almost three thousand people in the attacks on the World Trade Center and the Pentagon, the Bush administration, with the blessing of Congress and most Americans, went on an antiterrorist crusade. This meant beefing up security at home, adding to the defense budget, and ultimately conducting expensive wars and reconstruction in Afghanistan and Iraq (e.g., the cost to the United States in postwar Iraq was more than $1.5 billion a week). These costly efforts were coupled with several major tax cuts sponsored by the Bush administration and passed by Congress, resulting in a huge federal deficit. The result was continuous pressure to reduce or eliminate the programs making up the social safety net. So, too, the very expensive stimulus package, bailouts of banks and automobile manufacturers, and the resulting expanding debt incurred during the Obama administration applied pressure to cut safety net programs.

The economic slowdown and the federal and state slowdowns in spending for social programs have resulted in difficult times for the poor and near-poor. Consider homelessness, hunger, and unemployment, where the recession, a jobless recovery, the five-year cap on welfare benefits, the fraying of the social safety net, and the ever-higher cost of housing combine to place those previously on welfare at risk. From 2000 to 2009, government data show that:

- Homelessness was up, and the fastest growing segment of the homeless population is families.
- The demand for emergency food increased.
- Child poverty increased.
- The proportion of the poor who are very poor—i.e., they have half or less of the yearly income of those at the poverty line—had risen to its highest since 1975.
- The number of Americans without health insurance now numbered 46 million, the highest ever.

The question for policy-makers is, Are the poor, the hungry, the homeless, and those without health insurance responsible for their plight or are there structural arrangements and policy choices that affect them negatively? Social conservatives argue that the fault lies in individuals who do not work hard enough, have not sought out educational opportunities, have other shortcomings or pathologies, and who are enveloped by a culture of poverty. It is not society's problem but their problem. Thus, social policy should minimize or at the extreme eliminate the safety net and let the poor "sink or swim." Progressives feel that such an explanation "blames the victim." The poor are not responsible for the high cost of housing, the economic recession, and the shrinking job market. They are not responsible for the low wages and lack of benefits. Those who take this position seek social policies to expand the safety net because the members of society have a collective obligation to help people in need.

Working Parents

During the last half of the twentieth century, women entered the labor market in huge numbers. By 1998 the U.S. Census Bureau for the first time since it began tracking the numbers found that families with both parents in the labor force were now the majority (51 percent of married couples, up from 33 percent in 1976). Since then, the proportion has increased even more. Among the many problems facing working parents, two are critical: (1) obtaining job-protected leaves for family emergencies, including birth, and (2) finding and funding satisfactory care for children while parents are at work. In both instances, the policies of the federal and state governments lag behind the child support policies of other Western nations.

Parental Leave

Some businesses provide generous parental leave policies for their employees so that parents can have children, remain at home for some time after the birth of a child, or meet the emergency health needs of their families without losing their jobs, benefits, or sometimes even wages. Other employers have less generous programs or no programs at all for their employees (see Chapter 6). Some states require maternity leaves, whereas others do not.

Given the random nature of possible benefits in this area, some have advocated that the government mandate that businesses provide uniform benefits to their workers. In 1993, after seven years of legislative efforts and two presidential vetoes by conservative presidents, a federal policy concerning parental leaves was enacted. This policy required firms with more than 50 employees to provide their employees with unpaid maternity leaves of up to 12 weeks, guaranteed jobs (the same or an equivalent job after the leave), and the retention of job benefits during the leave.

Although this legislation is a progressive step, it is a relatively small step with two large problems. First, this policy does not cover 40 percent of the workers in the United States (those who work for businesses with fewer than 50 employees). Second, unpaid leave is a severe financial hardship for many mothers. Almost all other industrial countries provide new mothers and sometimes fathers with paid parental leave (a range of four months to a year at 80 to 90 percent of normal pay). The two biggest economic competitors of the United States—Japan and Germany—each guarantee at least three months of paid leave, with additional unpaid leave if desired. Moreover, most of the other industrial countries offer parental leave to care for sick children (from 10 weeks to 3 years, usually with low or no pay).

In 1997 President Clinton granted federal employees up to 24 hours of unpaid leave each year for family matters and emergencies. At the same time he urged Congress to extend the same benefit to all workers by expanding the Family and Medical Leave Act. Republicans have resisted this expansion, offering instead a bill that would allow employers to offer workers paid by the hour a chance to take comparable time off instead of the overtime pay they might otherwise be due. These contrasting positions represent the confrontation between the political interests of labor and those of business. Labor-friendly Democrats do not trust management, fearing that they will save money by cutting out the overtime they now must pay. Republicans and their business backers, on the other hand, do not trust ordinary workers, fearing that they will invent excuses to cheat employers out of the hired labor on which they depend (Means, 1997). The resulting impasse leaves workers without the necessary flexibility to meet their family demands.

Child Care

According to the Children's Defense Fund, about two out of three mothers of pre-school-age children and three out of four mothers of school-age children are in the labor force. Six in 10 preschool-age children and 7 in 10 school-age children have both parents in the labor force (2008:65). This creates a huge child-care problem, as noted by Suzanne W. Helburn and Barbara R. Bergman in their book *America's Childcare Problem* (2002).

> As we enter the twenty-first century, we haven't yet faced up to the child care needs created by women's large-scale entry into the labor market. The American child care system, in which parents, largely unassisted, must buy the care they need in the marketplace, has not worked well. It is in the public's interest that the services children receive be of good quality, but millions of parents are unable to pay what standard-quality services currently cost, much less what they would cost if quality improved. Parents need assistance in two ways: They need more help in meeting the cost of child care. And they need more help in assuring the safety and quality of the care their children get. (Helburn and Bergman, 2002:2)

Stated another way, the biggest problem facing most of these working parents is finding accessible and acceptable child care. The word *accessible* refers to cost, proximity, and compatibility with work schedules; *acceptable* refers to various dimensions of adequacy, such as sanitation, safety, stimulation, and caring supervision. Each of these variables is important, but the most immediate concerns are availability and cost: Child care is very expensive. It is the largest single work-related expense for working mothers. This means, of course, that the more affluent are able to take advantage of higher-quality facilities that emphasize child development and learning opportunities. Those less well off are more prone to use less costly child-care facilities that are likely to be overcrowded, unlicensed, and even unhealthy.

Despite the cost of child care, governments can provide such programs if they choose (the following examples are from Folbre, 2000). For example, in France, at an annual cost of $5,500 per child, there is a universal nursery for children ages 3 to 5. The cost is fully subsidized by the government, and nearly 100 percent of children attend. Within the United States, Georgia has a very progressive and universal prekindergarten program for four-year-olds, funded fully by money from the state lottery. This program serves 80 percent of the state's four-year-olds and has a robust public approval rating of 85 percent.

The United States has no comprehensive child-care system. This lack of a system differentiates us from the other industrialized nations. Currently, the federal government is involved modestly in providing for child care through two programs. First, it permits the deduction of child-care payments on income tax returns. This amounts to about a $4 billion tax credit, which is considerable. The problem, however, is that because it is tied to taxes, it has negligible effects on the poor because they do not earn enough to take advantage of it.

Second, the welfare legislation of 1996 included approximately $4 billion in new child-care funds over six years. "But the new law forces so many parents into the work force that this increase falls far short of what is needed to meet the new demand for child care generated by the law, much less to ensure that vulnerable children receive good care" (Children's Defense Fund, 1997:38).

The government's less-than-adequate child-care programs are fundamentally flawed in at least two respects. Foremost, they are underfunded. The amounts the federal government promised simply do not meet child-care needs. The other problem is that they rely on the states to implement the programs and to match the federal grants if they are to receive the monies. The states, through their governors, legislatures, and social service bureaucracies, vary greatly in their enthusiasm for child care, their licensing and monitoring of child-care programs, the standards they set to ensure quality in child care, and their ability to fund child-care programs. If history is a guide, then it is likely that many states will not commit the greater resources needed to receive the federal funds.

The decision makers at the state level vary in their views about child care. Some take the politically conservative position that the government should not interfere with parents' decisions regarding their children. Other conservatives object to the government's subsidization of child care because that encourages mothers to be in the workforce rather than at home with their children (a principle they are willing to overlook when it comes to poor single mothers). Libertarians would rely completely on the free market, free of government subsidies and regulations, to provide child care. In other words, where there is a need, entrepreneurs will meet it, driven by the profit motive. Progressives stand in strong opposition to the traditional laissez-faire government attitude regarding day care. Day-care centers, they argue, must be provided as the right of parents and children and as the obligation of society. Thus, there is need for a "large, active, and expensive federal program, providing both finance and a national framework for quality improvement, [to] serve the nation's purposes adequately" (Helburn and Bergmann, 2002:3).

The need for day care is obvious and is becoming greater as the proportion of mothers who have preschool children and who are employed in the labor force continues to grow. The need for subsidized child care for poor parents, who typically are single mothers, is especially acute.

The need for child care is not limited to preschool children. Working parents are also faced with taking care of their school-age children after school, but this usually conflicts with their work schedules. A common response is to let the children fend for themselves or be supervised by an older sibling until a parent gets home from work. The problem is exacerbated by schools that dismiss children at 2:30 or 3:00 p.m., hours before the end of the normal workday. The result is that about seven million **latchkey children** go home alone after school. Research shows that latchkey children are more likely than adult-supervised children to experiment with illicit drugs, to be sexually active, and to vandalize property and commit other crimes. Consider these facts: (1) The peak hour for violent crimes, including sexual assault, by juveniles is the first hour after school, from 3 p.m. to 4 p.m. (U.S. Department of Justice, 1999); and (2) the hours immediately after school are the peak hours for the conception of teenage pregnancies (Herbert, 1997). A report to the Attorney General said this:

> When we send millions of young people out on the streets after school with no responsible supervision or constructive activities, we reap a massive dose of juvenile crime. If, instead, we were to provide students with quality after-school programs, safe havens from negative influences, and constructive recreational, academic enrichment and community service activities, we would dramatically reduce crime while helping students develop the values and skills they need to become good neighbors and responsible adults (cited in Herbert, 1997:15).

Work-Related Policies and Gender Inequality

Businesses and governments in the United States have been slow to respond to the needs of women in the labor force. This reluctance on the part of those in power (almost always men) to provide support for parents (usually mothers) who need special help to combine the roles of worker and parent has two sources. One is a cultural attitude, the common belief that women really belong at home and should not be encouraged by government or their employers to have children and to work outside the home. Another source is structural: Women are relatively powerless, and it is to the advantage of the powerful to keep women in marginal and low-paying jobs. The irony, of course, is that Americans place the highest value on both work and family, yet they do little to help make the two compatible for women.

Women are also disadvantaged in the workplace when they use the work-related rules put in place by governments or businesses. Women are the ones taking leave for childbirth and staying with the newborn for the first weeks or months. Women also are the ones who typically request a leave to take care of sick family members. When these women take their leaves, they may have their job back (as now required by law for large firms), but they may also face two obstacles. One might be their co-workers, who may resent having to carry the load for them while they are absent. The second hindrance may come from management, which chooses men over women for promotions because men are more "reliable," and they appear to have a greater commitment to their careers than women appear to have.

Meeting the Needs of Disadvantaged Children

Poor children are at great risk in the United States and are the most neglected in the developed world. Compared to other industrial nations, the United States ranks (Children's Defense Fund, 2008:1):

- Twenty-second in low birthweight rates.
- Last in infant mortality rates.
- Last in relative child poverty.
- Last in the gap between the rich and the poor.
- Last in adolescent birth rates (ages 15–19).
- Last in protecting children against gun violence.

In 2007 one in six children (13.3 million) were below the poverty line (the following statistics are for 2007 and are from Children's Defense Fund, 2008). While only one-fourth of the total population, children represented a disproportionate share of the poor (34.9 percent). While only 15.0 percent of White children under age 18 were poor, 11.9 percent of Asian children were, as were 28.6 percent of Latino children and 33.7 percent of African American children. Finally, almost 1 in 13 children (5.8 million) lives in extreme poverty (at or below half of the official poverty line).

Poor Children at Risk

Each of the problems mentioned in this section hits poor children the hardest. They are more likely than privileged children to suffer from low birth weight, more likely to be exposed to toxic chemicals, and the least likely to receive good nutrition and decent medical care, including immunization against contagious diseases. They are also more likely to miss out on preschool education.

> Childhood poverty impairs physical growth, cognitive ability (e.g., reading ability), and socioemotional functioning (e.g., behavioral problems, depression)....The incidence, duration, and chronicity of childhood poverty also have large negative effects on children's IQ, educational achievement, and later adult productivity. (Lichter, 1997:122)

INFANT MORTALITY

Family poverty is strongly correlated with premature delivery; postnatal, infant, and childhood mortality; malnutrition; and ill health (Leach, 1994:188). The United States ranks low among the industrialized nations in infant mortality (an overall rate in 2005 of 6.86 deaths per 1,000 live births). Infant mortality is an important measure of the well-being of infants, children, and pregnant women because it is closely related to such factors as maternal health, quality of access to medical care, social class, and public health practices (the following data are from Children's Defense Fund, 2008). As a result of the confluence of these factors, African American babies are more than two times more likely to die as White infants (a rate of 13.26 for African Americans, compared with 5.73 for Whites). Among Latinos, the infant mortality rate for infants of Cuban and Central/South American origins was about half that for Puerto Ricans. Among Asians/Pacific Islanders, infant mortality rates for infants of Chinese origin was less than half that for Native Hawaiians.

Infant mortality results, for the most part, because children are born too soon or too small. Those who survive low birth weight are more likely to grow up deaf, blind, or mentally retarded than normal-birth-weight babies. Again, the rate of African American low birth weight is twice that of Whites. Among Latinos, women of Mexican origin have the lowest percentage of low-birth-weight infants and Puerto Ricans the highest. Among Asian Americans, low birth weight was lowest for births to women of Chinese origin and highest for women of Filipino origin.

Much of infant mortality is preventable. One-third of pregnant women (about 1.3 million women a year) receive inadequate prenatal care, mostly because they lack economic resources, including medical insurance. In 2007 nearly nine million children (about one in nine) were uninsured. By race/ethnicity, 20.7 percent of Latino children were not covered by health insurance and 12.8 percent of African American children were not covered, compared to 7.5 percent of White children who were uninsured (Children's Defense Fund, 2008:28).

INFECTIOUS DISEASES

The most recent data (2007) show that among two-year-olds, one in three was not fully immunized. Those children not immunized were disproportionately the poor and racial minorities and living in relatively poor states (e.g., South Dakota and West Virginia) (Children's Defense Fund, 2008:38). This situation has improved markedly since 1993, when Congress passed the Vaccines for Children program, which subsidized vaccinations for uninsured, Medicaid-eligible, and Native American children.

EXPOSURE TO TOXIC CHEMICALS

Poor children often live in environmentally unsafe situations. Affordable housing for the poor and the near-poor is often found where the air, water, and land are polluted. Especially dangerous for young children is exposure to lead, which is related to behavioral problems, reduced intelligence, and problems with speech. Substances such as PCBs (polychlorinated biphenyls) and mercury, the by-products of chemical and industrial production, not only cause cancer and birth defects, but there is evidence tying these compounds to lack of coordination, diminished intelligence, and poor memory in children (Kaplan and Morris, 2000). Children can also be exposed to pesticides and herbicides in the air or from the food they ingest.

HUNGER AND MALNUTRITION

The good health and development of children depend on a diet sufficient in nutrients and calories. Quality of food, as measured by the government's Healthy Eating Index, appears to be a problem for most U.S. children, a problem that worsens as they move toward adolescence. That is, most children do not eat enough fruits and vegetables and eat too much saturated fat and sugar. Children in families below the poverty level are less likely than higher-income families to have a diet rated as good.

Children living in poverty receive some food subsidies. In 2007, an average of 12.7 million children each month received food stamps and more than 17 million children received free or reduced-price school meals. The demand for both of these programs increased with the Great Recession—from April 2008 to April 2009 the applications for food stamps was up 16 percent and another three million children were added to school lunch programs.

EDUCATIONAL DEFICITS

One result of these problems—exposure to toxic chemicals, lack of adequate health care, inadequate diet—is that when poor children start school, they are already behind. "At age 5, poor children are often less alert, less curious, and less effective at interacting with their peers than are more privileged youngsters" (Hewlett, 1991:56). Moreover, poor children are more likely than privileged children to attend schools that are poorly staffed, overcrowded, and ill equipped, because schools are financed primarily through the property wealth of the districts. The consequence for them and for society is that they will likely be underachievers.

The Societal Response to Disadvantaged Children

What do we do about the 13.3 million impoverished children and the many millions more whose families are just above the government's poverty line? There is strong evidence that poor children—hungry, ill housed, and unhealthy—will not do as well as their more privileged peers in school and will be more likely to fall into self-destructive and nonproductive activities as they grow up. Clearly, the conditions of poverty will likely keep them from reaching their potential. These facts do not jibe with the great value Americans place on "equal opportunity."

If we choose, we can reduce or even eliminate poverty for children and their parents. Other societies have chosen to do this with success. The United States has actually taken the opposite position by eliminating AFDC payments, by cutting back on nutrition programs, by making only token efforts at job training, and by keeping the minimum wage too low.

REDUCING POVERTY FOR THE ELDERLY WHILE INCREASING POVERTY FOR THE YOUNG

As a nation, the United States has taken deliberate actions to reduce poverty among older Americans while simultaneously allowing childhood poverty to increase. In 1970, the proportion of elderly people in poverty was double the national average, yet by 2007 the poverty rate among the elderly was below the national average (9.7 percent compared to the national rate of 12.5 percent). The poverty rate for children under age 18 in 1970 was over one-third lower than that for the elderly. By 2007, this situation had changed, with 18.0 percent of children under age 18 living in poverty (DeNavas-Walt et al., 2008) (see Figure 13.1).

During the last 20 years, federal benefits to the elderly have risen from one-sixth of the federal budget to 30 percent (about $300 billion annually). This increase occurred because federal policy-makers created programs such as Medicare and Medicaid and because Social Security benefits were indexed to offset inflation. Conversely, however, these same decision-makers did not provide adequately for needy families with children. The government actually reduced or eliminated the programs targeted to benefit children (e.g., the children's share of Medicaid, Aid to Families with Dependent Children, Head Start, food stamps, child nutrition, and federal aid to education).

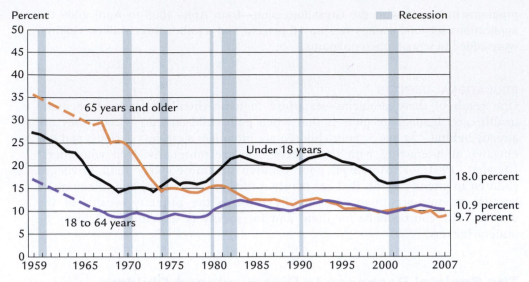

Figure 13.1   **Poverty Rates by Age: 1959–2007**

Note: The data points are placed at the midpoints of the respective years. Data for people 18 to 64 and 65 and older are not available from 1960 to 1965.

Source: DeNavas-Walt, Carmen, Bernadette D. Proctor, and Jessica C. Smith (2008). "Income, Poverty, and Health Insurance Coverage in the United States: 2007." In *Current Population Reports*, P60-235. Washington, DC: U.S. Census Bureau.

Childhood poverty is especially acute for racial minorities. The bias against children in federal programs is heightened for minority children. The late Senator Daniel Patrick Moynihan pointed out that there are two ways in which the federal government provides benefits to children in single-parent families. The first is Aid to Families with Dependent Children. The majority of the children receiving this type of aid are African American or Latino. Since 1970, the government has decreased the real benefits by 13 percent, and in 1996 it placed a two-year limit on benefits. The other form of assistance is Survivors Insurance (SI), which is part of Social Security. The majority of children receiving SI benefits are White, and these benefits have increased by 53 percent since 1970 (adjusted for inflation). Moynihan, writing eight years before the 1996 welfare legislation, said:

> To those who say we don't care about children in our country, may I note that the average provision for children under SI has been rising five times as fast as average family income since 1970. We do care about some children. Majority children. It is minority children—not only but mostly—who are left behind. (Moynihan, 1988:5)

Another telling illustration is that while Congress in 1996 eliminated AFDC and severely cut food stamps and school nutrition programs for the poor, it did not cut cash and food programs for poor senior citizens.

The decisions to help the elderly disproportionately reflect the electoral power that the elderly have compared to the young. The elderly are organized, with several national organizations dedicated to political action that will benefit their interests. The American Association of Retired Persons, for example, is the nation's largest special-interest organization, with over 40 million members. With the elderly making up 16 percent of the voting public (and much more in states such as Florida and Arizona, which have high concentrations of elderly people), politicians pay attention to their special needs.

Children, on the other hand, have no electoral power and few advocates (an exception is the Children's Defense Fund). Their parents, especially those who are poor, are not organized. So, in times of fiscal austerity, the needs of children—prenatal care for poor women, nutritional and health care, day care, and better schools—are underfunded. The irony is that political conservatives, who claim to be profamily, often ignore or resist government assistance to needy children and their struggling parents.

The argument here is not that the elderly and the young should compete for scarce resources and that one or the other should win. Rather, both age groups are dependents and have special needs. The test of a civilization is the condition of its dependents. So far the United States has opted to care moderately well for one and not at all well for the other.

INADEQUATE GOVERNMENT PROGRAMS FOR IMPOVERISHED YOUTH

Although the evidence is clear that investing in children saves money in the long run, government programs continue either to neglect the needs of poor children or to provide only modestly for them. Examples include the following:

- Government support for prenatal care among high-risk groups has declined significantly since 1980.

- The U.S. health care system is based on the principle that the users of services pay fees either directly or through insurance. Those who cannot afford these fees may seek public assistance. The services provided to those seeking assistance are defined differently by each state, as are the rules of eligibility. The result is that only about half of all poor children qualify for such help.

- The Centers for Disease Control has recommended that all children under the age of 6 be screened for lead in the blood, yet only 1 child in 10 receives such testing.

- The Special Supplemental Food Program for Women, Infants, and Children (WIC) provides mothers with vouchers to buy infant formula and wholesome foods (at a cost of about $30 a month), yet government funds support only about 60 percent of women and infants who qualify for the program.

The Children's Defense Fund has argued that government spending on poor children is actually sound fiscal policy (2001:xvii):

- A dollar invested in good early childhood programs for low-income children saves $7.00.

- A dollar invested in immunizations against diphtheria, tetanus, and whooping cough saves $23.00.

- A dollar spent in the Women, Infants, and Children (WIC) nutritional program saves $3.07 during a baby's first year.

- The average cost of providing a year of Head Start for one child is $5,403, while the average cost of keeping a person in prison for a year is $20,000.

THE SPECIAL CASE OF PRESCHOOL PROGRAMS TO ENHANCE COGNITIVE ABILITY

Children from impoverished backgrounds tend to do less well than their more privileged counterparts in school (grades, scoring on intelligence tests, deportment). This, of course, disadvantages them in school and in opportunities after they complete school. The reasons for this deficit are complex. Some of the possibilities are:

1. Their home environments are less likely to involve reading and other cognitive stimulation that is useful in school.

2. Their experiences outside the neighborhood are more limited (e.g., trips to museums, zoos, national parks, summer camps).

3. They are less likely to have computers and other recent technologies at home.

4. The language spoken at home may not be English, or if English is spoken it may not be grammatically correct.

5. The tests are biased for middle-class experiences.

6. Children of the affluent are more likely to attend early childhood development programs, which prepare them for school, than are children of the poor.

7. Poor children usually attend inferior schools.

8. Some would even argue that the poor are genetically disadvantaged. This last point is the old social Darwinism argument that the poor are poor because they do not have what it takes to succeed. In other words, in a competitive society they are where they should be.

This leads to a serious question: Is intelligence immutable, or is it possible to boost cognitive development? Head Start is one federally funded program that has documented positive effects for economically disadvantaged children. Lisbeth Schorr has summarized what is known about this excellent program:

> The basic Head Start model has proved to be sound. When three- to five-year-old children are systematically helped to think, reason, and speak clearly; when they are provided hot meals, social services, health evaluations, and health care; when families become partners in their children's learning experiences, are helped toward self-sufficiency, and gain greater confidence in themselves as parents and as contributing members of the community, the results are measurable and dramatic. (Schorr, 1988:192; see Schorr, 1997)

In effect, a number of studies have shown that Head Start programs raise IQ scores among poor children by as much as 10 points. These results, however, fade out entirely by the sixth grade. Yet this rise and fall of IQ scores makes the case for the role of environmental factors in cognitive development. As Maschinot has argued,

> [the critics of Head Start] ignore the obvious fact that once they leave Head Start, poor students typically attend substandard schools from the first grade onward. The fact that IQ scores drop again after this experience should lead one logically to conclude that intelligence as defined by IQ tests is highly responsive to environmental manipulations, not the reverse. (Maschinot, 1995:33)

Research outside of Head Start provides further justification for the Head Start model. The Abecedarian Project, conducted at the University of North Carolina, reinforces the belief that the early education of poor children pays off in cognitive advancement. This project has been rigorously researched (see Box 13.3) to assess the effects of assisting poor children in their preschool years and during their school years. By the time the children reached age 21, research shows that they benefited by

BOX
13.3

Researching Families

Nature Versus Nurture: Can IQ Be Raised?

There is a longstanding debate on the role of the environment on intelligence (see Herrnstein and Murray, 1994; Maschinot, 1995). Do impoverished children have different IQs than privileged children because of heredity, or is it environment? Let's examine one test to see whether environment makes a difference on IQ scores.

The Abecedarian Project used an experimental design to assess the effects of environment (the following information is from Campbell and Ramey, 1994). Ramey and his associates began with educationally high-risk children from 120 families. The IQs of the biological mothers averaged 85; 98 percent of the children were African American; the average maternal age was 19.9 years when the target child was born; maternal education averaged 10.6 years; the median earned family income was none; and three-fourths of the families were single-parent. From four months onward, half of these children (the experimental group) were randomly placed in a preschool where the staff focused on language development, preliteracy skills, and social development. The other half (the control group) stayed at home. When the children in the two groups reached kindergarten age, they were randomly divided again. Half of the experimental group received no further special treatment. The other half of the experimental group and half of the control group

received help in school for the next eight years. This help was a Home School Resource Teacher assigned to work with the parents of each child on individualized sets of educational activities to target basic skills. To summarize the procedures, there are four randomly selected groups: One received an enriched program for 12 years; another received this program for the first four years of life; another did not receive it for four years but did for the next eight; and one did not receive any enrichment at all. The results are as follows: (1) By age 3 the children in the experimental group averaged 17 points higher than the control group on IQ tests (101 versus 84); (2) these differences, although less pronounced, persisted more than a decade later (the difference was now about 10 IQ points). Campbell and Ramey concluded that for impoverished children, the earlier in the life span education occurs, the greater its benefit is likely to be.... The most important policy implication of these findings is that early educational intervention for impoverished children can have long-lasting benefits, in terms of improved cognitive performance. This underscores the critical importance of good early environments and suggests that the focus of debate should now be shifted from whether government should play a role in encouraging good early environments to how these environments can be assured (Campbell and Ramey, 1994:694–695).

delayed parenthood, higher IQs, higher reading and math scores, and more years of formal education (Ramey et al., 1999).

A second study, by the Robert Wood Johnson Foundation, of low-birth-weight infants followed their development for three years. The researchers found that the ones who had a stimulating day-care environment had, on average, a 13-point higher IQ score than the babies who did not receive those experiences (reported in Richmond, 1994).

As a final example, there is a study of high-risk African American children in Ypsilanti, Michigan. The children were divided randomly into two groups. One group received a high-quality active learning program as three- and four-year-olds. The other group got no preschool education. The groups were compared when they were age 40, with these results:

Their median income [of the group receiving preschool] is $20,800. That's 25 percent more than the average earnings of a matched group of children who didn't get this opportunity, the difference between an income that's above or below the poverty line. Not only earnings but life in general is better for the former preschoolers: 65 percent graduated from high school, compared with 45 percent of those who didn't go [to the preschool]; 57 percent of males raised their own children, versus 30 percent of the nonpreschool group; 36 percent had been arrested five or more times, versus 55 percent for the control group. That more than a third of the ex-preschoolers have been arrested at least five times is a useful reminder that pre-kindergarten is no panacea. *Still, the 2004 analysis finds a spectacular $17 return, to society as well as to the former [preschool] students, for every dollar spent on their early education.* (Kirp, 2005:26) (emphasis added)

The good news is that we know that early education helps poor youth prepare for school—and the earlier this education occurs, the better the results. The problem is that the majority of children from poor families do not have preschool programs to prepare them for school. Head Start, the major government program, reaches only about half of eligible four-year-olds and a smaller number of younger children (Gormley, 2005). At the state level, four states—Florida, Oklahoma, Georgia, and New York—formally guarantee universal preschool, and 37 others support some preschool programs.

The neglect of children, especially poor children, in their earliest years is a crisis, resulting in millions who grow up to live stunted lives. Lisbeth Schorr provides a fundamental reason for our neglect:

Our national failure to act on what we know about the early years is the product, at least in part, of our commitment to rugged individualism. The notion that every family should be able to care for its own, without outside help, has made the U.S. the only industrialized country in the world without universal preschools, paid parental leave, and income support for families with young children. (Schorr, 1997:235)

Funding Programs to Help Disadvantaged Children

Children's advocate Jonathan Kozol has said that "Children bless us with their mere presence on this earth. The great question is whether we will bless them" (quoted in Judson, 1997, 2A). Government policies, federal and state, can do much to provide a healthy environment for children and by increasing their life chances—lifting them out of poverty, providing health care, and eliminating educational deficits. The Children's Defense Fund has provided a list of child investments at the federal level that they felt were achievable by 2010 (2004:xxxiii):

- Get every child ready for school through full funding of quality care and Head Start, and new investments in universal preschool.
- Lift every child from poverty.
- Ensure that all children and their parents have health insurance.
- End child hunger through the expansion of food programs.
- Make sure every child can read by fourth grade and can graduate from school able to succeed in work and in life.
- Provide every child safe, quality after-school and summer programs.
- Ensure every child a place called home and decent affordable housing.
- Protect all children from neglect, abuse, and other violence and ensure they have the care they need.
- Ensure that families leaving welfare have the supports they need to be successful in the workplace, including health care, child care, education, and training.

The Children's Defense Fund argued that these goals were achievable by 2010 at a cost of $75 billion of new money annually (2004 through 2010) for a total cost of $525 billion. But the government did not act on these recommendations, once again leaving children behind.

Legislators and presidents make policy decisions that have fiscal consequences. For example, under George W. Bush and a Republican Congress, tax cuts were passed that will cost more than $1 trillion from 2001 to 2010, and those cuts benefited disproportionately the wealthiest 1 percent. More tax cuts are proposed, including ending the estate tax, which would reduce revenue by as much as $745 billion over 10 years (*USA Today*, 2006). Meanwhile, the United States is engaged in the Iraq and Afghanistan War, which costs, conservatively, $5 billion a month. To fund the war and to make up for the losses of tax revenues, the government actually has reduced programs that would benefit the economically disadvantaged. The government could enact and fund the programs suggested by the Children's Defense Fund easily by reversing the tax cuts. It has chosen, rather, to direct benefits to the wealthy and disregard the children of the disadvantaged.

The election of Barack Obama in 2008 and a Congress controlled by Democrats would seem to lead to a reversal of these policies. However, the Great Recession, the huge bailouts, and the stimulus packages have dramatically increased the government debt and lead, at least in the short run, to policies that limit the safety net.

Principles to Guide Family Policy: An Immodest Proposal

We have noted a number of structural problems affecting contemporary families. Although these problems are formidable, we can do something about them. If we, as a society, have the will, we have the resources to come to the aid of our children, provide universal health care, universal preschool training, day care and after-school care, job training, and other costly programs (Reich, 2001).

If we have the resources and the will, what steps should we take as a society to sustain and nourish families? The first step must be to determine the facts. This requires that we challenge the myths that often guide public opinion and our policy-makers. Providing the facts and demythologizing families have been major goals of this book.

The second step is to establish, as a society, principles that will guide family policies. This, we realize, is politically impossible at the moment, for at least two reasons. First, government decisions are determined largely by campaign contributions, gifts, lobbying, and media blitzes. Until the public demands effective campaign finance reform and lobbying reform, decisions will be made that benefit the most affluent among us and, conversely, work to the disadvantage of those who have no effective political voice (the poor, children, women, minorities). Second, the huge national debt and restricted state budgets keep them from enacting costly social programs.

Assuming that we can overcome the bias of money in politics and the political power of the moral right, dubious assumptions at best, let us propose some principles that we believe ought to guide family policies (we realize, of course, that this is a controversial exercise, but we ask you to ponder these proposals and improve on them).

1. We call for policies and behaviors that enhance our moral obligation to others, to our neighbors (broadly defined) and their children, to those unlike us as well as those similar to us, and to future generations. This principle runs counter to our heritage, since the Constitution of the United States is based on individualism.

Searching for a job at a community center.

The reigning philosophy of that time celebrated individualism, and the focus was on removing constraints on individual freedom. To this day, political quarrels about family policy can be traced to a conflict between concern for the individual and concern for the well-being of the family group (Anderson, 1991:237).

The celebration of individualism, we argue, leads to exacerbated inequality, the tolerance of inferior housing, schools, and services for "others," and public policies that are punitive to the disadvantaged. Moreover, exaggerated individualism is the antithesis of cooperation and solidarity—the requirements of community.

There is a flaw in the individualistic credo. We cannot go it alone entirely—our fate depends on others. Thus, it is in our individual interest to have a collective interest. As Alan Wolfe, discussing the Scandinavian countries, has put it:

> The strength of the welfare state—indeed, the accomplishment that makes the welfare state the great success story of modern liberal democracy—is the recognition that the living conditions of people who are strangers to us are nonetheless our business. (Wolfe, 1989:133)

There are two key issues that must be resolved. The first is where to place the blame. For social conservatives the poor are poor because of their lack of individual motivation and their cultural attitudes. We side with the progressives who argue that poverty has to do with

> the labor market that fails to produce enough decent paying jobs, and social policies that are unable to pull individuals and families out of poverty when unforeseen events occur. The United States has the means to alleviate poverty, and a range of models from other countries to borrow from. Allowing our policies to be mired in self-righteous moralism while millions of citizens suffer is unconscionable. It is time to shift the debate from one of blame, to one of justice and common concern. (Rank, 2003:48)

The second issue for U.S. society is: How much do we limit individual freedom for the collective good? Or, put another way, how willing are we to sacrifice (in taxes) so that the fate of others will be improved?

2. Acceptance of the first principle leads to the second, a call for government programs that provide for people who cannot provide for themselves. Economic inequality undermines the quality of family life—especially those living near or below the poverty line. Frank Furstenberg, Jr., says,

> The incivilities of poverty are evident in inner-city communities, blighted suburban areas and rural enclaves. They assume the form of inadequate housing, schools, social and recreational services, as well as the absence of commercial enterprises. The misallocation of resources in American society through a market system that provides unlimited rewards to the privileged at the same time as it excludes others from the benefits of prosperity is a potential problem for families struggling to maintain a decent life. (Furstenberg, 1999:37)

Thus, society must bring all members of society up to a minimum standard of dignity. At a minimum, this includes universal health insurance, jobs, a living wage that places one above the poverty line, and adequate pensions.

3. Acceptance of the preceding principles leads to a third, a special commitment to children (all children) and to implementing this commitment with viable, universal programs. In Jay Belsky's words:

> The time has come for this nation to regard child care as an infrastructure issue and make the same kind of investment in it that we talk about making in our bridges and roads and that we initially made in these vital transportation systems. We need to recognize that, in the same way that the massive capital investment in transportation and communication systems resulted in huge capital gains that we continue even to this day to realize, investment in child care can bring with it comparable long-term benefits. To gain insight into the costs, specifically foregone opportunity costs of not endeavoring to improve child care and increase options for families, imagine for a moment an America with the automobile but without paved roads. (Belsky, 1990:11)

Such a commitment to children involves providing prenatal and postnatal medical care, childhood immunization, protection from exposure to toxic chemicals, adequate nutrition, the elimination of child poverty, universal access to preschool programs, safe neighborhoods, and equally financed schools.

Most significant, children should be wanted by their parents. Unwanted pregnancies should be kept at a minimum through universal sex education in the schools and the easy availability of contraceptives. Abortion is legal. It should be readily available to those who choose this option and subsidized for those who cannot afford it.

4. A similar commitment to the one made for children must be made for women as well. Young single mothers need parenting skills, education, jobs, and subsidized day care. Divorced women need fair treatment by the courts, adequate child support from their former husbands, education, job skills, and jobs. All women in the labor force must have equity with men (equal pay for equal work, chance for promotion, and benefits), maternity leave with pay, reliable child care, and flexible work schedules without prejudice from management.

5. Although some family policies should be made and administered at the local and state levels, others must be largely financed and organized by the federal government.

This principle is based on the assumption that some issues are national in scope and require uniform standards (e.g., nutrition guidelines, immunization timetables, preschool goals, the certification of day care providers, and eligibility for health care). Other policies, such as reducing poverty, require the massive infusion of money and compensatory programs, coupled with centralized planning.

6. We call for "progressive family policies that reflect the realities of all kinds of families—including families of color, lesbian and gay families, single-parent and blended families, two-parent families, families in which a member has a disability, and families of all social classes" (Fried and Reinelt, 1993:66). This principle recognizes the family diversity present in contemporary society. The reality is that rather than return to the "modern family" of the 1950s, families have become more diverse. These diverse forms should be recognized and nurtured by society rather than vilified and denigrated, as is now often the case.

These may seem like radical proposals, but they are not. Most of these suggestions in one form or another are found in each of the Western democracies except the United States. Can we learn from them? Should we learn from them? Can we afford them? Can we afford not to adopt these proposals?

Chapter Review

1. Family policy refers to objectives concerning family well-being and the specific measures taken by governmental bodies to achieve them.

2. Conservatives and progressives differ in their concept of families: For the former, families are the building blocks of society; for the latter, families are socially and historically constructed. For conservatives, the traditional family, with working father, homemaker mother, and their children, is the way families are supposed to be. For progressives, families change as the society changes.

3. A central issue dividing cultural conservatives and progressives is whether same-sex marriage should be legitimized by the government. Conservatives oppose this because it is contrary to our heritage and what they consider the normal arrangement. Progressives argue that committed relationships are a good thing and that lesbians and gays should not be denied the rights and privileges accorded by the government to married couples.

4. Abortion was legalized by the U.S. Supreme Court in 1973. In 2005 approximately 1.2 million legal abortions were performed, terminating slightly less than one-fourth of all pregnancies. The annual abortion rate has been declining since 1980.

5. Reproductive rights policies are unfair to the poor, making it more likely that they will have unwanted babies. This bias takes two forms: (a) the relatively high cost of contraceptives and (b) federal law and many state laws that make it illegal for public money to be spent for abortions.

6. Although much less generous than found in other industrialized nations, the United States had a fairly comprehensive welfare program to help those in need from 1935 to 1996. This changed with the welfare legislation passed in 1996, which ended Aid to Families with Dependent Children, required welfare recipients to work within two years, placed a five-year lifetime limit on receiving welfare, required unmarried teen parents to live in an adult-supervised setting, gave the states great latitude in administering and funding welfare, cut $54.5 billion in funding over six years, and limited the benefits of legal immigrants. After 10 years, the results of the 1996 reform are mixed. It was successful in a growing economy, but the recessions of 2001 and 2007 showed how fragile these successes were.

7. Conservatives and progressives differ on the solution to welfare. Conservatives believe that the poor are to blame for their failure. Thus, they argue that

the safety net should be reduced further to encourage the poor to "sink or swim" on their own. Also, conservatives argue that if the poor married, this would lead them to be productive citizens. Progressives believe that a stronger social safety net is required to help the poor offset the structural conditions that make their lives so difficult.

8. Parental leave (for birth or sickness) is now federal policy for firms with more than 50 employees. Although this policy is progressive, it lags behind those of other industrial nations because the leave is unpaid and does not cover the 40 percent of U.S. workers who work for small businesses.

9. Unlike the other Western democracies, the United States has no comprehensive child-care system. Day-care provision for working parents is a special problem that is not met by government and many businesses.

10. Women are disadvantaged in the workplace when they use work-related rules such as family leave. Particularly, management may treat such women differently from men because managers assume that these women are less committed to their careers.

11. Some 13.3 million children (2007) are living below the poverty line. Racial minorities are disproportionately poor, with 33.7 percent of African American children and 28.6 percent of Latino children poor, compared to 15.0 percent of White children. The difference in child poverty by race is even greater when severe poverty is considered

(i.e., those families with incomes below one-half the poverty threshold).

12. Compared with other industrialized nations, the United States ranks relatively low in infant mortality (with African American babies more than two times more likely to die in their first year than White infants) and last in the number covered by health insurance.

13. Poverty among the elderly has been reduced by government programs (Social Security indexed for inflation), while poverty for children has increased because government actions have reduced programs to help children.

14. The unwillingness of society to help poor children is costly in the long run (cost of medical care, welfare, crime). Preschool programs for at-risk children are important for improving IQ scores and school performance.

15. We propose six principles to guide profamily policies: (a) policies and behaviors that enhance our moral obligation to others; (b) the government provision of benefits to people who cannot provide for themselves; (c) a special commitment to all children to ensure health, safety, preparation for school, and equal funding for schools; (d) a commitment to equality for women; (e) addressing many problems with federal money, standards, and administration; and (f) a recognition, acceptance, and nurturing of the diverse forms of families present in contemporary society.

Key Term

latchkey children   474

Related Websites

http://www.acf.hhs.gov/programs/ofa/welfare

ACF-Welfare Reform. This website is managed by the U.S. Department of Health and Human Services, Administration for Children and Families. It provides links to policy updates, recent reports, and current statistics related to welfare reform.

http://www.mathematica-mpr.com

Mathematica Policy Research, Inc. Founded in 1968, Mathematica Policy Research, Inc., has been known for its high-quality, objective research to support decisions about our nation's most pressing social policy problems. The firm has conducted some of the most

important studies of health care, welfare, education, employment, nutrition, and early childhood policies and programs in the United States. This research, which crisscrosses the human life span from children's health and welfare to long-term care for elderly people, provides a sound foundation for decisions that affect the well-being of Americans.

http://www.movingideas.org

Moving Ideas Network. Moving Ideas is a project of Care2.com. The website facilitates connections between activists and a wide variety of nonprofit organizations—from local to national—through discussion boards, blogs, events calendars, press releases, policy briefs, and scholarly publications. Issues covered on this site range from economic policy to civic participation, health care to foreign policy, and education to Social Security.

http://www.communitychange.org

Center for Community Change. CCC came out of the antipoverty movement and programs of the 1960s. Its mission is to help low-income people, especially people of color, build powerful, effective organizations through which they can change their communities and public policies for the better. Throughout the Center's history it has provided policy and organizing expertise on a range of issue areas, including community reinvestment, affordable and public housing, transportation, income support and job creation, economic development and housing production, hunger and malnutrition, immigrant rights and legislation, and community monitoring efforts to hold government agencies accountable to residents.

http://clasp.org

Center for Law and Social Policy. CLASP is a nonmember, nonprofit organization founded in 1968. Its work is concentrated on advancing the economic security, educational and workforce prospects, and family stability of low-income persons. To achieve this goal, CLASP promotes progressive policies on welfare reform, child support, child care, early education, workforce development, child welfare, low-income fathers, disconnected youth, and ex-offenders reentering society. In addition, CLASP has sought to secure equal justice for all Americans by promoting and protecting programs to expand access to our civil justice system for low-income persons by promoting racial justice and by stimulating innovations in the delivery of civil legal assistance.

http://www.kwru.org

Kensington Welfare Rights Union. KWRU is a multiracial organization of, by, and for poor and homeless people. KWRU is dedicated to organizing of welfare recipients, the homeless, the working poor, and all people concerned with economic justice. KWRU is the leading organization behind the Poor People's Economic Human Rights Campaign, a national effort led by poor and homeless women, men, and children of all races to raise the issue of poverty as a human rights violation.

http://urban.org

Urban Institute. Founded in 1968, the Urban Institute is a nonprofit, nonpartisan organization that analyzes policies, evaluates programs, and informs community development to improve social, civic, and economic

well-being. It works in all 50 states and abroad in over 28 countries. Its research findings are shared with policy-makers, program administrators, business, academics, and the public online and through reports and scholarly books.

http://www.prochoiceamerica.org

NARAL Pro-Choice America. The mission of NARAL Pro-Choice America is to support and protect, as a fundamental right and value, a woman's freedom to make personal decisions regarding the full range of reproductive choices through education, training, organizing, legal action, and public policy. The organization aims to develop and sustain a constituency that uses the political process to guarantee every woman the right to make personal decisions regarding the full range of reproductive choices, including preventing unintended pregnancy, bearing healthy children, and choosing legal abortion.

http://gseweb.harvard.edu/hfrp

Harvard Family Research Project. Founded in 1983 at the Harvard Graduate School of Education, HFRP strives to advance knowledge development by providing training, professional development, and technical assistance, and by offering strategies to encourage continuous learning and promote dialogue. The audiences for HFRP's work include policy-makers, practitioners, philanthropists, and concerned individuals.

http://www.equalrights.org

Equal Rights Advocates. Equal Rights Advocates has led the legal fight for women's equality for almost 30 years. Since 1974, ERA's mission has been to protect and secure equal rights and economic opportunities for women and girls through litigation and advocacy. Through the successful use of impact litigation, the ERA has brought an end to many systematic discriminatory practices and policies.

http://www.crlp.org

Center for Reproductive Rights. The Center for Reproductive Rights is a nonprofit legal advocacy organization dedicated to promoting and defending women's reproductive rights worldwide. The organization promotes universal access to safe and affordable contraception, including emergency contraceptives; works to make abortion safe and legal in the United States and, where appropriate, around the world; and strives to ensure that all women can freely exercise their basic human right to reproductive health, regardless of economic status.

http://www.epi.org

Economic Policy Institute. The Economic Policy Institute is a nonprofit, nonpartisan think tank that seeks to broaden the public debate about strategies to achieve a prosperous and fair economy. The mission of the Economic Policy Institute is to provide high-quality research and education in order to promote a prosperous, fair, and sustainable economy. The Institute stresses real-world analysis and a concern for the living standards of working people, and it makes its findings accessible to the general public, the media, and policy-makers.

http://www.nicwa.org/

The National Indian Child Welfare Association. NICWA is the most comprehensive source of information on American Indian child welfare and works on behalf of Indian children and families. NICWA provides public policy, research, and advocacy; information and training on Indian child welfare; and community development services to a broad national audience including tribal governments and programs, state child welfare agencies, and other organizations, agencies, and professionals interested in the field of Indian child welfare.

http://www.childrensdefensefund.org

The Children's Defense Fund is a nonprofit child advocacy organization for all children. It champions policies and programs that lift children out of poverty; protect them from abuse and neglect; and ensure their access to health care, quality education, and a moral and spiritual foundation.

Glossary

abortion   Expulsion of a fetus or embryo from the uterus, either spontaneously or via a medical procedure.

abuse   Behavior aimed primarily at hurting another person, either verbally or physically.

affect   Feeling or emotion; the degree of positive and negative affect in marital interaction is associated with relationship quality and stability.

ageism   Discrimination against the elderly.

agency   The ability of human beings to create viable lives even when they are constrained by social forces.

aggregate data analysis   A research technique that analyzes quantitative data at different times (e.g., births, deaths, work histories) in order to understand trends.

AIDS   Acquired immune deficiency syndrome, an incurable disease that attacks the immune system.

alienation   An individual's feeling of separation from the surrounding society.

alimony   Income paid to support a divorced spouse.

assimilation   Process by which individuals or groups voluntarily or involuntarily adopt the culture of another group, losing their original identity.

assortative mating   Addresses the question of who marries whom; in general, people marry individuals much like themselves (homogamy).

baby boom   A 15-year period in U.S. history following World War II when an extraordinary number of babies were born.

backstage behavior   Erving Goffman's term denoting that people act differently in private because they have fewer constraints.

beanpole family structure   A vertical, four-generation family structure (e.g., elderly parents living with adult children, as do their children and children's children).

bilateral model of parent–child relations   The assumption that there is an equal degree of agency to the parent and child.

binational family   Family of mixed legal status, such as an undocumented immigrant and a U.S. citizen or legal resident.

binuclear family   See *stepfamily*.

birth control   Any method used to avoid pregnancy.

birth order   Sibling position based on age.

blaming the victim   The belief that some individuals are poor, criminals, school dropouts, or otherwise deviant because they have a flaw within them.

blended family   See *stepfamily*.

boomerang generation   The present generation of youth, which is more prone then previous ones to have adult children move back in with their parents.

capital flight   Investment choices that involve the movement of corporate monies from one investment to another.

capitalism   Economic system based on private ownership of property, guided by the seeking of maximum profits.

capitalist patriarchy   Condition of capitalism in which male supremacy keeps women in subordinate roles at work and in the home.

chain migration   When migrating family members arrive at different times.

child abuse   "The distinctive acts of violence and nonviolence and acts of omission and commission that place children at risk" (Gelles, 1976:136).

civil union   One step removed from marriage but allows same-sex partners to have the same legal protections under state law as married couples.

class privilege   Advantages, prerogatives, and options available to those in an affluent economic situation.

cohabitation   Practice of living together as a couple without being married.

cohabitation (heterosexual)   Practice of sharing a household by an unmarried male and female in an emotional and physical relationship.

cohabitation (homosexual)   Practice of sharing a household by two persons of the same sex in an emotional and physical relationship.

cohort   Group of persons who are born at approximately the same time and who subsequently go through life stages together.

commuter marriage   A marriage in which spouses live apart because their jobs require that they live in different locations.

compulsory heterosexuality   The beliefs and practices that define and enforce heterosexual (other-sex attraction) behavior as the only natural and permissible form of sexual expression.

conflict perspective   View of society that posits conflict as a normal feature of social life, influencing the distribution of power and the direction and magnitude of social change.

consumption work   A form of invisible work for women as they select goods and make purchases for the family.

coping   The process by which individuals manage a set of demands that is perceived as excessive or experienced as stressful.

courtship Process of selection and attachment between potential mates that leads to the formation of strong emotional and sexual ties and possibly marriage.

cult of true womanhood Ideology by which women are judged by their piety, purity, submissiveness, and domesticity.

cultural approach View that assumes that families in society are the products of the culture in which they are embedded. Families, for example, differ by social class because of the distinctive values found in each class.

cultural tyranny Socialization process that forces narrow behavioral and attitudinal traits on persons.

culture Knowledge that the members of a social organization share.

culture of poverty View that the poor are qualitatively different in values and lifestyles from the rest of society and that these cultural differences explain continued poverty.

deindustrialization Widespread systematic diversion of capital (finance, plant, and equipment) from productive investment in the nation's basic industries into unproductive speculation, mergers, acquisitions, and foreign investment.

demography The study of population.

deskilling A consequence of job specialization and technological advances in which jobs require narrower and more repetitive tasks, resulting in lower pay, less prestige, and less autonomy.

deviance Behavior that violates the expectations of society.

differential fertility Variation in childbearing rates by social class or some other social characteristic.

discrimination Process of acting toward a person or group with partiality, typically because the individual or group belongs to a minority.

disengagement One response by the elderly in which they retreat from relationships, organizations, and society.

disinvestment Corporate decision to remove capital from an operation (e.g., shutting down a manufacturing plant).

divorce Legal termination of a marriage.

doctrine of two spheres The belief that married women should spend their lives within the home, while married men should devote their time outside the home to earning a living for the family.

domestic partner movement The effort to allow homosexuals to register as married; official recognition of gay partners provides them with the legal and economic benefits of marriage.

domestic partners Two individuals who are in a long-term committed relationship and are responsible for each other's financial and emotional well-being.

dual-earner marriage Marriage in which the husband and wife are both employed outside the home.

egalitarian Relationship in which the partners share equally in practical responsibilities and decision making.

emotion work Arlie Hochschild's term for the work that women do to keep right feelings in relationships.

empty nest syndrome State of psychological depression or search for new roles that occurs among many full-time housewives whose children have grown up and left home.

ethnic group Social group with a common culture distinct from the culture of the majority because of race, religion, or national origin.

ethnic stratification System of inequality in which race, religion, or national origin is the major criterion for rank and rewards.

ethnicity The condition of being culturally distinct on the basis of race, religion, or national origin.

exogamy The practice of marrying outside one's group.

extended family Several generations of kin that constitute a single family unit, in both living arrangements and obligations.

false consciousness In Marxian theory, the idea that the oppressed may hold beliefs damaging to their interests.

false universalization Incorrect generalization that people experience the family in uniform ways.

familism The attachment to one's nuclear family and to the extended family.

family Particular societal construct whereby persons are related by ancestry, marriage, adoption, or choice.

Family and Medical Leave Act of 1993 [FMLA] Federal law providing workers in establishments with more than 50 workers the right to unpaid job-protected leave to meet family health needs.

family-based economy Mode of production common in the colonial period wherein the household was the basic economic unit.

family cycle Changes that take place in the family unit as it moves from stage to stage as its members age.

family Darwinism The belief that families survive or sink by their own resources and fitness, not for structural reasons.

family household Persons who are related by birth, marriage, or adoption and share a residence.

family imagery An idealized picture of the family attained by distorting reality.

family policy Objectives concerning family well-being and the specific measures taken by governmental bodies to achieve them.

family reconstitution A research tool that uses every available fragment of information to reconstruct family and household patterns.

family strategies Conscious and unconscious solutions to the constraints imposed on families by economic and social structures.

"family values" The conservative term supporting the two-parent family, with the husband as the breadwinner and the wife as mother and homemaker. The implication is that all other family arrangements are the source of social problems.

family wage Income that men derive from work outside the home that is sufficient to allow women to stay home, raise children, and maintain a family.

family-wage economy Family members making a living by earning wages working outside the home, producing goods and services for employers.

fecundity Ability to have children.

feminization of poverty Rapid rise in the numbers of female-headed households living in poverty.

fertility Frequency of actual births in a population.

fictive kin People treated like family even though they are not related by blood or marriage.

flextime Employer–employee arrangement that permits the employee to choose his or her work schedule within specific limits.

frontstage behavior The formal playing of roles.

functionalism The dominant sociological paradigm of the 1950s and 1960s. It posited that the nuclear family was the basis of social organization and cohesion in society and essential for the socialization of children and for the division of labor that enabled women and men to perform their social roles in an orderly manner.

gay Male whose sexual preference is for someone of the same sex.

gender Cultural and social definition of feminine and masculine. It differs from sex, which is the biological fact of femaleness or maleness.

gender roles approach Males and females differ because of socialization. The assumption is that males and females learn to be different.

gender strategies Couples in relationships develop myths—versions of reality that emphasize sharing in order to preserve harmony and camouflage conflict.

gendered Behavior patterned according to sex.

gendered institution Gender is present in the processes, practices, images, ideologies, and distributions of power in the various sectors of social life.

gendered institutions approach Emphasizes the features of social organization that produce gender inequality.

gendered labor Work apportioned according to sex. Traditionally, this has meant that women do the household chores of cooking, cleaning, and child care, while men do yardwork and home repairs.

globalization The process by which the earth's peoples are increasingly interconnected economically, politically, culturally, and environmentally.

godly family The ideal colonial community based on patriarchy. The family was ruled by the father, who had authority over his wife, children, and servants, much as God the Father ruled over His children.

golden age of the family Mythical, idealized image of how the family once was.

graying of America Demographic trend toward an ever-increasing proportion of the population being old.

Head Start A federally funded program to educate disadvantaged preschool children.

"her" marriage Marriage as experienced by the woman.

heterogamy When the partners in a marriage differ on significant social variables, such as race, religion, or social class.

hidden economy Practice by which people work at legitimate occupations but evade taxes.

hidden labor Unpaid household labor performed by wives, which serves to reproduce the paid labor force.

"his" marriage Marriage as experienced by the man.

homogamous marriage A marriage of individuals who share similar social characteristics such as religion, race, age, and social class background.

homogamy When marriage partners are alike in various characteristics, such as race, ethnicity, religion, educational attainment, social class, and age.

homophobia Fear and hatred of homosexuals.

household Residential unit in which members share resources. These units vary in membership and composition. A household is not always a family (parents and children), and a family is not always a household (because it may be separated geographically).

household augmentation The strategy among the poor to double up in households to share expenses.

househusband A husband who stays home to care for the house and family while his wife works for pay outside the home.

human agency Individuals, acting alone or with others, shape, resist, challenge, and sometimes change their social environments.

hypergamy Marriage in which the female marries upward into a higher social stratum.

hypogamy Marriage in which the female marries downward into a lower social stratum.

ideology Shared beliefs about the physical, social, or metaphysical world.

illegitimacy Birth of a child to an unmarried woman.

immigrant analogy Assumption that racial minorities are just like European immigrants in that they will eventually become assimilated.

incest Sexual behaviors between persons so closely related that marriage between them is prohibited by law.

industrialization Process by which societies become increasingly organized around the production of goods and technology by machines.

inflation Situation in which too much money purchases too few goods, resulting in rising prices.

institution Social arrangement that channels behavior in an important area of societal life.

institutional racism Established and customary ways that exclude people of color from full and equal participation in the institutions of the dominant society. This occurs independent of prejudice or discrimination on the part of individuals.

institutional sexism Practice by which the social arrangements and accepted ways of doing things in society disadvantage females.

interaction work The effort by women to sustain communication with their mates.

intergenerational downward mobility Individuals who, when compared to the socioeconomic status of their parents, do not measure up.

internalization In socialization, the process by which society's demands become part of the individual, acting to control his or her behavior.

intimacy Emotionally charged relationship in which the participants are closely connected.

intimate terrorism The type of intimate partner violence—mostly perpetrated by men—characterized by attempt to completely dominate a partner using power and control tactics.

intragenerational downward mobility Individuals who, in the course of their adult lives, decline in socioeconomic status.

irregular economy Goods and services produced in unrecorded establishments to evade taxes.

kin Network of persons who are related by birth, adoption, or marriage.

kin work The work that women do to sustain family (visits, letters, telephone calls, presents, and cards).

latchkey children Children under age 13 who have no adult supervision after school.

latent function Unintended consequence of a social arrangement or social action.

learned helplessness Theory that when individuals perceive that the negative things happening to them are not their fault, they tend to give up trying to change the situation.

lesbian Female whose sexual preference is for someone of the same sex.

life chances   Opportunities throughout one's life cycle to live and experience the good things in society.

lifestyle   Relational patterns around which individuals organize their living arrangements.

machismo (macho)   Stereotypic description of Latino men, referring to male dominance, posturing, physical daring, and an exploitive attitude toward women.

macro level   Large-scale structures and processes of society, including the institutions and the system of stratification.

majority group   Social category in society holding superordinate power and successfully imposing their will on less powerful (minority) groups.

male chauvinism   Exaggerated beliefs about the superiority of the male and the resulting discrimination against females.

male privilege   Advantages and prerogatives that systematically benefit men and are denied to women.

manifest function   Intended consequence of a social arrangement or social action.

marianismo   A traditional socialization of Latina women to accept male domination.

marital contract   Legal document drawn up prior to a marriage, specifying rights and duties of the partners and especially the disposition of property in case of death or divorce.

marital power   Manner in which decision making is distributed between a husband and wife.

marital quality   A concept that refers to a couple's subjective evaluation of their marriage relationship.

marriage   Socially approved sexual union between two persons (monogamy) or more than two (polygamy).

marriage gap   Well educated and affluent couples tend to stay married, while the poor are more likely to divorce.

marriage squeeze   Excess of women at the most marriageable age.

mating gradient   Tendency for males to marry down and for females to marry up in age, education, and social class.

matriarchal family   A family form in which the woman holds the power.

matrix of domination   The systems of inequality (race, class, and gender) in which each of us exists.

micro level   Social organization and process of small-scale social groups.

minority   Social category composed of persons who differ from the majority, are relatively powerless, and are the objects of unfair and unequal treatment.

miscegenation laws   Laws forbidding people of different races from marrying. Abolished by the U.S. Supreme Court in 1967.

misogyny   Hatred of women.

modern family   The nuclear family that emerged in response to the requirements of an urban, industrial society consisting of an intact nuclear household unit with a male breadwinner, his full-time homemaker wife, and their dependent children.

mommy track   The employment of women in work positions that are less difficult but less prestigious, less lucrative, and limited in advancement potential. These positions do make it easier for women to care for their families.

monogamy   Form of marriage in which an individual cannot be married to more than one person at a time.

monolithic family form   Mythical belief that assumes a single, uniform family experience.

monopolistic capitalism   Form of capitalism prevalent in the contemporary United States in which a few large corporations control the key industries, destroying competition and the market mechanisms that would ordinarily keep prices low and help consumers.

moral right   A conservative political movement reacting to social changes that have taken place since World War II, especially in the areas of morality, welfare spending, and the role of women.

mores   Important societal norms, the violation of which results in severe punishment.

mortality rate   Frequency of actual deaths in a population.

mystification   Deliberate misdefinition of a situation.

myth   Idealized version about the way things are or were. These are beliefs that are held uncritically and without examination or scrutiny.

"myth of peaceful progress"   Erroneous belief based on two assumptions: (1) that the diverse groups in society have learned to compromise and live in harmony; and (2) that any group can gain its share of power, prosperity, and respectability merely by playing the game according to the rules.

"network families"   Support network of friends that some single people establish for themselves. These provide a familial alternative to those people without traditional families.

new federalism   Current federal policy of withdrawing monies for social programs for the needy, leaving states and local governments with the responsibility to provide for them.

new poor   Those who are downwardly mobile because their skills are no longer needed. They are much more trapped in poverty than were the "old poor" of previous generations.

no-fault divorce   Laws providing for divorce by mutual consent of the partners.

nonfamily household   Persons who live alone or with unrelated individuals.

norm   Part of culture that refers to rules that specify appropriate and inappropriate behavior; in other words, the shared expectations for behavior.

nuclear family   Kinship unit composed of husband, wife, and children.

nuptiality   The proportion of married persons.

offshoring   When a company moves its production to another country, producing the same products in the same way, but with cheaper labor, lower taxes, and fewer benefits to workers.

old poor   The poor of previous generations, who had more hope of upward mobility than the poor of today; the old poor had the advantages of an expanding economy and a need for unskilled labor.

order model   Conception of society as a social system characterized by cohesion, consensus, cooperation, reciprocity, stability, and persistence.

outsourcing   The offshore sourcing of information-based goods and service.

parachute children   Children who migrate alone, usually to pursue educational opportunities.

paradigm   The basic assumptions that scholars have of the social worlds they study.

parental leave   Policies of businesses that allow their employees to have children, take care of children, and meet emergency home needs without losing their jobs.

participatory socialization   Mode of socialization in which parents encourage their children to explore, experiment, and question.

patriarchal family   Family structure in which the father is dominant.

patriarchal terrorism   Violence initiated by men as a way of gaining and maintaining total control over their female partners.

patriarchy   Social relations in which men are dominant over women.

patriarchy (private)   Male dominance in the interpersonal relations between women and men.

patriarchy (public)   Male dominance in the institutions of the larger society.

pedophilia   Sexual interest in children.

peer group   Friends, usually of the same age and socioeconomic status.

peer marriage   A relationship organized around principles of equity and equality, and characterized by the sharing of economic, household, and child-rearing responsibilities.

pink-collar jobs   Low-status, low-paying jobs reserved primarily for women.

postmodern family   The multiplicity of family and household arrangements that has emerged as a result of a number of social factors, such as women in the labor force, divorce, remarriage, and cohabitation arrangements.

poverty   Standard of living below the minimum needed for the maintenance of adequate diet, health, and shelter.

power   Ability of one person or group to get another person or group to act on its wishes regardless of whether the other person or group agrees to.

prestige   Respect of an individual or social category as a result of social status.

primary group   Small group characterized by intimate, face-to-face interaction.

principle of least interest   Argument that the partner with the least interest in the relationship is the one who is more apt to exploit the other.

privilege   The distribution of goods and services, situations, and experiences that are highly valued and beneficial.

pronatalism   The strong positive value a society places on having children.

psychosocial interference   The transfer of moods from one social setting (e.g., work) to another (e.g., family).

qualitative methods   Research techniques based on subjective analysis.

quantitative methods   Research based on the analysis of numerical data.

quinceanera rites   This Mexican American ritual presents young women on their 15th birthday to the ethnic community as now eligible for marriage.

race   Socially defined category on the basis of a presumed common genetic heritage resulting in distinguishing physical characteristics.

racial-ethnic groups   Groups labeled as "races" by the wider society and bound together by their common social and economic conditions resulting in distinctive cultural and ethnic characteristics.

racial formation   The sociohistorical process by which races are continually being shaped and transformed.

racial stratification   System of inequality in which race is the major criterion for rank and rewards.

racism   Domination and discrimination of one racial group by the majority.

reconstituted family (blended family)   Family form created by a remarriage that involves one or more children from the previous marriage of either spouse.

remarriage   Marriage by anyone who has been previously married.

repressive socialization   Mode of socialization in which parents demand rigid conformity in their children, enforced by physical punishment.

revisionist perspective   New scholarship that challenges the traditional interpretations.

role   Behavioral expectations and requirements attached to a position in a social organization.

role performance (role behavior)   Actual behavior of persons occupying particular positions in a social organization.

sandwich family structure   A type of multigenerational household in which adults take care of their aging parents and their children simultaneously.

sandwich generation   A multigenerational household where adults are taking care of their aging parents and their children simultaneously.

second shift   The term referring to women's responsibilities for housework, child care, and home management that women must do in addition to their labor in the workforce.

secondary group   Large, impersonal, and formally organized group.

segmented labor market   The capitalist economy is divided into two distinct sectors: one in which production and working conditions are relatively stable and secure, the other composed of marginal firms in which working conditions are poor and wages and job security are low.

segregation   Separation of one group from another.

self-fulfilling prophecy   Event that occurs because it was predicted. The prophecy is confirmed because people alter their behavior to conform to the prediction.

sequencing   Adjusting the timing of events over the life course by eliminating or postponing activities in one sphere, either work or family, until a later stage.

severely poor   These families or individuals with incomes below one-half the poverty threshold.

sex-gender system   System of stratification that operates by ranking and rewarding women's and men's roles unequally (see *patriarchy*).

sex ratio   Number of males per 100 females in a population.

sex roles approach   Treats gender differences as learned.

sexism   Individual actions and institutional arrangements that discriminate against women.

sexual behavior   People's sexual acts and activities.

sexual identity   An individual's sexual self-classification as lesbian, gay, bisexual, or straight.

sexual orientation   The sex of those to whom one is attracted.

sexual scripts   Sexual behavior follows scripts that are learned by individuals and reflect society's expectations for appropriate sexual conduct.

sexual stratification   Hierarchical arrangement based on gender.

shared monopoly   Control by four or fewer firms of 50 percent or more of a particular market.

sibling   A brother or sister.

significant others   Those individuals who are most important to a person, such as parents and close friends.

situational couple violence   The type of intimate partner violence—perpetrated by both men and women—that occurs when a couple's conflicts escalate to violence.

social class   Number of persons who occupy the same relative economic rank in the stratification system.

social constructionist approach to families   The assumption that families are shaped by specific historical, social, and material conditions.

social constructionist approach to sexuality   This approach focuses on the social sources of sexuality; it concludes that diverse social arrangements produce variation in sexual desire and practice.

social control   Regulation of human behavior in any social group.

social Darwinism   The belief that the principle of the survival of the fittest applies to human societies, especially the system of stratification.

social differentiation   Process of categorizing persons by some personal attribute.

social inequality   Ranking of persons by wealth, family background, race, ethnicity, or sex.

social interaction   Process by which individuals act toward or respond to each other.

social location   One's position in society based on family background, race, socioeconomic status, religion, sexuality, or other relevant social characteristics.

social mobility   Movement by an individual from one social class or status group to another.

social movement   Collective attempt to promote or resist change.

social organization   Order of a social group as evidenced by the positions, roles, norms, and other constraints that control behavior and ensure predictability.

social production   The varied ways in which people make a living.

social reproduction   The maintenance of life on a daily basis, including food, clothing, shelter, and emotional activity.

social stratification   Ranking of people in a hierarchy that differentiates them as superior or inferior.

social structure   Patterned and recurrent relationships among people and parts of a social organization.

social system   Differentiated group whose parts are interrelated in an orderly arrangement, bound by geographic space or membership.

socialization   Process of learning the culture.

socialization agents   Those individuals, groups, and institutions responsible for transmitting the culture of a society to newcomers.

society   Largest social organization to which individuals owe their allegiance. The entity is located geographically, has a common culture, and is relatively self-sufficient.

socioeconomic status (SES)   The measure of social status that takes into account several prestige factors, such as income, education, and occupation.

sociology   Scholarly discipline concerned with the systematic study of social organizations.

spillover   Carrying over the concerns, responsibilities, and demands of one part of life to another (e.g., the conditions of work that affect family life).

split-shift parenting   When working parents share child care, one parent takes care of the children while the other works.

Standard North American Family (SNAF)   Dorothy Smith's concept for the glorified image of the family with a breadwinner husband and a wife whose primary responsibility is the care of husband, household, and children, even when she works for pay. This pervasive image serves an instrument of control by prescribing family structure in public policy.

status   Socially defined position in a social organization.

stepchild   Child of one's husband or wife by a former marriage.

stepfamily (reconstituted family, blended family, or binuclear family)   The family form created in a remarriage that involves one or more children from the previous marriage of either spouse.

stepparent   Person who occupies the parent role for the children by a former marriage of his or her spouse.

stereotype   Exaggerated generalization about some social category.

stigma   Label of social disgrace.

Stonewall riots   In 1969, after the police raided a gay bar in New York City, the homosexual patrons fought back. This event marks the beginning of the modern gay movement.

structural determinism   View that structural conditions control the destiny of individuals and groups.

structural diversity approach   Assumption that families are shaped by the structure of society (e.g., the availability of work, remuneration for work, opportunities by race and gender).

structural interference   Time constraints imposed by the demands of work and family roles.

structural transformation of the economy   Fundamental change of the economy resulting from powerful contemporary forces: technological breakthroughs in microelectronics, the globalization of the economy, capital flight, and the shift from a manufacturing economy to one based on information and services.

structured social inequality   Patterns of superiority and inferiority, the distribution of rewards, and the belief systems that reinforce the inequalities of society.

subculture   Relatively cohesive cultural system that varies in form and substance from the dominant culture.

sunrise industries   Sectors of economic potential, increased output, and rising employment.

sunset industries   Economic sectors experiencing declining output and employment.

transcultural adoption   When a child of one race or ethnic group is placed with adoptive parents of another race or ethnic group.

transience   Rapid turnover in things, places, and people.

transnational family   Family in which the members are located across national boundaries, but with a pattern of moving back and forth between countries.

transnational motherhood   Mothers live and work in one nation, while their children live in another nation.

transracial adoption   Placing a child of one race or ethnic group with adoptive parents of another race or ethnic group.

underclass   Assumption that the poor have a set of distinctively negative values, psychological attributes, and maladaptive behaviors (see *culture of poverty*).

underemployment   Being employed at a job below one's level of training and expertise.

underground economy   The hidden, irregular, and illegal economies.

undocumented immigrant   Immigrant who has entered the United States illegally.

urbanization   The movement of people from rural to urban areas.

value stretch   People in the lower classes sharing middle-class values but stretching them as they adjust to conditions of deprivation.

values   Shared criteria used in evaluating objects, ideas, acts, feelings, or events as to their relative desirability, merit, or correctness.

venereal diseases   Diseases transmitted by sexual contact.

voluntary childlessness   The decision by some couples not to have children.

welfare   Economic aid provided to those in need by the federal, state, and local governments.

widowhood   Loss of a spouse by death.

work–family interference   The ways in which the connections between jobs and family may be a source of tension for workers and family members.

work–family role system   Traditional uneven division of labor in which men's work role takes priority over the family role, and women, even those who work outside the home, are to give priority to the family role.

Bibliography

Bold entries indicate sources new to this edition.

Aaronson, Daniel, Kyung-Hong Park, and Daniel Sullivan (2006). "The Decline in Teen Labor Force Participation." *Economic Perspectives* (Q1): 2–18. Federal Reserve Bank of Chicago.

Abbott, Pamela, and Claire Wallace (1992). *The Family and the New Right*. London: Pluto Press.

Acker, Joan (1973). "Women and Stratification: A Case of Intellectual Sexism." *American Journal of Sociology* 78 (January): 936–945.

Acker, Joan (1980). "Women and Stratification: A Review of Recent Literature." *Contemporary Sociology* 9 (January): 25–39.

Acker, Joan (1992). "Gendered Institutions: From Sex Roles to Gendered Institutions." *Contemporary Sociology* 21 (September): 565–568.

Acock, Alan C., and David H. Demo (1994). *Family Diversity and Well-Being*. Thousand Oaks, CA: Sage.

Acs, Gregory (2007). Can We Promote Child Well-Being by Promoting Marriage?" *Journal of Marriage and Family* 26 (December): 1326–1344.

Adams, Bert W. (1980). *The Family*. Chicago: Rand McNally.

Aerts, Elaine (1993). "Bringing the Institution Back In." In *Family, Self, and Society: Toward a New Agenda for Family Research*, Philip A. Cowan, Dorothy Field, Donald A. Hansen, Arlene Skolnick, and Guy E. Swanson (eds.). Hillsdale, NJ: Erlbaum, pp. 3–41.

Ahlburg, Dennis A., and Carol J. De Vita (1992). "New Realities of the American Family." *Population Bulletin* 47 (August): entire issue.

Ahrons, Constance (1994). *The Good Divorce: Keeping Your Family Together When Your Marriage Comes Apart*. New York: Harper-Collins.

Aizenman, N. C. (2008). "Report: Hispanics in U. S. to Triple by 2050." *Wichita Eagle* (February 12): 4A.

Albelda, Randy (1992). "Whose Values, Which Families?" *Dollars & Sense* 182 (December): 6–9.

Albelda, Randy, and Heather Boushey (2006). "You Call This Reform?" *AlterNet* (August 24): Online: http://www.alternet.org/story/40732/

Alderman, Leslie (2009). "Uptick in Vasectomies Seen as Sign of Recession." *New York Times* (April 11). Online: http://www.nytimes.com/2009/04/11/health/11patient.html?

Aldous, Joan (1991). "In the Families' Ways." *Contemporary Sociology* 20 (September): 660–662.

Aldous, Joan, and Wilfried Dumon (1991). "Family Policy in the 1980s: Controversy and Consensus." In *Contemporary Families:* *Looking Forward, Looking Back*, Alan Booth (ed.). Minneapolis: National Council on Family Relations, pp. 466–481.

Ali, Lorraine, and Raina Kelley. (2008). "The Curious Lives of Surrogates." *Newsweek* (April 7): 45–51.

Allen, Katherine (1997). "Lesbian and Gay Families." In *Contemporary Parenting: Challenges and Issues*, Terry Arendell (ed.). Thousand Oaks, CA: Sage, pp. 196–218.

Allen, Katherine, and David H. Demo (1995). "The Families of Lesbians and Gay Men: A New Frontier in Family Research." *Journal of Marriage and the Family* 57 (February): 111–127.

Allen, Mike, and Nancy Burrell (1996). "Comparing the Impact of Homosexual and Heterosexual Parents on Children." *Journal of Homosexuality* 32 (2): 19–35.

Allen, Walter P. (1978). "The Search for Applicable Theories of Black Family Life." *Journal of Marriage and the Family* 40 (1): 117–129.

Alternatives to Marriage Project (2003). "Statistics About Unmarried Partners, Cohabitation, Living Together, and Marriage." Online: http://www.unmarried.org/statistics .html.

Alternatives to Marriage Project (2009). Online: http://www.unmarried.org.

Alvirez, David, and Frank D. Bean (1976). "The Mexican-American Family." In *Ethnic Families in America*, Charles H. Mindel and Robert W. Habenstein (eds.). New York: Elsevier, pp. 271–292.

Alwin, Duane F. (2004). "Parenting Practices." In *The Blackwell Companion to the Sociology of Families*, Jacqueline Scott, Judith Treas, and Martin Richards (eds.). Malden, MA: Blackwell, pp. 142–157.

Amato, Paul R. (2001). "The Consequences of Divorce for Adults and Children." In *Understanding Families into the New Millennium: A Decade in Review*, Robert M. Milardo (ed.). Minneapolis: National Council on Family Relations, pp. 1269–1287.

Amato, Paul R. (2004). "Divorce in Social and Historical Context." In *Handbook of Contemporary Families*, Marilyn Coleman and Lawrence H. Ganong (eds.). Thousand Oaks, CA: Sage, pp. 265–281.

Amato, Paul R., and Alan Booth (1996). "A Prospective Study of Divorce and Parent–Child Relationships." *Journal of Marriage and the Family* 58 (May): 356–365.

Amato, Paul R., and Danelle D. DeBoer (2001). "The Transmission of Marital Instability Across Generations." *Journal of Marriage and the Family* 63: 1038–1051.

Amato, Paul R., and Jacob Cheadle (2005). "The Long Reach of Divorce: Tracking Marital Dissolution and Child Well-Being

Across Three Generations." *Journal of Marriage and Family* 67: 191–206.

Amato, Paul R., David R. Johnson, Alan Booth, and Stacy J. Rogers (2003). "Continuity and Change in Marital Quality Between 1980 and 2000." *Journal of Marriage and Family* 65 (February): 1–22.

Amato, Paul R., Alan Booth, David R. Johnson, and Stacy J. Rogers. (2007). *Alone Together: How Marriage in America is Changing.* **Cambridge, MA: Harvard University Press.**

Ambert, Anne-Marie (1992). *The Effect of Children on Parents.* New York: Haworth Press.

American Medical Association (1993). "AMA Diagnostic and Treatment Guidelines on Child Sexual Abuse." *Archives of Family Medicine* **2(1): 19–27.**

American Sociological Association (2003). *The Importance of Collecting Data and Doing Scientific Research on Race.* Washington, DC: American Sociological Association.

AmeriStat (2003c). "Having Children Later or Not at All." Online: http://www.prb.org/AmeristatTemplate.cfm?Section=Fertility&template=/ContentManagement/ContentDisplay.cfm&ContentID=7964

AmeriStat (2003d). "More U.S. Women Outearning Their Husbands." Online: http://www.ameristat.org/Content/NavigationMenu/Ameristat/Topics1/MarriageandFamily/More_U_S_Women_Outearning_Their_Husbands.htm

Ammons, Paul, Josie Nelson, and John Wodarski (1982). "Surviving Corporate Moves: Sources of Stress and Adaptation among Corporate Executive Families." *Family Relations* 32 (April): 207–212.

Amott, Teresa (1993). *Caught in the Crisis: Women and the U.S. Economy Today.* New York: Monthly Review Press.

Amott, Teresa, and Julie Matthaei (1991). *Race, Gender, and Work: A Multicultural Economic History of Women in the United States.* Boston: South End Press.

Andersen, Margaret L. (1997). *Thinking about Women: Sociological Perspectives on Sex and Gender,* 4th ed. Boston: Allyn and Bacon.

Andersen, Margaret L. (2006). *Thinking About Women: Sociological Perspectives on Sex and Gender,* 5th ed. Boston: Allyn and Bacon.

Anderson, Margaret L. (2009). *Thinking About Women,* 8th ed. Boston: Allyn and Bacon.

Andersen, Margaret L., and Patricia Hill Collins, eds. (2007). *Race, Class, and Gender: An Anthology,* 6th ed. Belmont, CA: Wadsworth/Thompson.

Andersen, Margaret L., and Patricia Hill Collins, eds. (2010). *Race, Class, and Gender: An Anthology,* **7th ed. Belmont, CA: Wadsworth/Thompson.**

Andersen, Margaret L., and Patricia Hill Collins (2010). "Systems of Power and Inequality." In Margaret L. Andersen and Patricia Hill Collins, eds. *Race, Class, and Gender: An Anthology.* **Belmont, CA: Wadsworth/Thompson.**

Anderson, Elaine A. (1991). "The Future of Family Policy: A Postscript." In *The Reconstruction of Family Policy,* Elaine A. Anderson and Richard C. Hule (eds.). New York: Greenwood Press, pp. 237–240.

Anderson, Elijah (1990). *Streetwise.* Chicago: University of Chicago Press.

Anderson, Kristin L. (2002). "Perpetrator or Victim? Relationships Between Intimate Partner Violence and Well-Being." *Journal of Marriage and Family* 64 (November): 851–863.

Anderson, Kristin L. (2007). "Who Gets Out? Gender as Structure and the Dissolution of Violent Heterosexual Relationships." *Gender and Society.*

Anderson, Kristin L. (2008). "Is Partner Violence Worse in the Context of Control? *Journal of Marriage and Family* **70 (December): 1157–1168.**

Anderson, Michael A., Paulette Marie Gillig, Marily Sitaker, Kathy McClosky, and Nancy Grigsby (2003). "'Why Doesn't She Just Leave?': A Descriptive Study of Victim Reported Impediments to Her Safety." *Journal of Family Violence* 18 (June): 151–155.

Angel, Ronald J., and Marta Tienda (1982). "Determinants of Extended Household Structure: Cultural Pattern or Economic Need?" *American Journal of Sociology* 87 (6): 1360–1383.

Angier, Natalie (1991). "The Biology of What It Means to Be Gay." *New York Times,* September 1, pp. E1, E4.

Angier, Natalie (2000). "Scientists: DNA Shows Humans Are All One Race," *Denver Post* (August 22): 2A 5A.

Annin, Peter (1996). "Slumbering Around." *Newsweek,* November 4, p. 57.

Aponte, Robert (1991). "Urban Hispanic Poverty: Disaggregation and Exploration." *Social Problems* 38 (November): 516–528.

Aponte, Robert (2006). "Latinos: The Largest and Most Oppressed Minority," In *Race and Human Rights,* Curtis Stokes (ed.). East Lansing, MI: Michigan State University Press.

Appelbaum, Eileen, and Lonnie Golden (2003). "The Failure to Reform the Workday." *Challenge* 46 (January/February): 79–92.

Arendell, Terry (2000). "Conceiving and Investigating Motherhood: The Decade's Scholarship." *Journal of Marriage and the Family* 62 (November): 1192–1207.

Aries, Phillippe (1965). *Centuries of Childhood: A Social History of Family Life.* New York: Knopf and Random House.

Armas, Genaro C. (2000). "Asians, Hispanics Increase in U.S." *Rocky Mountain News,* August 30, p. 34A.

Armour, Stephanie (2003a). "Layoffs Can Stress Family Ties." *USA Today* (June 27): 1B–2B.

Armour, Stephanie (2008a). "Renters Can't Escape Housing Crisis." *USA Today* **(April 2): 1B–2B.**

Armour, Stephanie (2008b). "New Faces Join Ranks of Nation's Homeless." *USA Today* **(June 26): 1B–2B.**

Armour, Stephanie (2009). "More Families Move In Together." *USA Today* **(February 3): 1B–2B.**

Armour, Stephanie, and Michelle Kessler (2003). "USA's New Money-Saving Export-White Collar Jobs." *USA Today* (August): 1B–2B.

Arnett, Jeffrey Jensen (2000). "Emerging Adulthood: A Theory of Development from the Late Teens Through the Twenties," *American Psychologist* 55:469–480.

Arnst, Catherine (2001). "Being a Mother Just Doesn't Pay." *Business Week* (March 12): 22.

Arnst, Catherine (2006). "And Baby Makes ... a Market," *Business Week* (February 27): 100.

Arrighi, Barbara, and David J. Maume (2000). *Journal of Family Issues* 21 (May): 464–487.

Artis, Julie E., and Eliza K. Pavalko (2003). "Explaining the Decline in Women's Household Labor: Individual Change and Cohort Differences." *Journal of Marriage and the Family* 65 (August): 746–761.

Aschenbrenner, Joyce, and Carolyn Hamecdah Carr (1980). "Conjugal Relations in the Context of the Black Extended Family." *Alternative Lifestyles* 3 (4): 463–484.

Astone, Nan Marie (1993). "Thinking about Teenage Child-bearing." Report from the Institute for Philosophy and Public Policy, University of Maryland (Summer): 8–13.

Baber, Kristine M., and Katherine R. Allen (1992). *Women and Families: Feminist Reconstructions.* New York: Guilford Press.

Baca Zinn, Maxine (1975). "Political Familism: Toward Sex Role Equality in Chicano Families."*Aztlan* 6 (1): 13–26.

Baca Zinn, Maxine (1980). "Employment and Education of Mexican American Women: The Interplay of Modernity and Ethnicity in Eight Families." *Harvard Educational Review* 50 (1): 47–62.

Baca Zinn, Maxine (1989). "Family, Race, and Poverty in the Eighties." *Signs: Journal of Women in Culture and Society* 14 (4): 856–874.

Baca Zinn, Maxine (1990). "Family, Feminism, and Race in America." *Gender & Society* 14 (March): 62–86.

Baca Zinn, Maxine (1994). "Feminist Rethinking from Racial Ethnic Families." In *Women of Color in U.S. Society*, Maxine Baca Zinn and Bonnie Thornton Dill (eds.). Philadelphia: Temple University Press, pp. 303–314.

Baca Zinn, Maxine (2000). "Feminism and Family Studies for a New Century." *The Annals of the American Academy of Political and Social Science* 571 (September): 42–56.

Baca Zinn, Maxine, and Barbara Wells (2000). "Diversity within Latino Families: New Lessons for Family Studies." In *Handbook of Family Diversity*, David H. Demo, Katherine R. Allen, and Mark A. Fine (eds.). New York: Oxford University Press, pp. 252–273.

Baca Zinn, Maxine, and Bonnie Thornton Dill (1994). "Difference and Domination." In *Women of Color in U.S. Society*, Maxine Baca Zinn and Bonnie Thornton Dill (eds.). Philadelphia: Temple University Press, pp. 3–12.

Baca Zinn, Maxine, and Bonnie Thornton Dill (1996). "Theorizing Difference from Multicultural Feminism." *Feminist Studies* 22 (Summer): 1–11.

Baca Zinn, Maxine, and D. Stanley Eitzen (1998). "Missing Paradigm Shift in Family Sociology." *Footnotes* (American Sociological Association Newsletter) (January).

Baca Zinn, Maxine, Pierrette Hondagneu-Sotelo, and Michael A. Messner (2004). "Sex and Gender through the Prism of Difference." In *Through the Prism of Difference*, 2nd ed., Maxine Baca Zinn, Pierrette Hondagneu-Sotelo, and Michael A. Messner (eds.). Boston: Allyn and Bacon, pp. 1–8.

Baca Zinn, Maxine, Pierrette Hondagneu-Sotelo, and Michael A. Messner (eds.). (1997). *Through the Prism of Difference: A Sex and Gender Reader*. Boston: Allyn and Bacon.

Bachman, Ronet (1994). *Violence against Women*. Washington, DC: U.S. Department of Justice (NCJ-145325).

Bachman, Ronet, and L. E. Saltzman (1996). "Violence against Women." Rockville, MD: U.S. Department of Justice (NCJ-154348).

Bajaj, Vikas (2009). "Household Wealth Falls by Trillions." *New York Times* (March 13). Online: http://www.nytimes.com/2009/03/13/business/economy/13wealth.html.

Baker, Mike (2009). "Bankruptcies Surge in Spite of Law." Associated Press (April 19).

Bamshad, Michael J., and Steve E. Olson (2003). "Does Race Exist?" *Scientific American* (December): 78–85.

Barash, David P. (2006). "Sex Is Essential, Kids Aren't," *Los Angeles Times* (July 8): Online: http://www.latimes.com/news/opinion/commentary/la-oe-barash10may10,0, 7632432.story?t.

Barlett, Donald L. and James B. Steele. (2005). "The Broken Promise." *Time* (October 31): 33–38.

Barnett, Ola W., Cindy L. Miller-Perrin, and Robin D. Perrin (1997). *Family Violence across the Lifespan*. Thousand Oaks, CA: Sage.

Barnett, Rosalind Chait, and Karen C. Gareis (2006). "Role Theory Perspectives on Work and Family." In *The Work and Family Handbook: Multi-Disciplinary Perspectives and Approaches*, Marcie Pitt-Catsouphes, Ellen Crust Kossek, and Stephen Sweet (eds.). Mahway, NJ:

Barnett, Rosalind Chait, and Karen C. Gareis (2007). "Shift Work, Parenting Behaviors, and Children's Socioemotional Well-Being: A Within-Family Study." *Journal of Family Issues* 28(6): 727–748.

Barone, Michael (2001). "The Many Faces of America." *U.S. News & World Report* (March 19): 18–20.

Barrera, Mario (1979). *Race and Class in the Southwest*. South Bend, IN: University of Notre Dame Press.

Bartels, Diane M. (2004). "Brave New Families: Modern Health Technologies and Family Creation." In *Handbook of Contemporary Families*, Marilyn Coleman and Lawrence H. Ganong (eds.). Thousand Oaks, CA: Sage, pp. 493–505.

Bartfield, Judi (2000). "Child Support and the Postdivorce Economic Well-Being of Mothers, Fathers, and Children." *Demography* 37 (May): 203–213.

Bartholet, E. (1993). *Family Bonds: Adoption and the Practice of Parenting*. New York: Houghton Mifflin.

Bartik, Timothy (2002). "Poverty, Jobs, and Subsidized Employment." *Challenge* 45 (May/June): 100–111.

Barton, Jane Hughes (1994). *Remarriage after 50: What Women, Men and Adult Children Need to Know*. New York: Roger Thomas Press.

Bateson, Mary Catherine (2000). *Full Circles, Overlapping Lives: Culture and Generation in Transition*. New York: Random House.

Batson, Christie D., Zhenchao Qian, and Daniel T. Lichter (2006). "Interracial and Intraracial Patterns of Mate Selection Among America's Diverse Black Populations." *Journal of Marriage and Family* 68 (August): 658–672.

Bawley, Alan (2009). Many in U.S. Cutting Back on Health Care." *Kansas City Star*(March 15): 1A, 7A.

Bazar, Emily (2009). "Most Illegal Immigrants' Kids Legal." *USA Today* (April 15): 3A.

Beales, Jr., Ross W (1991). "The Preindustrial Family (1600–1815)." In *American Families: A Research Guide and Historical Guidebook*, Joseph M. Hawes and Elizabeth I. Nybakken (eds.). Santa Barbara, CA: Greenwood Press, pp. 35–84.

Bean, Frank D., Jennifer Lee, Jeanne Batalova, and Mark Leach (2004). *Immigration and Fading Color Lines in America*. New York: Russell Sage Foundation and Population Reference Bureau.

Beck, Ulrich, and Elizabeth Beck-Gernsheim (2004). "Families in a Runaway World." In *The Blackwell Companion to the Sociology of Families*, Jacqueline Scott, Judith Treas, and Martin Richards (eds.). Malden, MA: Blackwell, pp. 499–514.

Begley, Sharon (2001). "Brave New Monkey." *Newsweek* (January 22): 50–52.

Bell, Alan P., and Martin S. Weinberg (1978). *Homosexualities: A Study of Human Diversity*. New York: Simon & Schuster.

Belsky, Jay (1990). "Infant Day Care, Child Development, and Family Policy." *Society* (July/August): 10–12.

Belsky, Jay (1991). "Parental and Nonparental Child Care and Children's Socioemotional Development." In *Contemporary Families: Looking Forward, Looking Back*, Alan Booth (ed.). Minneapolis: National Council on Family Relations, pp. 122–140.

Belsky, Jay, and John Kelly (1994). *The Transition to Parenthood: How a First Child Changes a Marriage; Why Some Couples Grow Closer and Others Apart*. New York: Delacorte Press.

Benac, Nancy. (2006). "Americans' Views Resolute on Abortion." Associated Press (March 13).

Bengston, Vern L. (2001). "Beyond the Nuclear Family: The Increasing Importance of Multigenerational Bonds." *Journal of Marriage and Family* 63 (February): 1–16.

Bengtson, Vern L., Carolyn Rosenthal, and Linda Burton (1990). "Families and Aging: Diversity and Heterogeneity." In *Handbook of Aging and Social Sciences*, 3rd ed., Robert H. Binstock and Linda K. George (eds.). San Diego, CA: Academic Press, pp. 263–287.

Bengston, Vern L., Alan C. Acock, Katherine R. Allen, Peggye Dilworth Anerson, and David M. Klein (eds.) (2005). *Sourcebook of Family Theories and Research*. Thousand Oaks, CA: Sage Publications.

Berardo, Felix M. (1998). "Family Privacy: Issues and Concepts," *Journal of Family Issues* 19 (January): 4–19.

Berger, Peter L., and Hansfried Kellner (1975). "Marriage and the Construction of Reality." In *Life as Theatre*, Dennis Brissett and Charles Edgley (eds.). New York: Aldine De Gruyter, pp. 219–233.

Berk, Sarah Fenstermaker (1988). "Women's Unpaid Labor: Home and Community." In Women Working, Ann Helton Stromberg and Shirley Harkess (eds.). Mountain View, CA: Mayfield, pp. 287–302.

Bernard, Jessie (1971). "The Paradox of the Happy Marriage." In *Woman in Sexist Society*, Vivian Gornick and Barbara K. Moran (eds.). New York: Basic Books, pp. 145–162.

Bernard, Jessie (1972). *The Future of Marriage*. New York: Bantam Books.

Bernard, Jessie (1984). "The Good Provider Role: Its Rise and Fall." In *Work and Family*, Patricia Voydanoff (ed.). Palo Alto, CA: Mayfield, pp. 43–60.

Bernstein, Nina (2002). "More U.S. Kids Found Living in No Parent Homes." *Denver Post* (July 29): 3A.

Berrol, Selma (1991). "Immigrant Working Class Families." In *American Families: A Research Guide and Historical Handbook*, Joseph M. Hawes and Elizabeth I. Nybakken (eds.). Santa Barbara, CA: Greenwood Press, pp. 319–346.

Bianchi, Suzanne M. (1995). "Changing Economic Roles of Women and Men." In *State of the Union: America in the 1990s*, Vol. 1, Reynolds Farley (ed.). New York: Russell Sage Foundation, pp. 107–154.

Bianchi, Suzanne M. (2000). "Maternal Employment and Time with Children: Dramatic Change or Surprising Continuity?" *Demography* 37 (November): 401–414.

Bianchi, Suzanne M., John P. Robinson, and Melissa A. Milkie (2006). *Changing Rhythms of American Family Life*. New York: Russell Sage Foundation.

Bianchi, Suzanne M., and Daphne Spain (1996). "Women, Work, and Family in America." *Population Bulletin* 51 (December): entire issue.

Bianchi, Suzanne M., and Lynn M. Casper (2000). "American Families." *Population Bulletin* 55 (December): entire issue.

Bianchi, Suzanne M., L. Subaiya, and J. R. Kahn (1999). "The Gender Gap in the Economic Well-Being of Nonresident Fathers and Custodial Mothers." *Demography* 36: 195–203.

Biddlecom, Ann, and Steven Martin (2006). "Childless in America." *Contexts* 5 (Fall): 54.

Billingsley, Andrew (1992). *Climbing Jacob's Ladder*. New York: Simon & Schuster.

Birdwhistell, Ray L. (1980). "The Idealized Model of the American Family." In *Marriage and Family in a Changing Society*, James M. Henslin (ed.). New York: Free Press, pp. 562–567.

Bishaw, Alemayehu, and Jessica Semega (2008). "Income, Earnings, and Poverty Data from the 2007 American Community Survey." American Community Survey Reports ACS-09, U. S. Census Bureau. Washington, DC: U. S. Government Printing Service.

Biskupic, Joan (2003). "Same-Sex Couples Are Redefining Family Law in USA." *USA Today* (February 18): 1A–2A.

Blackwelder, Julia Kirk (1984). *Women of the Depression: Caste and Culture in San Antonio, 1929l–1939*. College Station, TX: Texas A&M University Press.

Blair-Loy, Mary, and Amy S. Wharton (2004). "Organizational Commitment and Constraints on Work-Family Policy Use: Corporate Flexibility Policies in a Global Firm." *Sociological Perspectives* 47(3): 243–267.

Blake, Judith (1989). Family Size and Achievement. Berkeley: University of California Press.

Blake, Judith (1991). "Number of Siblings and Personality." *Family Planning Perspectives* 23 (November/December): 272–274.

Blassingame, John (1977). *Slave Testimony: Two Centuries of Letters, Speeches, Interviews and Autobiographies*. Baton Rouge: Louisiana State University Press.

Blauner, Robert (1972). Racial Oppression in America. New York: Harper & Row.

Block, Sandra (1999). "Living Together? Commit to Contract." *USA Today* (October 15): 3B.

Block, Sandra (2006). "Boomer Inheritances Shrink as Parents Live Longer, Health Care Costs Rise." *USA Today* (June 27): 3B.

Blumberg, Paul M., and P. W. Paul (1975). "Continuities and Discontinuities in Upper-Class Marriages." *Journal of Marriage and the Family* 37 (December): 63–78.

Blumstein, Philip, and Pepper Schwartz (1983). *American Couples: Money, Work, Sex*. New York: William Morrow.

Bogart, Leo (2005). *Over the Edge: How the Pursuit of Youth by Marketers and the Media has Changed American Culture*. Chicago: Ivan R. Dee.

Bogenschneider, Karen, and Tom Corbett (2004). "Building Enduring Family Policies in the 21st Century." In *Handbook of Contemporary Families*, Marilyn Coleman and Lawrence H. Ganong (eds.). Thousand Oaks, CA: Sage, pp. 451–468.

Bohannan, Paul, and Rosemary Erickson (1978). "Stepping In." *Psychology Today* 11 (January): 53–54, 59.

Bolte, Angela (2006). "Do Wedding Dresses Come in Lavender? The Prospects and Implications of Same Sex Marriage." In Susan M. Ross, ed., *American Families Past and Present*. New Brunswick, NJ: Rutgers University Press, pp. 175–190.

Boo, Katherine (2003). "The Marriage Cure: Is Wedlock Really a Way Out of Poverty?" *The New Yorker* (August 18–25): 104–120.

Booth, Alan, and Paul R. Amato (1994). "Parental Gender Role Nontraditionalism and Offspring Outcomes." *Journal of Marriage and the Family* 56 (November): 865–875.

Bosman, Julie (2009). "Newly Poor Swell Lines at Food Banks." *New York Times* (February 20). Online: http://www.nytimes.com/2009/02/20/nyregion/20food.html.

Boston, Rob (2006). "The Top 10 Power Brokers of the Religious Right." *AlterNet*. Online: http://www.alternet.org/ story/ 38467

Boulding, Elise (1983). "Familia Faber: The Family as Maker of the Future." *Journal of Marriage and the Family* 45 (May): 257–266.

Boushey, Heather, and Christian E. Weller. (2005). "What the Numbers Tell Us." In *Inequality Matters: The Growing Divide in America and Its Poisonous Consequences*, James Lardner and David A. Smith (eds.). New York: The New Press, pp. 27–40.

Bradbury, Katherine, and Jane Katz (2005). "Wives' Work and Family Mobility." Federal Reserve Bank of Boston, Public Policy Discussion Papers No. 04-3. Online: www.bos.frb.org/economic/ppdp/2004/ppdp0403.pdf

Bradbury, Thomas N., Frank O. Fincham, and Steven R. H. Beach (2000). "Research on the Nature and Determinants of Marital Satisfaction: A Decade in Review." *Journal of Marriage and the Family* 62 (November): 964–980.

Bramlett, Matthew, and William D. Mosher (2001). *First Marriage Dissolution, Divorce, and Remarriage: Advance Data from Vital and Health Statistics*, No. 323. Hyattsville, MD: National Center for Health Statistics.

Brandon, Emily (2009). "When Retirement Means More Work." *U. S. News & World Report* (May): 40.

Breines, Wini, and Linda Gordon (1983). "The New Scholarship on Family Violence." *Signs* 8 (Spring): 490–531.

Brenner, Johanna, and Barbara Laslett (1986). "Social Reproduction and the Family." In Ulf Hammelstrand (ed.) *The Social Reproduction of Organization and Culture*. Newbury Park, CA: Sage pp. 117–131.

Brewer, Paul, and Clyde Wilcox (2005). "The Polls-Trends: Same-Sex Marriage and Civil Unions." *Public Opinion Quarterly* 69 (Winter): 599–616.

Brewster, Karin W., and Irena Padivac (2006). "No More Kin Care? Changes in Black Mothers' Reliance on Relatives for Child Care, 1977–1994." In *Race, Work and Family in the Lives of African American Families*. Lanham, MD: Rowman & Littlefield, pp. 97–116.

Bridenthal, Renate (1981). "The Family Tree: Contemporary Patterns in the United States." In *Household and Kin*, Amy Swerdlow, Renate Bridenthal, Joan Kelly, and Phyllis Vine (eds.). Old Westbury, NY: Feminist Press, pp. 47–105.

Brown, Brett V., and Sharon Bzostek (2003). *Violence in the Lives of Children*. Child Trends Data Bank Publication #2003-15. Online: http://www.childrensdatabank.org.

Brown, Susan L., and Alan Booth (1996). "Cohabitation versus Marriage: A Comparison of Relationship Quality." *Journal of Marriage and the Family* 58 (August): 668–678.

Brown, Susan L., and Alan Booth (2002). "Stress at Home, Peace at Work: A Test of the Time Bind Hypothesis." *Social Science Quarterly* 83 (December): 905–920.

Brown, Susan L., Gary R. Lee, and Jennifer Roebuck Bulanda (2006). *The Journals of Gerontology Series B: Psychological and Social Sciences* 61:571–579.

Browning, Christopher R., and Edward O. Laumann (1997). "Sexual Contact Between Children and Adults: A Life Course Perspective." *American Sociological Review* 62 (August): 540–560.

Brown-Smith, Naima (1998). "Family Secrets," *Journal of Family Issues* 14 (January): 20–42.

Bruce, Judith, Cynthia B. Lloyd, and Ann Leonard (1995). Introduction to *Families in Focus: New Perspectives on Mothers, Fathers, and Children*. New York: The Population Council.

Bruinsma, Beth H. (2006). "Flexible Families." In *Doing Without: Women and Work After Welfare Reform*, Jane Henrici (ed.) Tucson: University of Arizona Press, pp. 40–63.

Budig, Michelle (2004). "Feminism and the Family." In *The Blackwell Companion to the Sociology of Families*, Jacqueline Scott, Judith Treas, and Martin Richards (eds.). Malden, MA: Blackwell, pp. 416–434.

Bulcroft, Richard, and Jay Teachman (2004). "Ambiguous Constructions: Development of a Childless or Child-Free Life Course." In *Handbook of Contemporary Families*, Marilyn Coleman and Lawrence H. Ganong (eds.). Thousand Oaks, CA: Sage, pp. 116–135.

Bumpass, Larry L. (1990). "What's Happening to the Family? Interactions between Demographic and Institutional Change." *Demography* 27 (November): 483–498.

Bumpass, Larry, and Hsien-Hen Lu (2000a). "Cohabitation: How the Families of U.S. Children are Changing." *Focus* 21 (Spring): 5–8.

Bumpass, Larry, and Hsien-Hen Lu (2000b). "Trends in Cohabitation and Implications for Children's Family Contexts in the United States." *Population Studies* 54: 29–41.

Bunker, B. B., J. M. Zubek, V. J. Vanderslice, and R. W. Rice (1992). "Quality of Life in Dual-Career Families: Commuting versus Single-Residence Couples." *Journal of Marriage and the Family* 54: 339–406.

Burchinal, Margaret R. (1999). "Child Care Experiences and Developmental Outcomes." *The Annals* 563 (May): 73–97.

Burge, Kathleen (2003). "SJC: Gay Marriage Legal in Mass." *The Boston Globe* (November 18). Online: http://www.boston.com/news/local/massachusetts/articles/2003/11/18/sjc_gay_marriage_legal_in_mass/

Buriel, Raymond, and Terri De Ment (1997). "Immigration and Sociocultural Change in Mexican, Chinese, and Vietnamese American Families." In *Immigration and the Family*, Alan Booth, Ann C. Crouter, and Nancy Landale (eds.). Mahwah, NJ: Erlbaum, pp. 165–200.

Burr, Chandler (1993). "Homosexuality and Biology." *Atlantic Monthly* 271 (March): 47–65.

Bush, Kevin Ray, Stephanie A. Bohon, and Hyoun K. Kim (2005). "Adaptation Among Immigrant Families." In *Families and Change: Coping with Stressful Events and Transitions*, 3rd ed., Patrick C. McHenry and Sharon J. Price (eds.), Thousand Oaks, CA: Sage, pp. 307–322.

Business Week (2000a). "The New World of Work." (January 10): 36.

Buss, David M., Todd K. Shackelford, Lee A. Kirkpatrick, and Randy J. Larsen (2001). "A Half Century of Mate Preferences: The Cultural Evolution of Values." *Journal of Marriage and Family* 63 (May): 491–503.

Byrnes, Nanette, and Christopher Palmeri (2009). "Pensions Wage Into Toxic Assets." *Business Week* (April 27): 22.

Caffrey, Margaret M. (1991). "Women and Families." In *American Families: A Research Guide and Historical Handbook*, Joseph M. Hawes and Elizabeth I. Nybakken (eds.). New York: Greenwood Press, pp. 223–258.

California Employment Development Department (2005). "Paid Family Leave." Online: www.edd.ca.gov/fleclaimpf1.htm

Camarillo, Albert (1979). *Chicanos in a Changing Society: From Mexican Pueblos to American Barrios in Santa Barbara and Southern California, 1848–1930*. Cambridge, MA: Harvard University Press.

Campbell, Frances A., and Craig T. Ramey (1994). "Effects of Early Intervention on Intellectual and Academic Achievement: A Follow-up Study of Children from Low-Income Families." *Child Development* 65 (April): 684–698.

Campbell, Jacquelyn C., Linda Rose, Joan Kub, and Daphne Nedd (1998). "Voices of Strength and Resistance: A Contextual and Longitudinal Analysis of Women's Responses to Battering." *Journal of Interpersonal Violence* 13: 743–762.

Campo-Flores, Arian (2008). "A Gay Marriage Surge." *Newsweek*(December 5). Online: http://newsweek.com/id/172399.

Cancian, Francesca M. (1987). *Love in America: Gender and Self Development*. New York: Cambridge University Press.

Caplow, Theodore, Louis Hicks, and Ben J. Wattenberg (2001). *The First Measured Century*. Washington, DC: AEI Press.

Carey, Benedict (2007). "Research Finds Firstborns Gain the Higher I.Q." *New York Times* (June 22). Online: http://www.nytimes.com/2007/06/22/science/22sibling.html?_r=1&oref=slogin&pagewant.

Cargan, Leonard (1984). "Singles: An Examination of Two Stereotypes." In *Family in Transition*, 4th ed., Arlene S. Skolnick and Jerome H. Skolnick (eds.). Boston: Little, Brown, pp. 546–556.

Carlson, Allan (2005). *Fractured Generations*. New Brunswick, NJ: Transaction Publishers.

Carlson, Christopher (1990). *Perspectives on the Family: History, Class, and Feminism*. Belmont, CA: Wadsworth.

Carman, Diane (2000). "No Answer to Divorce Question." *Denver Post* (July 1): B1.

Carr, Lois Green, and Lorena S. Walsh (1979). "The Planter's Wife: The Experience of White Women in Seventeenth-Century Maryland." In *A Heritage of Her Own*, Nancy F. Cott and Elizabeth H. Pleck (eds.). New York: Simon & Schuster, pp. 25–58.

Carrington, Christopher (2002). "Domesticity and the Political Economy of Lesbigay Families." In *Families at Work: Expanding the Bounds*, Naomi Gerstel, Dan Clawson, and Robert Zussman (eds.). Nashville, TN: Vanderbilt University Press, pp. 82–107.

Carroll, Joseph (2007). "Most Americans Approve of Interracial Marriages." *Gallup News Service* (August 16). Online: http://www.gallup.com/poll/28417/Most-Americans-Approve-Interracial-Marriages.aspx.

Casper, Lynne, and Suzanne M. Bianchi (2002). *Continuity and Change in the American Family*. Thousand Oaks, CA: Sage.

Catalano, Shannan (2007). *Intimate Partner Violence in the United States*.

Catalyst (2008). *2008 Catalyst Census of Women Corporate Officers and Top Earners of the Fortune 500*. Online: http://www.catalyst.org/file/241/08_census_cote_jan.pdf.

Caulfield, Minna Davis (1974). "Imperialism, the Family, and Cultures of Resistance." *Socialist Revolution* 20: 67–85.

Center for Reproductive Rights (2003). *Roe v. Wade and the Right to Privacy*, 3rd ed. Online: www.reproductiverights.org/pdf/roeprivacy.pdf

Centers for Disease Control (2009). HIV/AIDS Surveillance Report, 2007. Vol. 19. Online: http://www.cdc.gov/hiv/topics/surveillance/resources/reports/.

Chafetz, Janet Saltzman (1997). "'I Need a Traditional Wife!': Employment-Family Conflicts." In *Workplace/Women's Place*, Dana Dunn (ed.). Los Angeles: Roxbury, pp. 116–123.

Chalk, Rosemary, Alison Gibbons, and Harriet J. Scarupa. (2002). "The Multiple Dimensions of Child Abuse and Neglect: New Insights into an Old Problem." Child Trends Research Brief: Online: http://www.childtrends.org/files/ChildAbuseRB.pdf

Chang, C. Y., and A. M. Wood (1996). "Dual-Career Commuter Marriages: Balancing Commitments to Self, Spouse, Family and Work." Paper presented at the National Conference of the American Counseling Association, Pittsburgh, PA.

Chauhan, Fazeel (2005). "Muslims Not Married in America." *Chowk* (June 28): Online: http://www.chowk.com/show_article.cgi?aid=00005325&channel=chaathouse

Chavez, Leo R. (1992). *Shadowed Lives: Undocumented Immigrants in American Society*. Orlando, FL: Harcourt Brace.

Cheal, David (1991). *Family and the State of Theory*. Toronto: University of Toronto Press.

Cherlin, Andrew J. (1978). "Remarriage as an Incomplete Institution." *American Journal of Sociology* 84 (November): 634–651.

Cherlin, Andrew J. (1981). *Marriage, Divorce, Remarriage*. Cambridge, MA: Harvard University Press.

Cherlin, Andrew J. (1992). *Marriage, Divorce, Remarriage*, revised and enlarged edition. Cambridge, MA: Harvard University Press.

Cherlin, Andrew J. (1999a). "Going to Extremes: Family Structure, Children's Well-Being and Social Science." *Demography* 36 (November): 421–428.

Cherlin, Andrew J. (1999b). *Public and Private Families*. Boston: McGraw-Hill.

Cherlin, Andrew J. (2000). "Generation Ex." *The Nation* (December 11): 62–68.

Cherlin, Andrew J. (2003). "What Do We Know About the Effects of Divorce on Children?" Council on Contemporary Families. Online: http://www.contemporaryfamilies.org/public/fact5.php

Cherlin, Andrew (2004). "The Deinstitutionalization of American Marriage." *Journal of Marriage and Family* 66 (November): 848–861.

Cherlin, Andrew J. (2009). *The Marriage-Go-Round: The State of Marriage and the Family in America Today*. New York: Alfred A. Knopf.

Chevan, Albert (1996). "As Cheaply as One: Cohabitation in the Older Population." *Journal of Marriage and the Family* 58 (August): 656–667.

Chideya, Farai (1999). "A Nation of Minorities: America in 2050." *Civil Rights Digest* 4 (Fall): 35–41.

Children's Defense Fund (1997). *The State of America's Children Yearbook: 1997*. Washington, DC: Children's Defense Fund.

Children's Defense Fund (2001). *The State of America's Children Yearbook: 2001*. Washington, DC: Children's Defense Fund.

Children's Defense Fund (2002). "Child Care Basics." Online: http://www.childrensdefense.org/cc_facts.htm

Children's Defense Fund (2004). *The State of America's Children 2004*. Washington, DC.

Children's Defense Fund (2005). *The State of America's Children 2005*. Online: http://www.childrensdefense.org/site/PageServer

Children's Defense Fund (2008). *The State of America's Children 2008*. Washington, D. C.

ChildStats.gov (2008). "America's Children at a Glance." Online: http://www.childstats.gov/AmericasChildren/glance.asp.

Child Trends (2006). "Facts at a Glance." Child Trends Publication #2006-03. Online: www.childtrends.org/Files/ FAAG2006.pdf

Child Trends (2007). "Dating." Child Trends Data Bank. Online: http://www.childtrends databank.org/pdf/73_PDF.

Child Trends (2008). "Sexually Experienced Teens." *Child Trends Data Bank*. Online: http://www.child trendsdatabank.org/indicators/24SexuallyExperienced Teens.cfm.

Child Trends Data Bank (n.d.). "Family Meals." Online: http://www.childtrendsdatabank.org/indicators/96FamilyMeals.cfm

Child Trends Data Bank (n.d.). "Percent of Children Living in the Home of Their Grandparents: 1970 to 2004." Online: http://www.childtrendsdatabank.org/tables/59_Table_2.htm

Christensen, A., and C. L. Heavey (1990). "Gender and Social Structure in the Demand/Withdraw Pattern of Marital Conflict." *Journal of Personality and Social Psychology* 59: 73–81.

Christensen, Andrew, Kathleen Eldridge, Adriana Bokel Catta-Preta, Veronica R. Lim, and Rossella Santagata (2006). "Cross-Cultural Consistency of the Demand/Withdraw Interaction Pattern in Couples." *Journal of Marriage and Family* 68 (November): 1029–1044.

Christopher, F. Scott, and Tiffani S. Kisler (2004). "Exploring Marital Sexuality: Peeking Inside the Bedroom and Discovering What We Don't Know—But Should!" In *The Handbook of Sexuality in Close Relationships*, John H. Harvey, Amy Wenzel, and Susan Specher (eds.). Mahwah, NJ: Lawrence Erlbaum, pp. 371–384.

Choice, Pamela, and Leanne K. Lamke (1997). "A Conceptual Approach to Understanding Abused Women's Stay/Leave Decisions." *Journal of Family Issues* 18 (May): 290–314.

Chow, Sue (2000). "The Significance of Race in the Private Sphere: Asian Americans and Spousal Preference." *Sociological Inquiry* 70 (1): 1–29.

Christensen, Kathleen (1988). *Women and Home-Based Work*. New York: Henry Holt.

Christensen, Kathleen (2006). "Leadership in Action: A Work and Family Agenda for the Future." In *The Work and Family Handbook: Multi-Disciplinary Perspectives and Approaches,*" Marcie Pitt-Catsouphes, Ellen Ernst Kossek, and Stephen Sweet (eds.). Mahway, NJ: Lawrence Erlbaum, pp. 705–733.

Chu, Kathy (2006). Parents of Teens Ride Waves of Expenses." *USA Today* (May 15): 1B–2B.

Ciabattari, Teresa (2007). "Single Mothers, Social Capital, and Work-Family Conflict." *Journal of Family Issues* 28(1): 34–60.

Clarksberg, Marin, and Phyllis Moen (2001). "Understanding the Time-Squeeze: Married Couples' Preferred and Actual Work-Hour Strategies." *American Behavioral Scientist* 44 (March): 1115–1135.

Coates, Joseph F. (2003). "What is Ahead for Families: Five Major Forces of Change." In *Annual Editions: The Family: 2003/04,* Kathleen R. Gilbert (ed.). Guilford, CT: McGraw-Hill/Dushkin, pp. 197–202.

Cockburn, Alexander (2002). "Blowback: From Unruh to Muhammed." *The Nation* (November 18): 8.

Cody, Cheryl Ann (1983). "Naming, Kinship and Estate Dispersal: Notes on Slave Family Life on a South Carolina Plantation, 1786 to 1833." In *The American Family in Social Historical Perspective*, 3rd ed., Michael Gordon (ed.). New York: St. Martin's Press, pp. 440–458.

Cohen, Phillip N. and Danielle MacCartney (2004). "Inequality and the Family." In *The Blackwell Companion to the Sociology of Families*. Jacqueline Scott, Judith Treas, and Martin Richards (eds.). Blackwell Publishing Ltd, pp. 181–192.

Cohen, Roger (2007). "Twixt 8 and 12, the Tweens." *New York Times* (July 12). Online: http://select.nytimes.com/iht/2007/07/12/opinion/12cohen.html?pagewanted= print.

Cohen, Susan A. (2009). "The Obama Administration's First Budget Proposal Prioritizes Sex Education and Family Planning but Not Abortion Access." *Guttmacher Policy Review* 12(2). Online: http://www.guttmacher.org/pubs/gpr/12/2/gpr120223.html.

Cohen, Theodore F. (1993). "What Do Fathers Provide? *Reconsidering the Economic and Nurturant Dimensions of Men as Parents*." In Men, Work, and Family, Jane Hood (ed.). Newbury Park, CA: Sage, pp. 1–22.

Coker, Donna (1999). "Enhancing Autonomy for Battered Women: Lessons from Navajo Peacemaking." *UCLA Law Review* 47 (1): 39–41.

Coker, Donna (2005). "Shifting Power for Battered Woman Law, Material Resources and Poor Women of Color." In *Domestic Violence at the Margins: Readings on Race, Class, Gender, and Culture*, Natalie J. Sokoloff (ed.). New Brunswick, NJ: Rutgers University Press, pp. 369–388.

Cole, David (1994). "Five Myths about Immigration." *The Nation*, October 17, pp. 410–412.

Coleman, Margaret (1998). "Homemaker vs. Worker in the United States." *Challenge* 41 (November/December): 75–87.

Coleman, Margaret, Lawrence H. Ganong, and Michelle A. Fine (2000). "Reinvestigating Remarriage: Another Decade of Progress." *Journal of Marriage and the Family* 62: 1288–1307.

Coleman, Marilyn and Lawrence H. Ganong (2004). *Handbook of Contemporary Families*. Thousand Oakes, CA: Sage Publications.

Coleman, Marilyn, Lawrence H. Ganong, and Mark Fine (2001). "Reinvestigating Remarriage: Another Decade of Progress." In *Understanding Families into the New Millennium: A Decade in Review*, Robert M. Milardo (ed.). Minneapolis: National Council on Family Relations, pp. 507–526.

Coleman, Marilyn, Lawrence H. Ganong, and Kelly Warzinik (2007). *Family Life in 20th Century America*. Westport, CT: Greenwood Press.

Collier, Jane, Michelle Z. Rosaldo, and Sylvia Yanagisako (1982). "Is There a Family? *New Anthropological Views*." In Rethinking the Family: Some Feminist Questions, Barrie Thorne and Marilyn Yalom (eds.). New York: Longman, pp. 25–39.

Collins, Chuck (2008). "The Visible Hand: Seven Government Actions that Have Worsened Inequality." Dollars

& Sense and United for a Fair Economy, eds. *The Wealth Inequality Reader*. **Boston: Economic Affairs Bureau, pp. 30–36.**

Collins, Chuck, Daniel Fireside, Amy Gluckman, Betsy Leondar-Wrightt, Meizhu Lui, James McBride, Amy Offner, Smiriti Rao, and Adria Scharf (2008). "The Racial Wealth Gap," in *The Wealth Inequality Reader*. Boston: Economic Affairs Bureau, pp. 14–15.

Collins, Chuck, Betsy Leondar-Wright, and Holly Sklar (1999). *Shifting Fortunes: The Perils of the Growing Wealth Gap*. Boston: United for a Fair Economy.

Collins, Patricia Hill (1990). *Black Feminist Thought*. Cambridge, MA: Unwin Hyman.

Collins, Patricia Hill (1997). "Comment on Heckman's 'Truth and Method: Feminist Standpoint Theory Revisited': Where's the Power?" *Signs: Journal of Women in Culture and Society* 22 (2): 375–381.

Collins, Patricia Hill (2000). *Black Feminist Thought: Knowledge, Consciousness, and the Politics of Empowerment*, 2nd ed. New York: Routledge.

Collins, Patricia Hill (2005). *Black Sexual Politics: African Americans, Gender, and the New Racism*. New York: Routledge.

Collins, Randall (1988a). *Sociology of Marriage & the Family*, 2nd ed. Chicago: Nelson-Hall.

Collins, Randall (1988b). "Women and Men in the Class Structure." *Journal of Family Issues* 9 (1) (March): 27–50.

Collins, Randall, and Scott Coltrane (1995). *Sociology of Marriage and the Family*, 4th ed. Chicago: Nelson-Hall.

Coltrane, Scott (1996). *Family Man: Fatherhood, Housework, and Gender Equity*. New York: Oxford University Press.

Coltrane, Scott (1998). *Gender and Families*. Thousand Oaks, CA: Pine Forge Press.

Coltrane, Scott (2000). "Research on Household Labor: Modeling and Measuring the Social Embeddedness of Routine Family Work." *Journal of Marriage and the Family* 62 (November): 1208–1233.

Coltrane, Scott (2004). "Fathering: Paradoxes, Contradictions, and Dilemmas." In *The Handbook of Contemporary Families*, Marilyn Coleman and Lawrence Ganong (eds.). Thousand Oaks, CA: Sage, pp. 224–243.

Coltrane, Scott, and Michele Adams (2008). *Gender and Families*, 2nd ed. Lanham, MD: Rowman and Littlefield.

Coltrane, Scott, and Elsa O. Valdez (1993). "Reluctant Compliance: Work-Family Role Allocation in Dual Earner Chicano Families." In *Men, Work, and Family*, Jane Hood (ed.). Newbury Park, CA: Sage, pp. 151–175.

Confessore, Nicholas (2002). "Swinging Seniors." *The American Prospect* (June 17): 10–11.

Conley, Dalton (2009). *Elsewhere, U. S. A.* New York: Random House.

Conlin, Jennifer (2009). "Living Apart for the Paycheck." *New York Times* (January 4): ST1.

Connell, R. W., D. J. Ashenden, S. Kessler, and G. W. Dowsett (1982). *Making the Difference*. Boston: Allen & Unwin.

Connell, Robert W. (1992). "A Very Straight Gay: Masculinity, Homosexual Experience, and the Dynamics of Gender." *American Sociological Review* 57: 735–751.

Cooney, Teresa M. and Kathleen Dunne. (2004). "Intimate Relationships in Later Life." In *Handbook of Contemporary Families*, Marilyn Coleman and Lawrence H. Ganong (eds.). Thousand Oaks, CA: Sage, pp. 136–152.

Coontz, Stephanie (1992). *The Way We Never Were: American Families and the Nostalgia Trap*. New York: HarperCollins.

Coontz, Stephanie (1997). *The Way We Really Are: Coming to Terms with America's Changing Families*. New York: Basic Books.

Coontz, Stephanie (1999a). "The American Family." *Life* (November): 79–94.

Coontz, Stephanie (1999b). "Introduction." In *American Families: A Multicultural Reader*, Stephanie Coontz, with Maya Polson, and Gabrielle Raley (eds.). New York: Routledge, pp. ix–xxix.

Coontz, Stephanie (2000). "Historical Perspectives on Family Diversity." In *Handbook of Family Diversity*, David H. Demo, Katherine R. Allen, and Mark A. Fine (eds.). New York: Oxford University Press, pp. 15–31.

Coontz, Stephanie (2001). "Historical Perspectives on Family Studies." In *Understanding Families into the New Millennium: A Decade in Review*, Robert Milardo (ed.). Minneapolis: The National Council on Family Relations, pp. 80–94.

Coontz, Stephanie (2002). "Nostalgia and Ideology." *American Prospect* 13 (April 18): 26–27.

Coontz, Stephanie (2005). *Marriage, a History: From Obedience to Intimacy or How Love Conquered Marriage*. New York: Viking Penguin.

Coontz, Stephanie (2007). "New Census Report on Marriage." Council on Contemporary Families List Serve (September 18). Online: http://www.census.gov/population/www/socdemo/marr-div.html.

Coontz, Stephanie (2008a). "Introduction to the Second Edition." In Stephanie Coontz, ed., *American Families: A Multicultural Reader*. New York: Routledge.

Coontz, Stephanie (2008b). "Stepdads are Fathers Too." Council on Contemporary Families Information Sheet (June 15). Online: SMintz@UH.edu.ccf@Listserve .UH.Edu.

Coontz, Stephanie, and Nancy Folbre (2002). "Marriage, Poverty, and Public Policy." Paper presented at the annual meetings of the Council on Contemporary Families (April 26–28). Online: www.contemporaryfamilies.org/ briefing.html

Cooper, Sheila McIssac (1999). "Historical Analysis of the Family." In *Handbook of Marriage and the Family*, 2nd ed., Marvin B. Sussman, Suzanne K. Steinmetz, and Gary W. Peterson (eds.). New York: Plenum Press, pp. 13–38.

Corliss, Richard (2002). "Does Divorce Hurt Kids?" *Time* (January 28): 40.

Cott, Nancy F. (1979). "Eighteenth-Century Family and Social Life Revealed in Massachusetts Divorce Records." In *A Heritage of Her Own: Families, Work, and Feminism in America*, Nancy F. Cott and Elizabeth H. Pleck (eds.). New York: Simon & Schuster, pp. 107–135.

Council on Contemporary Families (2009). "Are Babies Bad for Marriage." Research Update by Stephanie Coontz (January 9).

Cowdery, Randi S., Norma Scarborough, Carmen Knudson-Martin, Gita Seschadri, Monique E. Lewis, and Anne Rankin Mahoney (2009). Gendered Power in Cultural Contexts: Part II. Middle Class African American Heterosexual Couples with Young Children." *Family Process* 48(1): 25–39.

Crane, Mary Lou (1997). "Childhood Sibling Abuse: A Neglected Form of Maltreatment." *Progress: Family Systems Research and Therapy* 6: 27–41.

Crary, David (2005). "Strain of War Hits Home: Army Divorce Rates Soar." Associated Press (June 30).

Crittenden, Ann (2001). *The Price of Motherhood: Why the Most Important Job in the World Is Still the Least Valued.* New York: Metropolitan Books.

Crosby, John F. (1985). *Reply to Myth: Perspectives on Intimacy.* New York: Wiley.

Crowley, Martha (2002). "The National Low Income Housing Coalition." *Poverty and Race* 11 (January/February): 24–26.

Cuber, John F., and Peggy Haroff (1965). *Sex and the Significant Americans.* Baltimore: Penguin Books.

Cuber, John F., Martha Tyler John, and Kenneth S. Thompson (1975). "Should Traditional Sex Modes and Values Be Changed?" In *Controversial Issues in the Social Studies*, Raymond H. Muessig (ed.). Washington, DC: National Council for the Social Studies, pp. 87–121.

Cullen, Lisa Takeuchi (2007). "Till Work Do Us Part." *Time* (October 8): 63–64.

Currie, Elliott (1998). *Crime and Punishment in America.* New York: Metropolitan Books.

Curry, Timothy Jon (1991). "Fraternal Bonding in the Locker Room: A Profeminist Analysis of Talk about Competition and Women." *Sociology of Sport Journal* 8: 119–135.

Curwood, Jennifer Scott (2006). "What Does Sex Ed Have to Do with It?" *Wisconsin State Journal* (April 9): 11.

Dainton, Marianne, and Brooks Aylor (2001). "A Relational Uncertainty Analysis of Jealousy, Trust, and Maintenance in Long-Distance Versus Geographically Close Relationships." *Communication Quarterly* 49 (Spring): 178–188.

Daniels, Arlene Kaplan (1987). *Invisible Careers: Women, Civic Leaders.* Chicago: University of Chicago Press.

Darrah, Charles N., James M. Freeman, and J. A. English-Lueck (2007). *Busier Than Ever!: Why American Families Can't Slow Down.* Stanford, CA: Stanford University Press.

Davis, Robert (1994). "Abuse Knows No Social Boundaries." *USA Today* (June 20): 3A.

Davis, Shannon N., Theodore N. Greestein, and Jennifer P. Gerteisen Marks (2007). "Effects of Union Type on Division of Household Labor: Do Cohabiting Men Really Perform More Housework?" *Journal of Family Issues* 28(9): 1246–1272.

Degler, Carl (1980). *At Odds: Women and the Family in America from the Revolution to the Present.* New York: Oxford University Press.

Deitch, Cynthia H., and Matt L. Huffman (2001). "Family-Responsive Benefits and the Two-Tiered Labor Market." In *Working Families: The Transformation of the American Home*, Rosanna Hertz and Nancy L. Marshall (eds.). Berkeley: University of California Press, pp. 103–130.

Della Cava, Marco R. (2006). "When Mom (or Dad) Moves In." *USA Today* (May 15): 1A–2A.

Della Cava, Marco R. (2009). "Women Step Up as Men Lose Jobs." *USA Today* (March 19): D1–D2.

Dellinger, Walter (2009). "The Historian Who Lived What He Taught." *Washington Post National Weekly Edition* (March 30-April 5): 30.

D'Emilio, John (1996). "Commentary: What Is a Family?" Sociologists' *Lesbian and Gay Caucus Newsletter* (Summer): 3–4.

D'Emilio, John, and Estelle B. Freedman (1988). *Intimate Matters: A History of Sexuality in America.* New York: Harper & Row.

Demo, David H. (2000). "Children's Experience of Family Diversity." *Phi Kappa Phi Journal* 80 (Summer): 16–20.

Demo, David H., and Alan C. Acock (1991). "The Impact of Divorce on Children." In *Contemporary Families: Looking Forward, Looking Back*, Alan Booth (ed.). Minneapolis: National Council on Family Relations, pp. 162–191.

Demo, David H., and Martha J. Cox (2001). "Families with Young Children: A Review of Research in the 1990s." In *Understanding Families in the New Millennium*, Robert M. Milardo (ed.). Minneapolis: National Council on Family Relations, pp. 95–114.

Demo, David H., William S. Aquilino, and Mark A. Fine (2005). "Family Compositions and Family Transitions," In *Sourcebook of Family Theory and Research*, Vern L. Bengston, Alan C. Acock, Katherine R. Allen, Peggye Dilworth Anderson, and David M. Klein (eds.) Sage Publications, pp. 119–136.

Demos, John (1970). *A Little Commonwealth.* New York: Oxford University Press.

Demos, John (1972). "Demography and Psychology in the Historical Study of Family-Life: A Personal Report." In *Household and Family in Past Time*, Peter Laslett and Richard Wall (eds.). Cambridge, UK: Cambridge University Press, pp. 561–570.

Demos, John (1977). "The American Family of Past Time." In *Family in Transition*, 2nd ed., Arlene S. Skolnick and Jerome H. Skolnick (eds.). Boston: Little, Brown, pp. 59–77.

Demos, John (1979). "Images of the American Family, Then and Now." In *Changing Images of the Family*, Virginia Tufte and Barbara Meyerhoff (eds.). New Haven, CT: Yale University Press, pp. 43–60.

Demos, John (1981). "Family Membership in Plymouth Colony." In *Family Life in America*, 1620–2000, Mel Albin and Dominick Cavallo (eds.). St. James, NY: Revisionary Press, pp. 3–13.

Demos, John (1986). *Past, Present, and Personal.* New York: Oxford University Press.

Demos, John, and Virginia Demos (1973). "Adolescence in Historical Perspective." In *The American Family in Social Historical Perspective*, Michael Gordon (ed.). New York: St. Martin's Press, pp. 209–222.

DeNavas-Walt, Carmen, Bernadette D. Proctor, and Cheryl Hill Lee (2006). "Income, Poverty, and Health Insurance Coverage in the United States: 2005." *Current Population Reports*, P60–231. U. S. Census Bureau.

DeNavas-Walt, Carmen, Bernadette D. Proctor, and Jessica C. Smith (2008). "Income, Poverty, and Health Insurance Coverage in the United States:2007. *Current Population Reports*, P60-235. U. S. Census Bureau.

DeParle, Jason (2004). *American Dream: Three Women, Ten Kids, and a Nation's Drive to End Welfare.* New York: Viking.

DeParle, Jason (2009). "Welfare Aid Isn't Growing as Economy Drops Off." *New York Times* (February 2). Online: http://www.nytimes.com/2009/02/02/us/02welfare.html.

Deutsch, Francine M. (1999). *Halving It All: How Equally Shared Parenting Works.* Cambridge, MA: Harvard University Press.

DePaulo, Bella (2006). *Singled Out: How Singles Are Stereotyped, Stigmatized, and Ignored, and Still Live Happily Ever After.* New York: St. Martin's Griffin.

DeVault, Marjorie L. (1991). *Feeding the Family. The Social Organization of Caring as Gendered Work.* Chicago: University of Chicago Press.

Deveny, Kathleen (2003). "We're Not in the Mood." *Newsweek* (June 30): 41–46.

De Vita, Carol J. (1996) "The United States at Mid-Decade." *Population Bulletin* 50 (March): entire issue.

Dex, Shirley (2004). "Work and Families." In *The Blackwell Companion to the Sociology of Families,* Jacqueline Scott, Judith Treas, and Martin Richards (eds.). Malden, MA: Blackwell, pp. 435–456.

di Leonardo, Micaela (1987). "The Female World of Cards and Holidays: Women, Families, and the Work of Kinship." *Signs: Journal of Women in Culture and Society* 12: 440–453.

Dill, Bonnie Thornton (1983). "On the Hem of Life: Race, Class, and the Prospects for Sisterhood." In *Class, Race, and Sex: The Dynamics of Control,* Amy Swerdlow and Hanna Leisinger (eds.). Boston: G. K. Hall, pp. 173–188.

Dill, Bonnie Thornton (1988). "Our Mothers' Grief: Racial Ethnic Women and the Maintenance of Families." *Journal of Family History* 13 (4): 415–431.

Dill, Bonnie Thornton (1994). "Fictive Kin, Paper Sons, and Compadrazgo: Women of Color and the Struggle for Survival." In *Women of Color in U.S. Society*, Maxine Baca Zinn and Bonnie Thornton Dill (eds.). Philadelphia: Temple University Press, pp. 149–169.

Dill, Bonnie Thornton (1998). "Economic Disparity Is Key for Minorities." *Chronicle of Higher Education* (October 2): B7–B8.

Dill, Bonnie Thornton, Maxine Baca Zinn, and Sandra Patton (1993). "Feminism, Race, and the Politics of Family Values." *Report from the Institute for Philosophy and Public Policy,* University of Maryland 13 (Summer): 13–18.

Dobash, Russell P., and R. Emerson Dobash (1979). *Violence against Wives*. New York: Free Press.

Dobbs, Michael (2004). "They Don't Spare the Rod." *Washington Post National Weekly Edition* (March 1–7): 29.

Dodson, Lisa, and Ellen Bravo (2005). "When There is No Time or Money: Work, Family, and Community Lives of Low-Income Families." In Jody Heyman and Christopher Beem (eds.). *Unfinished Work: Building Equality and Democracy in an Era of Working Families.* **New York: The New Press, pp. 122–155.**

Dohm, Arlene, and Lynn Shniper (2007). "Occupational Employment Projections to 2016." *Monthly Labor Review* **130(11): 86–125.**

Domhoff, G. William (1970). *The Higher Circles: The Governing Class in America*. New York: Random House.

Donaldson, Evan B. (2006). Adoption Institute. Online: www.adoptioninstitute.

Dorfman, Dan (2009). "Will the Tanking Economy Ruin Your Sex Life?" *Huffington Post* **(March 30). Online: http://www.alternet.org/story/134205.**

Dorman, Patricia (2001). "Maternity and Family Leave Policies: A Comparative Analysis." *Social Science Journal* 38(2): 189–201.

Dorrington, C. (1995). "Central American Refugees in Los Angeles: Adjustment of Children and Families." In *Understanding Latino Families: Scholarship, Policy, and Practice*, R. Zambrana (ed.). Thousand Oaks, CA: Sage, pp. 107–129.

Douglas-Hall, Ayana, and Heather Koball (2006). "The New Poor." National Center for Children in Poverty. New York: Columbia University.

Douvan, Elizabeth, and Joseph Pleck (1978). "Separation as Support." In *Working Couples*, Robert and Rhona Rapoport (eds.). New York: Harper Colophon, pp. 138–146.

Downey, Douglas B. (1995). "When Bigger Is Not Better: Family Size, Parental Resources, and Children's Educational Performance." *American Sociological Review* 60 (October): 746–761.

Drucker, Peter F. (1993). *The Post-Capitalist Society*. New York: HarperCollins.

Drucker, Peter F. (1999). "Beyond the Information Revolution." *Atlantic Monthly* 284 (October): 47–57.

Drumm, Rene D., Marciana Popescu, and Matt L. Riggs (2009). "Gender Variation in Partner Abuse: Findings from a Conservative Christian Denomination." *Affilia: Journal off Women and Social Work* **24(1): 56–68.**

Dubeck, Paula J. (1998). "The Need and Challenge to Better Integrate Work and Family in the Twenty-First Century." In *Challenges for Work and Family in the Twenty-First Century*, Dana Vannoy and Paula J. Dubeck (eds.). Hawthorne, NY: Aldine de Gruyter, pp. 3–8.

Dunifon, Rachel, and Lori Kowaleski-Jones (2002). "Who's in the House? Race Differences in Cohabitation, Single Parenthood, and Child Development." *Child Development* 73 (August): 1249–1264.

Durose, Matthew R., Caroline Wolf Harlow, Patrick A. Langan, Mark Motivans, Ramona R. Rantala, and Erica L. Smith (2005). *Family Violence Statistics*. Washington, DC: U.S. Department of Justice.

Durr, Marlese and Shirley A. Hill (2006). "The Family-Work Interface in African American Households." In *Race, Work, and Family in the Lives of African American Families***, Marlese Durr and Shirley A. Hill (eds.). Lanham, MD: Rowman and Littlefield, pp. 73–85.**

Dworkin, Andrea (1981). *Pornography: Men Possessing Women*. New York: Perigree Books.

Dworkin, Shari L., and Lucia F. O'Sullivan (2007). "'It's Less Work for Us and It Shows Us She Has Good Taste:' Masculinity, Sexual Initiation, and Contemporary Sexual Scripts." In *The Sexual Self: The Construction of Sexual Scripts***, Michael Kimmel (ed.). Nashville, TN: Vanderbilt University Press, pp. 105–121.**

Dyer, Everett D. (1979). *The American Family: Variety and Change*. New York: McGraw-Hill.

Early, Frances H. (1983). "The French-Canadian Family Economy and Standard of Living in Lowell, Massachusetts, 1870." In *The American Family in Social Historical Perspective*, 3rd ed., Michael Gordon (ed.). New York: St. Martin's Press, pp. 482–503.

Ebeling, Ashlea (2007). "The Second Match." *Forbes* **(November 12): 86–91.**

Eby, Kimberly K. (2004). "Exploring the Stressors of Low-Income Women with Abusive Partners: Understanding Their Needs and Developing Effective Community Responses." *Journal of Family Violence* 19 (August): 221–232.

Eby, L. T., and J. E. Russell (2000). "Predictors of Employee Willingness to Relocate for the Firm." *Journal of Vocational Behavior* 57: 42–61.

Economist (1993). "The Other America." (July 10): 17–18.

***Economist* (2007a). "The Frayed Knot." (May 26): 23–25.**

***Economist* (2007b). "Skipping a Generation." (June 16): 39.**

***Economist* (2009a). "Money in Misery." (February 7): 21–24.**

***Economist* (2009b). "Shelter, or Burden?" (April 18): 76–78.**

Edelman, Peter (1997). "The Worst Thing Bill Clinton Has Done." *Atlantic Monthly* 279 (March): 43–58.

Edgar, Don (2004). "Globalization and Western Bias in Family Sociology." In *The Blackwell Companion to the Sociology of Families*. Jacqueline Scott, Judith Treas, and Martin Richards (eds.). Blackwell Publishing Ltd, pp. 3–16.

Edin, Kathryn (2000a). "Few Good Men." *The American Prospect* (January 3): 26–31.

Edin, Kathryn (2000b). "What Do Low-Income Single Mothers Say About Marriage?" *Social Problems* 47 (1): 112–133.

Edin, Kathryn, and Laura Lein (1997). *Making Ends Meet.* New York: Russell Sage Foundation.

Edin, Kathryn, and Maria Kefalas (2005). *Promises I Can Keep: Why Poor Women Put Motherhood Before Marriage.* Berkeley: University of California Press.

Edwards, Tamala (2000). "Flying Solo." *Time* (August 28): 47–53.

Ehrenreich, Barbara (1997). "When Government Gets Mean: Confessions of a Recovering Statist." *The Nation* (November 17): 11–16.

Ehrenreich, Barbara (2000b). "Will Women Still Need Men?" *Time*, Visions 21 issue (February 21): 62.

Ehrenreich, Barbara, and Arlie Russell Hochschild (2002). "Introduction." In *Global Woman,* Barbara Ehrenreich and Arlie Russell Hochschild (eds.). New York: Metropolitan Books.

Ehrenreich, Barbara, and Diedra English (1978). *For Her Own Good: 150 Years of the Experts' Advice to Women.* Garden City, NY: Doubleday/Anchor.

Ehrenstein, David (2006). "Gay Marriage Gets Even." *Los Angeles Times* (August 8): Online: http://www.latimes .com/news/opinion/commentary/la-oe-ehrenstein8aug08, 0,2343724

Eichler, Margrit (1981). "The Inadequacy of the Monolithic Model of the Family." *Canadian Journal of Sociology* 6 (Summer): 367–388.

Eitzen, D. Stanley (1974). *Social Structure and Social Problems.* Boston: Allyn & Bacon.

Eitzen, D. Stanley (1996). "Dismantling the Welfare State." *Vital Speeches of the Day* 62 (June 15): 532–536.

Eitzen, D. Stanley, and Maxine Baca Zinn (2007). *In Conflict and Order: Understanding Society,* 11th ed. Boston: Allyn and Bacon.

Eitzen, D. Stanley, and George H. Sage (2009). *Solutions to Social Problems: Lessons from State and Local Governments.* Boston: Allyn and Bacon.

Eitzen, D. Stanley, Maxine Baca Zinn, and Kelly Eitzen Smith (2010). *In Conflict and Order*, 12th ed. Boston: Allyn and Bacon.

Elias, Marilyn (2002). "Older Moms' Babies at Health Risk, Study Finds." *USA Today* (March 4): 1D.

Elias, Marilyn (2004). "Marriage Taken to Heart." *USA Today* (March 3): 3D.

Elliot, Sinikka, and Debra Umberson (2004). "Recent Demographic Trends in the U. S. and Implications for Well-Being." In *The Blackwell Companion to the Sociology of Families,* Jacqueline Scott, Judith Treas, and Martin Richards (eds.). Malden, MA: Blackwell, pp. 34–53.

Elliott, Michael (1994/1995). "Forward to the Past." *Newsweek* (December 26/January 2): 130–133.

Elliott, Pam (1996). "Shattering Illusions: Same-Sex Violence." In *Violence in Gay and Lesbian Domestic Partnerships*, Claire M. Renzetti and Charles Harvey Miley (eds.). New York: Harrington Park, pp. 1–8.

Elliott, Sinikka, and Debra Umberson (2008). "The Performance of Desire: Gender and Sexual Negotiation in Long-Term Marriages." *Journal of Marriage and Family* 70 (May): 391–406.

Ellison, Christopher G., and John P. Bartkowski (2002). "Conservative Protestantism and the Division of Household Labor Among Married Couples." *Journal of Family Issues* 23 (November): 950–985.

El Nasser, Haya (2006). "U. S.-Born Hispanics Drive Growth." *USA Today* (May 1): 1A.

El Nasser, Haya, and Lorrie Grant (2005). "Immigration Causes Age, Race Split." *USA Today* (June 9): 1A.

Emmers-Sommer, Tara M. (2004). "The Effect of Communication Quality and Quantity Indicators on Intimacy and Relational Satisfaction." *Journal of Social and Personal Relationships* 21(3): 399–411.

England, Paula (2004). "More Mercenary Mate Selection? Comment on Sweeney and Cancian (2004) and Press (2004)." *Journal of Marriage and Family* 66 (November): 1034–1037.

Epstein, Cynthia Fuchs, Carroll Seron, Bonnie Oglensky, and Robert Saute (2003). "The Family and Part-Time Work." In *Family in Transition*, 12th ed., Arlene S. Skolnich and Jerome H. Skolnick (eds.). Boston: Allyn & Bacon, pp. 335–349.

Epstein, Steven (1994). "A Queer Encounter: Sociology and the Study of Sexuality." *Sociological Theory* 12 (July): 188–202.

Erickson, Gabe (2008). "Military Divorce Rates at 16-Year High." *Minnesota Daily* (University of Minnesota), (December 12). Online: http://www.mndaily.com/2008/12/11/military-divorce-rates-16-year-high.htm.

Escoffier, Jeffrey (2007). "Scripting the Sex: Fantasy, Narrative, and Sexual Scripts in Pornographic Films." In *The Sexual Self: The Constructtion of Sexual Scripts,* Michael Kimmel (ed.). Nashville, TN: Vanderbilt University Press, pp. 61–79.

Eshleman, J. Ross, and Richard A. Bulcroft (2006). *The Family,* 11th ed. Boston: Allyn and Bacon.

Espiritu, Yen Le (1997). *Asian American Women and Men.* New York: Rowman and Littlefield.

Eve, Raymond A., and Donald G. Renslow (1980). "An Exploratory Study of Private Sexual Behaviors among College Students: Some Implications for a Theory of Class Differences in Sexual Behavior." *Social Behavior and Personality* 8 (1): 97–105.

Fackelmann, Kathleeen (2006). "Osteoarthritis Makes Its Move." *USA Today* (June 19): 1D–2D.

Falwell, Jerry (1980). *Listen America.* New York: Doubleday.

Families and Work Institute (2008). "New Study Shows Significant Changes Among Men and Women at Work and at Home." (March 26). Online: www.familiesandwork.org.

Faragher, Johnny, and Christine Stansell (1979). "Women and Their Families on the Overland Trail to California and Oregon, 1842–1868." In *A Heritage of Her Own*, Nancy F. Cott and Elizabeth H. Pleck (eds.). New York: Simon & Schuster, pp. 246–267.

Farber, Bernard (1973). "Family and Community Structure: Salem in 1800." In *The American Family in Social Historical Perspective*, Michael Gordon (ed.). New York: St. Martin's Press, pp. 100–110.

Faust, Kimberly A., and Jerome N. McKibben (1999). In *Handbook of Marriage and the Family,* 2nd ed., Marvin Sussman,

Suzanne K. Steinmetz, and Gary W. Peterson (eds.). New York: Plenum Press, pp. 475–499.

Feagin, Joe R., and Clairese Booher Feagin (1997). *Social Problems: A Critical Power-Conflict Perspective,* 5th ed. Upper Saddle River, NJ: Prentice Hall.

Federal Interagency Forum on Child and Family Statistics (2002). *America's Children: Key National Indicators of Well-Being, 2002.* Washington, DC: U.S. Government Printing Office.

Fenwick, Rudy, and Mark Tausig (2001). "Scheduling Stress: Family and Health Outcomes of Shift Work and Schedule Control." *American Behavioral Scientist* 44 (March): 1179–1198.

Ferguson, Susan (2007). *Shifting the Center: Understanding Contemporary Families,* 3rd ed. New York: McGraw-Hill.

Fernandez-Kelly, M. Patricia (1990). "Delicate Transactions, Gender, Home, and Employment among Hispanic Women." In *Uncertain Terms,* Gaye Ginsberg and Anna Lowenhaupt Tsing (eds.). Boston: Beacon Press.

Ferree, Myra Marx (1987). "Family and Job for Working-Class Women: Gender and Class Systems Seen from Below." In *Families and Work,* Naomi Gerstel and Harriet Engel Gross (eds.). Philadelphia: Temple University Press, pp. 289–301.

Ferree, Myra Marx (1991). "Feminism and Family Research." In *Contemporary Families: Looking Forward, Looking Back,* Alan Booth (ed.). Minneapolis: National Council on Family Relations, pp. 103–121.

Fetterman, Mindy (2006). "Retirement Unfolds in Five Stages for Healthy Boomers." *USA Today* (June 26): 1B–2B.

Fetterman, Mindy, Sandra Block, and John Waggoner (2006). "Navigating the 5 Phases of Retirement." *USA Today* (June 26): 5B.

Fields, Jason (2004). "America's Families and Living Arrangements." *Current Population Reports,* P20-553. Washington, DC: U.S. Bureau of the Census.

Fields, Jason, and Lynne M. Casper (2001). "America's Families and Living Arrangements: March 2000." *Current Population Reports,* P20-537. Washington, DC: U.S. Bureau of the Census.

Figart, Deborah M., and Ellen Mutari (1998). "Degendering Work Time in Comparative Perspective: Alternative Policy Frameworks." *Review of Social Economy* 56: 460–480.

Fine, Mark A., Lawrence H. Ganong, and David H. Demo (2005). "Divorce as a Family Stressor." In *Families and Change,* 3rd ed., Patrick C. McKenry and Sharon J. Price (eds.). Thousand Oaks, CA: Sage, pp. 227–252.

Finkelhor, David (1993). "Epidemiological Factors in the Clinical Identification of Child Sexual Abuse." *Child Abuse and Neglect* 17: 67–70.

Finkelhor, David, and Larry Baron (1986). "High-Risk Children." In *A Sourcebook on Child Sexual Abuse,* David Finkelhor (ed.). Newbury Park, CA: Sage, pp. 60–88.

Fireside, Daniel (2009). "Not Just Homeowners, But Renters Are Really Getting Screwed." *Dollars & Sense* (March 19). Online: http://www.alternet.org/ story/131384.

Fishman, Katharine Davis (1992). "Problem Adoptions." *Atlantic Monthly* 270 (September): 37–69.

Fishman, Pamela M. (1978). "Interaction: The Work Women Do." *Social Problems* 25 (April): 397–406.

Flanigan, Caitlin (2003). "The Wifely Duty," *Atlantic Monthly* (January/February): 171–182.

Fleck, Carole (2009). "All Under One Roof." *AARP Bulletin* (May): 24–25.

Folbre, Nancy (2000). "Universal Childcare: It's Time." *The Nation* (July 3): 21–23.

Forbes (2000). "Forbes 400 Richest in America, 1999." Online at: http://www.forbes.com/lists/home.jhtml?passListId=54& passyear=1999&PassListType=Person

Forbes. (2005). "The Forbes 400." (October 10): 89–320.

Forry, Nicole D., Leigh A. Leslie, and Bethany L. Letiecq (2007). "Marital Quality in Interracial Relationships: The Role of Sex Role Ideology and Perceived Fairness." *Journal of Family Issues* 28(12): 1538–1552.

Foster, John Bellamy (2006). "The Household Debt Bubble." *Monthly Review* 58 (May): 1–11.

Fowler, Ray (2008). "Statistics on Living Together Before Marriage." *Children and Marriage* (April 18). Online: RayFowler.org/2008/04/18/statistics-on-living-together-before-marriage.

Fowlkes, Martha R. (1987). "The Myth of Merit and Male Professional Careers." In *Families and Work,* Naomi Gerstel and Harriet Engel Gross (eds.). Philadelphia: Temple University Press, pp. 347–360.

Fowlkes, Martha R. (1994). "Single Worlds and Homosexual Lifestyles: Patterns of Sexuality and Intimacy." In *Sexuality across the Life Course,* Alice S. Rossi (ed.). Chicago: University of Chicago Press, pp. 151–184.

Fox, Greer Litton, Michael L. Benson, Alfred A. DeMaris, and Judy Van Wyk (2002). "Economic Distress and Intimate Violence: Testing Family Stress and Resource Theories." *Journal of Marriage and Family* 64 (August): 793–807.

Fox, Maggie (2002). "U.S. Falls Behind in Sex Education, Study Finds." Reuters News Service (April 26).

Franklin, Donna L. (1997). *Enduring Inequality: The Structural Transformation of the African American Family.* New York: Oxford University Press.

Frazier, E. Franklin (1939). *The Negro Family in the United States.* Chicago: University of Chicago Press.

Frey, William H. (2002). "'Multilingual America." *American Demographics* 24 (July/August): 20–23.

Frey, William H., Bill Abresch, and Jonathan Yeasting (2001). *America by the Numbers.* New York: New Press.

Fried, Mindy, and Claire Reinelt (1993). "A Family Policy for All Kinds of Families." *Social Policy* 23 (Summer): 64–71.

Friedman, Thomas L. (2005). *The World Is Flat.* New York: Farrar, Straus, and Geroux.

Fuchs, Rachel (1984). *Abandoned Children.* Albany: State University of New York Press.

Funderberg, Lise (2003). "Why We Break Up With Our Siblings," In *Annual Editions: The Family 2003/2004,* Kathleen R. Gilbert (ed.). Guilford, CT: McGraw-Hill/Dushkin, pp. 118–120.

Funk, Allie, and Margaret McLean Hughes (1996). "Shift Work and Child Care." In *Women and Work: A Handbook,* Paula J. Dubek and Katherine Borman (eds.). New York: Longman, pp. 406–407.

Furstenberg, Frank F., Jr. (1990). "Divorce and the American Family." *Annual Review of Sociology* 16: 379–403.

Furstenberg, Frank F., Jr. (1996). "The Future of Marriage." *American Demographics* 18: 34–40.

Furstenberg, Frank F., Jr. (1999). "Is the Modern Family a Threat to Children's Health?" *Society* 36 (July/August): 31–37.

Furstenberg, Frank F., Jr. (2000). "The Sociology of Adolescence and Youth in the 1990s: A Critical Commentary." *Journal of Marriage and the Family* 62 (November): 896–910.

Furstenberg, Frank F., Jr. (2001). "A Sociology of Adolescence and Youth in the 1990s." In *Understanding Families into the New Millennium*, Robert M. Milardo (ed.). Minneapolis: National Council on Family Relations, pp. 115–129.

Furstenberg, Frank F., Jr. (2003). "Teenage Childbearing as a Public Issue and Private Concern." *Annual Review of Sociology* 29:23–39.

Furstenberg, Frank F., Jr. (2004). "Mixed Messages on Marriage." Online: http://www.contemporaryfamilies.org.

Furstenberg, Frank F., Jr., and Andrew J. Cherlin (1991). *Divided Families: What Happens to Children When Parents Part*. Cambridge, MA: Harvard University Press.

Furstenberg, Frank F., Jr., and Julien O. Teitler (1994). "Reconsidering the Effects of Marital Disruption." *Journal of Family Issues* 15 (June): 173–190.

Gagnon, John (1983). "On the Sources of Sexual Change." In *Promoting Sexual Responsibility and Preventing Sexual Problems*, George W. Albee, Sol Gordon, and Harold Leitenberg (eds.). Hanover, NH: University Press of New England, pp. 157–170.

Gagnon, John H., and William Simon (1973). *Sexual Conduct: The Social Sources of Human Sexuality*. **Chicago: Aldine.**

Gaines, S. O., Jr., and Ickes, W. (1997) "Perspectives on Interracial Relationships." In *Handbook of Personal Relationships: Theory, Research and Interventions*. S. Duck (ed.). Chichester: Wiley, pp. 197–220.

Galinsky, Ellen (1986). "Family Life and Corporate Policies." In *Support of Families*, Michael Yogman and T. Berry Brazelton (eds.). Cambridge, MA: Harvard University Press.

Galinsky, Ellen (2001). "Toward a New View of Work and Family Life." In *Working Families: The Transformation of the American Home*, Rosanna Hertz and Nancy L. Marshall (eds.). Berkeley: University of California Press, pp. 207–226.

Galinsky, Ellen, and James T. Bond (1996). "Work and Family: The Experiences of Mothers and Fathers in the U.S. Workforce." In *The American Woman, 1996–97*, Cynthia Costello and Barbara Kivimae Krimgold (eds.). New York: Norton, pp. 79–103.

Galvin, Kathleen M., and Bernard J. Brommel (1999). *Family Communication: Cohesion and Change*, 5th ed. New York: Longman.

Gandel, Stephen, and Paul J. Lim (2008). "What Do I Do Now? *Money* **(November): 89–91.**

Gans, Herbert J. (1962). *The Urban Villagers*. New York: Free Press.

Gans, Herbert J. (1990). "Second Generation Decline." *Ethnic Racial Studies* 15: 173–192.

Garcia, Mario T. (1980). "La Familia: The Mexican Immigrant Family, 1900–1930. In *Work, Family, Sex Roles, Language*, Mario Barrera, Alberto Camarillo, and Francis Hernandez (eds.). Berkeley: Tonativa-Quinto Sol International, pp.117–140.

Gardner, Marilyn (2009). "Adult Children Back in the Nest." *Christian Science Monitor* **(February 24). Online: http://www.csmonitor.com/2009/0224/p17s02-lifp.html.**

Garey, Anita (1999). *Weaving Work and Motherhood*. Philadelphia: Temple University Press.

Garey, Anita, and Karen Hansen (1998). "Introduction: Analyzing Families with a Feminist Sociological Imagination." In *Families in the U.S.: Kinship and Domestic Politics*. Philadelphia: Temple University Press, pp. xii–xv.

Gates, Gary J. (2007). "Geographic Trends Among Same-Sex Couples in the U. S. Census and the American Community Survey." The Williams Institute. Online: http://repositories.cdlib.org/uclalalw/williams/census/gates_1.

Gaylord, Maxine (1979). "Relocation and the Corporate Family: Unexplored Issues." *Social Work* 24 (May): 186–191.

Gecas, Viktor, and Monica A. Seff (1991). "Families and Adolescents." In *Contemporary Families: Looking Forward , Looking Back*, Alan Booth (ed.). Minneapolis: National Council on Family Relations, pp. 208–225.

Gelles, Richard J. (1976). "Demythologizing Child Abuse." *The Family Coordinator* 24 (April) 135–141.

Gelles, Richard J. (1977). "No Place to Go: The Social Dynamics of Marital Violence." In *Battered Women*, Maria Roy (ed.). New York: Van Nostrand, pp. 46–62.

Gelles, Richard J. (1990). "Domestic Violence and Child Abuse." In *Violence: Patterns, Causes, and Public Policy*, Neil Alan Weiner, Margaret A. Zahn, and Rita J. Sagi (eds.). San Diego: Harcourt, Brace, Jovanovich.

Gelles, Richard J. (1993). "Family Violence." In *Family Violence: Prevention and Treatment*, Robert J. Hampton, Thomas P. Gullotta, Gerald R. Adams, Earl H. Potter, and Roger P. Weissberg (eds.). Newbury Park, CA: Sage.

Gelles, Richard J. (1995). *Contemporary Families: A Sociological View*. Thousand Oaks, CA: Sage.

Gelles, Richard J. (1997). *Intimate Violence in Families*, 3rd ed. Thousand Oaks, CA: Sage Publications.

Gelles, Richard J., and Claire Pedrick Cornell (1990). *Intimate Violence in Families*, 2nd ed. Newbury Park, CA: Sage.

Gelles, Richard J., and Murray A. Straus (1979). "Determinants of Violence in the Family." In *Contemporary Theories About the Family*, Vol. 1, Wesley R. Burr, Reuben Hill, F. Ivan Nye, and Ira L. Reiss (eds.). New York: Free Press, pp. 549–581.

Gelles, Richard J., and Murray A. Straus (1988). *Intimate Violence*. New York: Simon & Schuster.

Gelles, Richard J., Regina Lackner, and Glenn D. Wolfner (1994). "Men Who Batter: The Risk Markers." *Violence Update* 4 (August): 1–2, 4, 10.

Gelman, David (1992). "Born or Bred?" *Newsweek* (February 24): 46–53.

Genovese, Eugene D. (1981). "Husbands and Fathers, Wives and Mothers during Slavery." In *Family Life in America, 1620–2000*, Mel Albin and Dominick Cavello (eds.). New York: Revisionary Press, pp. 237–251.

Gerson, Kathleen (1993). *No Man's Land*. New York: Basic Books.

Gerson, Kathleen, and Jerry A. Jacobs (2001). "Changing the Structure and Culture of Work: Work and Family Conflict, Work Flexibility, and Gender Equity in the Modern Workplace." In *Working Families: The Transformation of the American Home*, Rosanna Hertz and Nancy L. Marshall (eds.). Berkeley: University of California Press, pp. 207–226.

Gerson, Kathleen, and Jerry A. Jacobs (2004). "The Work-Home Crunch." *Contexts* 3(4): 29–37.

Gerstel, Naomi R. (1977). "The Feasibility of Commuter Marriage." In *The Family: Functions, Conflicts, and Symbols*, Peter J. Stein, Judith Richman, and Natalie Hannon (eds.). Reading, MA: Addison-Wesley, pp. 357–365.

Gerstel, Naomi (2000). "The Third Shift: Gender and Care Work Outside the Home." *Qualitative Sociology* **23(4): 467–483.**

Gerstel, Naomi, and Harriet Engel Gross (1987a). "Commuter Marriage: A Microcosm of Career and Family Conflict." In *Families and Work*, Naomi Gerstel and Harriet Engel Gross (eds.). Philadelphia: Temple University Press, pp. 222–233.

Gerstel, Naomi, and Harriet Engel Gross (eds.) (1987b). *Families and Work*. Philadelphia: Temple University Press.

Gerstel, Naomi, and Natalia Sarkisian (2006a). "Sociological Perspectives on Families and Work: The Import of Gender, Class, and Race." In *The Work and Family Handbook: Multi-Disciplinary Perspectives and Approaches*, Marcie Pitt-Catsouphes, Ellen Ernst Kossek, and Stephen Sweet (eds.). Mahwah, NJ: Lawrence Erlbaum, pp. 237–265.

Gerstel, Naomi, and Natalia Sarkisian (2006b). "Marriage: The Good, the Bad, and the Greedy." *Contexts* 5(4): 16–21.

Gerstel, Naomi, and Natalia Sarkisian (2008). "The Color of Family Ties: Race, Gender, and Extended Family Involvement." In *American Families: A Multicultural Reader*, Stephanie Coontz (ed.). New York: Routledge, pp. 146–152.

Gerstel, Naomi, Dan Clawson, and Robert Zussman (2002). "Preface." In *Families at Work: Expanding the Bounds*, Naomi Gerstel, Dan Clawson, and Robert Zussman (eds.). Nashville, TN: Vanderbilt University Press, pp. vii–viii.

Giarrusso, Roseann, Merrel Silverstein, and Du Feng (2000). "Psychological Costs and Benefits of Raising Grandchildren." In *To Grandmother's House We Go and Stay*, Carole B. Cox (ed.). New York: Springer, pp. 71–90.

Gibbs, Nancy (2006). "The Magic of the Family Meal." *Time* (June 12): 51–54.

Gibbs, Nancy (2009). "Thrift Nation." *Time* (April 27): 20–27.

Giddens, Anthony (1992). *The Transformation of Intimacy: Sexuality, Love, and Eroticism in Modern Societies*. Stanford, CA: Stanford University Press.

Gilgun, Jane F. (1995). "We Shared Something Special: The Moral Discourse of Incest Perpetrators." *Journal of Marriage and Family* 57 (May): 265–281.

Gillis, John R. (1996). *A World of Their Own Making*. Cambridge, MA: Harvard University Press.

Gladin, Howard (1977). "Private Lives and Public Order: A Critical View of the History of Intimate Relations in the United States." In *Close Relationships*, George Levinger and Harold L. Rauch (eds.). Amherst: University of Massachusetts Press, pp. 33–72.

Glenn, Evelyn Nakano (1983). "Split Household, Small Producer and Dual Wage Earner: An Analysis of Chinese-American Family Strategies." *Journal of Marriage and the Family* 45 (1) (February): 35–46.

Glenn, Evelyn Nakano (1987). "Racial-Ethnic Women's Labor: The Intersection of Race, Gender and Class Oppression." In *Hidden Aspects of Women's Work*, Christine Bose, Roslyn Feldberg, and Natalie Sokoloff with the Women and Work Research Group (eds.). New York: Praeger, pp. 46–73.

Glenn, Evelyn Nakano (1992). "From Servitude to Service Work: Historical Continuities in the Racial Division of Paid Reproductive Labor." *Signs: Journal of Women in Culture and Society* 18 (1) (Autumn): 1–43.

Glenn, Evelyn Nakano (1994). "Social Construction of Mothering." In *Mothering, Ideology, Experience, and Agency*, Evelyn Nakano Glenn, Grace Chang, and Linda Rennie Forey (eds.). New York: Routledge, pp. 1–29.

Glenn, Evelyn Nakano (2002). *Unequal Freedom: How Race and Gender Shaped American Citizenship and Labor*. Cambridge, MA: Harvard University Press.

Glenn, Evelyn Nakano, with Stacey G. H. Yap (1992). "Chinese American Families." In *Minority Families in the United States: Comparative Perspectives*, Ronald L. Taylor (ed.). Englewood NJ: Prentice Hall.

Glenn, Norval D. (1996). "Values, Attitudes, and the State of American Marriage." In *Promises to Keep: Decline and Renewal of Marriage in America*, David Popenoe, J. B. Elshtain, and David Blankenhorn (eds.). Lanham, MD: Rowman and Littlefield, pp. 15–34.

Glenn, Norval D. (1997). "A Critique of Twenty Family and Marriage Textbooks." *Family Relations* 46 (July): 197–208.

Glenn, Norval D. (1998). "The Course of Marital Success and Failure in Five American 10-Year Marriage Cohorts." *Journal of Marriage and the Family* 60 (August): 569–576.

Glick, Jennifer E. (1999). "Economic Support From and To Extended Kin: A Comparison of Mexican Americans and Mexican Immigrants." *International Migration Review* 33 (Fall): 745–765.

Goffman, Erving (1959). *The Presentation of Self in Everyday Life*. Garden City, NY: Doubleday.

Goldscheider, Frances K., and Linda J. Waite (1991). *New Families, No Families? The Transformation of the American Home*. Berkeley: University of California Press.

Gonzalez-Lopez, Gloria (2005). *Erotic Journeys: Mexican Immigrants and Their Sex Lives*. Berkeley: University of California Press.

Goode, William J. (1963). *World Revolution and Family Patterns*. New York: Free Press.

Goode, William J. (1971). "Force and Violence in the Family." *Journal of Marriage and the Family* 33 (November): 624–636.

Goode, William J. (1983). "World Revolution in Family Patterns." In *Family in Transition*, 4th ed., Arlene Skolnick and Jerome Skolnick (eds.). Boston: Little, Brown, pp. 43–52.

Goodman, Ellen (1995). "Now We're Against Paying for Welfare and Abortions." *Coloradoan* (January 20): A8.

Goodman, Ellen (2002). "'Magical Thinking' Links Welfare Reform, Marriage." *Rocky Mountain News* (March 9): p. 5B.

Goodman, Peter S., and Jack Healy (2009). "660,000 Jobs Lost: Total Surpases 5 Million." *New York Times* (April 4): A1, A10.

Gordon, Michael (ed.) (1983). *The American Family in Social-Historical Perspective*. New York: St. Martin's Press.

Gordon, Milton (1964). *Assimilation in American Life: The Role of Race, Religion, and National Origins*. New York: Oxford University Press.

Gordon, Tula (1994). *Single Women: On the Margins?* New York: New York University Press.

Goreman, Patricia (2005). "Making Ends Meet: The Complex Household as a Temporary Survival Strategy among New Latino Immigrants to Virginia." *Complex Ethnic Households in America*, Laurel Schwede, Rae Lesser Blumberg, and Anna Y. Chan (eds.). Lanham, MD: Rowman and Littlefield, pp. 149–189.

Gorman, Anna (2007). "Immigrants' Children Grow Fluent in English, Study Says." *Los Angeles Times* (November 30). Online: http://www.latimes.com/news/local/la-me-english30nov30,0,1163558.story?coll=la-hom-center.

Gorman, Christine (1991). "Are Gay Men Born That Way?" *Time* (September 9): 60–61.

Gormley, William T., Jr. (2005). "The Universal Pre-K Bandwagon." *Phi Delta Kappan* 87 (November): 246–249.

Gorner, Peter (2006). "Equality Equates to Better Sex Life." *Chicago Tribune Online Edition* (April 19). Online: www-news.uchicago.edu/citations/06/060419.sex-ct.html

Gornick, Janet C., and Marcia K. Meyers (2001). "Support for Working Families: What the United States Can Learn from Europe." *American Prospect* 12 (January 1): 3–7.

Gosselin, Peter G. (2005). "Corporate America Pulling Back Pension Safety Net." *Los Angeles Times* (May 15). Online: http://www.latimes.com/business/specials/lal-na-risk151505,1,6671136,print.story?coll=.

Gottman, J., and R. W. Levenson (1999). "Dysfunctional Marital Conflict: Women Are Being Unfairly Blamed." *Journal of Divorce and Remarriage* 31 (3/4): 1–17.

Gover, Angela R., Catherine Kaukinen, and Kathleen A. Fox (2008). *Journal of Interpersonal Violence* 23(12): 1667–1693.

Gowen, Annie (2009). "Looking for Love: Immigrants' Children Seek Partners of Their Own Ethnicity to Date and, Perhaps Marry." *Washington Post National Weekly Edition* (March 16): 35.

Grabill, Wilson H., Clyde V. Kiser, and Pascal K. Whelpton (1973). "A Long View." In *The American Family in Social-Historical Perspective*, Michael Gordon (ed.). New York: St. Martin's Press, pp. 374–396.

Graff, E. J. (2002). "The Other Marriage War." *American Prospect* (April 8): 50–53.

Grall, Timothy S. (2006). "Custodial Mothers and Fathers and Their Child Support: 2003." U. S. Census Bureau. Online: www.census.gov/prod/2006pubs/p60-230.pdf.

Granrose, Cherlyn Skromme (1996). "Planning to Combine Work and Childbearing." In *Women and Work: A Handbook*, Paula J. Dubek and Katherine Borman (eds.). New York: Longman, pp. 401–403.

Green, Jennifer (2005). "Spain Legalizes Same-Sex Marriage." *Washington Post* (July 1): A14.

Greenberg, Susan H., and Karen Springen (2000). "Back to Day Care." *Newsweek* (October 16): 61–62.

Greenberger, Ellen, and Laurence Steinberg (1986). *When Teenagers Work: The Psychological and Social Costs of Adolescent Employment*. New York: Basic Books.

Greenhouse, Linda (2003). "Justices, 6–3, Legalize Sexual Conduct in Sweeping Reversal," *New York Times* (June 27). Online: http://www.nytimes.com/2003/06/27 .gays.html

Greenhouse, Steven (2009). *The Big Squeeze: Tough Times for the American Worker*. New York: Anchor Books.

Greenstein, Theodore N. (2000). "Economic Dependence, Gender, and the Division of Labor in the Home: A Replication and Extension." *Journal of Marriage and the Family* 62 (May): 322–335.

Greenwald, John (1999). "Elder Care: Making the Right Choice." *Time* (August 30): 52–56.

Gregory, Sean (2009). "Inside the Cocoon." *Time* (April 13): 59–60.

Greven, Phillip J. (1970). *Four Generations: Population, Land, and Family in Colonial Andover, Mass.* Ithaca, NY: Cornell University Press.

Greydanus, Donald E., Helen Pratt, C. Richard Spates, Anne E. Blake-Dreher, Marissa A. Greydanus-Gearhart, and Dilip R. Patel (2003). "Corporal Punishment in Schools." *Journal of Adolescent Health* 32(5): 385–393.

Grier, Peter (2009). "Ten Ways the New Economy Will Look Different." *Christian Science Monitor* (April 10). Online: http://www.csmonitor.com/2009/0412/p13501-usec.html.

Griffith, James, and Sandra Villavicienco (1985). "Relationships among Acculturation, Sociodemographic Characteristics, and Social Supports in Mexican American Adults." *Hispanic Journal of Behavioral Science* 7: 75–92.

Griswold del Castillo, Richard (1984). *La Familia*. South Bend, IN: University of Notre Dame Press.

Gross, Daniel (2008). "The New American Dream Isn't American." *Newsweek* (May 26): 30.

Gross, Daniel (2009). "The Quitter Economy." *Newsweek* (February 2): 31–32.

Gross, Harriet Engel (1984). "Dual-Career Couples Who Live Apart." In *Framing the Family*, Bert N. Adams and John L. Campbell (eds.). Prospect Heights, IL: Waveland Press, pp. 468–482.

Grossman, Lev (2005). "Grow Up? Not So Fast." *Time* (January 24): 42–53.

Grosswald, Blanche (2002). "'I Raised My Kids on the Bus': Transit Shift Workers' Coping Strategies for Parenting." *Journal of Sociology and Social Welfare* 29 (September): 29–49.

Groves, M. M., and D. M. Horn-Winegerd (1991). "Commuter Marriages: Personal, Family, and Career Issues." *Sociology and Social Research* 75 (4): 212–217.

Grundy, Lea, and Netsy Firestein (1997). *Work, Family, and the Labor Movement*. Cambridge, MA: Radcliffe Public Policy Institute.

Gruver, Deb (2006). "High Rates Likelier for Minorities." *Wichita Eagle* (June 1): 1A, 5A.

Guendelman, Sylvia (2003). "Immigrant Families." In *All Our Families: New Policies for a New Century*, 2nd ed., Mary Ann Mason, Arlene Skolnick, and Stephen D. Sugarman (eds.). New York: Oxford University Press, pp. 244–264.

Guo, Guang, and Kathleen Mullan Harris (2000). "The Mechanisms Mediating the Effects of Poverty on Children's Intellectual Development." *Demography* 37 (November): 431–447.

Gutman, Herbert (1976). *The Black Family in Slavery and Freedom, 1750–1925*. New York: Pantheon.

Gutman, Herbert (1983). "Persistent Myths about the Afro-American Family." In *The Family in Social-Historical Perspective*, Michael Gordon (ed.). New York: St. Martin's Press, pp. 458–470.

Haas, Linda (1999). "Families and Work." In *Handbook of Marriage and the Family*, 2nd ed., Marvin B. Sussman, Suzanne K. Steinmetz, and Gary Peterson (eds.). New York: Plenum, pp. 571–612.

Haberman, Clyde (2000). "NYC: Tips for Two Newly Parted by Their Jobs." *New York Times*, Archive (January 7).

Hacker, Andrew (1996). "The Racial Income Gap." In *The Meaning of Difference*, Karen E. Rosenblum and Toni-Michelle C. Travis. New York: McGraw-Hill, pp. 308–314.

Hacker, Andrew (2003). *Mismatch: The Growing Gulf Between Women and Men*. New York: Scribners.

Halgunseth, Linda Citlali (2004). "Continuing Research on Latino Families: El Pasado y el Futuro." In *Handbook of*

Contemporary Families, Marilyn Coleman and Lawrence H. Ganong (eds.). Thousand Oaks, CA: Sage pp. 333–351.

Halle, David (1984). *America's Working Man*. Chicago: University of Chicago Press.

Halpern, Diane (2005). "How Time-Flexible Work Policies Can Reduce Stress, Improve Health, and Save Money." *Stress and Health* 21: 157–168.

Hamburg, David A. (1993). "The American Family Transformed." *Society* 31 (January/February): 60–69.

Handlin, Oscar (1951). *The Uprooted*. Boston: Little, Brown.

Hansen, Karen V. (2005). *Not So Nuclear Families: Class, Gender, and Networks of Care*. New Brunswick, NJ: Rutgers University Press.

Hareven, Tamara K. (1975). "Family Time and Industrial Time." *Journal of Urban History* 1 (May): 365–389.

Hareven, Tamara K. (1976a). "Modernization and Family History: Perspectives on Social Change." *Signs: Journal of Women in Culture and Society* 2: 190–206.

Hareven, Tamara K. (1976b). "Women and Men: Changing Roles." In *Women and Men: Changing Roles, Relationships, and Perceptions*, Libby A. Cater, Anne Firor Scott, and Wendy Martyna (eds.). Queenstown, MD: Aspen Institute for Humanistic Studies, pp. 93–118.

Hareven, Tamara K. (1977). *Family and Kin in Urban Communities, 1700–1930*. New York: New Viewpoints.

Hareven, Tamara K. (1987). "Historical Analysis of the Family." In *Handbook of Marriage and the Family*, Marvin B. Sussman and Suzanne K. Steinmetz (eds.). New York: Plenum, pp. 37–57.

Hareven, Tamara K., and Maris A. Vinovskis (eds.) (1978). *Introduction to Family and Population in Nineteenth-Century America*. Princeton, NJ: Princeton University Press.

Harms, William (2006). "Gender Equality Leads to Better Sex Lives Among People 40 and Over." University of Chicago News Office (April 19). Online: www-news.uchicago.edu/releases/06/060419.sex.shtml.

Harris, Kathleen Mullan (1996). "The Reforms Will Hurt, Not Help, Poor Women and Children." *Chronicle of Higher Education* (October 4): 37.

Harry, Joseph (1983). "Gay Male and Lesbian Relationships." In *Contemporary Families and Alternative Lifestyles*, Eleanor D. Macklin and Roger H. Rubin (eds.). Beverly Hills, CA: Sage, pp. 216–234.

Hartley, Shirley Foster (1973). "Our Growing Problem: Population." *Social Problems* 21 (Fall).

Hartmann, Heidi I. (1981). "The Family as the Locus of Gender, Class, and Political Struggle: The Example of Housework." *Signs: Journal of Women in Culture and Society* 6 (3): 366–394.

Haskins, Cora (2003). "Treating Sibling Incest Using a Family Systems Approach." *Journal of Mental Health Counseling* 25(4): 337–350.

Hassouneh, Dena, and Nancy Glass (2008). "The Influence of Gender Role Stereotyping on Women's Experiences of Female Same-Sex Intimate Partner Violence." *Violence Against Women* 14(3): 310–325.

Hattery, Angela J., and Earl Smith (2007). *African American Families*. Los Angeles: Sage.

Hawes, Joseph M., and Elizabeth M. Nybakken (eds.) (2001). "Introduction." In *Family and Society in American History*. Urbana, IL: University of Illinois Press, pp. 1–8.

Hayes, Cherly D., John L. Palmer, and Martha J. Zaslow (eds.) (1990). *Who Cares for America's Children? Child Care Policy for the 1990s*. Washington, DC: National Academy Press.

Hays, Sharon (2003). *Flat Broke with Children: Women in the Age of Welfare Reform*. New York: Oxford University Press.

Health and Health Care in Schools (2001). "American Academy of Pediatrics Takes Position on School Condom Programs." (June). Online: www.healthinschools/org/ejournal/june01_1htm

Healy, Jack (2009). "Jobless Rate Hits 8.5% After 663,000 Jobs Lost in March." *New York Times* (April 4). Online: http://www.nytimes.com/2009/0404/business/economy/04jobs.html.

Healy, James R. (2006). "Oil Hits $70 a Barrel for the First Time." *USA Today* (April 18): 1B.

Healy, Melissa (1997). "Welfare 'Family Caps' Fail Test." *Denver Post* (September 12): 23A.

Healy, Michelle (2002). "Living Together Doesn't Mean Marriage," *USA Today* (November 20): 9D.

Heard, Holly (2007). "The Family Structure Trajectory and Adolescent School Performance: Difference Affected by Race and Ethnicity." *Journal of Family Issues* 28 (March): 319–354.

Heaton, Tim B. (1986). "How Does Religion Influence Fertility? The Case of Mormons." *Journal of the Scientific Study of Religion* 25: 248–258.

Heaton, Tim B. (1990). "Marital Stability Throughout the Child-Rearing Years." *Demography* 27 (February): 55–63.

Heaton, Tim B. (2002). "Factors Contributing to Increasing Marital Instability in the United States." *Journal of Family Issues* 23 (April): 392–409.

Heaton, Tim B., Karen Davis Boyd, Kennion D. Jolley, and Brent C. Miller (1996). "Influences of Children's Number, Age, Relatedness, Gender, and Problems on Parental and Marital Relationships." *Family Perspectives* 30 (2): 131–159.

Heaton, Tim B., and Cardell K. Jacobson (2000). "Intergroup Marriages: An Examination of Opportunity Structures," *Sociological Inquiry* 70 (Winter): 30–41.

Heins, Marjorie (2001). "Sex, Lies, and Politics." The Nation (May 7): 20–23.

Heintz, James, and Nancy Folbre (2000). *The Ultimate Field Guide to the U.S. Economy*. New York: New Press.

Helburn, Suzanne W. (1999). "The Silent Crisis in U.S. Child Care." *The Annals* 563 (May): 8–19.

Helburn, Suzanne W., and Barbara R. Bergman (2002). *America's Child Care Problem: The Way Out*. New York: Pallgrave.

Heller, Celia (1966). *Mexican American Youth: Forgotten Youth at the Crossroads*. New York: Random House.

Henretta, James A. (1973). *The Evolution of American Society, 1780–1815*. Lexington, MA: Heath.

Herbert, Bob (1996). "Taking Scissors to the Safety Net." *Rocky Mountain News* (December 14): 68A.

Herbert, Bob (1997a). "3:00, Nowhere to Go." *New York Times* (October 26): 15.

Herbert, Bob (2000b). "Working Harder, Longer." *New York Times* (September 4). Online: http://nytimes.com/library/opinion/herbert/090400herb.html

Herbert, Bob (2009a). "Reviving the Dream." *New York Times* (March 10). Online: http://www.nytimes.com/2009/03/10/opinion/10herbert.html,

Herbert, Bob (2009b). "Children in Peril." *New York Times* (April 21). Online: http://www.nytimes.com/2009/04/21/opinion/21herbert.html.

Herbert, Bob (2009c). "Far From Over." *New York Times* (May 9). Online: http://www.nytimes.com/2009/05/05/opinion09herbert.html.

Herbert, Tracy Bennett, Roxane Cohen Silver, and John H. Ellard (1991). "Coping with an Abusive Relationship: I: How and Why Do Women Stay?" *Journal of Marriage and Family* 53 (May): 311–325.

Herbert, Wray (1999). "Not Tonight Dear." *U.S. News & World Report* (February 22): 57–59.

Herman, Judith, and Lisa Hirschman (1981). *Father–Daughter Incest*. Cambridge, MA: Harvard University Press.

Herring, Cedric (2006). "Is Discrimination Dead?" In *Race, Work, and Family in the Lives of African Americans*, Marese Durr, and Shirley A. Hill (eds.). Lanham, MD: Rowman and Littlefield, pp. 3–11.

Herrnstein, Richard J., and Charles Murray (1994). *The Bell Curve: Intelligence and Class Structure in American Life*. New York: Free Press.

Hertzberg, Hendrik (2006). "Comment." *The New Yorker* (July 19): 29–30.

Hetherington, E. Mavis (2002). "Marriage and Divorce American Style." *American Prospect* (April 8): 62–63.

Hetherington, E. Mavis, and John Kelly (2002). *For Better or Worse*. New York: Norton.

Hetherington, E. Mavis, and Margaret Stanley-Hagan (2000). "Diversity among Stepfamilies." In *Handbook of Family Diversity*, David H. Demo, Katherine R. Allen, and Mark A. Fine (eds.). New York: Oxford University Press, pp. 173–196.

Hewlett, Sylvia Ann (1991). *When the Bough Breaks: The Cost of Neglecting Our Children*. New York: Basic Books.

Hewlett, Sylvia Ann (2002). *Creating a Life: Professional Women and the Quest for Children*. New York: Miramax Books.

Hewlett, Sylvia Ann, and Cornel West (1998). *The War against Parents: What We Can Do for America's Beleaguered Moms and Dads*. Boston: Houghton Mifflin.

Heyl, Barbara (1996). "Homosexuality: A Social Phenomena." In *The Meaning of Difference*, Karen E. Rosenblum and Toni-Michelle C. Travis (eds.). New York: McGraw-Hill, pp. 120–129.

Heymann, Jody. (2006). *Forgotten Families: Ending the Growing Crisis Confronting Children and Working Parents in the Global Economy*. New York: Oxford University Press.

Higginbotham, Elizabeth (1981). "Is Marriage a Priority?" In *Single Life: Unmarried Adults in Social Context*, Peter J. Stein (ed.). New York: St. Martin's Press, pp. 259–267.

Higginbotham, Elizabeth (2001). *Too Much to Ask: Black Women in the Era of Integration*. Chapel Hill: University of North Carolina Press.

Higginbotham, Elizabeth, and Margaret L. Andersen (2005). "Introduction." In Race and Ethnicity in Society, Elizabeth Higginbotham and Margaret L. Andersen (eds). Belmont, CA: Wadsworth.

Higginbotham, Elizabeth, and Margaret L. Andersen, eds. (2009). *Race and Ethnicity in Society: The Changing Landscape*. Belmont, CA: Wadsworth Cengage.

Hightower, Jim (2007). "Subprime Loans=Primetime for Vampire Lenders." *Hightower Lowdown* (August 22): 1.

Hill, Robert B. (1977). *Informal Adoption among Black Families*. Washington, DC: National Urban League Research Department.

Hill, Robert B. (1993). *Research on the African American Family*. Westport, CT: Auburn House.

Hill, Shirley A. (2005). *Black Intimacies: A Gender Perspective on Families and Relationships*. Thousand Oaks, CA: Alta Mira Press.

Himes, Christine L. (2001). "Elderly Americans." *Population Bulletin* 56 (December): entire issue.

Hirsch, Jennifer (2003). *Courtship After Marriage: Sexuality and Love in Mexican Transnational Families*. Berkeley: University of California Press.

Hobbs, Frank B., with Bonnie L. Damon (1996). "65+ in the United States." *Current Population Reports*, Series P23-290.

Hochschild, Arlie Russell (1975) "Inside the Clockwork of Male Careers." In *Women and the Power to Change*, Florence Howe (ed.). New York: McGraw-Hill, pp. 47–80.

Hochschild, Arlie Russell (1983a). "Attending to, Codifying and Managing Feelings: Sex Differences in Love." In *Feminist Frontiers*, Laurel Richardson and Verta Taylor (eds.). Reading MA: Addison-Wesley, pp. 250–262.

Hochschild, Arlie Russell (1983b). *The Managed Heart*. Berkeley: University of California Press.

Hochschild, Arlie Russell (1997). *The Time Bind*. New York: Metropolitan Books.

Hochschild, Arlie Russell (2000). "The Nanny Chain." *American Prospect* (January 3): 32–36.

Hochschild, Arlie Russell, with Anne Machung (1989). *The Second Shift*. New York: Viking Penguin, 1989.

Holahan, Catherine (2009). "The Real Unemployment Rate? Try 15.6%." *MSN Money* (April 3). Online: http://articles.moneycentral.msn.com/learnl-howo-to-invest/the-real-unemployment-rate.aspx.

Holland, Joshua (2006). "Prosperity in George Bush's Economy." *AlterNet* (January 6). Online: http://www.alternet.org/module/printversion/30447

Holmes, Mary (2004). "An Equal Distance? Individualization, Gender, and Intimacy in Distance Relationships." *Sociological Review* 52(2): 180–200.

Holstein, James A., and Jay Gubrium (1999). "What Is Family? Further Thoughts on a Social Constructionist Approach." *Marriage and Family Review* 28 (3/4): 3–20.

Hondagneu-Sotelo, Pierrette (1992). "Overcoming Patriarchal Constraints: The Reconstruction of Gender Relations among Mexican Immigrant Women and Men." *Gender & Society* 6 (September): 393–415.

Hondagneu-Sotelo, Pierrette (1994). *Gendered Transitions: Mexican Experiences of Immigration*. Berkeley: University of California Press.

Hondagneu-Sotelo, Pierrette (1995). "Women and Children First: New Directions in Anti-Immigrant Politics." *Socialist Review* 25 (1): 169–190.

Hondagneu-Sotelo, Pierrette (2001). *Domestica*. Berkeley: University of California Press.

Hondagneu-Sotelo, Pierrette, and Ernestine Avila (1996). "Transnational Motherhood: The Means of Spatial and Temporal Separations." (Unpublished manuscript.)

Hondagneu-Sotelo, Pierrette, and Ernestine Avila (1997). "I'm Here, But I'm There: The Meanings of Latina Transnational Motherhood." *Gender & Society* 11 (October): 548–571.

Hondagneu-Sotelo, Pierrette, and Michael A. Messner (1994). "Gender Display and Men's Power: The 'New Man' and the Mexican Immigrant Man." In *Theorizing Masculinities*, Harry Brod and Michael Kaufman (eds.). Newbury Park, CA: Sage, pp. 200–218.

Hooyman, N. R., and H. A. Kiyak (2002). *Social Gerontology*, 6th ed. Boston: Allyn and Bacon.

Hopkins, Jim (2006). "Egg-Donor Business Booms on Campuses." *USA Today* (March 16): 1A–2A.

Hopkins, Jim. (2005). "Wal-Mart Family Funds Causes, Candidates Backing Tax Cuts." *USA Today* (April 6): 1B–2B.

Horowitz, Bruce (2009). "A Year Later, Small Cuts Have Changed to Big Ones: Families Adjust Their Lifestyles During Recession." *USA Today* (March 19): 1A–2A.

Houseknecht, Sharon K., and Jaya Sastry (1996). "Family 'Decline' and Child Well-Being." *Journal of Marriage and the Family* 58 (August): 726–739.

Hovedt, M. E. (1982). "Life Adaptations." In *Homosexuality: Social, Psychological, and Biological Issues*. W. Paul, J. Weinrich, J. C. Gonsiorek, and M. E. Hovedt (eds.). Beverly Hills, CA: Sage, pp. 288–289.

Howe, Louise Kapp (1972). *The Future of the Family*. New York: Simon & Schuster.

Huber, Joan (1993). "Gender Role Change in Families: A Macro-Sociological View." In *Family Relations: Challenges for the Future*, Timothy H. Brubaker (ed.). Newbury Park, CA: Sage, pp. 41–58.

Hughes, Diane, Ellen Galinsky, and Anne Morris (1992). "The Effect of Job Characteristics on Marital Quality: Specifying Linking Mechanisms." *Journal of Marriage and the Family* 54 (February): 31–42.

Hulbert, Ann (2004). "Tweens 'R' Us." *New York Times Magazine* (November 28): 31–32.

Hull, Kathleen E. (2006). *Same-Sex Marriage: The Cultural Politics of Love and Law*. New York: Cambridge University Press.

Human Rights Campaign Foundation (2000). *The State of the Workplace for Lesbian, Gay, Bisexual, and Transgendered Americans*. Washington, DC: Human Rights Campaign Foundation.

Human Rights Campaign (2003). "Frequently Asked Questions on Domestic Partner Benefits." Online: http://www.hrc .org/worknet/dp/fed_overview.asp

Human Rights Campaign (2009a). "Domestic Partner Benefits." Online: http://www.hrc.org/issues/domestic_ partner_benefits.htm.

Human Rights Campaign (2009b). "Marriage Equality and Other Relationship Recognition Laws." Online: http://www.hrc.org/maps.

Human Rights Campaign (2009c). "The State of the Workplace for Lesbian, Gay, Bisexual and Transgender Americans, 2007-2008. Online: gyyp://www.hrc.org.

Hume, Deborah K., and Robert Montgomery (2001). "Facial Attractiveness Signals Different Aspects of Quality in Women and Men." *Evolution and Human Behavior* 22: 93–112.

Hunter, Andrea G. (2006). "(Re)Envisioning Cohabitation: A Commentary on Race, History, and Culture." In Marlese Durr and Shirley A. Hill (eds.). *Race, Work, and Family Life in the Lives of African Americans*. Lanham, MD: Rowman & Littlefield.

Hunter, A. G., and M. E. Ensminger (1992). "Diversity and Fluidity in Children's Living Arrangements." *Journal of Marriage and the Family* 54: 418–426.

Hurtado, A. (1995). "Variations, Combinations, and Evolutions: Latino Families in the United States." In *Understanding Latino Families*, R. E. Zambrana (ed.). Thousand Oaks, CA: Sage, pp. 40–61.

Huston, Ted L., and Heidi Melz (2004). "The Case for (Promoting) Marriage: The Devil Is in The Details." *Journal of Marriage and Family* 66 (November): 943–958.

Hutter, Mark (1981). *The Changing Family*. New York: Wiley.

Hutter, Mark (1991). "Immigrant Families in the City." In *The Family Experience*, Mark Hutter (ed.). New York: Macmillan, pp. 170–177.

Hyman, Batya (2000). "The Economic Consequences of Child Sexual Abuse for Adult Lesbian Women." *Journal of Marriage and Family* 62 (February): 199–211.

Hyman, Rebecca (2008). "America's Frightening Alzheimer's Epidemic." *AlterNet* (May 16). Online: http://www .alternet.org/story/85532/

Iglitzen, Lynne B. (1972). *Violent Conflict in American History*. San Francisco: Chandler.

Imber-Black, Evan (2000). "The Power of Secrets." In *Annual Editions: Marriage and the Family 2000/2001*, Kathleen R. Gilbert (ed.). Guilford, CT: Dushkin/McGraw-Hill, pp. 216–219.

Internal Revenue Service (2009). *Tax Guide for Seniors*, Publication 554. Washington, DC: U.S. Department of the Treasury.

Ishii-Kuntz, Masako (2000). "Diversity within Asian American Families." In *Handbook of Family Diversity*, David H. Demo, Katherine R. Allen, and Mark A. Fine (eds.). New York: Oxford University Press, pp. 274–292.

Ishii-Kuntz, Masako (2004). "Asian American Families: Diverse History, Contemporary Trends, and the Future." *The Handbook of Contemporary Families*, Marilyn Coleman and Lawrence H. Ganong (eds.). Thousand Oaks, CA: Sage.

Island, David, and Patrick Letellier (1991). *Men Who Beat the Men Who Love Them: Battered Gay Men and Domestic Violence*. New York: Harrington Park Press.

Jackson, Anita P., Ronald P. Brown, and Karen E. Patterson-Stewart (2000). "African Americans in Dual-Career Commuter Marriages." *The Family Journal: Counseling and Therapy for Couples and Families* 8 (January): 23–36.

Jackson, Patrick G. (1983). "On Living Together Unmarried: Awareness Contexts and Social Interaction." *Journal of Family Issues* 4 (March): 35–39.

Jackson, Stevi (2007). "The Sexual Self in Late Modernity." In *The Sexual Self: The Construction of Sexual Scripts*, Michael Kimmel (ed.). Nashville, TN: Vanderbilt University Press, pp. 3–15.

Jacobs, Jerry A., and Kathleen Gerson (1998). "Who Are the Overworked Americans?" *Review of Social Economy* 56 (Winter): 442–459.

Jacobs, Jerry A., and Kathleen Gerson (2004). *The Time Divide: Work, Family and Gender Inequality*. Boston: Harvard University Press.

Jacoby, Jeff (2001). "Threat Posed by Same-Sex Unions All Too Real." *Rocky Mountain News* (August 18): 4B.

Jagger, Alison M., and Paula S. Rothenberg (1984). *Feminist Frameworks*. New York: McGraw-Hill.

Jaipon, Sharon (2008). "Sex Education: There Appears to be Little Connection Between What Teens are Taught and Their Behavior." *USA Today* (September 8): 4D.

James, Kerrie, and Laurie MacKinnon (1990). "The 'Incestuous Family' Revisited: A Critical Analysis of Family Therapy Myths." *Journal of Marital and Family Therapy* 16 (January): 71–88.

Jarrett, Robin (1994). "Living Poor: Family Life among Single Parent African American Women." *Social Problems* 41 (February): 30–49.

Jarrett, Robin, and Linda Burton (1999). "Dynamic Dimensions of Family Structure in Low-Income African American Families." *Journal of Comparative Family Studies* 30 (Spring); 177–187.

Jayson, Sharon. (2005). "1.5 Million Babies Born to Unwed Moms in '04." *USA Today* (November 1): 7D.

Jayson, Sharon (2006a). "Merely Having an Older Sibling Can Be a Bad Influence." *USA Today* (April 25): 7D.

Jayson, Sharon (2006b). "Society Switches Focus Away from Children." *USA Today* (July 12): 1D.

Jayson, Sharon (2008). "Waiting for the Right Time." *USA Today* (November 10): 1D.

Jayson, Sharon (2009a). "Federally Funded Ad Campaign Holds Up Value of Marriage." *USA Today* (February 17): 1D.

Jayson, Sharon (2009b). "Obama Budget Shifts Money from Abstinence Only Sex Education." *USA Today* (May 12): 4D.

Jayson, Sharon (2009c). "Recession Redefines 'Necessities.'" *USA Today* (April 24): 1A.

Jefferson, David (2006). "How AIDS Changed America." *Newsweek* (May 15): 36–41.

Jefferson, David (2008). "The Divorce Generation Grows Up." *Newsweek* (April 21): 46–53.

Jeffries, Vincent, and H. Edward Ransford (1980). *Social Stratification, A Multiple Hierarchy Approach*. Boston: Allyn and Bacon.

Jencks, Christopher, Joseph Swingle, and Scott Winship (2006). "Welfare Redux." *American Prospect* 17 (March): 36–40.

Jepson, Lisa K., and Christopher A. Jepson (2002). "An Empirical Analysis of the Matching Patterns of Same-Sex and Opposite-Sex Couples," *Demography* 39 (August): 435–453.

Johnson, Dirk (1996). "No-Fault Divorce Is Under Attack." *New York Times*, "Themes of the Times" (Fall): 8.

Johnson, Michael P. (1995). "Patriarchal Terrorism and Common Couple Violence: Two Forms of Violence against Women." *Journal of Marriage and the Family* 57 (May): 283–294.

Johnson, Michael P. (2008). *A Typology of Domestic Violence: Intimate Terrorism, Violent Resistance, and Situational Couple Violence*. Boston: Northeastern University Press.

Johnson, Michael P., and Janel M. Leone (2005). "The Differential Effects of Intimate Terrorism and Situational Couple Violence." *Journal of Family Issues* 26 (April): 322–349.

Johnson, Michael P., and Kathleen J. Ferraro (2000). "Research on Domestic Violence in the 1990s: Making Distinctions." *Journal of Marriage and Family* 60 (November): 948–963.

Jones, Ann (1994). *Next Time, She'll Be Dead: Battering and How to Stop It*. Boston: Beacon Press.

Jones, Barry (1982). *Sleepers Awake! Technology and the Future of Work*. Melbourne, Australia: Oxford University Press.

Jones, Norrece J. (1991). *Born a Child of Freedom, Yet a Slave: Mechanisms of Control and Strategies of Resistance in Antebellum South Carolina*. Middletown, CT: Wesleyan University Press.

Jones, Rachel K., Mia R. S. Zolna, Stanley K. Henshaw, and Lawrence B. Finer (2008). "Abortion in the United States: Incidence and Access to Services, 2005." *Perspectives on Sexual and Reproductive Health* 40 (March): 6–16.

Judson, David (1997). "Neglect of Kids 'No Less than Collective.'" *Denver Post* (June 2): 2A.

Juster, Susan, and Maris A. Vinovskis (1987). "Changing Perspectives on the American Family in the Past." *Annual Review of Sociology* 13: 193–216.

Kagan, Jerome (1977). "The Child in the Family." *Daedalus* 106 (Spring): 33–56.

Kahl, Joseph A. (1957). *The American Class Structure*. New York: Holt, Rinehart.

Kain, Edward L. (1990). *The Myth of Family Decline: Understanding Families in a World of Rapid Social Change*. Lexington, MA: Lexington Books.

Kaiser Family Foundation (2003). *National Survey of Adolescents and Young Adults: Sexual Health Knowledge, Attitudes and Experiences*. Menlo Park, CA: Henry J. Kaiser Family Foundation.

Kaiser Family Foundation (2008). "Sexual Health of Adolescents and Young Adultls in the United States." Online: http://www.kff.org/womenshealth/upload/3040_04.pdf.

Kalb, Claudia (2004). "Brave New Babies." *Newsweek* (January 26): 45–53.

Kalb, Claudia, and Andrew Murr (2006). "Battling a Black Epidemic." *Newsweek* (May 15): 42–48.

Kalleberg, Arne L. (2009). "Precarious Work, Insecure Workers: Employment Relations in Transition." *American Sociological Review* 74 (February): 1–22.

Kamen, Paula (2002). *Her Way*. New York: Broadway Books.

Kammeyer, Kenneth C. W. (1981). "The Decline of Divorce in America." Paper presented at the meetings of the Midwest Sociological Society (April).

Kammeyer, Kenneth C. W., George Ritzer, and Norman R. Yetman (1990). *Sociology: Experiencing Changing Societies*, 3rd ed. Boston: Allyn and Bacon.

Kamo, Yoshinori, and Min Zhou (1994). "Living Arrangements of Elderly Chinese and Japanese in the United States." *Journal of Marriage and the Family* 56 (August): 544–558.

Kandiyoti, Deniz (1988). "Bargaining with Patriarchy." *Gender & Society* 2: 274–290.

Kanter, Rosabeth Moss (1984). "Jobs and Families: Impact of Working Roles on Family Life." In *Work and Family*, Patricia Voydanoff (ed.). Palo Alto, CA: Mayfield, pp. 111–118.

Kantrowitz, Barbara (2006). "Sex and Love: The New World." *Newsweek* (February 20): 51–60.

Kanuha, Valli Kalie (2005). "Compounding the Triple Jeopardy: Battering in Lesbian of Color Relationships." In *Domestic Violence at the Margins: Readings on Race, Class, Gender, and Culture*, Natalie J. Sokoloff (ed.). New Brunswick, NJ: Rutgers University Press, pp. 71–82.

Kaplan, Sheila, and Jim Morris (2000). "Kids at Risk." *U.S. News & World Report* (June 19): 47–53.

Karabell, Zachary (2009). "The Case for Derivatives." *Newsweek* (February 2): 35–36.

Karraker, Meg Wilkes (2008). *Global Families*. Boston: Allyn and Bacon.

Kass, Leon R. (2000). "The End of Courtship." *In the Public Interest* 141 (Fall). Online: http://www.thepublicinterest.com/main.html

Katz, Jonathan Ned (1990). "The Invention of Heterosexuality." *Socialist Review* 20 (January/March): 7–34.

Katzev, Aphra, Rebecca A. Warner, and Alan C. Acock (1994). "Girls or Boys? Relationship of Child Gender to Marital Stability." *Journal of Marriage and the Family* 56 (February): 89–100.

Kaukinen, Catherine (2004). "Status Compatibility, Physical Violence, and Emotional Abuse in Intimate Relationships." *Journal of Marriage and Family* 66 (May): 452–471.

Kawamoto, Walter T., and Tamara C. Cheshire (2004). "A Seven-Generation Approach to American Indian Families." In *Handbook of Contemporary Families*, Marilyn Coleman and Lawrence Gonong (eds.). Thousand Oaks, CA: Sage, pp. 385–393.

Kayyali, Randa A. (2006). *The Arab Americans*. Westport, CT: Greenwood Press.

Keefe, Susan (1984). "Real and Ideal Extended Familism among Mexican American and Anglo Americans: On the Meaning of 'Close' Family Ties." *Human Organization* 43: 65–70.

Keen, Judy (2008). "Pawnshops Doing Brisk Business." *USA Today* (November 10): 3A.

Keller, Josh (2007). "High-Tech Courtship." *Chronicle of Higher Education* (March 23): A6.

Kelly, Katy (2005). "Just Don't Do It!" *U.S. News & World Report* (October 17): 42–51.

Kelly, Katy, and Linda Kulman (2004). "Kid Power." *U.S. News & World Report* (September 13): 47–55.

Kendig, Sarah M., and Suzanne M. Bianchi (2008). "Single, Cohabiting, and Married Mothers' Time with Children." *Journal of Marriage and Family* 70 (December): 1228–1240.

Kennedy, David M. (1996). "Can We Still Afford to Be a Nation of Immigrants?" *Atlantic Monthly* (November): 51–80.

Kennedy, Randall (2002). *Sex, Marriage, Identity, and Adoption*. New York: Pantheon Books.

Kenniston, Kenneth (1977). *All Our Children: The American Family under Pressure*. New York: Harcourt Brace Jovanovich.

Kent, Mary Mo, Kelvin M. Pollard, John Haaga, and Mark Mather 2001. "First Glimpses of the 2000 U.S. Census." *Population Bulletin* 56 (June): entire issue.

Kenworthy, Tom. (2006). "Oversize Homes Wear Out Welcome." *USA Today* (February 21): 1A.

Kertzer, David I. (1991). "Household History and Sociological Theory." *Annual Review of Sociology* 17: 155–179.

Kibria, Nazli (1990). "Power, Patriarchy, and Gender Conflict in the Vietnamese Immigrant Community." *Gender & Society* 4 (March): 9–24.

Kibria, Nazli (1993). *Family Tightrope: The Changing Lives of Vietnamese Americans*. Princeton, NJ: Princeton University Press.

Kibria, Nazli (1994). "Migration and Vietnamese American Women: Remaking Ethnicity." In *Women of Color in U.S. Society*, Maxine Baca Zinn and Bonnie Thornton Dill (eds.). Philadelphia: Temple University Press, pp. 247–261.

Kibria, Nazli (1997). "The Concept of 'Bicultural Families' and Its Implications for Research on Immigrant and Ethnic Families." In *Immigration and the Family*, Alan Booth, Ann C. Crouter, and Nancy Landale (eds.). Mahwah, NJ: Erlbaum, pp. 205–210.

Kilborn, Peter T. (2004). "An All-American Town, A Sky-High Divorce Rate." *New York Times* (May 2): 20YT.

Kim, Hyoun K., Deborah M. Capaldi, and Lynn Crosby (2007). "Generalizability of Goffman and Colleagues' Affective Process Models of Couples' Relationship Outcomes." *Journal of Marriage and Family* 26 (February): 55–72.

Kim, Hyoun K., and Patrick C. McKenry (2002). "The Relationship Between Marriage and Psychological Well-Being: A Longitudinal Analysis." *Journal of Family Issues* 23 (November): 885–911.

Kimmel, Michael, and Michael A. Messner (2004). *The Gendered Society*, 2nd ed. New York: Oxford University Press.

Kinsey, Alfred S., Wardell B. Pomeroy, Clyde E. Martin, and the staff of the Institute for Sex Research (1948). *Sexual Behavior in the Human Male*. Philadelphia: Saunders.

Kinsey, Alfred S., Wardell B. Pomeroy, Clyde E. Martin, and the staff of the Institute for Sex Research (1953). *Sexual Behavior in the Human Female*. Philadelphia: Saunders.

Kirn, Walter (2000). "Should You Stay Together for the Kids?" *Time* (September 25): 75–88.

Kirp, David L. (2005). "Before School." *The Nation* (November 21): 24–30.

Kirschner, Bette Frankle, and Laurel Richardson Walum (1978). "Two-Location Families." *Alternative Lifestyles* 1 (November): 513–525.

Klein, Joe (2003). "Blessed Are the Poor—They Don't Get Tax Cuts." *Time* (June 9): 25.

Kluger, Jeffrey (2006). "The New Science of Siblings." *Time* (July 10): 47–55.

Kluger, Jeffrey (2007). "The Power of Birth Order." *Time* (October 29): 41–48.

Komorovsky, Mirra (1962). *Blue Collar Marriage*. New York: Vintage.

Kong, Deborah (2002). "24% of Domestic Help Undocumented." Associated Press (March 22).

Kornblum, Janet (2008). "More Women 40 to 44 Remaining Childless." *USA Today* (August 19): 12B.

Kornblum, William (1991). "Who Is the Underclass?" *Dissent* 38 (Spring): 202–211.

Koss-Feder, Laura (2003). "Providing for Parents." *Time*, bonus section (March), no pages given.

Kotkin, Joel, and Thomas Tseng (2003). "All Mixed Up." *Washington Post National Weekly Edition* (June 16–22): 22–23.

Krantz, Matt (2006). "Costs of Children." *USA Today* (May 15): 1B.

Kreager, Derek A. (2007). "Unnecessary Roughness? School Sports, Peer Networks, and Male Adolescent Violence." *American Sociological Review* 72 (October): 705–724.

Krim, Jonathan, and Griff Witte (2005). "Middle Class No More." *Washington Post National Weekly Edition* (January 10–16): 20–21.

Kristof, Nicholas D. (2005). "Bush's Sex Scandal." *New York Times* (February 16). Online: http//www.nytimes.com/005/02/16/opinion/16kristof.html?

Kristol, William, and Jeremy Rifkin (2002). "First Test of the Biotech Age: Human Cloning." *Los Angeles Times* (March 6). Online: http://latimes.com/news/opinion/commentary/lal-000016598mar06.story?coll=la%2Dnews%2Dc

Kruse, Douglas L., and Douglas Mahony (2000). "Illegal Child Labor in the United States: Prevalence and Characteristics." *Industrial & Labor Relations Review* 54 (October): 17–40.

Kuczynski, Leon, Lori Harach, and Silvia C. Bernardine (1999). "Psychology's Child Meets Sociology's Child: Agency, Influence and Power in Parent–Child Relationships." In *Contemporary Perspectives on Family Research*, Vol. 1. Stamford, CT: JAI Press, pp. 21–52.

Kulczycki, Andrzej, and Arun Peter Lobo (2002). "Patterns, Determinants, and Implications of Intermarriage Among Arab/Americans." *Journal of Marriage and Family* 64: 202–210.

Kulman, Linda (2005). "Get Married." *U. S. News & World Report* (January 3): 77.

Kurdek, Lawrence. (1993). "The Allocation of Household Labor in Gay, Lesbian, and Heterosexual Married Couples." *Journal of Social Issues* 49 (3): 127–139.

Kurdek, Lawrence A. (1998). "Relationship Outcomes and Their Predictors: Longitudinal Evidence from Heterosexual Married, Gay Cohabiting, and Lesbian Couples." *Journal of Marriage and the Family* 60 (August): 553–568.

Kurdek, Lawrence A. (2003). "Differences Between Gay and Lesbian Cohabiting Couples." *Journal of Social and Personal Relationships* 20(4): 411–436.

Kurdek, Lawrence A. (2004). "Gay Men and Lesbians: The Family Context." In *Handbook of Contemporary Families: Considering the Past, Contemplating the Future*, Marilyn Coleman and Lawrence H. Ganong (eds.). Thousand Oaks, CA: Sage.

Kurdek, Lawrence A. (2006). "Differences Between Partners from Heterosexual, Gay, and Lesbian Cohabitating Couples." *Journal of Marriage and Family* 68 (May): 509–528.

Kuttner, Robert (2003). "Welcome to the Amazing Jobless Recovery." *Business Week* (July 28): 26.

Lackey, Chad (2003). "Violent Family Heritage, the Transition to Adulthood and Later Partner Violence." *Journal of Family Issues* 24 (January): 74–98.

Ladner, Joyce A. (1971). *Tomorrow's Tomorrow: The Black Woman*. Garden City, NY: Doubleday.

Lagnado, Lucette (2009). "'Grandfamilies' Come Under Pressure." *Wall Street Journal* (April 4). Online: http://online.wsj.com/article/SB1238807041/19588951.html.

Laing, R. D. (1971). *The Politics of the Family*. New York: Random House.

Laird, Joan (2003). "Lesbian and Gay Families." In *Normal Family Processes: Growing Diversity and Complexity*, Froma Walsh (ed.). New York: Guilford Press, pp. 176–209.

Lamb, Michael E. (1987). *The Father's Role: Cross-Cultural Perspectives*. Hillsdale, NJ: Erlbaum.

Lamphere, Louise, Patricia Zavella, and Felipe Gonzales, with Peter B. Evans (1993). *Sunbelt Working Mothers*. Ithaca, NY: Cornell University Press.

Lampman, Jane (2003). "Shaping the Future of Marriage." *Christian Science Monitor* (October 2). Online: http://www.csmonitor.com/2003/1002/p12s02-lire.htm

Landry, Bart (2000). *Black Working Wives: Pioneers of the American Family Revolution*. Berkeley: University of California Press.

Laner, Mary Riege, and Nicole A. Ventrone (1998). "Egalitarian Daters/Traditionalist Dates." *Journal of Family Issues* 19 (4): 468–477.

Laner, Mary Riege, and Nicole A. Ventrone (2000). "Dating Scripts Revisited." *Journal of Family Issues* 21 (May): 488–500.

Langman, Lauren (1987). "Social Stratification." In *Handbook of Marriage and the Family*, Marvin B. Sussman and Suzanne L. Steinmetz (eds.). New York: Plenum, pp. 211–249.

Lannutti, Pamela (2005). "For Better or Worse: Exploring the Meanings of Same-Sex Marriage Within the Lesbian, Gay, Bisexual and Transgendered Community." *Journal of Social and Personal Relationships* 22(1): 5–18.

Lantz, Herman, Margaret Britton, Raymond L. Schmitt, and Eloise Snyder (1968). "Preindustrial Patterns in the Colonial Family in America: A Content Analysis of Colonial Magazines." *American Sociological Review* 33: 413–426.

Lareau, Annette (2008). "Introduction: Taking Stock of Class." In *Social Class: How Does It Work?*, Annette Lareau and Dalton Conley, (eds.). New York: Russell Sage, pp. 3–24.

Lareau, Annette (2003). *Unequal Childhoods: Class, Race, and Family Life*. Berkeley, CA: University of California Press.

Larkin, Jack (1988). *The Reshaping of Everyday Life*, New York: Harper & Row.

LaRossa, Ralph (1997). *The Modernization of Fatherhood: A Social and Political History*. Chicago: University of Chicago Press.

Larson, Reed, and Maryse Richards (1994). *Divergent Realities: The Emotional Lives of Mothers, Fathers, and Adolescents*. New York: Basic Books.

Lasch, Christopher (1975). "The Family and History." *New York Review of Books* 8 (November 13): 33–38.

Lasch, Christopher (1977). *Haven in a Heartless World: The Family Besieged*. New York: Basic Books.

Laslett, Peter (1971). *The World We Have Lost*, 2nd ed. New York: Scribners.

Latham, Lisa Moricoli (2000). "Southern Governors Declare War on Divorce." *Salon*. Online: http://salon.com/mwt/feature/2000/01/24/divorce/index.html

Laumann, Edward O., and Robert T. Michael (eds.). (2000). *Sex, Love, and Health in America: Private Choices and Public Policies*. Chicago: University of Chicago Press.

Laumann, Edward O., Anthony Paik, Dale B. Glosser, Jeong-Han Kang, Bernard Levinson, Edson Moreira, Alfredo Nicolosi, and Clive Gingell (2006). "A Cross-National Study of Subjective Sexual Well-Being among Older Women and Men: Findings and Behaviors." Online: www-news.uchicao.edu/releases/06/images/ 060419.sex.pdf

Laumann, Edward O., John H. Gagnon, Robert T. Michael, and Stuart Michaels (1994). *The Social Organization of Sexuality*. Chicago: University of Chicago Press.

Laumann, Edward O., Jenna Mahay, and Yoosik Youm (2007). "Sex Intimacy, and Family Life in the United States." In *The Sexual Self: The Construction of Sexual Scripts*, Michael Kimmel (ed.). Nashville, TN: Vanderbilt University Press, pp. 165–190.

Leach, Penelope (1994). *Children First: What Our Society Must Do—And Is Not Doing—for Our Children Today*. New York: Knopf.

Lee, Jennifer, and Frank D. Bean (2004a). "America's Changing Color Lines: Immigration, Race/Ethnicity, and Multiracial Identification." *Annual Review of Sociology* 30: 221–242.

Lee, Jennifer, and Frank D. Bean (2004b). "Intermarriage and Multiracial Identification: The Asian American Experience and Implications for Changing Color Lines." In *Asian American Youth*, Jennifer Lee and Min Zhou (eds.). New York: Routledge, pp. 51–63.

Lee, Sharon M. (1998). "Asian Americans: Diverse and Growing." *Population Bulletin* 53 (June): entire issue.

Lee, Sharon M., and Barry Edmonston (2005). "New Marriages, New Families: U. S. Racial and Hispanic Intermarriage." *Population Bulletin* 60 (2). Washington, DC: Population Reference Bureau.

Lehmann-Haupt, Rachel (2009). "Why I Froze My Eggs." *Newsweek* (May 11): 50–52.

Leibowitz, Lila (1978). *Females, Males, Families: A Biosocial Approach*. North Scituate, MA: Duxbury Press.

Leland, John (2000). "Silence Ending about Abuse in Gay Relationships." *New York Times* (November 6). Online: http://nytimes.com/2000/11/06/national/06ABUS.html

Lempert, Lora Bey, and Marjorie L. De Vault (2000). "Special Issue on Emergent and Reconfigured Forms of Family Life." *Gender & Society* 14 (February): 6–10.

Lerner, Gerda (1979). "The Lady and the Mill Girl: Changes in the Status of Women in the Age of Jackson 1800–1840." In *A Heritage of Her Own*, Nancy F. Cott and Elizabeth Pleck (eds.). New York: Simon & Schuster, pp. 182–196.

Lerner, Michael (1982). "Recapturing the Family Issue." *The Nation* (February): 141–143.

Lerner, Sharon (2005). "Post-Roe Postcard: Is Ole Miss Our Future?" *The Nation* (February 7): 14–19.

Levine, Heidi, and Nancy J. Evans (1996). "The Development of Gay, Lesbian, and Bisexual Identities." In *The Meaning of Difference*, Karen E. Rosenblum and Toni-Michelle Travis (eds.). New York: McGraw-Hill, pp. 130–136.

Levine, Jeffrey M. (2003). "Employment, Work Conditions, and the Home Environment in Single-Mother Families." *Journal of Family Issues* 29(10): 1268–1297.

Levine, Peter (2006). "Annette Lareau." (March 27). Online: http://www.peterlevine.ws/mt/archives/000823.html

Lewin, Tamar (2002). "A Frozen Sperm Riddle." *New York Times* (January 13). Online: www.nytimes.com/2002/01/13/weekin review/13LEWI..html

Lewis, Amanda, Maria Krysan, and Nakisha Harris (2004). "Introduction: Assesing Changes in the Meaning and Significance of Race and Ethnicity." In *The Changing Terrain of Race and Ethnicity*, Maria Krysan and Amanda Lewis, (eds.). New York: Russell Sage, pp. 1–24.

Lewis, Oscar (1959). *Five Families: Mexican Case Studies in the Culture of Poverty*. New York: Basic Books.

Lewis, Oscar (1966). *La Vida*. New York: Random House.

Lichter, Daniel T. (1997). "Poverty and Inequality among Children." *Annual Review of Sociology* 23: 121–145.

Lichter, Daniel T. (2001). *Marriage as Public Policy*. Washington, DC: Progressive Policy Institute.

Lichter, Daniel T., and Martha L. Crowley (2002). "Poverty in America: Beyond Welfare Reform," *Population Bulletin* 57 (June): entire issue.

Lichter, Daniel T., Diane K. McLaughlin, and David C. Ribar (2002). "Economic Restructuring and the Retreat from Marriage." *Social Science Research* 31: 230–256.

Lichter, Daniel T., and Zhenchao Qian (2004). *Marriage and Family in a Multiracial Society. The American People, Census 2000*. Washington, DC: Russell Sage Foundation/Population Reference Bureau.

Lichter, Daniel T., and Zhenchao Qian (2005). "Marriage and Family in a Multiracial Society." In *The American People: Census 2000*, Reynolds Farley and John Haaga (eds.). New York: Russell Sage Foundation, pp. 169–200.

Lichter, Daniel T., and Zhenchao Qian (2008). "Serial Cohabitation and the Marital Life Course." *Journal of Marriage and Family* 70 (November): 861–878.

Lichter, Daniel T., Deborah Roempke Graefe, and J. Brian Brown (2003). "Is Marriage a Panacea? Union Formation Among Economically Disadvantaged Unwed Mothers." *Social Problems* 50 (February): 60–86.

Lin, James, and Jared Bernstein (2008). "What We Need to Get By." *Economic Policy Institute*, Briefing Paper #224 (October 29).

Lleras, Christy (2008). "Employment, Work Conditions, and the Home Environment in Single-Mother Families." *Journal of Family Issues* 29(10): 1268–1297.

Lollock, L. (2001). "The Foreign-Born Population in the United States: March 2003." Washington, DC: U.S. Census Bureau.

LoPiccolo, Joseph (1983). "The Prevention of Sexual Problems in Men." In *Promoting Sexual Responsibility and Preventing Sexual Problems*, George W. Albee, Sol Gordon, and Harold Leitchberg (eds.). Hanover, NH: University Press of New England, pp. 39–65.

Lorber, Judith (1994). *Paradoxes of Gender*. New Haven, CT: Yale University Press.

Lord, Walter. (1955). *A Night to Remember*. New York: Henry Holt.

Lorentzen, Erlend, Havard Nilsen, and Bente Traeen (2008). "Will It Never End? The Narratives of Incest Victims on the Termination of Sexual Abuse." *The Journal of Sex Research* 45(2): 164–175.

Love, Alice Ann (2000). "Survey Shows 46% of Couples Work Different Shifts." *Albuquerque Journal* (March 10): A1.

Lowry, Rich (2006). "The Reform that Transformed America." *The Week* (September 8): 14.

Lozano-Bielat, Hope, David Masei, and Michelle Ralston (2009). "Same-Sex Marriage: Redefining Marriage Around the World." Pew Research Center. Online: http://www.perforum.org.

Lucal, Betsy (1996). "Oppression and Privilege: Toward a Relational Conceptualization of Race." *Teaching Sociology* 24 (July): 245–255.

Luker, Kristin (1996). *Dubious Conceptions: The Politics of Teenage Pregnancy*. Cambridge, MA: Harvard University Press.

Lundgren, Lena M., Jennifer Fleischer-Cooperman, Robert Schneider, and Theresa Fitzgerald (2001). "Work, Family, and Gender in Medicine: How Do Dual-Earners Decide Who Should Work Less?" In *Working Families: The Transformation of the American Home*, Rosanna Hertz and Nancy L. Marshall (eds.). Berkeley: University of California Press, pp. 251–269.

Lundquist, Jennifer Hickes (2006). "The Black-White Gap in Marital Dissolution Among Young Adults: What Can a Counterfactual Scenario Tell Us?" *Social Problems* 53(3): 421–441.

Luscombe, Belinda (2008). "Will the Market Kill Your Marriage?" *Time* (November 3): 62–63.

Lyness, J. F., M. E. Lipetz, and K. E. Davis (1972). "Living Together: An Alternative to Marriage." *Journal of Marriage and the Family* 34: 305–311.

Lytle, Tamara (2003). "Bush Open to Same-Sex Marriage Ban." *The Coloradoan* (July 31): 1A–2A.

Mabry, J. Beth, Rosean Giarruso, and Vern L. Bengston (2004). "Generations, the Live Course, and Family Change." In *The*

Blackwell Companion to the Sociology of Families, Jacqueline Scott, Judith Treas, and Martin Richards (eds.). Malden, MA: Blackwell, pp. 87–108.

Maciel, Jose A., Zanetta Van Putten, and Carmen Knudson-Martin (2009). "Gendered Power in Cultural Contexts: Part I. Immigrant Couples." *Family Process* **48(1): 9–23.**

Mackey, Richard A., Matthew A. Diemer, and Bernard A. O'Brien (2000). "Psychological Intimacy in the Lasting Relationships of Heterosexual and Same-Gender Couples," *Sex Roles* 43 (3/4): 201–227.

MacKinnon, Catherine A. (1989). *Toward a Feminist Theory of the State*. Cambridge, MA: Harvard University Press.

MacKinnon, Catherine (2007[1985]). "Pornography, Civil Rights, and Speech." In *Gender Violence: Interdisciplinary Perspectives*, **2nd ed., Laua L. O'Toole, Jessica R. Schiffman, and Margie L. Kiter (eds.). New York: New York University Press, pp. 374–388.**

Macklin, Eleanor D. (1983). "Nonmarital Heterosexual Cohabitation." In *Family and Transition*, 4th ed., Arlene S. Skolnick and Jerome H. Skolnick (eds.). Boston: Little, Brown, pp. 264–265.

Madden, Mary, and Amanda Lenhart (2006). *Online Dating. Pew Internet and American Life Project*. Online: www.pewinternet.org

Madsen, William (1964). *The Mexican-Americans of South Texas*. New York: Holt, Rinehart and Winston.

Mahoney, Sarah (2006). "The Secret Lives of Single Women." *AARP Magazine* (May/June): 70–109.

Malley-Morrison, Kathleen, and Denise A. Hines (2004). *Family Violence in a Cultural Perspective: Defining, Understanding, and Combating Abuse*. Thousand Oaks: Sage.

Malveaux, Julianne (2002). "More Jobs, Not More Marriages, Lift Poor." *Rocky Mountain News* (February 22): 15A.

Mandel, Michael (2009). "The Savings Surprise." *Business Week* **(April 13): 19.**

Mann, Susan A., Michael D. Grimes, Alice Abel Kemp, and Pamela J. Jenkins (1997). "Paradigm Shifts in Family Sociology? Evidence from Three Decades of Family Textbooks." *Journal of Family Issues* 18 (May): 315–349.

Manning, Stephen (2009). "A Make-Nothing Nation?" Associated Press (February 22).

Manning, Wendy D., and Pamela J. Smock (2000). "Swapping Families: Serial Parenting and Economic Support for Children." *Journal of Marriage and Family* 62: 111–122.

Manning, Wendy D., and Pamela J. Smock (2002). "First Comes Cohabitation and Then Comes Marriage?" *Journal of Family Issues* 23 (November): 1065–1087.

Mantsios, Gregory (1996). "Rewards and Opportunities: The Politics and Economics of Class in the U.S." In *The Meaning of Difference*, Karen E. Rosenblum and Toni-Michelle Travis (eds.). New York: McGraw-Hill, pp. 97–103.

March, Karen, and Charlene Miall (2000). "Adoption as a Family Form." *Family Relations* 49 (October): 359–362.

Marcus, Mary Brophy (2009). "Many Americans Say They Forgo Routine Dental Care." *USA Today* **(March 11): 4D.**

Marks, Carole (1991). "The Urban Underclass." *Annual Review of Sociology* 17: 445–466.

Marks, Loren D., Katrina Hopkins, Cassandraa Chaney, Pamela A. Monroe, Olena Nesteruk, and Diane D. Sasser (2008). "Together, We Are Strong?: A Qualitative Study of Happy, Enduring African American Marriages." *Family Relations* **57 (April): 172–185.**

Marks, Nadine F. (1996). "Flying Solo at Midlife: Gender, Marital Status, and Psychological Well-Being." *Journal of Marriage and the Family* 58 (November): 917–932.

Marks, Stephen R. (2006). "Understanding Diversity of Families in the 21st Century and Its Impact on the Work-Family Area of Study." In *The Work and Family Handbook: MultiDisciplinary Perspectives and Approaches,* **Marcie Pitt-Catsouphes, Ellen Ernst Kossek, and Stephen Sweet (eds.). Mahwah, NJ: Lawrence Erlbaum, pp. 41065.**

Marquardt, Katy, and Kirk Shinkle (2009). "Terrible Tale of the Tape." *U S. News & World Report* **(March): 54.**

Marsh, Kris, William A. Darity Jr., Philip N. Cohen, Lynne M. Casper, and Danielle Salters (2007). "The Emerging Black Middle Class: Single and Living Alone." *Social Forces* **86(2): 735–762.**

Marsiglio, William, Paul Amato, Ronald D. Day, and Michael E. Lamb (2001). "Scholarship on Fatherhood in the 1990s and Beyond." In *Understanding Families into the New Millennium: A Decade in Review*, Robert M. Milardo (ed.). Minneapolis: National Council on Family Relations, pp. 392–410.

Martin, Joyce A., Brady E. Hamilton, Paul D. Sutton, Stephanie J. Ventura, Fay Menacher, Sharon Kirmeyer, and T. J. Mathews (2009). "Births: Final Data for 2006." *National Vital Statistics Reports* **57(7). U. S. Department of Health and Human Services. Online: http://www.ecd.gov/nchs/data/nvsr/nvsr57/nvsr57_07.pdf.**

Martin, Karin A. (2002). "'I Couldn't Ever Picture Myself. Having Sex...': Gender Differences in Sex and Sexual Subjectivity." In *Sexuality and Gender*, Christine L. Williams and Arlene Stein (eds.). Malden, MA: pp. 142–167.

Martin, Michele T., Robert E. Emery, and Tara S. Peris (2004). "Single Parent Families." In *Handbook of Contemporary Families*, Marilyn Coleman and Lawrence H. Ganong (eds.). Thousand Oaks, CA: Sage, pp. 282–301.

Martin, Philip, and Elizabeth Midgley (1999). "Immigration to the United States." *Population Bulletin* 54 (June): entire issue.

Martin, Philip, and Elizabeth Midgley (2006). "Immigration: Shaping and Reshaping America." *Population Bulletin* 61 (December). Entire Issue.

Martin, Philip, and Gottfried Zurcher (2008). "Managing Migration: The Global Challenge." *Population Bulletin* **63 (March). Entire Issue.**

Maschinot, Beth (1995). "Behind the Curve." In *These Times* (February 6): 31–34.

Mason, Mary Ann (2003). "The Modern American Stepfamily: Problems and Possibilities." In *All Our Families*, 2nd ed., Mary Ann Mason, Arlene Skolnick, and Stephen D. Sugarman (eds.). New York: Oxford University Press, pp. 96–116.

Mason, Mary Ann, Arlene Skolnick, and Stephen D. Sugarman (1998). "Introduction." In *All Our Families: New Policies for a New Century*, Mary Ann Mason, Arlene Skolnick, and Stephen D. Sugarman (eds.). New York: Oxford University Press, pp. 1–12.

Mason, Mary Ann, Arlene Skolnick, and Stephen D. Sugarman (2003). "Introduction." In *All Our Families: New Policies for a New Century*, Mary Ann Mason, Arlene Skonick, and Stephen D. Sugarman (eds.). New York: Oxford University Press, pp. 1–12.

Mather, Mark (2009). "Children in Immigrant Families Chart a New Path." *Reports on America*. **Wahington, DC: Population Reference Bureau (February).**

Matthaei, Julie A. (1982). *An Economic History of Women in America*. New York: Schoken.

Matthews, Tony (1999). Online: http://3.ns.sympatico.ca/tands.matthews/christdivorce.html

Maume, David J., Jr., and Marcia Bellas (2001). "The Overworked American or the Time Bind? Assesssing Competing Explanations for Time Spent in Paid Labor." *American Behavioral Scientist* 44 (March): 1137–1156.

May, Martha (1990). "The Historical Problem of the Family Wage: The Ford Motor Company and the Five Dollar Day." In *Unequal Sisters: A Multi-cultural Reader in U.S. Women's History*, Ellen Carol DuBois and Vicki L. Ruiz (eds.). New York: Routledge, pp. 275–291.

McAdoo, Harriette Pipes (1978). "Factors Related to Stability in Upwardly Mobile Black Families." *Journal of Marriage and the Family* 40 (4): 761–776.

McCollum, Audrey T. (1990). *The Trauma of Moving*. Newbury Park, CA: Sage.

McCrate, Elaine (1997). "Hitting Bottom: Welfare 'Reform' and Labor Markets." *Dollars and Sense* 213 (September/October): 34–35.

McDonough, Siobhan (2005). "Housing Costing Americans More." Associated Press.

McEnroe, Jennifer (1991). "Split-Shift Parenting." *American Demographics* 13 (February): 50–52.

McFalls, Joseph A., Jr. (1998). "Population: A Lively Introduction." *Population Bulletin* 53 (September): entire issue.

McGinn, Daniel (2004). "Mating Behavior 101." *Newsweek* (October 4): 44–45.

McGraw, Lori A., and Alexis J. Walker (2004). "Gendered Family Relations: The More Things Change, the More They Stay the Same." In *Handbook of Contemporary Families*, Marilyn Coleman and Lawrence H. Ganong (eds.). Thousand Oaks, CA: Sage, pp. 174–191.

McIntosh, Peggy (1992). "White Privilege and Male Privilege: A Personal Account of Coming to See Correspondences through Work in Women's Studies." In *Race, Class, and Gender,* Margaret L. Andersen and Patricia Hill Collins (eds.). Belmont, CA: Wadsworth, pp. 70–81.

McKinley, Donald Gilbert (1964). *Social Class and Family Life*. Glencoe, IL: Free Press of Glencoe.

McLanahan, Sara, and G. D. Sandefur (1994). *Growing up with a Single Parent: What Hurts, What Helps*. Cambridge, MA: Harvard University Press.

McLanahan, Sara, and Karen Booth (1991). "Mother-Only Families." In *Contemporary Families: Looking Forward, Looking Back*, Alan Booth (ed.), Minneapolis: National Council on Family Relations, pp. 405–428.

McLanahan, Sara, and Lynne Casper (1995). "Growing Diversity and Inequality in the American Family." In *State of the Union: America in the 1990s*, Vol. 2, Reynolds Farley (ed.). New York: Russell Sage Foundation, pp. 1–46.

McLarin, Kimberly J. (1995). "For the Poor, Defining Who Deserves What." *New York Times* (September 17): 4E.

McLean, Elys A. (1995). "U.S. Children in Poverty." *USA Today* (January 31): 5A.

McLoyd, Vonnie C., Ana Mari Cauce, David Takeuchi, and Leon Wilson. (2001) "Marital Processes and Parental Socialization in Families of Color: A Decade Review of Research." In *Understanding Families into the New Millennium: A Decade in Review*, Robert M. Milardo (ed.). Minneapolis, MN: National Council on Family Relations, pp. 466–487.

Means, Marianne (1997). "Frazzled Families Could Use a Break." *Rocky Mountain News* (May 19): 39A.

Meckler, Laura (2002b). "Want a Stable Marriage? Be Rich, Religious, Over 20." Associated Press (July 25).

Meier, Diane E., and R. Sean Morrison (1999). "Old Age and Care Near the End of Life." *Generations* 23 (Spring): 6–11.

Melzer, Scott A. (2002). "Gender, Work, and Intimate Violence: Men's Occupational Violence Spillover and Compensatory Violence." *Journal of Marriage and Family* 64 (November): 820–832.

Menaghan, Elizabeth G. (1996). "Maternal Occupational Conditions and Children's Family Environments." In *Women and Work: A Handbook*, Paula J. Dubek and Kaktherine Borman (eds.). New York: Longman, pp. 409–412.

Messner, Michael A. (1996). "Studying up on Sex." *Sociology of Sport Journal* 13: 221–237.

Michael, Robert T., John H. Gagnon, Edward O. Laumann, and Gina Kolata (1994). *Sex in America*. Boston: Little, Brown.

Michigan State Medical Society (1993). *Reaching Out: Intervening in Partner Abuse*. East Lansing; Michigan State Medical Society.

Mignon, Sylvia I., Calvin J. Larson, and William M. Holmes (2002). *Family Abuse: Consequences, Theories, and Responses*. Boston: Allyn and Bacon.

Milkie, Melissa A., and Pia Peltola (1999). "Playing All the Roles: Gender and the Work–Family Balancing Act." *Journal of Marriage and the Family* 61 (May): 476–490.

Miller, Debra K. (2006). "The Effects of Childhood Physical Abuse or Childhood Sexual Abuse in Battered Women's Coping Mechanism: Obsessive-Compulsive Tendencies and Severe Depression." *Journal of Family Violence* **21(3): 185–195.**

Miller, JoAnn Langley, and Dean D. Knudsen (1999). "Family Abuse and Violence." In *Handbook of Marriage and the Family*, 2nd ed., Marvin Sussman, Suzanne K. Steinmetz, and Gary W. Peterson (eds.). New York: Plenum Press, pp. 705–741.

Miller, JoAnn, and Dean D. Knudsen (2007). *Family Abuse and Violence: A Social Problems Perspective*. **Lanham, MD: AltaMira Press.**

Miller, S. M., and F. R. Riessman (1964). "The Working Class Subculture: A New View." In *Blue Collar Worlds: Studies of the American Worker*, A. B. Shostack and W. Bomberg (eds.). Englewood Cliffs, NJ: Prentice Hall, pp. 24–36.

Millman, Marcia (1991). *Warm Hearts and Cold Cash: The Intimate Dynamics of Families and Money*. New York: Free Press.

Mills, C. Wright (1940). "Methodological Consequences of the Sociology of Knowledge." *American Journal of Sociology* 46 (November): 316–330. Reprinted (1963) in *Power, Politics and People: The Collected Essays of C. Wright Mills*, Irving L. Horowitz (ed.). New York: Ballantine, pp. 453–468.

Mindel, Charles H. (1980). "Extended Familism among Urban Mexican-Americans, Anglos and Blacks." *Hispanic Journal of Behavioral Sciences* 2: 21–34.

Minnotte, Krista Lynn, Daphne Pedersen Stevens, Michael C. Minnotte, and Gary Kiger (2007). "Emotion-Work Performance Among Dual-Earner Couples: Testing Four Theoretical Perspectives." *Journal of Family Issues* **28(6): 773–793.**

Mintz, Steven (2003). "Introduction: The Contemporary Crisis of the Family." New York: Council on Contemporary Families. Online: http://www.contemporaryfamilies.org/public/fact1.php.

Mintz, Steven (2004). "The Social and Cultural Construction of American Childhood." In *Handbook of Contemporary Families*, Marilyn Coleman and Lawrence H. Ganong (eds.). Thousand Oaks, CA: Sage, pp. 36–53.

Mintz, Steven (2006). "From Patriarchy to Androgyny and Other Myths: Placing Men's Family Roles in Historical Perspective." In *American Families: Past and Present*, Susan M. Ross (ed.). New Brunswick, NJ: Rutgers University Press, pp. 11–33.

Mintz, Steven (2008). "Excerpt from Huck's Raft: Laboring Children." In *American Families: A Multicultural Reader*, 2nd ed., Stephanie Coontz (ed.). New York: Routledge, pp. 96–106.

Mintz, Steven, and Susan Kellogg (1988). *Domestic Revolutions: A Social History of American Family Life*. New York: Free Press.

Mishel, Lawrence, Jared Bernstein, and Sylvia Allegretto (2007). *The State of Working America 2006/2007*. Ithaca, NY: Cornell University Press.

Mitchell, Juliett (1966) "Women, The Longest Revolution." *New Left Review* 44.

Moberg, David (1995). "Reviving the Public Sector." *In These Times* (October 16): 22–24.

Modell, John (1978). "Patterns of Consumption, Acculturation, and Family Income Strategies in Late Nineteenth-Century America." In *Family and Population in Nineteenth Century America*, Tamara K. Hareven and Maris A. Vinovskis (eds.). Princeton, NJ: Princeton University Press, pp. 206–240.

Modell, John, and Tamara K. Hareven (1977). "Urbanization and the Malleable Household: An Examination of Boarding and Lodging in American Families." In *Family and Kin in Urban Communities, 1700–1930*. New York: New Viewpoints, pp. 167–186.

Moen, Phyllis, and Elaine Wethington (1992). "The Concept of Family Adaptive Strategies." *Annual Review of Sociology* 18: 233–251.

Moen, Phyllis, and Kay B. Forest (1999). "Strengthening Families: Policy Issues for the Twenty-First Century." In *Handbook of Marriage and the Family*, 2nd ed., Marvin Sussman, Suzanne K. Steinmetz, and Gary W. Peterson (eds.). New York: Plenum, pp. 633–663.

Moen, Phyllis, and Yan Yu (2000). "Effective Work/Life Strategies: Working Couples, Work Conditions, Gender, and Life Quality." *Social Problems* 47 (August): 291–326.

Mohan, Geoffrey, and Ann M. Simmons (2004). "Diversity Spoken in 39 Languages." *Los Angeles Times* (June 16). Online: http://www.latimes.com/news/locak/la-me-mulltilingual16jun16,1,157

Mooney, Nan (2009). "Foreclosure Crisis Hits Warp Speed." *AlterNet* (March 30). Online: http:www.alternet.org/module/printversion/134003.

Moore, Joan W., and Raquel Pinderhughes (eds.) (1993). *In the Barrios: Latinos and the Underclass Debate*. New York: Russell Sage Foundation.

Moore, Kristin Anderson (2009). "Teen Births: Examining the Recent Increase." Child Trends Research Brief #2009-08. Online: www.childtrends.org/Files/Child_Trends_2009_03_13_FS_TeenBirthRate.pdf.

Morgan, David H. J. (2004). "Men in Families and Households." In *The Blackwell Companion to the Sociology of Families*, Jacqueline Scott, Judith Treas, and Martin Richards (eds.). Malden, MA: Blackwell, pp. 374–393.

Morin, Richard (2002). "Study Suggests Men Work Harder When They Have a Little One at Home, Especially If It's a Boy." *Coloradoan* (June 11): 5A.

Morisi, Teresa L. (2008). "Youth Enrollment and Employment During the School Year." *Monthly Labor Review* 131(2): 51–63.

Morone, James A. (1996). "The Corrosive Politics of Virtue." *American Prospect* 26 (May/June): 30–39.

Morris, Betsy (2002). "Trophy Husbands." *Fortune* (October 14): 78–98.

Mosley, Walter (2009). "Ten Things You Can Do to Stay in Your Home." *The Nation* (March 23): 10.

Moyers, Bill. (2005). "The Fight of Our Lives." In *Inequality Matters: The Growing Economic Divide in America and Its Poisonous Consequences*, James Lardner and David A. Smith (eds.). New York: The New Press, pp. 1–13.

Moyers, Bill, and Michael Winship (2009). "Changing the Rules of the Blame Game." *CommonDreams.Org* (April 8). Online: http://www.commondreams.org/print/40559.

Moynihan, Daniel P. (1965). *The Negro Family: The Case for National Action*. Washington, DC: Office of Policy Planning and Research, U.S. Department of Labor.

Moynihan, Daniel P. (1988). "Our Poorest Citizens—Children." *Focus* 11 (Spring): 5–6.

Mui, Ylan Q. (2009). "Home Economics in Anxious Times." *Washington Post National Weekly Edition* (March 2): 23.

Mukhopadhay, Carol, and Rosemary C. Henze (2003). "How Real Is Race? Using Anthropology to Make Sense of Human Diversity." *Phi Delta Kappan* (May): 669–678.

Mullings, Lieth (1986). "Uneven Development: Class, Race, and Gender in the U.S. before 1900." In *Women's Work*, Eleanor Leacock, Helen I. Safa, and contributors. South Hadley, MA: Bergin and Garvey, pp. 41–57.

Mullings, Lieth (1997). *On Our Own Terms: Race, Class, and Gender in the Lives of African American Women*. New York: Routledge.

Mulrine, Anna (2003). "Love.com." *U.S. News and World Report* (September 29): 52–58.

Murray, Charles (1984). *Losing Ground*. New York: Basic Books.

Murray, John E. (2000). "Marital Protection and Marital Selection: Evidence from a Historical-Prospective Sample of American Men." *Demography* 37 (November): 511–521.

Murray, Velma McBride, Gene H. Brody, Anita Brown, Joseph Wisenbaker, Carolyn E. Catrona, and Ronald L. Simmons (2002). "Linking Employment Status, Maternal Psychological Well-Being, Parenting, and Children's Attitudes About Poverty in Families Receiving Government Assistance," *Family Relations* 51 (1): 112–120.

Musick, Kelly (2002). "Planned and Unplanned Childbearing Among Unmarried Women," *Journal of Marriage and Family* 64 (November): 915–929.

Muwwakil, Salim (2008). "Come on Cosby, Stop Hatin." *In These Times* 32(January): 15.

Myers, Scott M., and Alan Booth (1996). "Men's Retirement and Marital Quality." *Journal of Marriage and the Family* 17 (May): 336–357.

Nagel, Joane (2003). *Race, Ethnicity, and Sexuality*. Oxford, UK: Oxford University Press.

Nakonezny, Paul A., Robert D. Shull, and Joseph Lee Rodgers (1995). "The Effect of No-Fault Divorce Law on the Divorce Rate across the 50 States and Its Relation to Income, Education, and Religiosity." *Journal of Marriage and the Family* 57 (November): 477–488.

Naples, Nancy A. (1992). "Activist Mothering: Cross Generational Continuity in the Community Work of Women from Low-Income Urban Neighborhoods." *Gender & Society* 6 (September): 441–463.

The Nation (1995). "Welfare Cheat." (October 9): 371–372.

The Nation (2008). "Stimulus from Below." (December 29): 3.

National Center on Addiction and Substance Abuse (2003). "The Importance of Family Dinners." Online: http://www.casacolumbia.org/absolutem/articlefiles/Family_Dinners_9_03_03.pdf

National Center on Elder Abuse (1998). National Elder Abuse Incidence Study: Final Report. Washington, DC: American Public Health Services Association.

National Conference of State Legislatures (2009). "Common Law Marriage." Online: www.ncsl.org/default.aspx?tabid=4265

National Institutes of Health (NIH) [2005]. "HIV Infection and AIDS: An Overview." Online: www.niaid.nih.gov/factsheets/hivinf.htm

National Marriage Project (2006). "The State of Our Unions 2006." Online: http://marriage.rutgers.edu/Publications/SOOU/SOOU2006.pdf.

National Marriage Project (2009). *The State of Our Unions 2008: The Social Health of Marriage in America*. Online: hyyp://marriage.rutgers.edu.

National Research Council (2003). *Elder Mistreatment: Abuse, Neglect, and Exploitation in an Aging America*. Washington, DC: The National Academics Press.

Naughton, Keith (2006). "The Long and Grinding Road." *Newsweek* (May 1): 53–60.

Navarro, Mireya (2004). "For Young Latinos, A Shift to Smaller Families." *New York Times* (December 5): 1,29.

Navarro, Vicente. (1991). "Class and Race: Life and Death Situations." *Monthly Review* 43 (September): 1–13.

Neergaard, Lauran (2000). "Alzheimer's Alarm Sounded." *Denver Post* (July 10): 2A.

Neugarten, Bernice L. (1980). "Grow Old Along with Me! The Best Is Yet to Be." In *Growing Old in America*, Beth Hess (ed.). New Brunswick, NJ: Transaction Books, pp. 180–197.

Newman, David and Liz Grauerholz (2002). *Sociology of Families*, 2nd ed. Thousand Oaks, CA: Pine Forge Press.

Newman, Katherine S. (1988). *Falling from Grace: The Experience of Downward Mobility in the American Middle Class*. New York: The Free Press.

Newman, Katherine S. (1993). *Declining Fortunes: The Withering of the American Dream*. New York: Basic Books.

Newman, Katherine S. (1994). "Troubled Times: The Cultural Dimensions of Economic Decline." In *Understanding American Economic Decline*, Michael A. Bernstein and David E. Adler (eds.). New York: Cambridge University Press, pp. 330–357.

New York Times (2002). "Don't Just Say No." (June 26). Online: www.nytimes.com/2002/06/26/opinion/26WED4.html

Nicholson, Linda (1997). "The Myth of the Traditional Family." In *Feminism and Families*, Hilde Lindemann Nelson (ed.). New York: Routledge, pp. 27–42.

Nock, Steven L. (2001). "The Marriages of Equally Dependent Spouses." *Journal of Family Issues* 22 (September): 756–777.

Nock, Steven L., James D. Wright, and Laura Saanchez (1999). "America's Divorce Problem." *Society* 36 (May/June): 43–52.

Noller, Patricia, and Judith A. Feeney (eds.) (2002). *Understanding Marriage: Developments in the Study of Couple Interaction*. New York: Cambridge University Press.

O'Connell, Martin, and Daphne Lofquist (2009). "Counting Same-Sex Couples: Official Estimates and Unofficial Guesses." U. S. Census Bureau Working Papers. Online: http//www.census.gov/population/www/socdemo/hh-fam-html.

O'Connor, Colleen (2009). *Denver Post* (February 26). Online: http://www.denverpost.com/fdcp?1235664096986.

O'Connor, Elaine (2003). "Easy Sex, Hard Fallout," *The Ottawa Citizen* (March 22). Online: http://www.canada.com/ottowa/ottowacitizen/specials/teensex/story.html.

O'Hare, William P. (1992). "America's Minorities: The Demographics of Diversity." *Population Bulletin* 47 (December): entire issue.

O'Hare, William P. (1996). "A New Look at Poverty." *Population Bulletin* 51 (September): entire issue.

O'Hare, William P. (2004). *The American People*. New York and Washington, DC: Russell Sage Foundation and the Population Reference Bureau.

Ohlemacher, Stephen. (2006). "Nation's Largest Food Bank Served More than 25 Million," Associated Press (February 23).

Okin, Susan Moller (1989). *Justice, Gender, and the Family*. New York: Basic Books.

Oliver, Melvin L., and Thomas M. Shapiro (1995). *Black Wealth/White Wealth: A New Perspective on Racial Equality*. New York: Routledge.

Omi, Michael, and Howard Winant (1994). *Racial Formation in the United States*, 2nd ed. London: Routledge.

Operation Comfort (2006). Online: http://www.operationcomfort.com

Ordonez, Jennifer (2007). "Baby Needs a New Pair of Shoes." *Newsweek* (May 14): 50–54.

Oropesa, Ralph, Daniel T. Lichter, and R. N. Anderson (1994). "Marriage Markets and the Paradox of Mexican American Nuptiality." *Journal of Marriage and the Family* 56 (November): 889–907.

Ortiz, Judith Coffer (2000). "The Myth of the Latin Woman: I Just Met a Girl Named Maria." In *Race, Class, and Gender: An Anthology*, 4th ed., Margaret L. Andersen and Patricia Hill Collins (eds.). Belmont, CA: Wadsworth, pp. 342–346.

Orsi, Robert A. (2001). "The Fault of Memory: Southern Italy in the Imagination of Immigrants and the Lives of Their Children in Italian Harlem, 1920-45." In *Family and Society in American History*, Joseph M. Hawes and Elizabeth M. Nybakken (eds.). Urbana, IL: University of Illinois Press, pp. 215–225.

Osmond, Marie Withers (1996). "Work-Family Linkages in Early Industrialization: The Public-Private Split." In *Women and Work: A Handbook*, Paula J. Dubek and Kathryn Borman (eds). New York: Longman, pp. 385–391.

Osmond, Marie Withers, and Barrie Thorne (1993). "Feminist Theories: The Social Construction of Gender in Families and Society." In *Sourcebook of Family Theories and Methods: A Contextual Approach*, P. G. Boss, W. J. Doherty, R. LaRossa,

W. R. Schumm, and S. K. Steinmetz (eds.). New York: Plenum, pp. 591–623.

Ostrander, Susan A. (1984). *Women of the Upper Class*. Philadelphia: Temple University Press.

Oswald, Ramona Faith (2002). "Resilience Within the Family Networks of Lesbians and Gay Men: Intentionality and Redefinition," *Journal of Marriage and Family* 64 (May): 374–383.

O'Toole, Laura L., Jessica R. Schiffman, and Margie L. Kiter Edwards (eds.) (2007). *Gender Violence: Interdisciplinary Perspectives*, **2nd ed. New York: New York University Press.**

Paetsch, Joanne J., Nicholas M. Bala, Lorne D. Bertrand, and Lisa Glennon (2004). "Trends in the Formation and Dissolution of Couples." In *The Blackwell Companion to the Sociology of Families*, **Jacqueline Scott, Judith Treas, and Martin Richards (eds.). Malden, MA: Blackwell, pp. 306–321.**

Page, Clarence (2006). "Guys in Real World Encounters 'Failure to Launch,' Too." *Hutchinson News* (April 10): A8.

Page, Susan (2009). "In One Year, 24 Million Slide from 'Thriving' to 'Struggling.'" *USA Today* **(March 10): 1A–2A.**

Palmer, Kimberly (2008). "The Day the Spending Stopped." *U. S. News & World Report* **(August 18): 41–43.**

Pann, Katrina McClintic, and Margaret Crosbie-Burnett (2005). "Remarriage and Recoupling." In *Families and Change*, Patrick McKenry and Sharon J. Price (eds.). Thousand Oaks, CA: Sage, pp. 253–264.

Parade **(2008). "The Truth About Teen Pregnancy." (October 5): 6.**

Parenti, Michael (1995). *Democracy for the Few*, 6th ed. New York: St. Martins Press.

Pargus, Damian Alan (2008). "Boundaries and Opportunities: Comparing Slave Family Formations in the Antebellum South." *Journal of Family History* **33: 316–345.**

Parker-Pope, Tara (2009). "The Myth of Rampant Teenage Promiscuity." *New York Times* **(January 27): D6.**

Parrenas, Rhacel Salazar (2000). "Migrant Filipina Domestic Workers and the International Division of Labor." *Gender & Society* 14 (August): 560–581.

Parrenas, Rhacel Salazar (2001). *Servants of Globalization: Women, Migration, and Domestic Work*. Stanford, CA: Stanford University Press.

Parrenas, Rhacel Salazar (2005). *Children of Global Migration: Transnational Families and Gendered Woes*. **Stanford: Stanford University Press.**

Parrenas, Rhacel Salazar (2007). "Mothering from a Distance: Emotion, Gender, and International Relations in Filipino Transnational Families." In *Shifting the Center: Understanding contemporary Families*, 3rd ed., Susan Ferguson (ed.). Boston: McGraw-Hill.

Parsons, Talcott (1955). "The American Family: Its Relations to Personality and the Social Structure." In *Family Socialization and Interaction Process*, Talcott Parsons and Robert F. Bales (eds.). New York: Free Press, p. 33.

Parsons, Talcott (1965). "The Normal American Family." In *Man and Civilization*, S. Farber, P. Mustaccht, and R. H. L. Wilson (eds.). New York: McGraw-Hill, pp. 31–50.

Pasley, Kay, and Brad S. Moorefield (2004). "Stepfamilies: Changes and Challenges." In *Handbook of Contemporary Families*, Marilyn Coleman and Lawrence H. Ganong (eds.). Thousand Oaks, CA: Sage, pp. 317–330.

Patterson, Charlotte J. (1992). "Children of Lesbian and Gay Parents." *Child Development* 63 (October): 1025–1042.

Patterson, Charlotte J. (2001). "Family Relationships of Lesbian and Gay Men." In *Understanding Families into the New Millennium: A Decade in Review*, Robert M. Milardo (ed.). Minneapolis: National Council on Family Relations, pp. 271–288.

Patterson, Charlotte J., and Richard E. Redding (1996). "Lesbian and Gay Families with Children." *Journal of Social Issues* 52 (Fall): 29–50.

Pattillo-McCoy, Mary (1999). *Black Picket Fences: Privilege and Peril Among the Black Middle Class*. Chicago: University of Chicago Press.

Paul, Elizabeth L., and Kristen A. Hayes (2002). "The Casualties of 'Casual' Sex: A Qualitative Exploration of the Phenomenology of College Students' Hookups." *Journal of Social and Personal Relationships* 19 (5): 693–661.

Paul, Elizabeth L., Brian McManus, and Allison Hayes (2000). "Hookups?: Characteristics and Correlates of College Students' Spontaneous and Anonymous Sexual Experiences." *Journal of Sex Research* 37 (February): 76–88.

Paul, Pamela (2002). *The Starter Marriage and the Future of Matrimony*. New York: Villard.

Pavetti, LaDonna (2000). "Welfare Policy in Transition: Redefining the Social Contract for Poor Citizen Families with Children." *Focus* 21 (Fall): 44–50.

Peplau, Letitia Anne (1981). "What Homosexuals Want." *Psychology Today* 15 (March): 28–38.

Peplau, Letitia Anne, Adam Fingerhut, and Kristin P. Beals (2004). "Sexuality in the Relatlionships of Lesbians and Gay Men." In *the Handbook of Sexuality in Close Relationships*, **John H. Harvey, Amy Wenzel, and Susan Sprecher (eds.). Mahwah, NJ: Lawrence Earlbaum, pp. 349–369.**

Perry-Jenkins, Maureen, and Elizabeth Turner (2004). "Jobs, Marriage, and Parenting: Working It Out in Dual-Earner Families." In *Handbook of Contemporary Families*, Marilyn Coleman and Lawrence H. Ganong (eds.). Thousand Oaks, CA: Sage, pp. 155–173.

Perry-Jenkins, Maureen, and Karen Polk (1994). "Class, Couples, and Conflict: Effects of the Division of Labor on Assessments of Marriage in Dual-Earner Families." *Journal of Marriage and the Family* 56 (February): 165–180.

Perry-Jenkins, Maureen, and Sonya Salamon (2002). "Blue Collar Kin and Community in the Small-Town Midwest," *Journal of Family Issues* 23 (November): 927–949.

Peters, Marie F., and Harriette P. McAdoo (1983). "The Present and Future of Alternative Lifestyles in Ethnic American Cultures." In *Contemporary Families and Alternative Lifestyles*, Eleanor D. Macklin and Roger Roben (eds.). Beverly Hills, CA: Sage, pp. 288–307.

Peterson, Karen S. (1993). "Guys Wed for Better, Wives, for Worse." *USA Today* (October 11): D1–D2.

Peterson, Karen S. (1996). "Typical Family Is a Modern-Day Oxymoron." *USA Today* (November 27): 4D.

Peterson, Karen S. (2000a). "Changing the Shape of the American Family." *USA Today* (April 18): 1D–2D.

Peterson, Karen S. (2000b). "Sex for Many Teens, Oral Doesn't Count." *USA Today* (November 16): 1D–2D.

Peterson, Karen S. (2001a). "43% of 1st Marriages end in 15 Years." *USA Today* (May 25): 2A.

Peterson, Karen S. (2002a). "Kids, Parents Can Make Best of Divorce." *USA Today* (January 14): 1A–2A.

Peterson, Karen S. (2002b). "'Market Work,' Yes; Housework, Hah!" *USA Today* (March 13): 6D.

Peterson, Karen S. (2003). "Stay Close By, for the Sake of the Kids." *USA Today* (July 7): 7D.

Pew Hispanic Center (2009). "Tabulations of 2000 Census and 2007 American Community Survey." *Statistical Portrait of Hispanics in the United States, 2007*. (March 5). Online: http://pewhispanic.org/factsheets/factsheet. php?FactsheetID=46.

Peyser, Marc (1999). "Home of the Gray." *Newsweek* (March 1): 50–53.

Phillips, Julie A. and Megan M. Sweeny (2005). "Premarital Cohabitation and Marital Disruption Among White, Black, and Mexican American Women." *Journal of Marriage and Family* (May): 296–314.

Pierce Transit (2006). "Your Driving Costs." Online: http://www.piercetransit.org/rideshare/costs.htm

Pinker, Steven (1997). "Why They Kill Their Newborns." *New York Times Magazine* (November 2): 52–54.

Piorkowski, Geraldine K. (2000). "Back Off." In *Annual Editions: Marriage and Family: 2000–2001*. Guilford, CT: Dushkin/McGraw-Hill, pp. 37–40.

Pixley, Joy E., and Phyllis Moen (2003). "Prioritizing Careers." In *It's About Time: Couples and Careers*, Phyllis Moen (ed.). Ithaca: Cornell University Press, pp. 183–200.

Pleck, Elizabeth H. (1973). "The Two-Parent Household: Black Family Structure in Late Nineteenth-Century Boston." In *The American Family in Social-Historical Perspective*, Michael Gordon (ed.). New York: St. Martin's, pp. 152–178.

Pleck, Joseph H. (1977). "The Work-Family Role System." *Social Problems* 24 (April): 417–427.

Polakow, Valerie (1993). *Lives on the Edge: Single Mothers and Their Children in the Other America*. Chicago: University of Chicago Press.

Pollard, Kelvin M., and William P. O'Hare (1999). "America's Racial and Ethnic Minorities." *Population Bulletin* 54 (September): entire issue.

Pollitt, Katha (1996). "Adoption Fantasy." *The Nation* (July 8): 9.

Popenoe, David (1993). "American Family Decline, 1960–1990: A Review and Appraisal." *Journal of Marriage and the Family* 55: 527–541.

Popenoe, David (1997). "Family Trouble." *The American Prospect* 34 (September/October): 18–19.

Popenoe, David (2005). *The War Over the Family*. New Brunswick, NJ: Transaction Press.

Portes, Alejandro, and Min Zhou (1993). "The New Second Generation: Segmented Assimilation and Its Variants." *Annals of the American Academy of Political and Social Science* 530: 74–96.

Portes, Alejandro, and Robert L. Beck (1985). *Latin Journey*. Berkeley: University of California Press.

Portes, Alejandro, and Rubén G. Rumbaut (1990). *Immigrant America: A Portrait*. Berkeley: University of California Press.

Potts, Laura (2001). "Contrary to 1981, Kids, Parents Today Doing More Together." Associated Press (May 7).

Powers, Kirsten A. (2007). "Immigrants Become Target for All of Society's Ills." *USA Today* (August 29): 13A.

Press, Julie E. (2004). "Cute Butts and Housework: A Gynocentric Theory of Assortative Mating." *Journal of Marriage and Family* 66 (November): 1029–1033.

Presser, Harriet B. (1999). "Toward a 24-Hour Economy." *Science* 284 (June 11): 1778–1779.

Presser, Harriet B. (2000). "Nonstandard Work Schedules and Marital Instability." *Journal of Marriage and the Family* 62 (February): 93–110.

Pressman, Steven, and Robert Scott (2007). "Three Million Americans are Debt Poor." *Dollars & Sense* #271 (July/August): 10–11, 13.

Previti, Denise, and Paul R. Amato (2003). "Why Stay Married? Rewards, Barriers, and Marital Stability." *Journal of Marriage and the Family* 65 (August): 561–573.

Prewitt, Kenneth (2003). *Politics and Science in Census Taking*. New York: Russell Sage Foundation.

Price, Christine A. (2005). "Aging Families and Stress." In *Families and Change*, 3rd ed., Patrick C. McHenry and Sharon J. Price (eds.). Thousand Oaks, CA: Sage, pp. 49–73.

Pryor, Jan, and Liz Trinder (2004). "Children, Families, and Divorce." In *The Blackwell Companion to the Sociology of Families*, Jacqueline Scott, Judith Treas, and Martin Richards (eds.). Malden, MA: Blackwell, pp. 306–321.

Pryor, John H., Sylvia Hurtado, Victor B. Saenz, Jennifer A. Lindholm, William S. Korn, and Kathryn M. Mahoney (2005). *The American Freshman: National Norms for Fall 2005*. Los Angeles: Higher Education Research Institute, UCLA.

Pugh, Tony (2001). "Mixed-Race Marriages Rising." *Denver Post* (March 23): 1.

Public Broadcasting System (2009). "Frontline: The Failure and Future of the Private Insurance Industry." (March 31).

Purdum, Todd S. (2000). "Shift in the Mix Alters the Face of California." *New York Times* (July 4). Online: http://nytimes.com/library/national/070400ca-latin.html

Pyke, Karen (2000). "The Normal American Family as an Interpretive Structure of Family Life Among Grown Children of Korean and Vietnamese Immigrants." *Journal of Marriage and the Family* 62 (February): 240–255.

Pyke, Karen (2004). "Immigrant Families in the U.S." In *The Blackwell Companion to the Sociology of Families*. Malden, MA: Blackwell, pp. 253–269.

Pyke, Karen (2008). "Immigrant Families in the U. S." In *American Families: A Multicultural Reader*, 2nd ed., Stephanie Coontz (ed.). New York: Routledge, pp. 210–221.

Qian, Zhenchao, and Jose A. Cobas (2004). "Latinos' Mate Selection: National Origin, Racial, and Nativity Differences." *Social Science Research* 33: 225–247.

Queen, Stuart A., and Robert W. Habenstein (1974). *The Family in Various Cultures*, 4th ed. Philadelphia: Lippincott.

Quindlen, Anna (2005). "Connecting the Dots." *Newsweek* (January 24): 76.

Quinn, Jane Bryant (2006). "New Math for College Costs." *Newsweek* (March 13): 43.

Raley, R. Kelly, and Jenifer Bratter (2004). "Not Even If You Were the Last Person on Earth! How Marital Search Constraints Affect the Likelihood of Marriage." *Journal of Family Issues* 25 (March): 167–181.

Raley, Sara B., Marybeth J. Mattingly, and Suzanne M. Bianchi (2006). "How Dual Are Dual-Income Couples? Documenting

Change From 1970 to 2001." *Journal of Marriage and Family* 68 (February) 11–28.

Rampell, Catherine (2009). "Shift to Saving May Be Downturn's Lasting Impact. *New York Times* **(May 9). Online: http://www.nytimes.com/2009/05/10/business/economy/10saving.html.**

Ramey, Craig T., F. A. Campbell, M. Burchinal, M. L. Skinner, D. M. Gardner, and S. L. Ramey (1999). "Persistent Effects of Early Intervention on High-Risk Children and Their Mothers." *Applied Developmental Science* 4: 2–14.

Ramirez, Oscar (1980). "Extended Family Support and Mental Health Status among Mexicans in Detroit." *La Red*, a monthly newsletter of the National Chicano Research Network, 28 (March 1980): 2.

Ramirez, Oscar, and Carlos H. Arce (1981). "The Contemporary Chicano Family: An Empirically Based Review." In *Explorations in Chicano Psychology*, Augustine Baron, Jr. (ed.). New York: Praeger, pp. 3–28.

Rampell, Catherine (2009). "As Layoffs Surge, Women May Pass Men in Job Force." *New York Times*

Rand, Michael R. (2008). *Criminal Victimization, 2007*. **U. S. Department of Justice. Online: http://www.ojp.usdoj.gov/bjs/abstract/ev07.htm.**

Rank, Mark R. (2000). "Poverty and Economic Hardship in Families." In *Handbook on Family Diversity*, David H. Demo, Katherine R. Allen, and Mark A. Find (eds.). New York: Oxford University Press, pp. 293–315.

Rank, Mark S. (2001). "The Effect of Poverty on America's Families," *Journal of Family Issues* 22 (October): 882–903.

Rank, Mark S. (2003). "As American as Apple Pie: Poverty and Welfare." *Contexts* 2 (Summer): 41–49.

Rank, Mark S. (2004). "The Disturbing Paradox of Poverty in American Families." In *The Handbook of Contemporary Families*, Marilyn Coleman and Lawrence H. Ganong (eds.). Thousand Oaks, CA: Sage, pp. 469–489.

Rank, Mark S., and Thomas A. Hirschl (2001). "The Occurrence of Poverty Across the Life Cycle: Evidence from the P. S. I. D." *Journal of Policy Analysis and Management* 20 (4): 737–735.

Rapp, Rayna (1982). "Family and Class in Contemporary America: Notes toward an Understanding of Ideology." In *Rethinking the Family: Some Feminist Questions*, Barrie Thorne and Marilyn Yalom (eds.). New York: Longman, pp. 168–187.

Rawlings, Steve (1995). "Households and Families: Population Profile of the United States: 1995." *Current Population Reports*, Series P1-23-189. Washington, DC: U.S. Government Printing Office, p. 28.

Rayman-Read, Alyssa (2001). "The Sound of Silence." *American Prospect*, Special Supplement (Fall): A21–A23.

Reagan, Leslie J. (1997). *When Abortion Was a Crime: Women, Medicine, and Law in the United States, 1867–1973*. Berkeley: University of California Press.

Reed, Betsy (2009). "Unemployment Is Hitting Men Particularly Hard—and Both Sexes Are Losing Out." *AlterNet* **(April 8). Online: http://www.alternet.org/story/135521/**

Reich, Robert B. (2000a). "It's the Year 2000 Economy, Stupid." *American Prospect* (January 3): 64.

Reich, Robert B. (2001). "The New Economy as a Decent Society." *American Prospect* (February 12): 20–23.

Reich, Robert B. (2008). "Totally Spent." *New York Times* **(February 13). Online: http://www.nytimes.com/2008/02/13/opinion/13reich.html?**

Renzetti, Claire M. (1992). *Violent Betrayal: Partner Abuse in Lesbian Relationships*. Newbury Park, CA: Sage.

Riche, Martha Farnsworth (2000). "America's Diversity and Growth: Signposts for the 21st Century." *Population Bulletin* 55 (June): entire issue.

Riche, Martha Farnsworth (2006). "Demographic Implications for Work-Family Research." In *The Work and Family Handbook: Multi-Disciplinary Perspectives and Approaches,* **Marcie Pitt-Catsouphes, Ellen Ernst Kossek, and Stephen Sweet (eds.). Mahwah, NJ: Lawrence Erlbaum, pp. 125–140.**

Richie, Beth E. (2005). "Foreword." In *Domestic Violence at the Margins: Readings on Race, Class, Gender, and Culture*, Natalie J. Sokoloff (ed.). New Brunswick, NJ: Rutgers University Press, pp. xv–xviii.

Richmond, Julius B. (1994). "Give Children an Earlier Head Start." *USA Today* (April 12): 13A.

Ridgeway, James (2009). "Who Shredded Our Safety Net? *Mother Jones* **34 (May/June): 28–33, 81–82.**

Riggle, Ellen D. B., Sharon Rostosky, and Robert Prather (2006). "Advance Planning by Same-Sex Couples." *Journal of Family Issues* 27 (June): 758–776.

Risman, Barbara J. (1998). *Gender Vertigo: American Families in Transition*. New Haven, CT: Yale University Press.

Risman, Barbara J., and Danette Johnson-Sumerford (1998). "Doing It Fairly: A Study of Postgender Marriages." *Journal of Marriage and the Family* 60 (February): 23–40.

Risman, Barbara J., and Pepper Schwartz (1988). "Sociological Research on Male and Female Homosexuality." *Annual Review of Sociology* 14: 125–147.

Risman, Barbara J., and Pepper Schwartz (2002). "After the Sexual Revolution: Gender Politics in Teen Dating." *Contexts* 1 (Spring): 16–25.

Rivera, Amaad, Jeannette Huezo, Christina Kasica, and Dedrick Muhammad (2009). *State of the Dream 2009: The Silent Depression*. **Boston: United for a Fair Economy.**

Rivers, Mary J. (2005). "Navaho Women and Abuse: The Context for Their Troubled Relationship." *Journal of Family Violence* 20 (April): 83–89.

Roberts, Dorothy (2009). "Child Welfare as a Racial Justice Issue." In *Race and Ethnicity in Society,* **Elizabeth Higginbottam and Margaret L. Andersen (eds.). Belmont, CA: Thompson Wadsworth, pp. 352–359.**

Roberts, Sam (2008). "In a Generation, Minorities May Be the U. S. Majority." *New York Times* **(August 14). Online: http://www.nytimes.com/2008/08/14/washington/14census.html?_r=1.**

Roberts, Sam (2009). "Slump Creates Lack of Mobility for Americans." *New York Times*. **(April 23). Online: http://www.nytimes.com/2009/04/23/us/23census.html.**

Robinson, Paul (1994). "The Way We Do the Things We Do." *New York Times Book Review* (October 30): 3, 22.

Rochelle, Ann (1997). *No More Kin: Exploring Race, Class, and Gender in Family Networks*. Thousand Oaks, CA: Pine Forge.

Rodman, Hyman (1964). "Middle-Class Misconceptions about Lower Class Families." In *Blue Collar World: Studies of the American Worker*, Arthur B. Shostak and William Gomberg (eds.). Englewood Cliffs, NJ: Prentice Hall, pp. 59–69.

Roehling, Patricia V., Phyllis Moen, and Rosemary Batt (2003). "Spillover." In *It's About Time: Couples and Careers*, Phyllis Moen (ed.). Ithaca, NY: Cornell University Press, pp. 101–121.

Rollins, Judith (1985). *Between Women: Domestics and Their Employers*. Philadephia: Temple University Press.

Romero, Mary (1992). *Maid in the U.S.A.* New York: Routledge.

Root, Maria (2002). *Love's Revolution: Interracial Marriage*. Philadelphia: Temple University Press.

Root, Maria, and P. P. Root (2001). "The Color of Love." *American Prospect*, April 8, pp. 54–55.

Rosenbluth, Susan C., Janice M. Steil, and Juliet H. Whitcomb (1998). "Marital Equality: What Does It Mean?" *Journal of Family Issues* 19 (May): 227–244.

Rosenfeld, Michael J. (2007). *The Age of Independence: Interracial Unions, Same Sex Unions, and the Changing American Family*. Cambridge: Harvard University Press.

Ross, Susan (ed.), (2006). "Introduction: Family Formations from a Sociological Perspective." In *American Families Past and Present*. New Brunswick, NJ: Rutgers University Press, pp. 2–10.

Rossi, Alice S. (1994). "Eros and Caritas: A Biopsychosocial Approach to Human Sexuality and Reproduction." In *Sexuality across the Life Course*, Alice S. Rossi (ed.). Chicago: University of Chicago Press, pp. 3–38.

Rouse, L. P. (1997). "Domestic Violence: Hitting Us Where We Live." In *Analyzing Social Problems: Essays and Exercises*, D. Dunn and D. V. Walker (eds.). Upper Saddle River, NJ: Prentice Hall, pp. 17–22.

Roy, Kkevin, and Linda Burton (2008). "Mothering Through Recruitment: Kinscription of Nonresidential Fathers and Father Figures in Low-Income Families." In *American Families: A Multicultural Reader*, Stephanie Coontz (ed.). New York: Routledge, pp. 341–365.

Roxburgh, Susan (2006). " 'I Wish We Had More Time to Spend Together': The Distribution and Predictors of Perceived Family Time Pressures Among Married Men and Women in the Paid Labor Force." *Journal of Family Issues* 27 (April): 529–553.

Ruane, Michael E. (2006). "For Better, for Worse." *The Washington Post National Weekly Edittion* (June 26): 6–7.

Rubel, Arthur J. (1966). *Across the Tracks: Mexican Americans in a Texas City*. Austin: University of Texas Press.

Rubin, Gayle (1984). "Thinking Sex: Notes for a Radical Theory of Politics and Sexuality." In *Pleasure and Danger*, Carol Vance (ed.). Boston: Routledge, pp. 267–320.

Rubin, Lillian B. (1976). *Worlds of Pain: Life in the Working-Class Family*. New York: Basic Books.

Rubin, Lillian B. (1983). *Intimate Strangers: Men and Women Together*. New York: Harper & Row.

Rubin, Lillian B. (1994). *Families on the Fault Line: America's Working Class Speaks about the Family, the Economy, Race, and Ethnicity*. New York: HarperCollins.

Ruggeri, Amanda (2008). "A Quiet Fight Over Gay Adoption." *U. S. News & World Report* (November 3):29.

Rumbaut, Ruben G. (1997). "Ties That Bind: Immigration and Immigrant Families in the United States." In *Immigration and the Family*, Alan Booth, Ann C. Crouter, and Nancy Landale (eds.). Mahwah, NJ: Erlbaum, pp. 3–46.

Rutenberg, Jim (2009). "Gay and Lesbian Leaders Say Federal Same-Sex Benefits Don't Go Far Enough." *New York Times* (June 18): A18.

Rutter, Virginia (1994). "Lessons from Step-Families." *Psychology Today* 27 (May/June): 30–33, 60, 62, 64, 66, 68–69.

Ryan, Mary P. (1983). *Womanhood in America: From Colonial Times to the Present*, 3rd ed. New York: Franklin Watts.

Saenz, Rogelio (2004). Latinos and the Changing Face of America. The American People, *Census 2000*. Washington, DC: Russell Sage Foundation/Population Reference Bureau.

Sanchez, George J. (1990). "Go after the Women: Americanization and the Mexican Immigrant Woman, 1915–1929." In *Unequal Sisters: A Multicultural Reader in U.S. Women's History*, Ellen Carol DuBois and Vicki L. Ruiz (eds.). New York: Routledge, pp. 250–263.

Sanchez, George J. (1999). "Excerpts from Becoming Mexican American: Ethnicity, Culture, and Identity in Chicano Los Angeles, 1900–1945." In *American Families: A Multicultural Reader*, Stephanie Coontz (ed.). New York: Routledge, pp. 128–152.

Sandberg, John F., and Sandra L. Hofferth (2001). "Changes in Children's Time with Parents: United States, 1981–1997." *Demography* 38 (August): 423–436.

Sanderson, Warren, and Sergei Scherbore (2008). "Rethinking Age and Aging." *Population Bulletin* 63 (December). Washington, DC: Population Reference Bureau.

Santelli, John, Mary A. Ott, Maureen Lyon, Jennifer Rogers, Daniel Summers, and Rebecca Schleifer (2006). "Abstinence and Abstinence-only Education: A Review of U. S. Policies and Programs." *Journal of Adolescent Health* 38: 72–81.

Santorum, Rick (2005). *It Takes a Family: Conservatism and the Common Good*. Wilmington, DE: ISI Books.

Sarkisian, Natalia, Mariana Gerena, and Naomi Gerstel (2007). "Extended Family Integration Among Euro and Mexican Americans: Ethnicity, Gender and Class." *Journal of Marriage and Family* 69 (February): 40–54.

Sarkisian, Natalia, and Naomi Gerstel (2004). "Kin Support among Blacks and Whites: Race and Family Organization." *American Sociological Review* 69 (December): 812–837.

Sarkisian, Natalia, and Naomi Gerstel (2006). "Ethnicity and Extended Families: Exploring Differences between Latinos/as and Euro Americans." Unpublished paper.

Savin-Williams, Ritch C., and Kristin G. Esterberg (2000). "Lesbian, Gay, and Bisexual Families." In *Handbook of Family Diversity*, David H. Demo, Katherine R. Allen, and Mark A. Fine (eds.). New York: Oxford University Press, pp. 197–215.

Sayer, Liana C., Philip N. Cohen, and Lynne M. Casper (2005). "Women, Men, and Work." In *The American People: Census 2000*, Reynolds Farley and John Haaga (eds.). New York: Russell Sage Foundation, pp. 76–106.

Scanzoni, John (2004). "Household Diversity: The Starting Point for Healthy Families." In *The Handbook of Contemporary Families*, Marilyn Coleman and Lawrence Ganong (eds.). Thousand Oaks, CA: Sage, pp. 3–11.

Scarr, Sandra (1997). "New Research on Day Care Should Spur Scholars to Reconsider Old Ideas." *Chronicle of Higher Education* (August 8): A48.

Scheper-Hughes, Nancy (1992). *Death without Weeping: Mother Love and Child Death in Northwest Brazil*. Berkeley: University of California Press.

Schmidt, Eric (2001). "For First Time, Nuclear Families Drop Below 25% of Households." *New York Times* (May 15): 17.

Schneider, Elizabeth M. (2000). *Battered Women and Feminist Lawmaking*. New Haven, CT: Yale University Press.

Schnittker, Jason (2007). "Working More and Feeling Better: Women's Health, Employment, and Family Life, 1974–2004." *American Sociological Review* 72: 221–238.

Schnurnberger, Lynn (2007). "The Truth About Family Dinners." *Parade* (November 11): 10–12.

Schor, Juliet B. (1991). *The Overworked American: The Unexpected Decline of Leisure*. New York: Basic Books.

Schorr, Lisbeth B. (1988). *Within Our Reach: Breaking the Cycle of Disadvantage*. New York: Doubleday Anchor Press.

Schorr, Lisbeth B. (1997). *Common Purpose: Strengthening Families and Neighborhoods to Rebuild America*. New York: Doubleday Anchor Books.

Schrag, Peter (2007). "As California Goes…" *The Nation* (April 9): 18–21.

Schulte, Brigid (2009). "We're Keeping Our Stuff." *Washington Post National Weekly Edition* (March 23): 35.

Schvaneveldt, Jay D., Robert S. Pickett, and Margaret H. Young (1993). "Historical Methods in Family Research." In *Sourcebook of Family Theories and Methods: A Contextual Approach*, P. G. Boss, W. J. Doherty, R. LaRossa, W. R. Schum, and S. K. Steinmetz (eds.). New York: Plenum, pp. 591–623.

Schwartz, John (1997). "The Sobering Impact of Marriage." *Washington Post National Weekly Edition* (February 10): 35.

Schwartz, Pepper (1994). "Modernizing Marriage." *Psychology Today* 27 (September/October): 54–59, 86.

Schwartz, Pepper (2000). "Creating Sexual Pleasure and Sexual Justice in the Twenty-First Century." *Contemporary Sociology* 29 (January): 213–219.

Schwartz, Pepper (2004). "What We Know About Sexuality in Intimate Relationships." In *The Handbook of Sexuality in Close Relationships*, John H. Harvey, Amy Wenzel, and Susan Specher (eds.). Mahwah, NJ: Lawrence Erlbaum, pp. 597–612.

Schwartz, Pepper, and Virginia Rutter (1998). *The Gender of Sexuality*. Thousand Oaks, CA: Pine Forge.

Schwede, Laurel, Rae Lesser Blumberg, and Anna Y. Chan (eds.) (2005). *Complex Ethnic Households in America*. Lanham, MD: Rowman & Littlefield.

Scommegna, Paola (2002). "Increased Cohabitation Changing Children's Family Settings," *Population Today* (October): 6–10.

Scott, Donald M., and Bernard Wishy (1982). *America's Families: A Documentary History*. New York: Harper & Row.

Scott, Jacqueline, Judith Treas, and Martin Richards (eds.) (2004). *The Blackwell Companion to the Sociology of Families*. Blackwell Publishing Ltd.

Scott, Janny (2008). "Reflection on Class Matters." In *Social Class: How Does It Work?*, Annette Lareau and Dalton Conley (eds.). New York: Russell Sage, pp. 354–358.

Seccombe, Karen (2007). *Families in Poverty*. Boston: Pearson, Allyn and Bacon.

Seccombe, Karen (2008). *Families and Their Social Worlds*. Boston: Allyn and Bacon.

Seery, Brenda L., and M. Sue Crowley (2000). "Women's Emotion Work in the Family: Relationship Management and the Process of Building Father-Child Relationships." *Journal of Family Issues* 21 (January): 100–127.

Seltzer, Judith A. (1994). "Consequences of Marital Dissolution for Children." *Annual Review of Sociology* 20: 235–266.

Seltzer, Judith A. (2001). "Families Formed outside of Marriage." In *Understanding Families into the New Millennium: A Decade in Review*, Robert M. Milardo (ed.). Minneapolis, MN: National Council on Family Relations, pp. 466–487.

Seltzer, Judith A. (2004). "Cohabitation and Family Change." In *The Handbook of Contemporary Families*, Marilyn Coleman and Lawrence A. Ganong (eds.). Thousand Oaks, CA: Sage, pp. 57–78.

Sengupta, Somini (1999). "Women Keep Garment Jobs by Sending Babies to China." *New York Times* (September 14): A1, A21.

Sennett, Richard, and Jonathan Cobb (1972). *The Hidden Injuries of Class*. New York: Vintage.

Settersten, Richard A., Jr., Frank F. Furstenberg, Jr., and Ruben G. Rumbaut (eds.) (2005). *On the Frontier of Adulthood: Theory, Research, and Public Policy*. Chicago: University of Chicago Press.

Seward, Rudy Ray (1978). *The American Family: A Demographic History*. Beverly Hills, CA: Sage.

Shanahan, Michael J., Erik J. Porfeli, Jeylan T. Mortimer, and Lance D. Erickson (2005). In *On the Frontier of Adulthood*, Richard A. Settersten, Jr., Frank F. Furstenberg, Jr., and Ruben G. Rumbaut (eds.). Chicago: University of Chicago Press, pp. 225–255.

Sharp, Elizabeth A., and Lawrence Ganong (2007). "Living in the Gray: Women's Experiences of Missing the Marital Transition." *Journal of Marriage and Family* 69 (August):831–844.

Shehan, Constance L. (1999). "No Longer a Place for Innocence: The Re-Submergence of Childhood in Post-Industrial Societies." *Contemporary Perspectives on Family Research*, Vol. 1. Stamford, CT: JAI Press.

Shehan, Constance L. (2003). *Marriages and Families*, 2nd ed. Boston: Allyn and Bacon.

Shelton, Beth Anne (1992). *Women, Men, and Time: Gender Difference in Paid Work, Housework, and Leisure*. New York: Glennwood.

Shelton, Beth Anne, and Daphene John (1993a). "Does Marital Status Make a Difference?" *Journal of Family Issues* 14 (3): 401–420.

Shelton, Beth Anne, and Daphene John (1993b). "Ethnicity, Race, and Difference: A Comparison of White, Black and Hispanic Men's Household Labor Time." In *Men, Work, and Family*, Jane Hood (ed.). Newbury Park, CA: Sage, pp. 1–22.

Sherif-Trask, Bahira (2004). "Muslim Families in the United States." In *The Handbook of Contemporary Families*, Marilyn Coleman and Lawrence H. Ganong (eds.). Thousand Oaks, CA: Sage, pp. 394–408.

Sherry, Allison (2001). "Experts: Domestic Violence Higher Among Police." *Denver Post* (June 24): 2B.

Shorter, Edward (1975). *The Making of the Modern Family*. New York: Basic Books.

Simon, Barbara L. (1987). *Never Married Women*. Philadelphia: Temple University Press.

Simpson, Bob (1998). *Changing Families: An Ethnographic Approach to Divorce and Separation*. Oxford, UK: Berg.

Simpson, Kevin (2000). "A Closet Is a Closet." *Denver Post* (August 20): 1A, 10A–11A.

Sklar, Holly (2003). "Imagine a Country: Life in the New Millennium." *Z Magazine* 16 (May): 53–59.

Sklar, Holly. (2006). "Happy New Year, American Dream." *The Progressive Populist* (February 1): 16.

Skolnick, Arlene (1983). *The Intimate Environment*, 3rd ed. Boston: Little, Brown.

Skolnick, Arlene S. (1987). *The Intimate Environment: Exploring Marriage and the Family*, 4th ed. Boston: Little, Brown.

Skolnick, Arlene S. (1993). "Changes of Heart: Family Dynamics in Historical Perspective." In *Family, Self, and Society: Toward a New Agenda for Family Research*, Philip A. Cowan, Dorothy Field, Donald A. Hansen, Arlene Skolnick, and Guy Swanson (eds.). Hillsdale, NJ: Erlbaum, pp. 43–68.

Skolnick, Arlene S. (1997b). "Family Trouble: Arlene Skolnick Responds." *American Prospect* 34 (September–October): 19–21.

Skolnick, Arlene S., and Stacey Rosencrantz (1994). "The New Crusade for the Old Family." *American Prospect* 18 (Summer): 59–65.

Skolnick, Arlene S., and Jerome H. Skolnick (eds.). (2007). *Family in Transition*, 14th ed. Boston: Allyn and Bacon.

SmartMoney.com (2008). "Long-Term Care." (September).

Smith, Daniel Blake (1983a). "Autonomy and Affection: Parents and Children in Chesapeake Families." In *The American Family in Social-Historical Perspective*, 3rd ed., Michael Gordon (ed.). New York: St. Martin's Press, pp. 209–228.

Smith, Dorothy (1993). "The Standard North American Family." *Journal of Family Issues* 14 (March): 50–65.

Smock, Pamela J. (1990). "Remarriage Patterns of Black and White Women: Reassessing the Role of Educational Attainment." *Demography* 27 (August): 467–473.

Smock, Pamela J. (2000). "Cohabitation in the U.S.: An Appraisal of Research Themes, Findings, and Implications." *Annual Review of Sociology* 26: 1–20.

Society (2003). "The Spread of the Divorce Bug." Vol. 40 (January): 2.

Sokoloff, Natalie J., and Ida Dupont (2005). "Domestic Violence: Examining the Intersection of Race, Class, and Gender: An Introduction." In *Domestic Violence at the Margins: Readings on Race, Class, Gender, and Culture*, Natalie J. Sokoloff (ed.). New Brunswick, NJ: Rutgers University Press, pp. 1–13.

Sowti, Naseem (2005). "Fewer Abortions." *The Washington Post National Weekly Edition* (July 25–31): 29.

Spain, Daphne, and Suzanne M. Bianchi (1996). *Balancing Act*. New York: Russell Sage Foundation.

Spitze, Glenna (1991). "Women's Employment and Family Relations." In *Contemporary Families: Looking Forward, Looking Back*, Alan Booth (ed.). Minneapolis: National Council on Family Relations, pp. 381–404.

Sprecher, Susan, and Rodney M. Cate (2004). "Sexual Satisfaction and Sexual Expression as Predictors of Relationship Satisfaction and Stability." In *The Handbook of Sexuality in Close Relationships*, John H. Harvey, Amy Wenzel, and Susan Sprecher (eds.). Mahwah, NJ: Lawrence Erlbaum, pp. 235–256.

Sprecher, Susan, Maria Schmeeckle, and Dine Felmlee (2006). "The Principle of Least Interest: Inequality in Emotional Involvement in Romantic Relationships." *Journal of Family Issues* 27(9): 1255–1280.

Sprey, Jetse (2001). "Theorizing in Family Studies: Discovering Process." In *Understanding Families into the New Millennium: A Decade in Review*, Robert M. Milardo (ed.). Minneapolis, MN: National Council on Family Relations, pp. 1–14.

Stacey, Carol, and Timothy J. Biblarz (2001). "(How) Does the Sexual Orientation of Parents Matter?" *American Sociological Review* 66 (April): 159–183.

Stacey, Judith (1990). *Brave New Families: Stories of Domestic Upheaval in Late Twentieth-Century America*. New York: Basic Books.

Stacey, Judith (1991). "Backward toward the Postmodern Family: Reflections on Gender, Kinship, and Class in the Silicon Valley." In *America at Century's End*, Alan Wolfe (ed.). Berkeley: University of California Press, pp. 17–34.

Stacey, Judith (1994). "The New Family Values Crusaders." *The Nation* (July 25/August 1): 119–122.

Stacey, Judith (1996). *In The Name of the Family: Rethinking Family Values in the Postmodern Age*. Boston: Beacon Press.

Stacey, Judith (1998). "Gay and Lesbian Families: Queer Like Us." In *All Our Families: New Policies for a New Century*, Mary Ann Mason, Arlene Skolnick, and Stephen D. Sugarman (eds.). New York: Oxford University Press, pp. 117–143.

Stacey, Judith (2001). "Family Values Forever." *The Nation* (July 9): 26–50.

Stacey, Judith (2003). "Gay and Lesbian Families: Queer Like Us." In *All Our Families*, 2nd ed., Mary Ann Mason, Arlene Skolnick, and Stephen D. Sugarman (eds.). New York: Oxford University Press, pp. 144–169.

Stacey, Judith, and Elizabeth Davenport (2002). "Queer Families Quack Back." *Handbook of Lesbian and Gay Studies*, Diane Richardson and Steven Seidman (eds.). Thousand Oaks, CA: Sage, pp. 355–374.

Stack, Carol (1974). *All Our Kin: Strategies for Survival in a Black Community*. New York: Harper & Row.

Stack, Carol, and Linda M. Burton (1994). "Kinscripts: Reflections on Family, Generation, and Culture." In *Mothering: Ideology, Experience, and Agency*, Evelyn Nakano Glenn, Grace Chang, and Linda Rennie Forcey (eds.). New York: Routledge, pp. 33–44.

Stafford, Laura, Susan L. Kline, and Caroline T. Rankin (2004). "Married Individuals, Cohabiters, and Cohabiters Who Marry: A Longitudinal Study of Relational and Individual Well-Being." *Journal of Social and Personal Relationships* 21(2): 231–248.

Stansell, Christine (1990). *In Unequal Sisters: A Multi-Cultural Reader in U.S. Women's History*, Ellen Carol DuBois and Vicki L. Ruiz (eds.). New York: Routledge, pp. 94–95.

Stanton, Glenn T. (2003). "How Cohabitation is Growing." *Focus on the Family*. Online: http://www.family.org/cforum/fosi/marriage/cohabitation/a0025612.cfm

Stapinski, Helene (1999). "Y Not Love?" *American Demographics* (February): 62–68.

Staples, Robert (1978). "The Myth of Black Sexual Superiority: A Re-examination." *Black Scholar* 9 (April): 16–23.

Staples, Robert, and Leonore B. Johnson (1993). *Black Families at the Crossroads: Challenges and Prospects*. San Francisco: Jossey-Bass.

State of Colorado (1999). "Common Law Marriage." Office of Legislative Legal Services. Online: http://www.state.co.us/gov_dir/leg_dir/olls/PDF/COMMON%20LAW%20MARRIAGE.pdf

Stayton, William R. (1985). "Lifestyle Spectrum 1984." In *Marriage and Family 85/86, Annual Editions*. Guilford, CT: Dushkin, pp. 17–20.

Stein, Peter, J., Judith Richman, and Natalie Hannon (1977). *The Family: Functions, Conflicts and Symbols*. Reading, MA: Addison-Wesley.

Steinberg, Stephen (1981). *The Ethnic Myth*. Boston: Beacon Press.

Steinmetz, Suzanne K. (1978). "Battered Parents." *Society* 15 (July/August): 54–55.

Steinmetz, Suzanne K., and Murray A. Straus (1974). *Violence in the Family*. New York: Harper & Row.

Stephen, Elizabeth Hervey (1999). "Assisted Reproduction Technologies: Is the Price Too High?" *Population Today* 27 (May): 1–3.

Sterling, Toby (2004). "The Global View of Gay Marriage." *CBS News* (March 4). Online: www.cbsnews.com/stories/2004/03/04/world/printable604084.shtml

Stevens, Heidi (2008). "Only Children Still Stung by Stereotypes." *Chicago Tribune* (August 18).

Stevenson, Betsey, and Justin Wolfers (2007). "Divorced From Reality." *New York Times* (September 29). Online: http://www.nytimes.com/2007/09/29/opinion/29wollfers. html?_oref=slogin

Stewart, Susan D. (2005). "How the Birth of a Child Affects Involvement with Stepchildren." *Journal of Marriage and Family* 67 (May): 461–473.

St. George, Donna (2007). "Feeling Guilty?" *Washington Post National Weekly Edition* (April 2): 35.

Stith, Sandra M., Karen H. Rosen, Kimberly A. Middleton, Amy L. Busch, Kirsten Lundeberg, and Russell P. Carleton (2000). "The Intergenerational Transmission of Spouse Abuse: A Meta-Analysis." *Journal of Marriage and the Family* 62 (August): 640–654.

Stone, Andrea (2009a). "Business Booming for Thrift Stores." *USA Today* (April 16): 3A.

Stone, Andrea (2009b). "Gay Marriage Ruling Sparks Anger." *USA Today* (May 27): 3A.

Strauchler, Orin, Kathy McCloskey, Kathleen Malloy, Marilyn Sitaker, Nancy Grigsby, and Paulette Gillig (2004). "Humiliation, Manipulation, and Control: Evidence of Centrality in Domestic Violence Against an Adult Partner." *Journal of Family Violence* 19 (December): 339–354.

Straus, Murray A. (1977). "A Sociological Perspective on the Prevention and Treatment of Wifebeating." In *Battered Women*, Maria Roy (ed.). New York: Van Nostrand.

Straus, Murray A. (1981). "Ordinary Violence Versus Child Abuse and Wife Beating: What Do They Have in Common?" Paper presented at the National Conference for Family Violence Researchers, Durham, NH.

Straus, Murray A., and Carrie L. Yodanis (1996). "Corporal Punishment in Adolescence and Physical Assaults on Spouses in Later Life: What Accounts for the Link?" *Journal of Marriage and the Family* 58 (November): 825–841.

Straus, Murray A., and Christine Smith (1990). "Family Patterns and Child Abuse." In Physical Violence in American Families. New Brunswick, NJ: Transaction Books, pp. 245–261.

Straus, Murray A., Richard Gelles, and Suzanne K. Steinmetz (1980). *Behind Closed Doors: Violence in the American Family*. New York: Anchor/Doubleday.

Stringer, Tiffany (2002). "Summertime, Summer Teens: What Do Teens Do All Summer?" *Occupational Outlook Quarterly* (2002–2003) 46 (Winter): 36–41. Washington, DC: U.S. Department of Labor, Bureau of Labor Statistics.

Surra, Catherine A. (1991). "Research and Theory on Mate Selection and Premarital Relationships in the 1980s." In *Contemporary Families: Looking Forward, Looking Back,* Alan Booth (ed.), Minneapolis, MN: National Council on Family Relations, pp. 54–75.

Sweeney, Megan (2002). "Remarriage and the Nature of Divorce." *Journal of Family Issues* 23: 410–440.

Sweeney, Megan M., and Maria Cancian (2004). "The Changing Importance of White Women's Economic Prospects for Assortative Mating." *Journal of Marriage and Family* 66 (November): 1015–1028.

Szegedy-Maszak, Marianne (2001). "Guess Who's Footing the 'Mommy Tax,'" *U.S. News & World Report* (March 19): 48.

Szinovacz, Maximiliane E. (1987). "Family Power." In *Handbook of Marriage and the Family*. New York: Plenum, pp. 651–693.

Tach, Laura, and Sarah Halpern-Meekin (2009). "How Does Premarital Cohabitation Affect Trajectories of Marital Quality." *Journal of Marriage and Family* 71 (May): 298–317.

Taft, Donald (1936). *Human Migration*. New York: Ronald Press.

Tahmincioglu, Eve (2008). "Paid Family Leave Becomes Hot Issue." *MSNBC* (June 2). Online: http://www. msnbc.com.

Talbot, Margaret (2000). "The Price of Divorce." *New York Times*. Online: http://nytimes.com/books/00/10/01/reviews/001001. 01talbot.html

Talvi, Silja J. A. (2005). "Alls or Nothings." *In These Times* (October 24): 10.

Tanner, Michael (2003). "Wedded to Poverty." *New York Times* (July 29). Online: www.nytimes.com/2003/07/29/opinion/29TANN.html

Taylor, Peggy (1992). "The Way We Never Were: A New Age Journal Interview with Stephanie Coontz." *New Age Journal* (September/October): 64–69.

Taylor, Ronald L. (2000). "Diversity Within African American Families." In *The Handbook of Family Diversity*, David H. Demo, Katherine R. Allen, and Mark A. Fine (eds.) New York: Oxford University Press, pp. 232–251.

Taylor, Ronald L. (2001). "Black American Families." In *Minority Families in the United States*, 3rd ed., Ronald L. Taylor (ed.). Englewood Cliffs, NJ: Prentice Hall.

Teachman, Jay (2003). "Premarital Sex, Premarital Cohabitation, and the Risk of Subsequent Marital Dissolution Among Women." *Journal of Marriage and Family* 65 (May): 444–455.

Teachman, Jay D., and Lucky Tedrow (2008). "Divorce, Race, and Military Service: More than Equal Pay and Equal Opportunity." *Journal of Marriage and Family* 70: 1030–1044.

Tentler, Leslie Woodcock (1979). Wage-Earning Women. Oxford, UK: Oxford University Press.

Thistle, Susan (2006). *From Marriage to the Market: The Transformation of Women's Work*. Berkeley: University of California Press.

Thompson, Cynthia Ak., Laura L. Beauvais, and Tommy D. Allen (2006). "Work and Family From an Industrial/Organizational Psychology Perspective." In *The Work and Family Handbook: Multi-Disciplinary Perspectives and Approaches*, Marcie Pitt-Catsouphes, Ellen Ernst Kossek, and Stephen Sweet (eds.). Mahwah, NJ: Lawrence Erlbaum, pp. 283–307.

Thompson, Linda, and Alexis J. Walker (1991). "Gender in Families." In *Contemporary Families: Looking Forward, Looking Back,* Alan Booth (ed.). Minneapolis, MN: National Council on Family Relations, pp. 76–102.

Thorne, Barrie (1982). "Feminist Thinking on the Family: An Overview." In *Rethinking the Family: Some Feminist Questions*, Barrie Thorne and Marilyn Yalom (eds.). New York: Longman, pp. 1–24.

Thorne, Barrie (1992). "Feminism and the Family: Two Decades of Thought." In *Rethinking the Family: Some Feminist Questions*, 2nd ed., Barrie Thorne and Marilyn Yalom (eds.) Boston: Northeastern University Press, pp. 3–30.

Thornton, Arland, and Linda Young-DeMarco (2001). "Four Decades of Trends in Attitudes Toward Family Issues in the United States: The 1960s Through the 1990s." *Journal of Marriage and the Family* 63 (November): 1009–1037.

Thornton, Arland, William G. Axinn, and Yu Xie (2007). *Marriage and Cohabitation*. **Chicago: University of Chicago Press.**

Thottam, Jyota (2003). "Where are the Good Jobs Going?" *Time* (August 4): 36–39.

Tichenor, Veronica J. (2005). *Earning More and Getting Less: Why Successful Wives Can't Buy Equality*. **New Brunswick, NJ: Rutgers University Press.**

Tilly, Louise, and Joan W. Scott (1978). *Women, Work, and Family*. New York: Holt.

Timmer, Doug A., D. Stanley Eitzen, and Kathryn D. Talley (1994). *Paths to Homelessness: Extreme Poverty and the Urban Housing Crisis*. **Boulder, CO: Westview Press.**

Tjaden, P., and N. Thoennes (2000). *Extent, Nature, and Consequences of Intimate Partner Violence*. Washington, DC: National Institute of Justice/Center for Disease Control and Prevention.

Tongue, Nance E. (2005). "I Live Here and I Stay There: Navajo Perceptions of Households on the Reservation." In *Complex Ethnic Households in America*, **Laurel Scwede, Rae Lesser Blumberg, and Anna Y. Chan (eds.). Lanham, MD: Rowman & Littlefield, pp. 39–93.**

Townsend, Nicholas W. (2002). *The Package Deal: Marriage, Work and Fatherhood in Men's Lives*. Philadelphia: Temple University Press.

Trejos, Nancy (2009). "The Boomerangs Return." *Washington Post National Weekly Edition* **(May 4): 23–24.**

Trenholm, Christopher, Barbara Devaney, Kenneth Fortson, Melissa Clark, Lisa Quay, and Justin Wheeler (2008). "Impacts of Abstinence Education on Teen Sexual Activity, Risk of Pregnancy, and Risk of Sexually Transmitted Diseases." *Journal of Policy Analysis and Management* **27(2):255–276.**

Trimberger, E. Kay (2005). *The New Single Woman*. Boston: Beacon Press.

Troy, Adam B., Jamie Lewis-Smith, and Jean-Philippe Laurenceau (2006). "Interracial and Intraracial Romantic Relationships: The Search for Differences in Satisfaction, Conflict, and Attachment Style." *Journal of Social and Personal Relationships* 23(1): 65–80.

Tucker, M. Belinda, Saskia K. Subramanian, and Angela D. James (2004). "Diversity in African American Families: Trends and Projections." In *The Handbook of Contemporary Families*, Marilyn Coleman and Lawrence H. Ganong (eds.). Thousand Oaks, CA: Sage, pp. 352–369.

Tufte, Virginia, and Barbara Meyerhoff (eds.) (1979). *Changing Images of the Family*. New Haven, CT: Yale University Press.

Turrell, Susan C. (2000). "A Descriptive Analysis of Same-Sex Relationship Violence for a Diverse Sample." *Journal of Family Violence* 15(3): 281–293.

Turse, Nick (2009). "Younger and Hungrier in America." *TomDispatch.com* **(March 9). Online:http://www.commondreams.org/print/39230.**

Twenge, Jean M., W. Keith Campbell, and Craig A. Foster (2003). "Parenthood and Marital Satisfaction: A Meta-Analytic Review." *Journal of Marriage and the Family* 65 (August): 574–583.

TwoOfUs.org (2009). National Healthy Marriage Resource Center. Online: htty://www.twoofus.org.

Tyre, Peg (2002). "Giving Lessons in Love." *Newsweek* (February 18): 64.

Tyre, Peg, and Daniel McGinn (2003). "She Works, He Doesn't." *Newsweek* (May 12): 45–52.

Tyson, Laura D'Andrea (2005). "Those Manufacturing Myths." *Business Week* (December 12): 130.

Uchitelle, Louis (2008). "The Wage That Meant Middle Class." *New York Times* **(April 20). Online: http://www.nytimes.com/2008/04/20/weekinreview/20uchitelle.html?**

Udel, Lisa J. (2001). "Revision and Resistance: The Politics of Native Women's Motherwork." *Frontiers: A Journal of Women Studies* 22(2): v–vi.

Uhlenberg, Peter (1972). "Marital Instability among Mexican-Americans: Following the Pattern of Blacks?" *Social Problems* 20 (Summer): 49–56.

UNAIDS/World Health Organization (2005). AIDS Epidemic Update: December 2005. Online: www.unaids.org/epi/2005/doc/report_pdf.asp

UNAIDS/World Health Organization (2007). *AIDS Epidemic Update: 2007*. **Online: http:data.unaids.org/put/EPISlides/2007/2007_epiupdate_en.pdf.**

Unmarried America (2009). Online: http://www.unmarried america.org.

U.S. Administration on Aging (1998). *The National Elder Abuse Incidence Study: Final Report*. Washington, DC: U.S. Department of Health and Human Services. Online: http://www.aoa.gov/eldfam/Elder_Rights/Elder_Abuse/AbuseReport_Full.pdf

U.S. Administration on Aging (2006). "Ageism." National Center on Elder Abuse, CANE Dataabase. Online: http://www.ncea.aoa.gov.

U.S. Administration on Aging (2007). "Major Types of Elder Abuse." National Center on Elder Abuse. Online: http://www.ncea.aoa.gov.

U.S. Bureau of the Census (1993). We the American . . . Foreign Born (September).

U.S. Bureau of the Census (1996). Current Population Reports, Series P25-1130.

U.S. Bureau of the Census (1999). Statistical Abstract of the United States, 1999, 119th ed. Washington, DC: U.S. Government Printing Office.

U.S. Bureau of the Census (2000). Online: http://www.census.gov/population/www/cen2000

U.S. Bureau of the Census (2002). *Statistical Abstract of the United States, 2002*, 122nd ed. Washington, DC: U.S. Government Printing Office.

U.S. Bureau of the Census (2003). *Current Population Survey*. Annual Social and Economic Supplement (September). Online: http://www.census.gov/population/socdemo/hh-fam/cps2003/tabAll-all.pdf

U.S. Bureau of the Census (2005a). "America's Families and Living Arrangements: 2004." Washington, DC: Author.

U.S. Bureau of the Census (2005b). Current Population Survey: 2004 and 2005. Annual Social and Economic Supplements "People and Families in Poverty by Selected Characteristics:

2003 and 2004. Online: http://www.census.gov/prod/2005.pubs/p60-229.pdf

U.S. Bureau of the Census (2005c). Current Population Survey. Annual Social and Economic Supplements (December). Online: http://www.census.gov/hhes/www/income/histinc/ f05.html

U.S. Bureau of the Census (2005d). "Income, Poverty, and Health Insurance Coverage in the United States: 2004." Current Population Reports, P60-229 (August)

U.S. Bureau of the Census (2006). *Statistical Abstract of the United States: 2006*, 26th ed.

U.S. Bureau of the Census (2006a). "Family and Living Arrangements: 2003." Online: http://pubdb3.census.gov/macro/032005/Famine/new07_000.htm. (January)

U.S. Bureau of the Census (2006b). "Families and Living Arrangements in 2003. Population Profile of the United States: Dynamic Version. Online: http://www.census.gov/population/pop-profile/dynamic/familiesLA.pdf

U.S. Bureau of the Census (2006c). "Table MS-2. Estimated Median Age at First Marriage, by Sex: 1890 to the Present." Online: www.census.gov/population/socdemo/hh-fam/ms2.pdf

U.S. Bureau of the Census (2006). *America's Families and Living Arrangements: 2005.* **Online: http://www.census.gov/populaltion/www/socdemo/bh-fam/cps2005.html.**

U.S. Bureau of the Census (2007a). *Current Population Survey.* **Annual Social and Economic Supplement. Online: http://www.census.gov/population/socemo/hh-fam/eps2007.**

U.S. Bureau of the Census (2007b). *Housing and Household Economic Statistics Division.* **Annual Statistics: 2007. Online: http://www.census.gov/hhes/www/housing/hus/annual6y/anno7-t20.html.**

U.S. Bureau of the Census (2008a). *American Fact Finder.* **Online:http://www.factfinder.census.gov.**

U.S. Bureau of the Census (2008b). *Statistical Abstract of the United States: 2009*, **128th ed. Washington, D. C.: U.S. Government Printing Office.**

U.S. Bureau of the Census (2009a). *America's Families and Living Arrangements: 2008.* **Online: http://www.census .gov/populaltion/www/socdemo/hh-fam/cps2008.html.**

U.S. Bureau of the Census (2009b). *Current Population Survey,* **Annual Social and Economic Supplement. FINC-01. Selected Characteristics of Families by Total Money Income in 2007.**

U.S. Department of Health and Human Services (1999). Health, United States 1999. DHHS publication 99–1232. Washington, DC: U.S. Government Printing Office.

U.S. Department of Health and Human Services (2002). Trends in the Well-Being of America's Children & Youth. Washington, DC: U.S. Government Printing Office.

U.S. Department of Health and Human Services (2007a). **"A Profile of Older Americans: 2007. Washington, DC: Administration on Aging.**

U.S. Department of Health and Human Services (2007b). *"A Statistical Profile of Hispanic Older Americans Aged 65+."* **Washington, DC: Administration on Aging.**

U.S. Department of Health and Human Services (2008). **"What is Child Abuse and Neglect?" Child Welfare Information Gateway. Online: http://www.childwelfare .gov/pubs/factsheets/whatiscan.pdf.**

U.S. Department of Health and Human Services (2009). *Child Maltreatment 2007.* **Washington, DC: U.S. Government Printing Office.**

U.S. Department of Justice (1999). "Violence After School." *Juvenile Justice Bulletin* (November).

U.S. Department of Labor (2007). "Employment Projections." Online: http://www.bls.gov/emp/empllab05.htm.

U.S. Department of Labor (2008a). *Highlights of Women's Earnings in 2007.* **Online: http://www.bls.gov/cps/cpswom2007 .pdf.**

U.S. Department of Labor (2008b). *Women in the Labor Force: A Databook.***Online: http://www.bls.gov/cps/wlf-databook-2008.pdf.**

U.S. Department of Labor (2009a). "Employment Situation: February 2009)." Online: http://www.bls.gov/news. release/archives/empsit_03062009.pdf.

U.S. Department of Labor (2009b). "DOL's Final rule on Family and Medical Leave." Online: http://www.dol. gov/esa/whd/fmla/finalrule/factsheet.pdf.

U.S. General Accounting Office (2004). *GAO-04-353R Defense of Marriage Act: Update to Prior Report.* **Online: http://gao.gov/new.items/d04353r.pdf.**

U.S. News & World Report (2001). "National Origin of Hispanics in U.S." (March 29).

USA Today (2000). "Aging-Parent Trap: Caregivers Feel Stress." (September 25): 9D.

USA Today (2002). "Quarter of Household Workers Called Illegal." (March 22): 3A.

USA Today (2006). "Wealthy Can't Avoid Death—But Will They Evade Taxes?" (June 6): 10A.

USA Today (2008). "Latino Numbers." (January 28): 7A.

University of Maine Center on Aging (2007). *Elder Abuse Screening Protocol for Phyicians: Lessons Learned from the Maine Partners for Elder Protection Pilot Program.* **Online: http://www.mainecenteronaging.org.**

Urban Institute (2006). "A Decade of Welfare Reform: Facts and Figures." Washington, DC: (June).

Uttal, Lynet (1999). "Using Kin for Child Care: Embedment in the Socioeconomic Networks of Extended Families." *Journal of Marriage and the Family* 61 (November): 845–857.

Valenzuela, Angela, and Sanford Dornbusch (1994). "Familism and Social Capital in the Academic Achievement of Mexican Origin and Anglo Adolescents." *Social Science Quarterly* 75: 18–36.

Vander Zanden, Ronald (1966). *American Minority Relations.* New York: Ronald Press.

Vanneman, Reeve, and Lynn Weber Cannon (1987). *The American Perception of Class.* Philadelphia: Temple University Press.

Vecoli, Rudolph J. (1964). "Contadini in Chicago: A Critique of the Uprooted." *Journal of American History* 51: 405–417.

Veevers, J. E. (1980). *Childless by Choice.* Toronto: Butterworths.

Vega, William A. (1990). "Hispanic Families in the 1980s: A Decade of Research." *Journal of Marriage and the Family* 52: 1015–1024.

Vega, William A. (1995). "The Study of Latino Families: A Point of Departure." In *Understanding Latino Families*, Ruth E. Zambrana (ed.). Thousand Oaks, CA: Sage, pp. 1–17.

Velez-Ibanez, Carlos G. (1996). *Border Visions.* Tucson: University of Arizona Press.

Vencat, Emily Flynn, and Ginanne Brownell (2007). "Ah, the Secluded Life." *Newsweek* **(December 10). Online: http://www.newsweek.com/id/72721/output/print.**

Verdin, Tom (2000). "Minorities in the Majority." Associated Press (August 31).

Vestal, Christine (2009). "States Coping with Rising Home-lessness." *Stateline.org*. (March 18). Online: http://www.stateline.org/live/details/story?ContentId=385137.

Vinovskis, Maris A. (2006). "Historical Perspectives on Parent-Child Interactions." In *Shifting the Center: Understanding Contemporary Families*, 3rd ed., Susan J. Ferguson (ed.). New York: McGraw-Hill, pp. 271–286.

Vinovskis, Maris, and Laura McCall (1991). "Changing Approaches to the Study of Family Life." In *American Families: A Research Guide and Historical Handbook*, Joseph M. Hawes and Elizabeth I. Nybakken (eds.). Santa Barbara, CA: Greenwood Press, pp. 3–14.

Visher, Emily B., John S. Visher, and Kay Pasley (2003). "Remarriage Families and Stepparenting." In *Normal Family Processes: Growing Diversity and Complexity*, 3rd ed., Froma Walsh (ed.). New York: Guilford Press, pp. 153–175.

Voydanoff, Patricia (1987). *Work and Family Life*. Beverly Hills, CA: Sage.

Waite, Linda (1995). "Does Marriage Matter?" *Demography* 32 (November): 483–507.

Waite, Linda (1999). "The Importance of Marriage Is Being Overlooked." *USA Today: The Magazine of the American Scene* (January): 46–48.

Waite, Linda (2000). "Trends in Men's and Women's Well-Being in Marriage." In *The Ties That Bind: Perspectives on Marriage and Cohabitation*, Linda Waite (ed.). New York: Aldine de Gruyter, pp. 368–392.

Waite, Linda, and Frances K. Goldscheider (1992). "Work in the Home: The Productive Context of Family Relationships." In *The Changing American Family*, Scott J. South and Stewart E. Tolnay (eds.). Boulder, CO: Westview Press, pp. 267–299.

Waite, Linda, and Maggie Gallagher (2000). *The Case for Marriage: Why Married People Are Happier, Healthier, and Better Off Financially*. New York: Doubleday.

Waite, Linda, G. Haggstrom, and D. E. Kanouse (1986). "The Effects of Parenthood on Career Orientation and Job Characteristics of Young Adults." *Social Forces* 65 (1): 28–43.

Waldfogel, Jane (2001). "Family and Medical Leave Evidence from the 2000 Surveys." *Monthly Labor Review* 124 (September): 17–23.

Waldron, Tom, Brandon Roberts, and Andrew Rearner (2006). *Working Hard, Falling Short: America's Working Families and the Pursuit of Economic Security*. Baltimore: Annie E. Casey Foundation.

Waller, Willard (1937). "The Rating and Dating Complex." *American Sociological Review* 2 (October): 727–734.

Wallerstein, Judith S. (2003). "Children of Divorce: A Society in Search of Policy." In *All Our Families*, 2nd ed. Mary Ann Mason, Arlene Skolnick, and Stephen D. Sugarman (eds.). New York: Oxford University Press, pp. 66–95.

Wallerstein, Judith S., Julia Lewis, and Sandra Blakeslee (2000). *The Unexpected Legacy of Divorce*. New York: Hyperion.

Walls, Melissa, Les B. Whitlock, Dan Hoyt, and Kurt Johnson (2007). "Early Onset Alcohol Use Among Native American Youth: Examining Female Caretaker Influence." *Journal of Marriage and Family* 69 (May): 451–464.

Wandersee, Winifred D. (1991). "Families Face the Great Depression (1930–1940)." In *American Families: A Research Guide and Historical Handbook*, Joseph M. Hawes and Elizabeth I. Nybakken (eds.). Santa Barbara, CA: Greenwood Press, pp. 125–156.

Warren, Elizabeth, and Amelia Warren Tyagi (2009). "Why Middle-Class Mothers and Fathers are Going Broke." In *Family in Transition*, 15th ed., Arlene S. Skolnick and Jerome H. Skolnick (eds.). Boston: Allyn and Bacon, pp. 399–417.

Watchful Shepherd (2005). Online: http://www.watchful.org.

Waters, Mary C., and Karl Eschbach (1995). "Immigration and Ethnic and Racial Inequality in the United States." *Annual of Review of Sociology* 21: 419–446.

Watts, Jerry (1997). "The End of Work and the End of Welfare." *Contemporary Sociology* 26 (July): 409–412.

Weber, Lynn (1998). "A Conceptual Framework for Understanding Race, Class, Gender, and Sexuality." *Psychology of Women Quarterly* 22: 13–32.

Weber, Lynn (2001). *Understanding Race, Class, Gender, and Sexuality: A Conceptual Framework*. New York: McGraw-Hill.

Websdale, Neil, and Byron Johnson (2005). "Reducing Woman Battering: The Role of Structural Approaches." In *Domestic Violence at the Margins: Readings on Race, Class, Gender, and Culture*, Natalie J. Sokoloff (ed.). New Brunswick, NJ: Rutgers University Press, pp. 389–415.

Weeks, Jeffrey, Brian Heaphy, and Catherine Donovan (2001). *Same-Sex Intimacies*. New York: Routledge.

Weeks, Jeffrey, Brian Heaphy, and Catherine Donoval (2004). "The Lesbian and Gay Family." In *The Blackwell Companion to the Sociology of Families*. Jacqueline Scott, Judith Treas, and Martin Richards (eds.). Blackwell Publishing Ltd, pp. 340–355.

Wegar, Katarina (2000). "Adoption, Family Ideology, and Social Stigma." *Family Relations* 49 (October): 363–370.

Weinbaum, Batya, and Amy Bridges (1979). "The Other Side of the Paycheck: Monopoly Capital and the Structure of Consumption." In *Capitalist Patriarchy and the Case for Socialist Feminism*, Zillah R. Eisenstein (ed.). New York: Monthly Review Press, pp. 190–205.

Weinstein, Miriam (2005). *The Surprising Power of Family Meals*. New York: Steerforth.

Weissbourd, Richard (1994). "Divided Families, Whole Children." *American Prospect* 18 (Summer): 66–72.

Weitzman, Lenore (1985). *The Divorce Revolution: The Unexpected Social and Economic Consequences for Women and Children in America*. New York: Free Press.

Welch, Liz (2003). "Grandparents to the Rescue." *Parade* (July 20): 4–5.

Wellner, Allison Stein (2005). "U.S. Attitudes Toward Interracial Dating Are Liberalizing." *Population Reference Bureau*. Online: http://www.prb.org

Wells, Barbara, and Maxine Baca Zinn (2004). "The Benefits of Marriage Reconsidered." *Journal of Sociology and Social Welfare* 31 (December): 59–80.

Wells, Miriam J. (1976). "Emigrants from the Migrant Stream: Environment and Incentive in Relocation." *Aztlan: International Journal of Chicano Studies Research* 7: 267–290.

Wells, Robert V. (1991). "Demographic Change and Family Life in American History: Some Reflections." In *The Family Experience*, Mark Hutter (ed.). New York: Macmillan, pp. 43–62.

Wellstone, Paul (1998). "The People's Trust Fund." *The Nation* (July 27/August 3): 4–5.

Welter, Barbara (1973). "The Cult of True Womanhood: 1820–1860." In *The American Family in Social-Historical Perspective*, Michael Gordon (ed.). New York: St. Martin's Press, pp. 224–250.

West, Carolyn M., Glenda K. Kantor, and Jana L. Jasinski (1998). "Sociodemographic Predictors and Cultural Barriers to Help-Seeking Behavior by Latina and Anglo American Battered Women." *Violence and Victims* 13(4): 361–375.

West, Cornel (2004). "Black Sexuality: The Taboo Subject." In *Race, Class, and Gender*, 5th ed., Margaret L. Andersen and Patricia Hill Collins (eds.). Belmont, CA: Wadsworth.

Wharton, Amy S. (2006). "Understanding Diversity of Work in the 21st Century and Its Impact on the Work-Family Area of Study." In *The Work and Family Handbook: Multi-Disciplinary Perspectives and Approaches*, Marcie Pitt-Catsouphes, Ellen Ernst Kossek, and Stephen Sweet (eds.). Mahwah, NJ: Lawrence Erlbaum, pp. 17–39.

Whitaker, Elizabeth Ann (2005). "Should I Stay or Should I Go Now: Wives Participation in the Decision to Move for their Spouses' Jobs." *Michigan Family Review* 10:88–109.

White, Lynn K. (1990). "Determinants of Divorce: A Review of Research in the Eighties." *Journal of Marriage and the Family* 52 (November): 904–912.

Whitehead, Barbara Dafoe (1993). "Dan Quayle Was Right." *Atlantic Monthly* 271 (April): 47–84.

Whyte, Martin King (1990). *Dating, Mating, and Marriage*. New York: Aldine De Gruyter.

Whyte, Martin King (1992). "Choosing Mates—The American Way." *Society* 29 (March/April): 71–77.

Wiehe, Vernon R. (1997). *Sibling Abuse: Hidden Physical, Emotional, and Sexual Trauma*. Thousand Oaks, CA: Sage.

Wienke, Chris, and Gretchen J. Hill (2009). "Does the 'Marriage Benefit' Extend to Partners in Gay and Lesbian Relationships?: Evidence from a Random Sample of Sexually Active Adults." *Journal of Family Issues* 30(2): 259–289.

Williams, Christine L., and Arlene Stein (eds.) (2002). *Sexuality and Gender*. New York: Blackwell.

Willetts, Marion C., Susan Sprecher, and Frank D. Beck (2004). "Overview of Sexual Practices and Attitudes Within Relational Contexts." In *the Handbook of Sexuality in Close Relationships*, John H. Harvey, Amy Wenzel, and Susan Sprecher (eds.). Mahwah, NJ: pp. 57–84.

Williams, Gertrude (1980). "Toward the Eradication of Child Abuse and Neglect at Home." In *Traumatic Abuse and the Neglect of Children at Home*, Gertrude Williams and John Money (eds.). Baltimore, MD: Johns Hopkins University Press, pp. 588–605.

Williams, Norma (1990). *The Mexican American Family: Tradition and Change*. Dix Hills, NY: General Hall.

Wilson, Craig (2001). "Singleness Not the Same as Not Settled." *USA Today* (October 23): 1D–2D.

Wilson, Everitt K. (1966). *Sociology: Rules, Roles, and Relationships*. Homewood, IL: Dorsey Press.

Wilson, James Q. (1993). "The Family-Values Debate." *Commentary* 95 (April): 24–31.

Wilson, William Julius (1987). *The Truly Disadvantaged: The Inner City, the Underclass, and Public Policy*. Chicago: University of Chicago Press.

Wilson, William Julius (1996). *When Work Disappears: The World of the New Urban Poor*. New York: Knopf.

Wilson, William Julius (2009). *More Than Just Race: Being Black and Poor in the Inner City*. New York: Norton.

Wolf, Rosalie S. (2000). "The Nature and Scope of Elder Abuse." *Generations* 24 (Summer): 6–12.

Wolfe, Alan (1989). *Whose Keeper? Social Science and Moral Obligation*. Berkeley: University of California Press.

Wolfe, Diane L. (1990). "Daughters, Decisions, and Domination: An Empirical and Conceptual Critique of Household Strategies." *Development and Change* 21: 43–74.

Wolfe, Diane L. (1992). *Factory Daughters*. Berkeley: University of California Press.

World Bank (2008). *World Development Indicators: 2008*. Washington, DC: World Bank Publications.

World Health Organization (2008). *2008 Report on the Global AIDS Epidemic* (July). New York: United Nations.

Wright, Erik Olin (2008). "Logics of Class Analysis." In *Social Class: How Does It Work?*, Annette Lareau and Dalton Conley (eds.). New York: Russell Sage, pp. 329–349.

Wright, Erik Olin, David Hachen, Cynthia Costello, and Joey Sprague (1982). "The American Class Structure." *American Sociological Review* 47 (December): 709–726.

Yancey, George (2002). "Who Interracially Dates: An Examination of the Characteristics of Those Who Have Interracially Dated," *Journal of Comparative Family Studies* 33 (Spring): 79–90.

Yans-McLaughlin, Virginia (1973). "Patterns of Work and Family Organization." In *The Family in History*, T. K. Rabb and R. I. Rotborg (eds.). New York: Harper & Row.

Ybarra, Lea (1977). "Conjugal Role Relationships in the Chicano Family." Ph.D. dissertation, University of California at Berkeley.

Yellowbird, Michael, and C. Matthew Snipp (2001). "American Indian Families." In *Minority Families in the United States*, 3rd ed., Ronald L. Taylor (ed.). Englewood Cliffs, NJ: Prentice Hall, pp. 227–249.

Yen, Hope (2009). "Minority Kids in Majority by 2023." Associated Press (March 5).

Yglesias, Matthew (2006). "$1.27 Trillion." *The American Prospect* 17 (July/August): 28–32.

Yllo, Kersti A. (2007). "Gender, Diversity and Violence: Extending the Feminist Framework." In *Shifting the Center: Understanding Contemporary Families*, 3rd. ed, Susan J. Ferguson (ed.). New York: McGraw-Hill, pp. 611–622.

Yoshioka, Marianne R., Louisa Gilbert, Naabila El-Bassel, and Malahat Baig-Amin (2003). "Social Support and Disclosure of Abuse: Comparing South Asian, African American, and Hispanic Battered Women." *Journal of Family Violence* 18 (June): 171–180.

Young, Iris Marion (1994). "Making Single Motherhood Normal." *Dissent* 41 (Winter): 88–93.

Zacks, E., R. J. Green, and J. Marrow (1988). "Comparing Lesbian and Heterosexual Couples on the Circumplex Model," *Family Process* 24: 487–507.

Zaretsky, Eli (1976). *Capitalism, the Family, and Personal Life*. New York: Harper & Row.

Zaslow, Martha J., and Kathryn Tout (2002). "Child-Care Quality Matters." *American Prospect*, April 8, p. 49.

Zavella, Patricia (1987). *Women's Work and Chicano Families*. Ithaca, NY: Cornell University Press.

Zhou, Min (1997). "Growing up American: The Challenge Confronting Immigrant Children and Children of Immigrants." *Annual Review of Sociology* 23: 63–95.

Zoroya, Gregg (2005). "Soldiers' Divorce Rates Up Sharply." *USA Today* (June 8): 1A.

Zuckerman, Mortimer B. (2006a). "Fairness and the Future." *U.S. News & World Report* (April 24): 60.

Zuckerman, Mortimer B. (2006b). "Rich Man, Poor Man." *U.S. News & World Report* (June 12): 71–72.

Zuckerman, Mortimer B. (2008). "The Haunted Housing Market." *U.S. News & World Report* (February 28): 64.

Zvonkovic, Anisa M., Megan L. Notter, and Cheryl L. Peters (2006). "Family Studies: Situating Everyday Family Life at Work, in Time, and Across Contexts." In *The Work and Family Handbook: Multi-Disciplinary Perspectives and Approaches*, Marcie Pitt-Catsouphes, Ellen Ernst Kossek, and Stephen Sweet (eds.). Mahwah, NJ: Lawrence Erlbaum, pp. 141–164.

Zweifel, Dave. (2005). "Super-Rich Leaving Even the Rich Behind." *The Progressive Populist* (July 15): 14.

Credits

Name Index

Subject Index

Birth Rates for Teenagers 15–19 Years by Race and Hispanic Origin: United States, 1991, 2000, 2005, and 2006

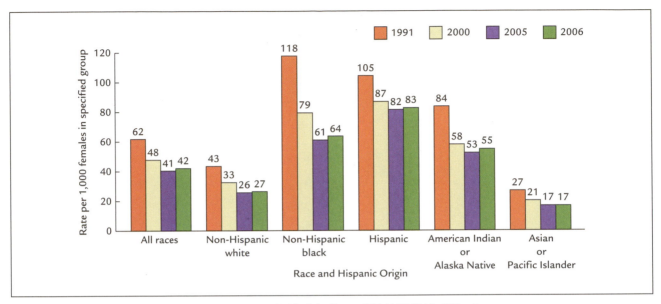

Source: Joyce A. Martin et al., "Births: Final Data for 2006." *National Vital Statistics Reports* 57(7). U.S.D.H.H.S., 2009, p 5.

Median Age at First Marriage by Sex: 1890–2008

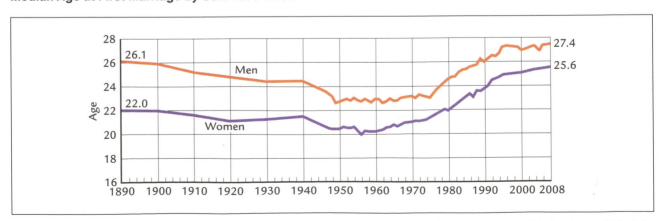

Source: "Marital Status and Living Arrangements: March 1998," *Current Population Reports,* Series P-20.514. Washington DC: U.S. Bureau of the Census, 1998; "Estimated Median Age at First Marriage, by Sex: 1890 to the Present" Table MS-2. U.S. Bureau of the Census, 2009. Online: www.census.gov/population/socdemo/hh-fam/ms2.xls.